GUNS IN AMERICAN SOCIETY

AN ENCYCLOPEDIA OF HISTORY, POLITICS, CULTURE, AND THE LAW

GUNS IN AMERICAN SOCIETY

AN ENCYCLOPEDIA
OF HISTORY, POLITICS,
CULTURE, AND THE LAW
VOLUME I: A–L

Edited by
Gregg Lee Carter

A B C ⬥ C L I O

Santa Barbara, California   Denver, Colorado   Oxford, England

Library of Congress Cataloging-in-Publication Data

Guns in American society : an encyclopedia of history, politics,
culture, and the law / edited by Gregg Lee Carter.
    p. cm.
  ISBN 1-57607-268-1 (hardcover : alk. paper)
 1. Gun control--United States--Encyclopedias. 2. Firearms--Law and
legislation--United States--Encyclopedias. 3. Firearms--Social
aspects--United States--Encyclopedias. 4. Violent crimes--United
States--Encyclopedias. 5. Social movements--United
States--Encyclopedias. I. Carter, Gregg Lee, 1951-

HV7436 .G8783 2002
363.3'3'097303--dc21
                        2002014682

07 06 05 04 03 02   10 9   8   7   6   5   4   3   2   1

This book is also available on the World Wide Web as an e-book. Visit abc-clio.com for details.

ABC-CLIO, Inc.
130 Cremona Drive, P.O. Box 1911
Santa Barbara, California 93116-1911

This book is printed on acid-free paper ∞.
Manufactured in the United States of America

CONTENTS

GUNS IN AMERICAN SOCIETY

ABOUT THE EDITORS

GENERAL EDITOR

Gregg Lee Carter (Ph.D., Columbia University, 1983) is a professor of sociology at Bryant College in Smithfield, Rhode Island. He has authored or edited nine books, including *The Gun Control Movement* (1997).

EDITORIAL BOARD

Walter F. Carroll (Ph.D., American University, 1983) is professor of sociology and chairperson of the Department of Sociology, Anthropology, and Criminal Justice at Bridgewater State College in Massachusetts. He is the coauthor of *Social Problems: Causes, Consequences, Interventions* (2000).

David B. Kopel (J.D., University of Michigan, 1985) is research director at the Independence Institute in Golden, Colorado, and a Fellow at the Cato Institute in Washington, D.C. He has written or edited ten books, including *The Samurai, the Mountie, and the Cowboy: Should America Adopt the Gun Controls of Other Democracies?* (1992), *Guns: Who Should Have Them?* (1995), *No More Wacos: What's Wrong with Federal Law Enforcement and How to Fix It* (1997), and *Gun Control and Gun Rights* (2002). He also serves as editor-in-chief of the *Journal on Firearms and Public Policy*.

Robert J. Spitzer (Ph.D., Cornell University, 1980) is Distinguished Service Professor of Political Science at the State University of New York–Cortland. He is the author of ten books, including *The Politics of Gun Control,* second edition (1998), and *The Right to Bear Arms: Rights and Liberties under the Law* (2001). He is also editor for the book series American Constitutionalism for the State University of New York Press.

Clyde Wilcox (Ph.D., Ohio State University, 1984) is professor of government at Georgetown University. He has authored or edited twenty books, including *The Changing Politics of Gun Control* (1998).

CONTRIBUTORS AND THEIR ENTRIES

Jonathan R. Almond
Pastor
Mathewson Street United Methodist Church
Providence, Rhode Island
Methodist Church, United

Thomas Altherr
Professor of History
Metropolitan State College
Denver, Colorado
*Dime Novels and the Sensationalization of
    Frontier Violence*
Hunting

Roseanna Ander
Joyce Foundation
Chicago, Illinois
Hemenway, David

James A. Beckman
Assistant Professor of Law and Justice
University of Tampa
Tampa, Florida
Antiterrorist Legislation
Articles of Confederation and Gun Control
Bailey v. United States
Barrett v. United States
Beecham v. United States
Bureau of Justice Statistics
Caron v. United States
Department of Justice, U.S.
Firearm Sentence Enhancement (FSE) Laws
Gun-Free School Laws
Lewis v. United States
National Firearms Act of 1934
Preemption Laws
Right-to-Carry Laws
Springfield, Inc. v. Buckles
Staples v. United States

Sullivan Law
United States v. Lopez
United States v. Powell

Murray S. Blackadar
Minister
Presbyterian Church (USA)
Providence, Rhode Island
Presbyterian Church (USA)

David I. Caplan
Attorney at Law
Delray Beach, Florida
Ammunition, Regulations of
Gun Registration
Liability of Gun Manufacturers
Magna Carta
Ninth Amendment
Perpich v. Department of Defense
Schubert v. DeBard
Tenth Amendment
United States v. Tot

Sue Wimmershoff-Caplan
Delray Beach, Florida
Magna Carta

Walter F. Carroll
Professor of Sociology
Bridgewater State College
Bridgewater, Massachusetts
American Academy of Pediatrics
Americans for Democratic Action
Americans for Gun Safety
*Association of American Physicians
    and Surgeons*
Borinsky, Mark
Campaign to Protect Sane Gun Laws
Cease Fire, Inc.

Northwest Missouri State University
Maryville, Missouri
Dodd, Thomas Joseph
Dole, Robert
Feinstein, Dianne
Lautenberg, Frank R.

Thomas Diaz
Violence Policy Center
Washington, D.C.
American Civil Liberties Union
Firearm Dealers
Firearm Industry
Video Games and Gun Violence
Violence Policy Center

John W. Dietrich
Assistant Professor of Political Science
Bryant College
Smithfield, Rhode Island
Craig, Larry E.
McCollum, William
National Tracing Center
Trigger Locks
Youth Crime Gun Interdiction Initiative
Youth Gun Control Legislation, The Juvenile
  Justice Bill of 1999

Keith Rollin Eakins
Assistant Professor of Political Science
University of Central Oklahoma
Edmond, Oklahoma
American Bar Association
Bryan v. United States
Congressional Voting Patterns on Gun Control
Interest Groups and Gun Legislation
Second Amendment
United States Congress and Gun Legislation
United States Supreme Court Decisions on
  Gun Control

Joanne Eisen
Research Associate
Independence Institute
Golden, Colorado
American Jewish Congress
American Medical Association and
  Gun Control
HELP Network

Kellermann, Arthur L.
National Center for Injury Prevention
  and Control

Elizabeth K. Englander
Associate Professor of Forensic Psychology
Bridgewater State College
Bridgewater, Massachusetts
Federal Bureau of Investigation
Firearms Owners Against Crime
Kennesaw, Georgia
Stevens v. United States

Michael Philip Fisher
American University
Washington, D.C.
State v. Boyce
State v. Kerner
State v. Kessler
State v. Rosenthal

T. Markus Funk
Assistant United States Attorney
Northern District of Illinois (Chicago)
Black Codes
NAACP and Gun Control
Racism and Gun Control
United States v. Hutzell

Eugene V. Gallagher
Rosemary Park Professor of Religion
Connecticut College
New London, Connecticut
Branch Davidians
Reno, Janet
Waco, Texas, Raid

Paul Gallant
Research Associate
Independence Institute
Golden, Colorado
American Jewish Congress
American Medical Association
HELP Network
Kellermann, Arthur L.
National Center for Injury Prevention
  and Control

Gilbert Geis
Professor Emeritus of Criminology, Law, and Society
University of California, Irvine
   Armijo v. Ex Cam, Inc.
   Aymette v. State
   Bernethy v. Walt Failor's Inc.
   Cases v. United States
   Commonwealth v. Davis
   Dickerson v. New Banner Institute, Inc.
   Farmer v. Higgens
   Fresno Rifle and Pistol Club, Inc. v. Van De Kamp
   Huddleston v. United States
   Merrill v. Navegar, Inc.
   Printz v. United States
   Robertson v. Baldwin
   Sklar v. Byrne
   Smith v. United States
   United States v. Adams
   United States v. Emerson
   United States v. Verdugo-Urquidez
   United States v. Warin

Marcia L. Godwin
Lecturer
Department of Political Science
California State University, Long Beach
Long Beach, California
   Citizens Committee for the Right to Keep and Bear Arms
   Doctors for Responsible Gun Ownership
   Gottlieb, Alan Merril
   Legal Community Against Violence
   Lott, John R., Jr.
   Roberti-Roos Assault Weapons Control Act of 1989
   Second Amendment Foundation
   Stockton, California, Massacre
   Women Against Gun Violence
   Women & Guns
   Zebra Killings

Linda Gorman
Senior Fellow
Independence Institute
Golden, Colorado
   Domestic Violence and Guns
   Gun Shows

Independence Institute
Kopel, David B.
National Firearms Association of Canada
United Kingdom—History of Gun Laws through 1900

Ellsworth S. Grant
West Hartford, Connecticut
   Colt, Samuel
   Ruger, William Batterman
   Winchester, Oliver Fisher

Stephen P. Halbrook
Attorney at Law
Fairfax, Virginia
   Switzerland, Gun Laws

David Harding
Associate Professor of Political Science
Arkansas State University
Jonesboro, Arkansas
   Attitudes toward Gun Control
   General Social Survey
   Ideologies—Conservative and Liberal

David T. Hardy
Attorney at Law
Tucson, Arizona
   Acquisition of Guns
   American Rifleman
   Ammunition, Types of
   Black Talon
   Cartridges
   Derringers
   Dum-Dum Bullet
   Gun Clubs
   Gun Owners of America
   Gunpowder
   Hammer, Marion P.
   Mail-Order Guns
   Minié Ball
   National Council to Control Handguns
   Orth, Franklin L.
   Pratt, Larry
   Spitzer Bullet
   Surplus Arms
   Williams Gun
   Zip Guns

Christopher Harris
Whittier College
Whittier, California
   Citizens Committee for the Right to Keep and
     Bear Arms
   Gottlieb, Alan Merril

F. Frederick Hawley
Professor of Criminal Justice
Western Carolina University
Cullowhee, North Carolina
   Boomtowns, Cowtowns, and Gun Violence
   Civil War and Small Arms
   Gun Culture
   Schoolyard Shootings
   South (U.S.) and Gun Violence

David Hemenway
Professor of Health Policy
Harvard School of Public Health
Boston, Massachusetts
   Accidents, Gun
   Firearm Injury Statistical Systems
   Gun Violence as a Public Health Problem
   Motor Vehicle Laws as a Model for Gun Laws
   Suicide, Guns and

Dennis A. Henigan
Director, Legal Action Project
Brady Center to Prevent Gun Violence
Washington, D.C.
   Brady Center to Prevent Gun Violence
   California Street (101) Massacre
   Dix v. Beretta USA Corp.
   Lawsuits against Gun Manufacturers
   Legal Action Project
   Nuisance Law and Gun Suits
   Smith & Wesson Settlement Agreement

Daniel Justin Herman
Assistant Professor of History
Central Washington University
Ellensburg, Washington
   Boone, Daniel
   Herbert, Henry William

Winny W. Hung
Senior Emergency Medicine Resident
Rhode Island Hospital

Providence, Rhode Island
   Gunshot Wounds (Wound Ballistics)

Jennifer Hurtarte
Special Projects Manager
American Academy of Pediatrics, Illinois
   Chapter
Chicago, Illinois
   Guns in the Home

Nancy M. Hwa
Brady Campaign to Prevent Gun Violence
Washington, D.C.
   Brady Campaign to Prevent Gun Violence

Ted G. Jelen
Professor of Political Science
University of Nevada at Las Vegas
   Collectors
   Gun Ownership

Don B. Kates
Research Fellow
Pacific Research Institute
San Francisco, California
   Alcohol and Gun Violence
   Availability of Guns, Effects on Crime
   Average-Joe Thesis
   Justifiable Homicides
   Lethality Effect of Guns

Jongsung Kim
Assistant Professor of Economics
Bryant College
Smithfield, Rhode Island
   Substitution Effects

Rebecca Knox
Associate Director, Public Health Education
Brady Center to Prevent Gun Violence
Washington, D.C.
   Project Lifeline

David B. Kopel
Research Director
Independence Institute
Golden, Colorado
   Bartley-Fox Carrying Law
   Beecher's Bibles

Jeffrey Kraus
Professor of Political Science
Wagner College
Staten Island, New York

Tom Lansford
Assistant Professor of Political Science
University of Southern Mississippi
Hattiesburg, Mississippi

Paul Lokken
Assistant Professor of History
Bryant College
Smithfield, Rhode Island

Nancy M. Lord
Bloomberg School of Public Health
Johns Hopkins University
Baltimore, Maryland

David S. Lux
Professor of History
Bryant College

Smithfield, Rhode Island
Brown Bess
Long Rifle (Pennsylvania/Kentucky)
Tommy Gun
Whitney, Eli

Kim A. Mac Innis
Associate Professor of Sociology and Criminal
 Justice
Bridgewater State College
Bridgewater, Massachusetts
Homicides, Gun
Mass Murder (Shootings)
Metal Detectors
Police Shootings

James Manning
Assistant Professor of Communication
Western Carolina University
Cullowhee, North Carolina
Civil War Reenactments

Wendy L. Martinek
Assistant Professor of Political Science
Binghamton University–State University of
 New York
Black Market for Firearms
Bureau of Alcohol, Tobacco, and Firearms

Gary A. Mauser
Professor of Marketing
Simon Fraser University
Burnaby, British Columbia, Canada
Canada, Gun Laws
Canadian Firearms Centre

Lorraine Mazerolle
Lecturer in Criminology
Griffith University
Mt. Gravatt Campus
Brisbane, Queensland, Australia
Gunshot Detection Technologies

Judith McDonnell
Associate Professor of Sociology
Bryant College
Smithfield, Rhode Island
Urbanism and Gun Violence
Women and Guns

David McDowell
Professor of Criminal Justice
State University of New York at Albany
National Crime Victimization Survey

Glenn E. Meyer
Professor of Psychology
Trinity University
San Antonio, Texas
Colleges and Gun Violence
Intervention Effects
Mental Disabilities and Gun Use and
 Acquisition
Weapons Instrumentality Effect

Jeffrey Miron
Professor of Economics
Boston University
Boston, Massachusetts
Drugs, Crime, and Guns: Cross-National
 Comparisons

Karen O'Connor
Professor of Government
American University
Washington, D.C.
State v. Boyce
State v. Kerner
State v. Kessler
State v. Rosenthal

Carol Oyster
Professor of Psychology
University of Wisconsin–La Crosse
Academics for the Second Amendment
Black Panthers
Centers for Disease Control
Columbine High School Tragedy
Gun News Digest
Hickok, James Butler "Wild Bill"
Hinckley, John Warnock, Jr.
Kleck, Gary
Metaksa, Tanya K.
National Association of School Psychologists
Ruby Ridge
Suicide, International Comparisons
Texas Tower Shooting
Violent Crime Rate

Kevin Pearce
Assistant Professor of Communication
Bryant College
Smithfield, Rhode Island
Media Violence
Paladin Press

Tiia Rajala
Research Fellow, Department of History
University of Turku
Henrikinkatu, Finland
Finland, Gun Laws
Firearms Coalition
Gritz, James "Bo"
Gun Magazines
Gun Owners of California
Gun Owners' Action League
Knox, Neal
Paul Revere Network
Russia, Gun Laws
Safety for Women and Responsible Motherhood
Second Amendment Committee
Student Pledge Against Gun Violence
Texans for Gun Safety
Women Against Gun Control
Women's Firearm Network

Saundra J. Reinke
Professor of Political Science
Augusta State University
Augusta, Georgia
Michigan Militia
Militia of Montana
Militia Watchdog Groups
Militias
Survivalism
Terrorism

Glenn Harlan Reynolds
Professor of Law
University of Tennessee
Knoxville, Tennessee
Federalism and Gun Control

Avid Reza
Resident Department of Emergency Medicine
Emory University School of Medicine
Atlanta, Georgia
Victimization from Gun Violence

G. Edward Richards
Assistant Professor of Criminology
University of Akron
Akron, Ohio
Dick Act (Militia Act of 1903)
Drive-by Shootings
Federal Law Enforcement Officers Association
International Association of Chiefs of Police
International Brotherhood of Police Officers
Law Enforcement for the Preservation of the
    Second Amendment
Lennon, John
Mailing of Firearms Act of 1927
McVeigh, Timothy
National Association of Police Organizations
National School Safety Center
National Sheriffs' Association
National Troopers' Coalition
Nichols, Terry L.
Police Executive Research Forum
Remington, Eliphalet, II
Sawed-off Shotguns
Thompson, Linda

Desmond Riley
Coalition to Stop Gun Violence
Washington, D.C.
Coalition to Stop Gun Violence

Robin L. Roth
Professor of Sociology
Lesley University
Cambridge, Massachusetts
Cease Fire, Inc.
Fraternal Order of Police
Pacific Center for Violence Prevention

Joseph F. Sheley
Dean, College of Social Sciences and
    Interdisciplinary Studies
California State University, Sacramento
Drugs, Crime, and Guns: United States

Lawrence Southwick, Jr.
Professor of Management
State University of New York–Buffalo
Enforcement of Gun Control Laws
Methodologies for Studying Gun Violence
Saturday Night Specials

Robert J. Spitzer
Distinguished Service Professor
State University of New York–Cortland
  Arming Women Against Rape and
    Endangerment
  Assault Weapons
  Assault Weapons Ban of 1994
  Automatic Weapons Laws
  Background Checks
  Brady Handgun Violence Prevention Act
    (Brady Bill)
  Carter, Harlon
  Eddie Eagle
  Federation for NRA
  Firearms Owners' Protection Act of 1986
  Institute for Legislative Action
  Lawyer's Second Amendment Society
  Licensing
  Million Mom March
  Mothers Against Violence in America
  National Board for the Promotion of Rifle
    Practice
  National Guard
  National Rifle Association
  Political Victory Fund
  Presser v. Illinois
  Quilici v. Village of Morton Grove
  Safety Courses
  Second Amendment Sisters
  Semiautomatic Weapons
  Speedloaders
  Turner Diaries
  Waiting Periods

Mary Zeiss Stange
Associate Professor of Women's Studies and
  Religion
Skidmore College
Saratoga Springs, New York
  Cowboy Action Shooting
  Izaak Walton League of America
  Oakley, Annie
  United States Conference of Catholic Bishops

Glenn H. Utter
Professor of Political Science
Lamar University
Beaumont, Texas
  Gun Control

Teri E. Vail
Tulane University
New Orleans, Louisiana
  Felons and Gun Control

Benjamin Webster
Georgetown University
Washington, D.C.
  Aborn, Richard
  Barr, Bob
  Berkowitz, Leonard
  Boxer, Barbara
  Brooks, Jack B.
  Bush, George H. W.
  Chaffee, John
  Chenoweth-Hage, Helen
  Conyers, John
  Dingell, John D.
  Hyde, Henry J.
  Kennedy, Edward M.
  Metzenbaum, Howard M.
  Schumer, Charles E.

Daniel W. Webster
Co-Director
Johns Hopkins Center for Gun Policy and
  Research
Baltimore, Maryland
  Child Access Prevention (CAP) Laws

Samuel C. Wheeler III
Professor of Philosophy
University of Connecticut
Storrs, Connecticut
  Genocide and Guns
  Jews for the Preservation of Firearms
    Ownership
  Right to Self-Defense

Clyde Wilcox
Professor of Government
Georgetown University
Washington, D.C.
  Aborn, Richard
  Barr, Bob
  Berkowitz, Leonard
  Boxer, Barbara
  Brooks, Jack B.
  Bush, George H. W.

Chaffee, John
Conyers, John
Dingell, John D.
Hyde, Henry J.
Kennedy, Edward M.
Metzenbaum, Howard M.
Schumer, Charles E.

Harry L. Wilson
Director of Center of Community Research

Roanoke College
Salem, Virginia
   Concealed Weapons Laws
   Uniform Crime Reports

James D. Wright
Provost and Distinguished Research Professor
University of Central Florida
Orlando, Florida
   Felons and Gun Control

PREFACE

Guns in American Society is the result of nearly three years of working with many of the most important researchers and writers on the role of guns in the contemporary United States. It covers all aspects of the issue: gun violence, gun control, government legislation, court decisions, gun organizations (both pro- and anti-control), gun owners, gun subcultures (for example, hunters and collectors), and attitudes toward guns. Many entries place the topics in historical and cross-cultural perspective.

The encyclopedia proposes no easy solutions to the problem of gun violence, and it is not "pro" or "anti" gun control. It does, however, map the social and political landscape of the gun issue in the United States—the key organizations and individuals, including their histories, their philosophies, and their tactics. It also analyzes American attitudes toward gun control and the degree to which these attitudes cohere with the agendas of important gun organizations on both side of the debate over gun control (those wanting stricter controls, such as are typical in Europe, or those wanting fewer controls, more in line with our colonial past). The encyclopedia provides ample data on gun violence, gun legislation, gun court decisions, gun prevalence, and gun attitudes. Entries have been carefully cross-referenced and are appended with suggested readings, representing the best of current scholarship. In short, there is more than enough information—for anyone who cares to do the perusing—for each reader to make up his or her own mind on the benefits or harms that the strict control of firearms may incur, as well as the obstacles facing those who would like to strengthen or weaken the current level of control.

The members of the Advisory Board for *Guns in American Society* are all first-rate scholars, and each one made a significant contribution to both volumes. I am grateful for their diligence, writing, and manifold editorial ef-forts. They are Walter F. Carroll of Bridgewater State College in Massachusetts, David B. Kopel of the Independence Institute in Colorado, Robert J. Spitzer of the State University of New York, Cortland, and Clyde Wilcox of Georgetown University in Washington, D.C. It has been my privilege to work with them.

My editing work benefited greatly from the Library staff at Bryant College. Reference librarians Colleen Anderson, Beth Ephraim, Paul Roske, and Heide-Lori Caiger were particularly helpful. The secretarial staff at Bryant is always ready to lend a hand. Elaine Lavallee and Joanne Socci performed many valued services, as did my student research assistants Travis Carter, Adam Graziano, and Olga Makovetskaya. My department chair, David Lux, was unfailing in his backing of this project—having approved several course releases to allow me the time to do my work and, indeed, even to the point of writing three important entries. The Bryant administration was also very cooperative and supportive, and I especially thank Earl Briden, John Tunney, V. K. Unni, and Ronald Machtley. My editors, James Ciment, Marie Ellen Larcada, and Susan McRory, were encouraging and enthusiastic from the moment each of them joined the project. On a personal note, I finally want to thank Lisa Harrington for her constant encouragement, and my children—Travis, Kurtis, and Alexis—for their love and forbearance.

Guns in American Society has been written for researchers, teachers, students, public officials, law-enforcement personnel, journalists, and members of the general public having an interest in this critical area of American life. I hope that it will stimulate and clarify every reader's thinking on the key issues surrounding guns in the contemporary United States, especially on the debate over gun control.

Gregg Lee Carter
Smithfield, Rhode Island

INTRODUCTION

The debate over gun control is often a war of statistics. What makes the wide use of statistics even more puzzling is that both sides in the debate often invoke the same statistics.

—James Lindgren and Frank E. Zimring,
Encyclopedia of Crime and Justice, 1983

Public debate and discussion about guns in American society are rarely guided by research. Based on personal experiences—for example, growing up in a home where firearms are used for hunting and recreation, or having a gut reaction of revulsion after reading about or seeing on television some horrific incident of gun violence—individuals tend to talk themselves into either a pro- or anti-gun position. There is good reason why most people do not rely on the relevant research: it represents a bog in which the average academic and the average public policy-maker, let alone the average citizen, can easily become mired. Indeed, at times it seems that both the research and the debate represent a morass that is so difficult to navigate that anyone unwilling to devote full-time study to it has little chance of making informed conclusions on the proper roles of firearms in our society.

Enter the present two-volume *Guns in American Society: An Encyclopedia of History, Politics, Culture, and the Law.* Its goal is help the reader navigate the research and become educated enough on any particular aspect of the gun issue to make an informed decision—for example, whether to support stricter or more lenient gun control, whether to become a gun owner, whether to support a particular political party, or whether to adopt or to refine a particular philosophy, simple or complex, regarding guns. The encyclopedia, the most comprehensive single source on the gun issue published to date, draws on a vast array of research in criminology, history, law, medicine, politics, and sociology. Its entries provide many cross-cultural and his-

torical comparisons to help place gun issues into broader contexts.

Guns and Violence

Of the many aspects of the gun issue, none is more important than whether there exists a causal link between gun prevalence and violence. Many people assume that such a link exists, yet establishing the validity of this link is much more difficult than the ordinary person might think.

The United States has weak national gun laws compared to almost all other economically developed, democratic nations, while U.S. gun violence is comparatively high. For example, Krug and his colleagues recently analyzed firearm-related deaths in the United States and twenty-five other high-income countries and found that the age-adjusted rate of firearm death (homicide, suicide, accident) "in the U.S. (14.24 per 100,000) is eight times the pooled rate for the other H[igh]-I[ncome] countries (1.76)" (Krug, et al., 1998; data are from the early- and mid-1990s). They also report that the U.S. crude homicide rate is six times higher than that for a typical economically developed country.

To gun control advocates, these two sets of facts are causally related, and the end result is nefarious: The more firearms circulating in a society, the more likely it is to suffer large numbers of violent crimes, suicides, and accidental deaths. Guns are not just another weapon: Assault with a gun, whether inflicted by another or self-inflicted, is many times more likely to result in death or serious injury than with any other weapon (Lindgren and Zimring, 1983). However, gun control opponents argue that the United States would be a violent and bloody society with or without the 200 million or so rifles, shotguns, and pistols currently in circulation. This argument is not groundless: The cross-national data of Krug and his colleagues reveal that even if we removed all of the firearm homicides for the United States, its rate would still be one and three-quarters times greater than the entire murder rate (gun- and non-gun-related) of the typical high-income country. Moreover, even if we eliminated all guns, surely some of the murders committed by guns would be committed by other means, so the net effect is that our murder rate would still actually be at least two to three times higher than our typical peer nation. In short, persuasive data can be marshaled to fit either side of the gun control debate; and, unfortunately, even when *tour de force* statistical analyses are carried out, the answers become no clearer.

While it may be hard to ascertain which side has the upper hand in the assessing of the guns-leads-to-violence data, it is clear that these varying assessments are at the heart of the gun control debate. Those working for stronger national gun laws, akin to the laws existing in most economically developed democracies, assume that such laws will reduce violence and save lives. As the Brady Campaign to Prevent Gun Violence (formerly known as Handgun Control, Inc.) states in many of its advertisements and communications with its supporters: "Our goal is to enact a comprehensive federal gun control policy to reduce gun violence." (The Brady Campaign is the largest and most important organization sustaining the movement to control guns.) Indeed, the organization argues that gun control works. In the fall of 2000, for example, it sent a letter to its supporters contending that the 1993 Brady Handgun Violence Prevention Act resulted in gun deaths dropping from 37,776 in 1992 to 32,436 in 1997 (Brady, 2000). On the other hand, progun groups challenge the premise that "a comprehensive federal gun control policy" will "reduce gun violence." In the words of the National Rifle Association

(NRA), "Guns don't kill, people do." In its flyers, the NRA repeatedly stresses that strict national gun laws, especially "registration and licensing," would have no effect on criminal violence, "as criminals, by definition, do not obey laws" (National Rifle Association, 1994, p. 9).

Cross-National Differences

As noted above, the United States has an overall murder rate that is six times higher than that of the average economically developed nation. Comparisons of murder-by-gun rates reveal an even more dramatic ratio: the U.S. rate of 7.07 is more than twelve times higher than the 0.58 average rate of its peer nations (Krug et al., 1998, p. 216). Concomitantly, this huge disparity in murder rates is accompanied by generally huge differences in gun prevalence: Killias (1993) reports that in the United States the percentage of households in the early 1990s with any type of gun was 48.0, which is three times that for the typical European country (16.2 percent), and twice as high as the rate of Australia and Canada (24.3 percent). (Note that the percentage of U.S. households with a firearm on the premises has dropped significantly in recent years—to about 35 percent; hunting has dropped in popularity, and millions of immigrants, relatively few of whom possess guns, have established households in the past decade.) Killias's data (N=13) reveal a strong correlation between gun prevalence and homicide. Hemenway and Miller (2000) confirm this correlation using the twenty-six high-income countries in the Krug et al. data set. On the other hand, Gary Kleck's (1997, p. 254) analysis of all of the nations (both high- and low-income) in that data set (N=36) reveals a much more modest correlation. Kleck believes that the entire Krug data set is a better indication of the truth, as a careful review of gun-prevalence/violent-crime studies on U.S. cities and counties show no consistent relationship (see Kleck, 1991, pp. 185–215). However, Mark Duggan (2001) believes that "previous research has suffered from a lack of reliable data on gun ownership." Using the level of sales of *Guns & Ammo* as an indicator of the level of gun ownership, Duggan finds that "changes in gun ownership are significantly positively related to changes in the homicide rate, with this relationship driven almost entirely by an impact of gun ownership on murders in which a gun is used" (Duggan, 2001, p. 1086).

Canada, Australia, New Zealand, Japan, and most European countries have much stricter gun regulations than the United States. Most importantly, these countries require that guns be registered, that gun owners be licensed, and that guns be stored and transported with utmost security. To get a license, a potential gun owner must typically pass an exam on gun safety. Also required are comprehensive background checks of individuals seeking to purchase guns, including any histories of criminality or mental incapacity. Although background checks are required by federally licensed firearms dealers when selling guns to their customers, sales between private individuals (including those at gun shows and flea markets) are not regulated by U.S. federal law, as they are in our peer nations. In the latter, of special interest to gun control advocates, because they consider these the most blameworthy weapons of violence, *handguns* are either outlawed or restricted so severely that ownership is extremely rare. This is reflected in the comparatively high percentage of households with a handgun present in the United States (about 22 percent) and the relatively tiny percentages elsewhere: 0.1 percent in the United Kingdom, 0.2 percent in the Netherlands, 2 percent in Australia, 2.5 percent in Spain, and 7 percent or less in Belgium, Canada, Finland, France, Norway, and Spain. The striking exception in Europe is Switzerland, which has a laxity in its gun laws comparable to that of the United States and a relatively high percentage of households where guns are present. Switzerland is the NRA's favorite example of the maxim "guns don't kill, people do" because it has low murder rates (both overall and by gun). However, gun control advocates are quick to point out that Switzerland's population is generally better trained than that of the United States in the safe use of firearms, as most adult Swiss men are members of the national militia.

The case of Switzerland alerts us not to oversimplify when making cross-national comparisons. Progun writers and groups have other favorite examples—Finland and Norway have high numbers of firearms but low rates of violence. On the other hand, Mexico and Russia have low numbers of firearms but high rates of violence. In short, there are forces beyond gun availability that influence the level of violence in any particular country. Most importantly, varying combinations of social heterogeneity and economic development have been linked to violence. For this reason, when countries are compared, they should be socioeconomically similar. Simplistic pair-wise comparisons are rarely useful, for as Kleck (1991, pp. 188-189) correctly argues "out of any large number of possible pairings, it is safe to say that at least a few pairs can be found to appear to support either side" of the gun control debate. For example, in recent years progun writers like to point out that Russia is extremely violent, yet has strict gun control and a relatively low percentage of households with guns, while in Switzerland gun prevalence is high but gun violence tends to be low (notwithstanding the massacre in the Swiss Canton of Zug in September of 2001, when a gunman broke into at a government building and shot fourteen people to death).

Reflections on the United States
Gun violence in the United States does not affect all segments of the population equally. African American males in their teens and early twenties are the most likely to suffer such violence. For example, in the 1990s, the rate of homicide due to firearms for black males in their early twenties was 140.7 per 100,000; the same rate for all individuals in their early twenties was 17.1. Similarly, the rate of homicide due to firearms for black teenagers was 105.3, while it was 14.0 for teenagers taken as a whole. Although the absolute numbers of victims involved has fallen in recent years, the racial slants in the data have not (see Carter, 1997, 2001; Fox, 2000).

These slants stand in contrast to the high media coverage of shootings involving teenage boys in the late 1990s and early 2000s. All but one of these high-profile incidents involved white male teens from small towns and suburbia (Springfield, Oregon; Pearl, Mississippi; West

Paducah, Kentucky; Jonesboro, Arkansas; Edinboro, Pennsylvania; Raleigh, Virginia; Santee, California; and most tragically, Littleton, Colorado). Except for the bloodbath at Columbine High School in Littleton, shootings of young people in the neighborhoods surrounding our inner-city schools are on par with these high-profile cases—although little publicized except in the local media. In short, white and minority gun violence are treated differently in the national media.

Establishing Causality—
No Easy Task

Whether a causal link exists between our society's high number of firearms and relatively lax federal gun laws, on the one hand, and our high rates of violence, on the other hand, represents the heart of the gun control debate. From the mid-1980s through early 1990s, guns diffused throughout the inner cities and many suburban communities of the United States. At the same time, these areas experienced growing rates of violence. Between 1984 and 1992, the FBI Uniform Crime Reports revealed that property crime was leveling off; on the other hand, violent crime continued to rise—steeply so between 1987 and 1993; and, most significantly, handgun violence catapulted from 589,000 murders, rapes, robberies, and assaults committed with handguns in 1988 to 1.1 million in 1993 (see Bastian and Taylor, 1994; Mackellar and Yanagishita, 1995). That crime rates—property, violent, gun-related—have fallen in the past decade to roughly those levels of the early 1980s does not negate the argument that the influx of guns was connected to the steep rise in violence in the late 1980s and early 1990s. Just as the riots of 1960s in African American neighborhoods were self-limiting (one can only burn down a neighborhood so many times), so too was much of the inner-city youth violence in 1980s and early 1990s. More specifically, the most violence-prone were the first to be cut down; those succeeding them were more mindful of the destructiveness of firearms; they also realized the benefits of a stabilized drug market. Alfred Blumstein (1995) offers this interpretation:

[Beginning in 1985,] in order to accommodate the increased demand, the drug sellers had to recruit a large number of new sellers.... The economic plight of many young urban African-American juveniles, many of whom see no other comparably satisfactory route to economic success or even sustenance, makes them particularly amenable to the lure of the drug markets. These juveniles, like many other participants in the illicit-drug industry, are likely to carry guns for self-protection, largely because that industry uses guns as an important instrument for dispute resolution.... Since the drug markets are pervasive in many inner-city neighborhoods, and the young people recruited into them are fairly tightly networked with other young people in their neighborhoods, it became easy for the guns to be "diffused" to other teenagers who go to the same school or who walk the same streets....In view of both the recklessness and bravado that is often characteristic of teenagers, and their low level of skill in settling disputes other than through the use of physical force, many of the fights that would otherwise have taken place and resulted in nothing more serious than a bloody nose can now turn into shootings as a result of the presence of guns. This may be exacerbated by the problems of socialization associated with high levels of poverty, high rates of single-parent households, educational failures, and a widespread sense of economic hopelessness. But those factors have been changing gradually over the years, and so they cannot readily provide the explanation for the sharp changes that began to take place in the mid-1980s.

Blumstein also contends that *white* juvenile homicide rates increased during the same era because of a "gun diffusion process" into suburbia (as guns crossed over into suburbia, guns begat guns in close-knit teenage circles). However, because national data, most importantly from the General Social Survey, reveal no increase in the percentages of individuals (including blacks and urban dwellers) or households possessing a gun, some analysts reject the notion that guns spread throughout the inner city and parts of suburbia during this period and accept the simpler "rise-in-gang-activity" interpretation (for example, see Kleck, 1997, pp. 72-74 and 256-258). Respondents to the General Social Survey are noninstitutionalized adults willing to take the survey. Not a very social scientific statement—but to those living in the streets of Boston, Chicago, Las Vegas, Los Angeles, Miami, New York, and other urban areas during the 1980s, the GSS data seem unable to detect or speak to the diffusion of guns they witnessed. Indeed, in line with the basic contours of the Blumenstein thesis (that is, that guns generate violence), recent work by Duggan (2001) reveals that part of the drop in violent crime and murder over the past decade in the United States reflects a falling proportion of gun-owning households.

Even if we find intuitive appeal in the Blumstein and Duggan line of reasoning and the correlations contained in the Killias cross-national data, correlation itself does not prove causality. Progun researchers and writers argue that the causal arrow might very well run the other way: that is, that rising rates of violence prompt citizens to arm themselves. Moreover, simple correlations do not take into consideration other variables that might be determinative of both these variables (implying that the guns/violence correlation is spurious). For example, rising immigration rates and subsequent rises in violence based on cultural conflict may account for the 1980s rise in gun violence. Or it may have been the growing presence of violent youth gangs—springing from low to high levels of salience with the introduction of crack cocaine in many urban areas—that produced the surge in violent crime. In short, the data do not fit neatly either the pro- or anti–gun control side of the debate. However, it is not unreasonable to hypothesize that the easy availability of guns, both legally and illegally, and their diffusion in urban areas during the 1980s greatly magnified the problems of violence associated with culture conflict and street gangs—even though some would argue that these forces would produce the same levels of violence even if guns were not on the scene.

The magnification hypothesis is supported when one considers that property crime (larceny, burglary, and auto theft) rates were flattening out in the United States during the late 1980s and early 1990s. Having ascertained that much of the rising crime rate in the 1960s and 1970s was due to the youthfulness of the population, demographers and criminologists had long ago predicted this flattening out. They predicted that as the post–World War II baby-boom generation aged, crime rates would fall (for crime is strongly correlated with youth: more than half of all street crime is committed by individuals under 25, with arrests peaking at age 18). If property crime was flattening out between 1984 and 1994, why wasn't violent crime (robbery, murder, aggravated assault) following a similar pattern? The diffusion of guns into urban areas—their availability, possession, and use—could account for the divergent trends in property crime and violent crime.

At the cross-national level, as noted earlier, one must also consider that the correlation between gun prevalence and violence can be accounted for by other factors, throwing suspicion on its causal nature. The two most important factors that must be taken into account are social homogeneity and economic inequality. Were the United States more socially and economically homogeneous, would its much greater prevalence of guns really matter that much? "A culture in which the citizens are very similar—sharing similar ethnicity, religious beliefs, income levels and values, such as Denmark—is more likely to have laws that represent the wishes and desires of a large majority of its people than is a culture where citizens come from diverse backgrounds and have widely disparate income levels and lifestyles, as in the United States" (Stephens, 1994, p. 23). For this reason, countries with a good deal of homogeneity normally have lower levels of law violation and violence than their heterogeneous counterparts. Kleck (1991, pp. 393-394) presents data in support of the notion that culture and not gun availability is what best distinguishes the United States from other developed countries that have much lower rates of violent crime. For example, Great Britain and Canada—two countries with low gun availability and low homicide rates—are often contrasted with the United States. In those societies, guns were not restricted in the early part of the twentieth century, yet their homicide rates were still extremely low (twelve to fourteen times lower than that of the United States).

As in the case of the United States taken by itself, it is difficult to rule out these alternative explanations for much greater levels of violence in the United States compared to other economically developed countries, though there is little doubt that heterogeneity plays a huge role in explaining the level of violence and crime in a nation. However, it is again not unreasonable to hypothesize that the easy availability of guns greatly magnifies the problems of crime and violence that are encouraged by the high levels of social/cultural heterogeneity and economic inequality in the United States.

The magnification hypothesis is further supported when one considers the "lethality" effect that assault by guns produces. Numerous studies confirm that gunshot wounds are much more likely to result in death than wounds inflicted by knife (the weapon generally assumed to be the next most lethal; see Cook and Ludwig, 2000, pp. 34–36). In comparing U.S. violence rates to those of our peer nations, gun control advocates observe that assaults in the United States are more likely to involve guns and that "guns kill." There is support for this position. A 1988 international crime survey—which asked the same questions in each country to obviate the problem of varying official national definitions of "assault"—revealed that the U.S. assault rate (5.4 percent of respondents reporting having been assaulted) is two and a third times greater than in other developed countries (average=2.9 percent), but the U.S. homicide rate is six times greater. Moreover, although several nations have assault-with-weapon rates on par with that of the United States—of those assaulted, 15 percent were attacked with weapons in the Netherlands and France, 14 percent in Northern Ireland and the United States, and 12 percent in Canada—the homicide rates of those same nations, where the weapon is much less often a gun, are many magnitudes smaller than that of the United States (Carter,

1997, p. 19). Such data support the argument that guns transform violent situations into lethal events. As epidemiologist David Hemenway phrases this notion, it is "the presence of a firearm [that] allows a petty argument to end tragically" (Henigan, Nicholson, and Hemenway, 1995, p. 57).

Law professor John R. Lott, Jr. (1998), disputes this conclusion, as well as most others concerning gun prevalence and violence. Indeed, the research of Lott and his colleague David Mustard (1997) has fueled one of the greatest debates on the issue of gun control and is closely related to the controversial research of Gary Kleck and Marc Gertz (1995) on the "good" effects of gun possession—that is, their usefulness in defending against criminal attack. In retort to Hemenway, Lott (1998, p. 8) observes that "few murderers could be classified as previously law-abiding citizens. In the largest seventy-five counties in the United States in 1988, over 89 percent of adult murderers had criminal records as adults"; indeed, what qualifies as an "acquaintance murder" is much less often a friend killing a friend, or a man killing his wife or girlfriend, than a gang member killing the member of another gang or one criminal killing another. Of even greater importance than this criticism are the meta-analyses conducted by Kleck and Lott of ecological and individual-level data. These reveal no consistent relationship between gun prevalence/ownership and violent crime; moreover, when individuals are freely allowed to carry concealed weapons, rates of violent crime drop. Their interpretation is straightforward and has intuitive appeal: criminals are rational, and they are less likely to rape, rob, or assault when they are fearful that a potential victim may be armed. For example, "in Canada and Britain, both with tough gun-control laws, almost half of all burglaries are 'hot burglaries' [in which a resident is at home when a criminal strikes]. In contrast, the United States, with fewer restrictions, has a 'hot burglary' rate of only 13 percent. Criminals are not just behaving differently by accident … The fear of potentially armed victims causes American burglars to spend more time than their foreign counterparts 'casing' a house to ensure that nobody is home" (Lott, 1998, p. 5). Just as alluringly in support of

Lott's argument is that the violent crime rates in those states allowing ordinary citizens to carry concealed handguns are significantly lower than in states where this is not the case.

However appealing, the research of Lott/Mustard and Kleck/Gertz has been assailed on a number of accounts, mainly methodological. Kleck's and Gertz's data, based on a 1993 national probability-sample telephone survey, lead them to estimate some 2.5 million defensive uses of guns per year. However, criminologists Philip J. Cook and Jens Ludwig (2000, p. 37) question this estimate because it is so far out of line with the estimate of 100,000 defensive gun uses that one gets using the "most reliable source of information on predatory crime because it has been in the field continuously since 1973 and incorporates the best thinking of survey methodologists," that is, the *National Crime Victimization Survey* (NCVS). And even though the 1994 National Institute of Justice survey on the "Private Ownership of Arms" (NSPOF) revealed a very high estimate for defensive gun use, 1.5 million uses (more in line with the Kleck and Gertz data than with the NCVS estimate), Cook and Ludwig (1997, p. 9) still contend the NCVS data are much more reasonable:

Some troubling comparisons: If the DGU [defensive gun use] numbers are in the right ballpark, millions of attempted assaults, thefts, and break-ins were foiled by armed citizens during the 12-month period. According to these results, guns are used far more often to defend against crime than to perpetrate crime. (Firearms were used by perpetrators in 1.07 million incidents of violent crime in 1994, according to NCVS data.) Thus, it is of considerable interest and importance to check the reasonableness of the NSPOF estimates before embracing them. Because respondents were asked to describe only their most recent defensive gun use, our comparisons are conservative, as they assume only one defensive gun use per defender. The results still suggest that DGU estimates are far too high.

For example, in only a small fraction of rape and robbery attempts do victims use guns in self-defense. It does not make sense, then, that the NSPOF estimate of the number of rapes in which a woman defended herself with a gun was more than the total number of rapes estimated from NCVS. For other crimes ... the results are almost as absurd.

As for the Lott/Mustard findings that the legalization of the carrying of concealed weapons has a significant marginal effect on the deterrence of violence crime, their complex statistical analyses of cross-sectional time-series data of more than 3,000 U.S. counties over an eighteen-year time span are far beyond the ken of most policymakers and others interested in the issue of gun control; thus, it is of no help to them to learn that several recent studies have poked holes in their findings (see, for example, Bartley and Cohen, 1998; Black and Nagin, 1998; Dezhbakhsh and Rubin, 1998; Duggan, 2000; and Ludwig, 1998, 2000). As economist William Shughart (1999, p. 659) observes, Lott and Mustard have "triggered a healthy econometric argument that is far from settled."

These complex data arguments regarding gun prevalence/violence have prompted some on the procontrol side to adopt a new view. They see the relevant data as not fitting neatly either side; moreover, they believe that it will be a long time before the question of whether gun prevalence/ownership/possession foments or thwarts violent crime is convincingly answered. They know that the elimination of guns can and does reduce violence: put metal-detectors in airports, and hijackings are reduced; put metal detectors in high schools, and shootings on school grounds disappear. However, with over 200 million guns currently in private hands in the United States, we are not going to eliminate our guns—not soon, not ever. Neither, given our great levels of heterogeneity and inequality, are we going to eliminate crime. But, by keeping guns out of our streets as much as possible—that is, by strictly controlling them—we can reduce the harm that they cause. This view is becoming increasingly popular among those examining the medical and other costs of gun violence. Philip J. Cook and Jens Ludwig express this best in noting that "guns don't kill people, but they make it real easy"; that is, controlling guns may not reduce violent crime but that it can reduce the harm done in such crime. Cook and Ludwig's recently published analyses of the medical, job-related/productivity, criminal-justice, school, and other costs of gun violence indicates that it costs the U.S. public "on the order of $100 billion per year, and affect[s] all of our lives in countless ways" (Cook and Ludwig, 2000, p. 117).

The Relevance of the Second Amendment
The fear of tyranny is still the primary motivator of those who oppose all forms of gun control in the name of the Second Amendment (which reads: "A well regulated Militia, being necessary to the security of a free State, the right of the people to keep and bear Arms, shall not be infringed."). They point to the lack of firearms in the general population that has allowed governments of some African and East European nations to brutalize their populaces throughout their histories, including the decade of the 1990s. On the other hand, political scientist Robert J. Spitzer (1998) makes a cogent argument that the United States is different. Indeed, there have been significant changes in our nation since late eighteenth century, when an armed population was critical to the defense of the new nation. In the past 220 years, the standing army has become entrenched in American life, and notions that it is a threat to personal liberty have long ago been dispelled. The concept of defense being limited to fighting at the borders of one's homeland repelling foreign invaders has been greatly broadened to the point where the defense business of America includes sending soldiers to Europe, Asia, Central America, and Africa; in short, the place of the United States in world affairs has changed dramatically. In the eighteenth century, the protection of the home, the farm, the village, the town, the city were left to the individual or to the militia; but by the middle of the nineteenth century, local police forces were the norm, and by the middle of the twentieth century, national law enforcement agencies (the FBI, Secret Service, Customs Service, Drug Enforcement Administration, Immigration and Naturalization Service) were well established.

In sum, eighteenth-century notions of the purpose and place of the militia in the community are out of step with the realities of the early twenty-first century, and so too, consequently, is the need to ensure the keeping and bearing of arms in private hands.

The Future of Guns and Their Control in the United States
Ultimately, the informed citizen must make up his or her mind on the issue of gun control on the basis of his or her fundamental values and view of human nature. For many, this choice can be made manifest in their voting—as, politically speaking, several features of American society ensure that the gun debate will continue to be salient, and often heated, in the decades to come. First, America is awash in guns—with over 200 million rifles, shotguns, and handguns as of 2002, with 2 to 3 million new firearms (a third of them handguns) being added to the total each year (Bureau of Alcohol, Tobacco and Firearms, 2001, 2002). Because guns don't wear out, the total number of firearms in the United States will exceed the size of its population in the not-too-distant future. Easy availability of firearms—through both legal and illegal means—is a fact of contemporary American life.

Second, crime rates in the United States have been falling for the past decade, partly in response to the baby boom generation growing up (youth and crime are significantly correlated). However, the children of the baby boom produced a baby boomlet, and individuals in this cohort—40 million strong—are now hitting their teens and early twenties, and street crime of all types is expected to rise in response. These two forces, youth and easy firearm availability, will keep gun violence alive and well.

Such violence will undoubtedly receive heavy media coverage, which will almost assuredly be slanted toward the procontrol side of the gun debate (those in the media overwhelmingly support gun control). Sympathetic media coverage will keep the Brady Campaign and its agenda for strict gun control in the limelight, and it would therefore be expected that membership rates and donations will remain high, if not grow outright. On the other side, the NRA's head start in membership and resources (in the late 1990s about an 8-to-1 advantage in membership and at least a 10-to-1 advantage in financial assets) will allow it to maintain a powerful presence on Capitol Hill no matter how much the Brady Campaign expands over the coming several years.

The trump card in this war over gun regulation will be the political makeup of the Congress and the presidency. As shown in various entries in this encyclopedia (e.g., Congressional Voting Patterns in Congress; Democratic Party and Gun Control; Ideologies—Conservative and Liberal; Republican Party and Gun Control; United States Congress and Gun Control), each side makes its greatest gains when political opportunity favors it. A conservative president and at least one house of Congress that is conservative favor the NRA and the progun side. In contrast, a liberal president and a liberal majority in at least one house favor the Brady Campaign and the antigun side. Any other combination—liberal president/conservative Congress or conservative president/liberal Congress—produces a standoff: the strong gun control legislation of 1993–1994 (the Brady law and the assault-weapons ban) will be neither dismantled nor built upon. With the Houses of Congress split between Republican and Democratic control, and with a Republican president, we can expect a standoff through the year 2004.

Nevertheless, the key political trend in the past thirty years has been toward conservatism. If the trend continues, and there is little reason to doubt that it will do so, then we might well find a conservative Republican (George Bush) in the White House in 2004 and a Republican retaking of the Senate. If this scenario unfolds, success for the gun control movement will be defined by what it does not lose (e.g., the assault-weapons ban) rather than by what it gains. However, the movement will be in a much better financial and organizational position to put up a good fight.

On the other hand, if some series of quirks places the presidency in the hands of the Democrats and elects a liberal Congress in 2004, then it would not be surprising to see American gun regulations coming closer to those of its peer nations in Western Europe. There would be a convergence of forces that has never occurred in U.S. history: a liberal Congress, a liberal president, public opinion strongly favoring gun control, and a powerful and well-organized gun control movement to counteract the NRA and others that prefer the status quo.

REFERENCES

Bartley, William Alan, and Mark A. Cohen. 1998. "The Effect of Concealed Weapons Laws: An Extreme Bound Analysis." *Economic Inquiry* 36: 258-265.

Bastian, Lisa D., and Bruce M. Taylor. 1994. "Young Black Male Victims." *Bureau of Justice Statistics Crime Data Brief, National Crime Victimization Survey, NCJ-147004.* Washington, D.C.: Bureau of Justice Statistics, U.S. Department of Justice. December.

Black, Dan A., and Daniel S. Nagin. 1998. "Do Right-to-Carry Laws Deter Violent Crime?" *Journal of Legal Studies* 27(January): 209-219.

Blumstein, Alfred. 1995. "Youth, Violence, Guns, and the Illicit-Drug Industry." *Journal of Criminal Law and Criminology* 86(Fall):10–36.

Brady, Sarah. 2000. *Letter to the HCI Membership.* Washington, DC: Handgun Control. November 7.

Bureau of Alcohol, Tobacco and Firearms. 2001. *Annual Firearms Manufacturers and Export Report, 2000.* http://www.atf.treas.gov/firearms/stats/afmer/afmer2000.pdf.

_____. 2002. "AFT Speech: National HIDTA Conference." http://www.atf.treas.gov/press/speech/fy01/120500hidtaconf.htm.

Carter, Gregg Lee. 1997. *The Gun Control Movement.* New York: Twayne Publishers.

_____. 2001. "Guns." Pp. 330–335 in *Boyhood in America: An Encyclopedia,* ed. Priscilla Ferguson Clement and Jacqueline S. Reinier. Santa Barbara, CA: ABC-CLIO.

Cook, Philip J., and Jens Ludwig. 1997. *Guns in America: National Survey on Private Ownership and Use of Firearms.* Research in Brief Report No. NCJ165476. Washington, DC: National Institute of Justice, Office of Justice Programs, U.S. Department of Justice. May.

_____. 2000. *Gun Violence: The Real Cost.* New York: Oxford University Press.

Dezhbakhsh, Hashem, and Paul H. Rubin. 1998. "Lives Saved or Lives Lost? The Effects of Concealed-Handgun Laws on Crime." *American Economic Review Papers and Proceedings* 88, 2:468-474.

Duggan, Mark. 2001. "More Guns More Crime." *Journal of Political Economy* 99 (October): 1086–1114.

Fox, James Alan. 2000. "Demographics and U.S. Homicide." Pp. 288–317 in *The Crime Drop in America*, ed. Alfred Blumstein and Joel Wallman. New York: Cambridge University Press.

Hemenway, David, and Matthew Miller. 2000. "Firearm Availability and Homicide Rates across 26 High-Income Countries." *Journal of Trauma* 49, 6:985–988.

Henigan, Dennis A., E. Bruce Nicholson, and David Hemenway. 1995. *Guns and the Constitution: The Myth of Second Amendment Protection for Firearms in America*. Northampton, MA: Aletheia Press.

Killias, Martin. 1993. "International Correlations between Gun Ownership and Rates of Homicide and Suicide." *Canadian Medical Association Journal* 148, 10:1721-1725.

Kleck, Gary. 1991. *Point Blank: Guns and Violence in America*. New York: Aldine de Gruyter.

_____. 1997. *Targeting Guns: Firearms and Their Control*. New York: Aldine de Gruyter.

Kleck, Gary, and Marc Gertz. 1995. "Armed Resistance to Crime: The Prevalence and Nature of Self-Defense with a Gun." *Journal of Criminal Law and Criminology* 86, 1: 150–187

Krug, E. G., K. E. Powell, and L. L. Dahlberg. 1999. "Firearm-Related Deaths in the United States and 35 Other High- and Upper-Middle-Income Countries." *International Journal of Epidemiology* 27, 2: 214-221.

Lindgren, James, and Franklin E. Zimring. 1983. "Regulation of Guns." Pp. 836–841 in *Encyclopedia of Crime and Justice*, ed. Sanford H. Kadish. New York: Free Press.

Lott, John R., Jr. 1998. *More Guns, Less Crime: Understanding Crime and Gun-Control Laws*. Chicago: University of Chicago Press.

Lott, John R., Jr., and David B. Mustard. 1997. "Crime, Deterrence, and Right-to-Carry Concealed Handguns." *Journal of Legal Studies* 261(January):1-68.

Ludwig, Jens. 1998. "Concealed-Gun-Carrying Laws and Violent Crime: Evidence from State Panel Data." *International Review of Law and Economics* 18: 239–254.

_____. 2000. "Gun Self-Defense and Deterrence." *Crime and Justice* 27: 363.

Mackellar, Landis F., and Machikio Yanagishita. 1995. *Homicide in the United States: Who's At Risk?* Washington, DC: Population Reference Bureau.

National Rifle Association. 1994. *Ten Myths about Gun Control*. Fairfax, VA: NRA Institute for Legislative Action.

Shughart, William F., II. 1999. "Review of *More Guns, Less Crime*." *Southern Economic Journal* 65, 3: 656–659.

Spitzer, Robert J. 1998. *The Politics of Gun Control*. 2d ed. New York: Chatham House.

Stephens, Gene. 1994. "The Global Crime Wave." *Futurist* 28, 4: 22–28.

GUNS IN AMERICAN SOCIETY

AN ENCYCLOPEDIA OF HISTORY, POLITICS, CULTURE, AND THE LAW

A

Aborn, Richard (1952–)

Richard Aborn served as president of Handgun Control, Inc. and of the Center to Prevent Handgun Violence from 1992 to 1996 (these organizations were renamed the Brady Campaign to Prevent Gun Violence and the Brady Center to Prevent Gun Violence, respectively, in June 2001). During his presidency, he lobbied and testified before Congress and a number of state legislatures and made numerous media appearances across the country. He helped mobilize support for the passage of the Brady Bill (Brady Handgun Violence Prevention Act), the ban on the import of assault weapons (Assault Weapons Ban of 1994), and the ban on large-capacity clips. He is among the most visible advocates of gun control and has been active in a variety of ways in many different arenas.

Aborn first became involved with gun control issues when he served from 1979 to 1984 in the Manhattan District Attorney's Office. In that capacity he investigated and prosecuted cases of gun violence and distribution and increasingly came to believe in the importance of restrictions on guns. After Aborn left the District Attorney's Office, he began work as a volunteer at Handgun Control, Inc. (HCI). His visible and effective advocacy led to his election to the Board of Trustees in 1988 and to the presidency of the organization in 1992.

While president of HCI, Aborn established a broad agenda. He lobbied the federal and state governments for laws mandating licenses to buy handguns, for mandatory fingerprint checks and safety training for those who apply for licenses, a mandatory seven-day cooling off period, and the registration of handgun transfers. He sought to ban possession of guns by those convicted of violent misdemeanors and to ban semiautomatic weapons and certain types of ammunition.

He served a concurrent term as president of the Center to Prevent Handgun Violence, which focuses on public education and community involvement. During his term he worked to develop and implement the STAR (Straight Talk About Risks) program, a curriculum for prekindergarten through twelfth grade that seeks to educate students about the risks of gun injuries. Aborn was instrumental in winning adoption for the program by the New York City public schools.

Aborn also served on a task force in New York State that focused on violent crime as a public health issue; he contributed to its published report, "New York State Strategy to Reduce Gun Violence." He was a Visiting Fellow at Columbia University, where he lectured on gun control, and has served as a consultant to the Ford Foundation project on violence, youth, and schools. In 2001, Aborn was senior counsel and director of policy at the Kamber Group, a media consulting group. He also serves on the board of New Yorkers Against Gun Violence.

Clyde Wilcox and Benjamin Webster

See also Assault Weapons Ban of 1994; Brady Campaign to Prevent Gun Violence; Brady Center to Prevent Gun Violence; Brady Handgun Violence Prevention Act

For Further Reading:

Time/AOL's on-line debate series on gun control: "Richard Aborn (HCI) v. Tanya Metaksa. (NRA's Institute for Legislative Action)." December 2, 1994. http://www.hoboes.com/html/Politics/Firearms.

Academics for the Second Amendment (A2A)

Academics for the Second Amendment (A2A) is a nonprofit corporation headquartered in St. Paul, Minnesota, whose purpose is to promote discussion of the Second Amendment and the right of individuals to keep and bear arms.

Founded in 1992, A2A's major activity is sponsoring seminars for academics, attorneys, journalists, and writers. Some A2A seminars are conducted jointly with the Second Amendment Foundation. While A2A seminars generally include a variety of speakers, they are usually chaired by attorney and writer Don Kates. The seminars often include an afternoon of target shooting at a nearby range. Except for the seminars themselves, the group does not sponsor academic research and does not support, financially or otherwise, the writing of articles. Besides its own seminars, A2A has also participated in conferences sponsored by the American Association of Law Schools.

A2A occasionally files *amicus curiae* briefs on legal cases dealing with firearm rights, such as the 1999 case *United States v. Emerson*. The lead author of that brief was Professor Nelson Lund of George Mason University School of Law. The brief was co-signed by over 100 scholars, as well as by former Attorney General Edwin Meese.

The organization sometimes takes out newspaper or magazine advertisements on Second Amendment issues. While A2A supporters agree that the Second Amendment protects an individual right, they have wide differences about the constitutionality or desirability of nonprohibitory forms of gun control.

A2A is headed by Joseph Olson, a tax and contracts professor at Hamline University School of Law in St. Paul. Olson has previously served on the National Rifle Association's Board of Directors.

Carol Oyster

See also Kates, Don B., Jr.; Second Amendment; Second Amendment Foundation; United States Supreme Court Decisions on Gun Control; *United States v. Emerson*

For Further Reading:

A2A brief to the U.S. Court of Appeals regarding *United States v. Emerson:* http://www.saf.org/pub/rkba/Legal/EMERSONacadsecd.htm.

Academics for the Second Amendment, Professor Joseph E. Olson, President, Box 131254, St. Paul, MN 55113.

Kaminer, Wendy. 1996. "Second Thoughts on the Second Amendment." *Atlantic* 277, 3 (March): 32–45; http://www.theatlantic.com/issues/96mar/guns/guns.htm.

Accidents, Gun

Unintentional firearm deaths, often called gun accidents in the popular press, are only a small fraction of gun suicides or gun homicides, but they still represent a substantial public health problem. Between 1965 and 1998, over 60,000 Americans died from accidental firearm shootings, more Americans than were killed in the Vietnam War. In the 1990s, an average of 1,200 Americans died each year from gun accidents, or over 3 people per day. Another 400 people each year were killed with guns in situations in which the shooter's intent was undetermined.

Primarily young people are dying. Over half of all unintentional firearm fatalities involve individuals under 25 years of age. Although relatively few adolescents own guns, the 15–19-year-old age group has by far the highest rate of unintentional firearm fatalities; second is the 20–24 age group, followed by the 10–14 age group. Children under age 15 in the United States have *nine* times the likelihood of dying from a fatal gun accident than similarly aged children in the rest of the developed world.

Not surprisingly, where there are more guns there are more accidental gun deaths. One study found that for every age group—men and women, blacks and whites—those living in states with more guns were far more likely to die of gun accidents. The differences were enormous. A typical resident from one of the four states with the most guns (Louisiana, Alabama, Mississippi, Arkansas) was *eight* times more likely to die in a gun accident than someone from one of the four states with the fewest guns (Hawaii, Massachusetts, Rhode Island, New Jersey). Although there were virtually the same number of children in both groups of states, between 1979 and 1997, 104 children aged 0–4 died from accidental gunshot wounds in the high-gun states, compared to only 6 in the low-gun states. Among 5–14 year olds, 565 children died from accidental gunshot wounds in the high-gun states compared to only 42 in the low-gun states. The fatal injury problem is, of course, only the tip of the iceberg. For every unintentional firearm fatality, there are approximately thirteen individuals injured seriously enough to be treated in hospital emergency rooms. In other words, about fifty people a day are shot unintentionally but do not die. This number does not include any of the more than eighty people each day who are treated in emergency rooms for BB/pellet gun wounds or the over fifty injured by firearms in other ways (e.g., powder burns, struck with a firearm, injured by the recoil of a firearm).

As with fatal firearm accidents, young males aged 15–24 are at highest risk for nonfatal accidental firearm injuries. Over one-third of unintended firearm wounds require hospitalization. The large majority of wounds are self-inflicted, and most are caused by handguns. Injuries generally occur during fairly routine gun handling—cleaning a gun, loading and unloading, hunting, target shooting.

Like death rates from most other types of unintentional injury, the U.S. unintentional firearm fatality rate has been falling over time. The accidental firearm fatality rate has also been falling in other developed nations; for example, while our rate fell 44 percent between 1970 and 1994, the Canadian rate fell 64 percent. The reduction in our accidental gun death rate is probably due to a rising standard of living (injury rates are lower among higher-income populations), improvements in emergency medicine (e.g., helicopter transport, prehospital advanced life support), and increased suburbanization (accidental gun fatality rates are over twice as high in rural than nonrural areas). Additionally, the percentage of households reporting at least one adult hunter fell from 37 percent in 1959 to 20 percent in 1993. The biggest drop in hunters has been among young people, who are at highest risk for accidental shootings.

Many policies can further reduce the number of accidental gun injuries. Currently, there are no federal safety standards for domestically manufactured firearms. New regulations might require that firearms do not go off when bumped or dropped and that guns have minimum trigger-pull standards to help prevent very young children from being able to pull a gun's trigger. A 1991 study of accidental firearm fatalities in ten cities by the U.S. General Accounting Office concluded that 8 percent of the unintentional firearm deaths could have been prevented by a child-proof safety device. An additional 23 percent of the deaths might have been prevented by load indicators that alert the user that the gun's chamber contains a bullet and by magazine disconnect devices (magazine safeties) that prevent a gun from firing once the ammunition magazine has been removed, even when a bullet remains in the chamber.

Prevention advocates argue that we have more safety standards for teddy bears and toy guns than we currently have for real guns. They find it difficult to justify why we do not child-proof guns when we know that child-resistant packaging of aspirin and prescription drugs has prevented hundreds of deaths among children. Since even the most basic camera indicates whether it is loaded, why can't the same determination be made by users of firearms? Such features could be readily available in almost all new handguns, at little cost.

David Hemenway

See also Firearm Injury Statistical Systems; Gun Violence as a Public Health Problem; Guns in the Home; Youth and Guns

For Further Reading:

Miller, Matthew, Deborah Azrael, and David Hemenway. 2001. "Firearm Availability and Unintentional Firearm Deaths." *Accident Analysis and Prevention* 33: 477–484.

Sinauer, Nancy, Joseph L. Annest, and James A. Mercy. 1996. "Unintentional, Nonfatal Firearm-related Injuries." *Journal of the American Medical Association* 275: 1740–1743.

Acquisition of Guns

Patterns of acquisition of guns have changed over the years. In the eighteenth century, civilian firearms were custom-made by gunsmiths and obtained directly from them. With the expansion of mass production in the nineteenth century, firearms were commonly ordered direct from the manufacturer. By the twentieth century, manufacturers had established marketing systems whereby the manufacturer sold to a wholesaler, or "jobber," who in turn sold to local dealers. An exception to this pattern was the mail-order house, which sold arms (mostly military surplus) and shipped them direct to its customers; mail-order houses vanished after the Gun Control Act of 1968, which generally prohibited interstate sales to nondealers.

A lively trade in used firearms, either person-to-person or through a dealer, exists in addition to these commercial outlets. Gun shows are especially popular, as many federal firearm regulations, e.g., background checks, are often sidestepped.

The total number of firearms acquired and owned by Americans can only be roughly approximated. Recent General Social Survey (2000) data reveal that about one-third of American households report owning a firearm, a figure that has fallen steadily over the past three decades (in the early 1970s, the figure was about one-half). However, studies of underreporting errors suggest the real figure may be considerably higher. Most households claiming to possess firearms report that they own several guns. The total number of firearms owned by Americans has been estimated at 235 million.

The acquisition of firearms by criminal elements has been the subject of a U.S. Bureau of Justice Statistics survey (2000, p. 10), which tallied responses from over 12,000 inmates who had used firearms while committing the criminal offense for which they were imprisoned. The inmates reported the following sources of the firearms they used: a friend or relative (35 percent), their drug dealer (15 percent), a licensed gun dealer (15 percent), a gun show or flea market (1.7 percent). Those groups suspicious of strong gun control efforts are especially quick to highlight these data, as they show that a large portion of the criminal population is able to sidestep regulations meant to keep guns out of their hands, while rarely resorting to gun shows.

David T. Hardy

See also Gun Control Act of 1968; Mail-Order Guns
For Further Reading:

Bureau of Justice Statistics. 2000. *Federal Firearms Offenders 1992–98.* Washington, DC: U.S. Department of Justice.
General Social Survey. 2000. "Do you happen to have in your home (or garage) any guns or revolvers?" If yes, "Is it a pistol, shotgun, rifle, or what?" Inter-University Consortium for Political and Social Research; http://www.icpsr.umich.edu/GSS/.
Kleck, Gary. 1997. *Targeting Guns: Firearms and Their Control.* Hawthorne, NY: Aldine de Gruyter.

African Americans and Gun Violence

Gun violence has disproportionately affected the African American community. For much of American history, firearms were used as a means to subjugate African Americans and deny them full economic and political rights. While overall crime rates, including gun-related crime, have declined among the general population during the past decade, gun violence has increased among African Americans. African American youths, especially young males, have been particularly affected by gun violence. In addition to higher rates of violent crime, suicide rates among the African American community have also increased. This has led community leaders to decry the self-destruction of younger generations and call for increased gun control measures.

In 1619, the first African Americans were brought as slaves to the region that would become the United States. Within the first few decades after the establishment of the initial colonies, laws were passed that denied African Americans, both slaves and freemen, access to firearms. In 1640, Virginia became the first colony to enact legislation that prohibited African Americans from carrying weapons in public. This was followed by legislation throughout the colonies that prohibited African Americans from even possessing firearms. The fear of a slave revolt was the main rationale for these laws. However, they also served to further disenfranchise and alienate African Americans from full participation in the socioeconomic mainstream.

Following the American Revolution, laws were passed at the national level to deny African Americans access to firearms. In 1792, Congress enacted the Uniform Militia Act. This legislation called upon every "able-bodied white citizen" to be a member of his respective state militia and possess a rifle, bayonet, and ammunition if called up for service. This effectively banned African Americans from service in the militias.

A suspect being searched by two armed police during the Watts race riots in Los Angeles, California, June, 1965. (Hulton / Archive by Getty Images)

Even as Northern states outlawed slavery, many continued bans or added new bans on gun ownership among the African American community. Concurrently, Southern states continued to restrict gun ownership. A law passed in 1825 even allowed the Florida militia and law enforcement to arbitrarily search African American homes for guns. As new slave states joined the Union, they also enacted bans on gun ownership by slaves. Texas passed such laws in 1840. When challenges to these laws were brought in state courts by free African Americans, they were uniformly rejected on the basis that African Americans, whether slave or free, were not considered to be citizens of the United States. Examples of these cases included the North Carolina case *State v. Newsom* in 1840 and Georgia's *Cooper v. Savannah* in 1848. In the infamous Supreme Court

case *Dred Scott v. Sandford* in 1857, the nation's highest court held that African Americans who were slaves or the descendants of slaves were not entitled to the rights of citizenship, including the right to carry or possess firearms.

Until the Civil War, guns were the primary tools used to keep African Americans in bondage. The inequity of power that resulted from the white monopoly on gun ownership meant that African Americans could not effectively resist slavery. The most significant slave revolt in American history, Nat Turner's Revolt in Virginia in 1831, demonstrated the inability of African Americans to overcome the well-armed state militia. Turner and his band of about sixty followers killed fifty-five white men, women, and children. However, within a week the revolt was put down by the militia. Turner and the majority of his supporters were either hanged or summarily executed. Whites throughout the state undertook reprisals against suspected sympathizers of Turner, killing dozens of innocent African Americans.

When the Civil War ended, various measures were passed in order to try to integrate African Americans into the broader society. However, in the immediate aftermath of the conflict, Southern states such as Mississippi, Louisiana, and Alabama again passed laws that forbade African Americans from owning or possessing weapons. Such laws were part of the "Black Codes," which were designed to restrict the newly won freedoms of African Americans. Congress attempted to overturn the Black Codes through the Civil Rights Act of 1866, which specifically stated that laws prohibiting African Americans from "having firearms" were illegal. The Civil Rights Act was bolstered by the ratification in 1868 of the Fourteenth Amendment. This amendment made African Americans full citizens of the United States and guaranteed all Americans equal protection of the law.

The passage of the Fourteenth Amendment led white supremacists to seek other means to prevent African Americans from having access to guns. From the end of the Civil War onward, African Americans faced terror and harassment from such groups as the Ku Klux Klan (KKK). These groups sought to intimidate African Americans into leaving the South or to keep them subservient by maintaining the prewar social order. If African Americans had been able to defend themselves, such intimidation would not have been successful. Therefore, state legislatures throughout the nation enacted legislation to deny access to weapons based on economic constraints. In 1870, Tennessee banned the sale of all handguns, except the expensive models (which most whites already owned as a result of their service in the Civil War). Other states, including Arkansas, Alabama, and Texas, passed similar laws. It is important to note that these laws affected new sales of weapons, so that the white population was able to retain the firearms it already possessed. African Americans suffered a further setback in their efforts to acquire firearms to protect themselves when the

Supreme Court ruled in *United States v. Cruikshank* (1875) that the national government did not have the power to stop the KKK from disarming African Americans. Instead, African Americans had to rely on state and local law enforcement to protect them. These institutions were often dominated by white supremacists or were unwilling to act for fear of alienating themselves from the white population.

Throughout the early period of the twentieth century, guns continued to be concentrated in the hands of white citizens and African Americans continued to face terror and oppression. The revival of the KKK in 1915 led to a renewed wave of lynchings and racially motivated killings in the South and Midwest. Such violence continued through the modern civil rights movement of the 1950s and 1960s. Efforts to empower African Americans in the South were met with resistance, often armed resistance, and those working to expand civil rights were frequently targeted for violence. The 1964 slaying of three civil rights workers in Mississippi exemplified this trend.

Frustration over continued discrimination and economic disparities sparked a series of race riots in the mid-1960s. For instance, the 1965 Watts riot in Los Angeles left thirty-four dead while riots in Newark, New Jersey, in 1967 killed twenty-six, and similar riots in Detroit killed at least forty. These dramatic periods of violence occurred simultaneously with a general rise in violent crime rates. From the end of World War II onward, the availability of inexpensive handguns, often called Saturday Night Specials, was partially responsible for this upswing in violence. Public reaction to the growth in crime rates and the 1968 assassinations of both Martin Luther King, Jr., and Robert F. Kennedy prompted Congress to pass the Gun Control Act of 1968. This was followed by a number of state Saturday Night Special laws that banned certain types of inexpensive handguns.

Violent gun crime in the United States peaked in the 1970s. However, while overall crime rates have declined since then, gun violence continued to increase in the African American community. The dramatic increase in violent crime as a result of the proliferation of certain illicit drugs, including crack cocaine, has been worsened by a new wave of inexpensive handguns. Since 1993, half of all new firearms have been handguns, and since 1973, more than 40 million new handguns have become available in the United States.

From 1985 through 1992, homicide rates and arrest rates for homicide among African American males doubled. Concurrently, homicide rates among the general population decreased by 27 percent. African Americans are three times as likely to be victims of handgun violence as are whites. In addition, rates of gun violence among African American youth increased by 300 percent and African American youth are four times as likely as their white counterparts to be victims of gun violence. These factors have partially contributed to a fourfold increase in the nation's prison population since 1980 (to a total of 1.3 million in 2001). By the 1990s, almost one-quarter of African American males between the ages of 18 and 30 were either in prison or had served time in prison. Although African Americans comprise about 12 percent of the population, almost 50 percent of homicide victims are African American. Significantly, the majority of gun violence that is now directed toward African Americans is perpetuated by African Americans. By 2000, almost 90 percent of gun violence suffered by African Americans was committed by other African Americans.

Tom Lansford

See also Black Codes; Black Panthers; Crime and Gun Use; Ku Klux Klan; NAACP and Gun Control; Poverty and Gun Violence; Vigilantism; Youth and Guns

For Further Reading:

Alexander, Rudolph, Jr., ed. 2000. *Race and Justice.* Huntington, NY: Nova Science Publishers.

Carter, Gregg Lee. 1997. *The Gun Control Movement.* New York: Twayne.

Kedia, P. Ray, ed. 1994. *Black on Black Crime: Facing Facts, Challenging Fictions.* Bristol, IN: Wyndham Hall Press.

Ogletree, Charles, Jr. 1995. *Beyond the Rodney King Story: An Investigation of Police Conduct in Minority Communities.* Boston: Northeastern University Press.

Sulton, Anne T., ed. 1994. *African-American Perspectives on Crime Causation, Criminal Justice Administration, and Crime Prevention.* Englewood, CO: Sulton Books.

Tolnay, Stewart E., and E. M. Beck. 1995. *A Festival of Violence: An Analysis of Southern Lynchings, 1882–1930.* Urbana: University of Illinois Press.

AK-47

The AK-47 is one of the most widely used assault rifles in the world. Millions of this model and its close cousins (such as the AKM, a modernized version of the AK-47 first produced in 1959, and the Norinco Type 56, a Chinese copy) were used as standard infantry weapons in the Soviet Union, the former Warsaw Pact countries, China, and others, starting in the late 1940s. The Israeli Galil and Finnish Valmet assault rifles use the same basic action. The AK-47 was replaced in Soviet service with the very similar AKM, which was subsequently replaced with the similar but smaller-caliber AK-74. The name AK-47 is short for "Avtomat Kalashnikova obrazets 1947g," which is Russian for "Automatic Kalashnikov model 1947."

The AK-47 is a selective fire (capable of semiautomatic or automatic fire at the flip of a switch), gas-operated assault rifle that feeds 7.62×39mm ammunition from a detachable 30-round magazine and has an effective range of about 300 meters. It weighs nearly 10 pounds, is about 34 inches long, and is generally regarded as robust and reliable.

AK-47s, like all automatic weapons, are subject to rigorous control in the United States. This has been the case since the passage of the National Firearms Act of 1934. Very few AK-47s are in civilian hands. However, thousands of semiautomatic derivatives of the AK-47 have been sold in the United States, including the Chinese Norinco Type 56S. Although the semiautomatic versions meet the definition of an "assault *weapon*" under U.S. and state statutes, they are not "assault *rifles*" per se—since an assault rifle is a selective-fire automatic rifle (Defense Intelligence Agency, 1988), a semiautomatic rifle cannot be an assault rifle. Conversely, an AK-47 assault rifle is not an "assault weapon" as the term is defined in the United States Code because an "assault weapon" is semiautomatic while an AK-47 is automatic.

A customer examines an AK-47 at a gun shop. (Nik Wheeler/Corbis)

Although semiautomatic derivatives of the AK-47 have a reputation for being particularly dangerous or lethal, this reputation is not entirely accurate. Semiautomatic versions of the AK-47 have a shorter range and less penetration and wound-causing potential than many ordinary center-fire hunting rifles. (The AK-47's intermediate-power 7.62mm cartridge produces wounds less serious than common deer-hunting cartridges such as the .308 Winchester or .30-06, especially when military-type full metal jacket bullets are used.) Their rate of fire is similar to that of other semiautomatic rifles and their rate of accurate, aimed fire is not dramatically higher than that of bolt-action rifles (Kopel, 1994).

In 1989, Patrick Purdy used a Norinco Type 56S, which looks like an AK-47 but is semiautomatic, in his infamous attack on an elementary school playground in Stockton, California. He killed five people and wounded thirty. As is not unusual in notorious mass shooting cases, the Stockton murders galvanized gun control efforts. California responded by passing the Roberti-Roos Assault Weapon Control Act of

1989, and President George Bush banned the importation of several kinds of semiautomatic weapons that same year, including the Norinco Type 56S.

Matthew DeBell

See also Assault Weapons; Assault Weapons Ban of 1994; National Firearms Act of 1934; Stockton, California Massacre

For Further Reading:

Defense Intelligence Agency. 1988. *Small Arms Identification and Operation Guide—Eurasian and Communist Countries.* Washington, DC: Government Printing Office.

Ezell, Edward. 1986. *The AK-47 Story.* Harrisburg, PA: Stackpole Books.

Kopel, David B. 1994. "Rational Basis Analysis of 'Assault Weapon' Prohibition." *Journal of Contemporary Law* 20: 381–417.

Alcohol and Gun Violence

Alcohol and gun violence have little to do with each other per se. Less than 4 percent of violent crimes involving alcohol also involve firearms (Bureau of Justice Statistics, 1998). But alcohol, drugs, and firearms are designated "criminogenic commodities" because they are each so frequently involved in crime, especially violent crime (Moore, 1983).

Since the failure of Prohibition, its proponents' identities and concerns have been obscured by decades of uncomprehending ridicule. Its proponents were truly the best and the brightest of three generations of humane and progressive Americans: William Lloyd Garrison, Horace Mann, Frederick Douglass, Susan B. Anthony, the Beechers (Harriet, Lyman, and Henry), Horace Greeley, Jane Addams, and William Jennings Bryan. Far from being narrowly religious, they were motivated by the involvement of alcohol in a vast amount of violent criminal behavior, including sex crimes and all varieties of homicide, particularly domestic homicide. "The Bottle," a late nineteenth-century cartoon by D. W. Moody, typifies their attitudes: It shows a husband being dragged off by the police in front of his children, who also witnessed the father beating their mother to death with the liquor bottle that now lies broken next to her head. The caption reads, "The husband in a state of furious drunkenness, kills his wife with the instrument of all their misery."

Indeed, the arguments for Prohibition closely parallel modern arguments for banning handguns. Comparatively, 28.7 percent of violent crimes involve firearms (primarily handguns) while roughly 35–40 percent of violent crimes are committed by offenders who were drinking. Handguns are the weapons used in 50–55 percent of murders, while nationally at least 37–44 percent of murderers were drinking (Bureau of Justice Statistics, 1998). Local and regional studies show from 19 up to 86 percent of offenders have been drinking when the murder was committed (Kates, 1984, pp. 143–144). Additionally, 35–72 percent of robbers were drinking, as were 33–50 percent of rapists and child molesters (Kates, 1984; Bureau of Justice Statistics, 1998). Roughly 25 percent of robbers use firearms (mostly handguns), as do 4 percent of rapists (Kleck, 1997, p. 217).

Beyond the toll of intentional crime is that from liquor-induced accidents. Drunk drivers kill over 13,400 people annually. There are roughly 850 accidental gun deaths each year; though there are no figures on how many of these are alcohol-related, the kinds of people who cause such accidents tend to have records of alcohol and drug abuse. Adding in alcohol-related illnesses, alcohol is involved in perhaps 10 percent of all American deaths annually, while handguns are involved in 1 percent or less.

At the same time, it should be emphasized that these problems are not associated with either drinking or gun ownership by ordinary people. If the incidence of alcohol-related criminal violence seems very large viewed on its own, it is minuscule compared to the vast number of Americans (roughly half of all adults) who drink without causing any harm. Alcohol-related crimes and accidents are usually linked to heavy drinkers. Even so, the great majority of heavy drinkers do not harm anyone.

By the same token, the incidence of gun violence (27.8 percent of all serious violent crime) is infinitesimal if viewed in the context of 250 million firearms contained in 33 percent of American households. Serious violent crime is not "caused" by the possession of alcohol or guns by normal people. Rather, violent crimes are committed by abnormal individuals as part of a pathology of highly aberrant behavior that includes regularly inebriating themselves (with alcohol or narcotics, or both) and inflicting harm on others with firearms or other weapons.

Another area in which firearms may be compared to alcohol is the ease with which restrictions, or total prohibition, of each are enforceable. Prohibiting or severely restricting guns among the general populace raises more or less the same enforceability problems as did alcohol prohibition—only more so. The single most important difference is that guns are not consumed by their use. Temperance advocates recognized that many drinkers might defy Prohibition, but nevertheless counted on the fact that continued drinking would expose drinkers to the risks of detection as they made repeated purchases of alcohol. But for the owners of the nation's 250 million guns, defying a ban would require merely doing nothing, i.e., the low-visibility, low-risk failure to turn in their guns. (Of course, for the gun to continue to be useful for either criminal activity or for self-defense, the owner would need to procure fresh ammunition at least once every 20–40 years.)

Motivations for gun owners to violate a ban in many ways parallel the motivations that impelled even otherwise law-abiding drinkers to violate Prohibition. One motivation for violation in each case is the feeling by responsible drinkers/gun owners that they are being blamed, and their liberty circumscribed, for the misbehavior of a tiny minority of highly aberrant drinkers/gun owners whom the responsible majority themselves despise and sharply differentiate from themselves. The outrage and anger this generates among the responsible majority inclines them to regard the ban as egregiously unjust. In the case of gun owners, anger and outrage are fueled by the deep belief (whether it is correct or not is irrelevant) that the ban is unconstitutional because the right to bear arms is guaranteed in the Bill of Rights. This argument was not available to drinkers because Prohibition was unquestionably legally valid, having been enacted by constitutional amendment.

Also crucially important is the immediate impetus for defying the law. Obviously, alcoholics during Prohibition experienced severe pressure to continue drinking, regardless of the law. For the great majority of drinkers, i.e., social drinkers, the pressure to continue drinking was far less. In contrast, those who believe a gun is a vital tool for defending themselves and their families clearly have a greater impetus for violating a gun ban.

None of this should be misunderstood as meaning that defiance of a firearms-confiscation measure would be universal. After all, despite the mythology that grew up after its repeal, many Americans did stop drinking in response to Prohibition. Unfortunately, in gun prohibition as in alcohol prohibition the result is likely to be less than desirable: The people most likely to comply are the responsible law-abiding people whose drinking or gun ownership represents no problem, while those most likely to resist are the people whom it is most desirable to affect.

Don B. Kates

See also Availability of Guns, Effects on Crime; Average-Joe Thesis

For Further Reading:
Bureau of Justice Statistics. 1998a. *Alcohol and Crime: An Analysis of National Data on the Prevalence of Alcohol Involvement in Crime.* Washington, DC: U.S. Department of Justice.
———. 1998b. *Sourcebook of Criminal Justice Statistics—1997.* Washington, DC: U.S. Department of Justice.
Kates, Don B. 1989. "Handgun Banning in Light of the Prohibition Experience." Pp. 139–165 in *Firearms and Violence: Issues of Public Policy,* ed. Don B. Kates. Cambridge, MA: Ballinger.
Kleck, Gary. 1997. *Targeting Guns: Firearms and Their Control.* Hawthorne, NY: Aldine de Gruyer.
Moore, Mark H. 1983. "Controlling Criminogenic Commodities: Drugs, Guns and Alcohol." Pp. 125–144 in *Crime and Public Policy,* ed. James Q. Wilson. San Francisco: Institute for Contemporary Studies.

American Academy of Pediatrics (AAP)

The American Academy of Pediatrics (AAP) is a nationwide medical association dedicated to the health of all children. The AAP takes one of the strongest firearm policy positions in the medical community, calling for the banning of handguns, assault weapons, and deadly air guns. The AAP's activities include supporting model gun control legislation, educating pediatricians and lay people about the dangers of firearms for children, and providing resources related to firearm injuries and violence.

Founded in 1930 by 35 pediatricians, the AAP today has 55,000 members, including 34,000 board-certified Fellows. The AAP is "committed to the attainment of optimal physical, mental, and social health and well-being for all infants, children, adolescents, and young adults." AAP programs in relation to firearms reflect that commitment and its position that gun violence is a public health issue. Through its "Periodic Survey of Fellows," the AAP gets feedback from members. The latest survey on guns and children indicates widespread agreement with AAP positions on gun control and on pediatricians educating parents about firearm safety.

In an updated policy statement in 2000, the AAP examined data on firearm-related deaths and injuries over the past decade. Although acknowledging slight decreases in gun violence in recent years, the AAP noted that 4,223 firearm-related deaths of children and adolescents occurred in 1997; 85 percent of all homicides and 63 percent of all suicides for adolescents aged 15–19 were committed with a firearm; 306 adolescents died from unintentional gun-related injuries in 1997; and the rates of firearm-related deaths for the United States are the highest among industrialized countries. In fact, the overall rate of firearm-related deaths for U.S. children under 15 is nearly twelve times greater than that for twenty-five other industrialized countries, and the rate of firearm-related homicide is nearly sixteen times higher than that in all the other countries combined.

Reaffirming its long-standing position that children are safest when there are no guns in their environment, the AAP policy statement renewed its support for banning handguns, semiautomatic assault weapons, and dangerous air guns. The policy states, "Because firearm-related injury to children is associated with death and severe morbidity and is a significant public health problem, child health care professionals can and should provide effective leadership in efforts to stem this epidemic." In supporting such bans, the AAP suggests that the Second Amendment does not grant individuals the right to bear arms.

Recommendations for firearm safety to parents stress that the safest thing is not to have a gun in the home, especially a handgun. For homes in which there are guns, the AAP emphasizes the importance of securely locking guns and ammunition in separate, secure places. The AAP also recommends ensuring that children do not have access to keys to the locations of guns and ammunition, asking police for advice on safe storage and gun locks, and talking with children about the risk of gun injury outside of the home. The AAP also strongly urges parents to work at making their homes safe, nonviolent places, discouraging overt displays of hostility between parents and among siblings.

The AAP has also expressed concern with the level of violence depicted in mass media, especially television. Reflecting this concern, the AAP made eleven recommendations for pediatricians in regard to media violence. These include recommending that pediatricians urge the entertainment industry to be more sensitive to media violence issues, contact local stations regarding violent programming, urge parents to monitor and limit their children's television viewing, and become better educated about media violence. In regard to parents, the AAP recommends limiting children's television watching to one to two hours a day, talking to children about television violence, and discussing with children nonviolent ways of resolving disagreements and solving problems.

The AAP provides additional resources on firearms, including a Speaker's Kit on "Preventing Firearm Injury: Protecting Our Children"; the brochure "Keep Your Family Safe from Firearm Injury" for distribution by pediatricians; the "Firearm Injury Prevention Resource Guide," a directory of groups working to prevent firearm injuries; and the "Steps to Prevent (STOP) Firearm Injury Kit," developed jointly with the Center to Prevent Handgun Violence and available to health care professionals. Many of these resources are available on the AAP website, although the Academy recently moved the public information section of its site to Medem.com, a website cosponsored by the AAP in cooperation with other national medical societies.

The AAP has supported various pieces of legislation aimed at preventing or reducing firearm injuries to children. These include the Children's Gun Violence Prevention Act of 1998, the Children Firearm Access Prevention Act, and a model bill, the Protection of Children from Handguns Act. The AAP also supported the Student Pledge Against Gun Violence and First Monday 2001, which focused on gun issues. The AAP is a member of the Coalition to Stop Gun Violence (CSGV).

Walter F. Carroll

See also Accidents, Gun; Assault Weapons Ban of 1994; Brady Handgun Violence Prevention Act (Brady Bill); Child Access Prevention (CAP) Laws; Coalition to Stop Gun Violence; HELP Network; Media Violence; Million Mom March; Suicides, Guns and; Trigger Locks; Youth Gun Control Legislation; Youth and Guns

For Further Reading:
American Academy of Pediatrics.
  http://www.aap.org.

———. 2000. "Firearm-Related Injuries Affecting
the Pediatric Population." *Pediatrics* 105 (April):
888–895.

———. 2001. "The New Morbidity Revisited: A
Renewed Commitment to the Psychosocial
Aspects of Pediatric Care." *Pediatrics* 108
(November): 1227–1230.

Medem, Inc. http://www.medem.com.

American Bar Association (ABA)

The American Bar Association (ABA), the national professional association for lawyers, consistently advocates the enactment of stronger gun control measures. The ABA's policymaking group, the House of Delegates, has drafted a number of positions in support of restricting the use and sale of guns. In addition to taking policy positions on gun control, the ABA has also been active in presenting its pro–gun control stances to congressional committees considering firearm-regulation bills. These actions have been somewhat controversial among some members of Congress. Some conservative lawmakers have expressed concern that the ABA has no special expertise in the issue of gun control and that it should not advocate positions on an issue divided along ideological lines. However, the ABA has remained committed to reducing gun violence in society through careful regulation of firearms. In fact, the ABA House of Delegates has deemed gun control to be one of its critical legislative priority issues.

After the assassination of President John F. Kennedy in 1963, the ABA responded to the tragedy by forming a task force to examine the regulation of firearms. As a result, the House of Delegates, in 1965, advocated requiring the licensing of firearm dealers; prohibiting sales to felons, mental incompetents, and minors; and controlling importation of firearms. In subsequent years, the House of Delegates continued to support a number of bills and proposals aimed at reducing gun violence in society by regulating the use and sale of guns.

In 1973, the House of Delegates supported legislation limiting the sale and possession of inexpensive imported handguns. In 1975, the ABA supported amending the Gun Control Act of 1968 to tighten up the licensing requirements of firearm dealers and to require background checks and waiting periods prior to firearm purchases. In 1983, the group opposed efforts to repeal parts of the Gun Control Act of 1968. In 1993, ABA policy supported legislation to regulate assault weapons. In 1994, the ABA endorsed providing the federal government authority to regulate firearms as consumer products, adopting required safety features such as gun locks and load indicators, and requiring gun owners to obtain and maintain a current handgun license. In 1996, the ABA supported amending the Gun Control Act of 1968 to include a private cause of action for persons suffering injury or damage as a result of a violation of gun control laws. And in 1998, they backed a program to address gun violence by youths at schools that included peer mediation programs, firearm education programs, and enforcement and enactment of gun laws emphasizing prevention, adult responsibility, and safety.

The ABA believes gun control provisions are consistent with a proper legal interpretation of the Second Amendment. In 1998, the chairperson of the ABA's Coordinating Committee on Gun Violence submitted to the Senate Subcommittee on the Constitution, Federalism, and Property Rights a statement of the ABA's views on issues arising under the Second Amendment. In it, the group wrote that federal and state court decisions have been consistent in the view that the Second Amendment gives all levels of government broad authority to limit private access to firearms. The statement closed by urging Congress to enact appropriate gun control measures to reduce tragic gun-related deaths and injuries in America, and emphasizing that the Second Amendment is not a valid reason for failing to adopt appropriate gun control measures.

However, the ABA's focus on reducing violent crime in society reaches beyond the advocacy gun control positions in Congress. For example, in 1994, the group committed to a joint effort with colleagues in the public health, law enforcement, and religious communities to reduce gun violence. The ABA held a "Summit on Crime and Violence" where leading members of the bar, representatives of other organizations, and government officials planned strategies on the war against crime and violence.

Keith Rollin Eakins

See also Assault Weapons Ban of 1994; Brady Handgun Violence Prevention Act (Brady Bill); Firearms Owners' Protection Act of 1986; Gun Control Act of 1968; Interest Groups and Gun Legislation; National Firearms Act of 1934; Second Amendment; United States Congress and Gun Legislation

For Further Reading:

American Bar Association. 2001a. "American Bar Association 2001 Legislative and Governmental Priorities: Federal Gun Control." ABA Network. http://www.abanet.org/poladv/priorities/guns.html.

———. 2001b. "American Bar Association Coordinating Committee on Gun Violence." ABA Network. http://www.abanet.org/gunviol/home.html.

———. 2001c. "Legislative and Governmental Advocacy: Letters and Testimony." ABA Network. http://www.abanet.org/poladv/letters.html.

Cottrol, Robert J., ed. 1994. *Gun Control and the Constitution: Sources and Explanations on the Second Amendment.* New York: Garland.

McMillion, Rhonda. 2000. "Targeting Gun Control Again." *ABA Journal* 86 (March): 104.

O'Connor, Karen, and Graham Barron. 1998. "Madison's Mistake? Judicial Construction of the Second Amendment." Pp. 74–87 in *The Changing Politics of Gun Control,* ed. John M. Bruce and Clyde Wilcox. Lanham, MD: Rowman & Littlefield.

Patterson, Samuel C., and Keith R. Eakins. 1998. "Congress and Gun Control." Pp. 45–73 in *The Changing Politics of Gun Control,* ed. John M. Bruce and Clyde Wilcox. Lanham, MD: Rowman & Littlefield.

Podgers, James. 1994. "Tackling Crime in the Streets." *ABA Journal* 80 (March): 104.

Spitzer, Robert J. 1995. *The Politics of Gun Control.* Chatham, NJ: Chatham House.

American Civil Liberties Union (ACLU)

Founded in 1920, the American Civil Liberties Union (ACLU) describes its mission as "to fight civil liberties violations wherever and whenever they occur" (American Civil Liberties Union, 1999). Its vigilance in litigating First Amendment issues of free speech and separation of church and state is well known. On the question of opposing gun control on Second Amendment grounds, however, the ACLU officially considers itself to be neutral. Even so, the organization has joined in recent years in ad hoc political coalitions with progun organizations on collateral issues, especially those involving questions of due process of law.

The ACLU was formed during a period when fundamental personal freedoms were under serious government attack. For example, in its first year it joined battle with U.S. Attorney General A. Mitchell Palmer over the rights of union and antiwar activists to organize, hold meetings, and distribute materials. In 1925 it arranged the services of renowned attorney Clarence Darrow to defend biology teacher John T. Scopes, charged for teaching evolution, in the famous criminal trial in Tennessee. The ACLU also was instrumental in overturning a U.S. Customs Service ban on importing James Joyce's novel *Ulysses,* fought the unconstitutional 1942 internment of Japanese Americans, supported the civil rights movement, opposes attempts to criminalize flag-burning, and litigates against racism, sexism, homophobia, religious intolerance, and censorship of unpopular speech.

A national board of directors in New York sets ACLU policy. The policy is implemented through a network of autonomous affiliate offices in the fifty states, staffed by about sixty staff lawyers and supplemented by the work of volunteer attorneys. ACLU lawyers take on about 6,000 cases each year. The organization receives no government funding.

The ACLU policy on gun control is a sore point with progun activists. It holds that "the individual's right to bear arms applies only to the preservation of efficiency of a well-regulated militia. Except for lawful police and military purposes, the possession of weapons by individuals is not constitutionally protected. Therefore, there is no constitutional impediment to the regulation of firearms" (ACLU Policy #47, quoted in American Civil Liberties Union, 2001b). To the ACLU, the question is not whether to restrict gun ownership, but how much to restrict, a question it concludes is for Congress to decide.

On the other hand, local affiliates of the ACLU occasionally involve themselves in proposed restrictions on firearm ownership when collateral civil liberties issues are implicated. For example, local affiliates opposed as excessive and ineffective the imposition of enhanced additional prison terms for use of guns in crimes in California as well as legislation in Connecticut authorizing law enforcement officials to confiscate the firearms of anyone found to be an immediate danger to himself and others.

At the national level, the ACLU joined forces in the 1990s with the militant Gun Owners of America (GOA), a group that relentlessly criticizes the National Rifle Association for being too soft. Headed by Larry Pratt, often credited with being one of the founders of the "militia" movement, the GOA forged a coalition with the ACLU and other civil libertarian groups to fight legislation perceived as infringing on other civil rights. Thus, for example, although the GOA and the ACLU opposed different parts of an omnibus antiterrorism bill, they joined forces and were thus able to lobby effectively conservative and liberal members of Congress whom one or the other would have had difficulty otherwise engaging.

Thomas Diaz

See also Gun Owners of America
For Further Reading:

American Civil Liberties Union. 1999. *ACLU Position Paper: The American Civil Liberties Union.* New York.
———. 2001a. "California Packs Toughest Gun-Sentencing Law," news release dated January 6, 1998, downloaded from ACLU Internet website, http://www.aclu.org, May 23.
———. 2001b. "Gun Control," downloaded from ACLU Internet Library, http://www.aclu.org/library/aaguns.html, May 23.
Diaz, Tom. 1999. *Making a Killing: The Business of Guns in America.* New York: New Press.
Mehren, Elizabeth, "Knocking Guns from the Hands of Potential Killers," *Los Angeles Times* (October 2, 1999), A1.

American Jewish Congress (AJC)

The American Jewish Congress (AJC) is a lobbying, legal, and cultural organization. In recent years, the AJC has become a strong proponent of restrictive gun laws.

World War I had a profound effect on Jewish life in the United States. The war was accompanied by a marked awakening of Jewish consciousness among those who had earlier stood aloof from their Jewish heritage. As the United States prepared to enter the war, a group of American Jews believed that a united American Jewish voice could best protect their convictions, desires, and dreams. This resulted in a preliminary conference held in Philadelphia in 1916. The first American Jewish Congress was convened in Philadelphia's Metropolitan Opera House in December 1918. In 1920, Rabbi Stephen Wise was charged with the task of transforming the succession of haphazardly planned Jewish gatherings into a permanent organization intended to safeguard Jews everywhere—in the United States, overseas, and especially in what was then the British colony of Palestine. After the threat of Nazi Germany had passed with the end of World War II, the AJC broadened its scope of activism to include extensive work on civil rights for blacks and many other issues.

The AJC has a membership of 50,000. Its headquarters are in New York and it maintains an Israeli office in Jerusalem. The AJC holds a convention every two years, at which time it sets the organization's agenda and elects a president who serves a two-year term. Policy is formulated in the interim by the AJC's Governing Council and the Executive Committee. The American Jewish Congress is sometimes confused with a separate group, the American Jewish Committee, which shares the same acronym.

The centerpiece of the AJC's antigun work is a petition campaign called "Stop the Guns: Protect our Kids!" The petitions demand that the U.S. Congress enact legislation to require that (1) all gun buyers pass a government test in order to receive a license; (2) all guns be registered with the government; (3) prospective gun buyers provide fingerprints and a photograph in order to receive a license; (4) firearm manufacturers be "required to install safety devices to prevent accidental and inadvertent firing"; and (5) licensing and registration rules that currently apply to retail firearm dealers be applied to all firearm transfers. The petition campaign is supported by a variety of gun prohibition and gun control organizations, and the AJC coordinates its work with other antigun lobbies and works in support of a wide variety of other proposed gun laws.

Opinion polls typically show that Jews are more supportive of gun control than are Gentiles, but some American Jews do not share the AJC's views on firearm ownership. For example, Jews for the Preservation of Firearms Ownership (JPFO) calls gun control "victim disarmament" and charges that the AJC's antigun activism undermines traditional Jewish values. The JPFO believes that "Jews, like everyone else, have a duty to protect and defend themselves and their families against violence." According to the JPFO, the AJC ignores both Jewish morality and the importance of armed self-defense, and from a historical perspective, that combination has been lethal for Jews.

Paul Gallant and Joanne Eisen

See also Jews for the Preservation of Firearms Ownership

For Further Information:

American Jewish Congress: 15 East 84th Street, New York, NY 10028; 212-879-4500; http://ajcongress.org.

Jews for the Preservation of Firearms Ownership: P.O. Box 270143, Hartford, WI 53027; 262-673-9745; http://www.jpfo.org.

American Medical Association (AMA)

The American Medical Association (AMA) is an organization of physicians whose goal is "to promote the art and science of medicine and the betterment of public health." The AMA believes that private firearm ownership is a public health menace and has consistently advocated strong gun control provisions in order to reduce citizen access to firearms.

The AMA was founded in 1847 by Nathan Davis at the Academy of Natural Sciences in Philadelphia. In 1999, it had a combined membership of 300,000 medical students and physicians. The AMA House of Delegates meets twice yearly to formulate AMA policy.

According to the AMA, the ownership and use of firearms, especially handguns, pose serious threats to public health. The AMA believes that handguns are one of the main causes of intentional and unintentional injuries and death in the United States.

In 1992, the AMA's Council on Scientific Affairs promulgated a report and position paper on assault weapons (guns with a military appearance), and declared them to be a public health hazard in the United States. It recommended legislation to restrict the sale and private ownership of such firearms.

Among the critics of the AMA report was Dr. Edgar A. Suter. In 1994 Suter said, "The AMA Council on Scientific Affairs did not conduct a rigorous scientific evaluation before supporting a ban on assault weapons. The Council appears to have unquestioningly accepted common misperceptions and even partisan misrepresentations regarding the nature and uses of assault weapons.... While an assault weapon ban may have appeared to the Council to be a simple solution to America's exaggerated 'epidemic' of violence, a scholarly review of the literature finds no reliable data to support such a ban. Unfortunately the Council's faulty call for prohibition may distract legislators and the public from addressing effective methods of controlling violence" (1994b).

The AMA encourages its members to use regular checkups as an opportunity to inquire from patients whether firearms are present in their household, to educate patients about the dangers of firearms, to advise patients to educate their children and neighbors about the dangers of firearms, and to remind patients to obtain firearm safety locks, lock up all firearms, and store ammunition separately.

The AMA supports numerous legislative initiatives dealing with firearms. These include: waiting periods and background checks for all handgun purchases; the requirement that manufacturers incorporate a variety of features in all firearms, including visible loaded-gun indicators, trigger locks, and an increased minimum force needed to activate a trigger; increased licensing fees for firearm dealers; increased federal and state surtaxes on manufacturers, dealers, and purchasers of handguns and semiautomatic firearms, as well as on the ammunition such firearm use, with the revenue allocated for health and law enforcement activities related to the prevention and control of violence in the United States; mandatory destruction of any firearms obtained in gun-surrender programs; a ban on certain types of bullets; and banning the possession and use of firearms and ammunition by unsupervised youths under the age of 18.

In his inauguration address delivered at its annual meeting on June 20, 2001, incoming president Richard F. Corlin renewed the AMA's push for more restrictive firearm laws. In a speech devoted entirely to the issue of firearm-related violence, Corlin declared that "gun violence—both self-inflicted and against others—is now a serious public health crisis," one that is "a uniquely American epidemic." According to Corlin, "The very language of the Second Amendment refutes any argument that it was intended to guarantee every citizen an unfettered right to any kind of weapon.... [W]e don't regulate guns in America. We do regulate other dangerous products like cars and prescription drugs and tobacco and alcohol.... In fact, no other consumer industry in the United States—not even the tobacco industry—has been allowed to so totally evade accountability for the harm their products cause to human beings. Just the gun industry."

Corlin called for re-funding of firearm research by the Centers for Disease Control and Prevention (CDC) and its National Center for Injury Prevention and Control, including the establishment of a National Violent Death Reporting System for both fatal and nonfatal gun injuries. (CDC funding for firearm research was terminated by Congress in 1996. While Corlin blamed the loss of funding on "heavy lobbying by the antigun control groups," critics had charged that the CDC's research on firearms was biased, promoted an antigun agenda, and failed to address any of the benefits accruing to private firearm ownership, such as self-defense. The outcome of the congressional action was a prohibition on public funding by the CDC "to advocate or promote gun control.")

Some physician groups have been highly critical of the AMA and its position on private firearm ownership. Doctors for Responsible Gun Ownership (DRGO), founded in 1994, believes that social activists in the medical and public health fields (including the AMA) have used their authority to misrepresent gun ownership as a "disease." According to DRGO, organized medical groups like the AMA use discredited advocacy research and poor medical scholarship to justify their political stand against firearms and gun owners. Furthermore, they ignore legitimate criminological research because it generally proves that good citizens use guns wisely.

DRGO has criticized the AMA's practice of encouraging doctors to use their professional authority and patient trust as a means of advancing a political agenda for gun control. A doctor's responsibility is to place the patient's needs above all else. However, a physician reverses this priority when, because of passionate political beliefs, he tries to influence a patient about guns and firearm ownership. In doing so, that doctor crosses the line from healer to political activist. DRGO maintains that this places such intervention in the area of unethical physician conduct called "boundary violations." The Association of American Physicians and Surgeons (AAPS) is another group that argues that the AMA's position on firearms is biased and politicized.

The AMA's best-known publication is the *Journal of the American Medical Association* (*JAMA*), published weekly. While *JAMA* explicitly states that its editorials do not reflect the views of the AMA, they nevertheless often mirror its philosophy. Each year, *JAMA* publishes a number of "theme" issues. One of these is usually on the subject of violence. The editorials accompanying these issues articulate the empathy, anguish, and frustration physicians face in the aftermath of violence, and their desire to prevent and eliminate violence.

However, while many of *JAMA*'s violence "theme" issues have contained articles dealing with guns and firearm-related violence, none of them have addressed the positive elements of firearm ownership (e.g., self-defense) that may prevent violence.

Although the vast majority of *JAMA* articles on firearms have supported gun control, a notable exception was an article in 2000 by Jens Ludwig and Philip Cook, which found that the Brady Bill had no significant effect on homicide rates or on overall suicide rates. A *JAMA* editorial that accompanied the study by Ludwig and Cook argued that the flaw in the Brady Bill was that its provisions applied only to sales by licensed gun dealers, and not to informal transactions among family, friends, or other acquaintances.

Paul Gallant and Joanne Eisen

See also Association of American Physicians and Surgeons; Doctors for Responsible Gun Ownership
For Further Reading:
American Medical Association. http://www.ama-assn.org.
Association of American Physicians and Surgeons. http://www.aapsonline.org.
Cook, Philip J., Bruce A. Lawrence, and Jens Ludwig. 1999. "The Medical Costs of Gunshot Injuries in the United States." *Journal of the American Medical Association* 282, 5 (August 4): 447–454.
Council on Scientific Affairs. 1992. "Assault Weapons as a Public Health Hazard in the United States." *Journal of the American Medical Association* 267, 22 (June 10): 3067–3070.
Doctors for Responsible Gun Ownership. http://www.claremont.org/1_drgo.cfm.
Faria, Miguel A., Jr. 2001. "Public Health and Gun Control—A Review." *Medical Sentinel* 6, 1: 11–18.
Ludwig, Jens, and Philip J. Cook. 2000. "Homicide and Suicide Rates Associated with Implementation of the Brady Handgun Violence Prevention Act." *Journal of the American Medical Association* 284, 5 (August 2): 585–591.
McAfee, Robert E. 1995. "Physicians and Domestic Violence: Can We Make a Difference?" *Journal of the American Medical Association* 273, 22 (June 14): 1790–1791.
Rosenfeld, Richard. 2000. "Tracing the Brady Act's Connection with Homicide and Suicide Trends." *Journal of the American Medical Association* 284, 5 (August 2): 616–618.
Suter, Edgar A. 1994a. "'Assault Weapons' Revisited—An Analysis of the AMA Report." *Journal of the Medical Association of Georgia* 83, 5 (May): 281–289.
———. 1994b. "Guns in the Medical Literature—A Failure of Peer Review." *Journal of the Medical Association of Georgia* 83 (March): 133–148.
Wheeler, Timothy. 1999. "Boundary Violations: Gun Politics in the Doctor's Office." *Medical Sentinel* 4, 4: 60–61.

American Revolution

Personal firearms were vitally important for the success of the American Revolution. The brunt of the initial fighting during the war was borne by state militias, composed of citizen-soldiers who carried their own hunting rifles and personal weapons into combat. However, ultimate victory over the British rested on the ability of the Continental Army to acquire heavy military weapons, including artillery. Nonetheless, the importance of a well-armed citizenry in the struggle for independence would continue to impact American politics as debate over the role and necessity of firearms in society continues into the twenty-first century.

In many ways, the American Revolution was an anomaly. Compared to people in Europe and other areas of the world, the white citizens of the British colonies of North America had greater political freedom and higher standards of living. Since their initial establishment, the various colonies had been granted considerable political latitude by the British Crown. In fact, the colonies were left essentially to run themselves, with the exception of trade with foreign nations. However, this tradition of "benign neglect" came to an end following the French and Indian War (1756–1763). The colonial militias had not been able to defend the thirteen colonies and London had been forced to send troops to North America and spend considerable sums on the defense of the colonies. Following the war, London attempted to recoup some of the funds it spent, but the British met considerable resistance from the colonies. Because the colonists had no direct representation in the British Parliament, many felt that it was unfair for them to be subject to "taxation without representation." The colonists undertook sporadic acts of civil disobedience against the new tax measures, including the famous Boston Tea Party. Colonists also opposed the issuance of writs and general warrants that allowed the British to search homes and seize property without specific search warrants. Finally, the quartering of British troops in personal homes, without the consent of the owners, was a source of resentment toward the Crown.

In response to British actions, the colonists established a Continental Congress in 1774 to organize their resistance efforts and coordinate their policies toward the Crown. The colonies had several significant advantages in their conflict with the British. The most obvious was the great distance between Great Britain and the colonies. In addition, since their formation, the defense of the colonies had rested on the white male population, rather than the regular British army. During instances of conflict with Native American tribes or when there were bandit gangs or pirates in operation or during episodes of civil disturbance, it usually fell to each colony's individual militia units to take action. All able-bodied white males over the age of 18 were liable for service in the militia. In addition, many colonies also mandated militia service by free African Americans and slaves under specific conditions. Each individual was expected to provide his own firearm, and mounted units required the militiaman to provide his own horse and equipment. Each colony maintained a variety of military equipment and supplies for use by the militia. Such equipment included cannon and artillery equipment, firearms, and such miscellaneous military supplies as tents, carriages, and entrenching equipment. The colonies also maintained supplies of ammunition.

As tensions grew between the colonies and London, the various militia units were reorganized. The main purpose behind the reforms was to ensure that the militia units would be loyal to the individual colonies and not to the Crown. The militias were also given expanded training to ready them for potential military action against regular British forces. There were alarm systems in place to alert the citizen-soldiers to hostile action so they could be called up and deployed quickly. Each individual militiaman was supposed to be ready to muster at a moment's notice. Because of this, the militia troops began to be popularly known as "minutemen."

The first shots of the American Revolution came during an attempt by the British to seize the ammunition and heavy weapons of the New England colonies' militias. In April 1775, British troops moved to confiscate the militia stores of the Massachusetts colony at the depot in Concord. On April 19, the first shot of the revolution was fired at Lexington and 8 minutemen were killed and 9 wounded during the ensuing skirmish with British regulars. The militia re-

treated and the British marched to Concord where they captured some minor equipment (the militia had hidden most of the supplies). After a second brief skirmish, the British marched back to Boston. However, during the British retreat, the minutemen used the unconventional guerrilla tactics that they employed against Native Americans and sniped at the British troops. The militia inflicted 273 casualties on the regulars while suffering 90 dead and wounded. In many ways, the battles at Lexington and Concord foreshadowed much of the combat of the coming war. The American forces were able to inflict significant casualties on the British, but had difficulty beating the regular British forces in pitched battles.

On July 4, 1776, the Continental Congress approved the Declaration of Independence from Great Britain. Following the Declaration, the Continental Congress dispatched envoys to Europe to seek support against the British. The Americans specifically sought foreign aid to help offset British naval superiority and to acquire military weapons, especially heavy artillery. The American forces also needed standard firearms, since the militia forces brought their own guns, which often used different ammunition. In addition, the American forces needed military training.

The minutemen had several distinct advantages over the British. They were more mobile than the British forces and could exist without the large supply infrastructure required by the Crown's forces. More significantly, many of the American forces had superior firearms. At the start of the war, the most common weapon was the smooth-bore Brown Bess musket. The highly disciplined British troops could fire three times as fast as their American counterparts, but the massed volley fire of the British was fairly inaccurate. Americans tended to have slower rates of fire, but they were more accurate. However, the accuracy range of the Brown Bess was only about 60 yards. As the revolution progressed, more and more Americans began using the Pennsylvania or Kentucky rifle. This firearm was rifled with twisting groves through the barrel, which made the bullet spin. It also has a longer barrel than the Brown Bess. These factors greatly

The Battle of Lexington. (Library of Congress)

increased the accuracy and range of the weapon. In the right hands, the rifled firearms of the minutemen were accurate at 200 yards and had an extreme range of 400 yards. These guns made American soldiers highly effective as snipers and irregular troops.

Throughout the American Revolution, the majority of American soldiers served in their respective state militia units. Usually, the troops preferred militia service because it kept them closer to their homes and they were only called to service for short periods of time. After the Battle of Bunker Hill, Gen. George Washington realized that in order to defeat the British, the Americans would need to establish a regular standing military force with the kind of training and discipline that was the hallmark of the British army. The result was the Continental Army. During the winter of 1777–1778, Washington camped his army in Valley Forge. With the aid of foreign soldiers who had been attracted to the American cause, Washington transformed the collection of militia units and volunteers into an effective fighting force.

The American victory at Saratoga in 1778 was a major turning point in the revolution since it demonstrated to the major European powers the capability of the Continental Army. After the victory, France and Spain began offering active support to the Americans. The French supplied the Americans with weapons and troops under the command of the Comte de Rochambeau. The French delivered thousands of Charleville muskets. These guns fired a smaller musket ball than the Brown Bess (.70 caliber versus the .75 caliber ball of the Brown Bess) and had a greater range and accuracy. In addition, the French muskets were fitted with bayonets whereas most of the Brown Bess muskets and Pennsylvania rifles had been the personal weapons of the Americans and did not have bayonets. The Charleville musket was so effective and popular with the American forces that it was widely copied and served as the basis for the Springfield Model 1795 musket, which became the standard weapon for the nation's regular army at the end of the eighteenth century.

The superior firearms of the Continental Army allowed the Americans to engage the British forces before the enemy could bring their own weapons to bear. In addition, the military intervention of the French expanded the American Revolution into a world war, which caused the British to have to defend their colonies around the globe. Following the British surrender at Yorktown in 1781, the two sides began to work toward a settlement of the conflict. The war ended with the Treaty of Paris in 1783. The importance of the militia units during the conflict and the fact that most of the firearms used by the American troops were privately owned have colored American attitudes toward gun ownership throughout the nation's history.

Tom Lansford

See also Brown Bess; Jefferson, Thomas; Militias; Second Amendment

For Further Reading:

Barnes, Ian. 2000. *The Historical Atlas of the American Revolution.* New York: Routledge.

Hoffman, Ronald, and Peter J. Albert, eds. 1981. *Diplomacy and Revolution: The Franco-American Alliance of 1778.* Charlottesville: University Press of Virginia.

Huston, James A. 1991. *Logistics of Liberty: American Services of Supply in the Revolutionary War and After.* Newark: University of Delaware Press.

Neimeyer, Charles Patrick. 1996. *America Goes to War: A Social History of the Continental Army.* New York: New York University Press.

Werner, Kirk D., ed. 2000. *The American Revolution.* San Diego: Greenhaven Press.

American Rifleman

American Rifleman is the principal publication of the National Rifle Association (NRA). It has been published since 1885 and is both the oldest and the largest circulation American firearm magazine. It was initially entitled *The Rifle;* in 1888 the title was changed to *Shooting and Fishing,* and in 1906 to *Arms and the Man.* In 1923 it assumed the present title of *American Rifleman.*

A copy of the monthly magazine is a benefit of NRA membership. Regular features include reports from the NRA's president, its executive vice-president, and the head of the Institute for Legislative Action, focusing on Second Amendment issues before the U.S. Congress and various state legislatures. Also included are two features: "The Armed Citizen," which summarizes reported uses of firearms in self-defense, product reviews, and reports of competitive firearm matches; and "From the Loading Bench," which presents cartridge reloading data.

In 1973, the NRA also began publishing *American Hunter* and, in the 1990s, *America's 1st Freedom* as alternatives for those members primarily interested in hunting or political activism. Currently, *American Rifleman* has a circulation of 1.6 million, *American Hunter* about 1.5 million, and *America's 1st Freedom* about 800,000.

David T. Hardy

See also Gun Magazines; *Gun Week; Women & Guns*

For Further Reading:

American Rifleman. http://www.american rifleman.org/site/index.asp.

National Rifle Association. http://www.nra.org/.

Americans for Democratic Action (ADA)

Americans for Democratic Action (ADA) is an independent, liberal, political organization founded in 1947. Among its founders were such leading political, academic, religious, and labor leaders as Eleanor Roosevelt, John Kenneth Galbraith, Arthur Schlesinger, Jr., Reinhold Niebuhr, Walter Reuther, and Hubert Humphrey. ADA has taken positions on a broad range of social and political issues, including strongly favoring gun control and opposing militarism. ADA is one of over forty religious, labor, medical, educational, and civic organizations that belong to the Coalition to Stop Gun Violence.

At the national level, ADA backs liberal candidates for Congress and rates legislators on their votes on important issues, with support for firearm-control legislation receiving a positive rating. The ADA Education Fund provides information on issues and legislation. The twenty-two local chapters of ADA carry out grassroots organizing efforts to reduce gun violence and lobby to elect liberal candidates.

ADA has consistently taken strong stands in favor of gun control measures. ADA strongly supported passage of the Brady Handgun Violence Prevention Act, and has defended the Brady Bill against attempts to weaken it. The association also supported a comprehensive ban on assault weapons. ADA sees the Brady Bill and the ban on assault weapons as the foundation of a national policy to reduce gun violence.

ADA also has supported legislation calling for child-safety locks on firearms, reasonable time periods for background checks for gun purchasers, and a minimum age of 21 for purchasing a handgun.

ADA emphasizes the importance of gun control by noting that the gun-related murder rate in the United States greatly exceeds those of other industrialized democracies. It argues that only effective firearm-related legislation can reduce high levels of firearm-related murders and injuries.

Walter F. Carroll

See also Assault Weapons Ban of 1994; Background Checks; Brady Handgun Violence Prevention Act (Brady Bill); Coalition to Stop Gun Violence; Democratic Party and Gun Control; Ideologies—Conservative and Liberal; Interest Groups and Gun Legislation; Lautenberg, Frank R.

For Further Reading:
ADA/ADAction. *http://www.adaction.org/.*
Brock, Clifton. 1985. *Americans for Democratic Action: Its Role in National Politics.* Westport, CT: Greenwood Press.
Gillon, Steven M. 1987. *Politics and Vision: The ADA and American Liberalism, 1947–1985.* New York: Oxford University Press.

Americans for Gun Safety (AGS)

Americans for Gun Safety (AGS) is a nonpartisan, not-for-profit organization that supports the rights of individuals to own guns while it advocates for stronger gun laws and tougher enforcement of current laws. AGS attempts to avoid what it sees as polarized positions in the gun control debate, in which one side argues that gun ownership is an absolute right with no restrictions and the other side attempts to massively regulate or ban guns. AGS supports the rights of individuals to own guns for sport, protection, and collecting, but emphasizes that with rights come responsibilities. The organization states that its goal is to "help keep guns out of the hands of criminals and kids, and to promote responsible gun ownership."

Andrew McKelvey, chief executive officer of TMP Worldwide, founded AGS in 2000 as a project of the Tsunami Fund, a Section 501(c)(4) nonprofit organization that works with progressive social-change organizations to enhance their ability to bring about political change through legislation. The Tsunami Fund is part of the Tides Foundation, which supports social change toward a society based on social justice, equitable economic opportunity, and a sustainable environment. Numerous media outlets have covered AGS, with the *Washington Post* referring to it as a "dominant force" for gun safety.

AGS notes that there are 300,000 gun-related crimes and 10,000 gun-related homicides each year in the United States. To deal with the proliferation of gun-related crimes, AGS stresses the importance of locking up criminals who use guns, enforcing existing gun laws, and closing loopholes that enable criminals and children to get guns. AGS lists its top priorities as supporting gun-safety ballot initiatives, improving background checks on potential gun purchasers, fighting illegal gun trafficking, promoting gun safety, and closing gun-show loopholes.

In 2000, AGS invested $3 million to help pass ballot initiatives in Colorado and Oregon. The initiatives closed the gun-show loopholes in those states by requiring that individuals purchasing guns at gun shows undergo a criminal background check. AGS also stresses the importance of improving and automating criminal history records to improve background checks. In six states, AGS is promoting enforcement packages to combat illegal gun trafficking. The AGS Foundation (AGSF), the educational arm of the organization, maintains a gun-safety website and has run a public service announcement promoting gun safety in 2,500 movie theaters. AGSF has also published *Playing with Firearms,* a report on video-game portrayals of guns. The report suggests that parents need to closely investigate video games before purchasing them for their children.

Emphasizing the importance of closing gun-show loopholes in the thirty-seven states where criminals can purchase guns at gun shows without background checks, AGS strongly supports the McCain-Lieberman gun-safety bill. The McCain-Lieberman bill would require criminal background checks for guns purchased at gun shows. To dispel myths about the gun-show loophole, AGS makes six key arguments. AGS maintains that: (1) criminals do get guns at gun shows; (2) background checks will not put gun shows out of business; (3) background checks will not prevent legitimate gun show sales; (4) background checks do deter criminals; (5) sales by unlicensed dealers are common; and (6) gun show operators will be able to carry out background checks.

Walter F. Carroll

See also Attitudes Toward Gun Control; Background Checks; Black Market for Firearms; Felons and Gun Control; Gun Shows; Medicine and Gun Violence; National Education Association; National Instant Criminal Background Check System; Video Games and Gun Violence

For Further Reading:

Americans for Gun Safety. http://ww2.americansforgunsafety.com/.
Americans for Gun Safety Foundation. 2001. "Playing with Firearms: What Parents Need to Know about Guns in Video Games." December. http://w3.agsfoundation.com/media/games_report.pdf.
Americans for Gun Safety Foundation. 2002. "Broken Records: How America's Faulty Background Check System Allows Criminals to Get Guns." January. http://w3.agsfoundation.com/media/BRReport.pdf.
Cook, Philip J., and Jens Ludwig. 2002. *Gun Violence: The Real Costs.* New York: Oxford University Press.

Ammunition, Regulations of

State and Local Regulations

Most states and localities do not regulate ordinary ammunition. A few, such as Massachusetts and Illinois, require a firearm identification card in order to purchase and possess any ammunition. A number of states have complex regulations on armor-piercing ammunition—California and New Jersey, for example—as well as on incendiary ammunition—California, for example. In addition, New Jersey bans hollow-point ammunition, but it still provides numerous exemptions for legitimate use. New York City regulates ordinary rifle and shotgun ammunition, banning the possession of all such ammunition except by those who hold a New York City rifle-shotgun license and prohibiting the purchase of such ammunition from a dealer unless the purchaser displays his or her license

to the dealer at the time of purchase. Other state laws and local regulations on tracer, incendiary, hollow-point, and armor-piercing ammunition vary considerably. Therefore, prudence dictates that a person become familiar with the laws of a particular state and locality on this subject before attempting to possess, acquire, or transfer ammunition in the particular state and locality.

Federal Regulations

The federal Gun Control Act of 1968 (GCA) originally required that licensed dealers must record sales of .22 rimfire ammunition. That recording requirement was deleted by a minor amendment to the GCA enacted in 1982.

Armor-piercing ammunition for rifles, shotguns, and pistols are addressed and regulated by federal law as part of the GCA. Federal law on armor-piercing ammunition explicitly refers only to such ammunition that can be used in a handgun; nevertheless, some armor-piercing rifle ammunition is automatically covered by federal law because some handguns can use rifle ammunition. Therefore, in any federal regulations on armor-piercing ammunition, such ammunition includes not only armor-piercing ammunition possessed for a handgun but also armor-piercing ammunition possessed for a rifle that any handgun can also use.

Federal law prohibits any person from manufacturing or importing armor-piercing ammunition usable in a handgun, but this does not apply to (1) the manufacture or importation of such ammunition for the use of the United States or any of its departments or agencies, or for the use of any state or any of its departments, agencies, or political subdivisions; (2) the manufacture of such ammunition for the purpose of exportation; and (3) the manufacture or importation for the purposes of testing or experimentation authorized by the secretary of the treasury. Federal law also prohibits any manufacturer or importer to sell or deliver armor-piercing ammunition, with the same use and purpose exceptions as for the manufacture or importation of such ammunition. At any rate, none of these prohibitions on armor-piercing ammunition applies to the mere private *transfer* of such ammunition.

In addition, federal law requires that licensed importers and licensed manufacturers mark all armor-piercing projectiles and packages containing such projectiles for distribution in the manner prescribed by the secretary of the treasury by regulation. The secretary must furnish information to each licensed dealer defining which projectiles are considered to be armor-piercing.

Furthermore, federal law makes it unlawful for a federal firearm-licensed dealer to deliver any firearm or armor-piercing ammunition to any person unless the dealer notes in his or her records either (1) the name, age, and place of residence of the person if the person is an individual; or (2) the identity and the local places of business of the person if the purchaser is a business entity.

Finally, federal law mandates an extra prison term of not less than five years for committing a federal crime of violence or a drug-trafficking crime by using or while carrying a firearm and at the same time possessing armor-piercing ammunition that can be fired in that firearm.

Constitutional Considerations

To investigate ammunition regulations in light of the U.S. Constitution, it is important to turn to the discussions in *United States v. Miller* (307 U.S. 174 [1939]) and in *The Federalist Papers* on the right of the people to keep and bear arms. *The Federalist* was published as newspaper articles during 1787–1788, and in a two-volume version in 1788, to encourage ratification of the Constitution proposed by the May-September 1787 Philadelphia Convention. The U.S. Supreme Court often approvingly quotes from and cites *The Federalist* to discern the structure of the American government created by the Constitution and to determine the intent and meaning of its provisions. For example, in the 1995 Supreme Court decision in *U.S. Term Limits, Inc. v. Thornton,* which involved the constitutionality of state-imposed term limits on members of Congress, the majority cited *The Federalist* at least thirty times and the minority cited it at least forty times. In *Term Limits,* moreover, both the majority and the minority recognized the ultimate sovereignty of the people. Here the Court was

echoing Alexander Hamilton's views expressed in *Federalist* no. 28. Hamilton wrote that, in the event of tyranny in the federal or a state government, the armed people would determine the issue and restore the Constitution and the rule of law by coming to the aid of the nontyrannical governmental entity.

In *Federalist* no. 29, Hamilton set forth the militia structure contemplated by the Constitution: (1) well-trained select or organized militias (today the state National Guards) and (2) general, unorganized, or sedentary militias that had been minimally trained—at most a few hours once or twice a year—composed of "the people at large … properly armed and equipped [with ammunition]" (p. 184). In *Federalist* no. 46, James Madison endorsed Hamilton's concept of an armed American populace to deter and, if necessary, overthrow tyranny. This concept derived from English history, including the English Bill of Rights (1689) and chapter 61 of the Magna Carta (1215).

United States v. Miller is the only twentieth-century U.S. Supreme Court opinion that deals directly with, and discusses in detail, the right to keep and bear arms. In that decision, the Court held that this right includes an individual right to keep arms suitable for militia or common-defense purposes. The Court pointed out that the militia comprises all citizens capable of bearing arms who—when called for service—are "expected to appear bearing arms supplied by themselves and of the kind in common use at the time." The Court noted that in all the American colonies as in England, the militia system was based upon the medieval principle of the assize of arms. This principle "implied the general obligation of all adult male inhabitants to possess arms" for the defense of country, community, and home (p. 179).

The principle of assize of arms grew out of the ancient *fyrd,* which preceded the 1066 Norman Conquest of England. This principle required every free man to possess ordinary arms of the time for "the defence of the country or of the peace" (Stubbs, 1905, p. 153). Before the Norman Conquest, the arms possessed by every freeman typically included the lance and the sword. When a starving person sold himself into slavery for sustenance, he gave up all his personal arms to his master. Upon freeing him, the master gave them back "as arms symbolical of liberty" (Crabb, 1831, p. 82). With them, the freed man could defend himself and his home, as well as his community and country. A century after the conquest, King Henry II updated the ancient *fyrd* by decreeing the 1181 Assize of Arms—a statute requiring, among other things, that every free man possess more up-to-date personal arms: a padded surcoat and an iron cap, as well as the lance.

As early as the fourteenth century, the common law of England considered everyone's home as "his castle and fortress, as well for his defence against injury and violence, as for his repose" (Coke, 1604, p. 91b)—"for the law wills that every man shall be as safe and sound in his own house as he shall be in the king's presence" (*Rex v. Slingesbie,* 1488). Thus, by the sixteenth century every free man had the right and duty to possess arms to defend against foreign enemies and domestic "evildoers" (*Statutes of England,* 1532).

In *Miller* (p. 180), the Court stressed that the "possession of arms also implied the possession of ammunition, and the authorities paid quite as much attention to the latter as to the former." The Court also pointed to seventeenth-century Massachusetts laws that provided that two-thirds of every militia company should be musketeers and that each of them should have not only a musket but also other equipment, including ammunition comprising "one pound of powder, twenty bullets, and two fathoms of match." The rest of the company were pikemen, each armed with "a pike, corselet, head-piece, sword, and knapsack."

To shed additional light on the principles governing the kinds of arms and ammunition protected by the right to keep arms, and to indicate a development of those arms from the more primitive to the more highly developed, the Court in *Miller* quoted from three state militia statutes adopted in the eighteenth century between the signing of the Declaration of Independence (July 4, 1776) and the ratification of the Constitution (1788). These statutes typically spoke in terms of requiring each militiaman to be armed with a firearm, a firelock, or a

musket, plus ammunition—in other words, ordinary personal arms and ammunition in common use at the time. In particular, a 1784 Massachusetts law directed that the militia comprise all able-bodied men under 60 years of age and required that every noncommissioned officer and private soldier of the militia "shall equip himself [with ammunition], and be constantly provided with a good fire arm ..." (p. 180). A 1786 New York law required that all militiamen—that is, all able-bodied male citizens of the state between 16 and 45 years of age residing within New York—had to provide themselves with a "good Musket or Firelock" as well as, among other things, "Twenty-four Cartridges ... each Cartridge containing a proper Quantity of Powder and Ball ..." (p. 181). And a 1785 Virginia militia statute required that every noncommissioned officer and private should appear at the appropriate muster field "armed, equipped, and accoutered ... with a good, clean musket carrying an ounce of ball ... a cartridge box properly made, to contain and secure twenty cartridges fitted to his musket ... and ... one pound of good powder, and four pounds of lead, including twenty blind cartridges ..." (pp. 181–182).

Thus, at the time of the adoption of the Constitution (1789), arms and ammunition were inextricably interwoven; that is to say, the right to keep constitutionally protected arms inherently included the right to keep ammunition suitable for those arms—namely, those arms that a militiaman at any given time would be expected to own and keep in his home.

It follows from the above discussion that the right to keep arms includes the possession by the people at large of all modern firearms that a relatively untrained person—that is, a person with no more training than that required for a musket or firelock—can be expected to use to good effect in defending home, community, or country. Such arms today would include, at a minimum, personal firearms such as ordinary semiautomatic rifles, shotguns, pistols, and revolvers—together with suitable ammunition. With these arms, the people at large can defend their homes and communities, as well as come to the aid of the organized militia when requested by either the federal or their state governments in case of emergencies.

The *Miller* decision further sheds light upon the scope of the right to possess ordinary ammunition. In support of its central holding that the Constitution protects the private possession of militia-type arms, the Court relied on and cited but one case, *Aymette v. State* (2 Humph. 154, 21 Tenn. 119, 124 [1840]), decided by the Tennessee Supreme Court in 1840. In that case, the Tennessee Supreme Court held that the "citizens have the unqualified right to *keep* [suitable arms].... But the right to *bear arms* is not of that unqualified character" (p. 160). The "unqualified" right to keep arms meant the individual right to possess suitable arms free from any regulations or restrictions, such as registration or licensing. It therefore follows that the right to keep, as opposed to bear, ordinary personal ammunition likewise would be an unqualified right.

As for the question of singling out ordinary ammunition for special taxation—that is, taxes imposed upon ammunition that discriminate against ammunition, or are not imposed across the board for all other items at the same tax rate, or are not related to the value of the ammunition—the *Miller* decision comes into play. It makes clear the proposition that if the firearm or ammunition fits into the category of a constitutionally protected type—that is, suitable for militia or common-defense purposes—then such a tax would be unconstitutional.

An explanation of the meaning of the right to keep arms, as well as a confirmation that this right includes the possession of ammunition, is provided by an often-cited 1871 Tennessee case, *Andrews v. State* (50 Tenn. 165, 8 Am. Rep. 8, 13 [1871]). In *Andrews,* the Tennessee Supreme Court ruled that, pursuant to a provision in the 1870 Tennessee Constitution (Article I, §24), all Tennessee citizens had a right "to keep and bear arms for their common defense." (*Andrews* further held that the "right to keep arms necessarily involves the right to purchase [suitable personal arms], to keep them in a state of efficiency for use, and to purchase and provide ammunition suitable for such arms, and to keep them in repair" (p. 178).

Under American colonial statutory and common law in effect at the time of the framing of the U.S. Constitution, the American colonists could lawfully keep firearms and ammunition free of any registration, special taxation, licensing, or disclosure to governmental authorities—except under some militia statutes and then only to prove the possession of only one firearm and a specified amount of ammunition. Thus, the structure of the American government laid down by the Constitution—with or without the Second Amendment—would appear to preclude the registration or licensing of ordinary ammunition. Narrowly tailored firecode provisions governing storage of ammunition, however, would constitute permissible safety regulation.

David I. Caplan

See also Ammunition, Types of; Anglo-Saxon Tradition of the Right to Keep and Bear Arms; *Aymette v. State;* Black Talon; Cartridges; *Cases v. United States;* Gun Control Act of 1968; Magna Carta; *Perpich v. Department of Defense; Schubert v. DeBard;* Second Amendment; *State v. Kessler;* Tenth Amendment; *United States v. Emerson; United States v. Miller; United States v. Tot*

For Further Reading:
Coke, Edward. 1604. *Semayne's Case in 5 Coke Reports 91a.* Reprinted in *Seventy-Seven English Reports,* Full Reprint 194, 195 (King's Bench, 1604).
Crabb, George. [1831] (1987). *A History of English Law.* Reprint, Littleton, CO: Fred B. Rothman & Co.
The Federalist. 1961. Edited by Jacob E. Cooke. Hanover, NH: Wesleyan University Press.
Rex v. Slingesbie. 1488. Translated in *The Publications of the Selden Society,* Vol. 115, Reports of Cases by John Caryll, Part I, 1485–1499, pp. 5–6. London: Selden Society, 1999.
Statutes of England. 1532. 24 Henry VIII chapter 5. Reprinted in *Statutes of the Realm,* Vol. 3, p. 422. London: Dawson of Pall Mall, 1963.
Stubbs, William. 1905. *Select Charters and Other Illustrations of English Constitutional History.* 8th ed. Oxford, UK: Clarendon Press.

Ammunition, Types of

Ammunition types can be classified roughly by rim design, ignition system, and projectile type. For four centuries, man has struggled to "marry" projectile, powder, and ignition system into a

A handful of rifle cartridges. (Michael Freeman/Corbis)

conveniently loaded unit. In the seventeenth century, musketeers carried bandoliers of wooden capsules filled with powder and ball; since the musketeer also carried a burning match, these proved extremely dangerous to the user. In the eighteenth and nineteenth centuries tubular paper cartridges, secured in a leather cartridge box, were employed; the user removed the cartridge, tore the paper open with his teeth, and emptied the contents down the barrel. As repeating firearms evolved in the nineteenth century, the modern "fixed" cartridge came into use, with powder contained in a brass case with the projectile held by friction at one end and the ignition system mounted at the other. Brass was used due to its springy nature; a brass cartridge would expand when the powder ignited, sealing the breech of the barrel, but spring back to nearly its original diameter to allow the fired cartridge to be easily removed from the gun. Mild steel has sometimes been used as a cartridge case material, but is much less satisfactory. Untreated steel cases will rust, and varnished ones can cause jamming as the varnish rubs off inside the chamber.

Fixed cartridges can be classified by their rim type, their ignition system, or their projectile. A repeating firearm must be able to mechanically extract and remove the empty cartridge after firing, a task accomplished by a metal hook-like device known as an extractor. The cartridge in turn must have a feature that the extractor can grasp. In a rimmed cartridge, the base of the cartridge extends outward in a disk, the rim, which the extractor can grasp. In a rimless cartridge, there is no protruding rim, but a groove is cut around the base of the cartridge, and the extractor grasps the groove. Variations include the semirimmed cartridge, which has a groove and a rim that protrudes only slightly, and the belted cartridge, in which the base of the cartridge case expands outward into a strengthening belt with a cut groove.

Cartridges can also be classed by their ignition system, the principal ones being rimfire and centerfire. Rimfire cartridges are rimmed, but the rim is hollow. An explosive primer compound is placed inside the rim and, when the firing pin strikes and crushes the rim, the compound explodes and ignites the powder. Since the metal of the rim must be quite thin to be crushable, rim-fire ignition is restricted to cartridges of very low power. Today only low-power .22 caliber cartridges are made in rimfire form. In the centerfire cartridge, the priming compound is placed in a metal capsule, the primer. The primer is mounted in the center of the cartridge's base; a cartridge of centerfire form can withstand considerably higher pressures than a rimfire.

In addition to these main types, there are some rare forms of ignition. A few modern rifles use electronic ignition, in which an electric current passes through the primer to detonate it. Early cartridges (ca. 1850) sometimes used a pin fire, in which the hammer struck a pointed pin extending sideways through the cartridge. The Prussian "needle gun" of the 1850s had a paper cartridge with primer located at the base of the bullet: a very long firing pin penetrated the cartridge and struck the primer.

Cartridges may further be classified by the nature of the projectile mounted in them. The earliest projectiles were simply solid lead or lead alloy. These materials were, however, too soft to take the higher velocities that arms designers reached in the late nineteenth century. At that point, jacketed bullets, with a lead core encased in a harder metal jacket, came into use; the harder jacket could take the higher velocities without smearing the inside of the barrel with lead. A copper-nickel alloy was first used for the jacket; it was found that this tended to leave hard-to-remove metal deposits inside the barrel, so "gilding metal," a copper alloy, then became standard jacket material. Mild steel has also been employed as a jacket material.

Jacketed bullets took several forms. In the full metal jacketed projectile, required for warfare by sundry international conventions, the copper alloy jacket covers the bullet's nose, inhibiting its expansion after impact. In the soft-point projectile, the jacket does not cover the nose; the exposed soft lead nose crushes upon impact and causes the projectile to expand. (The soft point originated as the military "Dum-Dum," whose use was subsequently outlawed in warfare.) In the hollow-point projectile, a hollow cavity of varying size is located in the nose, likewise promoting bullet expansion. Bullet de-

signers have also evolved variations on these forms, in which the bullet's point is composed of a plastic or bronze tip, enabling it to keep a sharp point but still expand.

Military cartridges take an even greater variety of projectiles. The full metal jacketed bullet, described above, is the traditional form. Armor-piercing projectiles contain a large, pointed, steel core; currently many forms of full metal jacketed ammunition also contain a small steel penetrator under the nose. Incendiary projectiles contain compounds that produce an incendiary flash when the bullet nose is crushed by impact. Tracer projectiles contain a manner of flare compound that burns during the bullet's flight, making its path visible so that a machine gunner can correct his aim. Additionally, there have been experiments with small-caliber explosive projectiles. Different features are sometimes combined, the ultimate combination being the armor-piercing incendiary tracer (APIT) projectile.

These essentially comprise the forms of ammunition used in rifles and handguns; shotgun ammunition takes different forms. The most commonly produced form has a plastic cartridge case on which a brass base and rim are mounted, strengthening it at the most critical areas. After powder, a plastic wad, and the shot are loaded, the forward end of the cartridge is sealed by folding it inward. On occasion, shotgun cartridges have also taken an all-brass or all-plastic form, and prior to the evolution of plastic cartridges, rolled paper shells were standard. Common loading material are birdshot (small pellets used for birds and small game), buckshot (larger pellets used for deer and large game), and a slug (a single large projectile, also used for large game). Specialty loads are also available—flares for signaling, firecrackers to drive birds away from crops, tear gas, tracer pellets, plastic pellets for riot control, incendiaries, tiny steel darts, and virtually anything else that can fit into a shotgun barrel.

Ammunition has generated fewer legislative controversies compared to firearms. In the 1970s, when efficient handgun soft-point and hollow-point ammunition became available, there were proposals to ban them on the ground that they were too deadly. In the 1990s, issues arose regarding armor-piercing handgun ammunition, whose projectile had a solid bronze core that increased its ability to penetrate. Critics charged that these projectiles would also pierce body armor and labeled them "cop-killer bullets." Congress ultimately outlawed civilian production of handgun ammunition with solid cores made of certain hard metals. A later controversy involved the "Black Talon" hollow-point produced by Winchester and aggressively marketed as an expanding projectile that inflicted greater injuries. After some of these rounds were used in the "101 California Street" murders, the marketing approach backfired on Winchester. The controversy ended after Winchester retitled the bullet the "Ranger Talon" and restricted sales to law enforcement personnel.

David T. Hardy

See also Black Talon; California Street (101) Massacre; Cartridges; Dum-Dum Bullet; Gunpowder; Minie Ball; Spitzer Bullet
For Further Reading:
Hogg, Ian, 1985. *Jane's Directory of Military Small Arms Ammunition.* New York: Jane's Publishing.
Logan, Herschel C. 1959. *Cartridges: A Pictorial Digest of Small Arms Ammunition.* Harrisburg, PA: Stackpole.

Amnesty Programs

Gun amnesty programs, often run in conjunction with gun buyback programs, have been used by law enforcement agencies to remove firearms from circulation. In such programs, weapons that are turned in (often for cash or some other material inducement) are accepted with "no questions asked." Also, those turning in illegal guns are not prosecuted for illegal possession of a firearm. Typically, no background checks or criminal investigations of participants are conducted.

Not all gun buyback programs include amnesty provisions. Individuals who turned in guns through local programs funded by the U.S. Department of Housing and Urban Development were required to show identification. The guns were then checked to determine whether they were stolen or used in a crime.

While amnesty and buyback programs have been politically popular (Callahan, Rivara, and Koepsell, 1994, p. 472), there is no empirical evidence that they actually succeed in reducing gun violence. Many of the guns that are turned into these programs are obsolete and therefore not likely to be used in criminal activity. Also, those who turn in guns tend to be older people, who are less likely to be engaged in criminal activity. A study of the gun amnesty program in Sacramento, California, found that 40 percent of the program participants were 55 years of age or older, and none were under the age of 25 (Romero, Wintemute, and Vernick, 1998).

There has also been some concern about amnesty programs where guns are not checked. A gun, used in a crime, might be turned in anonymously. The gun is then destroyed, depriving the authorities of evidence and allowing a criminal to escape prosecution.

Even gun control advocates have recognized the limitation of such programs. In a 1998 interview, Robin Terry, a spokesperson for Handgun Control, Inc., said that "any effort to get guns off the street is worthwhile. But I think they are more effective when they are used in connection with gun violence programs" (*Newark Star-Ledger*, 1998, p. 4).

Jeffrey Kraus

See also Availability of Guns, Effects on Crime; Crime and Gun Use; Gun Buyback Programs; Guns in the Home
For Further Reading:
Callahan, Charles M., Frederick P. Rivara, and Thomas D. Koepsell. 1994. "Money for Guns: Evaluation of the Seattle Gun Buy-Back Program." *Public Health Reports* 109: 470–477.
Newark Star-Ledger (from staff reports). 1998. "Newark Resurrects Gun Swap Program." February 10.
Plotkin, Martha, ed. 1996. *Under Fire: Gun Buy-Backs, Exchanges and Amnesty Programs.* Washington, DC: Police Executive Research Forum.
Romero, Michael, Garren Wintemute, and Jon Vernick. 1998. *Reduction in Prevalence of Risk Factors for Firearm Violence among Participants in a Gun Amnesty Program.* Monterey, CA: Program on Security and Development, Monterey Institute of International Studies; http://sand.miis.edu/research/1998/sept1998/sacgbb.pdf.

Van Horn, Dwight. 1992. "What's Wrong with Gun Amnesty Programs." *Law Enforcement Alliance of America Newsletter* (April): 2.

Anglo-Saxon Tradition of the Right to Keep and Bear Arms

The National Rifle Association, the Citizens Committee for the Right to Keep and Bear Arms, Gun Owners of America, and other key organizations opposed to gun control prefer to take the long view of history with regard to the Second Amendment. Supreme Court decisions between 1876 and 1938 contained language supporting the notion that the framers of the Constitution clearly intended ordinary citizens to possess arms and to be prepared to carry these arms into battle in defense of the state. However, the favorite starting point of gun control opponents is pre-Revolutionary America and even earlier—as far back as Saxon England in the seventh century. For then and thereafter, up through the ratification of the Second Amendment in 1791, various governments clearly intended that individual citizens have both the right *and the duty* to keep and bear firearms.

As early as the seventh century, there is strong evidence of an Anglo-Saxon legal tradition that not only allowed but required all free men (non-serfs) to keep and bear arms: "Every landowner was obliged to keep armor and weapons according to his rank and possessions; these he might neither sell, lend, nor pledge, nor even alienate from his heirs. In order to instruct them in the use of arms, they had their stated times for performing their military exercise; and once in a year, generally in spring, there was a general review of arms throughout each county" (Grose, 1812, pp. 1–2, as quoted in Hardy, 1986, p. 13).

Universal arms bearing for free men continued after the Saxons fell to the Normans in 1066. In 1181, Henry II authored the Assize of Arms, requiring all free men (most of whom were landowners) to own weapons: "Whosoever holds one knight's fee shall have a coat of mail, a helmet, a shield, and a lance; and every knight as many…. Every free layman having in chattels [movable property] or rent [land] to the value of 15 marks, shall keep a coat of mail, a helmet and shield and lance. Every free layman who shall have in chattels or rent 10 marks shall have a habergon [sleeveless armored coat], a chaplet [skullcap] of iron and a lance. Also all burgesses and the whole community of freemen shall have a wambais [leather body armor], a chaplet of iron, and a lance" (Grose, 1812, pp. 1–2, as quoted in Hardy, 1986, p. 14). While continental European society was split between an armed nobility and a disarmed peasantry, in England every free man had to possess and be willing to bear arms. For example, in France, between the fifteenth and eighteenth centuries, more than thirty different laws were enacted that prevented the population at large from possessing or using arms, especially firearms (Kennett and Anderson, 1975, p. 13).

This Anglo-Saxon tradition was broadened in 1285 with the Statute of Winchester, in which Edward I proclaimed that all men, not just free men, had the legal duty to maintain arms: "It is commanded that … every man between fifteen years of age and sixty years of age shall be assessed and sworn to armor according to the quantity of their Lands and Goods; that is, to wit, from Fifteen Pounds Lands and Goods Forty Marks, an Hauberke of iron, a sword, a knife, and a horse … he that hath less than Forty Shillings yearly, shall be sworn to keep Gisarmes [pole-axes], knives, and other less[er] weapons … and all others that may, shall have Bowes and Arrowes." (as quoted in Hardy, 1986, p. 15).

During the next 350 years, regulations in England concerning weapons and firearms were revised many times but they never denied both the right and necessity of all men to own and be willing to bear arms. However, matters changed abruptly during the English Civil Wars (1639–1689). Charles I, in trying to maintain his status as absolute monarch beholden to no one, least of all to members of Parliament, began a series of arms seizures from his parliamentarian enemies. To ensure that firearms did not fall into the hands of his foes, Charles ordered that gunsmiths produce "a record of all weapons they had manufactured over the past six months together with a list of their purchasers. In the future, they were commanded to report every Saturday night to the ordnance office the number of guns made and sold that week. Carriers throughout the kingdom were required to obtain a license if they wished to transport guns, and all importation of firearms was banned" (Malcolm, 1983, pp. 299–300, as quoted in Hardy, 1986, p. 29).

In retaliation, Parliament enacted a series of statutes that allowed it to confiscate arms from the citizenry and to deny the right of weaponry possession from those they thought loyal to Charles, including "Papists, and other persons who are voted to be Delinquents by both or either of the Houses of Parliament ... or that have been present with or aiding His Majesty ... or such Clergymen and others that have publicly preached or declared themselves to oppose, disgrace or revile the proceedings of both or either Houses of parliament." From such individuals, Parliament ordered that the "Arms, Ammunition, and Horses fit for Service in the War" were to be seized (Ordinance of 9 January 1642, as quoted in Hardy, 1986, p. 27). Parliament eventually banned all but the landed elite from owning firearms. In the Game Act of 1671, all persons not owning lands that produced at least 100 pounds in annual rental (which relatively few estates did) were barred from possessing firearms; moreover, those who qualified to own arms were given the power to search the premises of their tenants and to seize any firearms that might be found.

During his brief reign, James II, the son of Charles I, continued the practice of disarming citizens thought disloyal to the monarchy. However, the war between the Crown and Parliament ended with the Glorious Revolution in 1688 and the ascension of William and Mary to the throne. Because James II was not dead, but living in exile in France, William and Mary sought legitimacy from Parliament. After much debate, Parliament eventually ruled that James's living in exile was tantamount to his voluntarily having given up the throne; thus, the monarchy of William and Mary was rightful. The cost for receiving legitimacy was high, however, and William and Mary were forced to abide by Parliament's Declaration of Rights. The forerunner of the U.S. Constitution's Bill of Rights, this document outlined the basic rights of English-

men, among which was a clear restoration of the individual right to keep and bear arms (Malcolm, 1994).

The restored Anglo-Saxon tradition of all free men having the right, and even the duty, to keep and bear arms was transferred to colonial America, where all the colonies individually passed militia laws that required universal gun ownership. Hunting was essential to many families, and in light of immediate threats from the French, Dutch, Spanish, and Native Americans, it is not surprising that colonial militia statutes required that all able-bodied men be armed and trained. Intellectually, the colonial elite imbibed the writings of Whig political philosophers, who emphasized decentralized government, fear of a standing army, and the right of the common people to keep and bear arms in defense of themselves—against criminals, foreign powers, and especially the state itself (Colburn, 1965; Shalhope, 1982).

Gregg Lee Carter

See also Citizens Committee for the Right to Keep and Bear Arms; Gun Owners of America; Militias; Minutemen, Revolutionary; National Rifle Association; Second Amendment; United States Supreme Court Decisions on Gun Control

For Further Reading:
Carter, Gregg Lee. 1997. The *Gun Control Movement.* New York: Twayne.
Colburn, H. Treavor. 1965. *The Lamp of Experience: Whig History and the Intellectual Origins of the American Revolution.* Chapel Hill: University of North Carolina Press.
Grose, Francis. 1812. *Military Antiquities Respecting a History of the English Army.* London: Stockdale.
Hardy, David T. 1986. *Origins and Development of the Second Amendment.* Chino Valley, AZ: Blacksmith Publishers.
Kennett, Lee, and James LaVerne Anderson. 1975. *The Gun in America: The Origins of a National Dilemma.* Westport, CT: Greenwood Press.
Malcolm, Joyce Lee. 1983. "The Right of the People to Keep and Bear Arms: The Common Law Tradition." *Hastings Constitutional Law Quarterly* 10: 285–314.
———. 1994. *To Keep and Bear Arms: The Origins of the Anglo-American Right.* Cambridge, MA: Harvard University Press.
Shalhope, Robert E. 1982. "The Ideological Origins of the Second Amendment." *Journal of American History* 69 (December): 599–614.

Antiterrorist Legislation

As Americans have had to deal increasingly with the specter of armed terrorist activities and bombings on American soil in recent years, Congress has responded with antiterrorist legislation intended to more effectively deter and punish terrorists and strengthen the ability of federal law enforcement to investigate these acts of violence. While legislative attempts to control the threat of terrorism are not new and date as far back as the passage of the Alien and Sedition Acts in 1798, events of more modern origin such as the Oklahoma City and World Trade Center bombings have raised a host of new concerns and fears about how best to deter, investigate, prosecute, adjudicate, and punish terrorist acts that occur within the United States. Modern attempts at antiterrorist legislation have included provisions for the stricter control of guns, though such provisions have been deleted from any laws finally enacted.

On April 18, 1996, on the eve of the one-year anniversary of the bombing of the Alfred P. Murrah Federal Building in Oklahoma City, Congress submitted to President Bill Clinton for his signature the Antiterrorism and Effective Death Penalty Act (AEDPA) of 1996 (PL 104-132, 110n Stat. 1214). Although highly influenced by the Oklahoma City bombing, the AEDPA was also the result of other domestic bombings as well, notably the 1993 World Trade Center bombing in New York City. While not as sweeping as President Clinton and some congressional leaders had planned in the aftermath of the Oklahoma City bombing, Clinton signed the AEDPA into law on April 24, 1996, making the AEDPA the most prominent domestic antiterrorist legislation promulgated in recent years. Upon signing the act, Clinton stated that the AEDPA "stands as a tribute to the victims of terrorism and to the men and women in law enforcement who dedicate their lives to protecting all of us from the scourge of terrorist activity."

A large portion of the AEDPA provides new tools to enable law enforcement and administrative agencies to more effectively combat terrorism both at home and abroad. Key provisions of the AEDPA relating to domestic terrorism included increased funding for law enforcement organizations to study various antiterrorism programs, requiring that violators make restitution to their victims, criminalizing the use of chemical weapons in the United States or against American citizens abroad, requiring that plastic explosives contain chemical tagging material to make it easier for law enforcement to track its source, limiting a death row inmate's ability to use the federal habeas corpus process to appeal capital punishment sentences imposed in state courts, forbidding individuals from rendering aid to groups designated as terrorist, increasing the power of immigration authorities to prohibit entry into the United States of persons belonging to terrorist organizations, and deporting suspected alien terrorists and those already convicted of crimes. Dropped from the legislation prior to final enactment were Clinton-supported provisions that would have required tracing elements in explosive elements such as fertilizer, enhanced federal wiretapping capabilities regarding all telephones used by suspected terrorists, enabled the military to assist in cases involving biological and chemical weapons, lengthened the statute of limitations for firearm violations, and given the government access to consumer credit and other records of suspected terrorists.

Critics of antiterrorist legislation have decried the fact that the antiterrorist legislation risks jeopardizing basic constitutional rights and liberties. Aside from the increased police powers, the AEDPA raises a number of controversial issues. Challenges have been submitted on such things as the AEDPA's fund-raising ban on First Amendment free speech and association grounds and on the deportation components of the AEDPA on Fifth Amendment due process grounds—which, critics argue, may result in the removal of unwanted aliens from American shores without adequate proof or linkage to terrorist activities. Some of the original legislation's more stern provisions, including giving more leeway on the use of wiretaps and allowing greater use of military intervention to help in cases involving weapons of mass destruction, were removed prior to final enactment of the AEDPA for fear that the legislation would give the federal law enforcement community too much power and could result in the threatening of American civil liberties and more intrusive behavior by federal law enforcement agencies. Many of these concerns of the potential for federal overreaching were exacerbated by the congressional hearings on alleged federal agency abuses at Waco and Ruby Ridge, hearings that were occurring at the same time that the AEDPA was under consideration by Congress.

While the AEDPA is the latest in the long list of legislation in the United States dealing with terrorism, it will doubtfully be the last. The history of antiterrorist legislation in the United States dates as far back as the Alien and Sedition Acts of 1798, legislation enacted in part to stem the perceived problem of foreign political violence being imported to America's shores. Over the years, Congress has enacted other similar legislation, ranging from immigration legislation designed to exclude aliens from the United States based upon their belief or practice of anarchist principles, to legislation designed to allow for the prosecution and deportation of individuals in political groups engaged in what was perceived as "subversive" activities within the United States. While these various legislative initiatives in previous years were not directed to what is currently regarded and conceived as the modern terrorist threat and should not be characterized solely as antiterrorist legislation, such legislation has served as a clear precursor to such modern antiterrorist legislation as the AEDPA.

James A. Beckman

See also Bureau of Alcohol, Tobacco, and Firearms; Ruby Ridge; Waco, Texas, Raid

For Further Reading:

Kopel, David, and Joseph Olson. 1996. "Preventing a Reign of Terror: Civil Liberties Implications of Terrorism Legislation." *Oklahoma City University Law Review* 21: 247–347.

President's Statement on Signing the Antiterrorism and Effective Death Penalty Act of 1996, 32 Weekly Comp. Pres. Doc. 719, 721 (April 29, 1996).

Smith, Roberta. 1997. "Note: America Tries to Come to Terms with Terrorism: The United States Anti-Terrorism and Effective Death Penalty Act of 1996 v. British Anti-Terrorism Law and International Response." *Cardozo Journal of International and Comparative Law* 5 (Spring): 249–290.

Armijo v. Ex Cam, Inc. (1987)

The civil case of *Armijo v. Ex Cam, Inc.* resulted in a 1987 opinion by the United States District Court of New Mexico (656 F. Supp. 771) that was endorsed the following year by the United States Court of Appeals for the Tenth Circuit (843 F.2d 406). The case represented an attempt by the survivor of a person killed by an assailant armed with a Saturday night special to recover damages from the importer and manufacturer of the handgun used by the killer. The court, ruling against the plaintiff, declared that there was no precedent basis on which to collect damages from the commercial purveyor of a weapon and no basis in product liability law to support such a judgment.

The *Armijo* case was filed after the 1983 killing of Dolores Armijo's husband by her brother. Both Ms. Armijo and her daughter witnessed the shooting and were subject to an assault by Steven Armijo, who attempted to fire his gun at them. They were spared when the weapon did not go off.

The federal district court, obligated by law to determine what might have been decided had the case been heard in New Mexico (since the case involved parties from different states, it was tried in federal court as a diversity action; the second section of Article III of the U.S. Constitution provides for such a proceeding), where the killing occurred, concluded that the courts there had never been faced with an issue of this nature. Nor had the legislature ever addressed the subject. The district court therefore looked at four product liability rules under which the plaintiff Armijo might be entitled to a financial award: (1) strict product liability; (2) an "ultra hazardous product" principle; (3) negligence liability; and (4) a narrower form of strict liability pertaining to Saturday Night Specials. By a unanimous verdict, the court found that the requirements for none of these claims had been met. The decision focused on the fact that for Ms. Armijo to win her case the weapon itself had to be defective. Not without irony, the judge pointed out that the details of the case indicated clearly that this had not been so, at least in regard to the killing of the plaintiff's husband. In addition, there was a juridical stumbling block involved in holding a manufacturer and importer liable when the lethal act had been performed by a third party not under the defendant's control.

The only contrary case that the district court had to review was the 1985 decision in *Kelley v. R. G. Industries, Inc.* (497 A.2d 1143) in which the Maryland Supreme Court had held that a gun manufacturer was liable under the doctrine of "ultra hazardous activity" for selling a Saturday Night Special used in a murder. The district court in *Armijo* dismissed that case without offering any explanation beyond the statement that it did not "believe that the New Mexico courts would adopt any of these theories to recognize a cause of action in this case" (*Armijo,* 1987: 775). In any event, the Maryland legislature in short order had enacted a statute nullifying the *Kelley* decision.

Gilbert Geis

See also Lawsuits against Gun Manufacturers; Product Liability Lawsuits; Saturday Night Specials
For Further Reading:
Armijo v. Ex Cam, Inc., 843 F.2d 406 (10th Cir. 1988). http://www2.cs.cmu.edu/afs/cs/user/ wbardwel/public/nfalist/armijo_v_ex_cam.txt.
Kairys, David. 2000. "The Origin and Development of the Governmental Handgun Cases." *Connecticut Law Review* 32: 1163–1174.
Lytton, Timothy D. 1998. "Negligent Marketing: *Halberstam v. Daniel* and the Uncertain Future of Negligent Marketing Claims against Firearms Manufacturers." *Brooklyn Law Review* 44: 681–709.

Arming Women Against Rape and Endangerment (AWARE)

Arming Women Against Rape and Endangerment (AWARE) is a nonprofit organization formed to provide training, information, and support for women seeking to resist violence against them. The organization was founded by Nancy Biddle, whose personal experience with violence encouraged her to study women's self-defense options. AWARE says that it works to prevent violence against women through education and training, but it also seeks to empower women by offering information and training in a variety of self-defense techniques, from pepper spray to handguns and shotguns. AWARE retains instructors made available to interested persons and organizations. The organization is based in Bedford, Massachusetts

Robert J. Spitzer

See also Million Mom March; Second Amendment Sisters; Self-defense, Reasons for Gun Use; Women and Guns
For Further Reading:
Homsher, Deborah. 2001. *Women and Guns.* Armonk, NY: M. E. Sharpe.

Articles of Confederation and Gun Control

As the first written constitution of the United States, the Articles of Confederation neither contained any express provisions guaranteeing the alleged individual right to keep and bear arms nor gave to the new centralized government any means by which it could regulate guns or firearm possession or use. As the Articles of Confederation created only a league of thirteen sovereign independent states and a nominal centralized government, any constitutional protection for gun ownership was derived, if at all, from each of the thirteen state governments and constitutions. Similarly, any gun regulations or laws were instituted, if at all, on the state level as well. Under the Articles of Confederation, the centralized government lacked the basic authority to regulate interstate commerce and lacked a taxing power—two of the chief ways in which federal gun controls such as the National Firearms Act of 1934 and the Gun Control Act of 1968 have been enacted by the federal government in modern times. The centralized government also lacked the ability to enforce laws it could enact; there was no provision allowing for a chief executive or federal court system, and all "law enforcement" was left to the individual states. The centralized Congress, which was a unicameral body composed of delegates from each state, could not exert any of its limited powers over individuals. Lastly, in the only section in the Articles of Confederation to mention "arms," Article VI required that "every state shall always keep up a well regulated and disciplined militia, sufficiently armed and accoutred, and shall provide and constantly have ready for use, in public stores, a due number of field pieces and tents, and a proper quantity of arms, ammunition and camp equipage." This provision, which laid the foundation for the Second Amendment to the U.S. Constitution that followed later, illustrates the importance of the "militia" and the "collective right" theory to bear arms within the underpinnings of the Second Amendment.

Ratified in 1781 and remaining in effect until 1788, the Articles of Confederation established a loose confederation or league of states, rather than a strong centralized federal government as was eventually created by the U.S. Constitution in 1787. The Articles of Confederation were literally born from the conflict with Great Britain. From the onset of the American Revolution, influential state leaders stressed the need for a stronger government sufficiently powerful to defeat Great Britain and, presumably, defend against future aggressions. However, most Americans remained overly suspicious of a new powerful centralized state. Thus, each state retained its "sovereignty, freedom and independence." Article III of the Articles of Confederation illustrates this concept of a limited union best by describing the confederation of American states as "a firm league of friendship" of states "for their common defense, the security of their liberties, and their mutual and general welfare." While the new centralized government was given some limited enumerated powers, these powers largely dealt with the handling of foreign affairs issues (e.g., power to declare war, power to raise and support army and navy, and power to make treaties). Thus, regarding most domestic issues, the government created by the Articles of Confederation was largely a loose confederation or agency that enabled the actions of the individual states in their respective sovereign spheres.

James A. Beckman

See also Federalism and Gun Control; Gun Control Act of 1968; Militias; National Firearms Act of 1934; Second Amendment

For Further Reading:

Bellesiles, Michael. 2000. "Symposium on the Second Amendment: Fresh Looks: The Second Amendment in Action." *Chicago-Kent Law Review* 76: 61–102.

Bowen, Catherine. 1966. *Miracle at Philadelphia.* Boston: Little, Brown and Company.

Jensen, Merrill. 1940. *The Articles of Confederation: An Interpretation of the Social Constitutional History of the American Revolution, 1774–1781.* Madison: University of Wisconsin Press.

Assault Weapons

Assault weapons, first developed for military use, were designed as light machine guns, capable of firing in semiautomatic or fully automatic modes; they were subject to some federal regulation in the 1990s. Manufactured in rifle, pistol, and shotgun forms, these weapons began to come into civilian hands in large numbers with the sale of surplus M1 carbines in the 1960s, Chinese-made semiautomatic rifles (modeled after the Russian AK-47) in the 1980s, semiautomatic pistols like the MAC-10 in the 1980s, and the semiautomatic TEC-9 in the 1990s. A semiautomatic weapon fires one bullet with each pull of the trigger without manual rechambering; a fully automatic weapon fires bullets continuously and in rapid succession while the trigger is depressed until the bullet clip or magazine is empty.

American law dating to the 1930s has made possession of fully automatic weapons (usually called machine guns) difficult. Traditional machine guns were heavy, and required more than one individual to properly operate them. The first significant departure from the crew-operated machine gun was the Tommy gun, developed at the end of World War I for use by a single soldier and popularized by gangster use in the 1920s. While modern fully automatic assault weapons are relatively lightweight, they were already regulated if they fired in a fully automatic fashion. The spread of semiautomatic assault weapons in recent decades, and their increasing use in sensational crimes, such as the Stockton, California, schoolyard massacre in 1989, prompted calls for stricter regulation. Despite such incidents, civilian sales of semiautomatic assault weapons increased dramatically in the late 1980s and 1990s. They were popularized not only by manufacturers' intensive advertising, but also in movies and television programs. They also proved popular among right-wing survivalist and self-created militia movements. In some instances, legally obtainable semiautomatic weapons could be easily altered to fire in full automatic mode.

Critics of proposed new regulations of assault weapons argued that it was difficult to produce an acceptable definition of what constitutes an assault weapon. They also noted that the firing process for many hunting rifles was the same as that of military-style assault weapons, rendering the distinction between legitimate semiautomatic hunting rifles and allegedly illegitimate semiautomatic assault weapons merely cosmetic.

Some assault weapons were finally subjected to national regulation when Congress passed the Assault Weapons Ban of 1994. This law resolved the definition problem by defining an assault weapon, configured specifically for military use, as having such characteristics as a more compact design, a barrel less than twenty inches in length, extensive use of stampings and plastics in its construction, lighter in weight (six to ten pounds), a pistol grip or thumbhole stock, a folding or telescoping stock, a grenade launcher, a bayonet fitting, a barrel shroud, a threaded barrel for adding a silencer or flash suppressor, and the ability to receive a large clip that holds twenty to thirty bullets. Gun control supporters argued that these guns' lighter weight and smaller size made them more appealing for criminal use—especially in the case of semiautomatic pistols—because their design facilitated concealability and spray fire, a firing technique incompatible with typical hunting or sporting purposes. The Assault Weapons Ban of 1994, passed as part of the Violent Crime Control and Law Enforcement Act, banned nineteen named types of assault weapons and several dozen copycat weapons. It also specifically exempted 661 sporting rifles. Existing assault-style weapons were also exempted from the ban.

In 1998, President Bill Clinton directed the Bureau of Alcohol, Tobacco, and Firearms (BATF) to ban the import of fifty-eight models of semiautomatic firearms. Several studies of guns used in crimes supported the concern that assault weapons were appealing to criminals. While assault weapons accounted for only about 2–3 percent of all firearms owned in America, they accounted for 6–8 percent of gun crimes in the 1990s. Four states have also enacted assault weapons bans (California, Connecticut, New Jersey, and New York) as have several cities. The effectiveness of these bans has been questioned,

as manufacturers and dealers have been able to circumvent the ban by making minor or cosmetic changes in banned weapons to make them legal to sell.

Robert J. Spitzer

See also Assault Weapons Ban of 1994; Automatic Weapons Laws; Bureau of Alcohol, Tobacco, and Firearms; Semiautomatic Weapons; Sporting Purposes Test

For Further Reading:
Avery, Derek. 1995. *Firearms.* Ware, UK: Wordsworth.
Diaz, Tom. 1999. *Making a Killing.* New York: New Press.
Spitzer, Robert J. 1998. *The Politics of Gun Control.* New York: Chatham House.
Vizzard, William J. 2000. *Shots in the Dark.* Lanham, MD: Rowman and Littlefield.

Assault Weapons Ban of 1994

Enacted under Title XI as part of the Violent Crime Control and Law Enforcement Act of 1994 (PL 103-322; 108 Stat. 1796), this provision banned for ten years the future manufacture and transfer of nineteen named assault weapons and approximately 200 firearms covered by the law's generic definition of "assault weapon." Under the terms of the law, semiautomatic assault weapons were defined under three categories: rifles, pistols, and shotguns. Semiautomatic rifles and pistols fell under the law if they had the ability to accept a detachable magazine and possessed at least two other characteristics of such weapons; shotguns were considered assault weapons if they possessed at least two of the assault-weapon features. The law also specifically exempted 661 named weapons. In addition, it banned large-capacity ammunition-feeding devices (those that could hold more than ten rounds). The ban did not apply to assault weapons already in circulation. Guns neither banned nor protected by the law were exempted from its regulations.

In the 1980s, several factors converged to build support for some kind of legal restriction on assault weapons (firearms designed for military use), including spiraling crime rates, the increasing availability of such weapons, and the belief that such weapons served no legitimate hunting or sporting purpose. The key event spurring control supporters was a senseless January 1989 schoolyard massacre in Stockton, California, when five children were killed and twenty-nine others were wounded in a shooting spree by drifter Patrick Purdy, who used a Chinese AK-47 assault rifle. Within weeks, thirty states and many localities were considering bans on these weapons. Two years later, the worst such massacre in American history occurred in Killeen, Texas, when George J. Hennard killed twenty-two people and himself, and wounded twenty-three others, in a cafeteria. Several studies of guns used in crimes supported the concern that assault weapons were appealing to criminals. While assault weapons accounted for only about 2–3 percent of all firearms owned in America, they accounted for 6–8 percent of gun crimes in the 1990s.

Aside from the fierce political opposition to the ban from the National Rifle Association (NRA), regulation of such weapons posed a practical problem, since the definition of a semiautomatic weapon is one that fires a round with each pull of the trigger, which would include wooden-stocked hunting rifles. Assault-style semiautomatic weapons are distinguished from others in that they have large clips holding twenty to thirty bullets, are more compact in design, have barrels under 20 inches in length, take intermediate-sized cartridges, include extensive use of stampings and plastics, are lighter weight (about 6 to 10 pounds), and were designed for military use. In addition, they often have folding or telescoping stocks, heat-dispersing shrouds, pistol grips, grenade launchers, flash suppressors, and bayonet fittings.

President George Bush responded by passing an executive order in March 1989 placing a temporary ban on the import of certain assault rifles. The temporary ban became permanent and was later expanded to include a larger number of weapons, earning Bush the ire of the NRA. President Bill Clinton expanded the scope of the import ban in 1993, also by executive order, to include assault-style handguns, like the Uzi. Clinton expanded the order again in 1998.

In Congress, several bills aimed at curbing or banning assault weapons were introduced in 1989, but those bills languished in committee until 1990, when the Senate narrowly approved a provision to ban the production, sale, and possession of nine semiautomatic assault-type weapons. The provision was added to an omnibus crime bill. The House Judiciary Committee had approved a similar measure, but it never left committee. In conference committee, the assault-weapons ban was removed from the bill that was enacted into law. In 1991, the Senate again included an assault-weapons ban in a larger crime bill. A similar provision was included in the House version of the bill, but it was stripped out in a highly emotional floor vote that occurred one day after the massacre in Killeen, Texas.

In November 1993, the Senate passed a ban on the manufacture of nineteen assault weapons, but also included a provision allowing gun dealers to sell guns that had already been produced. The measure, added to a crime bill, also exempted over 650 types of hunting weapons. In the spring of 1994, the House took up the assault weapons ban. From the start, ban supporters shared little optimism that the House would approve the measure. While the majority Democrats in Congress were more sympathetic to the measure, some of their leaders, such as Speaker Tom Foley (D-WA), were not. In April, Clinton weighed in strongly for the ban, enlisting the help of several Cabinet secretaries, most notably Treasury Secretary and gun owner Lloyd Bentsen. Ban supporters received unexpected help from Rep. Henry Hyde (R-IL), a staunch conservative who had opposed gun measures in the past. Thanks in part to Hyde's support, the measure was approved by the Judiciary Committee on April 28, despite the opposition of Committee Chair Jack Brooks (D-TX).

Even though a final preliminary tally showed that the measure lacked the necessary votes for passage, the assault-weapons ban managed to pass in the House in a stunning finale by a two-vote margin, 216–214, on May 5. The drama was heightened when Rep. Andrew Jacobs, Jr. (D-IN), at the urging of several colleagues, switched his vote to support the ban in the final seconds of the roll-call vote. As with other gun control legislation, the political pressures were intense. A staff person for one freshman Republican representative who supported the bill commented, "You don't know the threats we received."

Because the assault-weapons ban was part of a larger crime bill that had passed in different versions in the two houses, a conference committee was called to iron out those differences. Typically, a bill that survives the legislative gauntlet up to the point of conference committee is all but assured final passage. Such was not the case for the assault-weapons ban. Bill supporters initially predicted that the conference committee would complete its work by the end of May. Yet it did not report a bill back to the House and Senate until the end of July, during which time Representative Brooks, a member of the House-Senate conference, attempted repeatedly to kill the assault-weapons ban. Brooks's efforts failed, but he did succeed in inserting provisions that exempted pawnbrokers from the Brady Bill and that barred all antihunting protests from taking place on federal lands. Meanwhile, Republican leaders launched a full-scale assault on the $33 billion crime bill, calling it a wasteful piece of legislation laden with pork-barrel spending. Anxious to win final approval, and with an eye toward the fall elections, Clinton and his congressional allies pushed for an early vote in the House. This proved to be a serious tactical blunder, however, because they had not lined up the necessary support. In a dramatic reversal on a procedural vote to adopt a rule for the bill, the House rejected the crime bill on August 11 by a vote of 225–210.

Under normal circumstances, a defeat on a rules vote would spell the end of the legislation. Yet Clinton would not accept the bill's defeat. He launched an intense public campaign, enlisting the assistance of police organizations and several members of his Cabinet. Congressional leaders vowed to bring the bill back, and in another departure from normal procedure, they negotiated a new version of the bill, this time cutting the bill's spending by about 10 percent.

On August 21, after three days and two nights of intense negotiation, the revised bill was again brought before the House in a highly unusual Sunday session. This time, with the help of moderate Republicans and four members of the black caucus who were persuaded to vote with the pres-

ident, the bill passed by a vote of 235–195. The bill then went to the Senate, where after considerable partisan wrangling, the bill was passed. Clinton signed the bill, HR 3355, on September 13. After the Republicans won control of Congress in the 1994 elections, party leaders promised to repeal the ban. In 1996, a measure to repeal passed in the House, but no Senate vote was taken, ending the effort to repeal.

The effectiveness of the ban was questioned by many, as manufacturers and dealers were able to make minor or cosmetic alterations to formerly banned weapons in order to avoid the regulations.

Robert J. Spitzer

See also Assault Weapons; National Rifle Association; Semiautomatic Weapons; Sporting Purposes Test

For Further Reading:
Spitzer, Robert J. 1998. *The Politics of Gun Control.* New York: Chatham House.
Vizzard, William J. 2000. *Shots in the Dark.* Lanham, MD: Rowman and Littlefield.
Windlesham, Lord. 1998. *Politics, Punishment, and Populism.* New York: Oxford University Press.

Assize of Arms
See Anglo-Saxon Tradition of the Right to Keep and Bear Arms

Association of American Physicians and Surgeons (AAPS)

The Association of American Physicians and Surgeons (AAPS) is a professional association of physicians founded in 1943 to further the practice of private, market-based medicine. The AAPS supports conservative, free-market positions on health care; strongly opposes government involvement in the health care system; and calls itself the "Delta Force" of private medicine. The organization also opposes Medicare and compulsory vaccination. In terms of gun control, it opposes the public health model of handgun violence, argues that the Second Amendment protects the right of individuals to own guns, and criticizes efforts to promote the regulation and control of firearms.

By the late 1970s, the Centers for Disease Control (CDC) had begun to emphasize a public health perspective on gun violence. In the early 1990s, the American Medical Association (AMA) and the American Academy of Pediatrics (AAP), along with more specialized medical organizations such as Doctors Against Handgun Injury (DAHI), began calling for more effective and restrictive gun controls. These organizations worked to define handgun violence as a public health issue. In the 1980s, medical journals had started publishing research on the causes and consequences of gun violence.

The AAPS, along with several other small medical associations such as Doctors for Responsible Gun Ownership (DRGO) and Doctors for Integrity in Policy Research (DIPR), vehemently opposes seeing handgun violence as a public health problem or as an epidemic. In addition to its criticism of the AMA, AAP, and DAHI, the organization also insists that gun research sponsored by the CDC and what it calls the public health establishment, is mostly politically motivated "junk science." The AAPS insists that handguns save lives and has published two special issues of its journal the *Medical Sentinel* focusing on the topic.

In the special issues of the *Medical Sentinel,* Dr. Miguel Faria, editor of the journal and the most visible spokesperson for the AAPS, argues that most gun violence studies have been methodologically flawed and politically motivated. Faria claims that (1) women are not endangered by carrying firearms, (2) easy access to guns does not cause crime, (3) mass killings are not due to the availability of guns, (4) gun violence is not the leading cause of death in children, and (5) the availability of guns actually saves both lives and money.

The AAPS also opposes efforts by other medical associations to encourage physicians to ask their patients about gun ownership. For example, the AAP advocates the removal of guns from homes and recommends that pediatricians ask parents whether they do have guns in the home. The AAPS criticizes the AAP recommendation for doctors to question parents about handguns in homes, suggesting that it may lead to "massive" legal liability.

Walter F. Carroll

See also American Academy of Pediatrics; American Medical Association; Centers for Disease Control; Doctors for Integrity in Policy Research; Doctors for Responsible Gun Ownership; Gun Violence as a Public Health Problem; Ideologies—Conservative and Liberal; Kates, Don B., Jr.; Kleck, Gary; Lott, John R., Jr.; Medicine and Gun Violence

For Further Reading:
Association of American Physicians and Surgeons. http://www.aapsonline.org/.
Bijlefeld, Marjolijn. 1999. "Miguel A. Faria, Jr." Pp. 86–89 in *People for and against Gun Control: A Biographical Reference.* Westport, CT: Greenwood Press.
DeConde, Alexander. 2001. *Gun Violence in America.* Boston: Northeastern University Press.
Kates, Don B., Jr., with John K. Lattimer and James Boen. 1997. "Sagecraft: Bias and Mendacity in the Public Health Literature on Gun Usage." Pp. 123–147 in *The Great American Gun Debate: Essays on Firearms and Violence,* eds. Don B. Kates, Jr. and Gary Kleck. San Francisco: Pacific Research Institute for Public Policy.

Attitudes toward Gun Control

Public opinion is a summary measure or description of the political attitudes of a group of persons on some public issue. In a democratic system, the opinion of the citizenry is to be the driving force behind public policy. Although there is evidence of longstanding support for strong gun control measures, and levels of support have increased in recent decades, elected officials have difficulties translating public opinion into public policy.

In a constitutional republic, the translation of public opinion into public policy is done by way of elected representatives and is limited by the constitutional framework, which places limits on the ability of the majority to enact its will in ways that would unduly harm the minority or jeopardize the system as a whole. However, even if one takes the simplistic adage "majority rules" as a guiding principle, there is no easy method of identifying majority public opinion in any policy area, let alone one as complicated as gun policy. Because public opinion is best thought of as a distribution, a conglomerate made up of the opinions of a group of individuals, one must usually consider the many points along a spectrum of opinion.

The ability to understand or even describe public opinion on an issue is closely tied to how one defines the issue and measures the individual opinions surrounding it. A statement such as "Public opinion supports gun control" hides much more than it reveals. It is true that many specific control proposals (e.g., a ban on the sale of assault weapons or the manufacture of plastic handguns) are supported by a clear majority of Americans. However, the issue of gun control is much broader than any of these specific measures, covering everything from universal bans on all civilian ownership of firearms to mandatory safety training before purchase. Thus, narrowly defined statements regarding public sentiment on specific public policy proposals are much more trustworthy than broad characterizations of support or opposition regarding controls, bans, permits, and the like.

Added to this are complications arising from the intensity with which individuals hold an opinion and the saliency of the issue in question. One person, when asked, might evince support for criminal background checks, but may not feel especially strong about it. Another might feel an almost religious fervor on the topic. For some, the issue of gun control hardly registers, while for others it is a topic worthy of daily thought, discussion, and action. Intensity and saliency are also related to the stability of individual opinion, which in turn shapes the stability of public opinion. Most research has indicated that, for the majority of Americans, opinions on guns and gun control are not very intensely held nor is the issue itself usually salient. This means that compelling events of the day, especially such high-profile national events as attempts at assassinating public officials or a spate of school shootings, often produce temporary shifts in public opinion.

Elected officials, especially members of the national legislature, are the most important audience for public opinion and are keenly aware of its ebbs and flows and the many nuances with which it is expressed. For a legislator, ever attuned to how an action will affect chances for success in an upcoming election, the question is not just how many people support a given policy, but how likely a person is to base actions (votes, donations, etc.) upon that issue. In essence, there is a complex calculus by which the politician weighs the opinions that reach his or her ears. Opinions that lack intensity, that are related to less salient issues, or that are likely to change in the near term, are given less weight. To put it another way, an intense, well-organized minority will usually overcome a marginally interested, easily distracted majority.

It is difficult to summarize the existing public opinion data on gun control without falling prey to charges of overgeneralization. However, there are some general patterns and statements that may be safely made. First, it is clear that there is widespread support for many specific proposals to regulate access to firearms, and majorities of Americans have expressed that support for several decades. In question after question, over a period of several decades, involving specific policies ranging from registrations and permits, to waiting periods, to limits on the number of guns that might be purchased, support levels usually hover near 75 percent.

Outright bans on guns of various types are among the least favored types of control measures. However, even gun bans, if they are targeted at particular types of firearms, often garnered between 55–75 percent support on surveys conducted throughout the 1990s and into the twenty-first century. The most often asked about type of firearm bans targeted so-called assault weapons, which were highly demonized by the press and gun control groups during the period in the wake of several high-profile mass shootings. Among the most palatable forms of controls are waiting periods and restrictions on classes of persons (such as convicted criminals and minors). Throughout the 1990s and early 2000s support for measures of these types approached or exceeded 90 percent.

From its nadir in the early 1980s, support for control measures has climbed steadily for the past two decades. The National Opinion Research Center, in its General Social Survey, has asked respondents the following question

Attitudes toward Gun Control

Characteristic	Percent in Favor of Requiring a Police Permit to Buy a Gun	Correlation (Gamma*)	Statistical Significance
Gender			
Male	72.7	0.44	<0.001
Female	87.1		
Race			
White	79.9	0.16	<0.009
Black	84.5		
Age			
18–39	80.7	0.02	>0.538
40–59	80.0		
60+	82.1		
Family Income per Year			
Less than $20,000	81.0	0.02	>0.535
$20,000–$50,000	80.1		
More than $50,000	82.3		
Occupational Prestige			
Lowest quartile	80.8	0.07	<0.027
Second quartile	77.6		
Third quartile	80.3		
Highest quartile	84.6		
Education			
Less than high school	79.9	0.10	<0.002
High school	79.3		
Junior college	80.3		
College degree	84.2		
Graduate degree	87.0		
Urbanization			
Rural	69.5	0.19	<0.001
Small town	77.0		
Suburb	81.7		
City	83.7		
Region			
Northwest	85.6	-0.12	<0.006
Midwest	81.0		
South	78.0		
Far west	78.8		
Foreign-born?			
No	80.4	-0.21	<0.006
Yes	86.4		
Political views			
Liberal	87.0	-0.25	<0.001
Moderate	81.6		
Conservative	75.4		
Political party			
Democrat	84.9	-0.19	<0.001
Republican	76.5		
Independent	79.3		
Burglarized in past year?			
No	81.5	-0.04	<0.688
Yes	80.2		

(continues)

Robbed in past year?			
No	81.3	0.19	<0.201
Yes	86.5		
Fears walking in own neighborhood?			
No	77.1	0.26	<0.001
Yes	85.2		
Hunter?			
No	86.2	-0.69	<0.001
Yes	53.3		
Gun-owning household?			
No	88.9	-0.55	<0.001
Yes	70.1		

Note: Correlation statistics summarize the strength of the relationship between two variables and can vary between −1 and +1. Gamma is a particular kind of correlational statistic appropriate for survey variables. As Gamma approaches zero, the relationship becomes increasingly less significant. As Gamma approaches either −1 or +1, the relationship becomes increasingly stronger. The sign (+ or −) indicates only the direction of the relationship, not its strength. For positive relationships, the variables are changing in the same direction. When statistical significance is <.05, conventional social science standards would deem the relationship as highly *significant.*
Source: Adapted from Carter, Gregg Lee. *The Gun Control Movement* (New York: Twayne, 1997), 53–54.

since 1972: "Would you favor or oppose a law which would require a person to obtain a police permit before he or she could buy a gun?" For almost twenty years, support for permits hovered between 70 and 75 percent. In 1989 it began to climb and has remained in the vicinity of 80 percent throughout the 1990s and early 2000s. Data on handgun registration, taken from numerous polls, indicate that support for this slightly more restrictive set of policies has risen from a low of about two-thirds of all Americans in the early 1980s to about 80 percent in the 1990s.

Some of the most irresolvable and contentious issues in American politics are those that coincide with existing divisions such as race, class, or culture. Gun control is certainly a perennial policy topic of long-standing and the partisans on both sides rate as among the most strident on any issue. As a political fault line, however, gun control does not closely parallel those other major dividing lines. By the 1990s, data on attitudes toward purchase permits, taken from such national surveys as the General Social Survey, showed no substantive differences by age, race, or household income. While males, hunters, and those living outside of cities and towns were less supportive of purchase permits,

in all of these groups clear majorities expressed support. Most interesting of all, there is widespread support among even gun owners for this type of control measure. This does, however, differ by type of gun ownership. Those who own long guns (rifles and shotguns) are far more resistant to the notion of gun control, whereas levels of support among those who own only handguns do not differ significantly from that found in the general population.

The accompanying table gives a detailed breakdown of the social and economic correlates of support for gun control as the issue is expressed in the General Social Survey ("Would you favor or oppose a law which would require a person to obtain a police permit before he or she could buy a gun?")

David Harding

See also Congressional Voting Patterns on Gun Control; General Social Survey; Gun Control; Ideologies—Conservative and Liberal

For Further Reading:

Asher, Herbert. 1992. *Polling and the Public.* Washington, DC: CQ Press.

Carter, Gregg Lee. 1997. *The Gun Control Movement.* New York: Twayne.

Crocker, Royce. 1982. "Attitudes toward Gun Control: A Survey." Pp. 229–267 in *Federal*

Regulation of Firearms, ed. Harry L. Hogan.
Washington, DC: Government Printing Office.

Mitchell, Susan. 1996. The Official Guide to
American Attitudes: Who Thinks What about the
Issues That Shape Our Lives. Ithaca, NY: New
Strategist Publications.

Tonso, William R. 1990. "Social Problems and
Stagecraft: Gun Control as a Case in Point." Pp.
35–53 in The Gun Control Debate: You Decide,
ed. Lee Nisbet. Buffalo, NY: Prometheus.

Automatic Weapons Laws

Federal government regulation of automatic weapons—those capable of firing bullets in rapid succession by depressing and holding down the gun trigger—dates to 1934. The use of submachine guns, such as the infamous Tommy gun, by gangsters in the 1920s and 1930s sparked public outrage and calls for government regulation.

Created for military use at the end of World War I, the Tommy gun was developed by U.S. Army Colonel John M. Thompson for use in trench warfare. Referred to by Thompson as a "trench broom," it was designed so that a single soldier could deliver numerous shots in a brief space of time, comparable to the heavier and more cumbersome machine guns used so devastatingly in the war. After the war, Thompson tried to market his gun, but had little success until Chicago gangsters began using the gun in 1925. Soon, other gangsters followed suit. Because automatic weapons could fire hundreds of rounds in a minute and produced a recoil that made aim and control difficult to impossible, they had no legitimate hunting or sporting use and posed a considerable danger to anyone in the vicinity of such a weapon.

In response, several states passed anti–machine gun laws, but the federal government failed to act until 1934. In a bill backed by President Franklin D. Roosevelt and referred to as the "Anti-Machine Gun Bill," Congress considered a measure that would have required national registration and taxation of several types of firearms that were considered appealing to criminals, including handguns, sawed-off shotguns, cane guns, and automatic weapons. The original proposal also called for fingerprinting individuals who purchased such weapons. This proposal drew opposition from the National Rifle Association and other gun interests. Responding to these pressures, the bill reported out of committee omitted pistols. As enacted, the National Firearms Act of 1934 (48 Stat. 1236) requires automatic weapons to be registered with the U.S. Treasury Department. The owner must be fingerprinted, undergo a background check, and pay a fee.

There were no major changes in the law until the Firearms Owners' Protection Act of 1986, which barred future possession or transfer of automatic weapons. However, pre-1986 weapons can be sold by federally licensed class III firearm dealers if the buyer passes the necessary background check and pays the federal tax. As of the mid-1990s, according to the U.S. government's Bureau of Justice Statistics, about 240,000 fully automatic weapons were registered in the United States. Half were owned by private individuals and the other half by various law enforcement and other government agencies. Law enforcement officials have noted that automatic weapons hold special appeal for criminals, especially those involved in drug trafficking, but crime statistics do not support the idea that such weapons are widely used by criminals, probably owing to the government's early and strict regulation of such weapons.

Robert J. Spitzer

See also Assault Weapons; Firearms Owners' Protection Act of 1986; Gun Control; National Firearms Act of 1934; Tommy Gun

For Further Reading:

Kennett, Lee, and James LaVerne Anderson.
1975. The Gun in America. Westport, CT:
Greenwood Press.

Leff, Carol Skalnik, and Mark H. Leff. 1981. "The
Politics of Ineffectiveness: Federal Firearms
Legislation, 1919–38." Annals of the American
Academy of Political and Social Science 455 (May):
48–62.

Vizzard, William J. 2000. Shots in the Dark.
Lanham, MD: Rowman and Littlefield.

Availability of Guns, Effects on Crime

Multiple theories have been offered as to the effect of gun availability on crime, including the following:

1. *Guns Facilitate Crime by Those Inclined to It:* Besides being almost self-evident, this is amply supported by empirical evidence. Gun robberies net far more than do robberies in which other weapons are used because without a gun, a robber is basically limited to attacking individuals. Also, guns allow robbers to attack such lucrative targets as banks and stores, whose proprietors might be armed (Kleck, 1997, p. 239).

By the same token, American and foreign data both show victims are less likely to suffer injury from robbers using guns. This is because victims are much more likely to comply if confronted with a gun; and robbers armed with lesser weapons may feel the need to start out by gratuitously hurting the victim in order to preempt resistance. Of course, if a gun robber actually shoots a victim, death is likelier than from injury with some lesser weapon (Cook, 1987 p. 361; Kleck, 1997, p. 238). Also, guns enable the weak to prey on the strong, though, in fact, criminals are mostly younger and stronger than victims.

2. *Guns Allow Victims to Resist Attack:* Neither martial-arts skills nor chemical sprays provide a real option for victims faced by attackers who are stronger or armed. Indeed, sprays like Mace are ineffective against attackers who are high on alcohol or drugs, or are intensely angry or excited, i.e., just the people who are most likely to attack and be the most dangerous (Jacobs, 1989).

It bears emphasis that those who deprecate self-defense with guns do *not* recommend using any other kind of weapon instead. Their advice to victims threatened with robbery or rape is "the best defense against injury is to put up no defense—give them what they want or run" (Shields, 1981; Zimring and Zuehl, 1986; Handgun Control Staff, 1976).

That advice is only partly supported by the evidence. Victims resisting with a lesser weapon than a gun are about twice as likely to suffer injury as victims who submit. But victims who pull guns find criminals generally flee. As a result, analysis of decades of national data shows victims who resist with a gun are only half as likely to suffer injury as those who submit—and of course, are much less likely to be robbed or raped (Kleck, 1997; Kates, 1991).

There is intense controversy as to just how often victims armed with guns actually do confront attacking felons. While the Federal Bureau of Investigation (FBI) compiles and publishes annual data on crimes, there is no protocol for self-defense incidents so, even when they are reported, police agencies do not record them as such. In surveys of prison inmates sponsored by the National Institute of Justice "[s]eventy percent of the respondents reported having been 'scared off,' shot at, wounded, or captured by a [gun-]armed crime victim" (Sheley and Wright, 1995, p. 63; Wright and Rossi, 1986, p. 154). From responses to more than fifteen national and state surveys in which the general populace was asked about defensive gun use, Gary Kleck (1995, 1997) estimated that 2–2.5 million victims annually use handguns to repel criminal attackers. Handguns are used by citizens to defend against crime about three times as often annually as by criminals to commit crimes. (Many of these incidents do not involve victims confronting criminals with guns, however. Less than 30 percent of all violent crime involves guns [Bureau of Justice Statistics, 1998, table 3-116]; for instance, guns are involved in only 25 percent of robberies and 4 percent of rapes [Kleck, 1997].)

Kleck's estimate has been vindicated by subsequent research (Southwick, 1997) and proved persuasive even to a criminologist who was deeply antipathetic to firearms (Wolfgang, 1995). Many others have felt Kleck's estimate highly exaggerated. But the principal critics' own national survey yielded the even higher figure of 3 million defensive uses annually. At that point they decided that surveys cannot provide a reliable index to defensive firearm use (Cook and Ludwig, 1998). They and other scholars opposed to defensive firearm ownership point to a different survey vehicle (the National Crime Victimization Survey) that suggests—but without directly posing the question—the incidence of defensive gun use is less than 100,000 annually (McDowall and Wiersema 1994; Cook and Ludwig, 2000; however, contrast Kleck and Kates, 2001).

3. *Guns Deter Criminal Attack:* The National Institute of Justice prison surveys found "36% of the respondents [imprisoned felons] in our study reported having decided at least 'a few times' not

to commit a crime because they believed the potential victim was armed." Between 34-36 percent of the inmates said that in contemplating a crime they either "often" or "regularly" worried they "Might get shot at by the victim." Fifty-seven percent of inmates agreed that "Most criminals are more worried about meeting an armed victim than they are about running into the police" (Sheley & Wright, 1995, p. 63; Wright & Rossi, 1986, p. 154).

Many American states now allow law-abiding, responsible adults to carry concealed handguns. From a study of twenty-five years of crime data in those states compared to states without such laws, University of Chicago economists concluded that the prospect of encountering an armed victim has deterred criminals from committing thousands of rapes, robberies, and/or murders. Predictably, this conclusion has been a subject of great controversy (see criticisms in Black and Nagin, 1998, and Dezhbakhsa and Rubin, 1998; for responses, see Shugart, 1999, and Lott, 2000).

4. *Firearm Availability "Causes" Violence:* The theoretical basis for seeing firearm availability as "causing" murder (rather than just facilitating it) is that law-abiding people kill because they have access to a gun in a moment of ungovernable passion. This is incorrect because murderers are almost never ordinary people. Rather, they are extreme aberrants with histories of violence, other crime, psychopathology, and substance abuse. Gun availability to such aberrants does facilitate their violence, but does not "cause" ordinary people to kill.

The theory that increased gun availability generally does increase homicide seemed plausible in the late 1960s when a substantial increase in guns coincided with a doubling of the American homicide rate. But correlation does not prove causation. Instead of more guns causing more crime, it appears that the vast crime increases of that era caused more people to buy guns. If more guns were, as is often asserted, "the major cause" of high American murder rates, the vast increases in guns since the 1960s should have coincided with vast increases in homicide. In fact, the reverse is true: Despite an approximately 160 percent increase in the number of handguns (from 36.9 million to 94.9 million) over the twenty-five-year

period 1973–1997 and a 103 percent increase in guns of all kinds (from 128 million to 254.5 million), the homicide rate actually dropped 27.7 percent (Kates and Polsby, 2000).

Nor do the much lower murder rates of Western Europe prove that it is widespread gun ownership that drives American homicide. When the twentieth century began, Western Europe had no gun laws, yet still had much lower homicide rates than the United States (where guns were more restricted legally). European gun laws were adopted in the tumultuous post–World War I era to prevent political crime, not curb apolitical homicide. Moreover Switzerland, where guns are nearly as widespread as in the United States—and even less legally controlled—has a lower homicide rate than most of its gun-banning neighbors (Barnett and Kates 1996, pp. 1236–42).

What all this suggests is that homicide rates reflect basic socioeconomic and cultural factors, not the mere availability of any particular form of weaponry. This is reinforced by two more facts. If gun availability accounted for the differences in national homicide rates, those differences should be confined to gun homicides, but they are not. Despite its lower population, the United States has more knife murders annually than Western Europe and Japan have murders committed with guns, knives, and every other kind of weapon combined. Once again, it is not the weaponry that makes the United States so violent, but the existence of a relatively larger number of violent aberrants in this country than in Western Europe and Japan.

This is further evidenced by the more relevant comparison of the United States to another extremely violent society, Russia, which remains violent despite many decades of laws and enforcement that have virtually eliminated gun ownership there. Citing data only recently available, Pridemore (2001) denies that the United States is the world's most homicidal society, claiming the Russian murder "rate has been comparable with or greater than in the United States for at least the past three and a half decades."

The Russian example also contradicts the idea that the 1960s–1970s doubling of the American homicide rate reflects the effect of increased gun ownership; for during that same period the Russian homicide rate also doubled, though virtually none of Russia's homicides were or are with guns. In 1965 the U.S. rate was 5.4 homicides per 100,000 population and the Russian rate was 5.9. By 1980 the U.S. rate was 10.5 homicides per 100,000 population, and Russia's was 13.0. When Russia went through its political chaos in the early 1990s, the Russian homicide rate almost tripled. Though Russian conditions had largely stabilized as of 1999, the Russian homicide rate "of a little more than 21 per 100,000 population was nearly 4 times greater than the [American] rate of 5.7" (Pridemore, 2001).

Don B. Kates

See also Average-Joe Thesis; Defensive Gun Use; Japan, Gun Laws; Lethality Effect of Guns; Mexico, Gun Laws; National Crime Victimization Survey; Switzerland, Gun Laws

For Further Reading:
Barnett, Randy E., and Don B. Kates. 1996. "Under Fire." *Emory Law Journal* 45: 1139–1259.
Black, Dan A., and Daniel S. Nagin. 1998. "Do Right-to-Carry Laws Deter Violent Crime?" *Journal of Legal Studies* 27: 209–219.
Bureau of Justice Statistics. 1998. *Sourcebook of Criminal Justice Statistics—1997.* Washington, DC: U.S. Department of Justice.
Cook, Philip J. 1987. "Robbery Violence." *Journal of Criminal Law and Criminology* 78: 357–376.
Cook, Philip J., and Jens Ludwig. 1998. "Defensive Gun Uses: New Evidence from a National Survey." *Journal of Quantitative Criminology* 14: 111–131.
———. 2000. *Gun Violence: The Real Costs.* Oxford: Oxford University Press.
Dezhbakhsha, Hashem, and Paul Rubin. 1998. "Lives Saved or Lives Lost: The Effects of Concealed Handgun Laws on Crime." *American Economic Review Papers and Proceedings* 88: 468–474.
Handgun Control Staff (Matthew G. Yeager, Joseph D. Alviani, and Nancy Loving). 1976. *How Well Does the Handgun Protect You and Your Family? Handgun Control Staff Technical Report 2.* Washington, DC: United States Conference of Mayors.
Jacobs, James B. 1989. "The Regulation of Personal Chemical Weapons: Some Anomalies in American Weapons Law." *University Dayton Law Review* 15: 141–159.
Kates, Don B. 1991. "The Value of Civilian Arms Possession as Deterrent to Crime or Defense against Crime." *American Journal of Criminal Law* 18: 113–167.
Kates, Don B., and Daniel D. Polsby. 2000. "Long Term Non-Relationship of Firearm Availability to Homicide." *Homicide Studies* 4: 185–201.
Kleck, Gary. 1995. "Guns and Violence: An Interpretive Review of the Field." *Social Pathology* 1: 12–47.
———. 1997. *Targeting Guns: Firearms and Their Control.* Hawthorne, NY: Aldine de Gruyter.
Kleck, Gary, and Don B. Kates. 2001. *Armed: New Perspectives on Gun Control.* Amherst, NY: Prometheus Books.
Lott, John R., Jr. 2000. *More Guns, Less Crime.* 2d ed. Chicago: University of Chicago Press.
McDowall, David, and Brian Wiersema. 1994. "The Incidence of Defensive Firearm Use by U.S. Crime Victims, 1987 through 1990." *American Journal of Public Health* 84: 1982–1984.
Pridemore, William A. 2001. "Using Newly Available Homicide Data to Debunk Two Myths about Violence in an International Context: A Research Note." *Homicide Studies* 5: 267–275.
Sheley, Joseph, and James D. Wright. 1995. *In the Line of Fire: Youth, Guns, and Violence in Urban America.* Hawthorne, NY: Aldine de Gruyter.
Shields, Pete. 1981. *Guns Don't Die—People Do.* New York: Arbor House.
Shugart, William F. 1999. "More Guns, Less Crime: Understanding Crime and Gun Control Laws." *Southern Economic Journal* 65: 978–981.
Southwick, Lawrence. 1997. "Do Guns Cause Crime? Does Crime Cause Guns? A Granger Test." *Atlantic Economic Journal* 25: 256–273.
Wolfgang, Marvin E. 1995. "A Tribute to a View I Have Long Opposed." *Journal of Criminal Law and Criminology* 86: 188–192.
Wright, James D., and Peter H. Rossi. 1986. *Armed and Considered Dangerous: A Survey of Felons and Their Firearms.* Hawthorne, NY: Aldine de Gruyter.
Zimring, Franklin E., and Gordon Hawkins. 1987. *The Citizen's Guide to Gun Control.* New York: Macmillan.
Zimring, Franklin E., and James Zuehl. 1986. "Victim Injury Death in Urban Robbery: A Chicago Study." *Journal of Legal Studies* 15: 1–40.

Average-Joe Thesis

The central conundrum of gun control is that those whom it is most urgent to disarm are at the same time least subject to being disarmed, while those most likely to comply are the law abiding whom it is least important to disarm. This conundrum is dismissed by those who assert that murderers are mostly law-abiding people ("average Joes") who would comply with a law banning firearms and who killed only because a gun was available in a moment of ungovernable anger (National Coalition to Ban Handguns, n.d.; Christoffel, 1991, p. 300).

If that were true, banning guns would be a cheap and effective way of reducing murder. However, murders are rarely, if ever, committed by ordinary, law-abiding persons. For as long as homicide studies have been done they have shown murderers to be people who are unlikely to comply with either gun laws or laws against violence in general. In almost every instance, murderers' lives are characterized by violence (often irrational) and other crime, substance abuse, psychopathology, and automobile, firearm, and other dangerous accidents (Mulvihill, Tumin, and Curtis, 1969, p. 532; Uniform Crime Reports, 1972, p. 38, and 1976, pp. 42ff; Straus, 1986; Robin, 1991, pp. 46–48; Dowd, Knapp, and Fitzmaurice, 1994, p. 872; Bureau of Justice Statistics, 1993; Kennedy, Piehl, and Braga, 1997; Kennedy and Braga, 1998; Braga, Piehl, and Kennedy, 1999; Rojek, 2000; Langford, Isaac, and Adams, 2000). Indeed, even those responsible for fatal gun accidents have a similar profile (Cook, 1982; Kleck, 1997, pp. 29–30). These are people having remarkably little concern for laws or lives, even their own lives.

Federal Bureau of Investigation (FBI) national data show homicide arrestees averaging a prior adult criminal career of at least six years, including four major felony arrests (Uniform Crime Reports, 1976, pp. 42ff.). Though only 15 percent of Americans have any kind of criminal record, national, state, and local studies consistently show criminal records for upward of 70–80 percent of arrested murderers. For instance, the federal Bureau of Justice Statistics study of "murder defendants [under indictment] in the nation's 75 largest counties" found 76.7 percent "had a criminal history" (Bureau of Justice Statistics, 1993). Moreover, murderers' criminal records tend to be robust. Without even considering other offenses they may have committed, 80 percent of Atlanta murder arrestees in 1997 had at least one prior drug offense; fully 70 percent had three or more prior drug offenses (Rojek, 2000).

Nor would it be correct to assume that if 70–80 percent of murderers have prior adult records, the other 20–30 percent must be the kind of ordinarily law-abiding people who would comply with a gun-confiscation order. In the first place, 10–15 percent of murderers are juveniles who, by definition, cannot have adult criminal records. But, insofar as their juvenile records are available, they show the same pattern as for adult murders. Researchers who have obtained access to criminal records for juvenile murderers in Minneapolis, Boston, Baltimore, and Kansas City describe them as "a relatively small number of very scary kids" (Kennedy, Piehl, and Braga, 1997; Kennedy and Braga, 1998; Dowd, Knapp, and Fitzmaurice, 1994). So extensive are their records that the combined priors of the 125 minors who killed other minors in Boston in the years 1990–1994 totaled 3 previous murder charges; 160 armed violent crimes; 151 unarmed violent crimes; 71 firearm offenses and 8 involving other weapons; and hundreds of property offenses, drug offenses, and other crimes (Kennedy, Piehl, and Braga, 1997).

Assuming adult murderers have juvenile crime records similar to these Boston juvenile murderers, their combined juvenile-cum-adult records would average ten to fourteen priors per murderer. Another reason 20–30 percent of murderers have no official record of prior crime is that much or all of their violence has been directed against their family members. Such victims are less likely to press charges and the police are loath to interfere in a family matter. A study of police responding to domestic disturbance calls in Kansas City found that 90 percent of all family homicides were preceded by previous disturbances at the same address, with a median of five calls per address. Thus homicide—of a stranger or someone known to the offender—is "usually part of a pattern of violence, engaged in by people who are known as violence prone" (Robin, 1991, pp. 47–48).

Perpetrator studies that delve beyond crime records find that, whether murderers also have such records of deviance, virtually all have life histories studded with violence and other crimes that may not have led to arrest. So, while a Massachusetts domestic murder study found at least 74.7 percent of perpetrators had priors, it also found 23.6 percent "were under an active restraining order at the time of the homicide. Forty percent of perpetrators had a history of having been under a restraining order at some time prior to the homicide, taken out by the victim or some other person" (Langford, Isaac, and Adams, 2000). Another form of aberrant behavior sharply distinguishing murderers from ordinary people is that often during childhood or adolescence the former tortured and/or killed animals.

To some extent, the myth that murderers are just "average-Joes" stems from a misunderstanding of the often-used description "domestic and acquaintance murder." That does not mean murderers are ordinary, law-abiding people. National data show the largest proportion of gun murders occurring in homes involving people who became acquainted through prior illicit drug dealings. Among New Orleans murder victims, 85 percent of those autopsied in 1992–1993 tested positive for metabolites of cocaine. In Los Angeles, 71 percent of minors injured in drive-by shootings "were documented members of violent street gangs." In Washington, D.C., 80 percent of all murders are estimated to be drug-related. Of Philadelphia murder victims in 1990–1996, between 84 percent and 93 percent tested positive for illegal drug use or had criminal histories (Kleck, 1997, p. 236; Hutson, Anglin, Pratts, 1994, p. 235; Cook and Ludwig, 2000, p. 23).

For several years a colloquium on juvenile murders in Boston has been conducted by a group consisting of academics, police, probation officers, and youth workers. Initially "the practitioners felt strongly that the youth homicide problem was almost entirely a gang problem." But on closer examination it was realized that a distinction had to be made. Yes, virtually all youth murders are committed by gang members. Yet many of these murders are unrelated to a gang, e.g., a gang member beating his girlfriend to death or shooting a drug dealer in the course of ripping him off (Braga, Piehl, and Kennedy, 1999, pp. 283–284).

In sum, while "domestic and/or acquaintance murder" literally describes many homicides, it does not refer to murders by "average-Joes" in ordinary neighborhoods and families. Typical domestic and/or acquaintance murders involve gang members; drug dealers, their competitors,

and/or customers; and men who kill women they have brutalized on prior occasions. While it is only sensible to prohibit firearm possession by such people, the fact that our laws already do so attests to the difficulty of disarming those who are inclined toward violence and determined to possess arms for that purpose.

Don B. Kates

See also Crime and Gun Use; Homicides, Gun; Women and Guns

For Further Reading:
Braga, Anthony, Anne M. Piehl, and David M. Kennedy. 1999. "Youth Homicide in Boston: An Assessment of the Supplementary Homicide Report Data." *Homicide Studies* 3: 277–299.
Bureau of Justice Statistics. 1993. "Murder Cases in 33 Large Urban Counties in the United States, 1988." Washington, DC: U.S. Department of Justice.
Christoffel, Katherine Kaufer. 1991. "Toward Reducing Pediatric Injuries from Firearms: Charting a Legislative and Regulatory Course." *Pediatrics* 88: 294.
Cook, Philip J. 1982. "The Role of Firearms in Violent Crime." Pp. 236–291 in *Criminal Violence,* ed. Marvin E. Wolfgang and Neil Alan Weiner. Beverly Hills: Sage.
Cook, Philip J. 1995. "Guns and Violence: An Interpretive Review of the Field." *Social Pathology* 1: 12–17.
Cook, Philip J., and Jens Ludwig. 2000. *Gun Violence: The Real Costs.* Oxford: Oxford University Press.
Dowd, M. Denise, Jana F. Knapp, and Laura S. Fitzmaurice. 1994. "Pediatric Firearm Injuries, Kansas City, 1992: A Population-Based Study." *Pediatrics* 94: 867–876.
Federal Bureau of Investigation. 1972. [Uniform Crime Reports.] *Crime in the United States 1971.* Washington, DC: Government Printing Office.
———. 1976. [Uniform Crime Reports.] *Crime in the United States 1975.* Washington, DC: Government Printing Office.
Hutson, H. Range, Deirdre Anglin, and Michael J. Pratts. 1994. "Adolescents and Children Injured or Killed in Drive-by Shootings in Los Angeles." *New England Journal of Medicine* 333: 326.
Kennedy, David, Anne M. Piehl, and Anthony Braga. 1997. "Youth Violence in Boston: Gun Markets, Serious Youth Offenders and a Use Reduction Strategy." *Law and Contemporary Problems* 59: 147–196.
Kennedy, David, and Anthony Braga. 1998. "Homicide in Minneapolis: Research for Problem Solving." *Homicide Studies* 2: 263–290.

Kleck, Gary. 1997. *Targeting Guns: Firearms and Their Control.* Hawthorne, NY: Aldine de Gruyter.

Langford, Linda, Nancy Isaac, and Sandra Adams. 2000. "Criminal and Restraining Order Histories of Intimate Partner-Related Homicide Offenders in Massachusetts, 1991–95." Pp. 51–61 in *The Varieties of Homicide and Its Research,* Paul H. Blackman et al. Quantico, VA: Federal Bureau of Investigation, FBI Academy.

Mulvihill, D. J., M. M. Tumin, and L. A. Curtis. 1969. *Crimes of Violence.* Washington, DC: Government Printing Office.

National Coalition to Ban Handguns. "A Shooting Gallery Called America." N.p., n.d.

Robin, Gerald D. 1991. *Violent Crime and Gun Control.* Cincinnati: Anderson Publishing.

Rojek, Dean G. 2000. "The Homicide and Drug Connection." Pp. 124–132 in *The Varieties of Homicide and Its Research,* Paul H. Blackman et al. Quantico, VA: Federal Bureau of Investigation, FBI Academy.

Straus, Murray A. 1986. "Domestic Violence and Homicide Antecedents." *Bulletin of the New York Academy of Medicine* 62: 446–461.

Aymette v. State (1840)

In 1840, the Tennessee Supreme Court in *Aymette v. State* (21 Tenn. 154, 3 Humphreys 154) declared that the state's legislature had the power to forbid the carrying of concealed weapons, despite the provision in the Tennessee constitution that guaranteed citizens (though only white citizens) the right to keep and bear arms "for their common defense." The court's conclusion took a position opposite to that decreed in an earlier Kentucky decision (*Bliss v. The Commonwealth*, 2 Ky. 90; 2 Littell Rep. 90, 1822). In that case, the state court of appeals overturned the conviction of a man who had carried a sword inside a cane on the ground that "whatever restrains the full and complete exercise [of the right to bear and keep arms] is forbidden by the explicit language of the [state] constitution" (*Bliss,* 1822: 91–92). The rationale set out in the *Aymette* decision would be employed ninety-nine years later by Justice James McReynolds in *United States v. Miller* (307 U.S. 174, 1939), the most recent U.S. Supreme Court case to adjudicate the reach of the Second Amendment of the federal Constitution.

The Tennessee case attended to the Second Amendment only obliquely, observing that the thrust of the Bill of Rights provision derived from the same English legal precedents as the Tennessee constitutional declaration. It would not be until 1932 that the U.S. Supreme Court in *Powell v. Alabama* (287 U.S. 145) first applied a guarantee in the Bill of Rights to the states, declaring that defendants had not received adequate legal counsel in a state court trial that involved the sentencing to death of eight African American men on trumped-up charges of raping two white women. Today, several of the first ten constitutional amendments—including the second—remain applicable only in federal jurisdictions.

The facts of the Tennessee weapons case were these: William Aymette had gone through the town of Pulaski seeking out a man he believed had wronged him. Aymette had a concealed weapon under his vest that resembled a bowie knife (also known as an Arkansas Tooth-Pick) and on occasion he waved the knife about openly. He was arrested and convicted of violating a law enacted during the 1837–1838 legislative session that forbade a person from carrying a concealed bowie knife. The offense was a misdemeanor and Aymette was sentenced to three months in jail and ordered to pay a $200 fine.

In its review of the *Aymette* case the Tennessee Supreme Court examined English precedents established during the reign of Charles II. In 1668, persons of high standing, as evidenced by how much money they possessed, were granted the right to bear and keep arms. Subsequently, James II disarmed the Protestants and quartered his Catholic troops among the people. William and Mary, his successors after James was forced to abdicate, reinstated the earlier arms provision.

The Tennessee judges were persuaded that the English law was meant to make certain that citizens would have the means to resist tyranny, such as that exercised by James II, who was said to have been able to "overawe" the people and make them submit to "the most arbitrary, cruel and illegal measures" (*Aymette,* p. 157). But Englishmen were accorded the right to keep and bear arms only for common defense purposes, that is, on occasions that the court labeled "civilized wars." Arms were not allowed for private defense; they could be employed legally only so that citizens as a body could rise up to defend their just rights. A concealed bowie knife could be outlawed without offending the state constitution, the Tennessee judges declared, because it was a weapon not traditionally used for military purposes and one that was dangerous to the peace and safety of the community; such a knife was "usually employed in private broils" and proved efficient "only in the hands of the robber and assassin" (*Aymette,* p. 158). A bowie knife would be mostly useless in war and the legislature had every right to declare its concealment on one's person a criminal offense.

Gilbert Geis

See also Anglo-Saxon Tradition of the Right to Keep and Bear Arms; *United States v. Miller*
For Further Reading:

Aymette v. State, 2 Humphreys 154 (Tenn. 1840). http://www–2.cs.cmu.edu/afs/cs/user/wbardwel/ public/nfalist/aymette_v_state.txt.
Reynolds, Glenn Hardin. 1995. "A Critical Guide to the Second Amendment." *Tennessee Law Review* 62: 461–512.

Background Checks

A background check entails an examination of the background of prospective gun buyers, conducted to determine whether the buyer has a criminal record, a history of mental illness, or other circumstances that should bar the individual from completing the gun purchase. The idea of conducting background checks of prospective gun buyers dates back at least to the 1930s, when a forty-eight-hour waiting period was applied in the District of Columbia; the drafting of that rule was assisted by the National Rifle Association (NRA), which continued to support the idea until the 1970s, when it reversed its position.

A concerted effort to enact a national waiting period for the purchase of a handgun in order to conduct background checks began in 1986. Those efforts succeeded in 1993 with the passage of the Brady Handgun Violence Prevention Act, which imposed a five-business-day waiting period for handgun purchases, during which time local law enforcement authorities were to conduct the necessary background checks. According to the law, handgun purchases are to be rejected if the applicant has been convicted of a crime that carries a sentence of at least a year (not including misdemeanors); if there is a violence-based restraining order against the applicant; or if the person has been convicted of domestic abuse, arrested for using or selling drugs, is a fugitive from justice, is certified as mentally unstable or is in a mental institution, or is an illegal alien or has renounced U.S. citizenship. Opponents of the law, including the NRA, filed suit against the Brady Bill, challenging its constitutionality—not as a violation of the Second Amendment's right to bear arms, but as a violation of states' rights under the Tenth Amendment. In 1997, a sharply divided U.S. Supreme Court struck down the law's provision requiring local police to conduct background checks in the case of *Printz v. United States* (521 U.S. 898). The ruling did not challenge the propriety of restricting handgun sales. Despite the ruling, handgun background checks generally continued on a voluntary basis.

In 1998, the five-day waiting period lapsed, as per the terms of the law, and was replaced by the Federal Bureau of Investigation's (FBI) National Instant Criminal Background Check System (NICS). This system is designed to allow an immediate background check to occur, although the system has been hampered by gaps in information and other technical problems. The check must be completed within three days, but 95 percent of the background checks are completed within two hours, according to a U.S. Justice Department report. From 1994 to 2000, almost 600,000 handgun purchases have been blocked as the result of background checks. This represented a rejection rate of about 2.5 percent of all handgun purchases. In 2000, twenty-six states conducted their own background checks; the rest relied on FBI data. State checks resulted in a slightly higher rejection rate, probably owing to better and more complete state data. Even though waiting periods are no longer required by the national government, nineteen states have their own, ranging from a few days to several months. They include Alabama, California, Connecticut, Florida, Illinois, Indiana, Kansas, Maryland, Massachusetts, Minnesota, Missouri, New Jersey, New York, North Carolina, Ohio, Rhode Island, South Dakota, Washington, and Wisconsin. Control proponents have argued for a restoration of a national three-day waiting period, in part because of the perceived value of a cooling-off period before handgun purchases.

One area of gun sales continues to be omitted from nationally mandated background checks. In most places, "secondary-market" gun sales by unlicensed individuals can occur without background checks. Referred to generally as the "gun-show loophole," these sales at gun shows, flea markets, and other unregulated venues account for as much as 40 percent of gun sales. As of 2000, eleven states required background checks for all handgun purchases, even those from unlicensed sellers. The tenth and eleventh states to close the gun-show loophole were Colorado and Oregon, where voters in the 2000 election approved statewide referenda requiring background checks for all gun-show purchases.

Robert J. Spitzer

See also Brady Handgun Violence Prevention Act (Brady Bill); Gun Shows; Licensing; National Rifle Association; *Printz v. United States;* Safety Courses; Waiting Periods
For Further Reading:
Spitzer, Robert J. 1998. *The Politics of Gun Control.* New York: Chatham House.
Vizzard, William J. 2000. *Shots in the Dark.* Lanham, MD: Rowman and Littlefield.

Bailey v. United States (1996)

In *Bailey v. United States* (516 U.S. 137 [1996]), the U.S. Supreme Court held that the government must show "an active employment" or active use of a firearm by a defendant in order for the defendant to be held criminally liable under a statute that makes it an offense to "use" or "carry" a firearm during a drug-trafficking crime. According to the Court, in order to be held criminally culpable under such a statute, the "Government must show that the defendant actively employed the firearm during and relation to the predicate crime." Hence, merely having the firearm stored in the trunk or glove compartment of a vehicle during the commission of a drug-trafficking offense would be insufficient, as the firearm was not being actively utilized during the commission of the crime. After *Bailey,* it has become much harder for prosecutors to win sentences under these criminal statutes, as the prosecutor must show actual use and employment of the weapon.

In *Bailey v. United States,* the petitioners Bailey and Robinson were both convicted of federal drug offenses and of violating section 924 (c)(1) of the Gun Control Act of 1968, which imposes a prison term upon a person who "during and in relation to any ... drug trafficking crime ... uses or carries a firearm." Bailey's conviction was based on a loaded pistol that the police found inside a bag in his locked car trunk after they arrested him for possession of cocaine found in the car's passenger compartment. Robinson's conviction was based on an unloaded, holstered firearm that was found in a trunk in her bedroom closet after she was arrested for a number of drug-related offenses. There was no evidence that either Bailey or Robinson actually employed or utilized the weapons in committing drug-related offenses.

The government had argued successfully on appeal to a lower court that the defendants should be held criminally responsible under the above statute if the guns were sufficiently accessible and proximate to the drugs so that the jury could potentially infer that the defendant had placed the gun in order to further the drug offenses or protect the possession of drugs. The Supreme Court, applying standard norms of statutory construction, rejected the government's arguments and held that the term "use" correctly connotes more than mere possession of a firearm. There must be an active employment of the weapon in the underlying crime. According to the Court, "use" would include such things as brandishing, displaying, bartering, striking with, and firing, or attempting to fire, a firearm, as well as making reference to a firearm in a defendant's possession. However, it does not include the mere placement or storage of the firearm at or near the site of crime, or at or near the proceeds, fruits or paraphernalia, of that crime.

James A. Beckman

See also *Beecham v. United States; Caron v. United States;* Enforcement of Gun Control Laws; Gun Control Act of 1968
For Further Reading:
Bettenhausen, Julie. 1998. "The Implications of Bailey v. United States on the Rise of the Convicted Criminal Claims and the Fall of 18 U.S.C. § 924(c)(1)." *Drake Law Review* 46: 677–715.

Barr, Bob

Bob Barr (R-GA) was elected to the U.S. House of Representatives in the Republican landslide of 1994. He has been perhaps the House's most outspoken critic of gun control. He has been one of the National Rifle Association's strongest supporters in Congress and sits on the organization's board of directors. Barr was named Gun Rights Legislator of the Year by the Citizens Committee for the Right to Keep and Bear Arms, in part because of his efforts to ban lawsuits against gun manufacturers. He has served as assistant majority whip and has a seat on the House Judiciary Committee, which deals with gun issues. On that committee, Barr earned national attention as a vehement critic of President Bill Clinton and a leading supporter of GOP impeachment efforts.

Barr worked with the Central Intelligence Agency in 1970–1978, earning during this time an M.A. from George Washington University in 1972 and a J.D. from Georgetown School of Law in 1977. He was appointed by President Ronald Reagan as U.S. attorney for the northern district in Georgia from 1986 through 1990. In 1990 he joined the conservative Southeastern Legal Foundation. He ran unsuccessfully for the U.S. Senate in 1992, but won a House seat in 1994 to represent Georgia's seventh congressional district.

Barr is chair of the Judiciary Subcommittee on Commercial and Administrative Law and is vice chair of the Government Reform Committee. He also serves on the Financial Services Committee. As assistant majority whip, Barr has functioned as a liaison between the party leadership and the party's social and cultural right. After the impeachment of Clinton in 1998, Barr emerged as one of the media stars of the Republican right and as an important player in GOP politics.

Barr has made opposition to gun control one of his defining issues. He has introduced national legislation to ban civil suits against gun manufacturers and worked to ensure passage of a similar law in Georgia. He has cosponsored laws to increase penalties for convicted felons who commit crimes using guns and been a leading critic of the Bureau of Alcohol, Tobacco, and Firearms.

Bob Barr. (U.S. House of Representatives)

In addition to the award as Gun Rights Legislator of the Year, Barr has been honored as Congressional Leader of the Year by the American Shooting Sports Council; named Freshman Legislator of the Year by the Conservative Political Action Committee; and received the Freedom Award from the Law Enforcement Alliance of America. He has received significant support from progun political action committees. Yet Barr is not personally a gun enthusiast.

Social conservative groups have also been enthusiastic supporters. Barr is a member of the prolife caucus and regularly wins plaudits from groups like the Christian Coalition, which has awarded him the Friend of the Family Award. Barr helped former Christian Coalition director Ralph Reed win the chair of the Georgia Republican Party, a move that is likely to help Barr if he decides to run for the U.S. Senate.

However, in 2002 Barr was defeated 2–1 in the congressional primary by another incumbent, John Lurder, whose position on gun control was more moderate (redistricting pitted the two against each other). Despite Barr's NRA support, he lost even among gun enthusiasts.

Clyde Wilcox and Benjamin Webster

See also Citizens Committee for the Right to Keep and Bear Arms; National Rifle Association; Republican Party and Gun Control

For Further Reading:
Barone, Michael, and Grant Ujifusa. 1999. *The Almanac of American Politics, 2000.* Washington, DC: National Journal.
Tapper, Jake. 1999. "The NRA's Big Guns: Meet the 10 Biggest Obstacles to Gun Reform Legislation." http://www.salon.com/news/feature/1999/08/12/nra/index.html.

Barrett v. United States (1976)

Barrett v. United States (423 U.S. 212 [1976]) is the U.S. Supreme Court case that held that a convicted felon's intrastate purchase from a retail dealer of a firearm that previously, but independently of the felon's receipt, had been transported in interstate commerce, is an unlawful criminal act under the Gun Control Act (GCA) of 1968. The Supreme Court interpreted the commerce clause nexus of the GCA to apply to a purchaser's intrastate acquisition of a firearm, even if the purchaser was not directly involved in the transportation in interstate commerce. Thus, according to the Supreme Court, the GCA's interstate commerce requirement is satisfied if the firearm at any point in its past had traveled in interstate commerce.

Petitioner was convicted of violating 18 U.S.C. Section 922(h), which makes it unlawful for a convicted felon "to receive any firearm or ammunition which has been shipped or transported in interstate or foreign commerce." No evidence was presented at the petitioner's trial to show that the defendant personally participated in the interstate movement of the firearm prior to its purchase. Evidence was presented to show that the firearm, independent of the petitioner's receipt, had been transported in interstate commerce from the manufacturer to the distributor and then from the distributor to the dealer. Petitioner appealed his conviction claiming that the GCA was not meant to reach an isolated intrastate receipt where the handgun was sold within the state by a local merchant to a local resident with whom the merchant was acquainted, and where the purchaser's transaction had no apparent connection with interstate commerce absent the handgun's attenuated out-of-state origin.

In rejecting the petitioner's claim, the Court opined that the GCA clause specifying that felons were prohibited "to receive any firearm or ammunition which has been shipped or transported in interstate or foreign commerce" was without ambiguity. The Court stated that this provision was directed unrestrictedly at the felon's receipt of any firearm that "has been" previously shipped in interstate commerce. Additionally, the Court ruled that had Congress intended to confine the GCA to direct interstate receipt, it would have so provided as it did in other sections of the GCA.

James A. Beckman

See also Gun Control Act of 1968
For Further Reading:
Streit, Kevin T. 1999. "Note: Can Congress Regulate Firearms? Printz v. United States and the Intersection of the Commerce Clause, the Tenth Amendment, and the Second Amendment." *William & Mary Bill of Rights Journal* 7: 645–670.

Barron v. Baltimore (1833)

The U.S. Supreme Court case *Barron v. Baltimore* (32 U.S. 243, 1833) set the precedent that the Bill of Rights only applied to the national government, not state and local governments. This left the individual states free to develop gun legislation without oversight from the federal government. *Barron v. Baltimore* would eventually be overturned through the incorporation doctrine that was a combination of congressional amendments and court action, including ratification of the Fourteenth Amendment and the Supreme Court case *Gitlow v. New York* (1925).

When the Bill of Rights to the Constitution was adopted in 1791, each state had its own bill of rights. Most people believed that the national Bill of Rights applied only to the federal government. Hence, a literal interpretation of the Constitution and the Bill of Rights would not prohibit state and local governments from passing legislation that infringed upon freedom of speech, religion, or the right to keep and bear arms. For instance, in 1813 Kentucky became the first state to pass a ban on concealed weapons.

In 1833, the Supreme Court affirmed the limitations on the Bill of Rights. The city of Baltimore was engaged in a series of infrastructure projects that diverted several streams from their natural courses. This caused a buildup of sand around John Barron's wharf that prevented ships from being able to approach the dock. Barron brought suit against the city claiming that since the Fifth Amendment forbade taking property without compensation, he ought to be reimbursed for the loss of business. Central to Barron's case was the notion that the Fifth Amendment should also apply to state and city governments.

Barron originally won his case and was awarded $4,500 in damages. However, the state court of appeals reversed the verdict and Barron appealed to the Supreme Court, which sided with the city. Led by Chief Justice John Marshall, the Court found that the Bill of Rights applied only to the national government.

In spite of *Barron v. Baltimore,* most states accepted the premise that the right to keep and bear arms was a fundamental right of citizenship. States such as Kentucky, Georgia, Louisiana, Tennessee, Texas, and Virginia all had legal or constitutional protections for gun ownership. Many states did, however, place limitations on the types of weapons, usually making a distinction between weapons "suitable" for use by the militia and those not fit for civilized warfare. For instance, in 1840 the Tennessee Supreme Court in *Aymette v. State* distinguished between civilized weapons, such as pistols and rifles, and uncivilized ones, such as bowie knives.

Prior to the Civil War, *Barron v. Baltimore* would be used as justification for unequal treatment of state citizens, mainly in the slave states. For instance, while most states allowed private ownership of firearms, there were restrictions against slaves or former slaves owning guns or other weapons. Following the Civil War and the ratification of the Fourteenth Amendment, such overtly racial restrictions could not be maintained. However, many Southern states used outwardly nonracial laws to restrict gun ownership. For instance, in 1881 Arkansas adopted legislation that limited the type of guns that could be owned to weapons that had military use. The practical impact of such laws was that former Confederate soldiers were able to keep their firearms from the war, but poorer citizens, including African Americans, were unable to purchase new weapons. Concerns over the ability of African Americans to arm themselves were

responsible for the passage of concealed-weapons legislation throughout the South. Concurrently, such sentiments also led many states to expand the legal doctrine of self-defense as a means to better protect specific classes.

Tom Lansford

See also *Aymette v. State;* Black Codes; Civil War and Small Arms; Fourteenth Amendment

For Further Reading:

Bland, Randall, and Joseph V. Brogan. 1999. *Constitutional Law in the United States: A Systematic Inquiry into the Change and Relevance of Supreme Court Decisions.* San Francisco: Austin & Winfield.

George, Robert P., ed. 2001. *Great Cases in Constitutional Law.* Princeton, NJ: Princeton University Press.

Harrison, Maureen, and Steve Gilbert, eds. 1991. *Landmark Decisions of the United States Supreme Court.* Beverly Hills, CA: Excellent Books.

Bartley-Fox Carrying Law

The 1974 Bartley-Fox law in Massachusetts imposed a mandatory one-year prison sentence for carrying a gun without a permit. This was the first law of its kind in the nation. The law is considered a model by gun control advocates and a horror story by gun-rights advocates.

The Bartley-Fox law became effective on April 1, 1975 (Mass. Statutes 1975, chapter 113, section 2). Although widely described as a carrying law, it actually applies to any unlicensed possession of any gun (whether loaded or unloaded)—or even a single round of ammunition—outside one's "residence or place of business" (Mass. Gen. Laws Ann. chapter 269, section 10, 2001 ed.). While one year is the mandatory minimum, the sentence can be up to two and a half years in city or county jail or from two and a half to five years in state prison.

In 1994, a White House working group convened by the Clinton administration issued a secret (but leaked) report setting forth objectives for future national gun control laws. Among the objectives was a national law modeled on Bartley-Fox, providing a mandatory sentence for carrying a gun without a permit. In Massachusetts, local police chiefs and sheriffs have complete discretion about the issuance of handgun carrying permits (Mass. Gen. Laws

Ann. ch. 140, section 131; *Chief of Police of Shelburne v. Moyer*, 16 Mass. App. 543, 453 N.E.2d 461, 1983; *MacNutt v. Police Com'r of Boston*, 30 Mass. App. 632, 572 N.E.2d 577, 1991). In practice, this means that in most jurisdictions no one can obtain a carry permit, while some jurisdictions issue to friends of the chief or people with other political connections.

The Massachusetts Civil Liberties Union (CLU) opposed Bartley-Fox because of the risk that nondangerous people might be sent to prison. The Massachusetts legislature's Black Caucus also opposed the bill, because of concern about discriminatory licensing and arrests.

The enactment of Bartley-Fox did generate some of the kinds of cases that the Massachusetts CLU had warned about. The first prosecution under Bartley-Fox was of an old woman who was passing out religious literature in a rough part of Boston.

An early test case of the law was the successful prosecution of a young man who had inadvertently allowed his gun license to expire. To raise money to buy his high school class ring, he was driving to a pawn shop to sell his gun. Stopping the man for a traffic violation, a policeman noticed the gun. The teenager spent the mandatory year in prison (*Commonwealth v. McQuoid*, 369 Mass. 925, 344 N.E.2d 179, 1976).

The most famous Bartley-Fox case, however, involved a man who started carrying a gun after a coworker assaulted him and repeatedly threatened to kill him. The coworker did attack later and the victim successfully defended himself. The crime victim was then sentenced to a mandatory one year in prison for carrying a gun without a permit. The Massachusetts high court summarized:

> The threat of physical harm was founded on an earlier assault by Michel with a knife and became a real and direct matter once again when Michel attacked the defendant with a knife at the MBTA [subway] station.... [D]efendant is a hardworking, family man, without a criminal record, who was respected by his fellow employees (Michel excepted).
> Michel, on the other hand, appears to have lacked the same redeeming qualities.

He was a convicted felon with serious charges pending against him.... It is possible that defendant is alive today only because he carried the gun that day for protection. Before the days of a one-year mandatory sentence, the special circumstances involving the accused could be reflected reasonably in the sentencing or dispositional aspects of the proceeding. That option is no longer available in the judicial branch of government in a case of this sort (*Commonwealth v. Lindsey*, 396 Mass. 840, 489 N.E.2d 666, 1986).

The *Lindsey* case generated such an outcry that defendant Lindsey was eventually pardoned by Massachusetts Governor Michael Dukakis, even though Dukakis was a staunch gun-prohibition advocate.

The Bartley-Fox law is vigorously enforced, regardless of the circumstances of possession. Even new residents have received the mandatory year sentence, including a college student from Louisiana (*Commonwealth v. Wood*, 398 Mass. 135, 495 N.E.2d 835, 1986). Although the law is, on its face, nondiscretionary, the effect has been to remove judicial discretion in sentencing, leaving prosecutors with discretion about whether to bring charges. Police, who lack the discretion about whether to make an arrest when they find a gun, will sometimes avoid conducting frisks on some persons who they do not believe deserve to be arrested.

Scholarly evaluations of Bartley-Fox have generated mixed results. Part of the problem is that studies assume that the only thing Bartley-Fox did was impose the mandatory sentence for unlicensed carrying. But in fact, Bartley-Fox also imposed mandatory sentences for use of a gun in a crime. Accordingly, it has been difficult to disentangle the effects of the two different parts of the Bartley-Fox law—one aimed at violent criminals, the other aimed at citizens who merely lack a permit.

One study was conducted by the U.S. Department of Justice, which concluded that "the effect may be to penalize some less serious offenders, while the punishment for more serious offenses is postponed, reduced, or avoided altogether" (Carlson, 1982, p. 15). The Wright, Rossi, and

Daly study *Under the Gun*—conducted under the auspices of the National Institute of Justice—found that the law reduced the casual carrying of firearms but did not significantly affect the gun-use patterns of determined criminals.

David B. Kopel

See also Gun Control; Massachusetts Gun Law; Wright, James D.

For Further Reading:

Beha, James A., II. 1977. "And Nobody Can Get You Out." *The Impact of a Mandatory Prison Sentence for the Illegal Carrying of a Firearm on the Use of Firearms and on the Administration of Criminal Justice in Boston—Part I & Part II.* *Boston University Law Review* 57: 96–146, 289; Part 1 available at: http://www.saf.org/LawReviews/JBeha1a.html; Part 2: http://www.saf.org/LawReviews/Beha1.html.

Carlson, Kenneth. 1982. "Mandatory Sentencing: The Experience of Two States." Department of Justice, National Institute of Justice Policy Brief. Washington, DC: Abt Associates.

Wright, James, Peter Rossi, and Kathleen Daly. 1983. *Under the Gun: Weapons, Crime and Violence in America.* Hawthorne, NY: Aldine de Gruyter.

Beecham v. United States (1994)

In *Beecham v. United States* (511 U.S. 368 [1994]), the U.S. Supreme Court held that a state restoration of civil rights does not invalidate a federal conviction under the Gun Control Act (GCA) of 1968, which requires that civil rights be restored under the law of the jurisdiction where the earlier proceedings were held. The Supreme Court unanimously indicated that the determination as to the restoration of civil rights is an issue of federal, not state, law when the federal firearm disability was imposed as a result of a federal conviction.

Petitioners in *Beecham* were each convicted of violating 18 U.S.C. Section 922(g), which makes it unlawful for a convicted felon to possess a firearm. While each petitioner was previously convicted of a federal felony offense, both of the petitioners had also obtained a restoration of their civil rights by their respective states. Under the definitional section of the GCA contained at 18 U.S.C. Section 921(a)(20), a conviction is determined in accordance with the law of the jurisdiction in which the proceedings were held (choice-of-law clause), and any conviction that has been expunged or set aside or for which a person has been pardoned or has had civil rights restored shall not be considered a conviction for purposes of the GCA (exemption clause). The petitioners construed these clauses as supporting the proposition that the restoration of civil rights related to state restoration procedures alone.

In rejecting the petitioners' claim, the Court utilized standard norms of statutory construction and held that the choice-of-law and exemption clauses should be read and construed in conjunction with each other, and not separately as claimed by the petitioners. The result of such statutory interpretation is that if "the law of the jurisdiction in which the proceedings were held" was a federal prosecution, any restoration of civil rights must be determined pursuant to that same jurisdiction, namely the federal government. Conversely, if the underlying proceedings were held in a state court, any restoration of civil rights must be determined by that state jurisdiction. In so ruling, the Supreme Court also rejected the notion that the arguable dearth of federal law procedure for restoring civil rights meant that Congress intended all felons to have access to all the procedures specified in the exemption clause at the state level.

While the Court expressed no opinion on whether or not a federal felon can have his civil rights restored under federal law, the law in this area is unsettled. However, two sets of federal procedure processes for the restoration of civil rights should be noted. First, under Article II of the Constitution, the president may pardon any offense, which would act as a restoration of civil rights under the GCA. Second, section 925(c) of the GCA allows the secretary of the treasury to accept applications and grant relief from the disability imposed by section 922(g). The secretary of the treasury has delegated this authority to the Bureau of Alcohol, Tobacco, and Firearms (BATF). However, this is largely an illusory right at present because the BATF has been prohibited by Congress in each of its annual appropriations since 1992 from taking any action on these applications.

James A. Beckman

See also *Bailey v. United States; Caron v. United States;* Enforcement of Gun Control Laws; Gun Control Act of 1968

For Further Reading:
Pals, Gregory. 1998. "Notes: Judicial Review under 18 U.S.C. § 925(c): Abrogation through Appropriations?" *Washington University Law Quarterly* 76: 1095–1119.

Beecher's Bibles

"Beecher's Bibles" was a nickname for rifles that were sent to Kansas by New England abolitionists in order to help antislavery settlers who were being persecuted and disarmed by the proslavery territorial government.

Pursuant to the 1854 Kansas-Nebraska Act, the question of slavery in the future states of Kansas and Nebraska was to be decided by a vote of the settlers. Both pro- and antislavery forces encouraged their allies to move into Kansas. The proslavery forces, with heavy support from "Border Ruffians" in Missouri, stuffed ballot boxes, violently drove Free Soilers away from the polls in 1855, disarmed the Free Soilers, and expelled all slavery opponents from the territorial legislature. (Free Soilers were immigrants from Northern states who wanted to prevent slavery in Kansas.)

The Free Soil settlers let their New England supporters know of their need for firearms. Among the strongest supporters of arming the settlers was the Reverend Henry Ward Beecher, one of eight children of the eminent preacher Lyman Beecher and brother of Harriet Beecher Stowe, whose sensational best-seller *Uncle Tom's Cabin* helped inflame the North against slavery.

In his *Ordeal of the Union,* historian Allan Nevins (1947, p. 431) writes that Beecher sent a letter to a Yale congregation of abolitionists, stating "there are times when self-defence is a religious duty. If that duty was ever imperative, it is now, and in Kansas." Nevins explains: "Beecher's remark that such weapons were a greater moral urgency among Border Ruffians than the Scriptures gave currency to the phrase 'Beecher's Bibles.'" According to one version of the story, Beecher and his church shipped twenty-five Sharps carbines (short rifles) in a crate concealed underneath twenty-five Bibles.

When the settlers opened the crate, they were disappointed to find Bibles, then delighted at what lay underneath. In any case, various groups in New England—such as the Massachusetts Emigrant Aid Company—began smuggling firearms to Kansas.

The Sharps were high-tech rifles invented in 1848, incorporating the new breech-loading design—as opposed to loading from the muzzle. They could fire five rounds a minute; they rapidly displaced muzzle-loading guns and were especially popular in the West. John Brown's raiders carried the Sharps carbine.

Not far from Lawrence, Kansas (the territorial capital), is the Beecher's Bible Church. During the territorial-era wars in Kansas, the church contributed a "Beecher's Bible Regiment" to the antislavery forces.

The Kansas state capitol in Topeka features a mural with a large picture of John Brown, and Henry Beecher in the background.

David B. Kopel

See also Civil War and Small Arms; *Dred Scott v. Sandford;* Frontier Violence

For Further Reading:
Beecher Bible and Rifle Church website. http://www.ksphototour.8m.com/beecher.htm.
Coates, Jerry, and John McAulay. 1996. *Civil War Sharps, Carbines, and Rifles.* Gettysburg, PA: Thomas Publications.
Kopel, David B. 1998. "The Second Amendment in the 19th Century." *Brigham Young University Law Review* 1998, 4: 1359–1545; http://www.davekopel.com/2A/LawRev/19thcentury.htm.
Nevins, Allan. 1947. *Ordeal of the Union: A House Dividing 1852–1857,* vol. 2. New York: Collier.

Beretta USA Corporation

See Dix v. Beretta U.S.A. Corp.

Berkowitz, Leonard (1926–)

Leonard Berkowitz is a social psychologist whose research has focused on the causes of aggression and violence. Berkowitz has proposed a "weapons effect," in which exposure to a weapon leads to aggressive feelings and behavior. Berkowitz argues that weapons can serve as conditioned stimuli, eliciting both the thoughts and motor responses associated with their use.

Berkowitz received his Ph.D. in social psychology from the University of Michigan in 1951 and began his academic career at the University of Wisconsin in 1955, where he taught until his retirement in 1993. During his career he wrote two major books on aggression. *Aggression: A Social Psychological Analysis* was published in 1962 and *Aggression: Its Causes, Consequences, and Control* was published in 1993. His research explored many sources of aggression: anger, frustration, exposure to violence in television and movies, and the presence of weapons.

Berkowitz argued that feelings, ideas, memories, and "expressive motor reactions" were linked associatively through an emotion-state network. If any of these elements were activated, the result would be some activation of the entire network. Berkowitz argued that aggressive feelings and behavior could be caused by exposure to cues that were associated with violence. In this way, the presence of a gun could arouse an emotional state that made the use of that gun more likely, because of associations between guns and violence from television, movies, and life.

He argues that "the finger pulls the trigger" but the trigger may also pull the finger. It's not just that having a gun is a convenient way of settling an argument. The weapon itself is a stimulant to violence (Kramer, 1995). Because guns are associated with violence and aggression, they stimulate violent thoughts and impulses.

Berkowitz's research was primarily experimental. A frequent protocol would involve a college student who might be exposed to some kind of frustration and then in some cases provided with additional stimuli that might be associated with aggressive responses. The student was then given the opportunity to exhibit a violent response, usually by administering electric shocks to subjects. The shocks were not real, but students were told that they were. Students might observe a short film in which a movie actor was involved in a violent altercation and then be offered the opportunity to shock a student whose name was similar to that of the movie actor. In some cases, weapons were present in the experimental laboratory or in the office in which students were initially briefed for the experiment.

In another experiment, students were permitted to throw wet sponges at clowns. The experimenters varied several conditions, including whether the clown insulted the subject. In one condition, a gun was visible in the booth; in another, it was absent. A clown who hurled insults did not incite more sponge throwing, but the presence of a gun did lead to a statistically significant increase.

Critics of Berkowitz's work have argued that the experiments evoked strong demand characteristics. Students could easily guess when they were expected to administer severe shocks and would be eager to please a professor by complying. Few would believe that a gun laying on a university desk or in a circus booth was accidental. Yet Berkowitz has varied his experimental protocols, always with the same result, and his experiments have been duplicated in other countries. Studies by other scholars have also shown that children who play with toy guns are more aggressive than those who do not.

Clyde Wilcox and Benjamin Webster

See also Media Violence

For Further Reading:
Berkowitz, Leonard. 1984. "Some Effects of Thoughts on the Anti- and Prosocial Influences of Media Events: A Cognitive Neoassociationistic Analysis." *Psychological Bulletin* 95: 410–427.
———. 1987. "Mood, Self-Awareness, and the Willingness to Help." *Journal of Personality and Social Psychology* 52: 721–729.
———. 1989. "The Frustration-Aggression Hypothesis: Examination and Reformulation." *Psychological Bulletin* 106: 59–73.
———. 1990. "On the Formation and Regulation of Anger and Aggression: A Cognitive-Neoassociationistic Analysis." *American Psychologist* 45: 494–503.
———. 1993. *Aggression: Its Causes, Consequences, and Control.* Philadelphia: Temple University Press.
Kramer, Michael. 1995. "Why Guns Share the Blame." *Time* 145, 19 (May 8): 48; http://www.time.com/time/magazine/article/0,9171,1101950 508–134132,00.html.

Bernethy v. Walt Failor's, Inc. (1978)

Robert Fleming, apparently heavily intoxicated, left a bar in Washington State, where he had been with his estranged wife, walked to Walt

Failor's gun shop and acquired a shotgun and ammunition. He immediately returned to the bar and shot Phoebe Fleming to death. Carolee Bernethy, on behalf of the three Fleming children, all minors, sued the gun shop and its owner for wrongful death damages. The trial court dismissed her case on the ground that she had no legal cause of action.

The Washington State Supreme Court, to which Bernethy appealed, noted that it was legally obligated to view the complainant's claims in their best light and concluded that there was at least a legal cause of action. It declared that the facts alleged by the plaintiff, if they could be proved to the satisfaction of a jury, would constitute negligence. The case therefore was sent back to the original court for a trial or a settlement (*Bernethy v. Walt Failor's, Inc.*, 653 P.2d 280, 1982).

The record showed that Robert Fleming had started drinking at 5:30 in the morning of the day that he killed his wife and that he drank continuously until 6:30 that evening, except for an hour when he passed out. When he left the bar, he walked to Walt Failor's gun shop, where Failor was working as a salesperson. He asked to look at a rifle for his son. Fleming agreed to buy the weapon and handed Failor a credit card. While Failor was checking his credit by telephone, Fleming picked up the rifle and ammunition that had been placed on the counter and left the shop. He threatened Failor when the owner sought to secure payment. Failor followed him to the tavern where the killing took place.

In defense of himself and his company, Failor unsuccessfully raised several issues before the state Supreme Court. First, he claimed that he did not realize that Fleming was drunk, though he granted that there was a scent of liquor about him. For support, Failor secured an affidavit from a customer who agreed with that judgment. But Fleming's blood alcohol was a high 0.23 percent. And apparently in an effort to mitigate his culpability for the killing of his wife, Fleming had told the police that he remembered wetting his pants before entering the gun store, staggering as he made the walk there, and having to rest his arms on the counter to support himself while he negotiated with Failor.

The judge thought it reasonable to presume that Fleming might well have appeared obviously intoxicated when he acquired the shotgun.

Failor also claimed that he owed no duty to Phoebe Fleming that he had breached. The judge thought that this was an arguable proposition that ought to be settled by a jury. While the state of Washington did not have a law specifically forbidding the sale of rifles to intoxicated people, it did have a statute disallowing such a sale to persons deemed incompetent, such as underage persons, habitual drunkards, or individuals of unsound mind. A jury, the court suggested, might reasonably find that Fleming fit into this grouping.

The court then reached back to an earlier decision to locate another possible ground for a successful damage action: "We consider it not only common sense, but common law and justice that one cannot let or loan to another, knowing that other to be reckless and incompetent, and in such a condition that he would be reckless and incompetent, an instrumentality which may be a very dangerous one in charge of that person" (*Mitchell v. Churches*, 206 P. 6, 1922).

Failor also insisted that Fleming had not been sold the gun but had stolen it. The judge again ruled that he would let this matter be decided by a jury. And so also would he allow the issue of whether the sale of the gun represented a "proximate cause" of the death of Phoebe Fleming. Other courts, facing essentially the same fact situation, later would disagree with this segment of the Washington decision. The Michigan Supreme Court, for instance, would note that a gun dealer in the case before it could not have known that the weapon he sold would be used in a lethal fashion; therefore, the requirement of "proximate cause" could not be met (*Buczkowski v. McKay*, 490 N.W.2d 330, 1992).

Gilbert Geis

See also *Merrill v. Navegar, Inc.*

For Further Reading:

Anstead, J. 1997. "Can a Seller of the Firearm to a Purchaser Known to the Seller to Be Intoxicated Be Held Liable to a Third Person Injured by the Purchaser?" Pp. 1–11 in *Deborah Kitchen v. K-Mart Corporation* (No. 86,812), July 17. Supreme Court of Florida, http://www.law.fsu.edu/library/flsupct/86812/op–86812.pdf.

Black Codes

After the Civil War, Southern legislatures determined to maintain their control over former slaves passed comprehensive sets of regulations known as "Black Codes" that deprived the freedmen of a variety of rights, including the right to travel, the right to serve on a jury, the right to engage in certain businesses, the right to testify against whites, and, perhaps most significantly, the right to possess firearms. These codes, which were drafted during a time that represents the dusk of slavery and the dawn of freedom, were passed by the legislatures of Mississippi, South Carolina, Alabama, and Louisiana in 1865, and Arkansas, Florida, Virginia, Georgia, North Carolina, Texas, and Tennessee in 1866. At their heart, Black Codes sought to ensure continued economic and social domination of white over black in the South.

Mississippi planter E. G. Baker wrote a letter to members of the state legislature on October 22, 1865, that provides an insight into the discriminatory mind-set that motivated the drafting of these codes: "It is well known here that our negroes through the country are well equipped with fire arms, muskets, double barrel shot guns, and pistols—and furthermore, it would be well if they are free to prohibit the use of fire arms until they had proved themselves to be good citizens in their altered state."

Mississippi was in fact the first state to adopt these means of social and economic control over the newly freed black population. Its code, tellingly titled an "Act to Regulate the Relation of Master and Apprentice Relative to Freedmen, Free Negroes, and Mulattoes," provided in part that "no freedman, free negro or mulatto, not in the military … and not licensed to do by the board of police of his or her county, shall keep or carry fire-arms of any kind, or any ammunition,… and all such arms or ammunition shall be forfeited to the former.…"

It is important to remember that the U.S. Constitution, as well as the various state constitutions, all guaranteed citizens the right to bear arms. Attempts by Southern legislators to use the Black Codes to disarm the South's black population were consequently a direct affront to those Northern and Southern abolitionists who sought equality, and they furthermore represented a willful blindness to the fact that the former slaves were now full citizens entitled to all of the rights held by their white countrymen.

Aside from the symbolic and theoretical impact of the racially discriminatory Black Codes, they also had a very direct impact on those who were prevented from lawfully arming themselves for purposes of self-defense. An 1867 Special Report of the Anti-Slavery Conference recognized that blacks were "forbidden to own or bear firearms, and thus were rendered defenseless against assaults." In fact, two weeks after the Mississippi code was enacted, Calvin Holly, a black private assigned to the Freedmen's Bureau in Mississippi, wrote a letter relating an article in the *Vicksburg Journal* to bureau commissioner Howard. In the letter, Holly said that "the Rebels are going about in many places through the State and robbing the colored people of arms, money and all they have and in many places killing."

The Southern legislators who proposed, drafted, and enacted the Black Codes knew well that an armed black populace was far less likely to be preyed upon by white mobs and would be in a position to prevent reenslavement by those white Southerners who were willing to use any means necessary to preserve antebellum social order. What is more, an armed black populace in the South could potentially play a part in maintaining the Union. While former Confederate soldiers could keep their firearms, Black Codes sought to disarm the one group with unionist sympathies, namely freedmen.

Northern Republicans, able to see clearly these discriminatory motivations reflected in the Black Codes, grew increasingly concerned and irritated. They considered these codes blatant attempts to de facto relegalize and relegitimize slavery in the South. Their concern over the South's perceived attempts to circumvent the freeing of slaves provided the backdrop to the 39th Congress's drafting of the Fourteenth Amendment to the U.S. Constitution. The Fourteenth Amendment was introduced in the Senate by Sen. Jacob Howard. He stated that the amendment would protect the personal rights in the Bill of Rights from state deprivation, specifically mentioning the right of the people to keep and bear arms. It was this period of congressional Reconstruction, fueled by Northern anger over Southern intransigence, that ultimately resulted in the repeal of the onerous Black Codes.

T. Markus Funk

See also African Americans and Gun Violence; Ku Klux Klan; NAACP and Gun Control; Racism and Gun Control; *United States v. Cruikshank*

For Further Reading:
Cottrol, Robert J., and Raymond T. Diamond. 1991. "The Second Amendment: Towards an Afro-Americanist Reconsideration." *Georgetown Law Journal* 80: 309–361.
Funk, T. Markus. 1995. "Gun Control and Economic Discrimination: The Melting-Point Case-in-Point." *Journal of Criminal Law and Criminology* 85: 764–806.
Halbrook, Stephen P. 1995. "Personal Security, Personal Liberty, and the Constitutional Right to Bear Arms: Visions of the Framers of the Fourteenth Amendment." *Seton Hall Constitutional Law Journal* 5: 341–434.

Black Market for Firearms

The black market for firearms in the United States consists of transactions in which stolen and/or purchased firearms (including both new and secondhand guns) are illegally transferred between buyers and sellers. Individuals who divert firearms from the legal to the illegal marketplace are engaged in firearm trafficking. While not all guns bought and sold on the black market are involved in the commission of crimes, firearm trafficking is the primary source of guns used in criminal activity. As many as one quarter of those identified as gun traffickers are convicted felons and almost half of all firearm-trafficking investigations involve convicted felons as either the buyer or seller.

The Bureau of Alcohol, Tobacco, and Firearms (BATF), an arm of the U.S. Department of the Treasury, is the agency with primary responsibility for combating gun trafficking and curtailing the black market for firearms. During the fiscal year 1999, the BATF brought to trial 2,161 defendants who were responsible for trafficking over 30,000 firearms on the black market.

There are four basic means by which firearms make their way onto the black market: licensed sellers selling to prohibited purchasers, unlicensed individuals selling to prohibited purchasers, individuals purchasing guns on behalf of prohibited purchasers, and firearm theft.

Federal law requires firearm dealers to obtain a federal firearm license from the National Licensing Center, a branch of the BATF. In addition to meeting federal regulations, gun dealers are required to abide by all local and state laws regarding the sale and possession of firearms. Firearm dealers are prohibited from selling firearms to certain classes of individuals, including convicted felons, those who have been adjudicated to be mentally defective, illegal aliens, and dishonorably discharged members of the armed services. Firearm dealers are also prohibited from selling guns (except for rifles and shotguns) to unlicensed individuals from outside their state.

Licensed dealers serve as a source of firearms for the black market when they choose to sell to purchasers without conducting the federally required background check (through the National Instant Criminal Background Check System operated by the Federal Bureau of Investigation) or knowingly sell to prohibited purchasers who have provided falsified information. While licensed firearm dealers were involved in less than 10 percent of the BATF firearm investigations during a recent two-year period, they accounted for almost half of all firearms recovered in the investigations.

Guns recovered from crime scenes are traced through the BATF's National Tracing Center. In 1996 and 1997, half of all guns successfully traced by the National Tracing Center were sold by 1 percent of all federally licensed dealers.

Not all individuals are required to obtain a federal dealer's license to sell firearms. Collectors and hobbyists who only make occasional sales and trades to enhance personal collections or who sell their collections in part or in whole are not required to do so. While such individuals are prohibited from knowingly selling guns to prohibited purchasers (including convicted felons, juveniles, and illegal aliens), they are not required to conduct background checks, as licensed dealers are required to do. Firearms make their way into the black market when unlicensed sellers knowingly sell guns from their private collections to prohibited buyers or legally purchase guns with the intention of reselling them illegally. Common venues for such illegal sales are gun shows, for both licensed and unlicensed individuals. The BATF reports that unlicensed sellers account for almost 27 percent of all firearms involved in BATF investigations.

Individuals who purchase guns on behalf of prohibited purchasers are called straw buyers and also contribute to the black market for guns. The straw buyer is legally eligible to purchase a gun but does so illegally by providing false information to the federally licensed seller regarding who the actual purchaser is. Friends (especially fellow gang members), relatives, and spouses are commonly used as straw buyers. As many as one quarter of straw buyers are juveniles. Individual straw buyers tend to be involved with the purchase of only one or a few firearms rather than the bulk purchase of firearms. However, the number of individuals who act as straw buyers can be quite substantial, leading to a heavy influx of firearms into the black market. Almost half of recent BATF firearm investigations involved straw buyers, accounting for approximately 30 percent of all BATF firearm investigations.

Recent figures from the National Crime Information Center report over 2.2 million stolen firearms. Not all stolen firearms make their way to the black market, but firearms stolen from individual owners as well as federally licensed dealers are an important source of guns for the black market. Less frequently, firearms are also stolen during shipping. However, though such transport thefts are relatively few in number compared to thefts from residences and licensed dealers, they typically involve large numbers of guns per incident.

The Bureau of Alcohol, Tobacco, and Firearms combats firearm trafficking and the black market for guns through a variety of programs administered by the agency's criminal enforcement division. Standard activities include inspection of federal licensees, background checks for gun purchasers, and criminal investigations of suspected firearm traffickers. Recent initiatives have included the Firearms License Compliance Program, the Firearms Investigative Task Force Program, and the Innovative Firearms Program.

The Firearms Licensee Compliance Program is aimed at enhancing compliance with federal firearm-sales regulations by federal licensees. The Firearms Investigative Task Force Program targeted groups and individuals involved in gun trafficking and the black market for firearms in several states. The Innovative Firearms Program provides assistance to state and local law enforcement organizations to develop and implement programs to reduce illegal firearm trafficking.

Wendy L. Martinek

See also Background Checks; Bureau of Alcohol, Tobacco, and Firearms; Felons and Gun Control; Firearm Dealers; Gun Shows; Licensing; National Instant Criminal Background Check System; National Tracing Center

For Further Reading:
Bureau of Alcohol, Tobacco, and Firearms. 2000a. *Commerce in Firearms in the United States.* Washington, DC: U.S. Department of the Treasury.
_____. 2000b. *Following the Gun: Enforcing Federal Laws against Firearms Traffickers.* Washington, DC: U.S. Department of the Treasury.
Bureau of Justice Assistance. 2000. *Reducing Illegal Firearms Trafficking: Promising Practices and Lessons Learned.* Washington, DC: U.S. Department of Justice.
Decker, Scott H., Susan Pennell, and Ami Caldwell. 1997. "Illegal Firearms: Access and Use by Arrestees." *National Institute of Justice Research in Brief,* January. Washington, DC: U.S. Department of Justice, Office of Justice Programs, National Institute of Justice.
Spitzer, Robert J. 1998. *The Politics of Gun Control.* 2d ed. New York: Chatham House.

Black Panthers

The Black Panther Party for Self Defense was founded in October 1966 in Oakland, California, by Huey P. Newton and Bobby Seale, based on the belief that only violent revolution would secure liberation for American blacks. To that end, all blacks were urged to arm themselves. The name was shortened to the Black Panthers and the ideology spread across the country to urban minority communities. The Black Panthers terrified mainstream America, which enacted gun control laws aimed directly at the Black Panthers.

In California in the mid-1960s, the Panthers began carrying rifles and shotguns openly—as

POLITICAL PRISONERS
OF USA FASCISM

A poster showing Black Panther leaders Bobby Seale and Huey P. Newton. (Library of Congress)

California law allowed—in order, the Panthers claimed, to protect victims of police brutality. The California legislature promptly enacted legislation restricting the carrying of long guns in public places. Governor Ronald Reagan, a strong opponent of the Black Panthers, signed the bill into law. More generally, the 1960s black militancy of which the Panthers were an especially visible element helped set the stage for the federal Gun Control Act of 1968, in which restrictions on inexpensive imported firearms were intended, in part, to prevent the urban unrest that was associated with the Black Panthers.

During the heyday of the Panthers, leaders were involved in a number of violent confrontations with police, resulting in deaths on both sides. Panthers believed that the Federal Bureau of Investigation's Counter Intelligence program was employed in an attempt to break the Black Panthers. Charges brought against Panthers failed to be substantiated in several high-profile cases. Newton was tried three times for killing a police officer in 1967. Each one resulted in a mistrial, the last in 1971. Seale was convicted as a codefendant in the "Chicago Eight" case of conspiracy to disrupt the Democratic Party con-

vention in Chicago in 1968. The conviction was later overturned. In 1971, Seale was acquitted on charges of murdering an alleged police informant. Finally, in 1971 thirteen Panthers were acquitted on charges of conspiracy to bomb public locations in New York City.

Sam Anderson claims to have been a founding member of the Harlem Panthers, whose founding in May 1966 predated the Oakland party. The Harlem party lasted only eighteen months, which Anderson claims was a result of media preference for the more militant Oakland branch.

In 1972, the Panthers experienced an ideological schism when Newton and Seale announced their intent to abandon violence as a Panther tenet. Former chief publicist Eldridge Cleaver resisted the change. The conflict was resolved in 1974 when Seale resigned as leader of the Panthers and Newton fled to Cuba to avoid drug charges. During the remainder of the 1970s, the Panthers refocused and provided services to the black community such as free breakfasts for children, free medical clinics, and free food and clothing to the homeless. The Black Panther Party continued to decline in influence and notoriety and essentially disappeared in the late 1970s.

Carol Oyster

See also Black Codes; Gun Control Act of 1968; NAACP and Gun Control; Racism and Gun Control

For Further Reading:
Leonardatos, Cynthia Deitle. 1999. "California's Attempt to Disarm the Black Panthers." *San Diego Law Review* 36: 947–996.
Pearson, H. 1994. *The Shadow of the Panthers: Huey Newton and the Price of Black Power in America.* Boston: Addison-Wesley.

Black Talon

The Black Talon (since renamed the Ranger Talon) is a jacketed hollow-point handgun bullet produced by the Winchester company. Like all such bullets, it is designed to expand upon impact, the lead core bulging at right angles to the bullet's axis to produce more shock and a larger wound channel, while the copper jacket splits and rolls back. A typical expanded bullet of this type assumes a mushroom shape, with the copper jacket rolled back behind the expanded, or mushroomed, lead core.

A unique feature of the Talon's design was that the copper jacket was thickened toward the point. Winchester advertised the Talon as possessing increased wounding power, since the thickened copper jacket would not roll back under the expanded lead core, but protrude at near right-angles to the bullet axis, making for a larger-diameter wound channel. Whether this actually made for increased lethality, or was merely an advertiser's puffing, was disputed by ballistics experts, but Winchester's ad copy showed the Talon's jacket assuming the form of sharp points extending outward from the expanding bullet to inflict additional damage.

In July 1993, gunman Gian Luigi Ferri killed six persons in an office shooting in San Francisco. Ferri used Black Talons for at least part of his murderous assault, and Winchester's publicity promptly rebounded upon the company. The design drew heavy media and political criticism, based both on its claimed lethality and the potential for points of the split jacket to penetrate surgical gloves during emergency surgery. In response, Winchester limited sales to law enforcement and renamed the projectile the Ranger Talon.

David T. Hardy

See also Ammunition, Types of; Dum-Dum Bullet
For Further Reading:
Peterson, Julie. 1993. "This Bullet Kills You Better." *Mother Jones* 18, 5 (September–October): 15; http://www.mojones.com/mother_jones/SO93/petersen.html.

Boomtowns, Cowtowns, and Gun Violence

Boomtowns and cowtowns possess similar characteristics. Cowtowns of the Old West (e.g., Fort Worth, Abilene, Wichita) were boomtowns in their beginnings. Some boomtowns that were mining-oriented, such as Tombstone, Arizona, are popularly and erroneously assumed to be primarily cowtowns. Some other celebrated boomtowns with a mining backdrop included San Francisco, Sacramento, and Virginia City. The economic bases of some cowtowns were

also somewhat more diverse, as a number were typified by such activities as gold mining and oil-well drilling. But there are many economic bases for boomtowns and they continue to exist on a number of "frontiers," including Brazil, the former Soviet Union, and the inner cities of today's United States.

Both boomtowns and cowtowns traditionally feature male-intensive industries (e.g., mining, the cattle industry, the sale of crack cocaine). Both involve the systematic exploitation of the male workforce through vice-related industries and costly provisioning and resupply. Boomtowns and cowtowns are both typified by extremely high ratios of young men to women and an absence of "respectable" women; both are environments where the use of alcohol and other intoxicants is common, encouraged, expected, and even demanded. Historically, in both sorts of towns, knives and firearms are frequently carried and used as weapons of first resort, at least in the early days of the boom. Accordingly, both are known as environments where violence flourishes, at least until tamed by "respectable" women. Indeed, the role of late-coming women "from back East" as "town tamers" is profound.

Although it may seem counterintuitive, by this set of criteria, certain American inner cities during the 1980s to the present might be thought of as boomtowns of a sort—places where young men and women of ill-repute sell drugs (a boom crop), other vice flourishes, respectable women are in short supply (as successful individuals of both sexes leave with the mass exodus of the middle class), the use of alcohol and other drugs is widespread, and advanced weaponry and their possession is not uncommon (Courtwright, 1996). In the early stages of the boom, violence is especially prevalent as different factions jockey for territorial dominance or exclusivity. Little legitimate activity occurs in some of these unhappy communities abandoned by the middle class and respectable poor and they become free-fire or combat zones, to use local and/or police parlance.

The role of law enforcement in boomtowns and cowtowns has traditionally been portrayed as heroic (to wit, the "Gunfight at O.K. Corral"), but more recent, revisionist interpretations

A saloon duel depicted in The Great Man's Lady. *(John Springer Collection/Corbis)*

show lawmen as opportunistic careerists—political animals, pimps, and gamblers protecting their own selfish interests (for example, in the Hollywood hit *Tombstone*). Far from being disinterested upholders of law and order or avatars of civilization, many lawmen in the Old West were, at best, little more than tools of the local mercantile and vice interests. While a few were primarily concerned with establishing order, justice was often incidental in that endeavor.

It was to this end that Dodge City, Kansas, established a "deadline" (in this case, the railroad tracks), north of which firearms could not be carried. In this and other cowtowns where this form of gun control operated, cowboys and drovers checked their weapons in at the sheriff's or town marshal's office, or at various kiosks built for that purpose, and received a numbered metal token. Upon leaving town, the weapons would be restored to them. This had the effect of allowing local law enforcement to both moni-

tor and temporarily disarm vice-bound potential troublemakers. Thus, they could be told to have a good time and also be warned "not to let the sun set" on them in that specific jurisdiction. The idea of town marshals or deputies facing down equally well-armed outlaws in fast-draw shoot-outs is the fiction of dime novels, the movies, and the television western of the 1950s and 1960s. Preemptive gun-possession ordinances in Dodge City, Kansas, for example, render the opening sequence of the popular television series *Gunsmoke* a gross inaccuracy.

Prostitutes and gamblers made life more tolerable for the male workforce but complicated law enforcement considerably. As both were seen as necessary, they were often protected industries. Even some lawmen, such as Wyatt Earp, were reputed to have interests in prostitution and other vice industries. Earp, along with his brothers, ran a gambling house during his off-and-on career in law enforcement. Brothels were common, sometimes in such numbers as to constitute a district. Several western cities claim the distinction of coining the term "red-light district" to refer to the practice of railroad brakemen leaving their lanterns outside prostitutes' "cribs" to prevent interruption, an act that apparently bathed entire streets in red light.

Prostitutes were often quite young and not particularly good-looking by the standards of that day or any other. However, reformed "soiled doves" and single women "visiting from back East" found plenty of eager suitors among the male population, and not a few married and vanished into respectable domesticity. Oftentimes in a boomtown, gamblers, prostitutes, and other residents would fall out, and feuding and violence might follow. In the river boomtown of Natchez, Mississippi, in 1835, a short-lived conflict developed and escalated rapidly, in which a hastily constituted "anti-gambling" society lynched five gamblers who had been involved in the killing of a local doctor. Sanity and gamblers returned soon after. Natchez-Under-the-Hill, as a vice district, remained a boomtown hot spot until river traffic lost its viability and cachet later in the century. Most violence involving prostitutes and cowboys/miners was considerably more prosaic and the circumstances not nearly as dramatic—resembling nothing more than a "Saturday Night" shooting on the "mean streets" of any major contemporary city. It should be added that boomtowns and cowtowns were not infrequently at ground zero in range "wars" that broke out in the West following the Civil War.

Boomtowns are an economic phenomenon that is not limited to the Old West or early American history. Rather, one can expect to find boomtowns wherever men work (in male-dominated industries) in predominately pastoral extractive industries, where paydays may be few but generally lucrative and where vice industries exist primarily to service and exploit those workers. Violence flourishes in boomtowns and cowtowns due to the widespread presence of weaponry, a subculture endorsing violent solutions to personal problems, and ambivalent law enforcement responses. The arrival of respectable women in force usually puts an end to boomtown vice and violence, be it

in Arizona, Mississippi, or Uganda—or in contemporary inner-city America.

F. Frederick Hawley

See also Dime Novels and the Sensationalization of Frontier Violence
For Further Reading:
Courtwright, David. T. 1996. *Violent Land: Single Men and Social Disorder from the Frontier to the Inner City.* Cambridge, MA: Harvard University Press.

Boone, Daniel (1734–1820)

Daniel Boone—arguably America's greatest culture hero of the Jacksonian and antebellum era—gained fame as a trailblazer, hunter, and Indian fighter. Boone's reputation rested, in part, on his contests with Indians in Kentucky and his participation in the Indian campaign known as Lord Dunmore's War of 1774 and then in the American Revolution. Indeed, on separate occasions Indians had killed one of Boone's sons, Israel, and had taken captive Boone's daughter, Jemima, who was rescued by her father and his friends. Yet in later life Boone said that he bore no ill will toward Indians. Some of the Shawnee who had once held Boone captive and who had adopted him into their tribe even came to visit Boone after both he and they had removed to Missouri.

At various times in his life, Boone also surveyed frontier lands, operated a country store, and tried his hand at planting tobacco. Never, however, did Boone prosper. After being sued by men who had lost their land because of his faulty surveying (and because of Kentucky's notoriously complicated land titles), Boone escaped his creditors by immigrating to Spanish-held Missouri in 1799. There the Spanish granted Boone about 8,500 acres of land and declared him a "syndic," an office comparable to justice of the peace. After Spain transferred the Louisiana Territory to the United States in 1803, Boone lost his Missouri lands because he had failed to cultivate them. In 1814, Congress finally stepped in to grant Boone, now in his seventies, a small plot of land as a reward for having played a critical role in the settlement of the West.

No doubt the dispossession of Indians and the settlement of the West by whites would have

Daniel Boone. (Library of Congress)

reprinted fourteen times between 1833 and 1868. Flint and others portrayed Boone as a "self-possessed" hero who rose to greatness solely through his own efforts. The wilderness that Boone inhabited—a place where men succeeded or failed through their individual initiative and energy—came to symbolize the libertarian values of the market revolution that transformed the United States during the Jacksonian and antebellum decades.

Whereas in the colonial era frontier hunters were frequently equated with savagery, the market revolution gave rise to a celebration of frontier individualists who epitomized desirable traits like "self-possession, self-control, and promptness in execution" (Peck, 1847, p. 15). The "most striking instance" of Boone's "peculiar self-possession," according to Flint, occurred when Boone, as a schoolboy, had coolly shot a panther while other boys had fled (Flint, 1847, p. 21). That event seemed to presage Boone's independence, wanderlust, skill with a gun, and love of hunting. Boone's "peculiar habits of character," waxed Flint, "were fortified by his long cherished habit of wandering for days together with no other companionship than his rifle and his own thoughts" (Flint, 1833, p. 51). To Francis Lister Hawks (1844), another Boone hagiographer, Boone was simply "the Kentucky Rifleman."

The particular gun with which Boone wandered was a Kentucky (or long) rifle, a small-bore (generally under .45 caliber), lightweight, long-barreled gun that was first produced by German gunsmiths who resided in western Pennsylvania. Though handmade by artisans and hence potentially expensive (gun prices varied greatly prior to the era of mass production), such guns became standard weapons among American farmers and frontiersmen. Fancier versions of the Kentucky rifle with gold and silver inlay—though still more expensive—appealed to a growing cadre of elite sport hunters in the early national era who identified themselves with both English aristocrats and with American frontiersmen like Boone.

If Boone's love for guns and hunting helped popularize sport hunting, it also helped popularize Manifest Destiny. Though earlier generations of Americans had claimed land through farming

proceeded apace without Daniel Boone. Congress awarded Boone a small parcel of land, however, because he—through the efforts of John Filson, a schoolteacher and land speculator whose promotional tract, *The Discovery, Settlement, and Present State of Kentucke,* was published in 1784—had become America's great hero of expansion. Filson attached to his promotional tract a so-called autobiography of Daniel Boone (the tale was based on Boone's reminiscences but written by Filson). Though the publication of Filson's Boone tale caused little stir in the United States, it caught the imagination of Europeans, leading Lord Byron to write stanzas about Boone in his poem *Don Juan.*

Americans became familiar with Boone's exploits through a condensed version of Filson's tale that was published by a Connecticut printer in 1786. Boone's popularity grew with each subsequent decade and peaked—judging by the output of art and literature on Boone—in the antebellum years. No less than seven Boone biographies appeared before the Civil War, one of which, Timothy Flint's *Biographical Memoir of Daniel Boone, the First Settler of Kentucky,* was (backwoods hunters could make no claim to lands that they failed to improve), Boone transformed expansion into a sort of jousting match. Through his battles with bear, buffalo, and Indian, Boone—like his fellow Americans—became the noble claimant of a vast domain.

In the Jacksonian and antebellum decades Daniel Boone became a new hero for a new era. Like Andrew Jackson, Boone became an icon of the self-made man. Just as important, Boone—or at least the Boone of literature—taught Americans that the use of guns had made them great, a lesson that would be remembered by writers, painters, and politicians. "Out of the long and brilliant list of patriots—whether orators, or warriors, or statesmen, or divines," wrote George Canning Hill in 1859, "no name shines with a purer lustre than that of Daniel Boone" (Hill, 1859, p. 59).

Daniel Justin Herman

See also Long Rifle (Pennsylvania/Kentucky)
For Further Reading:
Aron, Stephen Anthony. 1996. *How the West Was Lost: The Transformation of Kentucky from Daniel Boone to Henry Clay.* Baltimore: Johns Hopkins University Press.
Bakeless, John. 1939. *Daniel Boone: Master of the Wilderness.* Lincoln: University of Nebraska Press.
Faragher, John Mack. 1992. *Daniel Boone: The Life and Legend of an American Pioneer.* New York: Holt.
Flint, Timothy. 1833. *Indian Wars of the West.* Cincinnati: E. H. Flint.
———. 1847. *The First White Man of the West, or the Exploits of Col. Daniel Boone, the First Settler of Kentucky.* Cincinnati: G. Conclin. Originally published under the title *Biographical Memoir of Daniel Boone: The First Settler of Kentucky.* Cincinnati: N. & G. Guilford & Co., 1833.
Hawks, Francis Lister [Uncle Philip, pseud.]. 1844. *The Adventures of Daniel Boone, the Kentucky Rifleman.* New York: D. Appleton & Co.
Herman, Daniel Justin. 2001. *Hunting and the American Imagination.* Washington, DC: Smithsonian Institution Press.
Hill, George Canning. 1859. *Daniel Boone, the Pioneer of Kentucky.* Chicago: Donohue.
Lofaro, Michael A. 1978. *The Life and Adventures of Daniel Boone.* Lexington: University of Kentucky.
Peck, John Mason. 1847. *Life of Daniel Boone, the Pioneer of Kentucky.* Library of American Biography, ed. Jared Sparks. 2d ser., vol. 13. Boston: C. C. Little and J. Brown.
Slotkin, Richard. 1973. *Regeneration through Violence: The Mythology of the American Frontier, 1600–1860.* Middletown, CT: Wesleyan University Press.

Borinsky, Mark (1945–)

Dr. Mark Borinsky—a victim of gun violence—started the modern gun control movement when he founded the National Council to Control Handguns (NCCH) in Washington, D.C., in 1974 (Carter, 1997, p. 72). NCCH became Handgun Control, Inc. (HCI), the leading gun control advocacy organization in the country. In 2001, HCI changed its name to the Brady Campaign to Prevent Gun Violence.

While a psychology graduate student at the University of Chicago in 1973, Borinsky had a traumatic experience that led directly to his founding of NCCH. Borinsky and a friend were walking back to campus one evening when three young men robbed them at gunpoint. One of the young men kept urging the others to shoot their victims. Understandably shaken by this experience, Borinsky decided that after finishing his degree he would work to fight the problem of gun violence.

The next year Borinsky finished his Ph.D. and moved to Washington, D.C., to start a new job. Assuming that the assassinations of John F. Kennedy, Robert Kennedy, and Dr. Martin Luther King would have spawned numerous gun control groups, Borinsky searched for a gun-lobbying group to join, but found none that he thought were effective. Using his own money, Borinsky rented a tiny office at 1710 H Street, N.W., hired a secretary, and launched NCCH. Because he had a full-time job, he could not run the organization on a day-to-day basis. He placed an ad for someone to work with him in the *Northwest Current,* a small neighborhood newspaper.

Edward O. Welles, a retired Central Intelligence Agency officer, responded to the ad. Welles and Borinsky really were the organization until N. T. "Pete" Shields joined them in 1975. Shields, whose son had been killed by an assailant with a handgun, contributed greatly to the success of the organization. Most commentators acknowledge Shields's importance, but some minimize Borinsky's contribution,

Barbara Boxer. (U.S. Senate)

sometimes referring to Welles as the founder of NCCH. Welles and Shields were crucial to the success of NCCH and HCI, but Borinsky did initiate the organization. The three men all contributed greatly to HCI's success. That success was also due to the social and political environment within which they were working.

Carter (1997, p. 73) suggests that the mid-1970s was a propitious time for the "formation of HCI and the beginnings of the gun control movement." First, the social movements of the 1960s encouraged people to see personal troubles—such as being mugged at gunpoint—as public issues that would be amenable to solutions through social policy. Second, a huge lobbying industry had developed in Washington, D.C. That industry provided numerous opportunities for social issues-oriented organizations. Third, there was no effective interest group focused solely on gun control. Finally, the federal government provided opportunities for HCI. Congressional representatives, the Department of Justice's Bureau of Justice Statistics, and the Centers for Disease Control all worked with HCI in the 1970s.

Having founded the organization, Borinsky moved away from it in the 1970s and now works in the private sector.

Walter F. Carroll

See also Brady Campaign to Prevent Gun Violence; Brady Center to Prevent Gun Violence; Brady, James S.; Brady, Sarah Kemp; Gun Control; National Council to Control Handguns; Shields, Nelson T. "Pete"; Welles, Edward O.; Zebra Killings
For Further Reading:
Carter, Gregg Lee. 1997. *The Gun Control Movement.* New York: Twayne.
DeConde, Alexander. 2001. *Gun Violence in America.* Boston: Northeastern University Press.
Shields, Pete. 1981. *Guns Don't Die—People Do.* New York: Arbor House.

Boxer, Barbara (1940–)

Sen. Barbara Boxer (D-CA) has been a forceful advocate for gun control in the U.S. House of Representatives and now in the U.S. Senate. Boxer has used her position as a senator from the most populous state to garner media attention to her gun control policies, but has also worked quietly in the Senate to introduce bills and amendments, to alter language in bills, and to direct appropriations to gun control projects. When the Democrats regained the majority in the Senate in 2001, Boxer became an even more influential player in the gun control debate.

Working as a stockbroker and newspaper editor before entering politics, Boxer first served as a congressional aide during 1974–1976. She was elected to the Marin Board of Supervisors in 1976 and served for six years. She was elected to the House in 1983, where she served four terms. In 1992, she was elected to the Senate in the "Year of the Woman" (Cook, Thomas, and Wilcox, 1993), where she is currently serving in her second term. She sits on the Commerce Committee, the Public Works Committee, and the Foreign Affairs Committee.

Boxer supported the Brady Bill and the assault-weapons ban. She introduced the American Handguns Standards Act, which sought to ban Saturday Night Specials and other cheap handguns, in 1996. She introduced the Firearms Rights, Responsibilities, and Remedies Act in an effort to protect the ability of cities and groups to sue gun manufacturers, dealers, and importers for civil damages resulting from gun violence.

Much of Boxer's legislative activity has centered on protecting children from gun violence. In 1997 and again in 1999, she introduced with Sen. Herb Kohl (D-WI) the Child Safety Lock Act, which would require child-safety locks on all handguns sold in the United States. A version of this bill was adopted as an amendment to a Juvenile Justice Bill, but the legislation did not pass the House. She proposed another amendment to the Juvenile Justice Bill that directed the Federal Trade Commission to study manufacturers' efforts to market guns to children. This amendment was also adopted. In the floor debate, Boxer argued that gun manufacturers are targeting children as young as 4 years of age. She also introduced the Youth Access to Firearms Act, which would ban the sale or transfer of guns to people under 18, with exceptions for parents, grandparents, and guardians.

These efforts to control guns are part of a larger legislative agenda to reduce violence among youth. Boxer introduced the School Safety Fund Act, which would direct funds to local school districts for a variety of programs aimed at identifying and counseling potentially violent students, and for establishing violence prevention programs. She has also worked on funding for after-school programs, more police on campus, and more funding for hiring police.

Boxer is one of the most liberal members of the Senate. Although she has worked on military procurement issues (especially those dealing with California contractors), her greatest focus has been on women's issues. She sponsored the Violence against Women Act while serving in the House and helped to pass it in the Senate. She is also a strong supporter of abortion rights. Boxer is the author of one book, on women in politics.

Clyde Wilcox and Benjamin Webster

See also Assault Weapons Ban of 1994; Brady Handgun Violence Prevention Act (Brady Bill); Democratic Party and Gun Control; Lawsuits against Gun Manufacturers

For Further Reading:

Barone, Michael, and Grant Ujifusa. 1999. *The Almanac of American Politics, 2000.* Washington, DC: National Journal.

Boxer, Barbara. 1994. *Strangers in the Senate: Politics and the New Revolution of Women in America.* Washington, DC: National Press Books.

Cook, Elizabeth Adell, Sue Thomas, and Clyde Wilcox. 1993. *Women of the Year.* Boulder, CO: Westview Press.

Brady Campaign to Prevent Gun Violence

The Brady Campaign to Prevent Gun Violence is the nation's best-known citizens' organization working for stronger gun laws. The Brady Campaign works to prevent gun violence by supporting and defending sensible gun laws, regulations, and public policies; mobilizing grassroots activists; electing pro–gun control public officials; and increasing public awareness of the realities of gun violence. The Brady Campaign believes that a safer America can be achieved without banning all guns.

With its headquarters in Washington, D.C., and with regional staff in other parts of the country, the Brady Campaign works with allied organizations; victims of gun violence; law enforcement; the medical community; civic, educational, and religious groups; lawmakers; and citizens across the country who support stronger gun laws. It is a nonpartisan, not-for-profit organization funded mostly through membership and individual donations.

The Brady Campaign's most prominent spokespersons are former White House press secretary James Brady (for whom the Brady Bill is named) and his wife Sarah, who is the organization's chairperson. However, the Bradys did not start the organization. The Brady Campaign was established almost a decade before the Bradys became involved in the fight for stricter gun laws.

In the early 1970s, graduate student Mark Borinsky was held up at gunpoint and almost killed in Chicago. Determined to do something about gun crime after finishing his degree, Borinsky expected to find several gun control organizations in Washington, D.C., to which he could lend his support. Finding that there were none, he used his own resources to start the National Council to Control Handguns (NCCH) in 1974.

That same year, 23-year-old Nick Shields was shot and killed in San Francisco as he was preparing for lacrosse practice (one of the infamous Zebra Killings). Nick's father, N. T. "Pete" Shields, was an executive at the DuPont company. Wanting to do something to give meaning to his son's senseless murder, Shields became involved with NCCH in 1975 and soon took a year's leave of absence from his job to devote more time to NCCH. By the end of 1976, Shields took early retirement from DuPont to work full-time for NCCH as executive director.

By 1981, NCCH had been renamed Handgun Control, Inc. HCI and Shields was now chair of the organization. HCI had grown in membership and prominence as the leading lobby working to strengthen the nation's gun laws. On March 30, 1981, a mentally disturbed man, John Hinckley, Jr., tried to assassinate President Ronald Reagan, wounding the president, two law enforcement officers, and, most seriously, Press Secretary James Brady.

In 1983, realizing that legislation alone would not stem the nation's gun-violence epidemic, Shields founded HCI's sister organization, the Center to Prevent Handgun Violence, to change public attitudes and behavior surrounding guns. While the focus of HCI was on legislation and elections, the center's focus was on education, research, litigation, and outreach.

In 1985, another encounter with guns spurred Sarah Brady to join HCI. While vacationing in Illinois, the Bradys' 6-year-old son Scott found a loaded gun in the backseat of a friend's car and started playing with it. Thinking—as her son did—that the gun was a toy, Sarah took it from him and told him never to point a gun, toy or real, at another person. Then she realized that the gun her son had been holding was real—not unlike the one used to shoot James. She was outraged that firearms had become so common and accessible in our society that even a child could easily get hold of one. A few days later, her desire to do something became resolute when she read that the gun lobby, led by the National Rifle Association, was pushing a bill in Congress to roll back the nation's weaker gun laws. Sarah Brady called HCI and asked what she could do to help.

She quickly became the organization's most influential spokesperson, writing letters, lobbying members of Congress, appearing in the media, and testifying before congressional panels in support of common-sense gun laws. HCI achieved victories with the passage of legislation to ban armor-piercing ammunition and to ban guns that are not detectable by X-ray machines. When Shields retired in 1989, Sarah Brady became chair of HCI. She and James stepped up their advocacy for HCI's number-one priority: legislation to require background checks on gun purchasers—legislation that became known as the Brady Bill in James's honor.

The Brady Bill was eventually passed as the Brady Handgun Violence Prevention Act; it represented a landmark piece of legislation because it closed a gaping loophole in the nation's gun laws. Even though there were established categories of prohibited purchasers, such as felons, fugitives from the law, and drug abusers, there was no national requirement for background checks on gun purchasers. In most states, a gun buyer could simply sign a form, attesting that he or she was not a prohibited purchaser, and walk out with a gun. The form would simply get filed away with no follow-up or verification conducted to determine the accuracy of the information. John Hinckley, Jr., the man who almost killed James Brady, purchased his $29 gun at a gun store in Texas, where he was not a resident. Under the Gun Control Act of 1968, a gun purchaser must be a legal resident of the state in which the purchase is made. He was able to buy the gun because no background check was conducted.

The key provisions of the Brady Bill required a background check and a five-day waiting period on gun purchases from licensed gun dealers. After a seven-year battle, the bill was finally signed into law by President Bill Clinton on November 30, 1993, putting an end to the "lie-and-buy" system. In 1994, the federal assault-weapons ban was passed, limiting the availability of military weapons to the civilian market. While these two laws are landmarks in the history of gun laws, the work of the Brady Campaign is far from over.

The Brady Campaign is continuing the fight to close other loopholes in our gun laws and to pass measures that make it easier to enforce those laws. Its priorities include requiring comprehensive criminal background checks every time a gun is sold, including at gun shows, through classified ads, and over the Internet; requiring licensing and safety training for all new gun owners to ensure that they know proper handling of their weapons and the laws governing their use; requiring that records be kept every time a gun is sold, to catch gun traffickers and to enable law enforcement to trace guns recovered in crime; and setting consumer protection standards for firearms

On June 14, 2001, the boards of trustees of Handgun Control, Inc. and the Center to Prevent Handgun Violence officially changed the names of the organizations to the Brady Campaign to Prevent Gun Violence and the Brady Center to Prevent Gun Violence, respectively. The names were changed to honor James and Sarah Brady, who have been tireless champions for a safer United States. In October 2001, the Brady Campaign and the Brady Center entered into a historic partnership with the Million Mom March, a grassroots movement that started in 1999 in the wake of the Columbine High School massacre and other mass shootings. The union of these organizations makes the Brady Campaign the leader in the fight for a nation free from gun violence.

Nancy M. Hwa

See also Assault Weapons Ban of 1994; Borinsky, Mark; Brady Center to Prevent Gun Violence; Brady Handgun Violence Prevention Act (Brady Bill); Brady, James S.; Brady, Sarah Kemp; Gun Control; Hinckley, John Warnock, Jr.; Million Mom March; National Council to Control Handguns; Project Lifeline; Reagan, Ronald Wilson; Shields, Nelson T. "Pete"; Straight Talk About Risks; Welles, Edward O.; Zebra Killings

For Further Reading:
Brady Campaign to Prevent Gun Violence website. http://www.bradycampaign.org.
Carter, Gregg Lee. 1997. *The Gun Control Movement.* New York: Twayne.
Shields, Pete. 1981. *Guns Don't Die—People Do.* New York: Arbor House.

Brady Center to Prevent Gun Violence

The Brady Center to Prevent Gun Violence, founded in 1983 as the Center to Prevent

Handgun Violence, is a nonpartisan, nonprofit organization dedicated to reducing gun violence through litigation, educational initiatives, grassroots mobilization, and policy research. The Brady Center is an affiliate of the Brady Campaign to Prevent Gun Violence (formerly known as Handgun Control, Inc.), which works for the passage of local, state, and federal gun control laws.

The guiding principle of the Brady Center is that gun control legislation, although necessary, is not a comprehensive solution to the gun-violence problem. Thus, the activities of the Brady Center include such nonlegislative initiatives as providing pro bono legal representation to gun-violence victims, performing comprehensive policy research, and implementing educational programs in cooperation with teachers, parents, health care providers, and local law enforcement authorities.

The Legal Action Project (LAP) of the Brady Center seeks to use the courts to establish legal principles that will reduce gun violence. The LAP provides pro bono representation to individual gun-violence victims, as well as to cities and counties in lawsuits against the gun industry. LAP lawyers brought the first lawsuit against the industry by a city seeking to recover the public costs of gun violence, as well as the first suit seeking to hold a gun manufacturer liable for failing to personalize guns to prevent misuse by children and other unauthorized persons. Through the filing of "friend of the court" briefs and other assistance, the LAP also plays a key role in defending gun control laws under attack in the courts.

The Brady Center's education programs seek to increase awareness of gun violence through such grassroots efforts as implementing antiviolence school curricula, collecting and analyzing local gun-violence statistics, speaking at community events, organizing university students and health professionals, and assisting health care providers in counseling activities.

Project Lifeline, for instance, is a program that mobilizes and organizes health professionals in their efforts to educate the public about the costs of gun violence. Materials disseminated to Project Lifeline participants include information on the use of the media, literature on adopting institutional policy resolutions concerning guns and gun safety, and artwork to support local media campaigns. Straight Talk About Risks (STAR) is a gun-violence prevention curriculum that is implemented in over 100 school districts nationwide. Using a mixture of role-playing and other interactive activities, STAR is designed to combat gun violence by teaching children and teens social problem-solving and safety skills. Steps to Prevent Firearm Injury in the Home (STOP 2) assists health care providers in counseling and educating parents and children about the dangers of guns in the home. Other Brady Center programs include the Campus Alliance to Prevent Gun Violence, the Community Action Program, the Youth Action Network, the Parent Education Program, and the Hechinger Speakers Bureau.

Dennis A. Henigan

See also Gun Control; Lawsuits against Gun Manufacturers; Project Lifeline
For Further Reading:
Brady Center to Prevent Gun Violence. http://www.bradycenter.org/.
Carter, Gregg Lee. 1997. *The Gun Control Movement*. New York: Twayne.

Brady Handgun Violence Prevention Act (Brady Bill)

The Brady Handgun Violence Prevention Act (or Brady Bill) is a 1993 law passed by Congress (PL 103-159; 107 Stat. 1536) that required a five-business-day waiting period for the purchase of a handgun, for the purpose of conducting a background check on the prospective buyer and providing a cooling-off period in order to minimize impulse purchases that might lead to violence. Five years after enactment of the law, the five-day waiting period was eliminated and replaced by an instant background-check system.

From 1987 to 1993, gun control proponents, led by Handgun Control, Inc. (HCI), placed their primary political emphasis on the enactment of a national waiting period for handgun purchases. The purpose of such a rule was twofold: first, to provide authorities with the opportunity to conduct a background check on the prospective purchaser in order to void handgun purchases by felons, the mentally incompetent, or others who should not have handguns; and second, to provide a cooling-off period for those who seek to buy and perhaps use a handgun in a fit of temper or rage. On its face, such a procedure certainly represents a modest degree of government regulation, since it merely postpones a handgun purchase by a few days and denies handguns only to those whom everyone agrees should not have them. Yet the struggle over enactment of a waiting period took on epic proportions as a bitter power struggle between regulation opponents and proponents, where the ground being fought over was far less important than the struggle itself.

The Brady Bill was named after James Brady, the former White House press secretary and subsequent gun control advocate who was seriously injured in the assassination attempt against President Ronald Reagan in 1981. It was first introduced in Congress in 1987—in the Senate by Howard Metzenbaum (D-OH) and in the House of Representatives by Edward F. Feighan (D-OH). It quickly became the top priority of HCI and Sarah Brady, James Brady's wife and HCI leader. The National Rifle Association (NRA) opposed the measure, saying that it would merely be a prelude to stronger regulation, that it would not stop criminals from getting guns, and that it merely inconvenienced those entitled to guns. As late as the mid-1970s, however, the NRA had supported the idea of waiting periods.

The Brady Bill was put up to a chamber-wide vote in the House for the first time in September 1988, when opponents led by the NRA succeeded in defeating the bill by substituting an NRA-backed amendment for the waiting period, despite a concerted effort by HCI and a coalition of police organizations called the Law Enforcement Steering Committee. By its own account, the NRA spent from $1.5 million to $3 million in the successful effort to kill the bill, mostly on a media campaign and grassroots efforts. Assessing the failed effort, Representative Feighan noted that at least two dozen House members had privately spoken of their support for the bill, but had refused to vote for it not because they feared losing their seats, but because of "the aggravation" that accompanied opposing the NRA.

Two years later, both chambers voted to approve the Brady Bill. Initial House approval for a seven-day waiting period came in May 1991 (by a 239–186 vote), with Senate approval (by a 71–26 vote) following a month later. Before passing the Brady Bill, the House defeated an NRA-backed substitute, sponsored by Rep. Harley O. Staggers (D-WV), which called instead for an instant computerized background check of prospective handgun purchasers. Such a system would, in theory, eliminate the need for waiting, yet still bar gun purchases by those not eligible.

The problem with the proposal was that for such a system to work it would require that pertinent records from all the states be fully automated. Yet in 1991, only ten states had such automation; eight states still handled files manually and nine states did not even maintain the necessary felony records. Moreover, according to an analysis by Congress's Office of Technology Assessment, the time lapse between the conclusion of a criminal case and its logging in state records runs from weeks to months. Thus, the actual development of a viable system would take years and would cost hundreds of millions of dollars. The political motive behind the Staggers proposal was based on the principle that a motion is easier to defeat if the opposition has something to offer in its place. By proposing an alternative of little or no immediate feasibility, the NRA and its allies were proposing a plan that seemed to offer a meaningful reform, yet posed no actual change in gun-purchasing procedures for many years to come. The Staggers proposal would become Brady Bill opponents' chief rallying point. The Senate version differed from that of the House in that it called for a five-day waiting period instead of seven days and was attached to a controversial omnibus crime bill. A conference version was hammered out, but it was killed by filibuster in the Senate.

President George Bush publicly opposed the Brady Bill throughout 1991 and 1992, but linked it with the larger crime bill, saying that he would sign the measure even if Brady was included—but only if the larger crime bill was to his liking. Bush's veto threat hung over the bill, yet it also opened the door to presidential approval, since it provided a means whereby he could sign the measure into law without seeming to entirely abandon his inclination to oppose most gun control measures. In the end, Bush's qualified veto threat had little effect on the outcome, except to the extent that it buttressed the cause of Senate Republicans who succeeded in blocking the measure.

The Brady Bill struggle climaxed in 1993, when supporters promoted a five-business-day waiting period bill. House Judiciary Committee approval was won on November 4, despite the objections of committee chair and gun control opponent Jack Brooks (D-TX), who also boosted the bill's chances by reluctantly consenting to separate the measure from a new crime bill. Six days later, the full House approved the Brady Bill after fending off several amendments (sponsored by Republicans and Brooks) designed to weaken the bill. One such amendment, to phase out the waiting period after five years, was adopted. The final vote to pass the bill, H.R. 1025, was 238–189.

Following the lead of the House, the Senate separated the Brady Bill (S.R. 414) from the larger crime package. The bill faced a Republican filibuster almost immediately, but this move was forestalled by an agreement between the political party leaders to allow floor consideration of a substitute version that included two NRA-backed provisions. The first called for all state waiting periods to be superseded by the federal five-day waiting period (twenty-four states had waiting periods of varying lengths in 1993; twenty-three also had background checks). This was objectionable to Brady supporters because many states had waiting periods longer than five days, and the move was seen as a violation of states' rights. This amendment was stricken from the bill by a Senate floor vote. The second measure called for ending the five-day waiting period after five years. It survived a vote to kill it. The Senate then faced another filibuster, which looked as though it would be fatal to the bill. Brady supporters and congressional allies all conceded that the bill was dead for the year. The postmortems proved to be premature, however, because within a couple of days the Republicans decided to end their opposition on November 20, sensing a rising tide of impatience and no sense that they could win further concessions from Democratic leaders. The bill was passed that day by a 63–36 vote.

The bill then went to a contentious House-Senate conference on November 22. Opposing factions finally reached an accommodation and the bill was approved in the Senate by voice vote on November 24, with a promise to consider several modifications in early 1994. President Bill Clinton signed the bill into law on November 30.

As enacted, the Brady law codified a five-business-day waiting period for handgun purchases for the succeeding five years. According to the law, handgun purchases are to be rejected if the applicant has been convicted of a crime that carries a sentence of at least a year (not including misdemeanors); if there is a violence-based restraining order against the applicant; if the person has been convicted of domestic abuse, arrested for using or selling drugs, is a fugitive from justice, is certified as mentally unstable or is in a mental institution, or is an illegal alien or has renounced U.S. citizenship. The law also authorized $200 million per year to help states improve and upgrade their computerization of criminal records; increased federal firearm license fees from $30 to $200 for the first three years, and $90 for renewals; made it a federal crime to steal firearms from licensed dealers; barred package labeling for guns being shipped to deter theft; required state and local police to be told of multiple handgun sales; and said that police must make a "reasonable effort" to check the backgrounds of gun buyers. In addition, it provided for ending the five-day wait after five years, to be replaced with an instant background check, which began in December 1998. Such checks are conducted through information provided by the Federal Bureau of Investigation's National Instant Criminal Background Check System. The check must be completed within three days, but 95 percent of the background checks are completed within two hours, according to a U.S. Justice Department report. Even though waiting periods are no longer required by the national government, nineteen states have their own, ranging from a few days to several months. They include Alabama, California, Connecticut, Florida, Illinois, Indiana, Kansas, Maryland, Massachusetts, Minnesota, Missouri, New Jersey, New York, North Carolina, Ohio, Rhode Island, South Dakota, Washington, and Wisconsin.

Opponents of the law, including the NRA, challenged its constitutionality—not as a violation of the Second Amendment's right to bear arms, but as a violation of states' rights under the Tenth Amendment. In 1997, a sharply divided U.S. Supreme Court struck down the law's provision requiring local police to conduct background checks in the case of *Printz v. United States* (521 U.S. 898). The ruling did not challenge the propriety of restricting handgun sales. Despite the ruling, handgun background checks generally continued on a voluntary basis. From the time of the law's enactment through 2000, nearly 600,000 handgun sales were blocked as the result of the law (about 2.5 percent of all handgun purchases). In addition, the increase in federal firearm license fees helped reduce the number of license holders from nearly 300,000 to about 74,000 by 2000, as most license holders were not storefront dealers but private individuals who were willing to pay the low fee in order to save money on their own gun purchases. The Clinton administration issued regulations to monitor dealers more closely as well. Critics argued that the federal government failed to prosecute most Brady law violators. In response, the Clinton administration proposed hiring several hundred additional Bureau of Alcohol, Tobacco, and Firearms agents and federal prosecutors to focus on gun-law violators. Congress approved the proposal in 2000.

Brady law supporters also continued to note that the background-check provision only applied to licensed dealers. At gun shows and flea markets in most states, guns can be bought and sold by unlicensed individuals. An estimated 40 percent of gun sales occur at gun shows, flea

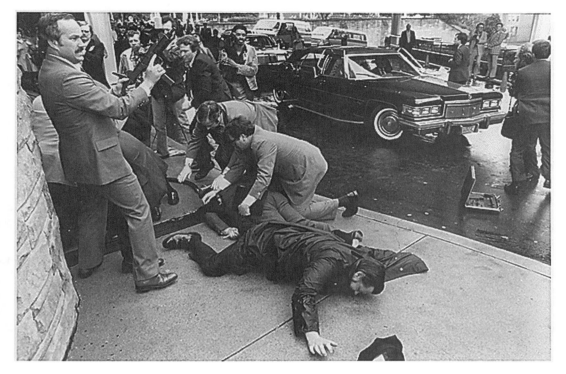

Two men tend to James Brady (lying face-down, center) while chaos erupts outside the Washington Hilton Hotel after the assassination attempt on President Reagan. (Ronald Reagan Library)

markets, and other unregulated "secondary market" venues (over 4,000 gun shows are held every year). National legislative efforts to close this so-called gun-show loophole failed in 1999 and 2000.

Robert J. Spitzer

See also Background Checks; Brady, James S.; Brady, Sarah Kemp; National Rifle Association; *Printz v. United States*

For Further Reading:

Bureau of Alcohol, Tobacco, and Firearms. 1997. *Gun Dealer Licensing and Illegal Gun Trafficking.* Washington, DC: U.S. Department of the Treasury.

———. *Gun Shows: Brady Checks and Crime Gun Traces.* 1999. Washington, DC: Department of the Treasury.

Spitzer, Robert J. 1998. *The Politics of Gun Control.* New York: Chatham House.

Brady, James S. (1940–)

James S. Brady was a lifelong member of the Republican Party and career public servant when he was wounded in the 1981 assassination at-

tempt on President Ronald Reagan. He subsequently became a staunch advocate for gun control. After he left public service in 1989, Brady and his wife, Sarah, led the effort to enact the Brady Bill, which mandated background checks and a waiting period before the purchase of a handgun. In 2001, the gun control advocacy organization Handgun Control, Inc. was renamed the Brady Campaign to Prevent Gun Violence and the Center to Prevent Handgun Violence was renamed the Brady Center to Prevent Gun Violence, in honor of the efforts of James and Sarah Brady.

James Scott Brady was born on August 29, 1940, in Centralia, Illinois. He attended the University of Illinois, where he majored in political science and communications. He graduated in 1962. Brady became interested in politics at an early age and was a staunch Republican. While in college he served as a staff member for Sen. Everett M. Dirksen, who was the Republican minority leader in the U.S. Senate. During the summer of 1962, Brady worked for the Justice Department's Antitrust Division as an honor intern.

After college, Brady worked for a number of private firms before reentering public service. In 1973, he married Sarah Kemp and the couple went on to have a son, James S. Brady, Jr. The same year that he married, Brady became a communications consultant for the U.S. House of Representatives. He soon joined the Nixon and Ford administrations, accepting the post of special assistant to the secretary of housing and urban development. This post was followed by a stint from 1975 to 1976 as special assistant to the director of the Office of Management and Budget. Brady finished out the Ford administration as an assistant to the secretary of defense. He then joined the staff of Sen. William V. Roth, Jr. (R-DE). Brady left Roth's staff in 1979 to serve as the press secretary of presidential candidate John Connally of Texas. He then joined the team of presidential candidate Ronald Reagan as the director of public affairs and research. Following Reagan's election, Brady was appointed spokesman for the office of the president-elect. In January 1981, Brady became the assistant to the president and White House press secretary.

On March 30, 1981, John Hinckley, Jr., tried to assassinate President Reagan. During the attempt, Reagan, Brady, and two others were wounded. Brady was seriously injured by a gunshot to the head, which struck him just above his left eye. The injury left Brady partially paralyzed and permanently disabled. Although Brady was unable to continue to carry out all of the functions of his demanding position, Reagan retained Brady as the official press secretary for the remainder of both of his terms in office. Brady left office on January 20, 1989.

Since the assassination attempt in 1981, Brady has worked with a number of groups that advocate for the disabled. He traveled the nation as a spokesperson for the National Head Injury Foundation. Brady eventually became vice chair of the organization as well as vice chairman of the National Organization on Disability. In 2000, President Bill Clinton named the White House Press Briefing Room the James S. Brady Press Briefing Room. This honor was in recognition of Brady's work on behalf of the disabled and his contributions to gun control efforts.

It was Brady's work on behalf of gun control legislation that led to his greatest impact on American politics. While he remained Reagan's press secretary, Brady supported the president's staunch anti–gun control stance. However, once out of office, Brady joined his wife in championing gun control legislation. The centerpiece of Brady's efforts was the bill that soon came to bear his name—the Brady Bill. Brady undertook a seven-year effort to gain passage of the bill. The Brady Bill was signed into law by Clinton on November 30, 1993. The law required a mandatory five-day waiting period and a background check before a handgun could be purchased. Brady later worked to secure passage of the federal Assault Weapons Ban of 1994, which forbade the manufacture and sale of such weapons. Brady continues to lobby on behalf of gun control efforts at both the state and national level. He serves on the boards of the two organizations that carry his name and continues to travel the country advocating on behalf of his twin causes—gun control and the rights of the disabled.

Tom Lansford

See also Assault Weapons Ban of 1994; Brady Campaign to Prevent Gun Violence; Brady Center to Prevent Gun Violence; Brady Handgun Violence Prevention Act; Brady, Sarah Kemp; Reagan, Ronald Wilson

For Further Reading:

Cook, Phillip J., and Jens Ludwig. 2000. *Gun Violence: The Real Costs*. New York: Oxford University Press.

DeConde, Alexander. 2001. *Gun Violence in America: The Struggle for Control*. Boston: Northeastern University Press.

Kleck, Gary, and Don B. Kates. 2001. *Armed: New Perspectives on Gun Control*. Amherst, NY: Prometheus Books.

Brady, Sarah Kemp (1942–)

Sarah Brady is the wife of former White House press secretary James S. Brady. After her husband was seriously wounded in an assassination attempt against President Ronald Reagan in 1981, Sarah became active in the gun control movement. She became the chair of Handgun Control, Inc. and later chair of the Center to

Sarah Brady, 1995. (James Leynse/Corbis SABA)

Prevent Handgun Violence. Sarah Brady is best known for her efforts to enact the Brady Bill, which mandated a waiting period and background check before the purchase of a handgun.

Sarah Kemp was born on February 6, 1942, in Missouri, although she grew up in Alexandria, Virginia. She attended the College of William and Mary. After graduation in 1964, she became a teacher in the Virginia public school system. However, in 1968 she began a career in politics, serving in a variety of positions within the Republican Party. From 1968 to 1970, she was an assistant to the campaign director of the National Republican Congressional Committee. She then accepted a position as an administrative aide for Rep. Mike McKevitt (R-CO). In 1972, she accepted the same position in the office of Rep. Joseph J. Maraziti (R-NJ) and held that post for the next two years. In 1973, she married James Brady. The couple have one son, James Scott Brady, Jr. From 1974 through 1978, Sarah held the posts of coordinator of field services and director of administration for the national Republican Party. She also served as

a delegate to five Virginia Republican Party conventions.

On March 30, 1981, Sarah's husband James was seriously wounded in an assassination attempt on President Reagan. He became partially paralyzed and remained disabled. The episode prompted Sarah to become active in the gun control movement. She advocated for what she termed "sensible" gun laws that did not infringe extensively upon the ability of responsible citizens to own or acquire weapons, but which limited access by criminals. As such, she initially sought to forge a compromise between the extremes of both sides of gun control issues.

In 1989, Sarah became the chair of Handgun Control, Inc. (HCI), an advocacy group that worked to promote gun control laws. While still in this capacity, Sarah became chair of HCI's sister organization, the Center to Prevent Handgun Violence (CPHV). Both organizations were private, nonprofit groups that lobbied on behalf of gun control legislation and supported educational programs. They also helped coordinate legal work in challenges against the gun industry and specific state and/or national laws through the CPHV's Legal Action Project.

Under Sarah's leadership, HCI worked to ensure passage of a 1993 measure in Virginia that limited handgun purchases to one per month. Both HCI and the CPHV also lobbied on behalf of the Assault Weapons Ban that was passed by Congress and signed into law by President Bill Clinton in 1994. However, the main effort of Sarah and both organizations was the passage of the Brady Bill, named in honor of her husband. The Brady Bill mandated background checks and required a five-day waiting or cooling-off period for those attempting to purchase handguns. After an intensive multiyear lobbying effort, the Brady Bill was passed in 1993.

In the wake of the Assault Weapons Ban of 1994 and the Brady Law, Sarah led the CPHV in an intensive campaign to develop a series of educational programs. For instance, the CPHV launched Steps to Prevent Firearm Injury (STOP) in coordination with the American Academy of Pediatrics in 1995 in order to train physicians to counsel families with small children on the potential risks of gun ownership. She also directed the CPHV to support legal action against the gun industry, including the 1998 lawsuit brought by New Orleans against firearm manufacturers. However, her increased efforts on behalf of gun control led many of her former supporters in the Republican Party to perceive that Sarah had abandoned her moderate position. When she spoke at the 1996 Democratic National Convention on gun control, her credibility as a moderate within the Republican Party was further eroded. In the 2000 election, HCI and the CPHV actively worked to defeat Republican presidential candidate George W. Bush.

In 2001, HCI and the CPHV were renamed in honor of Sarah and Jim Brady. Handgun Control, Inc. became the Brady Campaign to Prevent Gun Violence. The Center to Prevent Handgun Violence became the Brady Center to Prevent Gun Violence. Furthermore, on June 28, 2001, Sarah announced that the Brady Center and the Brady Campaign would merge with the organization behind the Million Mom March on Washington, D.C., in May 2000.

Tom Lansford

See also Brady Campaign to Prevent Gun Violence; Brady Center to Prevent Gun Violence; Brady Handgun Violence Prevention Act (Brady Bill); Brady, James S.; Legal Action Project; Project Lifeline

For Further Reading:

Cook, Phillip J., and Jens Ludwig. 2000. *Gun Violence: The Real Costs.* New York: Oxford University Press.

DeConde, Alexander. 2001. *Gun Violence in America: The Struggle for Control.* Boston: Northeastern University Press.

Kleck, Gary, and Don B. Kates. 2001. *Armed: New Perspectives on Gun Control.* Amherst, NY: Prometheus Books.

Branch Davidians

An obscure offshoot of the Seventh-day Adventist Church achieved sudden worldwide notoriety on February 28, 1993, when a bungled attempt by the Bureau of Alcohol, Tobacco, and Firearms (BATF) to serve a search and arrest warrant concerning illegal weapons went horribly wrong. The mismanaged raid and the intense firefight that it provoked resulted in the deaths of four agents and six residents of the Branch Davidians' Mount Carmel Center outside Waco, Texas.

BATF justified the raid with the claim that the residents of Mount Carmel were illegally converting semiautomatic weapons into machine guns, among other things. During the ensuing fifty-one-day siege, however, those inside Mount Carmel countered that many of them knew nothing at all about any illegal guns and that only a few of them were involved in the purchase and resale of firearms at local gun shows. In negotiations first with the BATF and then with the Federal Bureau of Investigation (FBI), the Branch Davidians portrayed themselves as a peaceful group of Bible students who had gathered at Mount Carmel to study with David Koresh, whom they believed to be the only man ever to unravel the mysteries of the biblical book of Revelation and its message about the imminent end of the world. Government agents, in turn, portrayed Koresh as a deranged con man who had duped gullible people into following him, exploited them for his own purposes, and would willingly lead them to their deaths.

The tense standoff ended on April 19, 1993, when, after a prolonged attempt by armored vehicles to punch holes in the rickety wood-framed building, the Mount Carmel Center was consumed in flames, taking the lives of seventy-four residents and leaving only nine survivors. Despite reports from the U.S. Departments of Treasury and Justice, hearings by Senate and House committees, a July 2000 report from Special Counsel John Danforth, and extensive reviews of the evidence by journalists and scholars, many aspects of the Waco incident remain in contention. Not the least of them is the role of firearms, and violence, in the beliefs and practices of the Branch Davidians and in the teachings of David Koresh.

History

The Branch Davidians and their predecessors the Davidians had been a presence in the Waco area for nearly sixty years at the time of the raid. For virtually all of that time they had lived in peaceful coexistence with their neighbors. They could trace their spiritual lineage to Victor Houteff, a dissident Seventh-day Adventist who preached about the imminent, literal establishment of a millennial "Davidian" kingdom in Palestine. In 1935 Houteff bought a 189-acre tract of land outside of Waco to serve as the headquarters for his tiny movement. He intended to gather together a group of 144,000 "servants of God," as mentioned in chapter seven of Revelation, and lead them to the land of ancient Israel where they would soon meet Christ at his messianic return. Although their move to Israel did not occur as soon as expected, throughout the 1940s Houteff's group conducted a vigorous international missionary enterprise from its Texas headquarters. That largely unsuccessful effort was funded in part by selling off sections of the original parcel of land. Houteff died in 1955 and was succeeded by his wife Florence. In 1957 she sold the original parcel of land and relocated the group to 941 acres of land in Elk, nine miles east of Waco. That was the same land on which Koresh would take up residence and eventually assume leadership of the group.

Florence became convinced that the end of the world and the dawning of the kingdom of God would begin during the Passover season in 1959. When her expectations went unfilled, the community was shattered and it dwindled to fewer than fifty people during the mid-1960s. The group was revivified under the leadership of first Ben and then Lois Roden during the 1970s and 1980s. Koresh, then known as Vernon Howell, came to Mount Carmel in 1981, an aimless high school dropout with twin passions for the electric guitar and the Bible. Like Houteff and the Rodens before him, Howell believed that the Seventh-day Adventist Church had become corrupted and could not claim to represent those who would be saved at God's imminent judgment. Lois Roden quickly recognized Howell's facility with the Bible and, to the dismay of her son George, recognized him as her successor. Lois Roden died in 1986 and by the summer of 1988, after several conflicts with George, Howell assumed the leadership of the community.

"David Koresh, the Lamb of God"

Soon after joining the group of bible students led by Lois Roden, the young man then known as Vernon Howell began to fashion a unique identity for himself. The turning point came during a 1985 visit to Israel, where Howell claimed to have had an extraordinary religious experience. Although his comments to those outside the group were very cryptic, it appears that he understood his experience as an ascent into the heavens, similar to the one recounted by the apostle Paul in II Corinthians 12 and to the "night journey" attributed to Muhammad in the Islamic tradition. On March 5, 1993, for example, he told one of the FBI negotiators that he had been taken up into the heavens, shown everything concerning the seven seals, and commissioned by God to spread the truth to all humanity. The 1985 experience thus lay behind Koresh's most provocative assertion, that he was a "Christ," an anointed one. That assertion, however, did not involve a claim of identity with Jesus Christ, but rather a similarity of function. Like Jesus and others who are called "Christs" or "messiahs" in the Bible, Koresh saw himself as having been chosen to execute God's will on earth. One of those "Christs," the sixth century B.C. Persian king Cyrus, who liberated the people of Israel from their captivity in Babylon, gave Howell the surname that he legally adopted in 1990, Koresh.

Koresh's specific task was to reveal, for the first time in human history, the message of the scroll sealed with seven seals that is mentioned in the book of Revelation, chapters four and five. Koresh's message concerned not only the imminent last judgment and the cataclysmic end of the world as we know it, but also the roles that he and his devoted followers would play in that apocalyptic scenario. Koresh identified himself as the Lamb of Revelation and his students fervently hoped that they would be among the 144,000 who would be saved. Revelation was the fixed point around which all Branch Davidian discourse revolved. All interpretive forays into the rest of the Christian scriptures, and Koresh ranged widely through the prophets and Psalms in his "Bible Studies," were explicitly designed to clarify and extend the message of the seven seals.

Koresh's message included references to all of the violent natural, social, and cosmic upheavals that are typical of biblical apocalypticism. He embraced Revelation's image of a climactic battle between the forces of good and evil at Armageddon and anticipated that he and his small band of followers might be called upon to fight on behalf of God. There is, however, no evidence that Koresh urged his followers to take matters into their own hands in order to hasten the apocalypse; nor is there evidence that the cache of weapons at the Mount Carmel Center was intended to be used to provoke the battle that would signal the end of the world. Koresh did not doubt that the day of judgment would hold terrible violence for those who have shunned the truth, but that violence would be enacted by God alone.

After Koresh

Only nine Branch Davidians survived the April 19 fire. Not many of those who were outside Mount Carmel at the time of the siege have kept the faith, and few new believers have been added since then. Nonetheless, two prominent representatives have emerged to continue, and even expand upon, Koresh's teachings. Livingstone Fagan, who had been sent out of Mount Carmel on March 23 to serve as a theological spokesperson for the community, has written several small tracts and a larger manuscript, *Mt. Carmel: The Unseen Reality,* during his incarceration on charges of conspiracy to commit murder. Fagan's writings constitute a faithful representation of Koresh's teachings. Another figure, known only as "The Chosen Vessel" but likely survivor Renos Avraam, has attempted to supplement Koresh's teachings with his own innovations. In neither body of writings, however, is there any endorsement of violence on the part of the faithful. The responsibility of the students of the seven seals is still to study the apocalyptic message of Revelation and prepare themselves for the imminent judgment of the Lord.

Eugene V. Gallagher

See also Bureau of Alcohol, Tobacco, and Firearms; Reno, Janet; Waco, Texas, Raid

For Further Reading:

Gallagher, Eugene V. 2000. "The Persistence of the Millennium: Branch Davidian Expectations of the End after Waco." *Nova Religio* 3: 303–319.

Moore, Carol. 1995. *The Davidian Massacre: Disturbing Questions about Waco Which Must Be Answered.* Franklin, TN: Legacy Communications; Springfield, VA: Gun Owners Foundation.

Reavis, Dick. 1995. *The Ashes of Waco: An Investigation.* New York: Simon & Schuster.

Tabor, James D., and Eugene V. Gallagher. 1995. *Why Waco? Cults and the Battle for Religious Freedom in America.* Berkeley: University of California Press.

Thibodeau, David, and Leon Whiteson. 1999. *A Place Called Waco: A Survivor's Story.* New York: PublicAffairs.

Wessinger, Catherine. 2000. *How the Millennium Comes Violently: From Jonestown to Heaven's Gate.* New York: Seven Bridges Press.

Wright, Stuart A., ed. 1995. *Armageddon at Waco: Critical Perspectives on the Branch Davidian Conflict.* Chicago: University of Chicago Press.

British American Security Information Council (BASIC)

The British American Security Information Council, commonly known as BASIC, is a nongovernmental research body that explores security and military issues and works to promote the nonproliferation of weapons. The organization produces a variety of publications on security and weapons issues and sponsors international forums to address these matters.

BASIC was founded in 1987. It has twin offices in London and Washington, D.C. When it was originally established, the Cold War was just beginning to wind down and arms control and nuclear nonproliferation dominated BASIC's activities. However, since the end of the superpower conflict in the early 1990s, BASIC has shifted to focus more on efforts to control the international arms trade and the traffic in light weapons. The organization brings together a variety of academics and policymakers who produce studies and analyze trends in weapons proliferation. BASIC also sponsors workshops and conferences on security and proliferation matters for government officials, scholars, and the general public. In addition, BASIC collaborates with other nongovernmental bodies to facilitate research and nonproliferation programs.

BASIC has a variety of specific programs that target areas of concern. For instance, the organization's Project on European Security has worked to coordinate arms-control cooperation between such international bodies as the North Atlantic Treaty Organization, the European Union, and the Organization for Security and Cooperation in Europe. One of BASIC's major programs is its Project on Light Weapons. This project seeks to evaluate the role and importance of light weapons in regional and substate conflicts. It further strives to counter the spread of small arms in all countries, including the United States. Specifically, BASIC has worked to decrease the number of weapons worldwide. Among the steps that BASIC has taken has been support for the destruction of weapons and strengthening gun control measures throughout the world. BASIC has also lobbied individual governments and such international organizations as the United Nations for more restrictive controls on the export of light weapons and bans on specific types of arms.

In the United States, BASIC has worked to limit the import of inexpensive handguns from such nations as Brazil and China. Furthermore, the organization has supported legislation that would limit the export of light weapons to na-

tions with high rates of gun violence as the result of the illicit drug trade or political instability. Finally, BASIC research and reports have been utilized as effective monitors of the domestic gun trade and both state and national endeavors to limit access to illegal weapons.

Tom Lansford

See also United Nations
For Further Reading:
British American Security Information Council website. http://www.basicint.org/.

Brooks, Jack B. (1922–)

Jack B. Brooks (D-TX) served in the U.S. House of Representatives from 1953 until his defeat in 1994. A conservative Democrat, Brooks generally opposed gun control legislation, including the Brady Bill, and had close ties to the National Rifle Association (NRA). In 1994, however, Brooks reluctantly supported President Bill Clinton's crime bill that included a ban on nineteen assault weapons and a limit on the number of rounds in gun magazines. Although the NRA did not oppose his election in 1994, Gun Owners of America (GOA) mobilized a fax alert that is widely credited with helping gun-rights advocate Steve Stockman defeat the "Dean of the House." Stockman served one term before being defeated in 1996.

After World War II, Brooks was elected in 1946 to the Texas House of Representatives, where he served for four years. He graduated from law school and worked as a lawyer and farmer until 1952, when he ran successfully for the U.S. House of Representatives. In 1990, Brooks became the chair of the House Judiciary Committee, which has jurisdiction over gun control issues.

He was widely regarded as smart and tough—his questioning of Nixon administration officials during the Watergate hearings won him the admiration of many Democrats and the enmity of the president. As chair of the Judiciary Committee, he battled with wily John Dingell (chair of the House Commerce Committee) over jurisdiction on telecommunications issues. Brooks's issue preferences defied easy categorization. He favored the death penalty, stiffer sentencing, and opposed gun control, but he also supported civil rights bills, labor initiatives, and other liberal measures.

While in the House, Brooks generally opposed gun control legislation. Brooks opposed the Brady Bill and Rep. Charles Schumer's ban on assault weapons. He was a gun owner, and enjoyed the support of the NRA throughout his career. In 1993, he was the chair of an important committee and the longest-serving member of the House of Representatives. He seemed unlikely to be defeated by repeat challenger Stockman and was not regarded by most observers as vulnerable.

But Brooks's Judiciary Committee was charged with bringing Clinton's crime bill to the floor in 1993. Although Brooks worked hard behind the scenes to remove gun control measures, he ultimately used his resources to help pass the final product, which included bans on assault weapons and certain magazines. The NRA and a number of gun manufacturers backed Brooks in his reelection bid; the NRA dispatched Tanya Metaksa to bolster Brooks's cause. But the more ideological GOA threw its support behind Stockman, who narrowly defeated Brooks. Stockman was an advocate for more radical gun groups, including militias, who favored conspiratorial accounts of the Federal Bureau of Investigation attacks on the Branch Davidian compound in Waco, Texas. Stockman served one term and was defeated for reelection.

Clyde Wilcox and Benjamin Webster

See also Gun Owners of America
For Further Reading:
Barone, Michael, and Grant Ujifusa. 1993. *The Almanac of American Politics, 1994.* Washington, DC: National Journal.

Brown Bess

"Brown Bess" is the familiar name for any one of several pattern muskets put into service by the British military between the 1720s and the 1840s. The "Bess" was the first of the eighteenth-century pattern muskets to gain adoption as a standard military weapon, and as such it was widely copied and imitated.

The Brown Besses were fabricated under the direction of the Board of Ordinance for the Land Service at the Tower of London. This close direction of arms production was a novelty in the early eighteenth century, and the British Board of Ordinance led the way in centralizing arms procurement (removing responsibility from the colonel commanding each local unit). In the process, the board developed a system to produce "pattern" arms. Private contractors fabricated components of the muskets (locks, stocks, and barrels) from patterns. The board inspected each lock and proved (test fired) each barrel. Separate contractors then took components from the board's inventory to assemble muskets of standardized specifications of bore, weight, furniture, lock design, and length. Although the parts in each individual weapon were fit by hand (not interchangeable), use of this pattern system made the completed weapons interchangeable in the hands of the soldiers who carried them. Individual differences in weight, balance, and handling were minimal. Every unit in the army could be equipped with weapons of standard bore, reliability, and handling characteristics. Moreover, the Board of Ordinance could control the supply of arms to ensure consistent quality and supply.

The development of pattern arms and centralized ordinance meant that soldiers could be trained to operate in very closely coordinated units firing virtually identical weapons. Technologically, the pattern musket and its associated socket bayonet provided the basis for the tactical revolution that finally banished the pike completely from European battlefields. As pattern muskets improved and their use in the hands of trained troops became the standard, the deadliness of coordinated fire from flintlock muskets put an end to the use of cavalry as shock troops on the battlefield. Thus, these flintlock muskets of the eighteenth century put an end to a tactical constant that dated to the eighth century.

Fitted with the socket bayonet, the Brown Bess was the first in a new class of weapons that provided the technological basis for establishing heavy infantry as the dominant force in tactical planning. Planning based on dominance of heavy infantry—massed formations of troops armed with a bayonet-equipped musket (or rifle)—lasted until World War I. At that point, the heavy machine gun and the artillery barrage changed tactical realities once again.

Strictly applied, the name Brown Bess refers only to the Long Land Pattern Musket produced for the British army from the 1720s to the 1790s. More commonly, however, the name appropriately describes the several variants based on the Long Land Musket that were in regular use until the 1840s. Less appropriately, the name Brown Bess is often applied as a more general term to describe eighteenth-century muzzle-loading flintlocks, especially the weapons carried by troops of the Continental Army during the American Revolution. In fact, the Bess was not standard issue among the Continentals, nor were the British Besses particularly popular with the Americans. They were among the heaviest, most cumbersome, and most difficult to use of the pattern muskets. The Bess called for real strength and highly trained skills.

The most important of the Brown Bess variants include the Short Land Pattern Musket and another model produced originally for the East India Company. The original Long Land Pattern Musket had a barrel length of 46 inches. The Short Land Pattern Musket introduced in the 1760s simply cut the barrel to 42 inches. That change may seem minor, but it had a real effect on the handing of the weapon in the close-packed ranks of troops who carried the Bess. This Short Land Musket, which is also called the New Land Pattern Musket, became the standard weapon for British troops in both the American Revolution and the Napoleonic Wars. Modified to accept percussion caps, the British Army carried on with the Bess until the 1840s. The East India Company's variant was a lighter, cheaper version of the rugged and reliable military weapons provided by the Board of Ordinance at the Tower. These less-rugged Besses, which had an even shorter barrel, are particularly known for their use as trade guns, especially in the North American fur trade.

The origins of the name Brown Bess are unclear and the term was never more than a nickname of familiar use, which accounts for its frequent misapplication as a generalized term applied to eighteenth-century flintlock muskets. The first appearances of the term Brown Bess in print occurred relatively late (1780s), but almost certainly the name was in common use among the troops who carried the weapon much earlier than the 1780s. The most widely accepted explanations for the name makes it a corruption of one of any number of Dutch or German terms related to guns and gun barrels: *bus, büsse, byssa,* or *busche.* The original name, then, would have meant nothing more than "brown barrel."

As a class, the weight and ruggedness of Brown Besses set them apart from other eighteenth-century military flintlocks. These were .75 caliber weapons weighing in excess of 10 pounds. Most other standard-issue pattern muskets from the period were of lesser caliber and somewhat lighter. French pattern muskets such as the Charlevilles, for example, were .69 caliber, and that was still widely considered a heavy infantry weapon. It was the 1763 Charleville that the French supplied in large quantities (over 80,000) to their American allies during the American Revolution. Thus, while the popular imagination has the Continentals of the American Revolution equipped with the Brown Bess, most American troops were actually issued the somewhat smaller-bore Charleville. The British had never allowed widespread distribution of the Besses in the colonies, even for militia use. The Brown Besses (about 17,000) actually used by Americans during the Revolutionary War were captured arms. The Charlevilles received from France beginning in 1777 supplied the American military needs for long arms well into the 1790s, and the first of the long arms produced at the Springfield Armory was a copy of the Charleville, not the Brown Bess. Indeed, the muskets on which Eli Whitney set out to perfect manufacturing by interchangeable parts was an American pattern based on the Charleville.

The Bess was considered heavy and difficult to master. It was designed to fire a very heavy ball, to stand up to violent use in bayonet charges, or to be turned end-for-end and used as a club. It fired with considerably more "kick" than such weapons as the Charleville, and it was thought that effective use required more highly trained and disciplined troops. The efficient use of the Bess, in fact, put the British regulars among the most effective and feared troops of the period. British regulars of the late eighteenth and early nineteenth century were particularly noted for their discipline and their coolness under fire. Equipped with the Brown Bess, their discipline and training gave them truly formidable military capability that is often underappreciated in light of the subsequent development of effective breech-loading and rifled weapons.

Looking back, especially in light of the mythology surrounding sharpshooters and the use of irregular troops armed with rifles, it is tempting to marvel at the foolishness of battlefield tactics that had red-coated regulars marching forward in their closely packed ranks. In fact, the red-coated regular marching forward in the serried ranks of the American Revolution had a better statistical chance of survival than did the combat infantryman crouching in the trenches of World War I or the GIs huddled in the foxholes of World War II. The British infantry square of the Napoleonic era was a truly formidable fighting formation, and its effectiveness was built on training and discipline designed to make the best use of the technical capabilities inherent in the Brown Bess. The Bess's ball was very large and heavy (sixteen balls to the pound) and it produced smashing and shattering effects in the wounds it created. Given the relatively low muzzle velocities possible with black powder, the inertia of this very large ball (3/4-inch in diameter) gave it considerably greater stopping power than what was possible with any weapon of lesser caliber.

The discipline and training of close-order drill for the redcoats was intended to pack the troops together to provide a formation with the maximum possible rate of fire. Three lines of troops firing in a coordinated fashion could effectively deploy one musket for each 14 inches of firing line. At least for short periods, coordinated fire from closely packed troops trained to use the Bess could produce a screen of projectiles that will bear comparison with the effects of modern automatic weapons. Even the use of the smooth-bore musket (as opposed to rifles) was calculated to increase the rate of fire. An effectively trained soldier equipped with smooth-bore muskets could fire at least three rounds per minute on command. In contrast, the muzzle-loaded rifles of the eighteenth century required several minutes of loading time for each round fired. Firing by platoons grouped into three lines, a well-trained battalion of soldiers equipped with the Brown Bess could keep a screen of musket balls in the air in front of their formation at all times. No contemporary formation of riflemen could produce anything comparable. Even when riflemen were used effectively during the American Revolution, as they were at the Battle of Saratoga, they were screened and protected from counterattack by troops armed with muskets and bayonets.

With a musket, even a good marksman could not expect to hit a man-sized target at any more than 40 to 50 yards. Individual aiming, however, was not called for. The Brown Bess, in fact, was not fitted with any sights at all; infantrymen were trained to point and shoot—not to aim at any individual target. A compact infantry formation could establish an effective screen of musket fire out to at least 150 yards—even on a battlefield swathed in black-powder smoke—simply by loading and firing on command. Such a screen of fire made it very dangerous for either cavalry or enemy infantry to approach a trained infantry formation, and it usually made it possible for a formation to move across a battlefield at will unless opposed by a comparably equipped and trained force or by massed artillery fire. It was the effectiveness of closely coordinated musket fire that finally ended any expectation that heavy cavalry could deliver a shock force capable of breaking massed infantry formations on the battlefield. The combination of the flintlock musket and the bayonet gave the battlefield advantage to the heavy infantry.

Despite several notorious incidents in the French and Indian War—and several others during the American Revolution—in which skirmishers, irregulars, or sharpshooters managed to break the discipline of British troops (or kill their officers), well-trained regulars equipped with muzzle-loading muskets dominated the wars of the late eighteenth and the early nineteenth centuries. The muzzle-loading pattern musket and its associated bayonet were key parts in a technology system that maximized the rate of fire and emphasized the need for highly skilled and trained infantrymen. As one of the heaviest and most rugged of the eighteenth-century pattern muskets, the Brown Bess was also among the most effective. It was also the first of the pattern muskets to be adopted as a standard weapon for a national army. Its weight, kick, and cumbersomeness made it more difficult to use than many other muskets, but in the hands of properly trained troops these same characteristics also made it just that much more deadly. The British army's reputation for reliance on a small number of long-service, highly trained professionals with particular expertise in the use of small arms was first established in the wars of the eighteenth and early nineteenth centuries. In that respect, the reputation of the modern British army was first built around the use of the Brown Bess.

David S. Lux

See also American Revolution; Long Rifle (Pennsylvania/Kentucky)

For Further Reading:

Jones, Archer. 1987. *The Art of War in the Western World.* New York: Oxford University Press.

Neumann, George C. 2001. "The Redcoat's Brown Bess." *American Rifleman Magazine* 149 (April): 49.

Wilkinson, Frederick. 1977. *The World's Great Guns.* London: Hamlyn Publishing Group.

Browning, John Moses (1855–1926)

John Browning revolutionized the gun industry. He was a productive inventor and one of the most successful gun manufacturers in modern history. Although he died in 1926, many of his weapons remain in use in the twenty-first century. Browning became noted for his innovations and the reliability of his designs. Among Browning's most celebrated designs were the Colt .45 caliber pistol, the Browning automatic rifle, and Browning automatic shotgun.

John Moses Browning was born on January 23, 1855, in Ogden, Utah, to Mormon parents. His father was a gunsmith and the younger Browning learned his trade working in his fa-

ther's shop. At age 14, John Browning built his first gun—a single-shot rifle that he gave to his brother Matt. After the death of their father in 1879, the two brothers opened their own gunsmith shop, which they named the Browning Arms Company. That same year, Browning married Rachel Teresa Child.

Soon after starting the company, Browning patented his first weapon, a single-shot rifle. While Browning created a variety of designs, the family arms business remained small and limited since the brothers could not expand their sales beyond their small town. However, in 1883 a representative of the Winchester Arms Company became interested in one of Browning's designs. Winchester paid Browning $8,000 for the rights to produce his rifle. This marked the start of a lengthy relationship between Browning and the Winchester Company. Ultimately, Browning gained forty-four patents for Winchester.

Browning utilized his genius to design a variety of weapons and different styles of firearms. Besides working for Winchester, Browning also designed guns for such firearm companies as Remington, Colt, and the Belgian company Fabrique Nationale (FN). Browning far preferred to work on his inventions rather than manage the family's company.

Browning's business relationship with Winchester proved fruitful for both parties. In 1887, Browning invented one of the most popular and widely used weapons in the American West, the Winchester Model 1887 lever-action repeating rifle. This gun used a lever to reload and cock the weapon prior to firing. This gave the gun a high rate of fire compared with the single-action rifles commonly in use at the time. Browning produced this design in a shotgun for Winchester as well. Browning followed these innovations with a pump-action mechanism for shotguns— the basic model for all pump-action shotguns manufactured through contemporary times.

One of Browning's most important innovations involved the use of compressed gas to operate weapons. Browning's inspiration for this new design came when he observed the tremendous amount of gas and air produced by the explosion that occurred when a bullet was fired. The gunsmith sought to utilize this power in such a way that would allow the gun to reload automatically. His design did just that. The gasses produced when a shell was fired created a recoil that moved the weapon's firing pin back. This allowed the spent bullet to be ejected and a new round to enter the chamber.

This automatic system was an integral component in the development of the modern machine gun. Browning personally designed two highly effective and popular machine guns. The first was the 1895 Colt Peacemaker, which became the standard heavy machine gun for the U.S. Army. His second design was the Browning automatic rifle (BAR), a lighter machine gun that could be fired by an individual. The BAR would be used in both world wars, Korea, and Vietnam.

One of Browning's greatest contributions to gunsmithing came with his development of automatic pistols. His first automatic handgun was a .32 caliber pistol that used a slide mechanism to automatically reload. This model was followed by a variety of weapons, including the famous Colt .45 caliber M-1911 government model. This heavy pistol became the standard sidearm for both the military and law enforcement. Browning also developed a lighter 9mm pistol known as the P-35 which was widely used by military and police forces around the world.

Browning also developed an automatic shotgun. However, Winchester decided not to produce the weapon because it was deemed too expensive to manufacture and the market was thought to be too small. Browning found a new partner in Belgium's FN. Not only did FN reap significant financial rewards by producing Browning's shotgun, but other companies, including Remington and Savage, contracted to use Browning's design in the production of their automatic shotguns. The Browning automatic–5 shotgun, which was first produced in 1902, is still produced and sold today. The association between the Browning Arms Company and FN survived long after Browning's death; in 1977 the Belgian corporation actually purchased the Browning Company. Browning has continued to operate under its own name and through the 1990s it recorded average annual sales of $100 million.

All of Browning's firearms were noted for both their reliability and their durability. The weapons were popular with the military and law enforcement because of their effectiveness and their consistency. The weapons were also marked by their simplicity of design and utility of function. The automatic weapons also provided far more firepower than contemporary firearms when Browning first introduced the weapons. Eventually Browning would patent over 100 different weapons. These ranged from pistols to artillery pieces for the army. A testament to Browning's design genius has been the continued manufacture of his weapons, decades after his death on June 21, 1926. In fact, at the time of his death there were still a number of new designs left that kept arms companies busy for a decade. It was not until 1935 that his final handgun design went into production.

Tom Lansford

See also Colt, Samuel; Firearm Dealers; Ruger, William Batterman; Smith & Wesson; Winchester, Oliver Fisher

For Further Reading:
Browning Company. 1942. *A History of Browning Guns from 1831.* Ogden, UT: Browning Company.
Winders, Gertrude Hecker. 1961. *Browning: The World's Greatest Gunmaker.* New York: John Day Co.

Bryan v. United States (1998)

The U.S. Supreme Court held in *Bryan v. United States* that under the Firearms Owners' Protection Act of 1986 (FOPA) a conviction for dealing in firearms without a federal license requires proof only that the accused knew his or her actions were illegal, not that he or she was aware of the federal licensing requirement. (A section of the FOPA prohibits the willful dealing in firearms without a federal license.) Sillasse Bryan was indicted and tried for violating that portion of the statute. There was enough evidence at his trial to prove that he was dealing in firearms and that he knew his actions were illegal, but there was no evidence that he was aware of the federal licensing requirement. After all the evidence was submitted, Bryan's attorney requested that the trial judge instruct the jury that Bryan could be convicted only if he knew of the federal licensing requirement, but the judge refused. Rather, the judge's jury instructions read, in part, that: "[a] person acts willfully if he acts intentionally and purposely and with the intent to do something the law forbids...." Bryan was found guilty. On appeal he argued that his conviction should be reversed because there was no proof that he had knowledge of the federal licensing requirement and the trial judge refused to instruct the jury that such knowledge was required for conviction. The court of appeals affirmed the trial court, stating that the trial judge's instructions were proper and that the U.S. government had proven that Bryan committed the criminal acts willfully. The U.S. Supreme Court affirmed the decision of the court of appeals, noting that Bryan's actions demonstrated that he knew he was engaging in illegal conduct.

In 1968, Congress enacted the Omnibus Crime Control and Safe Streets Act. Congress had determined that traffic in firearms increased lawlessness and violent crime, so it amended federal criminal laws to regulate the use and sale of firearms. For example, 18 U.S.C. § 923 established a federal licensing program and made it illegal to deal in firearms without a license. Section 924 imposed a fine of up to $5,000 or a prison sentence of not more than five years, or both, on anyone dealing in firearms without a license even if an individual believed he or she was acting lawfully. In 1986, anti–gun control proponents persuaded Congress to enact the FOPA, which added 18 U.S.C. § 924(a)(1)(D) to require knowledge of wrongdoing for conviction of illegal dealing in firearms. Specifically, the required element of knowledge for violation of Section 923 is that the suspect acts "willfully."

In upholding Bryan's conviction, the U.S. Supreme Court examined the meaning of "willful." The Court stated that a "willful" act is one done with a "bad purpose." Therefore, to show that the defendant violated the criminal statute the government need not prove that Bryan knew of the specifics of the law. The government simply had to prove that he acted knowing that his conduct was illegal. The Court found that the government met this requirement and the jury found that Bryan knew that his conduct was unlawful.

The Supreme Court also ruled that the legislative history of the bill is ambiguous. The evidence offered by Bryan of the legislative intent of members of Congress comes mainly from opponents of the bill and thus does not definitively suggest a different interpretation of "willfulness."

Finally, the Supreme Court held that although the trial court misstated the law in a jury instruction, after giving a correct instruction, the error was not severe enough to require a reversal of the decision. The trial court's instruction that "the government [need not] prove that [Bryan] had knowledge that he was breaking the law" was not a serious misstatement, and thus the Supreme Court declined to overturn Bryan's conviction for several reasons. First, Bryan did not object to the incorrect instruction at trial. Second, within the context of all of the instructions given, it was unlikely that the jury was misinformed. Third, Bryan did not raise this argument to the court of appeals. Fourth, the U.S. Supreme Court's decision to hear the case was limited to the narrow legal question of the definition of "willfulness."

Justice John Paul Stevens authored the majority decision of the Court, and was joined by Justices Stephen Breyer, Anthony Kennedy, Sandra Day O'Connor, David Souter, and Clarence Thomas. Justice Souter also wrote a concurring opinion. Justice Antonin Scalia wrote a dissenting opinion that was joined by Chief Justice William Rehnquist and Justice Ruth Bader Ginsburg.

Keith Rollin Eakins

See also Congressional Voting Patterns on Gun Control; Firearms Owners' Protection Act of 1986; Gun Control Act of 1968; United States Congress and Gun Legislation; United States Supreme Court Decisions on Gun Control

For Further Reading:

Bryan v. United States, 524 U.S. 184 (1998). http://supct.law.cornell.edu/supct/html/96–8422. ZO.html.

Firearms Owners' Protection Act, Pub. L. No. 99-308, 100 Stat. 449 (1986).

Bureau of Alcohol, Tobacco and Firearms (BATF)

The Bureau of Alcohol, Tobacco and Firearms (BATF) is a federal law enforcement organization within the Department of the Treasury. It is responsible for administering federal laws

Bureau of Alcohol, Tobacco and Firearms

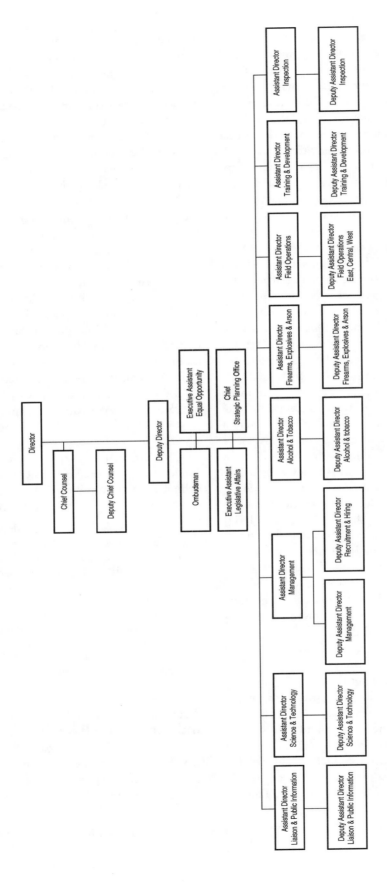

regulating alcohol, tobacco, firearms, and explosives. The BATF is also responsible for conducting arson investigations in conjunction with local, state, and national law enforcement agencies. The bureau is headquartered in Washington, D.C., with field offices located in various states as well as in a few other countries.

Its responsibilities regarding federal alcohol regulations include ensuring the collection of federal alcohol beverage taxes and monitoring the labeling of wine and distilled spirits, reviewing some 74,000 alcohol labels a year. Unlike the situation with regard to alcohol, the BATF is not involved with consumer protection issues (such as product quality or health warnings) related to tobacco. Instead, the bureau's mission with regard to tobacco centers on ensuring payment of federally mandated taxes on tobacco products. The BATF collected combined alcohol and tobacco tax revenues of over $12 billion in fiscal year 1999.

Firearm regulation and enforcement dominate the bureau's agenda, both in terms of expenditures and regulatory activity. The regulation of firearm possession (including licensing firearm dealers) and criminal investigations (including tracing guns used in criminal activity) are the bureau's major firearm-related activities.

The earliest incarnations of BATF agents were the individuals charged by Secretary of the Treasury Alexander Hamilton with collecting a federal spirits tax imposed in 1791, a levy that later gave rise to the Whiskey Rebellion. The first twentieth-century precursor to the BATF was the Prohibition Unit, an organization within the Bureau of Internal Revenue of the Treasury Department devoted to the enforcement of the Eighteenth Amendment and the Volstead Prohibition Enforcement Act. Perhaps the most colorful character in the bureau's history was Eliot Ness, whose story spawned both a television series and movies. Ness and his agents, nicknamed the Untouchables, became famous during the Prohibition period for pursuing gangster Al Capone and helping to build a successful case against him on tax-evasion charges. Tobacco came within the purview of the BATF during the 1950s when the bureau was given the responsibility to collect a federal

tobacco tax, but it has never commanded as much BATF attention as either alcohol or firearm regulation. Recently, the regulation of alcohol has receded in importance on the bureau's agenda as firearm regulation and enforcement has come to the fore.

The BATF underwent a series of name changes related to its expanding jurisdiction; successively, the Alcohol Tax Unit, the Alcohol and Tobacco Division, and the Alcohol, Tobacco, and Firearms Division. The National Firearms Act of 1934 (aimed at curtailing the easy availability of firearms for criminal activities) and the Federal Firearms Act of 1938 (prohibiting certain classes of people from owning firearms) gave the bureau its original entry into firearm regulation. Its current responsibilities with regard to firearms derive mostly from the Gun Control Act of 1968 and its subsequent amendments, including the Firearms Owners' Protection Act of 1986 and the Brady Handgun Violence Prevention Act of 1998.

The BATF is responsible for issuing federal licenses for gun manufacturers and dealers. The BATF's National Licensing Center is based in Atlanta and handles these licensing responsibilities. Dealers are required to maintain a permanent place of business from which to conduct their firearms business and are barred from selling to prohibited classes of individuals, including felons, juveniles, and those adjudicated to be mentally incompetent. Individuals who collect guns for personal collections and make sales only occasionally as part of their hobby are also required to obtain a federal collectors license.

To ensure compliance with licensing requirements, the BATF conducts occasional inspections of existing licensees but has historically been plagued with insufficient personnel for effective monitoring. The Brady Handgun Violence Prevention Act requires dealers obtain a criminal background check on a prospective buyer prior to making a sale. They do so through the National Instant Criminal Background Check System (NICS), which is operated by the Federal Bureau of Investigation (FBI). Though the BATF does not operate the NICS, it is responsible for ensuring dealer compliance with this provision of the Brady Bill.

The BATF also has responsibility for operating the National Tracing Center (NTC), which traces the ownership of guns recovered from criminal investigations. The NTC collects information on firearm sales, stolen guns, and chains of possession (from manufacturer to purchaser) to aid local, state, and national law enforcement agencies. Such information is part of a computerized database used to identify firearm-trafficking corridors and black markets for guns. In fiscal year 1999, the NTC traced over 200,000 firearms.

While the NTC is not limited to tracing guns involved in youth violence, it is closely associated with another program of the BATF: the Juvenile Firearms Violence Initiative. This initiative focuses on the use of firearms by juvenile offenders in the commission of violent crimes and is aimed at reducing the availability of guns to minors.

The BATF faces a unique situation with regard to the industries it regulates. The alcohol and tobacco industries have largely looked upon the bureau favorably. The firearm industry and gun control opponents, in particular the National Rifle Association (NRA), however, have viewed the BATF as an antagonist. In part this can be attributed to the different functions the BATF performs with regard to each industry. For the alcohol industry the BATF's regulatory activity serves to ensure compliance with federal standards and thus enhances the reputation of those alcohol products. Furthermore, the BATF is instrumental in securing entry for American alcohol products into foreign markets. With regard to the tobacco industry, the fact that the BATF does not regulate product quality and does little more than ensure compliance with federal tobacco tax regulations means that there is less opportunity for friction between the industry and the bureau. However, the relationship between the firearm industry and the BATF is much more volatile and is exacerbated by the intense opposition of anti–gun control groups such as the NRA.

The BATF has been the target of a number of intense attacks. When the bureau proposed to computerize records to facilitate meeting its regulatory obligations in the 1980s, Congress prohibited the BATF from spending any of its funds to do so and went so far as to cut the funds the BATF had estimated computerization would have cost from the bureau's budget. The bureau has also been the focus of several attempts at dismantlement, all of which have found the NRA (at least initially) arguing against the BATF's continued existence. Ronald Reagan included promises to dissolve the bureau during his 1980 presidential campaign, spurred in part by analyses conducted by conservative groups suggesting major budget savings from folding the BATF into other agencies, coupled with intense lobbying by the NRA.

Ironically, the NRA was subsequently instrumental in sparing the BATF when plans surfaced for the consolidation of the BATF with the Secret Service, a highly regarded organization. The bureau again became a target for dismantlement in the wake of its performance in the Ruby Ridge incident in 1992 and the raid on the Branch Davidian compound in 1993. Vice-President Al Gore, as part of his reinventing government initiative, recommended the merger of the BATF with the FBI, though the recommended merger never took place.

Wendy L. Martinek

See also Background Checks; Black Market for Firearms; Brady Handgun Violence Prevention Act (Brady Bill); Branch Davidians; Federal Firearms Act of 1938; Gun Control Act of 1968; Gun Registration; Gun Shows; National Firearms Act of 1934; National Instant Criminal Background Check System; National Rifle Association; National Tracing Center; Ruby Ridge; Youth Crime Gun Interdiction Initiative

For Further Reading:

Bureau of Alcohol, Tobacco and Firearms. 1998. *An Introduction to the Bureau of Alcohol, Tobacco, and Firearms and the Regulated Industries.* Washington, DC: U.S. Department of the Treasury.

Larson, Erik. 1994. *Lethal Passage.* New York: Crown.

Martinek, Wendy L., Kenneth J. Meier, and Lael R. Keiser. 1998. "Jackboots or Lace Panties? The Bureau of Alcohol, Tobacco, and Firearms." Pp. 17–44 in *The Changing Politics of Gun Control,* eds. John M. Bruce and Clyde Wilcox. Lanham, MD: Rowman and Littlefield.

Moore, James. 1997. *Very Special Agents: The Inside Story of America's Most Controversial Law Enforcement Agency—The Bureau of Alcohol, Tobacco, and Firearms.* New York: Pocket Books.

Spitzer, Robert J. 1998. *The Politics of Gun Control.* 2d ed. New York: Chatham House.

Bureau of Justice Statistics (BJS)

The Bureau of Justice Statistics (BJS), a component of the Office of the Justice Program in the U.S. Department of Justice, is the primary source for criminal justice statistics in the United States. The BJS collects, analyzes, publishes, and disseminates information to the criminal justice community on crime, crime rates, criminal offenders, victims, and the operation of the justice system at all levels of government. These data are critical to policymakers at all levels in promulgating legislation that ensures the administration of justice is efficient and fair while effectively combating crime.

The BJS annually publishes statistical findings on federal criminal offenders and case processing, correctional populations, and criminal victimization. The BJS periodically publishes statistical findings on a series of other topics, including felony convictions, practices and policies of state and federal prosecutors, the administration of law enforcement agencies and correctional facilities, and the characteristics of correctional populations. The BJS will also undertake special data collections and analyses to respond to the policy and legislative needs of the Department of Justice, the administration, Congress, and the criminal justice community. The BJS has made its data accessible in both print and digital format, with many of the BJS databases being accessible via the Internet. The BJS maintains more than two dozen major data collection series from which it publishes and distributes nationwide.

James A. Beckman

See also Department of Justice, U.S.

For Further Reading:

Bureau of Justice Statistics.
   http://www.ojp.usdoj.gov/bjs/.
Office of the Federal Register, National Archives and Records Administration. 1997. *The United States Government Manual*. Washington, DC: Government Printing Office.

Bush, George H.W. (1924–)

George Herbert Walker Bush was elected president of the United States in 1988. During the campaign he emphasized his opposition to gun control and his lifetime membership in the Na-

George H. W. Bush. (Library of Congress)

tional Rifle Association (NRA). As president, Bush provided rhetorical support for the NRA, but he also implemented a ban on imported assault rifles, along with other modest gun control measures. In 1994, Bush publicly resigned from the NRA and issued a letter denouncing fundraising efforts by the organization that described federal agents as "jackbooted government thugs." In 2000, his son, George W. Bush, was elected president of the United States. Like his father, Bush campaigned in opposition to gun control.

George H. W. Bush was born on June 12, 1924, in Milton, Massachusetts, to Dorothy Walker Bush and Prescott Bush (who later served as a Republican senator for Connecticut in 1952–1962). Bush ran unsuccessfully for the Senate in 1964, then won a seat in the House of Representatives in 1966 representing Texas's seventh district. Bush served on the Ways and Means Committee, and was reelected to the House in 1968 with no opposition. In 1970, he again lost a bid for the Senate.

During the 1970s Bush held a number of appointed positions. In 1971, he was named U.S. ambassador to the United Nations. In 1973, he was appointed chair of the Republican National

Committee. In 1974, he became chief of the U.S. Liaison Office in Peking during a period of normalizing relations between the United States and the People's Republic of China. In 1976, Bush became director of the Central Intelligence Agency.

Bush ran for the Republican presidential nomination in 1980. He won the Iowa caucuses but lost in New Hampshire to Ronald Reagan, who eventually won the nomination. Reagan picked Bush to be his running mate. Bush went on to serve two full terms as vice-president. As vice-president, Bush was in charge of the administration's antiterrorism policy and coordinated the war on drugs. He also headed a task force on regulatory relief.

In 1988, Bush won the GOP nomination for president and came from far behind to defeat Democrat Michael Dukakis in the general election. As president, he assembled an international coalition to drive Iraq from Kuwait in 1991, and for a time he enjoyed the highest popularity ratings of any incumbent president. But the economy slipped into recession and Bush was defeated in his bid for reelection by Bill Clinton in 1992.

As a candidate, Bush emphasized his opposition to gun control. He repeatedly claimed that states with the strictest gun controls had the highest crime rates and called for stricter sentencing for criminals. In 1988, Bush won the endorsement of the (NRA).

While in office, Bush introduced Operation Triggerlock, a program that directed U.S. attorneys to vigorously prosecute violations of gun laws committed by convicted felons and drug traffickers. This program provided increased support to the Bureau of Alcohol, Tobacco, and Firearms (BATF), an agency that had already benefited from Bush's backing as part of his strategy for the war on drugs as vice-president. This operation reinvigorated the BATF and changed their mission.

Bush's opposition to gun control was tested in 1989, when a gunman armed with a semiautomatic assault rifle massacred seventeen schoolchildren in Stockton, California. Two years later, a man killed twenty-three people (including himself) and wounded more than twenty others in a cafeteria in Killeen, Texas. Political pressure built during this period for controls on semiautomatic weapons and large weapon clips.

Bush's advisers were divided, with drug czar William Bennett and many police groups urging that limits be placed on the weapons, but others pushing Bush to focus instead on an anticrime policy. Bush waffled and vacillated on the subject before finally issuing an executive order in early 1989 temporarily banning the import of certain assault weapons. He later made the ban permanent and expanded the number of guns covered by the policy. The NRA reacted angrily and refused to endorse Bush in 1992. Yet Bush's ban did not cover domestically produced weapons, thereby avoiding a clash with gun manufacturers.

In May 1995, after the bombing in Oklahoma City, Bush made public a letter to the NRA in which he resigned his lifetime membership. Bush angrily denounced statements by NRA president Wayne LaPierre defending the group's characterization of federal law enforcement agents as "wearing Nazi bucket helmets and black storm trooper uniforms" and "attack[ing] law abiding citizens." The strongly worded letter served as a coda on Bush's complicated relationship with the NRA.

Clyde Wilcox and Benjamin Webster

See also Republican Party and Gun Control; Stockton, California, Massacre

For Further Reading:

Carter, Gregg Lee. 1997. *The Gun Control Movement.* New York: Twayne.

Davidson, Osha Gray. 1998. *Under Fire: The NRA and the Battle for Gun Control.* Iowa City: University of Iowa Press.

Duffy, Michael. 1992. *Marching in Place: The Status Quo Presidency of George Bush.* New York: Simon & Schuster.

Spitzer, Robert J. 1995. *The Politics of Gun Control.* Chatham, NJ: Chatham House.

Vizzar, William J. 2000. *Shots in the Dark: The Policy, Politics, and Symbolism of Gun Control.* New York: Rowman and Littlefield.

Buyback Programs

See Gun Buyback Programs

California Street (101) Massacre

On July 1, 1993, Gian Luigi Ferri entered the law offices of Pettit and Martin at 101 California Street in San Francisco, armed with three handguns and several hundred rounds of ammunition. Ferri was a former client who believed that the law firm had cheated him and contributed to his recent financial failures. He opened fire, killing eight people and wounding six more in the law firm and other offices before the police cornered him in a stairwell and he committed suicide. Public attention soon focused on a similarity between this mass killing and the Stockton schoolyard massacre of four years before: both gunmen had used assault weapons. Ferri used two TEC-DC9s, semiautomatic assault pistols manufactured by Navegar, Inc. of Miami, Florida, and equipped with military-style features that allow the user to fire many rounds of ammunition in a short period of time. Although California had banned the sale of assault weapons after the Stockton shooting, Ferri easily obtained his at a gun show and pawnshop in Nevada.

The 101 California Street massacre galvanized public opinion toward increased firearm regulation and contributed to the passage of the federal assault weapons ban the following year. Another important outgrowth of the massacre was *Merrill v. Navegar,* a historic lawsuit that produced the first appeals court decision to hold that a gun manufacturer may be held responsible for negligent conduct that increases the risk of criminal violence.

Navegar, doing business under the name Intratec, throughout the 1980s manufactured high-capacity assault pistols under the names KG-9 and TEC-9. The weapons quickly gained popularity among criminals. One study showed that the TEC-9 was the leading assault weapon

seized by law enforcement agencies in large cities in 1990 and 1991, accounting for 24 percent of all such weapons seized. When the District of Columbia and other jurisdictions enacted laws restricting the TEC-9 and other assault weapons by model name, Navegar made a minor alteration to the weapon and renamed it the "TEC-DC9" to evade the laws. The features that criminals found so appealing, however, remained the same: the ability to accept high-capacity magazines, which can hold fifty bullets or more; a barrel shroud, which cools the weapon so that the shooter can grasp it with both hands and spray-fire; and a threaded barrel to accommodate silencers. The company advertised in survivalist publications like *Soldier of Fortune* and *Combat Handguns,* touting the TEC-DC9's "firepower," "excellent resistance to fingerprints," and other features of little value to law-abiding gun purchasers.

In the lawsuit, filed in May 1994, massacre victims and their families argued that Navegar should be liable for negligence in selling assault weapons to the general public (rather than restricting sales to the military, police, and shooting ranges) and using advertising that increased the appeal of the guns to criminals and other high-risk gun buyers. Navegar executives testified that they were well aware of their product's stature as the preeminent assault weapon used in crimes and that they welcomed the publicity stemming from its use in notorious acts of violence because of the resulting spike in sales.

A California Superior Court judge dismissed the suit before trial, concluding that Navegar owed no duty to the victims because the weapons were legally manufactured and sold. In a landmark ruling in September 1999, the California Court of Appeals disagreed. The court held that although the manufacture and sale of a lawful firearm is not negligent in itself, Navegar owed the plaintiffs a duty to exercise reasonable care not to create risks above and beyond those inherent in the presence of firearms in society. It was the first appellate court decision imposing such a duty on a gun manufacturer.

On August 6, 2001, the California Supreme Court voted 5–1 to reverse the Court of Appeals ruling on other grounds, finding that a California statute, passed in 1983, barred the application of common law principles to impose liability on Navegar. The court held that the statute, Civil Code Section 1714.4, precluded any claim for negligence or strict liability against a gun manufacturer involving an assessment of the risks versus the benefits of a firearm. In dissent, Justice Kathryn Mickle Werdegar argued that the statute did not apply to the plaintiffs' claim because "[t]hough plaintiffs' claim does require a weighing of risks and benefits, the risk and benefits involved are not those *of the product as such,* but those created by defendant's choice of distribution channels" (emphasis in original). She further found that Navegar, under the common law, owed a duty of care in its "design, distribution and marketing activities." Largely as a result of the *Merrill* decision, in 2002 the California legislature repealed Section 1714.4, ending special immunity for the gun industry in California.

Dennis A. Henigan

See also Lawsuits against Gun Manufacturers; *Merrill v. Navegar, Inc.;* TEC-DC9 Pistol
For Further Reading:
Fried, Rinat. 1999. "California Lets Massacre Suit against Gunmaker Proceed: Ruling Is First to Green-Light Crime-Based Cause of Action." *National Law Journal* 7: A9.
Sward, Susan. 1998. "Legacy of Horror: Highrise Massacre Left Behind Change, Challenges." *San Francisco Chronicle* (June 30): A1.

Campaign to Protect Sane Gun Laws

The Campaign to Protect Sane Gun Laws is a coalition of national organizations that joined Handgun Control, Inc. (HCI) in 1995 to mobilize public opposition against attempts to weaken federal gun control laws, especially the Brady Bill and the assault weapons ban.

HCI (which later became the Brady Campaign to Prevent Gun Violence) viewed alliances with other organizations as a key to achieving its goals through influencing government. On March 30, 1995, the fourteenth anniversary of the shooting of President Reagan and James Brady, HCI joined with 108 national organizations to oppose efforts by the gun lobby to repeal the Brady Handgun Violence Prevention Act and the Assault Weapons Ban of 1994. The organizations joining the campaign represented some 140 million Americans and included such well-known organizations as the American Medical Association, the American Academy of Pediatrics, the NAACP, the United States Catholic Conference, and the United States Conference of Mayors.

Each of the organizations in the campaign pledged to oppose the repeal of sensible gun laws such as the Brady Bill and the assault weapons ban. At that time, progun groups were pressuring Congress to repeal and weaken both laws. In April 1995, Congress began hearings on a bill to repeal the assault weapons ban. The Campaign to Protect Sane Gun Laws successfully mobilized public opinion and generated intense lobbying pressure that helped prevent repeals.

Walter F. Carroll

See also American Academy of Pediatrics; American Medical Association; Assault Weapons; Assault Weapons Ban of 1994; Brady Campaign to Prevent Gun Violence; Brady Handgun Violence Prevention Act; Coalition to Stop Gun Violence; Interest Groups and Gun Legislation; National Rifle Association; United States Congress and Gun Legislation
For Further Reading:
Carter, Gregg Lee. 1997. *The Gun Control Movement.* New York: Twayne Publishers.
Spitzer, Robert J. 1998. *The Politics of Gun Control.* New York: Chatham House.

Canada, Gun Laws

Historically, Canada has had stricter gun control legislation than the United States, as well as lower rates of criminal violence and a higher suicide rate. As in the United States, Canada's urban areas have lower rates of legal gun ownership but higher rates of criminal violence than rural areas. But unlike in the United States, the responsibility for making criminal law lies with the federal government in Canada. Power is much more centralized there. For example, the prime minister unilaterally appoints all senators and all Supreme Court justices. Moreover, individual rights have less protection under the Canadian Charter of Rights and Freedoms than under the American Bill of Rights.

In 1995, the Canadian government passed the Firearms Act (Bill C-68), which mandated licensing firearm owners and universal firearm registration. This legislation is remarkable because Canada already had a strict firearm regime. Handguns had been registered since 1934, police scrutiny had been required for all firearm purchasers since 1977, a wide range of weapons were prohibited in 1977, and in 1991 a large number of semiautomatic rifles and large-capacity magazines were also prohibited or restricted. Opponents argue that such legislation is unworkable and just creates another costly bureaucracy.

The Firearms Act was forced though Parliament in 1995 by the Liberal Party. Three of the four opposition parties (Reform, Progressive Conservatives, and New Democrats) were united against Bill C-68. The only opposition party to support this legislation was the Quebec Party, possibly because Quebec was allowed to run a separate firearm registry. In 2000, a constitutional challenge by six provincial governments (including Ontario) was rejected by the Supreme Court of Canada.

When firearm registration was introduced, it was claimed that it would cost taxpayers $85 million (U.S.$55 million). By early 2001, the known costs had climbed to more than ten times that amount. Unfortunately, no solid evidence can be found linking Canadian gun laws to a decline in either crime rates or suicide rates (Dandurand, 1998).

The history of gun control in Canada demonstrates the "slippery slope" of gun control. Gun laws are passed during periods of fear and political instability. One question seems to never be asked: What is the most appropriate level of control for firearms? Politicians continually call for more gun laws and the bureaucracy continues to grow.

During the 1930s the Canadian government feared labor unrest as well as American rumrunners. As a result, in 1934 it passed firearm legislation that mandated handgun registration. There were separate permits for British subjects and for aliens. Before 1947, few Orientals or blacks qualified as British subjects. World War II introduced additional gun control laws. In 1941 Orientals were forbidden to own firearms and their firearms were confiscated.

Terrorism in Quebec dominated the late 1960s and the early 1970s. In 1969, another firearm law was introduced that created the categories of "restricted weapons" and "prohibited weapons" for the first time. "Restricted weapons" (e.g., handguns) had to be registered and their use was subject to strict conditions—including the requirement that a permit must be obtained to transport them. However, citizens were allowed to purchase a restricted weapon if the police judged them to be suitable owners.

"Prohibited weapons" (e.g., fully automatic firearms, silencers, switchblades, and rifles and shotguns shorter than 66 cm) were made subject to more stringent conditions than restricted weapons. (A fully automatic firearm continues to shoot as long as the trigger is held down—or until the magazine is empty.) It became illegal to purchase or sell a prohibited weapon, though individuals who happened to own them before the introduction of the legislation could keep them. The Royal Canadian Mounted Police (RCMP) was given the authority to attach any "reasonable conditions" to the "use, carriage or possession of the [restricted] weapon ... or ammunition, as he deems desirable in the interests of the safety of other persons." The government also gave itself the authority to restrict or prohibit, through Order-in-Council, any firearm "not commonly used in Canada for hunting or sporting purposes." (Orders-in-Council are decisions made at the cabinet level and therefore undergo no parliamentary review and are secret.)

In 1977 firearm legislation was amended again. A new permit was required to obtain "ordinary" rifles and shotguns (the Firearms Acquisition Certificate, or FAC). A new crime was introduced for "unsafe storage of firearms," although no definition of safe storage was provided. The

A mourner remembers the fourteen women slain at Montreal's École Polytechnique in 1989—an assault that galvanized support for a tougher gun control law in 1995. (AP Photo/CP, Ottawa Sun, Jonathan Hayward)

protection of property was eliminated as a suitable reason for acquiring a restricted firearm, and owners could no longer register handguns at their business address. The police began to refuse an FAC to anyone who indicated she or he desired to acquire a firearm for self-protection (even though in a typical year tens of thousands of Canadians claim to use firearms to protect themselves or their families from violence; see Mauser, 1996).

In 1991, significant changes were made in the firearm law in response to a horrific shooting that had shocked the country in 1989 in Montreal. After a lengthy investigation of the shooting, the Quebec coroner concluded that poor police response time rather than the particular weapon used was primarily responsible for the high number of deaths. The Conservative government decided there should be new firearm legislation. The 1991 legislation (Bill C-17) expanded the list of prohibited weapons to include converted full automatics and a large number of semiautomatic military-style rifles and shotguns. A semiautomatic firearm requires a separate press of the trigger for each shot, although it automatically readies itself for another shot. No empirical studies had been conducted to determine which, if any, types of firearms posed a threat to public security. Military-style firearms were restricted primarily because of their "cosmetic" differences from other firearms. This legislation changed the FAC system so that it now required applicants to provide a photograph and two references and imposed a mandatory twenty-eight-day waiting period and safety training before obtaining an FAC. At the same time, the application form was expanded to include thirty-five questions. If the applicant was married or divorced, one of their references was required to be a spouse or former spouse.

An applicant was now thoroughly screened by police. The screening often involved telephone checks with neighbors and spouses or ex-spouses. Other major changes included new Criminal Code offenses, new definitions of prohibited and restricted weapons, new regulations for firearm dealers, and clearly defined regulations for the safe storage, handling, and transportation of firearms.

A major focus of the new legislation was semiautomatic military-style guns. The class of prohibited weapons was expanded to include semiautomatic firearms that had been converted from fully automatic. Owners of the newly prohibited firearms were faced with eventual confiscation without compensation. The legislation also prohibited high-capacity cartridge magazines for automatic and semiautomatic firearms. A series of Orders-in-Council prohibited or restricted many semiautomatic rifles and some types of "nonsporting" ammunition.

Bill C-17's requirement for FAC applicants to show knowledge of the safe handling of firearms came into effect in 1994. To demonstrate such knowledge, applicants had to pass a test or a firearm safety course approved by a provincial attorney general, or a firearm officer had to certify that the applicant was competent in handling firearms safely. Bill C-17 also required that safety courses had to cover firearm laws as well as firearm safety.

Upon being elected in 1993 the Liberals proposed new gun laws. The government prohibited over half of all registered handguns in Canada and initiated plans to confiscate them. Most experts agree that these handguns had not been misused. In 1993, the auditor general of Canada reported that no evaluation of the 1991 firearm legislation had ever been undertaken (Auditor General, 1993, pp. 647–655). Bill C-68 became law on December 5, 1995.

In addition to requiring the licensing of owners and the registering of firearms, Bill C-68, known formally as the Firearms Act of 1995, broadened police powers of "search and seizure" and expanded the types of officials who could make use of such powers; weakened constitutionally protected rights against self-incrimination; and imposed stricter requirements for obtaining a firearm license (the application grew to six pages with forty-five questions and retained the personal questions included in the previous application).

Gary A. Mauser

See also Canadian Firearms Centre
For Further Reading:
Auditor General of Canada. 1993. *Report of the Auditor General.* Ottawa: Queen's Printer.

Canadian Firearms Centre: http://www.cfc-ccaf.gc.ca/en/default.asp.

Dandurand, Yvon. 1998. *Firearms, Accidental Deaths, Suicides and Violent Crime: An Updated Review of the Literature with Special Reference to the Canadian Situation.* Canadian Firearms Centre, Policy Sector, WD1998–4e, September.

Kopel, David B. 1992. *The Samurai, the Mountie, and the Cowboy. Should America Adopt the Gun Controls of Other Democracies?* Buffalo, NY: Prometheus Books.

Mauser, Gary A. 1996. "Armed Self-Defense: The Canadian Case." *Journal of Criminal Justice* 24, 5: 393–406.

———. 2001. *Misfire: Firearm Registration in Canada.* Vancouver: Fraser Institute.

Canadian Firearms Centre (CFC)

Created to implement and administer Canada's 1995 Firearms Act, the Canadian Firearms Centre is a branch of the Department of Justice in Canada. The CFC is responsible for licensing firearm owners; registering all firearms; coordinating with the Royal Canadian Mounted Police, the provincial police forces, and the Canadian Customs and Revenue Agency; and coordinating with provincial and territorial Chief Firearms Officers. The act does not generally apply to military or police personnel.

In principle, the Canadian federal government enacts criminal law and the provincial/territorial governments are responsible for enforcing it. Many Canadians, particularly rural and western Canadians, oppose licensing and registration. The provinces of Alberta, Saskatchewan, and Manitoba refused to cooperate with the CFC, forcing the CFC to directly administer the program in these provinces. Few hunting or shooting organizations agree with the Firearms Act or cooperate with the CFC.

Between 1977 and 1995 a police-issued Firearms Acquisition Certificate was required to acquire a firearm. Obtaining an FAC required passing a firearm safety course and a police background check. A license was not required to possess a firearm. The 1995 legislation mandated licenses for all firearm owners. Handguns have been registered since 1934. Registration of long arms began in 1998 and is to be completed in 2003.

The complexity of the 1995 law forced the Justice Department to create an extensive bureaucracy. In addition to the main office in Ottawa, the CFC has five other centers, including one for Quebec residents. The CFC quickly grew to 1,744 paid, full-time positions by July 2000. This does not include an unknown number of part-time employees.

The CFC has been plagued by serious problems. It was originally budgeted at U.S.$55 million, but the government is known to have spent more than U.S.$550 million on registering firearms by 2001. A 1999 review by Price-Waterhouse found the CFC to have exceeded its budget and to have a high error rate and unusually slow processing times. Average waits for licenses are over six months. In 2001, despite the huge backlog of applications, the CFC began to cut staff.

In a move to curb spiraling costs, in 2001 the government announced its intention to privatize many aspects of the CFC. This move will conveniently place the CFC outside the scrutiny of Canada's auditor general. Critics claim that privatization will lead to a lack of accountability and result in high costs for firearm licenses and further abuses of civil liberties. In 2001, a review by the privacy commissioner found that the CFC violated the Privacy Act due to unwarranted personal questions on applications.

In January 2001, the CFC announced that over 2 million owners were licensed or had applied for a license out of an estimated 2.4 million gun owners, and that there were 1.7 million firearms registered. In 1998, the CFC estimated that there were over 3.5 million firearm owners. In 1998, the Royal Canadian Mounted Police reported there were 272,837 people licensed and 1,204,998 firearms registered. Survey estimates of Canadian gun ownership vary widely from 2.4 million to over 5 million gun owners and between 6 million and 20 million firearms. The large majority of gun owners are hunters who own rifles or shotguns; few Canadians own handguns.

The RCMP has declined to take responsibility for enforcing the firearm legislation. In 2001, the CFC formed the National Weapons Enforcement Support Team (NWEST) to assist the police in enforcing the firearm laws. Critics claim NWEST will focus on enforcing registration, not illegal trafficking and smuggling.

Gary A. Mauser

See also Canada, Gun Laws
For Further Reading:
Breitkreuz, Garry. 2000. "The Canadian Firearms Act Means You Can't Take Your Fundamental Rights for Granted." http://www.whyfor.com/links/fundamental_rights.html.
Canadian Firearms Centre. 2000. "Canadian Firearms Program." http://www.cfc-ccaf.gc.ca/en/general_public/default.asp.
Kopel, David B. 1992. *The Samurai, the Mountie, and the Cowboy. Should America Adopt the Gun Controls of Other Democracies?* Buffalo, NY: Prometheus Books.
Mauser, Gary A. 2001. *Misfire: Firearm Registration in Canada.* Vancouver, BC: Fraser Institute.
Privacy Commissioner of Canada. *Review of the Personal Information Handling Practices of the Canadian Firearms Program.* http://www.privcom.gc.ca.
Royal Canadian Mounted Police. *Annual Firearms Report to the Solicitor General of Canada.* http://www.cfc-ccaf.gc.ca/en/research/publications/stats/default/aspTable4.

Caron v. United States (1998)

This U.S. Supreme Court case (524 U.S. 308) held that the federal law forbidding felons from possessing firearms and enhancing criminal sentences for violations of this prohibition can be applied to someone who is allowed under state law to possess rifles and shotguns but not handguns. The Supreme Court interpreted the felon-in-possession prohibition and the sentence enhancement provision of the Gun Control Act (GCA) of 1968 to apply to a felon who under state law was forbidden to have some guns after his original conviction but was permitted to possess other guns. Thus, if the state placed any restrictions on the types of guns the felon could possess when his civil rights were restored, such restrictions had the effect of making the felon fully accountable to the firearm possession prohibition and the enhanced punishment provisions of the GCA.

A petitioner was convicted of violating 18 U.S.C. Section 922(g)(1), which forbids a per-

son convicted of a serious offense to possess any firearm and requires that a three-time violent felon who violates this provision receive an enhanced sentence. The GCA further specifies that a person cannot be held to the above standard if the offender's civil rights have been restored, "unless such ... restoration ... expressly provides that the person may not ... possess ... firearms." The petitioner claimed that he should not be accountable under this law, as he had his civil rights restored with respect to his ownership of rifles and shotguns. The state at issue permitted a convicted felon to possess rifles but restricted possession of handguns to inside one's home or business.

In rejecting the petitioner's claim, the Court opined that the petitioner's restoration of civil rights was a defense to the GCA, as the state in question placed some restrictions on what sort of firearms he could possess. The Court stated that the restoration of civil rights has no effect on the GCA even if the state allows the possession of certain types of guns, some long, as possession of at least some categories of guns is not permissible. The Court further held that it was the likely congressional intent of the GCA to prohibit felons from possessing any guns if the state restoring the felon's civil rights forbade the possession of any type of gun.

James A. Beckman

See also *Bailey v. United States; Beecham v. United States;* Enforcement of Gun Control Laws; Gun Control Act of 1968

Carter, Harlon (1913–1991)

A lifelong gun activist and National Rifle Association (NRA) leader who spearheaded the organization's extremist and more political turn in the 1970s, Carter was born in a small Texas town in 1913, where guns were a part of his early life. He became a skilled marksman and joined the NRA at the age of 16. A year later, Carter was charged with murder for shooting and killing a 15-year-old with a shotgun. Carter claimed self-defense, as the murdered boy had a knife. A jury found Carter guilty of murder without malice and sentenced him to a maximum of three years in prison. Carter appealed the conviction, which was reversed on procedural grounds. The appeals court cited incorrect instructions by the judge to the jury regarding self-defense as the justification for reversal. The charges were eventually dropped.

In 1951, Carter won election to the NRA's national board of directors. He served as the organization's vice president from 1963 to 1965 and as president from 1965 to 1967; he then became a member of the NRA's executive council. Carter's professional career fell outside of the NRA. He worked for the U.S. Border Patrol for many years and became its head in 1950. Eleven years later he became a regional commissioner for the Immigration and Naturalization Service (of which the Border Patrol was a part), a position from which he retired in 1970.

In 1975, Carter was named head of the newly created NRA Institute for Legislative Action (ILA). From that position, he, along with other hard-liners, argued for a tougher, less compromising, and more political role for the NRA. For example, Carter voiced his opposition to any restriction on the availability of cheap handguns, called Saturday night specials. In response, in 1976, the ruling NRA old guard leaders fired seventy-five hard-liners, who were also critical of old guard plans to build a World Sports Center in Colorado Springs, move the NRA there, and place greater organizational emphasis on hunting and sporting activities. Carter resigned in protest in 1976. He and his allies, including gun activist Neal Knox, plotted to win control of the NRA at its 1977 annual convention in Cincinnati. In what was later dubbed the Cincinnati Revolt, the hard-line (also called "new guard") faction won some key procedural changes, which they then used to their advantage. By the end of the convention, the hard-liners had prevailed, and Carter was elected NRA executive vice president. Carter appointed Neal Knox to head the ILA after the short tenure of Robert Kukla.

From this point forward, the NRA adopted a no-compromise approach to any and all gun control proposals. It also adopted a more strident and heated rhetorical style, and focused ever more organizational resources on its anti–gun control political efforts. Its immediate priority was to repeal the Gun Control Act of 1968, an effort that partially succeeded with enactment of the Firearms Owners' Protection Act of 1986, also known as the McClure-Volkmer bill. Under Carter, the NRA also pressed to increase its membership and began extensive merchandising efforts. It also decided that its new, harsher image needed softening, which led to the launching of its "I'm the NRA" advertising campaign in 1982. These ads featured women, actors, politicians, and others in order to portray gun ownership and gun sports as a less threatening, and more mainstream activity. In 1982, Carter fired Knox, who had become too radical even for Carter. In ailing health, Carter left the NRA presidency in 1985. He died in 1991.

Robert J. Spitzer

See also Firearms Owners' Protection Act of 1986; Institute for Legislative Action; National Rifle Association; Revolt at Cincinnati

For Further Reading:

Davidson, Osha Gray. 1993. *Under Fire: The NRA and the Battle for Gun Control.* New York: Henry Holt.

LaPierre, Wayne. 1994. *Guns, Crime, and Freedom.* Washington, DC: Regnery.

Spitzer, Robert J. 1998. *The Politics of Gun Control.* New York: Chatham House.

Sugarmann, Josh. 1992. *National Rifle Association: Money, Firepower and Fear.* Washington, DC: National Press Books.

Cartridges

Cartridge names follow one of two broad customs. Nonmetric cartridges are commonly referred to by their caliber (in theory, in hundredths or thousandths of an inch). Metric cartridges are commonly referred to by their caliber in millimeters followed by the case length in millimeters: thus a 7 x 57 mm refers to a cartridge with a 7 mm diameter bullet and an empty cartridge case 57 mm long. Some American metric cartridges are used with an additional designation (e.g., the 6 mm Remington).

The nonmetric designation has a problem in that there may be a multitude of cartridges firing bullets of the same diameter, so an additional designation is needed. This takes a near-universe of forms. In cartridges of the black powder era, it was customary to hyphenate the weight of black powder that the cartridge would hold. Thus a .30-30 and a .45-70 held thirty and seventy grains of black powder, respectively. More modern cartridges were often named for the company that first introduced them (e.g., the .280 Remington, .308 Winchester, and .45 ACP, or Automatic Colt Pistol), the nation or group that adopted them (the .303 British, 7.62 mm Russian, and .223 NATO), or sometimes for its individual inventor (the .257 Roberts). The venerable .30-06, on the other hand, takes its descriptor from the date of its introduction (1906). Sometimes the designation is simply a trade label suggesting velocity: the .22 Hornet, the .220 Swift, the .219 Zipper, or the .250-3000 (the first factory cartridge to exceed 3,000 feet per second velocity). Particularly high-power cartridges may be designated "magnum"; when that description is already used in a given caliber, "maximum" is sometimes used to designate an even more powerful round.

From time to time individual gunsmiths or enthusiasts have created "wildcat" cartridges, a type not made by any factory, usually by taking a factory cartridge and "necking it down" to fire a smaller caliber bullet, "necking it up" to take a larger one, or "blowing it out" to reduce its taper and increase its powder capacity. These may be designated in a variety of ways, such as by hyphenating its original caliber (e.g., .22-250 refers to a .25 caliber cartridge necked down to .22), using its inventor's name (e.g., .35 Whelen), or in other ways (e.g., a .30-06 necked down to .25 becomes the .25-06, and if "blown out" becomes the .25-06 Improved).

As if the above were not sufficiently complicated, it must be noted that a given cartridge may have multiple names. For example, the .308 Winchester, .308 NATO, and 7.62 x 51 all refer to the same cartridge, and the .22-250 began its life as the .22 Varminter.

A further complication is that the cartridge name may not reflect the actual bullet diameter! Most .38 and .44 handguns fire bullets of .357 and .429 diameter. The .38-40 is actually .40 caliber. The .219 Zipper, .222 Remington, .223 Remington, and .224 Weatherby all fire bullets of the same diameter, but the .45-70, .45 ACP,

Filling cartridges at the U.S. Arsenal at Watertown, Massachusetts. From Harper's Weekly, 1861. *(Library of Congress)*

and .45 Long Colt use three slightly different bullet diameters.

David T. Hardy

See also Ammunition, Types of; Black Talon; Dum-Dum Bullet; Gunpowder; Minie Ball; Spitzer Bullet
For Further Reading:
Hogg, Ian. 1985. *Jane's Directory of Military Small Arms Ammunition.* New York: Jane's Publishing.
Logan, Herschel C. 1959. *Cartridges: A Pictorial Digest of Small Arms Ammunition.* Harrisburg, PA: Stackpole.

Cases v. United States (1942)

On August 27, 1941, a friend of Jose Cases Velazquez purchased ten rounds of .38 caliber revolver ammunition for him at a hardware store. Three days later, Velazquez went to the Annandale's Beach Club in Carolina, Puerto Rico, and shot another patron with a .38 Colt–type revolver of Spanish manufacture. Since Velazquez had a recorded criminal conviction for aggravated assault, he was charged with violation of sections 2e and 2f of the Federal Firearms Act of 1938, which prohibit a person who has been convicted of a crime of violence to receive a firearm or ammunition that has been shipped in interstate or foreign commerce. The federal court of appeals for the first circuit court denied Velazquez's appeal (*Cases v. United States,* 1942).

Velazquez challenged the conviction primarily on the ground that the statute represented ex post facto legislation; that is, he claimed that he was being charged in regard to a situation—his previous criminal conviction—that had occurred before the passage of the Federal Firearms Act. He also claimed that the act itself was unconstitutional because it infringed on peoples' right to keep and bear arms.

The appellate court ruled that the Federal Firearms Act of 1938 did not violate Second Amendment constitutional guarantees since "the government can limit the keeping and bearing of arms by a single individual as well as by a group of individuals, though it cannot prohibit the possession or use of any weapon which has a reasonable relationship to the preservation or efficiency of a well regulated militia" (*Cases,* 1942, p. 922). The judge noted, with a trace of sarcasm, that "there was no record that the appellant was or ever had been a member of any military organization or his use of the weapon under the circumstances was in preparation for a military career" (*Cases,* 1942, p. 923).

At the same time, the court felt that the reach of the Second Amendment needed contemporary refinement. As it now stood, the judge declared, it was so broad that a literal reading might indicate that the federal government was restricted to regulating only archaic weapons such as flintlock muskets or matchlock harquebuses.

In regard to the claim that the act imposed an ex post facto penalty on the defendant, the court ruled that the requirement of a nonviolent record before a person legally could purchase firearms or ammunition was a reasonable way to define unfitness, and a sensible procedure to afford protection to the community.

Gilbert Geis

See also Federal Firearms Act of 1938
For Further Reading:
Cases v. United States, 131 F. 2d 916 (1st Cir. 1942). http://www–2.cs.cmu.edu/afs/cs.cmu.edu/user/wbardwel/public/nfalist/cases_v_us.txt.

Cease Fire, Inc.

Cease Fire, Inc., a national, not-for-profit organization, aimed to save lives by reducing the number of handgun-related deaths and injuries in the United States, especially among children. The organization focused on the public health implications of handgun violence and strove to educate people about the dangers of keeping firearms in the home. Jann Wenner—founder, editor-in-chief, and publisher of *Rolling Stone* magazine—founded Cease Fire, Inc. in 1996.

Wenner had been a good friend of John Lennon. Lennon's murder in 1980 impelled Wenner to become active in the gun control movement and to eventually found Cease Fire. After three years the financial drain of the organization led Wenner to shut it down. While it operated, Cease Fire, in conjunction with other organizations, ran advertising campaigns and developed public awareness of the impact of firearm violence on children.

In 1997, Cease Fire launched a national awareness campaign that included TV public service announcements (PSAs) and print ads. The PSAs and print ads noted that ten children were killed by a gun every day. Each ad or PSA presented the true story of a child who had been killed by a handgun in his or her home. The focus on the tragic death of one child made these ads and PSAs very powerful. The print ads showed a picture of a small child or children with captions such as "John Higgins hid his handgun so well, it took his son three years to find it." The ad then explained the circumstances in which the child found the gun and the ensuing tragedy. In the case of the John Higgins ad, Billy Higgins accidentally shot and killed his 2-year-old sister.

The actor Michael Douglas narrated the television PSAs. One ad showed a young boy who was perhaps 5 or 6 years old standing on a stack of boxes on a chair to reach a box that contained a gun. The child plays with the gun, the scene fades to black, and a shot is heard. Other PSAs were similar; some featured a group of children playing and then gaining access to a gun in the home. In all of the ads, the message is "Think your kids don't know where your gun is? Think again."

Cooperating with Cease Fire on the campaign were the American College of Emergency Physicians, the National Association of Children's Hospitals and Related Institutions, the National Association of County and City Health Officials, the National Association of Secondary School Principals, and the National Education Association. Cease Fire also worked with leaders from a variety of other organizations and industries, including those in law, law enforcement, entertainment and media, and academia.

Cease Fire launched the campaign in Boston, in conjunction with the unveiling of Stop Handgun Violence's huge billboard drawing attention to handgun-related deaths of children. The campaign then moved to Albuquerque, Austin, Cleveland, Miami, Portland, and Salt Lake City. Cease Fire also worked with Parent-Teacher Associations to promote the campaign.

When Cease Fire stopped operating in 1999, Jann Wenner gave Physicians for Social Responsibility (PSR) the rights to use the powerful Cease Fire ads and PSAs. PSR added its name to the materials and continued to distribute them as part of its "Risk: Gun in the Home" public awareness campaign. The print ads could be downloaded from the PSR website and the PSAs still appeared on television.

Walter F. Carroll and Robin L. Roth

See also Accidents, Gun; Child Access Prevention Laws; Children's Defense Fund; Doctors Against Handgun Injury; Guns in the Home; Lennon, John; National Education Association; National SAFE KIDS Campaign; Physicians for Social Responsibility; Smart Guns; Stop Handgun Violence; Trigger Locks; Victimization from Gun Violence; Youth and Guns

For Further Reading:
Physicians for Social Responsibility. 2000. "PSR Violence Prevention Program: Risk: Guns in the Home." http://www.psr.org/riskguns.html.

Center for Gun Policy and Research

The Center for Gun Policy and Research is dedicated to preventing gun-related injuries and deaths through the application of a public health perspective to the issue of gun violence

prevention. Its faculty and affiliated experts pursue strategies for reducing gun violence.

The center is based at the Johns Hopkins Bloomberg School of Public Health in Baltimore, Maryland. The School of Public Health is the oldest and largest school of public health in the country and is an academically acclaimed international resource with 400 full-time faculty and 1,800 students a year from eighty countries worldwide.

Investigation into the cause and prevention of gun injuries and fatalities began at the Bloomberg School of Public Health more than twenty years ago as part of an overall injury prevention research effort. Center Co-Directors Jon Vernick and Daniel Webster have worked on gun violence prevention research for the past decade. In 1995, the center was formally established with funding from the Joyce Foundation.

The center examines the public health effects of guns in society and serves as an objective resource for the media, policy makers, advocacy groups, and attorneys. For the past two decades its faculty have helped shape the public agenda in the search for solutions to gun violence. Graduates of the school's academic programs hold leadership positions in the field of gun violence prevention worldwide.

The center is engaged in a broad range of activities including original scholarly research, policy analysis, and agenda-setting public discourse. Its activities strive to bring public health expertise and perspectives to the complex policy issues related to gun violence prevention. Center priority areas of activity include the following:

Guns as Consumer Products: The center redefined the debate on gun violence prevention by proposing that the safe design of guns could be regulated in much the same way as the safety of cars, toys, and other consumer products. This new approach opened the way for legislation and litigation to protect consumers. The center's research interests also include the marketing of guns and the regulation of gun sales.

Restricting Gun Access among Youth and Other High-Risk Users: The center studies policies and behaviors related to gun access and carrying among youth. The center also designs and evaluates interventions and other policies designed to keep guns from criminals and other high-risk groups.

Monitoring the Effectiveness of Gun Laws: The center monitors and evaluates the effectiveness of major gun laws, including laws banning Saturday night specials, concealed weapons laws, handgun registration laws, handgun licensing laws, and child firearm access prevention laws.

Firearm Litigation: The center holds to the position that litigation is an important tool for protecting the public's health. Center faculty assist with litigation designed to change the way guns are designed, marketed, distributed, and sold.

Technology for "Safer" Guns: The center pioneered the concept of "personalized" guns that can only be fired by their intended owner. Such guns could potentially prevent childhood gun deaths, youth suicides, and homicides committed with stolen guns. The center promotes incorporating "safer gun" technology into the design and manufacture of all guns through litigation, legislation, regulation, and public education.

Model Legislation: In 1996 the center developed a model law that would require all new handguns to be personalized. This model law, revised in 1998, has been used by Pennsylvania, New Jersey, New York, and other states in their efforts to draft effective legislation.

Tracking Public Opinion on Gun Use and Prevention Strategies: Since 1996 the center has annually conducted a national poll in conjunction with the National Opinion Research Center to assess public attitudes toward guns and prevention strategies. The findings provide an important basis for the development of new public policies.

Testimony and Expertise: Center faculty and affiliated experts are frequently invited to advise federal, state, and city legislators on gun laws and regulations, and regularly testify at congressional and state hearings.

Public Education: A key center function is providing the public with accurate information about gun injuries and prevention strategies. Fact sheets as well as center publications, bibliographies, published articles, and information for the media and general public are available by contacting the center.

Nancy Lord Lewin

See also Child Access Prevention Laws; Gun Violence as a Public Health Problem; Lawsuits against Gun Manufacturers; Medicine and Gun Violence; Motor Vehicle Laws as a Model for Gun Laws; Product Liability Lawsuits; Smart Guns; Trigger Locks; Violence Prevention Research Program

For Further Reading:
Johns Hopkins Center for Gun Policy and Research home page: http://www.jhsph.edu/gunpolicy/.

Center for the Study and Prevention of Violence (CSPV)

The Center for the Study and Prevention of Violence assists individuals and groups seeking to understand and prevent violence, especially adolescent violence. Acting as a bridge between researchers and practitioners and policy makers, CSPV acts as an information clearinghouse, provides technical assistance, and carries out research on the causes and prevention of violence. Although the center does provide information on firearms and their role in violence, it does not emphasize gun and gun control related issues.

Founded in 1992 with a grant from the Carnegie Corporation, CSPV is a research center within the Institute of Behavioral Science at the University of Colorado at Boulder. University of Colorado sociologist Delbert S. Elliot directs the center, which has a three-fold mission. First, and most basic, its Information House is a central location for collecting, evaluating, storing, and disseminating violence-related information. Focusing primarily on youth violence, Information House acts as a clearinghouse providing bibliographic information to the public. It also provides fact sheets and position papers. For example, the Fact Sheet on Youth Handgun Violence provides basic information on youth handgun violence in Colorado and the United States. The fact sheet notes that handgun homicides by males aged 15–18 increased by over 150 percent from 1980 to 1995. The CSPV "Position Summary on Gun Control Prevention Efforts" suggests that research on the effectiveness of gun control laws is inconclusive.

The second part of the CSPV mission is providing technical assistance in evaluating and developing violence prevention programs. For example, in 1996 CSPV received funding from the Colorado Division of Criminal Justice, the Centers for Disease Control and Prevention, and the Pennsylvania Commission on Crime and Delinquency to develop "Blueprints for Violence Prevention," a national project to identify and replicate effective violence prevention programs. The project has reviewed over 500 programs, identifying 11 effective violence prevention programs, called Blueprints, and 19 promising programs. CSPV provides technical assistance and training to these programs. CSPV also provides technical assistance to sixteen Colorado schools and school districts as part of the Safe Communities–Safe Schools Initiative.

Third, CSPV carries out research and data analysis. For example, CSPV is conducting research on youth and guns sponsored by the Colorado Trust, a private foundation dedicated to the health and well-being of the people of Colorado. In this research CSPV will document the nature of the problem nationally and in Colorado, review existing programs focusing on youth access to handguns, conduct focus groups, and identify promising strategies to reduce handgun violence in Colorado. The research program will not address the issue of handgun control or advocate for or against any type of handgun control policy or legislation.

The CSPV website allows online database searches. It also provides extensive links to other violence resources on the internet.

Walter F. Carroll

See also Centers for Disease Control; Children's Defense Fund; Columbine High School Tragedy; Gun Violence as a Public Health Problem; Media Violence; National School Safety Center; Schoolyard Shootings; Student Pledge Against Gun Violence; Youth Gun Control Legislation, the Juvenile Justice Bill of 1999; Youth and Guns

For Further Reading:

Arredondo, Sabrina, et al. 1999. *Preventing Youth Handgun Violence: A National Study with Trends and Patterns for the State of Colorado.* Boulder, CO: Center for the Study and Prevention of Violence. CSPV home page: http://www.colorado.edu/cspv/.

Center to Prevent Handgun Violence

See Brady Center to Prevent Gun Violence

Centers for Disease Control (CDC)

The Centers for Disease Control is a federal agency—in the Department of Health and Human Services—supported by tax revenues. Its mission is to monitor health problems; conduct research on the prevention of health problems; develop, advocate, and implement public health solutions to health problems; and promote healthy behaviors and safe and healthy environments. The Intentional Injuries section of the CDC's National Center on Injury Prevention and Control (NCIPC) is the division of CDC that deals with firearms. The reports to Congress, newsletters, and published articles based on CDC-supported research identify firearm ownership as a public health problem. This position is contested by researchers such as Gary Kleck (1997) and John R. Lott, Jr. (1998), whose findings indicate either that firearms are not causally related to violence or that firearm ownership is associated with a reduced risk of violence.

The antifirearm position of the CDC (although denied by Dr. Mark Rosenberg, head of NCIPC since the mid-1980s) has been identified by criminology researchers as representing a series of violations of the usual research conventions. Criminologist Gary Kleck identified the existence of "sample censoring" in the types of information the CDC reports. Whenever levels of gun violence increase, according to Kleck, the CDC is very vocal in calling this to the attention of the public. When levels of gun violence decrease, however, as has been true for the past decade, the CDC fails to call attention to this fact.

A similar problem was identified in CDC publications by Don B. Kates, Jr. (1995), and his colleagues in papers published by the CDC. The literature reviews of publications from this agency exhaustively account for the antifirearm literature but virtually ignore the presence of a scholarly literature that fails to support this position (for example, see Mercy et al., 1993). Kates also identified situations in which statistically weak data were interpreted by CDC-supported authors such as Arthur Kellermann (Kellermann et al., 1990) as providing unambiguous proof of the inherent dangers of firearms. It is difficult to conclusively determine whether there is systematic bias introduced into the analysis and interpretation of data such as that collected by Kellermann (with CDC support), because CDC policy does not require researchers to share their data with other investigators, and Kellermann has declined to do so, despite the fact that this is customary research practice.

Finally, the NCIPC definition of the term "children" in its literature, though commonly employed in the public health literature, includes individuals from birth to the age of 19. As has been pointed out by Kleck and others, this includes children under the age of 15, who have an extremely low rate of accidents or deaths associated with firearms, along with the cohort from 15 to 19 years of age, who rank near the top in the frequency of almost every type of accident or crime, including those involving firearms. This results in apparent high frequencies of firearm-related accidents and deaths for "children."

Carol Oyster

See also Gun Violence as a Public Health Problem; Kellermann, Arthur L.; Kleck, Gary; Lott, John R., Jr.; Methodologies for Studying Gun Violence; Victimization from Gun Violence

For Further Reading:

Kates, Don B., Jr., Henry E. Schaffer, John K. Lattimer, George B. Murray, and Edward H. Cassem. 1995. "Guns and Public Health: Epidemic of Violence or Pandemic of Propaganda?" *Tennessee Law Review* 62: 513–596.

Kellermann, Arthur L., Frederick P. Rivara, Joyce Banton, Donald T. Reay, and Corinte L. Flegner. 1990. "Validating Survey Responses to Questions about Gun Ownership among Owners of Registered Handguns." *American Journal of Epidemiology* 131: 1080–1084.

Kleck, Gary. 1997. *Targeting Guns: Firearms and Their Control.* Hawthorne, NY: Aldine de Gruyter.

Mercy, J. A., et al. 1993. "Public Health Policy for Preventing Violence." *Health Affairs* 12: 7.

Chaffee, John H. (1922–1999)

The late John H. Chaffee, a Republican senator from Rhode Island, was a pivotal supporter of the Lautenberg amendment, which passed in 1999 in the aftermath of the Columbine High School shootings. Chaffee was also known as a strong environmentalist, an advocate of expanding the government's role in health care, and a supporter of civil liberties.

Chaffee came from one of Rhode Island's "Five Families" and attended Yale University before leaving to serve in the marines in World War II and later in Korea. Chaffee was elected to the state legislature in 1956 and quickly became the leader of the Republican Party. In 1962 he challenged an incumbent Democratic governor and won. He was defeated in his bid for a fourth term for governor in 1968, and served for three years as secretary of the navy under Richard Nixon. He lost a Senate bid in 1972, but won an open seat in the Senate in 1976, where he served until his death in 1999.

As a moderate Republican in a chamber that became increasingly polarized during his tenure, Chaffee became a key player in brokering bipartisan compromises. Chaffee was often the "median voter"—the fifty-first vote that decided winning coalitions. During the 1990s he was instrumental in compromises on health care, welfare reform, and environmental regulations. He stood out among an increasingly conservative Republican caucus as a social liberal—ardently prochoice on abortion, supportive of gay rights, and opposed to the flag amendment. These positions cost him his position in the Republican Party leadership; he lost his post as chair of the Republican conference in 1990.

Chaffee was also a supporter of gun control—one of only a handful of Republican senators who backed such legislation during the 1990s. In 1992, Chaffee wrote a passionate op-ed column in the *Washington Post* calling for a ban on the manufacture, sale, and possession of handguns. As the Senate worked through various gun control measures in the 1990s, Chaffee's support was often critical. For example, in the 1994 debate on the ban on assault weapons, Republican Party leader Robert Dole announced a filibuster of the bill that would have spelled the bill's death. Yet at the cloture vote (to end the debate and move to passage of the crime bill that contained the assault weapons ban) the filibuster failed by a single vote. John Chaffee was one of only six Republicans to vote to end the filibuster. In 1999, the Lautenberg amendment that required instant background checks for purchasers at gun shows and pawnshops passed with Vice President Al Gore's tie-breaking vote. Chaffee was one of only six Republicans to support the measure. Chaffee withstood strong pressure from party leaders to oppose the measure.

Chaffee's death in 1999 ended a distinguished twenty-three-year Senate career. He was succeeded in office by his son, Lincoln Chaffee, who has continued his father's tradition of support for gun control.

Clyde Wilcox and Benjamin Webster

See also Assault Weapons Ban of 1994; Lautenberg, Frank R.

For Further Reading:

Barone, Michael, and Grant Ujifusa. 1999. *The Almanac of American Politics, 1998.* Washington, DC: National Journal.

Spitzer, Robert J. 1995. *The Politics of Gun Control.* Chatham, NJ: Chatham House.

Chenoweth-Hage, Helen (1938–)

Helen Chenoweth-Hage, a Republican, represented the first district of Idaho in the U.S. House of Representatives for three terms, from 1995 to 2001, in the 104th through 106th Congresses. She was among the most conservative members of a relatively conservative House and provoked controversy by using the title "congressman," mocking efforts to protect endangered species, supporting the federal government shutdown of 1995, defending right-wing militias, strongly opposing gun control, and attacking President Clinton's affair with Monica Lewinsky despite her own affair with a married man.

Chenoweth was born in Kansas in 1938, lived in California and Oregon as a child, attended Whitworth College in Washington, and moved to Idaho in 1964. Prior to her service in Congress, Chenoweth worked as a visiting instructor at the University of Idaho School of Law, as executive director of the Idaho Republican Party (1975–1977), as chief of staff for Congressman Steve Symms, and as a consultant. In Congress she focused her attention on natural resources and agricultural issues and served on the Second Amendment Rights and Firearms Legislation Task Force of the Republican Policy Executive Committee. She chaired the subcommittee on Forestry and Forest Health. Fulfilling

Helen Chenoweth-Hage. (U.S. House of Representatives)

a campaign promise, she did not seek reelection after her third term.

Chenoweth was among the most anti–gun control members of the House; she received an NRA Legion of Honor Award, was named Gun Rights Defender of the Year by the Citizens Committee for the Right to Keep and Bear Arms, and received an "A+" rating from the Gun Owners of America, an organization even less receptive to gun control than the NRA. In 1995 she introduced an amendment, which was defeated 317–111, to prevent "any member of ATF from receiving any bonuses or salary rewards [that] year until the Waco and Ruby Ridge and other investigations have been concluded." She voted to repeal the semiautomatic assault-style weapons ban that took effect in 1994 and to withdraw the United States from the United Nations. She voted against a bill to require background checks for gun purchases at gun shows, and she sponsored a bill to require federal law enforcement officers to get permission from local authorities before making arrests. In 1997 she cosponsored legislation to repeal a ban on gun ownership by persons convicted of a misdemeanor crime of domestic violence.

Matthew DeBell

See also Assault Weapons Ban of 1994; Citizens Committee for the Right to Keep and Bear Arms; Gun Owners of America; National Rifle Association; Ruby Ridge; Waco, Texas, Raid

For Further Reading:

Barone, Michael, and Grant Ujifusa. 1999. *The Almanac of American* Politics, 2000. Washington, DC: National Journal.

Child Access Prevention (CAP) Laws

In 1989, Florida became the first U.S. state to pass a child access prevention gun law. Also known as safe gun storage laws, CAP laws require gun owners to store their firearms in a manner that would prevent children and teens from gaining unauthorized access. The laws vary in how "safe storage" is defined, but generally require firearms to be securely locked in a cabinet or gun safe, or, in some states, with a trigger lock. Some CAP laws only hold gun owners criminally liable if unsafe storage leads to an injury, while others are not dependent upon injurious outcomes. Another way in which state CAP laws vary is in the maximum penalty allowed for law violations. As of January 2000, only three of the seventeen U.S. states with CAP laws allowed for felony prosecutions.

The first study of such laws used data through 1994 to estimate the effects of the first twelve state CAP laws that went into effect (see Cummings et al., 1997). The authors estimated that these laws were associated with a significant reduction (41 percent) in the rate of unintentional firearm deaths among youths up to age 14, but only in states with felony prosecution. Data from this study also indicated that there was a negative association between the adoption of these laws and teen firearm suicide rates that approached statistical significance.

Webster and Starnes (2000) conducted a subsequent study with data through 1997 that assessed the effects of CAP laws on unintentional firearm deaths among youth under age 15 in the first fifteen states to adopt these laws. They found that CAP-law effects were not uniform across states. Florida's CAP law was associated with a 51 percent drop in the rate of unintentional firearm deaths to youths, but there

was no effect of the law in the other fourteen CAP-law states.

The most recent study has examined the effects of CAP laws on crime as well as on unintentional firearm deaths and suicides among youth. Lott and Whitley (2001) hypothesized that CAP laws could increase criminal victimization within the home by making guns less accessible for home occupants to defend themselves against home intruders. Despite the relative rarity of unintentional firearm deaths to youths under age 15 in most states in a given year, the authors estimated CAP laws' effects within five-year age groups. They report no statistically significant CAP-law effects on unintentional firearm deaths or suicides across all CAP-law states, among those that allow felony prosecutions for CAP-law violations, or in any single state that adopted a CAP law. The study also found that the introduction of CAP laws were associated with statistically significant increases in police-reported rapes (9 percent), robberies (8–10 percent), and burglaries (4–6 percent). Under various assumptions about prelaw trends, the authors report even greater law-associated increases in crime, including increases in aggravated assaults.

It is difficult to discern exactly why Lott and Whitley do not find significant CAP-law effects on unintentional firearm deaths when such effects were so striking in Webster and Starnes's research. Breaking up the 0–14 age group into three five-year subsets weakens statistical power to detect statistically significant effects. Lott and Whitley also use a statistical model (Tobit) not typically used to study data with many zero values for specific states and years, because the model can be highly sensitive to model specification. Model specification is also at issue in the derivation of the laws' effects on crime, as no specification tests are offered and some of the findings are difficult to reconcile. For example, their models also reveal that laws prohibiting individuals from bulk handgun purchases increase crime in both the state that adopts the measure as well as in adjacent states. The findings on CAP laws' effects on crime are also not consistent with other relevant research findings. Kellermann et al. (1995) found that citizens attempted to use a gun in defense in less than 2 percent of home invasion crimes. The 8–10 percent increase in total robberies associated with the adoption of CAP laws does not seem plausible given that only 11 percent of *all* robberies occur in residences (Federal Bureau of Investigation, 1998), most of which will not have either children or guns. If such effects were true, CAP laws would have to double the number of robberies in residences. The reduction in burglaries also seems implausible. By definition, such crimes do not involve criminal contact with victims and most criminals are unlikely to be aware of laws concerning firearm storage.

Daniel W. Webster

See also Defensive Gun Use; Gun Control; Gun Violence as a Public Health Problem; Kellermann, Arthur L.; Lott, John R., Jr.; Motor Vehicle Laws as a Model for Gun Laws; Victimization from Gun Violence; Youth and Guns

For Further Reading:

Cummings, Peter, David C. Grossman, Frederick P. Rivara, and Thomas K. Koepsell. 1997. "State Gun Safe Storage Laws and Child Mortality Due to Firearms." *Journal of the American Medical Association* 278: 1084–1086.

Federal Bureau of Investigation. 1998. *Crime in the United States, 1997: Uniform Crime Reports.* Washington, DC: U.S. Department of Justice.

Kellermann, Arthur L., Lori Westphal, Laurie Fischer, and Beverly Harvard. 1995. "Weapon Involvement in Home Invasion Crimes." *Journal of the American Medical Association* 273: 1759–1762.

Lott, John R., Jr., and John E. Whitley. 2002. "Safe Storage Gun Laws: Accidental Deaths, Suicides, and Crime." *Journal of Law and Economics* 44: 659–689.

Webster, Daniel W., and Marc M. Starnes. 2000. "Reexamining the Association between Child Access Prevention Gun Laws and Unintentional Firearm Deaths among Children." *Pediatrics* 106: 1466–1469.

Childproof Guns

See Smart Guns

Children's Defense Fund (CDF)

A private, nonprofit child advocacy group, the Children's Defense Fund is a vocal proponent of strict gun control measures in the United States. The organization was founded in 1973 by Mar-

ian Wright Edelman, an African American lawyer closely involved in civil rights activism in the South during the 1960s. Under Edelman's leadership, the Washington, D.C.–based CDF has sought to provide information to the U.S. public on the state of children's health, welfare, and education, and to lobby government at all levels in favor of policy initiatives aimed, for example, at expanding access to early childhood education and health insurance. Its primary focus is on issues affecting poor children, minority children, and children with disabilities, with improvement in the health indices of these groups being a central goal of the organization. Evidence indicating that Americans under the age of 19—especially African Americans—are far more likely than children and youth in other industrialized nations to suffer firearm-related injury or death has led the CDF to argue that the prevention of gun violence is a vital issue of children's health in the United States.

For the CDF, a lack of regulations on firearms in the United States is directly responsible for high numbers of gun-related homicides, suicides, and accidental deaths among young people in the country. In the organization's estimation, a preventive approach to the problem of gun violence among children and youth in the United States entails tight restrictions on the ownership and availability of firearms. The CDF calls for the registration of all firearms in order to facilitate police tracking of guns that end up in the hands of children, and licensing requirements for potential gun owners to ensure firearms competency and knowledge of safe storage. It also supports measures such as requirements that trigger locks or other safety devices be sold with all new guns, state legislation severely penalizing adults found guilty of allowing children access to firearms, the application of consumer safety regulations to the gun industry, and a limit on the purchase of handguns to one per month per individual.

In addition to its national headquarters, the CDF maintains fourteen offices in eight states and encourages a wide range of activism in support of its legislative and policy agenda. It works particularly closely with organizations that combine a strong religious orientation with a commitment to social activism. The CDF sponsors such programs as Child Watch Visitation, which aims to introduce community leaders and elected officials to constituencies that have been directly affected by gun violence and other issues of concern to the Fund. The group's major effort to provide statistical and other information on those issues to policy makers and the public is an annual report on the status of children and youth in the United States.

Paul Lokken

See also Youth and Guns
For Further Reading:
Children's Defense Fund. 2002. "About Us." http://www.childrensdefense.org/aboutus.php.
———. 2002. "Protect Children Instead of Guns, 2001." http://www.childrensdefense.org/pdf/gunreport_2001.pdf.
———. 2001. *The State of America's Children: A Report from the Children's Defense Fund.* Boston: Beacon Press.
Edelman, Marian Wright. 2001. "Leave No Child Behind." *Black Collegian* 31, 3: 126–127.

Citizens Committee for the Right to Keep and Bear Arms (CCRKBA)

The Citizens Committee for the Right to Keep and Bear Arms is a nonprofit organization that describes itself as "the common sense gun lobby." With an estimated membership of 650,000, an advisory board that includes members of Congress, and an affiliated political action committee, the CCRKBA aggressively promotes gun rights. The CCRKBA serves mainly to promote political activities in support of gun rights while its companion organization, the Second Amendment Foundation, focuses more on education and publications.

The CCRKBA is part of a network of gun rights organizations overseen by Alan Gottlieb. As of 2001, Gottlieb served as chair of the CCKRBA and Joe Waldron, a retired Marine Corps officer, acted as executive director. According to the *Encyclopedia of Associations,* the organization had a staff of forty and a $3.6 million budget, although the extent to which staff and resources were shared with other organizations is unclear.

CCRKBA and the Second Amendment Foundation have shared offices in Bellevue, Washington. The two organizations cosponsor an annual Gun Rights Policy Conference. They also share ownership of several talk radio stations, with the CCRKBA having significant ownership in stations in Winchester, Nevada; Portland, Oregon; and Spokane, Washington. Additionally, Gottlieb chairs the Talk America Radio Network, which broadcasts on a number of affiliated stations.

The CCRKBA itself publishes a monthly newsletter, *Point Blank,* with an estimated circulation of 100,000. Its affiliated political action committee, the Right to Keep and Bear Arms Political Victory Fund, supports progun candidates in both federal and state campaigns. In the wake of the September 11, 2001, terrorist attacks on the World Trade Center in New York City and the Pentagon, the CCKRBA supported legislation proposed by Rep. Ronald Paul (R-TX) to prohibit federal agencies from enacting regulations to forbid pilots from being armed.

While the CCRKBA generally supports a gun rights agenda, it has been criticized by some activists for compromising with gun control supporters. For example, in 1999 Gottlieb and the CCRKBA supported legislation in Washington State related to storage of unlocked guns. In addition, the CCRKBA, via press release, has offered to work with Rep. Carolyn McCarthy (D-NY), a staunch gun control advocate, on gun show legislation.

Marcia L. Godwin
and Christopher Harris

See also Gottlieb, Alan Merril; *Gun News Digest;* Gun Rights Policy Conference; Gun Shows; *Gun Week;* Second Amendment Foundation; *Women & Guns*
For Further Reading:
Ballard, Patricia Tsune, ed. 2001. *Encyclopedia of Associations.* 37th ed. Farmington Hills, MI: Gale Group.
Citizens Committee for the Right to Keep and Bear Arms. Liberty Park, 12500 N.E. Tenth Place, Bellevue, WA 98005, (800) 426-4302. Internet site: http://www.ccrkba.org.
Utter, Glenn H. 2000. *Encyclopedia of Gun Control and Gun Rights.* Phoenix, AZ: Oryx Press.

City of Las Vegas v. Moberg (1971)

City of Las Vegas v. Moberg (82 N.M. 626, 1971) was the first of several 1970s decisions that reversed a several-decade decline in the use of state constitution right-to-keep-and-bear-arms provisions. Perhaps unsurprisingly—because of the increasing disorder of the 1960s—by the time the *Moberg* case was decided the guarantees of a right to keep and bear arms had been disregarded by most state courts. The *Moberg* decision, while agreeing that *concealed* carrying of arms could be regulated or completely prohibited, also found that a law that prohibited the *open* carrying of arms was unconstitutional, since it violated Article 2, Section 6 of the New Mexico Constitution.

Leland James Moberg had entered a police station in Las Vegas, New Mexico, wearing a holstered pistol, to report a theft from his automobile. A city ordinance prohibited carrying of any deadly weapon, openly or concealed, including "guns, pistols, knives with blades longer than two and half inches, slingshots, sandbags, metallic metal knuckles, concealed rocks, and all other weapons, by whatever name known, with which dangerous wounds can be inflicted."

Moberg appealed his conviction based on Article 2, Section 6 of the New Mexico Constitution: "The people have the right to bear arms for their security and defense, but nothing herein shall be held to permit the carrying of concealed weapons." The New Mexico Court of Appeals agreed that "ordinances prohibiting the carrying of concealed weapons have generally been held to be a proper exercise of police power," but also asserted that "as applied to arms, other than those concealed, the ordinance under consideration purports to completely prohibit the 'right to bear arms.' It is our opinion that an ordinance may not deny the people the constitutionally guaranteed right to bear arms, and to that extent the ordinance under consideration is void."

The court of appeals cited *State v. Rosenthal* (Vt. 1903), *In re Brickey* (Idaho 1902), *State v. Woodward* (1937), and *State v. Kerner* (1921) as precedents for its position. With the exception of the *Woodward* case, this list of decisions was perfectly appropriate for the facts in *Moberg*.

Each decision involved a state constitution's guarantee of a right to keep and bear arms; each involved a person charged with violating a local ordinance (not a state law) that prohibited the carrying of a pistol; and each involved a peaceful person carrying a gun openly.

The *Woodward* decision was the oddball case in the list, however, because Woodward was on trial for assault with a deadly weapon, and the dispute was not whether he was lawfully carrying a weapon at the time of the incident but whether the judge's instructions had prejudiced the jury against Woodward by implying that carrying a gun was unlawful. While the Idaho Court of Appeals ordered Woodward to be retried with different jury instructions, there was no statute or ordinance struck down by the decision—unlike *Rosenthal, Brickey,* and *Kerner,* each of which had found a local ordinance unconstitutional.

The *Moberg* decision was short and contained little in the way of analysis, historical evidence, discussions of original intent, or appeals to pragmatic arguments for or against gun control.

Clayton E. Cramer

See also Concealed Weapons Laws; *State v. Kerner; State v. Rosenthal*

For Further Reading:

City of Las Vegas v. Moberg, 82 N.M. 626, 627, 628, 485 P. 2d 737 (App. 1971).

Commonwealth v. Ray, 218 Pa. Super. 72, 272 A. 2d 275 (1970).

Davis v. State, 146 So. 2d 892, 893, 894 (Fla. 1962).

Grimm v. City of New York, 56 Misc. 2d 525, 289 N.Y.S. 2d 358 (1968).

In Re Brickey, 8 Ida. 597, 70 Pac. 609, 101 Am. St. Rep. 215 (1902).

Photos v. City of Toledo, 19 Ohio Misc. 147, 250 N.E. 2d 916, 918, 919, 920, 921 (Ct. Comm. Pleas 1969).

State v. Bolin, 200 Kan. 369, 436 P. 2d 978, 979 (1968).

State v. Dawson, 272 N.C. 535, 545, 546 (1967).

State v. Kerner, 181 N.C. 574, 107 S.E. 222 (1921).

State v. Rosenthal, 75 Vt. 295, 55 Atl. 610 (1903).

State v. Schutzler, 249 N.E. 2d 549 (Ohio Ct. Comm. Pleas 1969).

State v. Woodward, 58 Ida. 385, 74 P. 2d 92 (1937).

City of Salina v. Blaksley (1905)

The 1905 Kansas Supreme Court decision *City of Salina v. Blaksley* (83 P. 619, 72 Kan. 230,

1905) is the foundation of the theory that the Second Amendment does not guarantee an individual right. As such, *Salina* is perhaps the most important state court decision involving the Second Amendment, although *Salina* was overruled by implication in a 1979 Kansas Supreme Court decision.

In 1842, a concurring opinion by an Arkansas Supreme Court judge said that the Second Amendment right was merely "an assertion of that general right of sovereignty belonging to independent nations, to regulate their military force" (*State v. Buzzard*, 4 Ark. 18, 32, 1842; Dickinson, concurring). This is the only known document from the nineteenth century asserting that the Second Amendment does not guarantee a right of individuals to possess firearms. The concurring opinion was not cited by any other nineteenth-century courts. Even in Arkansas, subsequent case law in the nineteenth century regarded the Second Amendment as an individual right (*Fife v. State*, 31 Ark. 455, 456, 1876).

In the town of Salina, Kansas, James Blaksley was convicted of carrying a pistol while intoxicated. When he appealed his conviction, neither Blaksley nor the prosecutor argued that the right to arms did not pertain to individuals, and the matter was therefore never briefed. The government attorney had simply argued that the local law was a reasonable gun control. Nevertheless, the Kansas Supreme Court chose to issue a decision announcing that the Second Amendment, and the right to arms in the Kansas state constitution, did not belong to citizens.

According to the *Salina* court, the "right to arms" meant only that the state militia, in its official capacity and while in actual service, could not be disarmed. The *Salina* court rejected or misdescribed every nineteenth-century source of authority that it used. (No eighteenth-century or prior sources were cited.)

The Kansas court rejected the Kentucky case of *Bliss v. Commonwealth* (12 Ky., 2 Litt, 90, 1822) and the long line of cases holding that in order to secure a well-regulated militia, individual citizens needed to be able to own and practice with guns. The court quoted a sentence from Bishop's *Statutory Crimes* that "the keeping and bearing of arms has reference only to war,

and possibly also to insurrections." The quote was accurate, but the Kansas court neglected the language surrounding the quote and other writings by Bishop, which made it clear that Bishop thought the right to arms was "declaratory of personal rights" and therefore belonged to individuals, not the state.

Lastly, the court quoted *Commonwealth v. Murphy*, an 1896 decision that had upheld, against a state constitutional claim, a Massachusetts law (similar to the Illinois law upheld by the U.S. Supreme Court in *Presser v. Illinois*) that banned mass parades with weapons. The Massachusetts court had written: "The right to keep and bear arms for the common defense does not include the right to associate together as a military organization, or to drill and parade with arms in cities or towns, unless authorized so to do by law" (44 N.E. 138, Mass. 1896). But holding that the right to arms does not authorize individuals to behave in a certain manner is not the same as the Kansas ruling that there is no individual right at all.

The *Salina* court did not discuss the pre–Civil War history of Kansas, when the proslavery government's disarmament of individual citizens was denounced nationally as a violation of the Second Amendment. The main basis of the *Salina* holding is the Kansas court's textual analysis of the implications of the Kansas arms right provision and of the Second Amendment. The Second Amendment was not at issue in the case and was simply analyzed as a guide to textual analysis of the Kansas provision. The court did not explain why the framers of the Kansas Constitution, in the middle of an article titled "Bill of Rights," suddenly inserted a provision that had nothing to do with rights but instead tautologically affirmed a power of the state government: in essence, that the militia is under the complete power of the state government.

Decades later, the Kansas Supreme Court moved away from *Salina* by declaring a local gun control ordinance unconstitutional (*Junction City v. Mevis*, 601 P.2d 1145, Kan. 1979). By then, however, *Salina*'s no-right theory had spread far beyond the Kansas state line. The next case to adopt a nonright theory was *United States v. Adams* (11 F. Supp. 216, S.D. Fla.

A row of stacked Union rifles at Petersburg, Virginia, April 3, 1965. (Library of Congress)

1935), which stated that the Second Amendment "refers to the militia, a protective force of government; to the collective body and not individual rights." The *Salina* nonrights position was widely adopted by federal district and appellate courts in the last three decades of the twentieth century, although the *Salina* case itself was not always acknowledged.

David B. Kopel

See also *Presser v. Illinois;* Second Amendment
For Further Reading:
Kopel, David B. 1998. "The Second Amendment in the Nineteenth Century." *BYU Law Review* 1998: 1359–1545; http://www.davekopel.com/2A/LawRev/19thcentury.htm.
Kruschke, Earl R. 1985. *The Right to Keep and Bear Arms.* Springfield, IL: Charles C. Thomas.

Civil War and Small Arms

The American Civil War has been characterized as the first "modern" war. One of the most important changes was the shift from the Napoleonic tactics in the field. The practice of massing infantry for frontal assaults (which often involved firing a volley at point-blank range and then resorting to the bayonet and/or using the musket as a club) proved disastrous in the face of new firearm technology and munitions that were brought to bear in this conflict. Specifically, the use of the "minie ball," the replacement of the musket with the rifle, and the supplanting of the single-shot rifle with the breech-action, rapidly firing carbine all led to the demise of tactic of frontal assault.

It seemed to take commanders on both sides a while to learn this lesson, however. Lee, looking for a decisive victory on Northern soil and buoyed by the fighting spirit and mettle of his troops, made the same fundamental error at Gettysburg that Burnside had made against the Army of Northern Virginia in 1862, at Fredericksburg. Grant, although thought of today as one of the first of the modern commanders from that war, made the same mistake in 1864 at Cold Harbor, a catastrophe that cost the North 13,000 casualties to the South's 2,500.

The arms and munitions that spelled the end of the "age of frontal assault" were mass-produced in the North but hard to come by in the South. At the beginning of the war both sides were using single-shot muzzle-loading rifles that were very similar. Early in the war, the North used the Springfield (.58 cal.) musket while the South, habitually very short on military ordnance of every kind, relied on the British Enfield (.577 cal.) or other arms secured in Europe. The efforts of agents of the Confederate government, such as Caleb Huse, a Massachusetts native, were crucial in this regard. Increasingly a wide variety of weapons salvaged from the battlefield proved critical to Southern armies as the Northern blockade became more effective.

The North, also initially short of arms, used numerous European suppliers as well. By the time production at Northern armories reached capacity late in the war, Union forces were well armed indeed. Northern armories produced 3 million firearms during the war and Union agents purchased another million in Europe. Of the total of 500,000 guns in Confederate hands, well over two-thirds had been purchased in Europe. The greater part of the remainder was provided by the battlefield or seized from Union facilities occupied by the Confederate government immediately following secession. Southern armories, at Richmond and Fayetteville, North Carolina, produced only a few firearms

Union forces also benefited from innovative rapid-fire firearms such as the Sharps (.52 cal.) and Spencer (.52 rimfire) carbines and the Henry (.44 cal.) rifle, all of which found service during the war. Only the innate conservatism of Union army ordnance office bound the Union troops to the less efficient Springfield until relatively late in the war. Colt's revolvers found favor with both sides; the Navy model (.36 cal.) was especially popular in the South. Union forces favored the .44 caliber in this revolver and it was later almost supplanted by the sturdier and more inexpensive Remington .44 Army. Numerous revolvers made by other manufacturers, domestic and European, were obtained by both government and individuals throughout the war. Rudimentary but very functional machine guns, Gatling guns, and other precursors made their appearance in the war but played no major part.

The importance of the Civil War for the history of firearms and the development of the gun culture in the United States is that after the Union's huge advantage in industrial weapons production crushed the agrarian South, huge numbers of used and surplus weapons went home with both victor and vanquished. A generation of combat-hardened young men had learned the relatively new lesson that firepower prevails. Disastrous and abortive Reconstruction-era violence followed, and much of the "wildness" in the West can be attributed to these young men and their arsenal. Furthermore, the gun manufacturers of the Connecticut Valley, who had profited mightily from federal contracts, sold the surplus inexpensively and began to advertise and dump their wares to those in the cities and on the frontiers. The government itself engaged in sales of large lots of this surplus in the postwar period. Some of the sales were at government facilities in the United States, and many of these arms and gun parts found their way to private owners and gunsmiths. (A surprising amount of U.S. surplus firearms was offered on the international market, being sold to the French and ending up as Prussian war booty following the Franco-Prussian War. The Prussians sold much of it to Turkey.) Immigrants and those on the way west made heavy emotional investment in the incipient gun mythos. With highly accurate rifles like those developed during the war, professional hunters exterminated the buffalo, and the forces of the victorious Union, with massive firepower, including the Gatling gun, firmly put the remaining Native-Americans in their place—reservations. The aftermath of the war allowed the innovations in weaponry of the first modern war to be carried by all and sundry, and according to some historians, was the critical period in the formation of an American gun culture (see Bellesiles, 1996, 2000).

F. Frederick Hawley

See also

Civil War Reenactments; Colt, Samuel; Gun Culture; Minie Ball; Remington, Eliphalet, II; Surplus Arms; Williams Gun

For Further Reading:

Bellesiles, Michael A. 1996. "The Origins of Gun Culture in the United States, 1760–1865." *Journal of American History* 83, 2 (September): 425–455.

_____. 2000. *Arming America: The Origins of a National Gun Culture.* New York: Knopf.

Edwards, William B. 1962. *Civil War Guns.* Harrisburg, PA: Stackpole Press.

A group of men dressed as Civil War soldiers stand to attention during a reenactment of the Battle of Bull Run, Virginia, 1986. (Joseph Sohm: Chromo Sohm Inc./Corbis)

Civil War Reenactments

Civil War reenactment regiments are largely composed of civilian hobbyists and historians whose aim is to recreate landmark Civil War battles with replica and authentic black powder weapons once used by the infantry, artillery, and cavalry during the four-year American conflict of 1861–1865. Standard-issue small arms play a vital yet fairly uniform role in many of today's Civil War reenactments.

The actual conflict between the Northern and Southern states served as a technological catalyst for modern weaponry, introducing a range of small-arm developments from smaller yet more accurate ballistics to the prototype of today's machine gun. However, reenactors personally finance their pastime and generally stick with a greatly modified arsenal, placing more emphasis on safety and battlefield tactics than on a wide range of firepower.

Enlisted men in the infantry are required to purchase a .58 caliber, percussion cap, muzzle-loading long arm. The most commonly used

weapons during the war and those found in today's reenactments are the 1861 or 1863 models of the Springfield-rifled musket and an Americanized version of the British 1853 Enfield-rifled musket. All of these weapons must be "three-band," or have three metal bands securing the metal barrel to the wooden stock. "Three-band" denotes a weapon of greater length and prevents ear damage to a comrade when shooting over his shoulder in a firing line. Another safety feature is the prohibition of bullets and ramrods lest they are accidentally left in a barrel charged with black powder. Infantry officers carry a percussion cap sidearm modeled on early 1860s issuances such as the .36 caliber Colt and the Remington .44 caliber pistols, both six-shot revolvers.

For safety reasons, of course, reenactments do not feature "bayonet charges" into opposing trenches. The initial designs of Civil War–rifled muskets, such as the .58 caliber Springfield and Enfield, required weapons to be almost five feet in length, thus greatly improving shooting accuracy and bayonet thrusting distance. The artillery, however, typically did not share these concerns. Operating from a relatively immobile position and ideally at great distance from the enemy, artillerists placed less value on large infantry weapons. Today's artillery reenactors are lightly armed with the Remington or Colt revolvers or the short, two-band, .58 caliber artillery carbine.

Conversely, the general thrust of the cavalry was mobility and its purpose to outpace the enemy. Many cavalry reenactors are terrific horsemen and quite adept at staged swordplay. Most are also armed with the Colt or Remington revolvers or the much larger and heavier .44 caliber Dragoon pistols that serve as "clubs" when out of ammunition. The cavalry also totes the .54 caliber Sharps carbine, a short, breech-loading rifle that is much easier to load and fire on horseback.

Much like the tack taken by Civil War reenactors who recreate four years of varied warfare that took place in many locales, this essay necessarily generalizes their small-arms use. Though there are some basic requirements based on the company's role in the regiment (e.g., rifle for infantryman, horse if cavalry), the reenactor is welcome to accrue as much authentic or replicated weaponry as he or she can afford—again provided it meets safety and company standards. Reenactment publications such as the *Camp Chase Gazette* provide reviews on weapon usage, and most authentic and reproduced weapons are purchased through Dixie Gun Works in Union City, Tennessee, a company dedicated to black powder and Civil War weapons.

James Manning

See also Civil War and Small Arms
For Further Reading:
American Civil War Reenactor Images: A
    Photographic Gallery. http://www.
    wildwestweb.net/cw.html.
Dixie Gunworks. 2001. Catalog issue no. 150.
    Union City, TN.
Horwitz, Tony. 1999. *Confederates in the Attic.*
    New York: Vintage Books.

Civilian Marksmanship Program

See National Board for the Promotion of Rifle Practice

Bill Clinton. (Library of Congress)

Clinton, William J. (1946–)

In 1992, William Clinton became the first president of the United States to be elected with a public stance that was antithetical to the National Rife Association (NRA). During his first term (1993–1997) significant gun control legislation was enacted, and after his party lost control of Congress in 1994, the president continued to propose additional legislation while also pursuing nonlegislative means.

With Clinton's support, the "Brady Bill" (named for the James Brady, President Reagan's press secretary, who was shot and seriously wounded along with Reagan and two law enforcement officers in 1981) was enacted by Congress after seven years of debate under previous administrations (including a veto by President George Bush)and signed into law by Clinton in November 1993 (PL 103-159). The law established a five-business-day waiting period for handgun sales through licensed dealers. The statute also required local law enforcement authorities to conduct background checks on handgun purchasers (this provision was declared unconstitutional by the Supreme Court in *Printz v. United States* [95-1478], 521 U.S. 98

[1997]). In 1994, Congress enacted the administration's crime bill (PL 103-322). The statute's key gun control provision was a ban on the manufacture, sale, and importation of nineteen assault weapons. Congress also passed the Gun-Free Schools Act of 1994 (PL 103-382), which required schools receiving federal funds to expel for at least one year any student who brought a weapon to the school.

After the Democratic Party lost control of Congress in the 1994 election, Clinton resorted to nonlegislative means to pursue his gun control policies. In 1997, Clinton and the nation's eight largest gun manufacturers agreed that they would include child safety locks with all new handguns. Clinton had previously issued an executive memorandum ordering federal law enforcement authorities to provide child safety locks for their officers' firearms.

In March 2000, the Clinton administration announced that Smith & Wesson, the nation's largest gun manufacturer, had agreed to reform the way it designed, distributed, and marketed the company's products. The agreement settled a number of lawsuits brought by the U.S. Department of Housing and Urban Development (HUD) and a number of local jurisdictions against major U.S. gun manufacturers. The suits sought compensation for the damages that the guns produced by the manufacturers had inflicted upon the aggrieved communities. Smith & Wesson became the first defendant to settle.

In April 2000, in the aftermath of a shooting at the National Zoo, where seven children were wounded, Clinton announced that HUD and the District of Columbia government would spend $350,000 to buy 7,000 guns as part of a local gun buyback program. The Washington program was the largest of HUD's BuyBack America program, a $15 million initiative that more than eighty local jurisdictions had already joined.

Clinton's efforts to convince a Republican-controlled Congress to enact additional gun control legislation were unsuccessful. After the Columbine High School massacre in April 1999, the president proposed raising the legal age for owning a gun from 18 to 21 and extending the Brady Law waiting period requirement to weapons sold at gun shows. These measures were rejected by Congress, many of the opponents arguing that additional gun control legislation would not prevent incidents like that at Columbine and that more effective enforcement of existing gun laws could have a more significant impact.

Jeffrey Kraus

See also Antiterrorist Legislation; Assault Weapons Ban of 1994; Background Checks; *Bailey v. United States;* Brady Handgun Violence Prevention Act (Brady Bill); Branch Davidians; Bush, George H. W.; Columbine High School Tragedy; Democratic Party and Gun Control; Dole, Robert; McVeigh, Timothy; Reno, Janet; Waco, Texas, Raid; Waiting Periods

For Further Reading:
Clinton, William Jefferson. 1995. *Proposed Legislation: 'Saving Law Enforcement Officers' Lives Act of 1995': A Message from the President of the United States Transmitting a Draft of Proposed Legislation to Save the Lives of America's Law Enforcement Officers.* Washington, DC: U.S. Government Printing Office.
U.S. Congress. House of Representatives. Committee on the Judiciary. 1993. *Brady Handgun Violence Prevention Act: Report Together with Additional and Dissenting Views to Accompany H.R. 1025.* Washington, DC: U.S. Government Printing Office.
———. Subcommittee on Crime. 2000. *Implementation of the National Instant-Check System for Background Checks of Firearm Purchasers: Hearing Before the Subcommittee on Crime of the Committee on the Judiciary, House of Representatives,* 105th Cong., 2d sess., June 11, 1998. Washington, DC: U.S. Government Printing Office.
———. 1999. *Pending Firearms Legislation and the Administration's Enforcement of Current Gun Laws: Hearing Before the Subcommittee on Crime of the Committee on the Judiciary, House of Representatives,* 106th Cong., 1st sess., May 27, 1999. Washington, DC: United States Government Printing Office.
———. Subcommittee on Crime and Criminal Justice. 1994. *Brady Handgun Violence Protection Act: Hearing Before the Subcommittee on Crime and Criminal Justice of the Committee on the Judiciary, House of Representatives, 103rd Congress, 1st Session on H.R. 1025, September 30, 1993.* Washington, DC: U.S. Government Printing Office.
———. 1993. *Federal Firearms Licensing: Hearing Before the Subcommittee on Crime and Criminal Justice of the Committee on the Judiciary, House of Representatives, 103rd Congress, 1st Session, June*

17, 1993. Washington, DC: U.S. Government Printing Office.

U.S. Department of Justice, Office of Justice Programs, Office of Juvenile Justice and Delinquency Prevention. 1996. "Reducing Youth Gun Violence: An Overview of Programs and Initiatives: Program Report." Washington, DC: U.S. Department of Justice, Office of Justice Programs, Office of Juvenile Justice and Delinquency Prevention.

U.S. General Accounting Office. 1996. *Gun Control: Implementation of the Brady Handgun Violence Prevention Act: Report to the Committee on the Judiciary, U. S. Senate, and the Committee on the Judiciary, House of Representatives.* Gaithersburg, MD: U.S. General Accounting Office.

Coalition to Stop Gun Violence (CSGV)

The Coalition to Stop Gun Violence was founded in 1974 to combat the problem of gun violence in the United States. CSGV represents a coalition of more than 40 religious, professional, labor, medical, educational, and civic organizations and comprises more than 120,000 individual members nationwide. CSGV's mission is to stop gun violence by fostering effective community and national action.

Organizational History

Galvanized by the assassinations of President John F. Kennedy in 1963 and Robert Kennedy and Martin Luther King, Jr., in 1968, many individuals and organizations recognized the destructive role that firearms, especially handguns, played in American society. These concerned citizens formed a loose coalition of gun control advocates to lobby for stricter controls on handguns, an effort that resulted in passage of the historic Gun Control Act of 1968.

Many of the supporters of the Gun Control Act united to build a movement to counterbalance the gun lobby, fight for stricter gun control laws, and lobby for better enforcement of existing legislation. In 1974, this loose coalition of groups tapped Michael Beard to become the first executive director and eventual president of the National Coalition to Ban Handguns. The National Coalition to Ban Handguns eventually became the Coalition to Stop Gun Violence.

Legislative Agenda

CSGV's legislative agenda is to close illegal markets for firearms. Illegal markets place firearms into the hands of criminals, youths, and other prohibited purchasers. These sales are made possible by lax gun laws that allow transfers from the primary market, where background checks are required, to the secondary market, where anything goes. Background checks are currently conducted only at licensed dealers, leaving nearly 4 million firearm transactions to be conducted with no questions asked. CSGV contends that this secondary market is a haven for criminals, terrorists, and others intent on destruction.

Licensing and registration form the essential basis of a modern gun violence prevention policy—they provide the foundation for the gun laws of other nations, all of which have lower levels of gun death and injury than the United States. Not only can licensing and registration save lives by stopping the flow of new firearms to criminals and youth, they also allow more effective enforcement of existing gun laws.

Licensing for firearm owners ensures that they are not prohibited from purchasing firearms and are adequately trained. Licensing also permits more accurate identification of a purchaser at the point of purchase and ensures that prospective firearm purchasers must have contact with local law enforcement. Firearm registration provides a mechanism for stopping the flow of firearms from the legal market (licensed dealers) to the criminal and youth markets. Registration prevents illegal transfers by making the owner responsible for what happens to his or her firearm and by making owners periodically take responsibility for their guns by renewing each gun's registration (similar to the registration of motor vehicles).

In addition to lobbying for a licensing and registration system, CSGV helped secure passage of the 1993 Brady Bill, which provides for background checks during firearm purchases, and the 1994 assault weapons ban.

Grassroots Organizing

CSGV supports a range of organizations and individuals who are fighting to reduce gun violence. CSGV provides technical advice, training seminars, and practical skills to ensure that concerned individuals and organizations are up to speed on the latest developments in firearm legislation and educational initiatives. In addition, CSGV partners with state and local organizations to lobby for effective gun laws.

Educational Goals

CSGV seeks to educate Americans about the dangers that firearms pose. Just as Americans have woken up to the dangers of smoking, now people are realizing how guns are damaging the United States. Gun violence costs the country an estimated $100 billion per year (Cook and Ludwig, 2000). Far from making a home safe, a gun kept there is more likely to be used to kill a family member or friend than to be used against an intruder (Cummings and Koepsell, 1998; Kellermann and Reay, 1986). The CSGV contends that one of its central messages—that a gun endangers rather than protects a home—is being heard. From 1993 to 1999 handgun production dropped 52 percent in the United States, and the percentage of households possessing a gun dropped from 42 percent in 1993 to 33 percent in 2000 (General Social Survey, 2000). Accompanying this drop in handgun production and gun ownership has been a 27 percent decline in firearm deaths.

CSGV counteracts what it contends is the myth that the Second Amendment is a barrier to tough gun control laws. In fact, no gun control law has ever been overturned on Second Amendment grounds, including bans on handguns, sawed-off shotguns, automatic weapons, and assault weapons. Most courts have ruled that the Second Amendment guarantees a collective right, not an individual right as argued by the gun lobby.

Youth Work

The CSGV works with young people, attempting to determine how gun violence affects their lives and helping them find positive alternatives to violence. Although the media tend to focus on school shootings, the vast majority of young people do not carry guns. The National Longitudinal Survey of Youth reveals that only one in every eleven boys between the ages of 12 and 16 carries a handgun at some point during any twelve-month period, and the rate is much lower for girls (*Juvenile Offenders and Victims*, 1999).

CSGV's sister organization, the Educational Fund to Stop Gun Violence, works to decrease gun violence through research, education, and litigation.

Desmond Riley

See also Assault Weapons Ban of 1994; Brady Handgun Violence Prevention Act; Gun Control; Gun Control Act of 1968; Gun Registration; Gun Shows; Licensing; Motor Vehicle Laws as a Model for Gun Laws; Second Amendment; Youth and Guns

For Further Reading:

Cook, Philip J., and Jens Ludwig. 2000. *Gun Violence: The Real Costs*. New York: Oxford University Press.

CSGV website: http://www.csgv.org.

Cummings, Peter, and Thomas D. Koepsell. 1998. "Does Owning a Firearm Increase or Decrease the Risk of Death?" *Journal of the American Medical Association* 280 (August 5): 471–473.

General Social Survey. 2000. "Do you happen to have in your home (or garage) any guns or revolvers? If yes, Is it a pistol, shotgun, rifle, or what?" Inter-University Consortium for Political and Social Research. http://www.icpsr.umich.edu/GSS/.

Kellermann, Arthur, and Don Reay. 1986. "Protection or Peril? An Analysis of Firearms Related Deaths in the Home." *New England Journal of Medicine* 314: 1557–1560.

Office of Juvenile Justice and Delinquency Prevention. 1999. *Juvenile Offenders and Victims, 1999: National Report*. Washington, DC: U.S. Department of Justice.

Cocaine and Gun Violence
See Drugs, Crime, and Guns

Cody, William "Buffalo Bill" (1846–1917)

William "Buffalo Bill" Cody was one of the most famous Americans of his era. He served as a member of the Pony Express, a scout for the army, and a buffalo hunter. His exploits were dramatized and immortalized in a series of novels. Cody also managed the traveling Wild West

Lithograph of Buffalo Bill on horseback, holding a smoking rifle. (Library of Congress)

After his hunting expedition, Cody returned to service with the army for the next four years as chief of scouts with the Fifth Cavalry. During this period Cody took part in sixteen battles against Native Americans, culminating in the defeat of the Cheyenne at Summit Springs, Colorado. In 1872, Cody was awarded the Medal of Honor for his service.

Meanwhile, Ned Buntline began to write a series of dime novels based on the exploits of Cody. Buntline created "Buffalo Bill" as the alter ego to the real-life Cody. Buntline eventually wrote 550 of these novels, which were packed with violence and gunplay. They were enormously popular and made Buffalo Bill a household name. Although only 26 years old, Cody was already a national folk hero.

In 1872, Buntline convinced Cody to portray his character in a stage play, *Scouts of the Prairie*. In between occasional periods of service with the army, Cody continued acting in the show for the next eleven years. The success of this venture led Cody to establish his own show, "Buffalo Bill's Wild West Show," in 1883. The Wild West Show combined theater and historical drama. Cody used live animals, including buffalo. He employed a number of the Old West's most famous people, including Annie Oakley and Chief Sitting Bull (who had led the attack against Custer). Cody used Native Americans from government reservations and often used his show to speak out about the treatment of the various tribes. In fact, after the Massacre at Wounded Knee in 1890, Cody and a number of the Native American performers in his show traveled to the reservation to help restore order and prevent further violence.

Meanwhile, both of the great herds of buffalo, the southern and northern groups, had been hunted to extinction by the year that Cody launched his extravaganza. In addition, the frontier had begun to close and open spaces were quickly being fenced in and settled. Cody bemoaned the loss of the frontier in his shows, which were becoming increasingly popular. In 1887, the Wild West Show was part of the American Exposition at Queen Victoria's Silver Jubilee in London. For ten years, the show made regular appearances in Europe. Cody used the

Show, which brought the frontier to Americans in the eastern areas of the nation. For many Americans, Cody remains the symbol of the West and the embodiment of the importance of guns in the settlement of the nation.

William Frederick Cody was born on February 26, 1846, near Le Claire, Iowa. His father died in 1857 and the family subsequently moved from Iowa to Kansas. At age 11, Cody began working as a mounted messenger for Majors and Russell Company. When gold was discovered two years later in Colorado, Cody moved west to prospect. The following year, at age 14, Cody joined the Pony Express as a rider. In 1860, he made the third longest trip in the organization's history (some 322 miles).

In 1863, Cody volunteered for the Seventh Kansas Cavalry and fought in Missouri and Tennessee. After the Civil War, he continued to work for the army as a scout and dispatch rider. In 1866, Cody married Louisa Frederici in St. Louis. From 1867 to 1868, Cody was contracted to provide buffalo meat for the Kansas Pacific Railroad. By his own account, Cody shot 4,280 buffaloes in seventeen months and earned the nickname "Buffalo Bill."

Gun collectors looking at a shotgun. (Peter Johnson/Corbis)

financial bonanza produced by his show to fund a variety of projects. His concern with the loss of wildlife and habitat led him to establish game preserves in Colorado and Wyoming. He also worked to limit the length of hunting seasons in a number of states. Cody served as a model of the later hunter-conservationist and would inspire figures such as Theodore Roosevelt.

Cody also sought to develop his own town. Along with a group of investors, he established a town that bore his name in Wyoming in 1896. Cody had grand visions for his town, but they never matured. Still, three major canals and two dams were built and 16,200 acres were placed under irrigation. While Cody was a master showman, he was a poor businessman. By the end of his life, he had lost most of his fortune. Cody died on January 10, 1917.

Tom Lansford

See also Boomtowns, Cowtowns, and Gun Violence; Frontier Violence

For Further Reading:

Blackstone, Sarah J. 1986. *Buckskins, Bullets, and Business: A History of Buffalo Bill's Wild West.* Westport, CT: Greenwood Press.

Cody, William F. 1998. *Buffalo Bill's Life Story: An Autobiography.* Reprint. Mineola, NY: Dover Publications.

Wetmore, Helen Cody. 1998. *Last of the Great Scouts: The Life Story of Col. William F. Cody.* Charlottesville: University of Virginia Library.

Collectors

Collecting firearms appears to be one of the more popular hobbies in the United States. While it is difficult to produce a precise estimate of the number of gun collectors in the United States, the activity is sufficiently widespread to support a very large number of publications, websites, and chat rooms. These communications outlets are organized in almost every conceivable fashion. While some publications, such as the National Rifle Association's quarterly journal, *Men at Arms,* are intended for general audiences, other magazines and websites cater to much narrower clienteles. Some publications target readers interested in particular time periods, such as those of the Old West, the American Civil War, or World War II, while others focus attention on collectors of specific brands of firearms, such as Browning, Winchester, Colt, or Smith & Wesson. Still others are organized around a geographical unit, such as the Dallas Arms Collectors' Association or the New Mexico Gun Collectors' Association.

While it is difficult to generalize about such a diverse group of communications outlets, these magazines and websites tend to emphasize four different types of messages. First, these media constitute an important means of exchange. Information about gun sales, shows, and innovations are spread to interested readers through both substantive articles and paid advertisements. In addition to providing information about the purchases of guns and ammunition, these publications also provide access to further information. Some of these, such as *Men at Arms* or the more specialized *Guns of the Old West,* contain reviews of books on topics of interest to gun collectors.

Second, many of the articles in publications for gun collectors consist of descriptions of historical events in which firearms played important roles. These might include accounts of battles, military and scientific expeditions, or the depiction of firearms in the general media culture. The emphasis on history appears to fulfill an important rhetorical purpose, which involves pointing out the constructive use of guns in significant events in U.S. and world history.

Third, many of the articles in gun-oriented publications focus on the technical, performance-related characteristics of various weapons. Often, several different firearms of the same general type (such as revolvers, rifles, or shotguns of a particular caliber) are tested and compared to one another along different technical criteria. These might include accuracy, durability, aesthetics, and reliability. The theme of safety is often emphasized in articles of this type, since associations of gun owners and collectors are often eager to live down a perceived reputation for recklessness.

Finally, some of these publications and sites carry explicit political messages. These are generally labeled clearly and set off from the rest of the publication in question. Explicitly political communications seem generally to fall into one of two distinct types. One set of messages emphasizes the legitimacy of gun ownership and the folly of gun control. These will often contain messages about the Constitution generally (or, more specifically, the Second Amendment) or about American history. The American Revolution is a popular theme in these communications, as the notion of a "citizen militia" is a very powerful rhetorical symbol to members of these groups. The connection between this type of political socialization and the historical articles described above is quite obvious, and there is considerable overlap between the two categories. Somewhat more rarely, other political messages will emphasize short-term tactics and will contain descriptions of candidate positions on firearm-related issues, information about pending legislation in Congress or in state legislatures, or analyses of recent court decisions.

The general point is that gun collecting is far from a private activity. Although individual collections may appear isolated from one another, gun collectors have created elaborate communications networks, which in turn promote shared cultural values and ideological perspectives.

Ted G. Jelen

See also Gun Culture; *Gun News Digest;* Gun Ownership; Gun Shows; *Gun Week;* Recreational Uses of Guns; Target Shooting
For Further Reading:
R. L. Wilson. 2000. *R. L. Wilson Price Guide to Gun Collecting.* 3d ed. New York: House of Collectibles.

Colleges and Gun Violence

The issue of guns on campus is of concern to educators and the broader community. In general, the carrying and possession of firearms on college campuses is forbidden by state law or institutional rules. Even colleges that support the shooting sports typically store the guns away from students.

Some people view colleges as safe havens from violence, but that is not always the case. According to the *Chronicle of Higher Education* ("Facts and Figures," 2000), there has been a slow rise in weapons arrests on campuses in recent years. In 1996 there was a 1 percent increase and in 1998 there was a 0.5 percent increase.

There are three sources of violence and thus concern. Colleges, like the rest of society, may suffer acts of workplace violence. Violent behavior by disgruntled employees, family members, significant others, and stalkers could occur on college campuses. In this way, colleges seem no different from other work environments.

The second concern is the possibility of drug-related gun violence spreading to college campuses, especially to schools that are close to urban centers with many gun-related crimes. Neighborhood residents may wander onto campus or engage in drug dealing. Relatedly, there is a risk associated with outreach programs: students involved in gangs may carry weapons on campus for personal protection. Many high school students cite personal protection as a reason for carrying a weapon to school, and there is no reason to think the urban college campus may be different. There is also concern that drug and alcohol usage on campus may lead to violent behavior. The *Chronicle of Higher Education* has discussed this issue in some depth. Some critics, however, have criticized such reports as focusing on minority institutions and students to a much greater extent than necessary and for being unduly alarmist.

A third major risk is that of rampage shootings, which have been prominent in the media. One of the most infamous incidents was the Texas Tower Massacre committed by Charles Whitman at the University of Texas, Austin, in 1966, when he killed fourteen out of the forty-five people he shot. Other incidents have included the slaying of fourteen women at the University of Montreal's Ecole Polytechnique. However, in recent times the killings at elementary and secondary schools, such as in Littleton, Colorado (Columbine), or Springfield, Oregon, have had more impact on society. The focus has been on the nature of the killers (due to their ages, environmental contexts, mental illnesses, and previous warnings to their peers) and whether gun control laws would have had any effect in preventing their crimes. The youth of the offenders and the victims seems to have more impact on society than do the college cases. Fortunately, such events are rare and there is nothing to suggest that a college is at greater risk that any other public place. One must note that current laws deprive educators and staff of any option for armed self-defense.

Other issues relevant to guns on campus are college student opinions about firearms and the rate of possession of firearms. A study by Miller, Hemenway, and Wechsler (1999) found that 3.5 percent of college students nationally reported having a handgun with them at college. This is probably an underestimate of ownership given college possession restrictions. Meyer (2001) found that 12 percent of men and 3.5 percent of women in a Texas and Oregon sample reported owning handguns. Surveys about gun laws themselves are always suspect, as it is easy to manipulate answers through the forms of questions asked (see Kleck, 1991; Vizzard, 2000). Nevertheless, it is clear that the college-educated population does not dramatically differ from other segments of the public on these issues. Kleck (1991) summarizes data indicating that most people in the United States favor weak to moderate controls on gun purchases (i.e., waiting periods and background checks) but not outright bans. Meyer (2001) found a similar pattern, with some support for licensing requirements but not for outright bans. Interestingly, about 48 percent of that sample (whose members did not own a handgun) indicated that they might buy one in the future. In comparison, the Meyer sample of faculty found that about 20 percent owned a handgun, with about 15 percent not owning one but contemplating a future purchase.

The last issue is the status of firearms research on college campuses. To the gun world, academics are seen as mostly wild-eyed liberals who strongly oppose the Second Amendment. Redding (2001) documents such liberal tendencies in psychology. Certainly, most academic writings tend to focus on the problems of firearms in society. However, some of the most serious support for the Second Amendment has come from liberal scholars such as Lawrence Tribe of Harvard Law School. The work of John Lott, Jr. (1998), and Gary Kleck (1991) on the utilitarian value of guns in society has bolstered the case for a strong defense of the Second Amendment. Such works have even led to calls for liberal scholars to censor themselves because their analyses hurt the gun control cause (Etzioni, 2001). Organizations do exist to support Second Amendment rights that are oriented toward academics. The best known of these is the Academics for the Second Amendment group, which holds a yearly meeting where members of the scholarly community can be informed of the latest scholarship on the issues as well as attend a background tutorial.

Glenn E. Meyer

See also Academics for the Second Amendment; Attitudes toward Gun Control; Columbine High School Tragedy; Schoolyard Shootings; Texas Tower Shooting; Youth and Guns

For Further Reading:

Etzioni, Amitai. 2001. "Are Liberal Scholars Acting Irresponsibly on Gun Control?" *Chronicle of Higher Education* 47: B14–B15; http://www.gwu.edu/~ccps/B350.html.

"Facts & Figures: A Look at Campus Crime." 2000. *Chronicle of Higher Education* (June 9); http://ericcass.uncg.edu/virtuallib/violence/3004.html.

Kleck, Gary. 1991. *Point Blank.* Hawthorne, NY: Aldine de Gruyter.

Lott, John R., Jr. 1998. *More Guns, Less Crime: Understanding Crime and Gun Control Laws.* Chicago: University of Chicago Press.

Meyer, Glenn E. 2001. "Campus Weaponry: Student and Faculty Attitudes." Paper presented at the meeting of the American Society of Criminology, Atlanta, GA.

Miller, Matthew, David Hemenway, and Henry Wechsler. 1999. "Guns at College." *Journal of American College Health* 48, 1 (July): 7–12.

Redding, Richard E. 2001. "Sociopolitical Diversity in Psychology: The Case for Pluralism." *American Psychologist* 56, 3: 205–215.

Vizzard, William J. 2000. *Shots in the Dark.* Lanham, MD: Rowman & Littlefield.

Colt, Samuel (1814–1862)

For more than a century, beginning in 1855, Colt revolvers were manufactured in the brownstone armory that Samuel Colt built near the Connecticut River in Hartford. At the time it was the largest private armory in the world, crowned with a blue, onion-shaped dome, which has been a Hartford landmark ever since.

Inventor, entrepreneur, promoter, Samuel Colt was born in Hartford in 1814, the son of Christopher and Sarah Caldwell Colt. As a youngster his passion for firearms and explosive devices made him an indifferent student, to the chagrin of his father, who in desperation apprenticed him as a sailor on the brig *Corvo,* sailing from Boston to Calcutta and back. While aboard, the 16-year-old youth conceived of the revolutionary idea of the revolver by watching the action of the ship's wheel and carved a wooden model of a six-shooter. His father financed the making of two prototypes. Both failed.

Undeterred but penniless, Colt decided to earn money to carry on his experiments by becoming a performer billed as "the celebrated Dr. Coult of New York, London, and Calcutta." Using his knowledge of nitrous oxide, he toured Canada and the east coast for three years giving demonstrations of "laughing gas." He engaged a competent mechanic, John Pearson, to make improved models and, borrowing $1,000 from his father, sailed to Europe to apply for patents. Still only 21, he received patents in London (December 8, 1835) and France—and U.S. Patent no. 138 the following February. On the strength of these he obtained $200,000 in capital from New York and New Jersey investors.

His first attempt at manufacturing took place in Paterson, New Jersey, in a leased section of a silk mill. The company failed in 1842, however, even though 100 of his revolvers had met with success against the Seminole Indians in Florida and in the hands of Texas Rangers against the Comanches. Five years later, seeking good firearms for use in the Mexican War, the army gave him an order for 1,000 revolvers. Still "poor as a churchmouse," as he said, and lacking production facilities, Colt turned to Eli Whitney, Jr., in Whitneyville, Connecticut, where the Colt-Whitney-Walker model was manufactured.

Now on his way to fame and fortune, Colt returned to Hartford, rented quarters, and produced the Colt Dragoon model. In 1852, he purchased 250 acres of flood-prone land in the South Meadows and began planning not only the construction of a great armory but also a self-sufficient community called Coltsville. Ignoring the skepticism and hostility of the city fathers, he built a dike along his property for flood protection, laid out streets, erected houses for his employees, and even built a hall for their entertainment.

Always on the lookout for more business, Colt saw an opportunity to furnish guns for both sides in the Crimean War. The first American to manufacture abroad, he in 1853 opened a factory in London to make the Model 1849 Pocket and the Model 1851 Navy. Unfortunately, the plant was mismanaged and closed in 1857.

The operating genius of the Colt Armory was Elisha K. Root, the most brilliant machinist of his era in New England. Adapting the system of interchangeable parts pioneered by Eli Whitney and the Springfield Armory, Root developed equipment and processes that made possible the mass production of firearms on machines, except for the finishing and final assembly. By 1857 the armory turned out 250 guns a day. It also became a training center for a succession of gifted mechanics, like Pratt and Whitney, who went on to apply Root's methods in companies of their own. It is said that Root was the inspiration for the hero in Mark Twain's novel *A Connecticut Yankee in King Arthur's Court.*

Colt himself functioned as president and salesman extraordinary by aggressive marketing and close relations with military officials, legislators, and foreign heads of state. Thousands of his revolvers were shipped to California during the Gold Rush. He traveled abroad, wangling introductions to government officials and making them gifts of beautifully engraved weapons.

In less than a decade, Colt had become America's first tycoon, a millionaire and rather bibulous, cigar-smoking bachelor who had everything but a wife and home. These he acquired with his usual dispatch and pomp. He chose as his bride the gracious and gentle Elizabeth Jarvis, daughter of a Middletown minister. At age 30, she was twelve years younger. The extravagance of their wedding on June 5, 1856, shocked Hartford's staid society, as did Colt's building of the palatial *Armsmear* on the western end of his domain.

As North and South raced toward the cataclysm, Colt was busy making enormous profits by filling the demands of both sides right up to the firing on Fort Sumter that started the Civil War. A Democrat, he opposed the election of Lincoln for fear the Union would be destroyed—and a lucrative market thereby lost. In his view, slavery was not a moral wrong but an inefficient economic system. Anticipating the onset of conflict, he shrewdly prepared the armory for a five-year struggle and the arming of a million men by erecting a duplicate of the H-shaped factory.

By then his immense business responsibilities began to wear down his seemingly inexhaustible energies. Bothered by frequent attacks of inflammatory rheumatism, he drove himself as if he knew his days were numbered. At the age of 47 he died on January 14, 1862, leaving his widow and son Caldwell an enormous estate for that time.

Samuel Colt had adopted as his motto "Vincit qui patitur" (he conquers who suffers). But a more apt key to his character is the remark he once wrote to his half brother William: "It is better to be at the head of a louse than at the tail of a lion … If I can't be first I won't be second in anything."

A catastrophe almost put an end to the armory two years after his death when 1,500 men were working two ten-hour shifts to keep General Grant's troops supplied with muskets and revolvers. Fire destroyed the original factory and most of the machines. Elizabeth Colt ordered the building of a new armory. At the height of the Civil War annual production had reached 100,000 revolvers and nearly 50,000 muskets. During peacetime, however, the military's demand for munitions declined sharply. The company tried to keep its work force busy making machine tools, steam engines, sewing machines, printing presses, and both the Gatling and Browning machine guns. In 1872 appeared the six-shot Colt .45, or "Peacemaker," the gun that became a legend among cowboys and frontiersmen. It was said that while Lincoln made all men free, Colt made all men equal.

In 1901, four years before her death, Mrs. Colt, the grande dame of Hartford society, sold Colt Armory to Boston and New York financiers. The company earned huge profits until the end of World War I, paying its investors annual dividends averaging 22 percent. Making and selling munitions was a business like any other, and the moral aspects of being "dealers in death" did not disturb the conscience of management. Certainly, Hartford did not regard gun making as a sin—not in a state that had been the arsenal of the nation since colonial times. Furthermore, though the founder made millions, none of his successors became rich.

During World War I the Colt Armory achieved the best records in its history. Before America's entry in the war, because of demand from Canada and Great Britain its order backlog extended to three years, employment rose to nearly 4,000, and its stock quintupled in value. By the end of the war in 1918 it had delivered 425,500 automatic pistols, 151,700 revolvers, 13,000 Maxim-Vickers machine guns, and 10,000 new Browning machine guns, while handling smoothly the subcontracting of nearly 100,000 more. Employment peaked at 10,000. The three most responsible for this spectacular achievement were President William C. Skinner; Fred Moore, head of production; and the inventor John Browning, whose .45 pistol was the army's standard sidearm. Besides his .30 caliber machine gun, he also invented a lightweight automatic rifle. His son, Lt. Val A. Browning, was the first to fire both weapons in France.

Peacetime called for a different strategy. Anticipating a severe drought in military sales, Skinner and his successor, Samuel Stone, set in motion a diversification program, as was done after the Civil War. They obtained contracts for adding machines and commercial dishwashers to be marketed under the name of someone other than Colt. Stone acquired a company engaged in molding hard plastics, which he renamed "Colt rock," and another company that made electrical products.

Colt weathered the Great Depression better than the other Hartford manufacturers, reducing the work week, cutting salaries, keeping more men on the payroll than were needed, and eating up surplus. On Pearl Harbor Day in 1941, the company was still the largest private armory in the United States and the only one turning out machine guns. As it had in two previous conflicts, Colt Armory stretched itself to the limit, winning the army-navy "E" for outstanding pro-

duction in 1942. But a few months later it was evident that the armory was in the incipient stage of its eventual downfall. It began losing money every month. The root of the trouble was partially its fatigued and strife-torn labor force, but more importantly the obsolescence of both management and manufacturing techniques.

In September 1955 the directors voted to merge Colt Armory with an upstart conglomerate called Penn-Texas, which had acquired Pratt & Whitney Machine Tool the same year. Under the new ownership the most significant achievement was the introduction of the M-16 automatic rifle, which became the standard army and air force weapon. In recent years Colt Armory suffered one blow after another: more mismanagement, heavy deficits, obsolete products, loss of markets and contracts, defense cutbacks, a four-year strike, another buyout, and bankruptcy. Yet it recovered from all of these reversals and now operates, not in the old downtown armory but in a modern plant in West Hartford. The departure in 1994 marked the end of 147 years of gun making in Hartford, during which not only Colt Armory but also Sharps, Pope Manufacturing, and Pratt & Whitney Machine Tool had led the state to an unprecedented era of power and prosperity. The armory is being renovated for small businesses, artists' studios, and possibly a museum of industrial technology.

Ellsworth S. Grant

See also Browning, John Moses; Remington, Eliphalet, II; Ruger, William Batterman; Whitney, Eli; Winchester, Oliver Fisher

For Further Reading:

Barnard, Henry. 1866. *Armsmear—The Home, the Arm, and the Armory of Samuel Colt: A Memorial.* New York: Alvord.

Edwards, William B. 1953. *The Story of Colt's Revolver.* Harrisburg, PA: Stackpole.

Grant, Ellsworth S. 1995. *The Colt Armory.* Lincoln, RI: Andrew Mowbray.

Haven, Charles T., and Frank A. Belden. 1997. *A History of the Colt Revolver.* Special edition. Fairfax, VA: National Rifle Association (Odysseus Editions).

Hosley, William. 1996. *Colt—The Making of an American Legend.* Amherst: University of Massachusetts Press.

Rohan, Jack. 1948. *Yankee Arms Maker: The Story of Sam Colt and His Six-Shot Peacemaker*. Rev. ed. New York: Harper.

Wilson, Robert Lawrence. 1979. *The Colt Heritage: The Official History of Colt Firearms, from 1836 to the Present*. New York: Simon and Schuster.

Columbine High School Tragedy

On April 20, 1999, Eric Harris and Dylan Klebold, both seniors at Columbine High School in Littleton, Colorado, entered the school and killed twelve fellow students and one teacher before taking their own lives. An additional twenty-three students were injured in the shooting spree. Arguably the Columbine murders shook the American psyche more than any shooting since the 1968 assassination of Sen. Robert F. Kennedy. While Columbine deeply unsettled the United States initially, the crime's long-term impact on gun policy was much smaller than had originally been expected. The Columbine events did, however, have a variety of positive and negative long-term impacts on some parts of American society, and the debate that followed revealed one of the fundamental fault lines within the country.

A year's worth of planning came to culmination when Harris and Klebold entered Columbine High School early on the morning of April 20 and deposited duffel bags containing twenty-pound propane tanks in the cafeteria, with a timer set to detonate the tanks at 11:17 A.M. According to the report released by the Jefferson County Sheriff's Office, the tanks contained sufficient explosive power to "kill the majority of students" who would be in the cafeteria for lunch. But the tanks did not detonate as planned.

Harris and Klebold returned to the school at 11:00 A.M. and began shooting at 11:19. The first five students shot (two of whom were

A security video shows Dylan Klebold (right) and Eric Harris in the Columbine High School cafeteria on the day they killed twelve students and one teacher. (AP Photo/Jefferson County Sheriff's Department)

killed) were sitting on the steps outside the school cafeteria. Seventeen-year-old Rachel Scott was murdered specifically because she had witnessed her Christian faith to one of the killers several weeks before. When one of the killers put a gun to her head and tauntingly asked if she still believed in God, she replied, "You know I do." "Go be with Him, then," he answered, and pulled the trigger.

At 11:24 the school resource officer, Deputy Sheriff Neil Gardner, returned from lunch and exchanged fire in a long-distance gun battle with Harris and Klebold before they entered the building. Deputy Gardner did not enter the building to pursue the killers, nor did any of the other Jefferson County sheriff's deputies, who arrived within minutes. A SWAT team quickly assembled outside the school, but the team did not enter the building until approximately 12:06 P.M.

In the meantime, Klebold and Harris were shooting people inside the school. Among their victims was teacher Dave Sanders (age 47), who was holding a door open so that students could flee. Harris and Klebold entered the school library where students were hiding under desks and library tables. Inside the library, a teacher had called 911 on a portable phone, and the 911 operator had told the teacher to keep the students in the library because help was on the way. Because Columbine High School sits on a sloping hill, students could have fled the library through an exit door on an outside wall.

Another 911 call revealed that Harris and Klebold had entered the library. Inside, they taunted students as they shot them one by one. The police remained outside.

The last victim in the library was killed at about 11:35 A.M. Klebold and Harris returned to the now-empty cafeteria, shooting randomly and hurling pipe bombs, most of which failed to detonate. While Harris and Klebold had used a variety of explosives with which a skilled bomb-maker could have killed hundreds, the two murderers failed to kill anyone with their homemade devices—although shrapnel from the explosives did cause a number of injuries. Columbine demonstrated it is easy to kill people with firearms, but while a trained person (like Timothy McVeigh) can kill hundreds of people with explosives, it is difficult for an untrained person to do so.

Harris and Klebold attempted to enter a locked room where a large number of students had hidden. An open 911 line made it clear to law enforcement precisely where the killers were. But acting under orders from Jefferson County Sheriff John Stone, the police did not attempt to enter. One Denver SWAT team member who tried to go in on his own initiative was ordered down and forced to remain outside.

Harris and Klebold returned to the now-empty library (the surviving students had fled), where they shot and killed themselves at 12:08 P.M. Based on the final positions of the murderers' guns and bodies, it appears that Harris killed Klebold and then himself.

The first SWAT personnel entered the east side of the school (far from where the killers were known to be) at 12:06 p.m. For the next several hours the police continued to "contain the perimeter"—searching and securing one room at a time, starting with the rooms farthest from where the killers had last been spotted.

Every injured person who received prompt medical care survived. But police did not reach the room where teacher Dave Sanders was bleeding for nearly three hours, despite pleas from cellular phone callers in the room with him. He eventually bled to death; he was the only teacher killed that day. SWAT team personnel entered the library for the first time at 3:22 P.M.

The murderers' weapons consisted of an Intratec TEC-DC9 semiautomatic pistol, obtained from Mark Manes, son of a gun control activist, who was later sent to prison for knowingly providing a handgun to minors in violation of Colorado law and for using a sawed-off shotgun (during target practice with the killers) in violation of federal law. The other three weapons were a Hi-Point 9 mm carbine, a Savage 67H pump-action shotgun, and a Savage 311-D twelve-gauge shotgun. These were obtained from Robyn Anderson, a friend of Harris, who had bought them for the youths at the Tanner Gunshow in December 1998 from a private individual.

Anderson's purchase of the long guns was lawful, and it would have been lawful for Harris or Klebold to have bought the long guns directly. After the murders, Anderson stayed quiet about her role as a gun supplier (until an anonymous person turned her in), and some people were suspicious that she had left the Columbine campus in a great hurry a few minutes before the shootings began.

Later, she told conflicting stories about whether gun controls would have affected her decision to buy the guns for Harris and Klebold. One version, offered in testimony before the Colorado legislature in January 2000, was that she would not have bought the guns if there had been background checks on gun buyers, even though she had a clean record. This contradicted the story she told *Good Morning America* in June 2000. Unlike Mark Manes and Philip Duran (who introduced the killers to Manes and was sent to prison), Anderson has never apologized for her role as a gun supplier to the murderers.

Harris and Klebold were perceived by both themselves and others as the butt of teasing and bullying. As detailed by the Denver weekly newspaper *Westword* and by the *Washington Post*, Columbine High School had a culture in which favored athletes were allowed to bully others and violate rules with impunity.

Harris and Klebold had earlier been arrested in 1998 and pled guilty to first-degree criminal trespass, theft, and criminal mischief for breaking into a parked van and stealing some of the contents. They spent one year in a juvenile diversion program consisting of community service and anger management classes, from which they were released on February 3, 1999.

At approximately that same time, Harris was reported to the police by Judy Brown, the mother of a classmate, as a suspect in a case of vandalism. After Harris discovered Brown's identity, he broke the car windshield of Brown's son Brooks and posted a death threat to Brooks Brown on his website. Judy Brown provided ten pages of material from the website, including the death threat, to police, who filed a report of a "suspicious incident" on March 18, 1999. The Jefferson County Sheriff's Department prepared a search warrant application for Harris's home, but never took the warrant to court.

Five days before the shooting at Columbine High School, Harris was denied entry into the U.S. Marines because he was taking the antidepressant medication Luvox. Harris was one of several recent mass killers who were using antidepressants that appeared to cause extreme paranoid reactions in a small number of users. Klebold, in contrast, was "drug free," according to his autopsy.

The societal reaction to Columbine fit the pattern of classic "moral panics," which sociologists have described as hysterical community reactions designed to reestablish norms of control by cracking down on outcasts—regardless of whether the outcasts are really the cause of the alleged problem.

Although preliminary reports identified the killers as members of the "Trench Coat Mafia," a group of no more than twelve students who regularly wore black trench coats to school, the group credibly denied that Harris and Klebold were members. The incorrect reports led some school districts to ban the wearing of trench coats, and many schools began to crack down on "Goth" culture. ("Goth" is a youth subculture with an interest in Dark Ages imagery and other forms of darkness, including dark clothing.)

Corrupting music was also blamed, particularly the groups Marilyn Manson and KMFDM. But the connection between the killers and music was found to be much more tenuous than originally thought. Nevertheless, Columbine spurred many movie theaters to begin strict enforcement of the rule against unaccompanied minors viewing R-rated movies.

Video games also came in for scrutiny, since the killers spent a great deal of time playing "first-person-shooter" games like Doom and Quake. But no substantial changes in marketing or sales resulted, and video game defenders pointed out that the vast majority of people who play such games do not commit violent crimes, just as the vast majority of children in earlier generations who played "cowboys and Indians" did not later shoot real people with bows or guns.

Over the next two years, a number of Columbine copycat crimes were attempted at schools around the nation by disgruntled students. No fatalities resulted, except at Santana

High School outside San Diego, where two people were killed in March 2001. Some media critics charged that excessive, sensational coverage of Columbine and other school shootings was an important cause of additional school shootings.

While media practices remained largely unchanged after Columbine, many schools—especially high schools—became notably more authoritarian and began in some cases to share characteristics with minimum security prisons.

Most schools already had "zero tolerance" policies forbidding students from carrying firearms on school grounds, but these policies were now enforced in ways that would have seemed absurd a decade before. Children were suspended or expelled for playing "cops and robbers" on the playground, for playing with "finger guns," for drawing pictures of soldiers, for making cutout guns from paper, for expressing support for the Second Amendment, and for other activities not involving real weapons. Other students were disciplined for possessing Swiss army knives in the trunks of their cars parked on school grounds, for possessing a photograph of a shooting session at a target range, or for having a kitchen knife in their car that had fallen out of a box while the family was moving. A student in Brooklyn was suspended for carrying a metal ruler, which was required by his shop class. The enforcement of antiweapons policies against students who did not possess weapons was, in part, a reflection of the determination of the American school establishment to "do something." Locker and automobile searches and other invasions of student privacy also became more common.

Some people, including conservative radio commentator Paul Harvey, House of Representatives Majority Whip Tom Delay (R-TX), and Darrell Scott (the father of slain student Rachel Scott), blamed the absence of school prayer and, more broadly, the decline of religious values. Whether organized school prayer would have made any difference for Harris and Klebold is unclear, but it is plain that they were nihilistic. In the videotapes they made of themselves and on Harris's website, they claimed to be accountable to no one and entitled to enforce their will against everyone else. One videotape expressed

their views of the afterlife that Klebold expected, which involved floating in limbo.

Columbine spurred a surge of activism among Christian youth groups. Many young Christians were inspired by Rachel Scott and Cassie Bernall, evangelical Christians who were murdered at Columbine, and by Valeen Schnurr, a Catholic who was severely wounded but who made a quick recovery that defied medical explanation.

In a videotape made a month before the killings, Eric Harris expressed his desire to "get a chain reaction going," and indeed copycat crimes followed Columbine, although the death toll appears to be far lower than Harris would have preferred. Rachel Scott, who had made a point of showing kindness to outcasts, the handicapped, and others at Columbine, hoped for a different kind of chain reaction: "I have a theory that if one person can go out of their way to show compassion, then it will start a chain reaction of the same," she had written in her diary. Scott's diary had been in her backpack and was held by the Jefferson County Sheriff's Office for many months after the shooting; when it was finally released to her family, it was discovered that for over a year she had been expecting to die. On the morning that she died, she drew a picture of a rose shedding thirteen tears.

Harris and Klebold, in contrast, had spent the last two years of their lives increasingly enraged and narcissistic. Some people traced the Columbine murders to grossly negligent or detached parenting, but the Harris and Klebold families refused to speak to the media (partly out of fear of civil or criminal liability), thus making any assessment of the quality of their parenting difficult. Reports from neighbors and friends who knew the families when the children were younger did not reveal notably deficient parenting. Klebold's parents refused to let him play with toy guns as a child. A number of states passed laws designed to reinforce parental or teacher authority to control or discipline children.

Within police ranks, debate began over the "perimeter control" tactics that had resulted in the police staying outside the building while people were being murdered inside. Perimeter control was a standard tactic for SWAT teams, based on the principle that officer safety is the most important goal. Over the next two years, many, but not all, police departments decided that perimeter control was an inadequate response to an "active shooter." Thus, in the March 22, 2001, shootings at Granite Hills High School in El Cajon, California, a policeman ended the shootings by quickly confronting the killer. This was the first time that a school shooting in progress had been stopped by police intervention. (In a little-reported Texas case, a policeman had engaged in a shoot-out with a would-be killer who was on the way to school.)

Not all police changed their tactics, however. In December 2000, a disgruntled employee murdered seven people at an office in Wakefield, Massachusetts. The police stayed outside until the employee sat down on a couch and waited to be arrested.

In response to the questionable police response at Columbine, some public safety advocates pointed out that two previous school shootings (in Pearl, Mississippi, and Edinboro, Pennsylvania) had been stopped by armed adults. It was urged that schools authorize selected teachers or other responsible and trained adults to possess concealed handguns at school. The advocates argued that laws forbidding adult possession of weapons turned schools into safe zones for murderers, and they pointed to research by John Lott and William Landes (1999) showing that mass shootings in public places drop precipitously after the enactment of handgun-carrying laws; Lott and Landes suggested that even though most mass killers expect to die at the end of their spree, they may be deterred by the risk that armed victims may terminate the killing spree before it even begins. In support of this thesis, Lott pointed to a highly publicized shooting at the Los Angeles Jewish Community Center preschool in August 1999; the killer, an anti-Semite and racist, had scouted out several Jewish institutions and decided not to attack them after discovering that they had security guards. He settled on the preschool only after determining that it was undefended. At the Wakefield, Massachusetts, shootings, an employee who had tried to stop the killer but was murdered had a permit to carry a handgun in his home state of New Hampshire, but, in conformity with Massachusetts law, had not been carrying his gun at work. Opponents of teacher possession of handguns objected that the necessary training would be too expensive and that teachers owning guns would set a bad example for students.

Columbine set off the worst month in the National Rifle Association's history. The group's annual meeting had been scheduled to begin in Denver in late April. Politicians who had promised to speak at the event withdrew. The NRA leadership began to scale down the meeting, eventually leaving only the legally required membership meeting on a Saturday afternoon.

Even so, Denver Mayor Wellington Webb (who had courted the NRA's huge convention business several years earlier, when the meeting place was being decided) publicly urged the NRA not to come to Denver. Gun control advocates placed newspaper ads telling the NRA to stay away, and set plans for an antigun rally. Meanwhile, the NRA maintained a self-imposed silence until the convention day.

On that day the NRA and the antigun rally each drew about 6,000 enthusiasts. The antigun rally featured Tom Mauser, father of slain Columbine student Daniel Mauser. The elder Mauser joined the staff of a new Colorado gun control organization, SAFE (Sane Alternatives to the Firearms Epidemic), as its top professional lobbyist.

At the NRA convention, NRA President Charlton Heston rebuked Mayor Webb: "Don't come? We're already here," Heston invoked, pointing to the large number of NRA members in Colorado and in the Columbine community. The speech was in keeping with Heston's long-standing efforts to portray the NRA as a pervasive part of mainstream America.

Heston's speech, though well received by its audience, was instantly overshadowed by the surprise appearance of the next speaker, Colorado Secretary of State Vikki Buckley (a black Republican). Buckley spoke about her own past as a victim of gun violence, described Columbine as "a New Age hate crime," excoriated Wellington Webb for attacking constitutional amendments, and demanded that the gun prohibition advocates spend less time obsessing about guns and more time preventing children from being born out of wedlock. The crowd gave her a standing ovation, and a few days later the *Wall Street Journal* suggested that Republicans consider Buckley for national office. Buckley died in July 1999, however.

When Utah Republican Sen. Orrin Hatch brought his juvenile justice bill to the floor of the U.S. Senate in mid-May, the NRA was forced to refrain from opposing several antigun amendments so as to conserve its political capital. Even after acquiescing to an amendment to impose background checks on sales by private individuals at gun shows, the NRA was defeated 51–50 (with Vice President Gore casting the tie-breaking vote) on a much harsher amendment that gave the Bureau of Alcohol, Tobacco, and Firearms the regulatory authority to abolish or severely curtail gun shows.

After the juvenile crime bill, which was laden with antigun amendments, passed the Senate, House sponsors wanted to bring it to a quick vote. But the House Republican leadership decided to wait until after the Memorial Day recess. One antigun representative objected, warning, "It's doesn't take the NRA long to reload."

When the full House voted on the juvenile justice bill in mid-June, the gun measures had been split off into a separate bill. The final version of the bill included a gun show background check measure that the NRA could live with (no extra regulatory power granted to the BATF), some additional gun restrictions (including on imports of certain magazines and on long-gun possession by people under 18), as well as repeal of the 1976 Washington, D.C., municipal handgun ban. A surprise coalition of mostly Republican gun rights supporters (who thought the bill went too far) and mostly Democratic gun control advocates (who thought the House bill did not go nearly far enough) ended up killing the House gun bill.

Back in Colorado, the aftermath of Columbine blocked the NRA's efforts to pass legislation for a concealed handgun carry law, and for a state law prohibiting most local gun control laws. In the summer of 1999, Governor Bill Owens endorsed a variety of gun controls.

The focus of the 2000 legislative session was on guns more than any other issue. By the time the session was over, all gun control proposals had been defeated, except for some "tough-on-crime" measures that the NRA had supported. The legislature passed and the governor signed the broadest law in the nation prohibiting lawsuits against gun manufacturers.

That fall, SAFE brought a "gun show" initiative on the statewide ballot and passed it with 70 percent of the vote. A similar measure was passed by Oregon voters with 60 percent of the vote.

Columbine changed, probably permanently, the dynamics of the debate on gun shows, turning them from an obscure issue of interest only to gun control activists into a well-known national issue.

A second effect was to energize, at least temporarily, antigun activists. The most famous of these was talk show host Rosie O'Donnell, who declared the day after Columbine that there ought to be a mandatory jail sentence for gun ownership.

In one of the presidential debates, the Columbine issue was raised. Vice President Gore pointed to guns, and Governor Bush pointed to values. The two answers exemplified the cultural divide revealed by the gun debate in general and so sharply intensified by the horror of Columbine. Is human evil a product of a wicked character, or of a bad environment in which dangerous objects like guns are available?

Thus, even as Columbine was a uniquely traumatizing mass shooting, it ultimately revealed the same philosophical fault lines that have characterized the gun debate from the very beginning. Indeed, the "material versus spiritual" debate is as old as philosophy itself.

Carol Oyster and David B. Kopel

See also Gun Control; Gun Shows; Gun-Free School Laws; Heston, Charlton; Mass Murder; Media Violence; National Rifle Association; Schoolyard Shootings; Video Games and Gun Violence; Youth Gun Control Legislation, The Juvenile Justice Bill of 1999; Youth and Guns

For Further Reading:

Bernall, Misty, Madeleine L'Engle, and Michael W. Smith. 2000. *She Said Yes: The Unlikely Martyrdom of Cassie Bernall.* Nashville, TN: Word Publishing.

Buckley, Vikki. 1999. "Welcoming Remarks of the Colorado Secretary of State to the NRA Convention." http://nrawinningteam.com/meeting99/buckleysp.html.

Civil Rights Project, Harvard University. 2000. "Opportunities Suspended: The Devastating Consequences of Zero Tolerance and School Discipline Policies." http://www.law.harvard.edu/civilrights/conferences/zero/zt_report2.html.

Governor's Columbine Review Commission Report. May 2001. http://www.state.co.us/columbine/.

Independence Institute. 2001. Columbine resources. http://i2i.org/suptdocs/crime/columbine.htm.

Kopel, David B. 2000. "What If We Had Taken Columbine Seriously?" *Weekly Standard* (April 24).

Lott, John R., Jr., and William Landes. 1999. "Multiple Victim Public Shootings, Bombings, and Right-to-Carry Concealed Handgun Laws." University of Chicago Law School, John M. Olin Law and Economics Working Paper no. 73 (April). http://papers.ssrn.com/sol3/papers.cfm?abstract_id=161637. Revised version in John R. Lott, Jr., *More Guns, Less Crime.* 2d ed. Chicago: University of Chicago Press, 2000.

National Center for Education Statistics. Statistics on school safety and zero tolerance. http://nces.ed.gov/.

SAFE Colorado. 2001. "Sane Alternatives to the Firearms Epidemic." http://www.safecolorado.com/.

Scott, Darrell. 2001. *Chain Reaction: A Call to Compassionate Revolution.* Nashville, TN: Thomas Nelson Publishers.

Scott, Darrell, et al. 2000. *Rachel's Tears: The Spiritual Journey of Columbine Martyr Rachel Scott.* Nashville, TN: Thomas Nelson Publishers.

Westword. 2001. "Columbine Extra." Collected Columbine stories. http://www.westword.com/columbine/index.html.

"Zero Tolerance = Zero Common Sense = Zero Justice." http://www.crossmyt.com/hc/zerotol/zero-tol.html.

Zoba, Wendy M. 2000. *Day of Reckoning: Columbine and the Search for America's Soul.* Grand Rapids, MI: Brazos Press.

Commonwealth v. Davis (1976)

The question before the Massachusetts appellate court in *Commonwealth v. Davis* was this: Did a Massachusetts law that forbade the possession of a shotgun with a barrel less than eighteen inches long violate protections guaranteed in the state's Declaration of Rights and in the Second Amendment to the U.S. Constitution? The Supreme Judicial Council of Massachusetts answered both these questions in the negative. The state statute, it decreed, conflicted neither with the Declaration of Rights nor the Constitution.

The shotgun had been discovered when police, having secured a warrant, searched the apartment of Hubert Davis and found firearms and ammunition, including a shotgun banned under state law. Davis's appeal cited Article 17 of the Massachusetts Declaration of Rights, which said: "The people have a right to keep and bear arms for the common defense. And as, in time of peace, armies are dangerous to liberty, they ought not be maintained without the consent of the legislature; and the military power shall always be held in an exact subordination to the civil authority, and be governed by it."

The court said that the historical record indicated that the Declaration was a product of colonists' distrust of standing armies and their preference that their protection be entrusted to a militia made up primarily of ordinary citizens. The Declaration was interpreted as giving only members of organized militia groups the absolute right to keep arms for the common defense. It did not guarantee individual weapon ownership or possession.

The judge included one qualification to the foregoing rule. Militiamen in earlier times, he pointed out, customarily furnished their own equipment and might have been under an obligation to do so. Had a law at that time, such as the article under which Davis was convicted, been reviewed, it likely would have been rejected as interfering with a militia duty. But "the situation no longer exists; our militia, of which the backbone is the National Guard, is now equipped and supported by public funds" (*Davis,* 1976, p. 888).

The opinion dismissed the objection raised on Second Amendment grounds with the observation that the amendment's guarantee was binding only on the federal government. The Massachusetts judge believed it unlikely that the provisions of the Second Amendment would ever be applied to the states, since they did not refer to individuals but rather to groups of persons. Even so, the judge noted, congressional bans on certain weapons involved in interstate commerce had been approved by the United States Supreme Court, and, even with a particularly broad reading of the Second Amendment, the states likely would retain the right to outlaw specified weapons within their own borders.

Gilbert Geis

See also *Cases v. United States;* Second Amendment; *United States v. Miller; United States v. Tot*
For Further Reading:
Commonwealth v. Hubert Davis. 1976. Supreme Judicial Court of Massachusetts, Suffolk. 343 N.E. 2d 847. http://www.abanet.org/gunviol/cases/commonwealth.html.

Concealed Weapons Laws

Concealed weapons laws are one of the most common forms of gun control regulation throughout the states. Adopted by most states in the early twentieth century as alternatives to a total ban of weapons, they were often backed by opponents of gun control such as the National Rifle Association.

They reemerged as an important part of the gun control debate in the 1980s and 1990s as gun control opponents organized to modify most of the laws to end the discretion of local police chiefs and sheriffs to require mandatory issuance of permits to those who meet certain requirements. Before 1987, only Georgia, Indiana, Maine, New Hampshire, North Dakota, South Dakota, Vermont, and Washington had "shall issue" laws requiring law enforcement officials or courts to issue firearm-carrying permits to the average citizen. In 1987, Florida enacted a "shall issue" right-to-carry law that eventually served as the framework for twenty-four other states that passed similar laws in the late 1980s and 1990s. At present, thirty-three states have such laws.

The most common requirements are demonstration of a minimum level of proficiency with a firearm (usually through completion of a training course or passing a test) and a criminal background check that reveals no felony convictions. Some states also include any convictions for domestic abuse or sex offense in the category of disqualifying events.

It is interesting that the opponents of gun control sparked the movement to change the laws they helped craft decades earlier. In some states,

such as Virginia, they responded to sentiment that some of the judges were improperly exercising their discretion in denying permits to qualified citizens. In many cases it was simply a preference to fight the legislative battles at the state level. State laws generally prohibit local jurisdictions from passing their own gun control measures (so-called preemption laws). This means that the interest groups involved in trying to influence policy can focus their attention on the state legislatures rather than concerning themselves with a much larger number of city councils.

In 2000, it seemed that the trend toward adoption of more liberal laws (ones that granted more permits) had stopped or at least slowed with the defeat of bills in several key states, including California. An exception was New Mexico, where a right-to-carry law was signed into law on April 3, 2001.

The debate over these laws hinges largely on whether one believes that they increase the safety of the carrier by giving her or him the opportunity to fend off would-be assailants and deter potential criminals because they know their intended victim might be armed, or whether one believes that they lead to an increase in the crime rate because more people own and carry guns. Researchers have found evidence that bolsters each argument, and the debate has yet to be settled, despite several academic studies and numerous sets of statistics from both sides (compare Lott and Mustard, 1997, and Lott, 1998, with Black and Nagin, 1998, and Dezhbakhsh and Rubin, 1998). Some academics even argue that the laws seem to have little impact on the crime rate. This dispute parallels that over the benefits of the defensive use of guns (as touted by Kleck, 1997) versus the actual costs to society of gun ownership (as decried by Cook and Ludwig, 2000, and Ludwig, 2000). This discussion is also conducted in the halls and on the floors of state legislatures throughout the country whenever such a bill comes before a legislature.

In general, as evidenced in Virginia, there is a brief spike in the number of individuals applying for a permit to carry a concealed weapon as soon as the more lenient laws are implemented, but this increase levels off after about a year.

Harry L. Wilson

See also Cook, Philip J.; Defensive Gun Use; Gun Control; Hemenway, David; Kleck, Gary; Lott, John R., Jr.; Preemption Laws; Right-to-Carry Laws; Self-Defense, Legal Issues; Self-Defense, Reasons for Gun Use; Substitution Effects

For Further Reading:

Black, Dan, and Daniel Nagin. 1998. "Do 'Right to Carry' Laws Deter Violent Crime?" *Journal of Legal Studies* 27: 209–219.

Cook, Philip J., and Jens Ludwig. 2000. *Gun Violence: The Real Costs.* Oxford and New York: Oxford University Press.

Dezhbakhsh, Hashem, and Paul Rubin. 1998. "Lives Saved or Lives Lost? The Effects of Concealed-Handgun Laws on Crime." *American Economic Review* 88, 2 (May): 468–474.

Kleck, Gary. 1997. *Targeting Guns: Firearms and Their Control.* Hawthorne, NY: Aldine de Gruyter.

Kleck, Gary, and Marc Gertz. 1995. "Armed Resistance to Crime: The Prevalence and Nature of Self-Defense with a Gun." *Journal of Criminal Law and Criminology* 86: 150–187.

Lott, John R. 1998. "The Concealed Handgun Debate." *Journal of Legal Studies* 27: 221–243.

Lott, John R., and David B. Mustard. 1997. "Crime, Deterrence, and Right-to-Carry Concealed Handguns." *Journal of Legal Studies* 26: 1–68.

Ludwig, Jens. 2000. "Gun Self-Defense and Deterrence." *Crime & Justice* 27: 363–381.

Vizzard, William J. 2000. *Shots in the Dark: The Policy, Politics, and Symbolism of Gun Control.* Lanham, MD: Rowman & Littlefield.

Wilson, Harry L., and Mark J. Rozell. 1998. "Virginia: The Politics of Concealed Weapons." Pp. 125–138 in *The Changing Politics of Gun Control*, ed. John M. Bruce and Clyde Wilcox. Lanham, MD: Rowman & Littlefield.

Congressional Voting Patterns on Gun Control

Members of the U.S. Congress demonstrate three predictable patterns of voting on gun control issues. First, regional voting differences are evident. Southern members of Congress are notably inclined to vote against gun regulation, whereas eastern members of Congress largely favor firearms regulation. Second, urban-rural differences are striking. Members of Congress representing rural constituents are much more likely to oppose gun control measures than are their colleagues who represent urban populations. Third, party cleavage is prominent. Particularly in recent years, gun control proposals typically find Democrats in support of firearms regulation and Republicans against it.

Regional Differences

Congressional decision making on gun control bills aligns closely with regional origins. This regional cleavage is most notable between the South and West and the rest of the country. Southern members of Congress are notably inclined to disfavor firearms regulation. This is not surprising, since, relative to the East, private ownership of guns is particularly high in the South. And although midwesterners and westerners have similar levels of gun ownership, the proportion of multiple gun owners is substantially higher in the West (and in the South) than in the Midwest and East.

Reviewing the voting patterns for the Brady Act of 1993 and the Assault Weapons Ban of 1994 illustrates these regional differences. The Brady Act of 1993 required a background check and waiting period for gun purchasers, and the Assault Weapons Ban of 1994 prohibited the manufacture and importation of certain semiautomatic weapons. Southern members of Congress were relatively unreceptive to these gun control measures. Only about 42 percent of the southern representatives and 46 percent of the southern members of the Senate voted in favor of the Brady Bill. Southern congressional support of the Assault Weapons Ban of 1994 was even more anemic. Only 34 percent of the southern representatives favored the bill, and a mere 31 percent of southern senators voted for its passage.

In sharp contrast to their southern colleagues, eastern members of Congress overwhelmingly supported these measures. A sizable 79 percent of eastern senators voted in favor of the Brady Bill as did approximately 75 percent of eastern representatives. Support for the Assault Weapons Ban was similarly robust. Seventy-five percent of eastern senators approved the bill, and 70 percent of eastern representatives gave it the nod.

Among western and midwestern legislators, patterns of support for the Brady and assault weapons bills fell mostly between the solid backing from eastern members of Congress and the relatively weak support from southern congresspersons. Midwestern and western representatives were strikingly close in their voting preferences. Fifty-six percent of both groups assented to the Brady Bill. Fifty-two percent of the western House members voted for the assault weapons bill, and a nearly identical 51 percent of the midwestern House members approved the measure. But midwestern and western senators were not so homogeneous in their voting—largely because of party differences. Midwestern senators staked their positions closer to their eastern comrades, whereas western senators aligned more closely to their southern colleagues. A hefty 87 percent of midwestern senators favored the Brady Bill while only 46 percent from the West did so. And in contrast to the 42 percent of western senators' votes, 78 percent of midwestern senators approved of the Assault Weapons Ban.

Urban-Rural Differences

Regional voting differences partly reflect urban-rural cleavages. Irrespective of regional and party differences, urban legislators are much more likely to favor gun control measures than are their rural counterparts. This urban-rural difference reflects distinct patterns of gun ownership. Studies consistently report that the incidence of gun ownership is highest in rural areas and lowest in cities. Many more guns are used for hunting and sporting purposes in rural areas than in cities, so rural citizens, not surprisingly, are much less amenable to gun regulation than are urbanites. Moreover, because cities tend to have high rates of violent crime compared to rural America, urban legislators strongly support gun control bills to try to keep guns out of the hands of criminals.

Examining the congressional votes on the Brady and Assault Weapons Ban bills reveals the urban-rural split over positions on gun control. Urban House members overwhelmingly supported both measures; rural representatives strongly opposed them. Nearly all urban House Democrats voted for the Brady and Assault Weapons Ban bills. And although urban House Republican support of the Brady and Assault Weapons Ban bills was far weaker (hovering just

below 50 percent) than that of urban House Democrats, it was nearly double that of the rural House Republicans. The urban-rural voting differences on these bills also existed when controlling for regions of the country, although it was strongest in the South and West.

Party Differences

Political party differences in gun control politics have increased markedly in recent years. In 1968, both the Republican and Democratic parties had platforms expressing some support for federal gun regulation. When the Gun Control Act of 1968 went to the floors of Congress for vote, overwhelming majorities of both parties in the House and Senate expressed their support for the bill. The little opposition to the bill that existed was similarly bipartisan, coming mainly from the South. By the 1990s, gun control had become a beacon to illuminate the difference between the Republican and Democratic parties. Gun control had become a polarizing issue in Congress, with Republicans predominantly opposing controls and Democrats favoring them.

Congressional voting patterns on the Brady and Assault Weapons Ban bills reflected this divide. House Democratic support for the bills exceeded House Republican support by margins of 42 and 48 percentage points, respectively. These sizable party differences remained across all regions. Although support for gun control in the South was lower than in other regions, the difference between the party's yes-vote percentages on these measures was still greater than 30 percentage points in both the House and Senate.

Keith Rollin Eakins

See also Assault Weapons Ban of 1994; Brady Handgun Violence Prevention Act; Democratic Party and Gun Control; Firearms Owners' Protection Act of 1986; Gun Control; Gun Control Act of 1968; Gun Ownership; Republican Party and Gun Control; United States Congress and Gun Legislation

For Further Reading:

Davidson, Osha Gray. 1993. *Under Fire: The NRA and the Battle for Gun Control.* New York: Henry Holt.

Jelen, Ted G. 1998. "The Electoral Politics of Gun Ownership." Pp. 224–246 in *The Changing Politics of Gun Control,* ed. John M. Bruce and Clyde Wilcox. Lanham, MD: Rowman & Littlefield.

Lambert, Diana. 1998. "Trying to Stop the Craziness of This Business: Gun Control Groups." Pp. 172–195 in *The Changing Politics of Gun Control,* ed. John M. Bruce and Clyde Wilcox. Lanham, MD: Rowman & Littlefield.

Langbein, Laura I. 1993. "PACs, Lobbies, and Political Conflict: The Case of Gun Control." *Public Choice* 77, 3: 551–572.

Patterson, Samuel C., and Keith R. Eakins. 1998. "Congress and Gun Control." Pp. 45–73 in *The Changing Politics of Gun Control,* ed. John M. Bruce and Clyde Wilcox. Lanham, MD: Rowman & Littlefield.

Spitzer, Robert J. 1995. *The Politics of Gun Control.* Chatham, NJ: Chatham House.

Conservatism and Gun Control

See Ideologies—Conservative and Liberal

Consumer Product Safety Laws

Consumer product safety policy aims to protect consumers from certain types of hazards. For firearms, product safety has been pursued by firearms industry standard setting; by tort lawsuit; by focused legislative statutes; and by administrative implementation of broad, general statutes.

Two controversies predominate: whether particular requirements that claim to promote safety actually do so, and whether administrators should have the power to ban guns without legislative consent. At the federal level, the Consumer Product Safety Commission is forbidden to regulate guns, precisely because of fears of indirect gun prohibition. In Massachusetts, the attorney general, claiming authority from a consumer fraud statute, has imposed a wide variety of gun restrictions.

The original consumer safety regulations for American firearms were the standards set for the firearms industry by the Sporting Arms and Ammunition Manufacturers Institute (SAAMI), an industry trade association. SAAMI was created in 1926, pursuant to a request from the federal government. SAAMI has created over 700 standards, which are updated every five years. SAAMI standards are examined and reviewed by the American National Standards Institute (ANSI) and by the National Institute of Standards and Technology.

Although SAAMI standards are not legally binding, manufacturers who wish to obtain government contracts must meet the standards, since the FBI, the U.S. military, and many state or local government agencies often require that procured firearms meet SAAMI specifications.

In American law, the most traditional form of consumer safety protection is the right of a consumer to bring a tort lawsuit against the manufacturer of a defective product. Consumer lawsuits against manufacturers of defective guns (e.g., the gun's barrel explodes, or the gun discharges when accidentally dropped) have helped improve the quality of firearms sold and driven many substandard guns off the market. In contrast to lawsuits brought against makers of properly functioning guns (e.g., lawsuits filed in 1998–1999 by big-city mayors), consumer lawsuits against genuinely defective guns are uncontroversial.

Legislatures may also choose to enact firearms laws designed to protect consumers (as opposed to firearm laws intended to prevent gun crime, the more common objective). For example, in 2000 Maryland enacted legislation requiring that all guns sold in the state beginning on January 1, 2003, be equipped with internal locking devices (Md. Ann. Code § 442c[d]).

The Maryland law is an example of consumer legislation that is premised on the idea that many consumers are incapable of judging their own best interests. Currently, some guns have internal locks and some do not. The Maryland law assumes that consumers who choose guns without locks are making a mistake.

Some states have enacted bans on so-called junk guns or Saturday night specials. The bans are often touted as protecting consumers from unreliable guns, although this claim is not entirely consistent with the fact that all the gun bans contain an exemption allowing police possession of the banned guns. If the banned guns really are unreliable and dangerous to the user, then it is difficult to see why anyone would want the police to have such guns.

Another proposal, not currently enacted in any state, would require that all guns (or all handguns, or all self-loading handguns) have a "loaded indicator." Lawsuits have been brought against manufacturers of guns without a loaded indicator, although none of the lawsuits so far have succeeded.

As the name suggests, a "loaded indicator" shows that a firearm is loaded. Advocates of mandatory loaded indicators, such as Jon S. Vernick and Stephen P. Teret of Johns Hopkins University, argue that loaded indicators would reduce accidents involving the handling of firearms that the user mistakenly thought was unloaded. The issue is particularly relevant for self-loading firearms that use detachable ammunition holders, or magazines. If the magazine is removed from the gun, the firearm can still hold one round of ammunition in the firing chamber—although the user might think that the gun was safe because the magazine was removed.

Opponents of the Teret/Vernick proposal argue that mandatory loaded indicators would actually increase gun accidents. The critics argue that reliance on loaded indicators is contrary to the first rule of gun safety: "Treat every gun as if it's loaded." Relying on loaded indicators might also encourage people to violate the second and third rules: "Always point the gun in a safe direction" and "Keep your finger off the trigger until you are ready to shoot." If people believe that some mechanical device has rendered a gun harmless, they may be more careless about following the safety rules, and more accidents would result.

Critics also point out that even if loaded indicators became mandatory immediately, most firearms in the existing American supply of approximately 250 million guns would not have them. A person who got used to relying on a loaded indicator on a new gun might presume that all guns have such devices, and then presume that an older gun was unloaded simply because there was no loaded indicator visible.

Similar debates exist for almost all the "consumer safety" proposals offered by gun control advocates. The controversy over "smart gun" mandates involves a debate between those who believe that new technologies will reduce gun accidents and those who believe that the technologies will make guns less reliable for protection.

Even more controversial than the substance of "consumer safety" controls is how they should be created. At the national level, Congress has granted the Consumer Product Safety Commission (CPSC) broad powers to impose standards, recall consumer products, or ban them. The three CPSC commissioners are appointed by the president and assisted by a professional staff.

If the CPSC decides that there is no feasible standard by which a product can be made safe (meaning that in the CPSC's view the benefits of the product exceed the risks), then the CPSC may ban the product. For example, in 1990 the CPSC banned the sale of lawn darts.

Rather than outlawing the sale of an entire category of product, the CPSC may instead choose to order the recall of certain versions of a product. Often, a manufacturer will voluntarily recall a product and provide replacements rather than force the CPSC to issue a formal order. For example, in July 2000 the Master Lock company recalled 752,000 gun locks after the CPSC determined that the locks were too easy to defeat. (No accidents had been reported involving the locks; see http://www.cpsc.gov/cpscpub/prerel/prhtml00/00149.html.)

The CPSC's jurisdiction covers "consumer products." The statutory definition of consumer products specifically excludes a wide variety of items, including food, drugs, cosmetics, medical devices, tobacco products, motor vehicles, pesticides, aircraft, boats, and fixed-site amusement rides. Also excluded are firearms and ammunition (15 U.S.C. § 2052[a][1][E] and 2080[d] and [e]).

It is sometimes said that there are numerous consumer safety regulations for teddy bears and toy guns but no such regulations for real guns. Within the ambit of CPSC regulations this is true, although it would be just as accurate to say that there are no consumer safety regulations for food or automobiles. But once one looks beyond CPSC regulations, one finds that food is extensively regulated by the Department of Agriculture, that automobiles are extensively regulated by the National Highway Traffic

Safety Administration, and that firearms are extensively regulated by the Bureau of Alcohol, Tobacco, and Firearms (which has promulgated over 150 pages of small-type regulations about firearms manufacture, sale, and possession).

Putting aside administrative regulations, federal legislative statutes impose more restrictions on the sale of firearms than on any other common consumer product, except for prescription drugs. Manufacturing, wholesaling, or retailing of a firearm requires a federal license. For a retail sale to be consummated, the retailer must obtain permission from the FBI via the National Instant Check System. No other consumer product requires federal government approval for every single retail transaction.

While the CPSC has the authority to ban the sale or manufacture of products, the BATF cannot ban the sale or manufacture of firearms (although the BATF can ban some kinds of imports and has the power in a few special categories to classify firearms or ammunition in ways that amount to de facto bans). Congress, of course, can and does ban guns, as with the federal assault weapons prohibition. Some states have enacted their own assault weapons bans, and some have also banned small, inexpensive guns (i.e., Saturday night specials). A few cities, including Chicago and Washington, D.C., have banned handguns.

But the nub of the controversy is that it is extremely difficult to pass gun bans, even in states that are generally favorable to gun control, such as New Jersey and Illinois. Thus, the Violence Policy Center (VPC) argues that the Bureau of Alcohol, Tobacco, and Firearms should be given the authority to ban guns administratively whenever the BATF decides that the guns are too dangerous for consumers to have. The VPC believes that the BATF ought to ban all handguns and most self-loading (i.e., semiautomatic) rifles and shotguns.

Alternatively, Sen. Howard Metzenbaum (D-OH), the leading gun control advocate in Congress during the 1980s and early 1990s, proposed that the Consumer Product Safety Commission be given authority over firearms, thereby allowing the CPSC to ban whatever guns it chooses.

Besides making the usual arguments against gun control, opponents of administrative bans argue that prohibition of some or all guns is an important policy issue that ought to be decided by elected officials after full and open debate and public input—rather than decided by three unelected members of an administrative agency.

Critics also argue that Article 1 of the United States Constitution states that "all legislative powers herein granted" are granted to the Congress, and therefore Congress cannot delegate law-making power to executive branch agencies such as the CPSC or BATF. Since the New Deal, however, courts have been very permissive in allowing Congress to delegate power. (For an argument that delegating too much law-making power to administrative agencies allows Congress to dodge tough decisions, see Schoenbrod, 1993.)

In 1997, the Massachusetts attorney general imposed sweeping gun controls based on a statute against "unfair or deceptive trade practice." The attorney general claimed that it was unfair or deceptive to sell handguns that (1) did not have tamper-resistant serial numbers, (2) did not meet standards that the attorney general created for durability and for being dropped on hard surfaces, (3) did not have the types of locks that the attorney general thought best, (4) did not have heavy trigger pulls that would make the guns impossible for an average 5-year-old child to fire, and (5) had a barrel less than three inches long. For the last requirement, the manufacturer could sell short-barreled guns as long as certain disclosures about accuracy were made. (See 940 Code Mass. Regs. §§ 16.00 et seq.)

The American Shooting Sports Council (a trade association, which later merged with the National Shooting Sports Foundation) filed suit, claiming that the Massachusetts law against "unfair and deceptive trade practice" did not give the attorney general the authority to invent a detailed code of gun manufacture. The lawsuit also argued that particular details of the attorney general's regulations were illogical, nearly impossible to meet, or counterproductive. The attorney general lost in the trial court but won in the Massachusetts Supreme Court (*American Shooting Sports Council, Inc. v. Attorney General,*

711 N.E.2d 899 Mass. 1999). The Massachusetts legislature mooted the issue by enacting a law granting the attorney general the power to create the regulations he had created.

When the regulations initially went into effect in Massachusetts, the result was to bar the sale of all handguns except those made by Smith & Wesson, which is based in Springfield, Massachusetts.

After the 2000 election of George Bush reduced the prospects for broad new federal gun controls, the Center to Prevent Handgun Violence (which later changed its name to the Brady Campaign to Prevent Gun Violence) urged state attorneys general to follow the lead of the Massachusetts attorney general. The CPHV suggested that twenty states had consumer protection laws that could be used to impose gun controls.

Another consumer-related issue bears not only on firearms themselves but on their advertising. In 1996, the Center to Prevent Handgun Violence filed a petition (consisting of a request letter and supporting documentation) with the Federal Trade Commission (FTC) asking the FTC to ban gun advertising that encourages defensive gun ownership. A similar petition was filed by Professors Teret and Vernick in conjunction with Dr. Garen Wintemute of the University of California. The CPHV petition asked that defensive gun ads be banned as "deceptive" because gun ownership does not increase safety in the home but in fact is very dangerous.

Under current FTC policy, an advertisement is "unfair" if it causes "substantial injury to consumers which is not reasonably avoidable by consumers themselves and not outweighed by countervailing benefits to consumers or to competition." The CPHV argued that the defensive gun advertisements are unfair because they encourage people to own guns for protection. Gun ownership leads to injuries and deaths, the CPHV pointed out. There are no countervailing benefits, the organization argued, since defensive gun use is very rare.

Opponents of the advertising ban argued that defensive gun ownership does increase safety among lawful gun owners; that harm from guns is "reasonably avoidable by consumers themselves" because consumers can obey gun safety rules and laws against committing gun crimes; and that the FTC should not censor speech on a controversial policy topic. As of mid-2002, the FTC had not ruled.

David B. Kopel

See also Bureau of Alcohol, Tobacco, and Firearms; Lawsuits against Gun Manufacturers; Saturday Night Specials; Smart Guns; Sporting Arms and Ammunition Manufacturers' Institute

For Further Reading:

Bejar, Benjamin. 1998. "Wielding the Consumer Protection Shield: Sensible Handgun Regulation in Massachusetts: A Paradigm for a National Model." *Boston University Public Interest Law Journal* 7: 59–91; http://www.saf.org/LawReviews/Bejar1.html.

Center to Prevent Handgun Violence. Material on firearm advertising. http://www.gunlawsuits.org/reform/advertising.asp.

Dobray, Debra, and Arthur J. Waldrop. 1991. "Regulating Handgun Advertising Aimed at Women." *Whittier Law Review* 12: 113–129; http://www.saf.org/LawReviews/DobrayAndWaldrop1.htm.

Johns Hopkins Center for Gun Policy and Research, School of Public Health. 624 N. Broadway, Baltimore, MD 21205, (410) 955-3995; http://support.jhsph.edu/departments/gunpolicy/default.cfm.

Kopel, David B. 2000. "Treating Guns like Consumer Products." *University of Pennsylvania Law Review* 148: 1213–1246.

Sporting Arms and Ammunition Manufacturers Institute: http://www.saami.org/.

Vernick, Jon S., and Stephen P. Teret. 2000. "Public Health Approach to Regulating Firearms as Consumer Products." *University of Pennsylvania Law Review* 148: 1193–1212.

Conyers, John (1929–)

John Conyers (D-MI) has served in the House of Representatives since 1965. He is the ranking member of the House Judiciary Committee and the second most senior member of the House. Conyers has emerged as one of the leading advocates of gun control in the House. He helped found the Congressional Black Caucus and is generally considered to be dean of the group.

After a four-year stint in the army in Korea in the early 1950s, Conyers received a law degree in 1958. He served for three years as legislative assistant to John Dingell and was active in civil rights and labor groups before he won a seat in

John Conyers. (U.S. House of Representatives)

guns out of the hands of juveniles, especially those with criminal records. He also introduced the Gun Safety Act, a companion to the Schumer-Boxer Senate bill, which would have introduced more stringent safety regulations for domestic handguns and required trigger locks. In the early days of the George W. Bush administration, Conyers was vocal in his criticism of proposals by Attorney General John Ashcroft that would shorten the retention of background check records in the Brady Bill.

Should the Democrats recapture control of the House of Representatives, Conyers would assume the chairmanship of the Judiciary Committee. Legislation relating to gun control is assigned to the Judiciary Committee, so Conyers would be in a strong position to articulate his views and bring legislation to the floor of the chamber.

Clyde Wilcox and Benjamin Webster

See also Boxer, Barbara; Democratic Party and Gun Control; Schumer, Charles E.
For Further Reading:
Barone, Michael, and Grant Ujifusa. 1999. *The Almanac of American Politics, 2000.* Washington, DC: National Journal.
John Conyers's home page: http://www.house.gov/conyers/.

the House as part of the Democratic landslide of 1964, representing northern Detroit. Conyers was one of only a handful of African Americans in Congress in the 1960s, and was a vocal opponent of the Vietnam War and a supporter of a guaranteed income and racial reparations. He has one of the most liberal voting records in Congress—often receiving ratings of 100 from the liberal political organization Americans for Democratic Action and 0 from the American Conservative Union. Conyers's greatest visibility came during the Judiciary Committee hearings on the impeachment of President Bill Clinton. As ranking minority member of the committee, Conyers presented the Democratic arguments clearly and with a subtle sense of humor.

Conyers has been active in the area of criminal justice. He introduced the Hate Crimes Act, the Violence Against Women Act, the Public Safety Officers Benefits Act (which doubled survivor benefits to families of police officers killed in action), and legislation barring the use of racial profiling.

Conyers has been an active advocate of gun control. He cosponsored an amendment to a juvenile justice bill in 1997 that sought to keep

Cook, Philip J. (1946–)

Philip J. Cook, one of the leading public policy researchers in the United States, has made major contributions to research on gun violence and policy. He is the ITT/Sanford Distinguished Professor of Public Policy at the Terry Sanford Institute of Public Policy at Duke University. He is also a professor of economics and sociology at Duke and a research associate of the National Bureau of Economic Research.

Born in Buffalo, New York, Cook received his B.A. from the University of Michigan and his Ph.D. in economics from the University of California, Berkeley, in 1973. Cook went to Duke as an assistant professor of economics in 1973 and has been there ever since. His research has focused on the regulation of unhealthy and unsafe behavior. In addition to his work on the costs and consequences of gun availability, he has carried out studies on numerous other policy issues,

Philip J. Cook. (courtesy of author)

ried out the National Survey of Private Ownership of Firearms (NSPOF), the most comprehensive overview of gun inventory and gun ownership in the country. The survey generated numerous important findings related to the size, composition, and ownership of the nation's gun inventory; the methods of and reasons for firearm acquisition; the storage and carrying of guns; and DGUs (Cook and Ludwig, 1997).

In 1995, Cook chaired a symposium sponsored by the Guggenheim Foundation on youth violence. The symposium focused on the role of guns in homicides, especially among young inner-city men. The Duke University School of Law journal *Law and Contemporary Problems* published the papers from the conference in 1996 under the title *Kids, Guns, and Public Policy.* Cook edited the issue and emphasized that although homicide rates in general had been falling, those for youths had greatly increased and all of that increase had been due to guns.

Cook's research on the effects of gun availability on robberies and murders committed during robberies helps us understand the "instrumentality effect." This effect suggests that the instrument used in a crime influences whether the crime is lethal. Cook's research on robbery showed that robbers who chose to use firearms in committing their crime did so in order to ensure control and compliance on the part of their victims. When robbers used guns there was less likely to be a physical attack, but if there was a physical attack the victims were more likely to be killed. In fact, "the case-fatality rate for gun robbery is three times as high as for robberies with knives and ten times as high for robberies with other weapons" (Cook and Ludwig, 2001, p. 35).

Cook also studied the fifty largest cities in the United States to find out whether gun availability influences crime. He found that in cities with low gun ownership rates, the percentage of homicides and suicides involving guns is low. In cities with many guns, robbers are more likely to use guns in their crimes and the robberies are more likely to be lethal than in cities with fewer guns (Cook, 1979).

Cook has also made important contributions to the discussion of DGUs, taking issue with

including alcohol-related problems, state lotteries, sources of inequality in earnings, and the costs of the death penalty. Cook has written widely on guns and gun violence, and his work has focused on some of the most important and controversial issues in the gun control debate. His research includes studies on the effects of gun availability on violence, instrumentality effects, gun markets, defensive uses of handguns against criminal attacks (DGUs), the tracing of guns used in crimes, and the real costs of gun violence.

Cook has received numerous academic honors, fellowships, and grants, including grants to investigate major issues in firearm policy. For example, in 1979–1980 the Center for the Study and Prevention of Handgun Violence funded his study of the causal linkages between gun control ordinances and crime. In 1993–1994, the Harry Frank Guggenheim Foundation supported his study of stolen-gun markets. In 1994, the National Institute of Justice provided a grant to the Police Foundation for a study of guns in the United States. Cook and Jens Ludwig car-

Kleck and Gertz's estimate of 2.5 million DGUs annually (Kleck, 1997; Kleck and Gertz, 1995). Kleck and Gertz argue that there are more DGUs than crimes committed with handguns. If true, this might weaken arguments for gun control, although Cook points out that, aside from the dispute over the numbers, it is not clear that all these DGUs add to public safety. Cook and his colleagues refer to the estimate of 2.5 million DGUs as "the gun debate's new mythical number" (Cook, Ludwig, and Hemenway, 1997). The National Crime Victimization Survey (NCVS) generates an estimate of about 100,000 DGUs a year. Cook and his colleagues suggest that the higher estimate is at least partly due to the likelihood of having many more "false positives"—those who did not use a gun for self-defense during the period studied but say that they did—than "false negatives"—those who did use a gun for self-defense but did not report it (Cook and Ludwig, 2001; Cook, Ludwig, and Hemenway, 1997; Hemenway, 1997).

Cook and Ludwig's own National Survey of Private Ownership of Firearms (NSPOF) generates an estimate of about 1.5 million DGUs. Cook and Ludwig suggest that this figure is an overestimate and that accurate estimates of DGUs are unlikely to emerge from such large sample surveys because of the likelihood of false positives outweighing false negatives. Progun groups have gleefully seized on Cook and Ludwig's suggestion that their own survey overestimated DGUs and suggested that the results prove Kleck and Gertz's estimate. In fact, Cook and Ludwig exercise sound methodological judgment in reaching their cautious conclusions.

Sociologist Tom Smith (1997) has urged a "truce in the DGU war," arguing that the Kleck and Gertz estimate of 2.5 million DGUs annually is too high and that the NCVS estimate of about 100,000 DGUs is too low. He suggests a possible figure of 1,210,000 DGUs per year. Smith argues that the debate would benefit from more data and less speculation.

In a major contribution to thinking about gun policy, Cook and Ludwig have estimated the net costs of gun violence in the United States (Cook and Ludwig, 2001). Rather than focusing only on the costs of handgun violence in terms of the medical costs and lost productivity associated with gun injuries and deaths, Cook and Ludwig develop an economic-cost framework to calculate the *full* or *real* costs of handgun violence. Their goal is "to document how gun violence reduces the quality of life for everyone in America" (Cook and Ludwig, 2001, p. viii), and they estimate that gun violence costs about $100 billion. They derive most of this estimate, which is much higher than most such figures, from a "contingent-valuation" survey. The National Opinion Research Center (NORC) of the University of Chicago asked the questions in its 1998 General Social Survey (GSS). The survey asked respondents what they would pay to reduce gun crime in their communities. Extrapolating from those figures, Cook and Ludwig reached an estimated cost of $80 billion a year, to which they added additional costs to arrive at the $100 billion figure. This research broadens the debate over gun violence and gun control by emphasizing that all Americans are potential victims of gun violence.

Walter F. Carroll

See also Acquisition of Guns; Availability of Guns, Effects on Crime; Black Market for Firearms; Crime and Gun Use; Defensive Gun Use; General Social Survey; Guggenheim Foundation, Harry Frank; Gun Ownership; Gun Violence; Gun Violence as a Public Health Problem; Kleck, Gary; Lethality Effect of Guns; National Institute of Justice; Weapons Instrumentality Effect; Zimring, Franklin

For Further Reading:
Bijlefeld, Marolijn. 1999. "Philip J. Cook." Pp. 64–68 in *People for and against Gun Control: A Biographical Reference.* Westport, CT: Greenwood Press.
Cook, Philip J. 1979. "The Effect of Gun Availability on Robbery and Robbery Murder: A Cross-Section Study of Fifty Cities." *Policy Studies Review Annual* 3: 743–781.
Cook, Philip J., and Jens Ludwig. 1997. *Guns in America: National Survey on Private Ownership and Use of Firearms.* Research in Brief. Washington, DC: Department of Justice, National Institute of Justice (May).
———. 2000. *Gun Violence: The Real Costs.* New York: Oxford University Press.
Cook, Philip J., Jens Ludwig, and David Hemenway. 1997. "The Gun Debate's New Mythical Number: How Many Defensive Gun Uses Per Year?"

Journal of Policy Analysis and Management 16: 463–469.

Cook, Philip J., Mark H. Moore, and Anthony A. Braga. 2002. "Gun Control." Pp. 291–330 in *Crime: Public Policies for Crime Control*, 2d ed., ed. James Q. Wilson and Joan Petersilia. San Francisco: ICS Press.

Kleck, Gary. 1997. *Targeting Guns: Firearms and Their Control*. New York: Aldine de Gruyter.

Kleck, Gary, and Marc Gertz. 1995. "Armed Resistance to Crime: The Prevalence and Nature of Self-Defense with a Gun." *Journal of Criminal Law and Criminology* 86: 150–187.

Smith, Tom. 1997. "A Call for a Truce in the DGU War." *Journal of Criminal Law and Criminology* 87: 1462–1469.

Corporation for the Promotion of Rifle Practice and Firearms Safety

See National Board for the Promotion of Rifle Practice

Cowboy Action Shooting (CAS)

Participants in Cowboy Action Shooting wear costumes inspired by the Old West and shoot replica or vintage firearms in events organized according to a specific set of rules established by the Single Action Shooting Society (SASS). Similar to tactical shooting exercises on the one hand and historical reenactments on the other, CAS imitates real-life shooting situations and aims for historical accuracy. However, unlike most other simulations, Cowboy Action shooters use live ammunition—heavy loads and lots of them—in their shooting events. CAS is a combination of both competitive and recreational shooting. By the close of the twentieth century, it had become the fastest growing outdoor shooting sport in the United States, popular among both men and women.

Participants in CAS span all walks of life and income levels. What brings them together is a common interest in the history and traditions of the American West: what SASS refers to as "The Spirit of the Game." They wear accurate reproductions of Old West attire in fabrics available in the nineteenth century (no synthetics or vinyl) and authentic styles (most women eschew pants for skirts and bustles). Some wear vintage

Ricky Nelson and John Wayne as archetypal cowboy shooters in the 1959 Howard Hawks movie Rio Bravo. *(Corbis/Sygma)*

clothes and shoot antique guns. Most of the guns used, however, are replicas of firearms produced before 1900: single-action revolvers, black-powder or lever-action rifles, and pump or lever-action shotguns. The only concession to modernity is that all shooters must wear eye and ear protection.

Shooters are required to adopt aliases, some of which recall heroic western figures or types (Judge Roy Bean, Wyatt Earp, Bounty Hunter), while others are clever plays on frontier themes (Aimless Annie, Buck Roo, Chili King), and still others on participants' real-life identities (a biochemist named "Lady Doc," an attorney named "Lilly Lawless"). They get together for shooting matches in which the various tests of skill conform to scenarios based on famous incidents of western history or in classic western films (stage coach robberies, saloon shoot-outs, shooting from horseback—the horse generally, in this case, being a mechanical breed), pitting shooters against wooden or steel targets. Prizes are awarded in different shooting classes, as well as for the best costumes; in order to qualify for the costume competition, one must be an active shooter.

The Single Action Shooting Society is the largest association of CAS shooters, with a membership that approached 40,000 in 2001 and more than 350 local affiliates nationwide. Club presidents are called territorial governors, and clubs bear names like the Alamo Moderators, the Hole in the Wall Gang, and Doc Holliday's Immortals. At shooting matches, groups of contestants are organized into posses. Major CAS shooting events have evocative names like Helldorado, Range War, and Mule Camp. The world championship CAS event is End of Trail, held annually in April in southern California.

Mary Zeiss Stange

Larry E. Craig. (U.S. Senate)

For Further Reading:

Anderson, Hunter Scott. 2000. *The Top Shooter's Guide to Cowboy Action Shooting.* Iola, WI: Krause Publications.

Laws, Susan. 2000. *Cowgirl Action Shooting.* Wimberly, TX: Aimless Annie Enterprises.

Taffin, John. 1999. *Action Shooting: Cowboy Style.* Iola, WI: Krause Publications.

Cowtowns and Gun Violence

See Boomtowns, Cowtowns, and Gun Violence

Craig, Larry E. (1945–)

Larry Craig, a Republican senator from Idaho, has been a leading advocate for gun rights during his years in the House of Representatives and Senate. A member of the National Rifle Association Board of Directors since 1983, Craig firmly believes that most gun control measures are unconstitutional limits on a citizen's right to bear arms and that they aid criminals by denying citizens the ability to defend themselves. Craig's most important legislative initiative on gun issues was an amendment to the 1999 Juvenile Justice Bill. The amendment, which would have established a system for conducting background checks on purchasers at gun shows, was initially passed by the Senate, but later was replaced by a tougher, Democratically supported amendment.

Craig was born, raised, and educated in Idaho. After working as a rancher, Craig entered politics at the age of 29. He served in the Idaho Senate for six years before being elected to the U.S. House of Representatives in 1981. After five terms in the House, Craig ran for the Senate in 1990. He won the election quite easily and was reelected with no major difficulty. He has been particularly active on the Appropriations and Energy Committees and joined the party leadership in 1996 by becoming chairman of the Republican Policy Committee. He also serves on the Congressional Advisory Board of the Second Amendment Foundation and on the Congressional Sportsman's Caucus.

Throughout his time in Congress, Craig has established a conservative voting record. He often receives close to perfect voting scores from conservative groups and has close to 100 percent party unity scores. He was a major figure in efforts to pass a balanced budget constitutional amendment. While serving on the Energy Committee, he has repeatedly sought to establish a permanent nuclear waste repository. He has also been very active on land use and environmental issues; Craig has strongly opposed the Forest Service's handling of land issues and has sought to cut their budget, reduce the number of agents, and deny them permission to carry weapons.

Craig strongly supports gun ownership by hunters and sportsmen and broadly supports the right of citizens to bear arms. Craig argues that the Second Amendment to the Constitution unambiguously gives private citizens the right to own guns and be free of government regulation. Furthermore, he argues that gun ownership is a part of the inalienable right to self-defense. Thus, any effort to restrict that right calls the democratic system of the United States into question by allowing excessive government power. He has repeatedly spoken on the Senate floor to explain his interpretation of protections afforded by the Bill of Rights.

Craig also opposes many gun control laws because he feels criminals will never abide by restrictions like registration. Instead, he believes that these laws only complicate the lives of law-abiding citizens and make them less likely to be prepared in case they are attacked. Craig argues that statistics showing the number of crimes committed with guns and the number of people killed by guns hide the fact that many more people may be preventing crimes or killings by using their guns to deter crime. He has called for citizens around the country to write to him with stories of how they used weapons to stop or prevent crimes.

Craig has voted against most major gun control legislation. In 1999, he drew attention by submitting an amendment to the Juvenile Justice Bill. The amendment would have allowed, but not required, private gun sellers at gun shows to conduct background checks on purchasers. The amendment would also have granted immunity from future civil prosecution to any dealer who conducted a check, and called for the immediate destruction of most sensitive information found during the check. The amendment was passed 53–45 on May 12, 1999, only one month after the Columbine shootings. However, in the following days, sharp criticism was voiced by Democratic leaders, gun control advocates, and even many Republicans who felt that the measure should require checks. The Senate therefore reversed itself and supported a tougher, Democratically supported amendment. Ultimately, the House rejected the Senate's language on gun shows and other issues and no final bill was ever passed.

John W. Dietrich

See also Congressional Voting Patterns on Gun Control; Defensive Gun Use; National Rifle Association; Second Amendment; United States Congress and Gun Legislation; Youth Gun Control Legislation, The Juvenile Justice Bill of 1999

For Further Reading:
Craig, Larry E. 2002. "Policy Statements: The Second Amendment." http://www.senate.gov/~craig/frontpage.htm.

Crime and Gun Availability
See Availability of Guns, Effects on Crime

Crime and Gun Use
Throughout its history, the United States has had a relatively high rate of violent crime compared with other nations of equivalent economic and political development. During the early years of the country, the inexpensiveness and widespread availability of guns were major contributing factors to crime. In addition, disadvantaged groups in society traditionally had limited access to firearms and were therefore more often the victims of violent crime and intimidation. Gun use as a factor in committing crimes peaked in the 1980s and has steadily declined since then.

During the early era of colonization in North America, effective law enforcement was rare. Along the frontier regions of the nation, guns were used to commit a variety of crimes ranging from murder to theft. Law enforcement was the responsibility of local sheriffs recruited from the community. If there were large bands of bandits, the militia would be called out. The result of all this was that law enforcement was reactive, though if criminals were caught, justice was often severe, with what would be considered harsh penalties by today's standards.

This pattern of crime and gun use continued as the frontier moved west. The massive influx of people into California in the wake of the discovery of gold in 1849 led to a dramatic rise in crime as people fought over claims to land. Strikingly, the homicide rate in the region tripled between 1849 and 1850. In the aftermath of the Civil War there was a corresponding rise in crime and gun use in the West as renewed waves of settlers moved westward, many carrying the firearms that they had used during the war between the states. The influx of well-armed people and the lack of effective law enforcement in areas of the West caused increases in a variety of crimes and ushered in the era of the gunfight. There were several bands of well-organized and armed bandits that robbed trains and banks. Many of these groups, including the James Gang, were comprised of veterans of the Civil War who had served in irregular guerilla units such as Quantrill's Raiders. Meanwhile, the gunfight became a relatively common means for men to settle disputes, though the practice was not as widespread as popular fiction would later portray it to be.

The closing of the frontier in the 1890s and the subsequent increase in both the scale and scope of law enforcement brought a decline in gun-related crimes in the West. However, large-scale immigration in the East and the extreme poverty faced by many immigrants drove crime rates higher in the East, although gun use was not as widespread as it had been in the West. In addition, the municipal police forces of the urban areas of the East were more efficient than their counterparts in the South and West.

The establishment of Prohibition in 1920 with the ratification of the Twenty-third Amendment led to the outbreak of another era of serious crime. Organized crime gangs came to dominate the procurement and illegal sale of alcohol. The spread of speakeasies (illegal bars that served alcohol) brought enormous profits to organized crime and facilitated its spread. Mobsters such as Al Capone built immense empires (Capone's organization brought in an estimated $60 million per year). The rise of the Mafia led to bitter and often bloody turf wars over control of territory and markets. During the 1920s, in Chicago alone there were 500 Mafia-related murders. Crimes such as racketeering and extortion also

rose. In the aftermath of World War I, many former servicemen had experience with automatic weapons. The introduction of such firearms as the Thompson submachine gun and automatic handguns, including the .45 caliber Colt Model 1911A, greatly exacerbated the level and proliferation of violence.

Other factors also influenced crime and gun use during the 1920s and 1930s. The proliferation of automobiles increased the mobility of criminals. The onset of the Great Depression in 1929 added vast numbers of Americans to the unemployment rolls. By 1930 there were some 3 million Americans out of work. With bank and business failures, the number of homeless people increased dramatically. Petty theft, mainly of food and other sundries, grew more common, as did more serious crime, especially bank robberies. The widespread poverty and despair provoked a backlash against disadvantaged groups in the United States, including recent immigrants and African Americans. Throughout the nation, hate groups such as the Ku Klux Klan grew dramatically during the late 1920s and the 1930s. In addition, the number of hate crimes, including lynchings, tripled. In the South, lynchings became an all-too-frequent occurrence as well-armed gangs terrorized African Americans. During the 1920s and 1930s the nation's homicide rate rose to a level that would not be seen again until the 1980s.

The advent of World War II led to a drop in violent crime, and the prosperity of the 1950s served to continue this trend. However, racial violence continued throughout the South as the civil rights movement gained momentum and white supremacists sought to intimidate the pro-integrationists. Crime rates in the United States increased in the early 1960s, for despite the affluence of the period a significant proportion of the population lived below the poverty line. The 1960 census showed that 25 percent of the nation, or about 40 million Americans, were poor.

As the nation's social fabric began to come apart because of the shocks of Vietnam, drug use increased, the counterculture grew, and crime rose dramatically. This last trend was exacerbated by the influx of relatively inexpensive handguns known as Saturday night specials. Violent race riots in major cities such as Detroit, Los Angeles, and Newark left scores dead and hundreds injured from gunshots. In the South, political violence related to the civil rights movement continued, while the assassinations of John F. Kennedy in 1963, Martin Luther King, Jr., in 1968, and Robert F. Kennedy in 1968 brought gun violence to the forefront of the public's attention. Meanwhile, groups from both the political left and right began to engage in antigovernment activities, including bombings of public buildings and bank robberies. The rise in gun crime led Congress to enact the nation's first federal firearm control law in over three decades, the Gun Control Act of 1968.

Throughout the 1970s crime continued to increase as drug use expanded, especially in urban areas. Furthermore, there were turf wars between organized crime organizations and a rise in gang-related violence. The introduction of a powerful new form of cocaine, known as crack, accelerated the violence as gangs fought each other for control of the market. Many police forces were unprepared to deal with the violence and increased gun use that was engendered by the spread of crack. Between 1985 and 1991 homicides among African American males under the age of 20 doubled, while overall homicide rates involving the use of a gun climbed by 71 percent. Between 1960 and 2000, 1 million Americans died from firearms (including in homicides, suicides, and accidental shootings). The rise in gun violence corresponded with the dramatic increase in guns. By 2000 Americans owned an estimated 200 million guns. This figure included an estimated 40 million handguns that had been produced since 1973. The guns used in crimes came from a variety of sources, but the majority were purchased legally. According to a 1991 survey by the Justice Department, 10 percent of guns used in crimes were stolen while 28 percent were bought or acquired illegally (the remainder were purchased through legitimate sources).

The rates of gun use in nonfatal crimes, such as theft, sexual assault, and aggravated assault, also increased dramatically during the late 1980s. About one-third of these crimes were committed by perpetrators using firearms. In comparison, approximately 70 percent of homicides were committed with firearms. Handguns were the weapons of choice because they were easy to conceal and relatively inexpensive. Handguns accounted for 86 percent of all gun-related crimes (3 percent were perpetrated with rifles, 5 percent with shotguns, and 5 percent with undetermined types of firearms). In 1992, a record 931,000 crimes were committed with handguns.

After the surge in gun violence during the late 1980s, gun crime began to decline significantly in the 1990s. Between 1993 and 2000, crimes perpetrated with firearms declined by almost 40 percent. This drop was the result of a variety of factors. First, tougher sentencing laws were enacted by a number of states and the federal government. These new measures expanded the length of prison time for those convicted of violent crime. By 2000, the nation's prison population had expanded to 1.3 million people, four times the number of inmates in 1980. Second, new legislation made it more difficult to obtain guns. The Brady Handgun Violence Prevention Act, which went into effect in 1994, placed limitations on people's access to guns. The law required background checks and waiting periods before handguns could be purchased. In addition, the 1994 Violent Crime Enforcement Act made the possession of semiautomatic assault weapons manufactured after the act illegal. Third, the maturation of the crack cocaine market and the growing popularity of other illicit drugs caused a decrease in the gun violence related to the sale and importation of illicit drugs. Fourth, new methods of policing have improved the efficiency of law enforcement. Programs such as community policing have improved relations between law enforcement and the communities it serves while buyback programs have had minor success in reducing the number of weapons available. Fifth, the economic expansion of the 1990s brought more people into the workforce and like other periods of economic expansion led to a general decrease in the crime rate. While the 1990s witnessed a general decline in gun crime, this decline was not uniform. Specific segments of the nation continued to experience high rates of gun violence. This was especially true of African American and Hispanic males under the age of 20.

Tom Lansford

See also African Americans and Gun Violence; Availability of Guns, Effects on Crime; Black Market for Firearms; Brady Handgun Violence Prevention Act; Concealed Weapons Laws; Drive-by Shootings; Drugs, Crime, and Guns, United States; Federal Firearms Act of 1938; Felons and Gun Control; Frontier Violence; Gun Buyback Programs; Gun Violence; National Firearms Act of 1934;

For Further Reading:

Carter, Gregg Lee. 1997. *The Gun Control Movement.* New York: Twayne Publishers.

Cook, Phillip J., and Jens Ludwig. 2000. *Gun Violence: The Real Costs.* New York: Oxford University Press.

DeConde, Alexander. 2001. *Gun Violence in America: The Struggle for Control.* Boston: Northeastern University Press.

Kleck, Gary, and Don B. Kates. 2001. *Armed: New Perspectives on Gun Control.* Amherst, NY: Prometheus Books.

Miller, Maryann. 1995. *Drugs and Gun Violence.* New York: Rosen Publishing Group.

U.S. Department of Justice. 2001. *National Crime Victimization Survey, 2000.* Washington, DC: GPO.

Cross-National Comparisons of Gun Violence

See Victimization from Gun Violence

Defensive Gun Use (DGU)

Defensive gun use is the use of a firearm for defensive purposes against an immediate threat. The "use" may involve firing the gun, but more commonly it amounts to simply brandishing a gun. Scholarly research suggests that the overwhelming majority of DGUs are "successful"—although whether such successes are morally legitimate is a subject of controversy. There is a heated dispute about how many DGUs take place in the United States annually; Kleck's (1997) National Self-Defense Survey suggests 2.5 million or more, whereas the National Opinion Research Center (Smith, 1997) estimates that a figure of several hundred thousand is more plausible.

Defensive gun use should be distinguished from the deterrent effects of firearm ownership. DGUs involve crimes-in-progress, whereas deterrence involves crimes that are never attempted because the criminal fears that the victim might be armed. Thus, Lott's *More Guns, Less Crime* (2000), which finds that violent crime drops 5–8 percent and that mass murders in public places drop about 90 percent after the enactment of "shall issue" handgun carry licensing laws, is not really part of the DGU debate, since Lott's research involves deterrence much more than the thwarting of attempted crimes.

The National Crime Victimization Survey (NCVS) is conducted annually by the U.S. government to estimate the prevalence of crime and to study related matters. Examining survey results from 1979 to 1985, Kleck (1997) found that respondents who reported using a firearm to resist a violent crime were injured less often than were people who resisted by other means or who did not resist at all.

The lowest crime completion rates were found when the victim used a firearm. For example, when robbery victims did not resist, the robbery succeeded 88 percent of the time and the victim was injured 25 percent of the time. If the victim resisted with a gun, the robbery success rate fell to 30 percent and the victim injury rate to 17 percent. In fewer than 1 percent of DGUs did the criminal take the gun away from the victim. Other forms of resistance (e.g., shouting for help or using a weapon other than a firearm) had crime success rates somewhere in between the extremes of nonresistance and resistance using a firearm. All other forms of resistance had higher victim injury rates than did nonresistance or firearm resistance.

Many gun control advocates argue that DGUs are harmful to society. For example, the United Methodist Church, which founded the National Coalition to Ban Handguns (now named the Coalition to Stop Gun Violence) declares that people should submit to rape and robbery rather than endanger the criminal's life by shooting him (Kates, 2002). Opposing gun ownership by battered women, Betty Friedan argues that "lethal violence even in self-defense only engenders more violence" (Japenga, 1994, p. 54). Under this view, violence is per se evil and it is irrelevant whether that violence is used to perpetrate a crime or to prevent one.

The only national study of how frequently firearms are used against burglars was conducted by Ikeda (1997) and four other researchers for the Centers for Disease Control and Prevention (CDC). In 1994, random digit dialing phone calls were made throughout the United States, resulting in 5,238 interviews. The interviewees were asked about use of a firearm in a burglary situation during the last twelve months.

The CDC researchers found that 6 percent of the sample population had used a firearm in

Defensive Gun Use

Survey	Field	Bordua	DMI one	DMI two	Hart	Ohio
Area	California	Illinois	U.S.	U.S.	U.S.	Ohio
Year of interviews	1976	1977	1978	1978	1981	1982
Gun type covered	Handguns	All guns	All guns	All guns	Handguns	Handguns
Recall period	Ever/1, 2 years	Ever	Ever	Ever	5 years	Ever
Excluded uses against animals?	No	No	No	Yes	Yes	No
Excluded military, police uses?	Yes	No	Yes	Yes	Yes	No
DGU question refers to	Respondent	Respondent	Household	Household	Household	Respondent
% who used gun	1.4/3/8.6[a]	5.0	15	7	4	6.5
% who fired gun	2.9	n.a.	6	n.a.	n.a.	2.6
Implied number of defensive gun uses	3,052,717	1,414,544	2,141,512	1,098,409	1,797,461	771,043

Survey	Mauser	Gallup	Gallup	Kleck & Gertz	L.A. Times	Tarrance	Police Foundation
Area	U.S.	U.S.	U.S.	U.S.	U.S.	U.S.	U.S.
Year of interviews	1990	1991	1993	1993	1994	1994	1994
Gun type covered	All guns	All guns	All guns	All guns	All guns	All guns	All guns
Recall period	5 years	Ever	Ever	1 year	Ever	5 years	1 year
Excluded uses against animals?	Yes	No	No	Yes	No	Yes	Yes
Excluded military, police uses?	Yes	No	Yes	Yes	Yes	Yes	Yes
DGU question refers to	Household	Respondent only	Resp.	Resp.	Resp.	Resp./ Household	Resp.
% who used gun	3.79	8	11	1.326	8[c]	1/2[d]	1.44
% who fired gun	n.a.	n.a.	n.a.	0.63	n.a.	n.a.	0.70
Implied number of defensive gun uses[b]	1,487,342	777,153	1,621,373	2,549,862	3,609,682	764,036	2,730,000

[a] 1.4% in past year, 3% in past two years, 8.6% ever.

[b] Estimated annual number of DGUs of guns of all types against humans, excluding uses connected with military or police duties, after any necessary adjustments were made, for United States, 1993.

[c] Covered only uses outside the home.

[d] 1% of respondents, 2% of households.

[e] 9% fired gun for self-protection, 7% used gun to "scare someone." An unknown share of the latter could be defensive uses not overlapping with the former.

Source: Adapted from Kleck, Gary. *Targeting Guns: Firearms and Their Control* (Hawthorne, NY: Aldine de Gruyter), pp. 187–188.

a burglary situation in the last twelve months. Extrapolating the polling sample to the national population, the researchers estimated that in the last twelve months there were approximately 1,896,842 incidents in which a householder retrieved a firearm but did not see an intruder. There were an estimated 503,481 incidents in which the armed householder *did* see the burglar, and 497,646 incidents in which the burglar was scared away by the firearm. As detailed by Kleck (1997), other research suggests that there are about two dozen cases annually in which an innocent person is fatally shot after having been mistaken for a burglar.

While the CDC burglary data have attracted little controversy, estimates of the total number of DGUs are the subject of great debate. The accompanying table, adapted from Kleck (1997), summarizes all American studies aimed specifically at estimating DGU numbers. The later studies tend to be considerably more sophisticated methodologically than the earlier surveys and include various safeguards to weed out respondents who might invent a DGU story.

Gun control advocates argue that all of the above surveys are wrong and that the only correct figure for DGUs comes from the NCVS. That survey suggests 55,000 to 108,000 DGUs annually (depending on the year). Kleck and other critics respond that the NCVS never directly asks about DGUs (but instead asks an open-ended question about how the victim responded), and that because the NCVS is nonanonymous and is conducted by U.S. Department of Justice officials, respondents may be reluctant to disclose DGUs.

Hemenway (1997) and Kleck have engaged in an extended debate about the validity of Kleck's figures (and the other surveys) versus those of the NCVS. Smith (1997) of the National Opinion Research Center concludes that the NCVS's figures probably are too low (partly because it only asks about some crimes, and not the full scope of crimes from which a DGU might ensue), and that the Kleck figure is too high. Smith estimates that the true number of DGUs annually is somewhere between 256,500 and 1,210,000.

David B. Kopel

See also Coalition to Stop Gun Violence; Cook, Philip J.; Kleck, Gary; Lott, John R., Jr.; National Crime Victimization Survey; Right to Self-Defense; Self-Defense, Legal Issues; Self-Defense, Reasons for Gun Use

For Further Reading:

Hemenway, David. 1997. "Survey Research and Self-Defense Gun Use: An Explanation of Extreme Overestimates." *Journal of Criminal Law and Criminology* 87: 1430. http://www.saf.org/LawReviews/Hemenway1.htm.

Ikeda, Robert M., Linda L. Dahlberg, Jeffrey J. Sacks, James A. Mercy, and Kenneth E. Powell. 1997. "Estimating Intruder-Related Firearms Retrievals in U.S. Households, 1994." *Violence and Victims* 12: 363.

Japenga, Anne. 1994. "Would I Be Safer with a Gun?" *Health* (March/April): 54.

Kates, Don B. 2002. "Endnotes for Reflections on Gun Control and Holocausts." http://www.donkates.com/genendnotes.html.

Kleck, Gary. 1997. *Targeting Guns: Firearms and Their Control.* Hawthorne, NY: Aldine de Gruyter.

———. 1999. "Degrading Scientific Standards to Get the Defensive Gun Use Estimate Down." *Journal on Firearms and Public Policy* 11: 77. http://www.saf.org/journal/10_gun.html.

Lott, John R., Jr. 2000. *More Guns, Less Crime: Understanding Crime and Gun-Control Laws.* 2d ed. Chicago: University of Chicago Press.

Smith, Tom W. 1997. "A Call for a Truce in the DGU War." *Journal of Criminal Law and Criminology* 87: 1462. http://www.saf.org/LawReviews/SmithT1.htm.

Democratic Party and Gun Control

Since the early 1970s, the Democratic Party at the national level has been committed to supporting gun control, earning it the enmity of the National Rifle Association and, until the Clinton administration (1993–2001), a perception among some voters as being "soft on crime."

The Democratic Party committed itself to gun control in its 1972 platform. Baer (2000) notes that Sen. George McGovern, with the assistance of the party's left faction, secured the Democratic presidential nomination. This faction was able to force the regular Democratic Party and its white working-class supporters out of the convention (symbolic of this was the refusal to seat Chicago Mayor Richard Daley's

Illinois delegation because of an insufficient number of African American and female delegates; in their place, a delegation headed by Jesse Jackson was seated). The faction also forced the party to adopt a platform that reflected its viewpoint. On domestic issues, that platform "supported amnesty for draft evaders, gun control legislation, busing to achieve school integration, abolition of the electoral college, and ratification of the Equal Rights Amendment (ERA)" (Baer, 2000, p. 24).

In contrast, the Republican Party remained opposed to gun control (Congressional Quarterly, 1994, p. 139). The party's opposition to gun control, as well as its movement to the right on a number of other issues, helped it make significant inroads in the Democratic Party's white-ethnic working-class constituency. For twenty years, the Democratic Party found itself in the political wilderness. During that period (1972–1992), it elected one president (Jimmy Carter in the post-Watergate election of 1976), watched its electoral dominance of the old confederacy evaporate, and saw its white working-class constituency transformed into "Reagan Democrats" (Greenberg, 1995). President Reagan recognized this phenomenon. In his 1984 campaign, he reached out to the disaffected: "To all the good Democrats who respect their tradition, I say: You are not alone and you are not without a home.... We're putting out our hands and we're asking you to come walk with us" (Noonan, 1990, pp. 127–128). In white-ethnic strongholds in Democratic bastions like Brooklyn, New York, where Adlai Stevenson received 80 percent of the vote in 1956 and Hubert Humphrey polled 75 percent in 1968, Ronald Reagan would defeat Jimmy Carter (Rieder, 1985, p. 259).

In February 1985, a new faction of the Democratic Party, the Democratic Leadership Council (DLC), emerged. The DLC's membership included elected public officials, financial contributors, and political operatives who were hoping to move the Democratic Party's political philosophy back to the ideological center. In establishing this organization, these "New Democrats" were trying to counter Reagan by attempting to "change the party rather than changing

parties" (Attlesey, 1985, p. 52). While the DLC broke with the liberals who had come to dominate the party on a number of key issues, gun control was a point of agreement for the party's two factions. At the DLC's convention in Cleveland in 1991, the group backed a seven-day waiting period for buying a gun and stronger mandatory sentences for those who committed crimes with guns (DLC, 1991, pp. 38–39).

The keynote speaker at the Cleveland convention was Governor Bill Clinton of Arkansas. Eighteen months later, Clinton would be elected president, becoming the first Democrat in almost a generation to be elected to the office. Under Clinton, the Democratic Party would become even more closely identified with gun control, since, with control of the White House and Congress for the first time since 1980, the party would be in a position to enact its gun control proposals.

With support from Clinton, a Democratic Congress passed the Brady Bill, named for James Brady, President Reagan's press secretary, who after being shot and seriously wounded along with Reagan and two law enforcement officers in 1981 had become active in the gun control movement. Essentially the same bill had been debated for seven years during prior Republican administrations. Signed by Clinton in November 1993, the bill (PL 103-159) mandated a five-business-day waiting period for handgun sales through licensed dealers (the DLC had advocated a seven-day waiting period in its 1991 policy document). The statute also required local law enforcement authorities to conduct background checks on handgun buyers (this provision was declared unconstitutional by the U.S. Supreme Court in *Printz v. United States* [95-1478], 521 U.S. 98 1997). In 1994, the Democratic-majority Congress enacted the Clinton administration's crime bill (PL 103-322). The law's major gun control provision was a ban on the manufacture, sale, or importation of nineteen assault weapons. Also that year, Congress approved the Gun-Free Schools Act of 1994 (PL 103-382), which required schools receiving federal funds to expel for one year any student caught with a weapon in the school or on school grounds.

NRA Political Victory Fund Independent Expenditures, 1989–1999

Years	For Democrats/ Against Republicans	%	For Republicans/ Against Democrats	%	Other Expenditures	Total Expenditures
1989–1992	$454,588	41	$659,477	59	0	$1,114,065
1993–1996	$196,670	6	$3,044,766	93	$22,848	$3,264,284
1996–1999	$59,914	4	$1,621,214	92	0	$1,681,128

Source: Data drawn from campaign finance disclosure reports filed by the NRA Political Victory Fund with the Federal Elections Commission.

In 1994, the Republicans gained control of both houses of Congress, picking up nine Senate seats and fifty-three in the House of Representatives. This overwhelming defeat represented a repudiation of Clinton and the Democratic Congress's policies in the first two years of the administration, including the Democratic Party's position on gun control. A 1992 Clinton voter, interviewed by *Time* magazine, offered some insight into the 1994 midterm defeat: "I voted for him, but he's just got it all wrong about where we all stand on gays and guns and taxes" (Stacks, 1994, p. 46).

Clinton would also acknowledge the role that the party's gun control position played in 1994. In an April 1995 press conference, the president stated: "There are some who would be on this platform today who lost their seats in 1994 because they voted for the Brady Bill and they voted for the assault weapons ban" (White House Press Office, 1995).

Clinton would recover and be reelected in 1996. However, his party would remain the congressional minority. While Clinton would pursue nonlegislative avenues to continue his gun control agenda, congressional Democrats found that they could push neither Clinton's nor their own legislative proposals through a Republican-controlled Congress.

While there has been strong support for gun control within the Democratic Party, it is not unanimous. One longtime opponent of gun control in the party had been U.S. Rep. John D. Dingell of Michigan. First elected to Congress in 1955, he opposed gun control for many years, but voted for the 1994 Crime Bill and resigned his seat on the board of the NRA (Barone and Ujifusa, 1999, p. 860). In 1999, Dingell and forty-five House Democrats voted against the Ju-

venile Justice Bill, which would have required mandatory background checks of buyers at gun shows and child safety locks on handguns.

The Democratic Party's position on gun control has resulted in increased opposition to the party by gun rights groups, notably the NRA. Campaign finance data offer one indicator of this growing opposition (see accompanying table). Between 1989 and 1992, Democrats were the beneficiaries of 41 percent of the independent expenditures made by the NRA Political Victory Fund. After the 1992 presidential election, the pattern of independent expenditures by the group became more skewed against the Democrats. During President Clinton's first term (1993–1996), the amount of money spent nearly tripled, and Democrats were beneficiaries of 6 percent of the independent expenditures made by gun rights groups. In the first three years of President Clinton's second term (1997–1999), independent expenditures made on behalf of Democrats dropped to 4 percent of the total. In the 2000 presidential election, the NRA Political Victory Fund spent $817,562 on behalf of George W. Bush, the Republican Party's presidential candidate (Federal Elections Commission, various dates). As governor of Texas, Bush had signed laws making it legal to carry concealed weapons and difficult for cities to sue gun manufacturers.

In the 2000 presidential election, the Democratic Party continued to adhere to the view that strengthening gun control reduced gun violence. On gun control, the party's platform (2000) stated: "Democrats passed the Brady Law and the Assault Weapons Ban. We increased federal, state, and local gun crime prosecution by 22 percent since 1992. Now gun crime is down by 35 percent. Now we must do even more. We need mandatory child safety locks. We should require a photo license identification, a background check, and a gun safety test to buy a new handgun. We support more federal gun prosecutors and giving states and communities another ten thousand prosecutors to fight gun crime."

In the 2000 Republican Party platform, the only reference to gun control at all was that the party asserted that "any juvenile who commits any crime while carrying a gun should automatically be detained."

Bush's election and the Democratic Party's failure to regain control of Congress may lead to a reconsideration of the party's stance. President Clinton, in an election post mortem, stated that the NRA "probably had more to do than anyone else with the fact that we didn't win the House this time, and they hurt Al Gore" (Dao, 2001, p. 1).

Max Sardin, a Democratic congressman from Texas, offered a similar assessment: "If the Democrats and the Gore campaign had not been so strident in opposition to gun rights … there's absolutely no doubt that Vice President Gore would be president … It cost him a tremendous amount of support across the South. It cost him support in his home state of Tennessee. It was a big issue in West Virginia, Arkansas … and hurt him in voter turnout throughout the country with the labor vote" (Moscoso, 2001). Steve Cobble, director of the Campaign for a Progressive Future, a liberal political action committee, said that "gun control has become the shorthand for why Democrats don't do well" (Dao, 2001, p. 1).

In the post-Clinton era it remains to be seen whether the Democrats will continue, as a party, to strongly support gun control. In the mid-1980s a group of centrist Democrats, including Clinton, attempted to move their party back to the center ideologically in order to strengthen the party's electoral base. One of the few "old" Democrat positions that these "new" Democrats embraced was gun control. With a growing concern about the party's inability to attract votes from white male voters in the rural South and Midwest, the party may consider distancing itself from a position it has been associated with for more than thirty years.

Jeffrey Kraus

See also Americans for Democratic Action; Assault Weapons Ban of 1994; Boxer, Barbara; Brooks, Jack B.; Clinton, William J.; Congressional Voting Patterns on Gun Control; Conyers, John; Dingell, John D.; Johnson, Lyndon B.; Kennedy, Edward M.; Metzenbaum, Howard M.; Political Victory Fund; Republican Party and Gun Control; Schumer, Charles E.

For Further Reading:

Attlesey, Sam. 1985. "Both National Parties Focusing on Texas." *Dallas Morning News* (June 30): A52.

Baer, Kenneth S. 2000. *Reinventing Democrats: The Politics of Liberalism from Reagan to Clinton.* Lawrence: University Press of Kansas.

Barone, Michael, and Grant Ujifusa. 1999. *The Almanac of American Politics, 2000.* Washington, DC: National Journal.

Congressional Quarterly. 1994. *Guide to U.S. Elections.* Washington, DC: Congressional Quarterly.

Dao, James. 2001. "New Gun Control Politics: A Whimper, Not a Bang." *New York Times* (March 11), sec. 4: 1.

Democratic Leadership Council. 1991. *The New American Choice: Opportunity, Responsibility, Community.* Washington, DC: Democratic Leadership Council.

Democratic National Committee. 2000. *Party Platform.* Washington, DC: Democratic National Committee.

Federal Elections Commission. Various dates. Disclosure reports filed by the NRA Political Victory Fund. http://www.fec.gov.

Greenberg, Stanley B. 1995. *Middle Class Dreams: The Politics and Power of the New American Majority.* New York: Times Books/Random House.

Moscoso, Eunice. 2001. "Some Democrats Advise Their Party to Drop Gun Control Efforts." Cox Newspapers News Service (February 25).

Noonan, Peggy. 1990. *What I Saw at the Revolution: A Political Life in the Reagan Era.* New York: Random House.

Republican National Committee. 2000. *Republican Platform 2000: Renewing America's Purpose Together.* Washington, DC: Republican National Committee.

Rieder, Jonathan. 1985. *Canarsie: The Jews and Italians of Canarsie against Liberalism.* Cambridge, MA: Harvard University Press.

Stacks, John F. 1994. "The Election Stampede!" *Time* 144, 21: 46–52.

White House Press Office. 1995. "Transcript of President Clinton's Statement." April 27.

Department of Justice, U.S.

Often described as the largest law firm in the nation, the Department of Justice (DOJ) arguably serves as counsel for the citizenry and the public at large by representing them in enforcing the federal civil and criminal laws of the land. The DOJ is specifically responsible for enforcing all federal criminal prosecutions regarding guns, weapons, and explosive violations in the federal courts. The DOJ also conducts all cases in the Supreme Court in which a federal issue is at stake and represents the government in legal matters generally. The DOJ is charged with enforcing the laws and defending the interests of the United States according to the law, providing federal leadership in deterring and controlling crime, punishing those guilty of illegal behavior, and administering and enforcing the nation's immigration laws.

In September 1789, the office of the attorney general was created and the occupant accorded membership in the president's cabinet. It was not until June 1870, however, that the attorney general became the head of the Department of Justice, as the department was first established by an act of Congress on June 22, 1870. Since 1870 the attorney general has presided over the Department of Justice and served as the chief law enforcement officer of the federal government. The mission of the office of the attorney general is to supervise and direct the administration and operation of the Department of Justice, including the Federal Bureau of Investigation, Drug Enforcement Administration, Immigration and Naturalization Service, Bureau of Prisons, and Office of Justice Program, which are all within the DOJ. The attorney general also supervises and directs the various activities of the DOJ as represented by the U.S. attorneys and U.S. marshals in the various judicial districts around the country. Since 1870 the DOJ has been a cabinet-level department of the federal government.

James A. Beckman

See also Bureau of Justice Statistics; Federal Bureau of Investigation

For Further Reading:

Bureau of Justice Statistics website: http://www.usdoj.gov.

Connor, Roger, Michael Dettmer, and Redding Pitt. 2000. "The National Symposium on the Changing Role of U.S. Attorneys' Offices in Public Safety: A Brief History Prepared for the Changing Role of U.S. Attorneys' Offices in Public Safety Symposium." *Capital University Law Review* 28: 753–773.

U.S. Government Printing Office. 1997. *The United States Government Manual.* Washington, DC: Office of the Federal Register, National Archives and Records Administration. Pp. 328–365.

Derringers

Derringers are very small one- or two-shot pistols designed to be carried in the pocket and used for defense at very close quarters. The derringer originated from a one-shot, muzzle-loading pistol designed by Henry Deringer of Philadelphia in the 1850s. The design quickly became popular and Deringer faced many competitors. Deringer's gun was high in both quality and price, and many of his competitors put out cheaper models stamped with his name. He responded with trademark infringement suits; in an attempt to evade them, the competitors began to stamp their firearms "Derringer" (with two *r*'s), and this spelling became generally accepted as the name of the firearm type. Deringer's original guns were of relatively large caliber, .33 to .52, whereas the modern derringer is most commonly chambered for .22 rimfire. An authentic Henry Deringer pistol is today a collector's item commanding a high price.

David T. Hardy

See also Handguns

For Further Reading:

Eberhardt, L. D., and Robert L. Wilson. 1985. *The Deringer in America.* New York: Andrew Mowbray.

Parsons, John E. 1952. *Henry Deringer's Pocket Pistol.* New York: William Morrow.

Dick Act (Militia Act of 1903)

American mobilization during the Spanish-American War demonstrated weaknesses in the U.S. military apparatus, in particular the state militias. In addressing these deficiencies, Secretary of War Elihu Root began a program of military reform. This program led to the Militia Act of 1903, better known as the Dick Act.

U.S. Sen. Charles Dick, a major general in the Ohio National Guard, sponsored this legislation. It was the beginning of the federalization of the state militia system. Under this bill, all state organized militias were required to conform to regular army organization within five years of its passage. It required units to attend twenty-four drills and five days of annual training each year. The Dick Act also provided pay for annual training. In return for federal funding, militia units were subject to inspection by regular army officers and forced to meet certain standards of military professionalism.

Federal funding for the state militias, also known as National Guard units, increased dramatically. In 1887, Congress had appropriated only $400,000 to arm state militias. Between 1903 and 1916, the federal government spent over $53,000,000 on state guard units.

With reorganization came changes in the bureaucratic machinery responsible for overseeing militia affairs. Until the passage of the Militia Act, individual bureaus of the War Department had handled militia affairs. After the bill's passage, a department was created within the office of the adjutant general whose sole purpose was to coordinate and oversee National Guard affairs.

The Dick Act has been of particular interest to those involved in the debate over gun control in the United States. For gun control advocates, it "eliminated any notion of universal citizen membership in the militia and with it the claim that citizens in general have a right to bear arms of at least the 'unorganized militia'" (Utter, 2000, p. 76). This contention is completely rejected by gun rights and militia groups. A central theme running throughout the progun/promilitia ideology is a fear of what they perceive as the federal government's increasing involvement in local and state affairs. This involvement is seen as both tyrannical and dictatorial, as well as contrary to U.S. constitutional guarantees. Gun rights advocates are adamant in their belief that a central purpose of a state or local militia is to be ready to oppose, forcefully if need be, the unjust actions by the federal government, and thus the state National Guards represent only a federalized

military reserve force and not true militias of the general populace.

G. Edward Richards

See also Michigan Militia; Militia of Montana; Militias; National Guard; Second Amendment
For Further Reading:
Spitzer, Robert J. 1995. *The Politics of Gun Control.* Chatham, NJ: Chatham House.
Utter, Glenn H. 2000. *Encyclopedia of Gun Control and Gun Rights.* Phoenix, AZ: Oryx Press.

Dickerson v. New Banner Institute, Inc. (1983)

David F. Dennison, the chairman of the board of the New Banner Institute, had been charged in Iowa with violating a state law prohibiting the carrying of concealed weapons. The original charge had involved the kidnapping by Dennison of his estranged wife, but a plea bargain resulted in the weapons allegation. Dennison pled guilty. The offense carried a possible five-year prison term, but the judge instead sentenced Dennison to a period of probation. If he completed that probation satisfactorily, which he did, then his conviction was to be expunged from the records.

Subsequently, the New Banner Institute applied to the secretary of the treasury for three federal licenses to engage in firearm transactions. They were granted. On the basis of advice from the trial judge and from Dennison's own attorney, his weapons offense was not noted in response to a direct question in the application about previous gun law violations. The Bureau of Alcohol, Tobacco, and Firearms subsequently learned of Dennison's record and began a license revocation process. After a hearing before an administrative judge, G. R. Dickerson, the BATF chief, determined that regardless of what Dennison's sentence had been, his admission of guilt for an act involving a weapon permitted the government to revoke his company's license to deal in firearms.

The U.S. Supreme Court in *Dickerson v. New Banner Institute, Inc.* (460 U.S. 103, 1983) thus found itself confronted with a definitional dilemma: Had the chairman been convicted of a criminal offense carrying a sentence of a year or more, which would disqualify his company from manufacturing weapons, or did the fact that the offense was wiped from the records after a successful period of probation indicate that what he had done could not form a basis for revoking the company's license?

The district court in South Carolina, where New Banner was located, had upheld the license revocation. The court of appeals for the fourth circuit reversed that decision (649 F. 2d 216, 1981). Finally, by a 5–4 vote, the U.S. Supreme Court reversed the court of appeals: the company's license, it declared, could be revoked on the basis of the chairman's offense.

The majority opinion in the Supreme Court put great stress on the fact that Dennison had admitted guilt. It declared that the sentence was beside the point, noting that it was federal law, not Iowa law, that was to prevail in deciding the merits of the case, and that a similar sentence of probation and expungement would not have been accorded by a federal court. Besides, even the existence of an outstanding indictment (in contrast to a guilty plea) would constitute sufficient grounds for a license revocation. The Court emphasized what it saw as the clear aim of the Congress in enacting the provision under review: it was to keep unsavory characters out of the gun business. To do so, the opinion said, "Congress was reaching far and wide and did so intentionally" (*Dickerson,* 1983, p. 115). Rather gratuitously, the opinion also noted that earlier Dennison had been arrested for aggravated assault and child abuse, though he was not tried for either offense.

A short dissent, written by Chief Justice William Rehnquist and endorsed by three of his colleagues, maintained that there had been no conviction, as necessary under the revocation law. In Dennison's case an actual conviction, the minority maintained, would have required a guilty plea that was officially accepted and/or that was entered into the court record as a formal judgment.

Gilbert Geis

See also Bureau of Alcohol, Tobacco, and Firearms; Concealed Weapons Laws

For Further Reading:

Dickerson v. New Banner Institute, Inc., 460 U.S. 103, 103 S. Ct. 986 (1983); http://www–2.cs.cmu.edu/afs/cs/usr/wbardwel/public/nfalist/dickerson_v_newbanner.txt.

Dime Novels and the Sensationalization of Frontier Violence

By the eve of the Civil War, American publishers discovered the "dime novel" (or "half dime novel," which sold for a nickel), a form of fiction that excited the reading public with its rambunctiously violent plots. Advancements in printing and papermaking allowed for drastic drops in price for cheaply printed, portable books for a booming (and increasingly literate) urban population hungry for rousing stories about the trans-Mississippi West. Over the next few decades, the dime novel flourished and became one of the most important influences on American perceptions of the "Wild West."

The publisher Erastus Beadle led the way in 1860 by reprinting an 1839 magazine serialization entitled *Malaeska: The Indian Wife of the White Hunter* by Ann S. Stephens. The book sold at least half a million copies. Later that year, Edward A. Ellis established the typical dime novel plot with *Seth Jones; Or, The Captives of the Frontier.* Overnight the dime novel western became male centered and Eurocentric, adding dash and thrilling exploits to the old captivity narrative motif. Now a white hunter rescued the captives in the name of white westward progress.

The dime novel format hit the peak of its popularity with the arrival of "Buffalo Bill" Cody novels in 1869. E. Z. C. Judson, better known by his pen name, Ned Buntline, discovered Cody, who was a scout and bison hunter for the railroads, and fashioned him as the legendary hero. Ten years later, Prentiss Ingraham picked him as the author of the series, which cemented "Buffalo Bill" in the national imagination as the embodiment of the spirit of the West. This blended with Cody's own commercialization of the western imagery in his enormously popular Wild West Shows that toured the United States and Europe into the 1910s. "Buffalo Bill" relied constantly on

Cover art for Gentleman Joe, the Bonanza King—*a classic example of the dime novel. (Library of Congress)*

his rifle to produce food or for protection, or on his Colt pistols to establish law and order or to rescue white captives. Other dime novel heroes, such as Edward Wheeler's "Deadwood Dick," added some slight variations on the theme, but basically by the 1880s the formula of the genre was set. Later dime novel western series in the twentieth century repeated the familiar themes almost to the point of exhaustion. In their pages, far many more instances of gun-related violence, murder, and retribution occurred than could have ever happened in the actual West.

In the movie *Unforgiven,* Clint Eastwood's 1992 antiwestern masterpiece, Richard Harris played a gunslinger whose reputation was the product of dime novels, but who, according to his own answers to an eager young journalist, had not performed even one of those fantastic literary exploits. The movie's irony is obvious, but in the nineteenth century many Americans believed fervently in the violent imagery of the dime novels. Central to that violence were the ever-present six-shooters and repeater rifles. Many a cover featured "Buffalo Bill" or "Deadwood Dick" locked in combat with a fearsome Indian or rapscallious rustler, the hero having just fired his trusty Colt or Spencer at close range into the villain's body. Even before reading a single word, the reader knew that Anglo-American civilization was safe for another day, that Manifest Destiny was becoming more of a reality each month in the American West. The prose, full of shootouts, hairbreadth escapes, and revenge killings, simply confirmed for late-nineteenth-century Americans the righteousness of the American conquest westward.

Thomas Altherr

See also Boomtowns, Cowtowns, and Gun Violence; Cody, William "Buffalo Bill"; Frontier Violence; Hickok, James Butler "Wild Bill"

For Further Reading:

Bold, Christine. 1987. *Selling the Wild West: Popular Western Fiction, 1860 to 1960.* Bloomington: Indiana University Press.

———. 1996. "Malaeska's Revenge; or, The Dime Novel Tradition in Popular Fiction." Pp. 21–42 in *Wanted Dead or Alive: The American West in Popular Culture,* ed. Richard Aquila. Urbana: University of Illinois Press.

Carter, Gregg Lee. 1997. *The Gun Control Movement.* New York: Twayne Publishers.

Jones, Daryl. 1978. *The Dime Novel.* Bowling Green, OH: Bowling Green State University Press.

Slotkin, Richard. 1992. *Gunfighter Nation: The Myth of the Frontier in Twentieth-Century America.* New York: HarperCollins.

Tompkins, Jane. 1992. *West of Everything: The Inner Life of Westerns.* New York: Oxford University Press.

John D. Dingell. (U.S. House of Representatives)

Dingell, John D. (1926–)

John Dingell (D-MI) is one of the staunchest opponents of gun control in the U.S. House of Representatives. A master tactician, Dingell has frequently used procedural maneuvers and amendments to defeat or weaken gun control legislation. In June 1999, after the Senate had approved a gun control measure, Dingell managed to block legislation by use of a killer amendment. Dingell served for many years on the NRA Board of Directors, and once referred to BATF agents as "fascists."

The son of a congressman, Dingell received his law degree from Georgetown Law School in 1952. He served as assistant prosecuting attorney for Wayne County, Michigan, from 1954 to 1955, and then won a special election to succeed his father, who died in office in 1955. Dingell won reelection in each succeeding election from 1956 through 2000. He served as chair of the powerful House Committee on Energy and Commerce from the 97th through the 103d Congresses.

Dingell represents Detroit and thus has been a staunch supporter of the auto industry. He has consistently fought against stricter air pollution controls for cars and trucks, often clashing with members of his own committee. Dingell has never shied away from political conflict, however, and he has earned a reputation as a master strategist. In one highly publicized incident, Dingell was told by a colleague on the Energy and Commerce Committee that he lacked the votes to win on an issue. Dingell retorted, "Yeah, but I've got the gavel," and banged it down to adjourn the meeting.

For many years Dingell used his powerful position as chair of Energy and Commerce to bottle up gun control legislation in the House. In 1981 he was part of an effort to shut down the BATF, and was quoted in an NRA-produced film as referring to BATF agents as "a jack-booted group of fascists who are … a shame and a disgrace to our country." Dingell used his power in the House to effectively block gun control legislation during the 1980s and 1990s. When the Republicans took control of the chamber in 1995, Dingell took a low profile on gun control. But in 1999 he managed to insert an amendment in a House bill that would have weakened regulations on background checks of those who sought to buy guns at gun shows. The Dingell amendment would have given officials just twenty-four hours to conduct a background check and permitted the sale to be completed if officials had failed to finish their investigation. The amendment was a "killer amendment" because it sufficiently weakened the provisions of the overall bill that gun control advocates voted against final passage, and it permitted gun control opponents a "free vote" in favor of gun control.

Despite Dingell's earlier strong language about BATF agents, he resigned his seat on the NRA board after the organization mailed fundraising letters accusing the BATF of using "storm trooper" tactics and being "jack-booted thugs." Dingell's resignation came at a time when former president George Bush resigned his membership and General H. Norman Schwarzkopf criticized the NRA publicly. But Dingell has never backed away from his strong support for NRA policies, often leading him to conflict publicly with John Conyers, who once served as his aide.

Clyde Wilcox and Benjamin Webster

See also Bureau of Alcohol, Tobacco, and Firearms; Conyers, John

For Further Reading:

Anderson, Jack. 1996. *Inside the NRA: Armed and Dangerous, an Exposé.* Beverly Hills, CA: Dove Books.

Martinek, Wendy, Kenneth J. Meier, and Lael Keiser. 1998. "Jackboots or Lace Panties? The Bureau of Alcohol, Tobacco, and Firearms." Pp. 17–44 in *The Changing Politics of Gun Control,* ed. John M. Bruce and Clyde Wilcox. Lanham, MD: Rowman & Littlefield.

Spitzer, Robert J. 1995. *The Politics of Gun Control.* Chatham, NJ: Chatham House.

Dix v. Beretta U.S.A. Corp.

Dix v. Beretta U.S.A. Corp. is the first lawsuit ever filed seeking to establish the liability of a gun manufacturer for failing to "personalize" guns to prevent their use by children, teenagers, and other unauthorized persons.

Brought in April 1995 in Alameda County Superior Court in northern California, the *Dix* case arose from the tragic shooting a year earlier of 15-year-old Kenzo Dix by his friend Michael S. Michael had taken a 9 mm Beretta 92 Compact L pistol from a bag beside his father's bed, replaced the gun's full magazine with an empty one, and brought the gun to his room to show to his friend Kenzo. Michael did not know that a bullet remained hidden in the pistol's firing chamber. Thinking the gun was unloaded, Michael pointed the gun at Kenzo and pulled the trigger, inflicting a fatal wound.

Kenzo's parents, Griffin and Lynn Dix, filed suit against Michael's father and stepmother for leaving the pistol accessible to Michael. The claims were settled for $100,000. The suit also included a groundbreaking product liability claim against Beretta that asserted that the Beretta pistol was defective because it was designed without personalized safety features, such as internal locking devices, that would prevent its unauthorized use. Other product liability claims asserted that the gun lacked an effective chamber-loaded indicator and that the warnings accompanying the gun were insufficient. The filing of the lawsuit commenced a protracted legal battle in the California courts.

Following discovery proceedings, in May 1998 a California trial judge denied Beretta's motion for summary judgment in the first court, ruling that a gun maker can be strictly liable for failing to personalize guns. Beretta's petition for review of this decision to the California Court of Appeals failed, thus clearing the way for a jury trial.

In November 1998, a deeply divided jury returned a 9–3 verdict in favor of Beretta. Following an investigation of juror misconduct and bias, the Dixes moved for a new trial, which was denied by the trial judge. However, in June 2000 the California Court of Appeals reversed the judgment against the Dixes, finding that the trial judge had improperly failed to consider the evidence of juror bias offered by the Dixes. Following remand to the lower court, the trial judge ordered a new trial, concluding that at least one juror had prejudged the case in favor of Beretta. The new trial order was upheld by the Court of Appeals in February 2002. As of this writing the case is awaiting a second trial.

The *Dix* case became prominent in the national debate over the feasibility and wisdom of requiring guns to have safety mechanisms to prevent misuse by children and teenagers. Most of the lawsuits filed by municipalities against the gun industry have made claims, modeled after *Dix,* that the manufacturers should be liable for failing to incorporate feasible personalization systems and seek to recover the public costs of gun violence that could have been prevented by such systems. These lawsuits assert that personalization of guns would not only prevent unintentional shootings by juveniles, but would also reduce the number of teenage suicides committed with guns stored in the home and deter theft of guns by making stolen guns unusable by thieves or by purchasers of stolen guns.

Regardless of the ultimate outcome of the *Dix* case and similar litigation, the threat of liability for failing to personalize guns is having an impact on gun design. Since the *Dix* case was filed, several major gun makers have begun to market guns with personalization systems, such as combination locks or key-operated locks integral to the firearm. The March 2000 settlement agreement between Smith & Wesson, various cities, and the Clinton administration, a version of which was entered as a consent decree in the litigation brought by Boston against the gun industry, requires the company to install such internal locks within two years.

Dennis A. Henigan

See also Lawsuits against Gun Manufacturers; Product Liability Lawsuits; Smith & Wesson Settlement Agreement
For Further Reading:
http://www.gunlawsuits.org.

Doctors Against Handgun Injury (DAHI)

Doctors Against Handgun Injury is a coalition of twelve medical societies, organized and sponsored by the New York Academy of Physicians. About two-thirds of America's physicians belong to at least one of the DAHI member societies. DAHI defines handgun injury as a public health problem. Therefore, the organization does not define itself as a gun control organization, but brings a public health perspective to handgun injury in order to reduce the level of death and injury. DAHI is committed to drawing on its medical expertise and the best available scientific evidence to reduce firearm injuries.

Drawing on Centers for Disease Control and Prevention data, DAHI notes that in 1998, 17,420 Americans used firearms to commit suicide; 11,798 died from homicide with firearms; unintentional firearm deaths claimed the lives of 866; and probably at least 90,000 suffered non-fatal, firearm-related injuries. Focusing on homicide, suicide, and unintentional deaths and injuries, the organization acknowledges the complexity of such public health problems, but argues that reducing the availability of handguns would save lives and prevent injuries.

In order to promote public safety, DAHI proposes (1) collecting comprehensive, detailed data on firearm-related injuries; (2) improving gun safety by treating guns as consumer products; (3) expanding Brady background checks to gun shows; (4) supporting limits on how many guns a person can buy during a specific time period; (5) restoring a waiting period between the time an individual purchases a gun and the time he or she takes possession of the gun; (6) aggressively enforcing current laws against the illegal possession, purchase, and sale of handguns; (7) requiring that doctors ask their patients about gun ownership and provide them with information about the risks of firearms in the home; and (8) carrying out additional research on suicide prevention.

The DAHI member societies as of early 2002 are the American Academy of Pediatrics, American Association for the Surgery of Trauma, American College of Emergency Physicians, American College of Physicians, American Society of Internal Medicine, American College of Preventive Medicine, American College of Surgeons, American Medical Women's Association, Eastern Association for the Surgery of Trauma, National Hispanic Medical Association, National Medical Association, Physicians for Social Responsibility, and Society of Critical Care Medicine. Additional societies will probably join the organization.

Walter F. Carroll

See also Accidents, Gun; American Academy of Pediatrics; American Medical Association; Availability of Guns, Effects on Crime; Background Checks; Brady Handgun Violence Prevention Act; Centers for Disease Control; Consumer Product Safety Laws; Crime and Gun Use; Enforcement of Gun Control Laws; Firearm Injury Statistical Systems; Gun Shows; Gun Violence as a Public Health Problem; Gunshot Wounds; Lethality Effect of Guns; Medicine and Gun Violence; One-Gun-per-Month Laws; Physicians for Social Responsibility; Suicide, Guns and

For Further Reading:

Benson, Josh. 2001. "Medical *Machers* Ask: Should Guns Be Part of Patient Profile?" *New York Observer* (March 19): 1.

Cole, Thomas B. 2001. "Medical Societies Unite against Firearm Injuries." *Journal of the American Medical Association* 285, 16 (April 25): 2068–2069.

Cook, Philip J., and Jens Ludwig. 2000. *Gun Violence: The Real Costs.* New York: Oxford University Press.

Doctors Against Handgun Injury website: http://www.doctorsagainsthanduninjury.org/.

Doctors for Integrity in Policy Research (DIPR)

Doctors for Integrity in Policy Research, Inc. is a conservative organization that defines itself as a national think tank of medical professionals. DIPR exposes what it sees as biased and incompetent research related to public policy. DIPR reviews research, publishes and publicizes its findings, testifies before congressional and other legislative committees, and participates in litigation. DIPR takes strong stands against gun control and opposes the public health perspective on gun violence as a medical epidemic.

Originally named Doctors for Integrity in Policy and Research, the California-based DIPR has taken stands on various areas of medical research, including what it calls the politicization of AIDS research. However, the organization focuses most closely on the medical and public health research literature on guns and violence. Other anti–gun control organizations refer to DIPR as a Right to Keep and Bear Arms (RKBA) organization. Dr. Edgar A. Suter, a California physician, established DIPR and acts as national chair of the organization, which has approximately 500 members.

In the late 1970s, the Centers for Disease Control (CDC) had begun to take a public health perspective on gun violence. Later the CDC's National Center for Injury Prevention and Control (NCIPC) funded research on the causes and consequences of gun violence. Much of this research, which appeared in medical journals such as the *Journal of the American Medical Association (JAMA)* and the *New England Journal of Medicine (NEJM),* emphasized the role of firearms in contributing to violence in the United States. In the early 1990s, the American Medical Association (AMA) and the American Academy of Pediatrics (AAP), along with more specialized medical organizations such as Doctors Against Handgun Injury, began to call for more effective and restrictive gun controls and worked to define handgun violence as a public health issue.

DIPR, along with several other small medical associations, such as the American Association of Physicians and Surgeons (AAPS) and Doctors for Responsible Gun Ownership (DRGO), vehemently opposes the view of handgun violence as a public health problem or as an epidemic. Suter was harshly critical of the medical and public health research on guns and gun violence, and cited social science research suggesting that firearms have positive consequences in society. DIPR insists that NCIPC-sponsored gun research was "results oriented," politically motivated "junk science." This view led DIPR to become actively involved in efforts to cut congressional funding for NCIPC because of what the organization sees as its support for incompetent, biased, and politicized research. Indeed, Congress defunded NCIPC's gun research in 1996 on grounds that it was "biased and unscientific."

DIPR takes stands similar to those of AAPS and DRGO. It argues for the Second Amendment as conferring an individual right to own guns, claims that the costs of firearm violence are much lower than suggested by gun control advocates, and argues that medical costs saved by the legitimate use of guns far outweigh those due to criminals using firearms.

Walter F. Carroll

See also American Academy of Pediatrics; American Medical Association; Association of American Physicians and Surgeons; Centers for Disease Control; Cook, Philip J.; Doctors Against Handgun Injury; Doctors for Responsible Gun Ownership; Gun Violence as a Public Health Problem; Ideologies—Conservative and Liberal; Kates, Don B., Jr.; Kleck, Gary; Lott, John R., Jr.; Medicine and Gun Violence; National Center for Injury Prevention and Control

For Further Reading:

Cook, Philip J., and Jens Ludwig. 2000. *Gun Violence: The Real Costs.* New York: Oxford University Press.
DeConde, Alexander. 2001. *Gun Violence in America: The Struggle for Control.* Boston: Northeastern University Press.
Kates, Don B., Jr., with John K. Lattimer and James Boen. 1997. "Sagecraft: Bias and Mendacity in the Public Health Literature on Gun Usage." Pp. 123–147 in *The Great American Gun Debate: Essays on Firearms and Violence,* ed. Don B. Kates, Jr., and Gary Kleck. San Francisco: Pacific Research Institute for Public Policy.
Suter, Edgar A. 1994. "Guns in the Medical Literature—A Failure of Peer Review." *Journal of the Medical Association of Georgia* 83 (March): 137–148.

For Further Information

DIPR: Edgar A. Suter, M.D., national chair, 5201 Norris Canyon Road, Suite 220, San Ramon, CA 94583, (925) 277-0333, (925) 277-1568 (fax).

Doctors for Responsible Gun Ownership (DRGO)

Doctors for Responsible Gun Ownership is an organization that promotes the "safe and legitimate" use of firearms and opposes attempts by public health professionals and organizations to classify gun violence as a medical epidemic. The organization is a project of the Claremont Institute for Statesmanship and Political Philosophy, a nonprofit, politically conservative research institution. Although based in California, it has a national and international membership.

By the early 1990s, medical journals were increasingly publishing research on the causes of gun violence. Organizations such as the American Medical Association and the American Academy of Pediatrics also began advocating more directly the adoption of gun control restrictions. The AAP currently advises that doctors ask parents questions about gun storage and advise parents to remove weapons from residences. In California these efforts became especially visible when the California Wellness Foundation, established by a health maintenance organization, began funding a multimillion-dollar violence prevention initiative.

DRGO was formed in late 1993 by Dr. Timothy Wheeler and other doctors concerned about these activities. Wheeler is a full-time surgeon in Fontana, California, and serves as director and spokesperson for the organization. The organization became a project of the nearby Claremont Institute in 1994. The membership numbers approximately 1,300.

About 60 percent are physicians; most other members are scientists and medical professionals. Most of the membership is from the United States, but there are a few members from other countries.

DRGO focuses on educational activities and policy advising. It has prepared amicus briefs for legal cases, written position papers, and testified before medical organizations and elected officials. Dr. Wheeler himself has twice testified before Congress, written opinion articles for major newspapers across the United States, and made numerous radio and television appearances, including on *60 Minutes*.

Marcia L. Godwin

See also American Academy of Pediatrics; American Medical Association; Association of American Physicians and Surgeons; Doctors for Integrity in Policy Research; Health Care Professionals; Medicine and Gun Violence

For Further Reading:

Godwin, Marcia L., and Jean Reith Schroedel. 2000. "Policy Diffusion and Strategies for Promoting Policy Change: Evidence from California Local Gun Control Ordinances." *Policy Studies Journal* 28, 4: 760–776.

Kates, Don B., Jr., with John K. Lattimer and James Boen. 1997. "Sagecraft: Bias and Mendacity in the Public Health Literature on Gun Usage." Pp. 123–147 in *The Great American Gun Debate: Essays on Firearms and Violence,* ed. Don B. Kates, Jr., and Gary Kleck. San Francisco: Pacific Research Institute for Public Policy.

Wheeler, Timothy. 2000. "The AMA's Epidemic of Deceit" and "The Social Hygiene of Gun Control." Claremont, CA: Doctors for Responsible Gun Ownership. http://www.claremont.org.

For Further Information:

Doctors for Responsible Gun Ownership. The Claremont Institute for Statesmanship and Political Philosophy, 250 First Street, Suite 330, Claremont, CA 91711, (909) 621-6825. Internet site: http://www.claremont.org.

Doctors for Sensible Gun Laws (DSGL)

Doctors for Sensible Gun Laws is one of several small organizations of medical professionals that criticize the antigun positions taken by major medical organizations and publications such as the American Medical Association, the American Academy of Pediatrics, and the *New England Journal of Medicine.* DSGL argues that these organizations and publications ignore and misinterpret data, reach illogical conclusions, and use unsound scientific methods. DSGL and like-minded groups emphasize the benefits of private firearm ownership and point out data that they feel are ignored or denied by those opposed to their position. In this regard, DSGL is similar to the American Association of Physicians and Surgeons, Doctors for Integrity in Policy Research, and Doctors for Responsible Gun Ownership.

DSGL's mission statement is "to provide a healthy dose of common sense and honesty to the national debate over gun laws and the role of guns in society. DSGL is especially concerned with the way that medical organizations have allowed their names and professional publications to be used to promote the agenda of the anti-gun/anti-self-defense lobby."

DSGL was founded in 2000 through the collaborative efforts of several doctors. Their original intent was to create a web-based resource site for the presentation of accurate information that could be used by fellow physicians and other health care professionals to educate health care consumers and colleagues.

As of the winter of 2002, DSGL has approximately 250 members from most U.S. states and Canada. DSGL is not affiliated with other organizations, but its members belong to national, state, and county medical societies, as well as scientific organizations, across the United States.

Physicians, other health care providers, and scientists affiliated with DSGL have published several articles offering a different perspective than that offered by the mainstream medical organizations (Blanks, 2002; Johnstone, 2001; http://www.dsgl.org).

David Cowan

See also American Academy of Pediatrics; American Medical Association; Association of American Physicians and Surgeons; Centers for Disease Control; Doctors for Integrity in Policy Research; Doctors for Responsible Gun Ownership; Gun Violence as a Public Health Problem; Kates, Don B., Jr.; Kellermann, Arthur L.; Medicine and Gun

Violence; National Center for Injury Prevention and Control

For Further Reading:

Blanks, Jeremy D. 2002. "Does Gun Control Equal Crime Control?" http://www.keepandbeararms. com/newsarchives/XcNewsPlus.asp?cmd=view& articleid=409.

Doctors for Sensible Gun Laws home page: http://www.dsgl.org.

Johnstone, Andrew A. 2001. "Why Barbara Carries a Gun." *Medical Economics* (February 5); http://www.claremont.org/publications/wheelerjo hnstone010213.cfm.

Dodd, Thomas Joseph (1907–1971)

As a Democratic representative (1953–1957) and senator (1959–1971) from Connecticut, Thomas Dodd evolved toward supporting gun control throughout much of his congressional career. Although his legislative legacy on firearm issues probably rested mainly on his prominent role in helping win passage of the Gun Control Act of 1968, Dodd devoted much of his career to helping the domestic gun industry. As a legislator representing a prominent gun manufacturing state, Dodd's early Capitol Hill reputation was one of protecting and promoting weapons manufacturers. In the Senate he became known especially for efforts to eliminate the importation of guns. He focused his initial efforts on winning bans of both the importation of surplus foreign military guns and of inexpensive Saturday night specials. Dodd was chairman of the Senate's Subcommittee on Juvenile Delinquency, whose jurisdiction was particularly well suited to his increasing efforts to ban the sale and distribution of guns to minors (a key approach to reducing violent juvenile crime). He also began proposing a ban on the mail-order purchase of handguns and later expanded his campaign to include banning the mail-order sale of rifles and shotguns. Dodd renewed his efforts with increased determination following the assassination of President John Kennedy in November 1963. Lee Harvey Oswald was thought to have murdered the president with an Italian-manufactured rifle purchased through the mail.

However, it was not until the assassinations of the Rev. Martin Luther King, Jr., and Sen. Robert Kennedy in 1968 that Dodd's long-standing efforts to ban the mail-order sale of firearms finally began paying off. Later that year, with Dodd playing a key role in the Senate, Congress passed the Gun Control Act of 1968, the first significant gun control measure approved in thirty years. The new law, although greatly weakened through compromises made to assure its passage, placed new restrictions on the sale of firearms, particularly handguns. The restrictions included either limiting or prohibiting both the interstate and foreign sale of some weapons, and banning the sale of firearms and ammunition to minors, felons, persons declared mentally incompetent, and drug addicts. The law also increased federal license fees and record-keeping provisions for dealers.

Further gun control efforts by Dodd were cut short by his reelection defeat in 1970. Although the National Rifle Association claimed credit for his defeat because of his increased gun control activities, other observers said at the time that his censure by the Senate in 1967 over financial misconduct allegations was probably the prime cause of his defeat.

Robert Dewhirst

See also Gun Control Act of 1968; Saturday Night Specials

For Further Reading:

Sherrill, Robert. 1973. *The Saturday Night Special.* New York: Charterhouse.

Dole, Robert (1923–)

A native of rural Kansas, Robert Dole has been a consistent opponent of gun control, an issue seldom debated among his constituents because gun control measures traditionally lacked even minimal support in midwestern states. Hence, Dole remained a strong opponent of gun control throughout his political career, both as the county attorney in his home of Russell County, Kansas, and later as a member of the state legislature. Upon arriving in Washington, D.C., first as a U.S. representative (1961–1969) and then as a U.S. senator (1969–1996), Dole focused most of his attention on agricultural and balanced

Robert Dole. (Library of Congress)

budget concerns and on gaining influence on Capitol Hill. In the Senate this intensely partisan Republican became a key member of the Agriculture and Finance committees. However, when gun control proposals did arise, particularly in the 1980s and 1990s, Dole was seen as a consistent opponent of such measures. These occasions, most commonly proposals to control or restrict gun sales, provided Dole with opportunities to oppose gun restrictions. Initially, he was best known for his committee and floor votes opposing gun control measures. In the mid-1970s the National Rifle Association presented Dole a "Defender of Individual Rights" award for his efforts to help block a federal Bureau of Alcohol, Tobacco, and Firearms plan to establish national firearm registration.

Later, after he became Senate minority leader and then chamber majority leader, Dole several times played key roles in procedural maneuvers on gun control proposals. In 1985, as majority leader, Dole helped maneuver through the Senate the McClure-Volkmer bill (the Firearms Owners Protection Act), a measure that sought to repeal major parts of the Gun Control Act of 1968. He did so by routing the bill directly to the chamber floor instead of first going to the Judiciary Committee. This rare maneuver allowed bill supporters to defeat several prominent amendments made by gun control advocates.

In 1991 Dole helped negotiate a compromise to untangle a legislative logjam and help assure passage of the Brady Bill, which reduced the waiting period to buy handguns from seven to five days. The waiting period would then expire after a national computer background check was in place two years later. The bill subsequently died at the hands of a Republican filibuster on the Senate floor. However, in 1993 Dole opposed compromising on a similar Brady gun control bill before the Senate. The efforts of Dole and other gun control opponents failed, though, and the measure passed Congress and was signed into law by President William Clinton.

Robert Dewhirst

See also Brady Handgun Violence Prevention Act; Firearms Owners' Protection Act of 1986; Gun Control Act of 1968

For Further Reading:

Cramer, Richard Ben. 1995. *Bob Dole.* New York: Vintage Books.

Thompson, Jake H. 1996. *Bob Dole: The Republicans' Man for All Seasons.* New York: D. I. Fine Books.

Domestic Violence and Guns

The debate over the role that firearms play in domestic violence is fueled by disagreements over the benefits arising from defensive gun use, different views on the level of control that normally law-abiding people exercise over their aggressive impulses, controversial research findings from small samples of relatively unrepresentative individuals, and doubts about the extent to which statistical techniques designed for the relatively controlled environment of medical research adequately compensate for the notorious data problems inherent in any coherent study of gun use in the general population.

Those who believe that gun ownership makes already volatile domestic situations even more dangerous worry that having a gun in a household increases the likelihood that an enraged spouse will impulsively commit murder. In 1976, "intimates" (defined as spouses, ex-

Richard Goodwin holds a pistol aimed at his wife, Mickey, while holding her hostage for several hours. Shortly after this dramatic photo was taken, Goodwin agreed to be interviewed by a television reporter. As he stepped from the house using his wife as a shield, Goodwin apparently tripped, causing the gun to discharge. A bullet struck her in the neck. After the shot, police fired at Goodwin. Mickey Goodwin died at Maine Medical Center. Richard Goodwin survived. (Bettmann/Corbis)

spouses, and former or current boyfriends or girlfriends) committed 13.6 percent of all homicides, killing 2,957 people, 54 percent of whom were women. By 1999, 11 percent of homicides were by intimates, who killed 1,642 people, 74 percent of whom were women.

The decline in homicides by intimates during this period was largely attributable to a decrease of 52 percent in murders by spouses, and to the fact that the rate of murders by intimates among blacks, which was about eleven times that of whites in 1976, fell to about four times that of whites by 1996 (Bureau of Justice Statistics, 2001a; Greenfeld et al., 1998, pp. 5–7). In 1996, the number of murders by intimates per 100,000 persons aged 20–44 was 0.85 for whites and 3.73 for blacks. Rates for women alone were higher, 1.34 for whites and 4.51 for blacks (Greenfeld et al., 1998, p. 40).

People who abuse their intimate partners are not typical Americans. Evidence from the National Crime Victimization Survey, the Uniform Crime Reporting Program, and the National Incident-Based Reporting Program suggests that abusers are far more likely to drink to excess, use illegal drugs, and have a past history of crime and of brutalizing others. Divorced, separated, and never-married women appear significantly more likely to be targets of violence by intimates than married women or men. From 1993 to 1999 the number of victims per 1,000 women aged 20–24 was 19.7 for never-married women, 151.0 for separated women, 77.6 for divorced women, and 8.0 for married women. The overall rate of victimization by intimates for all women during this period was about 8 per 1,000 (Rennison, 2001, p. 10). As one would expect, strangers and acquaintances, friends, roommates, people known by sight only, and coworkers were more dangerous than intimates. Victimization rates by strangers and acquaintances were 11.8 and 13.7 per 1,000 women in 1996 (Greenfeld et al., 1998, p. 38).

Firearms are underrepresented in incidences of violence by intimates. In 1994, roughly 1.3 million victims were treated in hospital emergency rooms for injuries resulting from intimate violence. Among the 1 million people who were willing to report the victim-offender relationship, firearms accounted for just 1 percent of all injuries. In 74 percent of the cases, injuries were inflicted without using a weapon, in 10 percent of the cases injuries were inflicted using an object such as a club, and in 7 percent of the cases injuries were inflicted with a knife (Greenfeld et al., 1998, p. 22). And though firearms were used in 65 percent of all homicides in 1999, they were used in only 59 percent of intimate homicides that year (Bureau of Justice Statistics, 2001a, 2001b).

Those who hypothesize that a gun in the home increases the risk that someone will be killed or injured typically cite a series of studies published by Kellermann and others in the medical literature in the 1990s. All of those studies exaggerate the risk of owning a firearm because their results rely on official reports of deaths that fail to take into account the benefits that accrue when guns are used for self-defense.

Studies that rely on official statistics on deaths or injuries underestimate the benefits of defensive gun use because many such cases do not make their way into official crime statistics. If no one is hurt because the attackers run when a gun is brandished, the incident may not be reported. In those cases that are reported, people using illegal guns for protection may fear arrest and decide not to mention their gun use. Finally, routine police reports may not include information on weapon use by victims.

In pioneering work aimed specifically at estimating unreported defensive gun use, Kleck and Gertz (1995) found an estimated 2.5 million cases of defensive gun use in the United States each year, a number substantially higher than the roughly half a million cases in which criminals used guns to commit a crime. Though critics of the methodology of surveys on defensive gun use by its proponents have been concerned about error rates caused by false positives, false negatives, and inaccurate memories (Cook and Ludwig, 1997), Kleck and Gertz's results have been replicated in independent surveys. At present, scholars in the field generally accept that the best empirical evidence shows that defensive

gun use is far more common than previously thought. The limited existing data on outcomes when victims use guns to resist attacks suggest that those resisting with guns are less likely to be injured than those who submit to their attackers or resist with other weapons (Kleck, 1991, pp. 123–126).

In addition to ignoring the benefits of defensive gun use, much of the medical literature on the risks associated with having guns in the home analyzes unrepresentative samples with statistical techniques ill suited to distinguishing between cause and effect. Though widely cited as evidence that firearms are likely to contribute to impulsive murders, the 1993 paper on guns and the risk of homicide in the home by Kellermann and his colleagues profiled an aberrant, particularly violent subculture. Of the 420 homicides in which the victims were killed in their homes, 30 percent were felony (involving, for example, a spouse killing another spouse who is in the act of assaulting him or her) or drug related, 31 percent occurred in households with a history of illicit drug use, and 32 percent occurred in homes with a history of fights between members. Fifteen of the victims were killed by police acting in the line of duty.

The authors' calculations yielded primary risk factors similar to those indicated by the aggregate statistics on intimate partner violence. Using illicit drugs, having a history of family violence or arrests, living in rental housing, and living alone were associated with a greater risk of homicide than keeping a gun in the house, and more victims were murdered by acquaintances and strangers than by spouses or intimates. Though the authors asserted that "our results suggest that they [guns] actually pose a substantial threat to members of the household," they admitted that their interpretation of causation might be incorrect given that "people may have acquired a gun in response to a specific threat."

As constructed, the study could not tell whether the correlation between gun ownership and homicide was a risk in and of itself or whether the murder victims' households were more likely to contain guns simply because their occupants, knowing that they were at risk from their criminal associates, bought guns to defend themselves. Although women are disproportionately represented in intimate homicides, 63 percent of the victims in the Kellermann sample were men. Gunshot wounds were the cause of death in 50 percent of the cases, and knives were used to kill in 26 percent of them. Victims resisted in 44 percent of the cases. In 14 percent there was evidence of forced entry. In only eight cases could it even be established that the gun used in the homicide was the one kept in the home (Lott, 1998, p. 24).

Similar weaknesses plague many of the studies in the medical literature, making it impossible to draw broad conclusions on the role of guns in domestic violence. Guns in the hands of a drunken abuser are no doubt dangerous. But guns in the hands of potential victims have been used to drive off or kill enraged intimates bent on murder. Because women typically have less physical strength than men and are more likely to be victimized, the benefits of defensive gun use may be especially important in cases of domestic violence.

Linda Gorman

See also Defensive Gun Use; General Social Survey; National Crime Victimization Survey; Right to Self-Defense; Self-Defense, Legal Issues; Self-Defense, Reasons for Gun Use; Uniform Crime Reports; Victimization from Gun Violence

For Further Reading:

Blackman, Paul H. 1995. "The Federal Factoid Factory on Firearms and Violence." *Journal on Firearms and Public Policy* 7 (Fall): 21–74.

Bureau of Justice Statistics. 2001a. *Homicide Trends in the U.S., Intimate Homicide.* January 4. Washington, DC: Bureau of Justice Statistics. http://www.ojp.usdoj.gov/bjs/homicide/tables/intimatestab.htm.

———. 2001b. *Homicide Trends in the U.S., Weapons Used.* January 4. http://www.ojp.usdoj.gov/bjs/homicide/tables/weaponstab.htm.

Cook, Philip J., and Jens Ludwig. 1997. *Guns in America: National Survey on Private Ownership and Use of Firearms.* Research in Brief report no. NCJ165476. Washington, DC: National Institute of Justice, Office of Justice Programs, U.S. Department of Justice.

General Social Survey. 2001. Cumulative General Social Survey, 1972–2000. http://www.icpsr.umich.edu/GSS/.

Greenfeld, Lawrence A., et al. 1998. *Violence by Intimates: Analysis of Data on Crimes by Current or Former Spouses, Boyfriends, and Girlfriends.* March. NCJ-167237. Washington, DC: Bureau of Justice Statistics.

Kellermann, Arthur L. 1995. "Weapon Involvement in Home Invasion Crimes." *Journal of the American Medical Association* 273, 22: 1759–1762.

———. 1998. "Injuries and Deaths Due to Firearms in the Home." *Journal of Trauma* 45, 2: 263–267.

Kellermann, Arthur L., et al. 1992. "Suicide in the Home in Relation to Gun Ownership." *New England Journal of Medicine* 327: 467–472.

Kellermann, Arthur L., et al. 1993. "Gun Ownership as a Risk Factor for Homicide in the Home." *New England Journal of Medicine* 329: 1084–1091.

Kleck, Gary. 1991. *Point Blank: Guns and Violence in America.* Hawthorne, NY: Aldine de Gruyter.

Kleck, Gary, and Marc Gertz. 1995. "Armed Resistance to Crime: The Prevalence and Nature of Self-defense with a Gun." *Journal of Criminal Law and Criminology* 86: 150–187.

Lott, John R. 1998. *More Guns, Less Crime: Understanding Crime and Gun Control Laws.* Chicago: University of Chicago Press.

Rennison, Callie Marie. 2001. *Intimate Partner Violence and Age of Victim, 1993–1999.* October. NCJ-187635. Washington, DC: Bureau of Justice Statistics.

Domestic Violence Offender Gun Ban

See Lautenberg, Frank R.

Dred Scott v. Sandford (1856)

Dred Scott was an intensely controversial 1856 Supreme Court case involving slavery, the citizenship of free blacks, and the Missouri Compromise. Chief Justice Roger Taney's opinion for the majority of the Court addressed the Second Amendment in two ways: First, the Court said that if free blacks were American citizens, state laws would not be able to prevent them from carrying guns. Second, the Court said that Congress could not violate the Bill of Rights by disarming American citizens who lived in territories that were not yet states.

Dred Scott was the slave of a federal army officer who had taken Scott to live with him in an army post in the state of Illinois and later to

Dred Scott. (Library of Congress)

arms." The new nation's federal militia law of 1792 had enrolled only free white males in the militia of the United States, and blacks had been excluded from the New Hampshire militia. These facts suggested to Chief Justice Taney that free blacks were not recognized as citizens, since they were not in the militia.

In dissent, Justice Benjamin Curtis retorted by pointing to the language of the 1792 Militia Act, which enrolled "every free, able-bodied, white male citizen." Justice Curtis noted the implication of the language that "citizens" included people who were not able-bodied, male, or white; otherwise, there would have been no need to limit militia membership to able-bodied white males.

The *Dred Scott* majority offered a list of the allegedly unacceptable consequences of black citizenship: Black citizens would have the right to enter any state, to stay there as long as they pleased, and within that state they could go where they wanted at any hour of the day or night, unless they committed some act for which a white person could be punished. Further, black citizens would have "the right to … full liberty of speech in public and private upon all subjects which [a state's] own citizens might meet; to hold public meetings upon political affairs; and to keep and carry arms wherever they went." Thus, Chief Justice Taney claimed that the "right to … keep and carry arms" (like "the right to … full liberty of speech" and "the right to … hold public meetings on political affairs") was a right of American citizenship.

Most of the rights mentioned by Chief Justice Taney appear to be rephrasings of explicit rights contained in the Bill of Rights. Instead of "freedom of speech," Justice Taney discussed "liberty of speech"; instead of the right "peaceably to assemble," he discussed the right "to hold meetings"; and instead of the right to "keep and bear arms," he discussed the right to "keep and carry arms."

Although resolution of the citizenship issue was sufficient to end the *Dred Scott* case, the Taney majority decided to address what it considered to be an error in the opinion of the circuit court. The Court ruled that Congress had no power to outlaw slavery in a territory, as

an army post in part of a territory comprising the future state of Wisconsin. Slavery had been outlawed there by Congress when it passed the Northwest Ordinance; Congress extended the slavery ban to new territories with the 1820 Missouri Compromise.

Ownership of Scott eventually passed to someone in Missouri (Sanford, but misspelled in the case name as "Sandford"). Scott sued in federal court to be declared free, since he had resided on free soil, having been brought there by his master.

A divided Supreme Court ruled that Scott could not sue in a federal court, because he was not a U.S. citizen. The majority opinion was written by Chief Justice Roger Taney, a Maryland Democrat with strong Southern sympathies.

Among Taney's proofs that free blacks were not citizens was the fact that blacks were often excluded from militia service. The Taney opinion explained that the parties to the original American social compact were only those "who, at that time [of American independence], were recognized as the people or citizens of a State, whose rights and liberties had been outraged by the English Government; and who declared their independence, and assumed the powers of Government to defend their rights by force of

Congress had done in the 1820 Missouri Compromise for the future territory of Nebraska.

Chief Justice Taney's treatment of the territories question began with the universal assumption that the Bill of Rights constrained congressional legislation in the territories: "No one, we presume, will contend that Congress can make any law in a territory respecting the establishment of religion, or the free exercise thereof, or abridging the freedom of speech or of the press, or the right of the people of the territory peaceably to assemble and to petition the government for redress of grievances. Nor can Congress deny to the people the right to keep and bear arms, nor the right to trial by jury, nor compel anyone to be a witness against himself in a criminal proceeding." From the universal assumption that Congress could not infringe the Bill of Rights in the territories, Taney concluded that Congress could not infringe the property rights of slaveowners by abolishing slavery in the territories.

It is sometimes argued that the Second Amendment right does not belong to individual citizens but instead protects a "state's right" to have a militia. This argument is not consistent with *Dred Scott,* because *Dred Scott* viewed the amendment as enforceable in the territories—which of course are not states and therefore cannot exercise state's rights. Chief Justice Taney's list of the rights of territorial citizens that could not be infringed by Congress included only individual rights.

The Supreme Court's opinion in *Dred Scott* (which was shared by six members of the seven-member Court on the citizenship issue, and by five on the territories issue) was not casual. The Court knew that *Dred Scott* would be one of the most momentous cases ever decided, as the Court deliberately thrust itself into the raging national controversy over slavery. The case was argued in two different terms, and the chief justice's opinion began by noting that "the questions in controversy are of the highest importance." Unlike most Supreme Court cases, *Dred Scott* became widely known and was hotly debated among the general population. The Court majority's statement listing the right to arms as one of several individual constitutional rights that Congress could not infringe was widely

quoted during antebellum debates about congressional power over slavery (see, for example, Douglas, 1859). *Dred Scott's* holding about black citizenship was implicitly overruled by the first sentence of the Fourteenth Amendment, which declares that all persons born in the United States are citizens of the United States and of the state in which they reside.

David B. Kopel

See also Second Amendment; United States Supreme Court Decisions on Gun Control; *United States v. Emerson*

For Further Reading:

Douglas, Stephen. 1859. "The Dividing Line between Federal and Local Authority: Popular Sovereignty in the Territories." *Harper's* (September).

Dred Scott v. Sandford, 60 U.S. (19 How.) 393 (1856).

Fehrenbacher, Don E. 2001. *The Dred Scott Case: Its Significance in American Law and Politics.* New York: Oxford University Press.

Finkelman, Paul, ed. 1997. *Dred Scott v. Sandford: A Brief History with Documents.* Boston: Bedford Books.

Kopel, David B. 1999. "The Supreme Court's Thirty-Five *Other* Gun Cases: What the Supreme Court Has Said about the Second Amendment." *St. Louis University Public Law Review* 18: 99.

Drive-by Shootings

Drive-by shootings, or "drive-bys," have most often been associated with gang violence. A drive-by shooting occurs when a firearm is discharged from a vehicle. The vehicle is usually in motion during the commission of the crime. Besides harming the intended victim, drive-by shootings sometimes inflict collateral damage by harming innocent bystanders, thus making the crime especially heinous. While the motivation behind the commission of the crime is usually to inflict harm on a specific person or group, this is not always the case. Sometimes the perpetrators simply target a person fitting a general description or someone who is part of a physically identifiable group.

Drive-by shootings have helped focus national attention on gun-related violence and have fueled the desires of gun control advocates for stricter gun control measures. The senseless loss of life associated with drive-by shootings has garnered support among those sympathetic to the plight of the victims.

Basketball coach Ricky Birdsong of Northwestern University was killed in 1999 in a Chicago drive-by shooting. Birdsong, an African American, was shot by 21-year-old white supremacist Benjamin Nathaniel Smith. Smith died after a high-speed chase near Salem, Illinois. After his car crashed, Smith shot himself.

G. Edward Richards

See also Crime and Gun Use; Drugs, Crime, and Guns, United States

For Further Reading:
Sanders, William B. *Gangbangs and Drive-Bys: Grounded Culture and Juvenile Gang Violence.* Hawthorne, NY: Aldine de Gruyter.

Drugs, Crime, and Guns: Cross-National Comparisons

Violence rates differ dramatically across countries. Each year there is roughly one homicide per 100,000 persons in England or Japan but six per 100,000 in the United States. A common view is that these differences are a result of differences in gun control and gun availability (e.g., Killias, 1993a, 1993b), and some evidence appears consistent with this hypothesis. Most notably, England and Japan have restrictive gun control laws that border on complete prohibition of handguns, and they appear to have relatively low numbers of guns per capita. The United States, in contrast, allows legal ownership of a broad range of firearms and appears to have the highest rate of gun ownership in the world.

A more detailed examination of the evidence, however, suggests a weaker effect of gun control and gun availability on violence (Kopel, 1992; Kleck, 1997). Several countries (e.g., Israel, Switzerland, New Zealand) have relatively lax gun control laws and/or high firearm availability, yet their homicide rates differ little from those in England or Japan. More generally, cross-national studies of the relationship between homicide rates and gun control and gun availability suffer numerous deficiencies, including small samples, sensitivity to outliers, and a paucity of control variables. Perhaps most importantly, existing analyses fail to identify the direction of causation

between guns and violence; a positive correlation might indicate that violence creates a demand for guns rather than that guns cause violence. The existing literature thus fails to make a convincing case that guns and gun control are important determinants of violence rates across countries.

The question remains, however, as to what factors do explain cross-national differences in violence. The evidence suggests that enforcement of drug prohibition is an important determinant of violence rates across countries and that omission of this factor from previous analyses explains much of the apparent effect of guns or gun control.

Prohibitions and the Demand for Violence

The hypothesis that prohibitions can increase violence is based on the following reasoning. Prohibitions of goods for which there is substantial demand and imperfect substitutes generally give rise to black markets, and in such markets participants cannot resolve disputes via standard nonviolent mechanisms. For example, black market producers cannot use the legal system to adjudicate commercial disputes such as nonpayment of debts. Black market employers risk legal penalties if they report their employees for misuse of "company" property. Purchasers of black market goods cannot sue for product liability, nor can sellers use the courts to enforce payment. And rival firms cannot compete via advertising and thus might wage violent turf battles instead. In black markets, disagreements are more likely to be resolved with violence.

The hypothesis that prohibitions increase violence is consistent with a number of facts. Numerous sources, anecdotal and otherwise, report the use of violence in the alcohol trade during Prohibition (1920–1933) but not before or after. Violence committed by pimps or johns against prostitutes is widely regarded as a feature of prostitution markets, in which prostitutes cannot easily report violence without risking legal sanctions themselves. Similarly, violence was an important feature of the gambling industry during its early years in the United States, when entry was prohibited in most places; the incidence has decreased as legal gambling has mushroomed.

Yet many prohibitions are associated with minimal levels of violence. For example, compulsory schooling laws are prohibitions against not attending school, but there is little violence associated with them. Minimum wage laws are prohibitions against hiring employees at subminimum wages, yet at least in the United States there is little violence associated with them too. More generally, a broad range of regulatory polices (e.g., environmental, occupational health and safety, labor market) can be characterized as prohibitions but do not appear to generate violence. And the pre-1920 state prohibitions of alcohol and the federal prohibitions of drugs in the 1940s and 1950s were not associated with nearly the levels of homicide experienced in the last several decades. Most relevant to this analysis, western European countries have drug prohibition laws similar to those in the United States, yet substantially lower rates of violence.

There are several reasons why some prohibitions might not generate violence. The most important of them is that prohibitions are unlikely to create violence unless there is substantial enforcement. And the amount of violence will increase with the degree of enforcement (Miron, 1999). There are two parts to this argument. Prohibitions are unlikely to create substantial black markets unless there is a substantial degree of enforcement, and the size of the black market will increase with the degree of enforcement. The reason is that prohibitions generally contain exceptions that permit legal or quasi-legal production and consumption of the good, thus allowing use of nonviolent mechanisms to resolve many disagreements. But increased enforcement in the form of new laws that decrease the scope of the exceptions, or increased monitoring of existing exceptions, places some additional transactions outside the mechanisms for resolving legal disputes.

Enforcement is also critical to the degree of violence under prohibition because participants in black markets are likely to develop mechanisms for avoiding violence, but enforcement makes this more difficult. For example, rival suppliers might agree to cartelize a market, thus reducing the need for advertising, but the arrest of one supplier generates violence among the remaining suppliers, who attempt to capture new market shares. Alternatively, black market suppliers can create private, nonviolent mechanisms for resolving disputes, but enforcement that creates turnover among suppliers makes such arrangements difficult to maintain. Still another mechanism is that, given higher dispute resolution costs, black market participants can choose production and distribution methods that minimize transactions (e.g., home production), but heightened enforcement makes this difficult. Likewise, consumers of the prohibited commodity can purchase repeatedly from a reliable supplier, but enforcement that generates turnover among suppliers makes this harder, increasing the scope for disagreements.

This reasoning suggests the following hypotheses for empirical examination. First, differences in the degree of drug prohibition enforcement across countries might explain differences in violence. Second, greater gun control might itself increase violence by driving gun markets underground; thus, differences in gun control across countries might also explain differences in violence.

Evidence

The accompanying table presents average homicide rates across countries for the period of 1990–1996. The U.S. rate is approximately 9 per 100,000 people, which is five to nine times the average rate in most other western democracies. Yet the U.S. rate is similar to or less than that in many countries. Seven Central or South American countries have homicide rates greater than the U.S. rate, and several others have rates that are close. Every country in this group has a homicide rate higher than the average rate for the rich western countries other than the United States. Similarly, ten of the twenty former Soviet bloc countries have rates that exceed the U.S. rate, with practically every country in this group having a homicide rate greater than the average of the rich countries excluding the United States. Thus, the level of homicide in the United States stands out in comparison to other rich democratic countries, but not in comparison to the world as a whole.

This overview of homicide rates is partially, but not entirely, supportive of the hypotheses

Average Homicide Rates across Countries, 1990–1996

Country	Homicide	Country	Homicide
U.S.	9.30	Argentina	4.40
Austria	1.17	Chile	2.75
Canada	1.73	Colombia	83.50
Denmark	1.21	Ecuador	12.63
Finland	3.13	Guyana	4.60
France	1.10	Paraguay	9.80
Germany	1.15	Venezula	15.30
Greece	1.33	Azerbaijan	29.85
Iceland	0.13	Belarus	10.40
Ireland	0.65	Bulgaria	5.00
Italy	1.70	Croatia	4.05
Luxembourg	0.80	Czech Republic	2.10
Malta	1.20	Estonia	24.03
Netherlands	1.20	Hungary	3.70
Norway	0.93	Kazakhstan	18.43
Portugal	1.50	Kyrgyzstan	12.35
Spain	0.93	Latvia	21.97
Sweden	1.18	Lithuania	11.73
Switzerland	1.32	Moldova	14.50
U.K.	1.00	Poland	2.78
Australia	1.73	Romania	4.15
New Zealand	1.75	Russia	29.98
Hong Kong	1.23	Slovakia	2.40
Japan	0.60	Slovenia	1.98
Korea	1.60	Turkmenistan	4.50
Singapore	1.55	Ukraine	15.00
Bahamas	16.17	Uzbekistan	4.30
Barbados	7.33	China	1.13
Costa Rica	5.55	Israel	1.73
Cuba	7.83	Kuwait	1.60
Mexico	17.27	Macau	3.20
Nicaragua	5.30	Mauritius	2.10
Trinidad & Tobago	10.75	Philippines	11.50

Source: Miron (2001a).

described above. On the one hand, violence rates are high in the countries of the Caribbean and Latin America, most of which are key producers of, or transit points for, illegal drugs. Colombia's homicide rate, in particular, is roughly ten times the U.S. rate. The fact that these countries produce and ship illegal drugs does not necessarily mean they will be violent; the hypothesis is that the degree of enforcement plays the crucial role. But the existence of a substantial amount of black market activity is a necessary condition for enforcement to encourage violence.

On the other hand, violence rates are also high in the countries of the former Soviet bloc, which are less substantial (though still significant) producers or transshippers of illegal drugs.

This does not mean that enforcement of drug prohibition is not playing a role in these elevated violence rates; these countries have illegal drug markets that are potentially violent. But much of their violence likely reflects ethnic conflict or the lack of an effective criminal justice system; either possibility implies that the high violence rates are unrelated to drug prohibition or gun control. If the violence is due to either of these two mechanisms, however, it is still consistent with the broader perspective described, which is that violence is high when alternative dispute resolution mechanisms are not readily available.

To examine the key hypotheses more explicitly, Miron (2001a) reports analyses of homicide rates using measures of drug prohibition enforcement and gun control, with and without standard control variables. The dependent variable in these analyses is the average homicide rate during the 1993–1996 period. The measure of drug prohibition enforcement is the average quantity of drugs seized per capita in each of nine different categories over the 1994–1996 period. The measure of gun control comes from the United Nations International Study on Firearms Regulation. The questions used asked countries whether they have regulations that prohibit the ownership of long guns or handguns. The measure of gun control is the sum of the responses to these two questions (see Miron, 2001b, for details and caveats regarding the data).

The analyses reveal that drug seizure rates and homicide rates are positively related in most cases, often at a statistically significant level. The results also show that greater prohibition of guns is associated with a higher level of homicide, and the relationship is statistically significant in most cases. Additional results in Miron (2001a) show that controlling for other determinants of homicide rates yields similar, though less significant, results. The empirical findings are therefore consistent with the hypotheses outlined above.

Discussion

The empirical results summarized here provide a possible explanation for the large differences in violence rates across countries, and they suggest that previous analyses might have spuriously attributed these differences to gun control or availability. According to the analyses discussed here, differences in drug prohibition enforcement explain differences in violence, which in turn explain differences in gun ownership that correlate positively with violence even though gun ownership does not cause that violence. Further, the results provide a hint that restrictive gun control regimes can increase violence.

These results must be interpreted with caution, however. Beyond the data weaknesses highlighted in Miron (2001b), there are several issues of interpretation that arise in evaluating the results (see Miron, 2001a, for details). But the results provide no evidence that stricter gun control is associated with lower rates of violence across countries, and they do provide evidence that is consistent with an alternative explanation for the observed correlation between violence and gun ownership.

Jeffrey A. Miron

See also Drugs, Crime, and Guns: United States; Gun Control; Victimization from Gun Violence
For Further Reading:
Killias, Martin. 1993a. "International Correlation between Gun Ownership and Rates of Homicide and Suicide." *Canadian Medical Association Journal* 148: 1721–1725.
_____. 1993b. "Gun Ownership, Suicide, and Homicide: An International Perspective." Pp. 289–306 in *Understanding Crime: Experiences of Crime and Crime Control,* ed. Anna del Frate, Uglijesa Zvekic, and Jan J. M. van Dijk. Rome: UNICRI.
Kleck, Gary. 1997. *Targeting Guns: Firearms and Their Control.* New York: Aldine de Gruyter.
Kopel, David. 1992. *The Samurai, the Mountie, and the Cowboy.* Buffalo, NY: Prometheus.
Miron, Jeffrey A. 1999. "Violence and the U.S. Prohibitions of Drugs and Alcohol." *American Law and Economics Review* 1, 1–2 (Fall): 78–114.
_____. 2001a. "Violence, Guns, and Drugs: A Cross-Country Analysis." *Journal of Law and Economics* 44, 2: 615–633.
_____. 2001b. "Violence, Guns, and Drugs: A Cross-Country Analysis." Industry Studies Working Paper no. 107, Boston University.

Drugs, Crime, and Guns: United States

Presumed links between drugs, crime, and guns are staples of public perceptions and governmental and media analyses of urban social problems. Yet studies show that popular understanding is much in need of qualification and specification. Not all criminals use or sell drugs, not all drug users and sellers are criminal predators, and neither violent offenders nor drug users and sellers necessarily employ firearms in the conduct of their activities. And while many people would argue that gun possession fosters social problems, especially among the young, few would accord gun possession the status of the single cause of either drug-related activity or predatory criminal behavior.

Much about drug use and firearms is inferred from positive associations between hard-drug abuse (primarily of heroin and cocaine but in some places also methamphetamine) and predatory crime. Fourteen percent of juveniles incarcerated for robbery in long-term, state-operated facilities in 1987, for example, had committed their crimes under the influence of drugs, excluding alcohol (Beck, Kline, and Greenfeld, 1988). Twenty-five percent of jail inmates charged in 1996 with robbery and 40 percent of state prison inmates serving time for robbery and surveyed in 1997 reported committing their offenses while under the influence of drugs, again excluding alcohol (U.S. Department of Justice, 1998, 1999). An average of 55 percent of those charged in 2000 with violent offenses among recently booked adult male arrestees in thirty-four metropolitan areas tested positive for cocaine, heroin, marijuana, methamphetamine, or PCP, with marijuana and cocaine generally exhibiting the strongest relationship to the alleged offenses (National Institute of Justice, 2001). Presumably, the violent offenses referred to in these studies included many committed with firearms.

Does drug use or abuse foster violent behavior? Evidence that use of illegal substances has a direct pharmacological effect on criminal violence (and aggression in general) is far from definitive. An indirect association between drug abuse and violence, primarily through criminal activity conducted to support a drug habit, seems more likely. Robbery using some sort of weapon and often a gun, for example, is apparently not uncommon among serious users of hard drugs and especially those whose addictions require daily or even more frequent use (Anglin and Speckart, 1986; Johnson et al., 1990; Nurco et al., 1988). There is also evidence that drug use fosters the carrying of weapons for protection, at least among youths (Lizotte et al., 1994; Sheley and Wright, 1995, 1998), who are the subjects of the vast majority of research in this area.

Experienced students of the relationships among drugs, crime, and firearm-related activities direct their attention more to potential links between violence and drug trafficking than to those between violence and drug use. (Importantly, a strong relationship between use and sales should not be assumed.) A number of studies have found higher levels of personal crime and the carrying and use of guns and other weapons among drug-selling youths than among drug-using ones, though the latter are more likely to be involved in property crime (Altschuler and Brounstein, 1991; Callahan and Rivara, 1992; Lizotte et al., 1994; Sheley and Wright, 1995, 1998). Drug use and sale combined is more often associated with gun-related activity and violent offending than is either taken separately (Sheley and Wright, 1995). Persons who sell drugs publicly (that is, those whose clientele extends beyond friends) appear to commit violent offenses with firearms at higher rates than do persons who do not sell drugs yet commit violent offenses. Involvement in robberies and assaults increases when offenders move from independent to group sales of drugs (Fagan, 1992).

Tendencies toward predatory behavior notwithstanding, most of the violence related to drug trafficking appears systemic, a function of establishing, maintaining, and expanding drug-sale territories, controlling the sales force, assuring the quality of supply, and collecting payments from customers (Goldstein, 1985). Firearms are utilized to intimidate workers, competitors, clients, and neighborhood residents. Drug trafficking disputes, by definition irresolvable through resorting to tort law and other legally framed mediation processes, not surprisingly are addressed through violence (Staley, 2000). The utilization of firearms in these contexts by persons with little training in their use increases the risk of injury to innocent bystanders and thus especially evokes public ire.

A considerable amount of media and government attention has been focused on the *types* of firearms associated with drug-related activity. That such activity may increasingly involve the use of more sophisticated, assault-type firearms is a source of exceptional public concern. The single study to date to examine the issue in depth (Sheley and Wright, 1995) centered on possession of revolvers, automatic or semiautomatic handguns, military-style automatic or semiautomatic rifles, regular shotguns, and sawed-off shotguns by juvenile males incarcerated for serious offenses and by male students in especially troubled inner-city high schools. Possession of any of these firearms, save regular shotguns, was found to be unrelated to increased involvement in the use of hard drugs for both samples. As drug use increased among those who later were incarcerated, possession of a regular shotgun became more likely (to a statistically significant degree); exactly the opposite outcome was found among the high school sample.

It was only when the student sample was divided into exceptionally heavy drug users (only 5 percent of the students) and all others that a pattern arose: possession of every type of firearm was more common among the former group, with the highest percentages of students possessing military-style assault rifles and sawed-off shotguns. This relationship did not hold for the inmate sample, which suggests that movement to frequent and serious crime (which did not characterize even the most drug-involved students) will have the same effect on firearm possession as crossing into the world of decidedly heavy drug use.

Drug distribution activity tended to increase the likelihood of possession of firearms of all types among the inmate sample. Revolvers and automatic and semiautomatic handguns tended especially to be weapons of choice among inmate drug sellers, whether or not sellers also were users of drugs. Students who sold but did not use drugs were as likely to possess firearms as were students who used drugs heavily. Sellers who were nonusers were especially more likely to possess automatic or semiautomatic handguns.

In sum, while it is indisputable that activities involving drugs, crime, and firearms are interrelated, the nature of those interrelationships is not clear. Though there is little evidence to suggest a linear relationship between involvement in drug activity and either criminal or firearm-related behavior, it is nonetheless clear that heavy drug users and persons seriously involved in drug sales (especially those who combine these activities) are, by any contemporary standard, troublesome to society.

Importantly, the strength of the associations at issue is insufficient to constitute a basis for prediction; it merely improves our ability to understand them. To the extent that a youth enters into either criminal or drug-related behavior, the odds of possessing, carrying, and using firearms increases. Most researchers are careful to state that there clearly is no certainty that relationships between drug activity and gun activity are *causal*. Though an argument might easily be made that involvement in drug activity leads one to possess, carry, and use firearms, it is obvious that such an involvement is not a *necessary* precondition of involvement in gun-related activity. All studies of these phenomena find substantial proportions of those involved in one such activity uninvolved in the other.

It might also be argued that drug- and gun-related activities are both manifestations of an emerging normative structure, perhaps even a subculture, and that participation in this structure is what is most telling. The suggestion, in other words, is not that some youths become involved in drug activities, which causes them to engage in gun-related behaviors, but that these youths become involved with peer structures and values whereby "hanging out," using (and perhaps selling) drugs, and carrying and using guns become part and parcel of the daily routine of existence (Fagan, 1990). Thus, no one element is causally prior to the other.

Notable as well, neither drug-related nor criminal activity is the primary motivator of gun possession and carrying among youths. The average youth who possesses and carries firearms (even the average youth involved in crime or drugs) does so because he views himself as in need of protection in a hostile social environment (Decker et al., 1997; Sheley and Wright, 1995, 1998). By most accounts, serious and frequent involvement as a seller or buyer in drug exchanges places one in dangerous situations. Areas where such exchanges occur appear to be more dangerous than those where they do not occur. Heavy drug use also places one in the company of others whose substance abuse level is sufficient to promote armed exploitation of peers. Finally, firearms carried for protection in the conduct of life in the world of drugs translate to weapons at hand in what otherwise would be social conflicts played out with less violence. They also lead to chance encounters where people are relieved of property. In this sense and those noted above, the association between drug-related and firearm-related activities is considerably more complicated than commonly expressed in the public debate.

Joseph F. Sheley

See also Availability of Guns, Effects on Crime; Crime and Gun Use; Drugs, Crime, and Guns: Cross-National Comparisons; Felons and Gun Control; Youth and Guns

For Further Reading:
Altschuler, David M., and Paul J. Brounstein. 1991. "Patterns of Drug Use, Drug Trafficking, and Other Delinquency among Inner City Adolescent Males in Washington, D.C." *Criminology* 29: 589–621.
Anglin, M. Douglas, and George Speckart. 1986. "Narcotics Use, Property Crime, and Dealing: Structural Dynamics across the Addiction Career." *Journal of Quantitative Criminology* 2: 355–375.
Beck, Allen, Susan Kline, and Lawrence Greenfeld. 1988. *Survey of Youth in Custody, 1987.* Washington, DC: Bureau of Justice Statistics.
Callahan, Charles M., and Frederick P. Rivara. 1992. "Urban High School Youth and Handguns." *Journal of the American Medical Association* 267: 3038–3042.
Decker, Scott H., Susan Pennell, and Ami Caldwell. 1997. *Illegal Firearms: Access and Use by Arrestees.* Washington, DC: National Institute of Justice.
Fagan, Jeffrey. 1990. "Social Processes of Delinquency and Drug Use among Urban Gangs." Pp. 183–219 in *Gangs in America,* ed. C. Ronald Huff. Newbury Park, CA: Sage.
———. 1992. "Drug Selling and Illicit Incidents in Distressed Neighborhoods." Pp. 99–146 in *Drugs, Crime, and Social Isolation,* ed. A. Harrell and G. Peterson. Washington, DC: Urban Institute Press.
Goldstein, Paul J. 1985. "The Drugs/Violence Issue: A Tripartite Conceptual Framework." *Journal of Drug Issues* 15: 493–506.
Johnson, Bruce D., Terry Williams, Kojo A. Dei, and Harry Sanabria. 1990. "Drug Abuse in the Inner City: Impact on Hard-Drug Users and the Community." Pp. 9–67 in *Drugs and Crime,* ed. Michael Tonry and James Q. Wilson. Chicago: University of Chicago Press.
Lizotte, Alan J., James M. Tesoriero, Terence P. Thornberry, and Marvin D. Krohn. 1994. "Patterns of Adolescent Firearms Ownership and Use." *Justice Quarterly* 11: 51–73.
National Institute of Justice. 2001. *Annual Report on Drug Use among Adult and Juvenile Arrestees.* Washington, DC: National Institute of Justice.
Nurco, David N., Thomas E. Hanlon, Timothy W. Kinlock, and Karen R. Duszynski. 1988. "Differential Criminal Patterns of Narcotic Addiction over an Addiction Career." *Criminology* 26: 407–423.
Sheley, Joseph F., and James D. Wright. 1995. *In the Line of Fire: Youth, Guns, and Violence in Urban America.* Hawthorne, NY: Aldine de Gruyter.
———. 1998. *High School Youths, Weapons, and Violence: A National Survey.* Washington, DC: National Institute of Justice.
Staley, Samuel R. 2000. "Same Old, Same Old: American Drug Policy in the 1990s." Pp. 543–559 in *Criminology: A Contemporary Handbook,* ed. Joseph F. Sheley. 3d ed. Belmont, CA: Wadsworth.
U.S. Department of Justice. 1998. *Profile of Jail Inmates, 1996.* Washington, DC: U.S. Department of Justice.
———. 1999. *Substance Abuse and Treatment, State and Federal Prisoners, 1997.* Washington, DC: U.S. Department of Justice.
Wright, James D., and Peter H. Rossi. 1994. *Armed and Considered Dangerous: A Survey of Felons and Their Firearms.* Hawthorne, NY: Aldine de Gruyter.

Dueling

During the early period of American history, dueling was relatively common in the country. Both swords and guns were used, but pistols emerged as the weapon of choice. By the 1800s, the rules and customs surrounding dueling had become codified and the practice was deemed an acceptable means for gentlemen to settle their differences. Following the deaths of several prominent Americans, however, including Alexander Hamilton, public pressure began to mount to abolish the practice. But it was not until the Civil War that dueling came into disfavor in the South.

Dueling had its roots in medieval European practices whereby noblemen would fight to avenge their honor or to prove their innocence. The concept behind such judicial combat centered around the belief that God would only allow the person who was in the right to win. This legitimized the violence and even gave it state sanction. Later attempts to ban dueling during the 1600s and 1700s met with little success, despite efforts by the Church to suppress the practice.

The first recorded duel in American history occurred in 1621 in Massachusetts. The combatants fought with swords, but pistols quickly be-

The duel between Aaron Burr and Alexander Hamilton, July 11, 1804, in Weehawken, New Jersey. (Hulton/Archive by Getty Images)

came the favorite weapons in the British North American colonies. By the time of the American Revolution (1775–1783), dueling had become widespread, but it was particularly popular among the landed gentry of the South. In 1777, the "Code Duello" was published by a group of Irish dueling enthusiasts. The code contained specific rules of conduct for duels, including stipulating the number or severity of wounds or the number of shots that were necessary to satisfy the honor of the grieved party. In 1838, John Lyde Wilson, the governor of South Carolina, published an American version of the code.

Dueling customs and the "Code Duello" mandated that once a grievance had been registered, all action was coordinated through seconds. The second was usually a close friend or relative. Ideally, the seconds were supposed to try to mediate the dispute before violence ensued. If a reconciliation was not possible, the seconds arranged the meeting time, place, and other details. The party that was accused of the grievance chose the weapons used. The accused could apologize at any point prior to the duel and the mat-ter would be dropped, but once the encounter began it could only be stopped with the consent of the grieved party or when specific injury or death was inflicted on either party. The most common weapon used was a smoothbore flintlock pistol. Most wealthy American men owned a matched set of these guns. They were often given as presents and many were exquisitely crafted. Nonetheless, these weapons were relatively inaccurate and unreliable. In addition, custom dictated that duelists had to fire their gun within three seconds. These factors were probably the key to the popularity of the flintlock pistols since their drawbacks usually meant that few people were killed in duels. In fact, it was very uncommon for duelists to be seriously wounded. For instance, in a celebrated duel in North Carolina in 1797, the two duelists exchanged twelve rounds apiece without hitting each other.

Still, many men died in duels and the societal costs of this practice led a variety of prominent Americans to oppose dueling. Benjamin Franklin and George Washington, as well as a host of religious leaders, led the movement to ban dueling.

Partially as a result of such leadership, many states outlawed dueling soon after the Revolutionary War. By 1800, dueling was illegal in most northern states. However, such bans were not uniform and were often ignored. For instance, while dueling was illegal in Washington, D.C., it remained legal in Maryland. Consequently, men would cross the border into the neighboring state to duel. Likewise, although dueling became illegal in North and South Carolina soon after 1800, the gentry of these states would travel to isolated areas to fight. In South Carolina, the duelists would leave areas such as Charleston and go to the state's barrier islands for their combat. Tybee Island, off the coast of South Carolina, became noted as an area for duels.

Society's acceptance of dueling began to decline after a number of famous Americans were killed in altercations and following a number of grisly encounters that seemed to the public to be executions rather than legitimate efforts to settle disputes. The infamous 1804 duel between Alexander Hamilton and Aaron Burr, which resulted in the death of Hamilton, horrified many in the nation. Other prominent Americans of the period who were killed in duels included Button Gwinnett, who was one of the signers of the Declaration of Independence, and Commodore Stephen Decatur. As late as 1859, dueling continued to take its toll on American politics. That year, California Sen. David Broderick was killed in a duel.

As more and more states outlawed dueling, its adherents found increasingly innovative methods to avoid prosecution. For example, in cases where two neighboring states both outlawed dueling, for a time the duelists would stand on opposite sides of the state border and fire. This made it very difficult to prosecute because of the different jurisdictions. In the aftermath of the Civil War, dueling dramatically declined. States developed an ingenious tactic to combat the practice when they began enacting legislation that prohibited convicted duelists from holding public office. California enacted such a law in 1849, while North Carolina did not follow suit until 1868. Through such measures, states undermined the appeal of dueling by striking at the livelihood of the southern gentry and thereby responding to the widespread public dissatisfaction

with the practice. Dueling would continue to be practiced during the westward expansion in the form of gunfights, but it was not formalized in the manner of the ritualized duels of the South.

Tom Lansford

See also Frontier Violence
For Further Reading:
Baldick, Robert. 1965. *The Duel: A History of Dueling.* New York: C. N. Potter.
Melville, Lewis. 1974. *Famous Duels and Assassinations.* New York: J. H. Sears.
Quinn, Arthur. 1997. *The Rivals: William Gwin, David Broderick, and the Birth of California.* Lincoln: University of Nebraska Press.

Dum-Dum Bullet

In the early twentieth century, "dum-dum" was employed as a slang term for all expanding bullets. The original dum-dum was a British .303 rifle bullet with the hard metal jacket removed from the tip, thus exposing the soft lead core. Upon impact, the bullet tended to expand, imparting greater shock; it was adopted in the belief that the tribal enemies faced by the British were fanatics who could not be stopped by an ordinary rifle bullet. The design was created by a Captain Bertie Clay and produced at the Dum-Dum Arsenal in India, hence its name.

The original dum-dum bullet was dangerous to its user as well as to its recipient; with the lead core exposed both at the base and at the nose, the gas pressures of firing sometimes blew the lead core out and left the copper jacket lodged in the barrel, leading to catastrophic failure of the rifle when the next bullet fired hit the jacket remnants. It was subsequently replaced by a hollow-point design with the copper jacket enclosing the base. This was the ancestor of all modern hollow-point projectiles.

The dum-dum and all similar designs were forbidden for wartime use by the Hague Declaration of 1899, which prohibited use of bullets designed to flatten or expand in the human body.

David T. Hardy

See also Ammunition, Types of; Black Talon
For Further Reading:
Hogg, Ian. 1985. *Jane's Directory of Military Small Arms Ammunition.* New York: Jane's Publishing. Pp. 13–14.

E

Eddie Eagle

This program was created by the National Rifle Association (NRA) in 1988 to teach children to avoid gun accidents. The core of the program, symbolized by the costumed cartoon character Eddie Eagle, consists of a four-line slogan designed to tell children from prekindergarten to sixth grade how to react if they encounter a gun: "Stop! Don't touch. Leave the area. Tell an adult." The NRA makes available various instructional materials, including workbooks, posters, and an animated video. According to the NRA, the program has been used in all fifty states and has reached more than 12 million children. The NRA says that Eddie Eagle offers no value judgments about whether guns are good or bad.

Critics of the program argue that it has less honorable purposes. In its report "Joe Camel with Feathers," the Violence Policy Center (VPC), a pro–gun control research organization, argues that the program was developed by the NRA as a lobbying tool to defeat gun child-safety legislation then being considered in Florida by offering the program as a voluntary, NRA-controlled substitute for government regulation. The VPC further criticizes the program for failing to include information about the dangers of guns, and charges that the program is really a backdoor method for recruiting children into gun use. The VPC also says that there is no proof that the program has been effective in reducing gun-related harm to children. The NRA says its program has been effective, however, and denies that it is designed to promote firearm use.

Robert J. Spitzer

See also National Rifle Association; Safety Courses; Violence Policy Center

For Further Reading:
Spitzer, Robert J. 1999. "The Gun Dispute." *American Educator* (Summer): 10–15.
Violence Policy Center. 1997. "Joe Camel with Feathers." Washington, DC: Violence Policy Center (November).

Education Fund to End Handgun Violence

See Coalition to Stop Gun Violence

Emergency Committee for Gun Control

In 1968, the National Council for a Responsible Firearms Policy (NCRFP) founded the Emergency Committee for Gun Control to lobby on behalf of the Gun Control Act of 1968 (GCA). The Emergency Committee supported national gun registration, national gun licensing, a ban on interstate gun sales, and a ban on mail-order sales of long guns. The bipartisan committee—headed by former astronaut and future senator John Glenn—played an important role in getting the GCA passed.

In the late 1960s, the NCRFP was the only lobbying or advocacy group focusing specifically on gun control. However, the organization was underfunded and not very effective. President John F. Kennedy's assassination in 1963 had engendered some support for gun control, but that support did not generate any gun control legislation. The climate for gun control changed dramatically in 1968, however, with the murders of the Reverend Martin Luther King, Jr., and Robert Kennedy. Those assassinations opened up the possibility of gun control legislation (Vizzard, 2000, p. 102). On June 6, 1968, the day after Robert Kennedy died, President Lyndon Johnson went on national television to call for

Congress "to enact a strong and effective gun law governing the full range of lethal weapons" (De-Conde, 2001, p. 183). Several days later, he created the National Commission on the Causes and Prevention of Violence.

On May 24, 1968, the Senate had passed and sent to the House of Representatives Title IV of the Omnibus Crime Control and Safe Streets Act. Title IV was the gun control section of the act. Although Title IV banned felons and a few other categories of people from receiving, possessing, or transporting firearms, Johnson was not satisfied with it. He signed the bill into law but continued to work on getting Congress to pass his own more comprehensive gun control bill—the Gun Control Act of 1968 (DeConde, 2001; Vizzard, 2000).

The Emergency Committee for Gun Control played a crucial role in getting the GCA passed. Attorney General Ramsey Clark had gone to the NCRFP to request that it set up a broader, more effective group. The NCRFP then met with representatives of thirty-eight groups that favored comprehensive gun control. The groups included the AFL-CIO, the American Bar Association, the National Council of Churches, and the American Civil Liberties Union. Individual members included New York Mayor John Lindsay, Johnny Carson, Joe DiMaggio, Ann Landers, Vince Lombardi, and Frank Sinatra. These groups and individuals established the Emergency Committee. To head the committee, the group chose John Glenn. The former astronaut was a close friend of the Kennedy family and a staunch supporter of gun control.

The Emergency Committee effectively lobbied Congress and publicized the need for more comprehensive gun control. In October, Congress passed the Gun Control Act of 1968. The more comprehensive GCA replaced Title IV of the Omnibus Crime Control and Safe Streets Act. Having been formed to lobby on behalf of the GCA, the Emergency Committee did not operate long after the bill passed. Despite its brief existence, the committee played a key role at an important point in the development of gun control legislation and policy in the United States.

Although the GCA was the first important gun control legislation passed since the Federal Firearms Act of 1938, gun control supporters felt that in order to gain passage the bill had been substantially weakened. And, indeed, in a standard pattern, gun control opponents succeeded in weakening the bill and then later argued that the weakened law was ineffective.

Walter F. Carroll

See also Brady Campaign to Prevent Gun Violence; Coalition to Stop Gun Violence; Dodd, Thomas Joseph; Gun Control Act of 1968; Methodist Church, United; National Council for a Responsible Firearms Policy; Omnibus Crime Control and Safe Streets Act

For Further Reading:

DeConde, Alexander. 2001. *Gun Violence in America.* Boston: Northeastern University Press.
Patterson, Samuel C., and Keith R. Eakins. 1998. "Congress and Gun Control." Pp. 45–73 in *The Changing Politics of Gun Control,* ed. John M. Bruce and Clyde Wilcox. Lanham, MD: Rowman & Littlefield.
Vizzard, William J. 2000. *Shots in the Dark: The Policy, Politics, and Symbolism of Gun Control.* Lanham, MD: Rowman & Littlefield.

Enforcement of Gun Control Laws

The issue of enforcement of gun laws is really a cover for opposing new gun laws. Those on one side of the issue argue that "we need to make a law restricting guns" while those on the other side say "we don't need new laws—we need enforcement of existing gun laws." Though there is always, of course, some enforcement of existing laws, it is a relevant issue whether the amount of enforcement is optimal. The rate of arrests by both state and federal agencies for weapons offenses is shown in the accompanying figure (p. 187).

The rate of arrests per 1,000 people increased substantially from the mid-1980s through about 1993 and decreased thereafter. The number of arrests ranged from about 150,000 to 200,000 per year. There are two competing explanations for the later decline in the number of arrests. First, enforcement was first increased and then decreased. Second, because of increased enforcement earlier, the criminal activity that leads to arrests decreased since

Arrests for Weapons Offenses

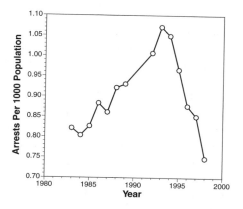

Source: Statistical Abstract of the United States (various issues).

it no longer paid off for the offenders. Either of these explanations may be correct. Note that the federal arrests are a small fraction of the state arrests, so the decline had nothing to do with policies made in Washington.

An optimal amount of gun law enforcement would be at a level at which the marginal cost of reducing a crime by enforcement equaled the marginal social cost of the crime prevented by that enforcement. Generally, that means, in effect, deterring crime. In order to know whether the level of enforcement is optimal, we need to know the costs of enforcement and the effect of enforcement on crime as well as the social cost of that crime. None of these issues are usually very well analyzed, however, because the production relations have not been agreed upon generally or estimated acceptably.

We have some idea of the costs of police, courts, and corrections, but we do not know with any accuracy the degree to which crimes are deterred by these factors. This is unlike the private sector, where we can generally calculate how much it costs to produce an additional unit of a product, given the labor, capital, materials, and so forth that go into that product.

It is difficult to obtain a valid measure of the costs of a crime. There is the value placed on the goods stolen by a thief or robber, presuming we do not count the value to the criminal as a gain,

but what about the psychic costs to the victim or the reduced feeling of safety among other potential victims? In business, we have a good idea of the value of an additional unit of the product; it is the price at which it can be sold.

Presumably, the purpose of the laws and their enforcement is to attempt to strike this balance between the marginal costs and the marginal benefits. There are at least three types of gun control laws in the United States. First, there are those laws that restrict the importation of guns and equipment. Second, there are laws that affect manufacturing or sales within U.S. borders. Third, there are laws on ownership and use by the individual. (There are also laws regulating the armed services and police, but these are not generally of interest directly to the public.)

The first two types of laws may be thought to be relatively easy to enforce, but generally their enforcement is more efficient at the federal level. There are relatively few importers or manufacturers compared to the number of consumers who own guns or might own them. That does not mean that there are no violators of the law, but the inspections needed to ensure compliance are fewer in number. The number of retail dealers is larger. They may be more tempted to violate the laws, especially if doing so is profitable.

Individual gun owners are much more numerous. According to the national polls, some one-third to two-fifths of households own guns of one sort or another (General Social Survey, 2000). The law that is most likely to be violated is one that forbids a convicted felon from owning a gun. In many cases, convicted felons are career criminals who feel the need to have a gun in the performance of their profession. Their victims are more compliant and consequently more profitable to them. Further, criminals may well be potential victims of other criminals and consequently feel the need for self-defense. Until a person uses a gun in some fashion, how can we tell that the person has an illegal gun? The intrusiveness of the personal inspections needed to ensure that each person does not have an illegal gun is simply incompatible with a free society.

Most arrests for weapons-related crimes are

made by local or state police. In 1998, federal arrests in this category numbered 3,549 while state and local arrests totaled 190,600 (*Sourcebook of Criminal Justice Statistics, 1999,* 2000, tables 4.1 and 4.36). Consider the data on firearm arrests in 1996 shown in Table 1:

The conviction-to-arrest ratio is important

Table 1. 1966 Data on Firearms Arrests

	State	Federal	Total
Arrests	212,357	3,843	216,200
Convictions	33,337	3,310	36,647
Sentenced to incarceration	22,413	3,030	25,443
Prison	13,302	2,811	16,113
Jail	9,111	219	9,330
Sentenced to probation	10,924	280	11,204
Percent probation	32.8	8.5	30.6
Mean prison sentence (months)	45	107	56
Percentage of sentence expected to serve	56	85	61
Expected time served (months)	25	91	37
Expected prison time per conviction (months)	9.98	77.28	16.27

Sources: Bureau of Justice Statistics, 2001 (www.ojp.usdoj.gov/bjs/); *Sourcebook of Criminal Justice Statistics 1999* (Washington, DC: U.S. Department of Justice, Office of Justice Programs, Bureau of Justice Statistics).

because those not convicted, either because the cases are weak or because there are insufficient resources to pursue them, are given little incentive to change their behavior. Of course, if their illegal weapons are confiscated, that does impose a cost. For those without a criminal history, the cost of the arrest is higher, particularly in terms of their reputations. The conviction-to-arrest ratio is about 16 percent for states and 88 percent for federal cases.

Once a person is convicted, the next step is sentencing. As shown in Table 1, more than 30 percent of convicted firearm felons are given probation. This is even more pronounced at the state level. Also, a substantial fraction of those convicted at the state level are sentenced to jail

rather than prison, and the sentences are considerably shorter there, averaging five months in state courts and eight months in federal courts (probably, in many cases, equal to the time served before the trial; state courts average 217 days between arrest and sentencing in weapons offenses. (See *Sourcebook of Criminal Justice Statistics, 1999,* 2000, table 5.55.)

Of those sentenced to prison, the average sentence is 45 months at the state level and 107 months at the federal level. The fraction of the sentence actually served is also shorter at the state level. The result is that a person convicted of a felony gun crime (when that crime is the most serious part of the conviction) can expect to serve an average of 10 months in prison if in a state court or 77 months if in a federal court. The average across all such convictions is 16 months in prison. Since only about 17 percent of those arrested are actually convicted and, of course, only a small percentage of those who violate the gun laws are unlucky enough to be arrested and charged, the expected cost of violating the gun laws in terms of prison time is very small.

Suppose that all of those arrested were actually guilty but were not prosecuted due to a weak case, lack of importance, or other factors. (Of course, some are not guilty. About 18 percent of federal arrestees are determined not to have committed a crime.) The expected prison time for a person arrested in the jurisdiction of a state is 1.6 months but for federal cases is 68 months. Overall, the expected prison time for an arrestee is 2.8 months.

For violent crimes where the weapons offense is not the most serious charge, the sentence for the more serious crime may be enhanced by a penalty for using or possessing a firearm in the offense, such as a robbery. That is not counted in the weapons arrests noted above. However, the average enhancement in the federal courts has been about a hundred months in recent years.

While inspecting people to ensure that they do not have illegal firearms is infeasible, increasing the sentences for illegal use of those firearms is not. It should be possible, if desired by society, to substantially increase the penalties, especially at the state level. Further, enhancement of the sentences for other crimes when they are done with illegal guns should help reduce the incentive to use guns in committing such crimes.

When considering the violation of gun laws, note that the "little old lady" who lives in a crime-prone area and who has a handgun as an equalizer is unlikely to be arrested even if her gun is illegal. Her purpose is self-defense and few juries would convict her even if she uses the gun to shoot an intruder. It might be legal for her to have a long gun, such as a shotgun, but that would not serve as well for self-defense inasmuch as the intruder might take it away, a task that is more difficult with a handgun. Also, keeping a handgun handy and using it is easier than it is for a longer gun. Of course, the handgun is less deadly, but the intruder is more likely to be frightened off rather than shot in any such confrontation.

The real concern is keeping the guns out of the hands of criminals or other persons who should not be trusted with guns because of the danger they pose. To that end, numerous laws have been passed to keep guns out of such hands. The Bureau of Justice Statistics lists some fifty different categories under which felony charges on the federal level may be made (Bureau of Justice Statistics, 2001). These are divided into three major categories: transfer, regulatory, and possession. In 1998, some 6,397 defendants were charged with 7,144 firearm-related crimes. The top fifteen categories are listed in Table 2.

This set of categories includes about 96 percent of all the federal charges, with about 89 percent of these being possession charges. The first two comprise about 69 percent of all federal charges. These are charges against a person, generally a convicted felon, who cannot legally possess a gun but who has one anyway, and charges against a person for using a gun during a violent crime or drug crime. In about twenty of the crimes no person was charged. The prison sentences are generally greater for those who violated the possession laws (averaging 105 months) as compared to violators of transfer laws (62 months) and regulatory laws (33 months).

Table 2. Largest Categories of Federal Firearms Charges, 1998

Category	Major Category	Number of Charges
1 Possession of a firearm by a prohibited person	Possession	2,513
2 Use or possession of a firearm during the commission of a violent or drug trafficking offense	Possession	2,386
3 Receipt or possession of an unregistered firearm	Possession	302
4 Unlawful importation, manufacture, distribution, shipment, or receipt of firearms	Transfer	301
5 Shipment, transportation, or receipt of firearms by a person under indictment for a felony offense	Possession	281
6 Possession of stolen firearms	Possession	222
7 Transportation, shipment, or receipt of firearms with obliterated or altered serial numbers	Possession	149
8 Possession of a machine gun	Possession	144
9 Distribution of firearms to prohibited persons	Transfer	103
10 Shipment, transportation, or receipt of a firearm with the intent to commit a felony or with reasonable knowledge that a felony will be committed	Transfer	97
11 Possession of a firearm in a school zone	Possession	80
12 Distribution of firearms to a person not present in the business establishment where they were sold	Transfer	73
13 U.S. Code, vol. 26, (section) 5841, Registration of Firearms	Regulatory	72
14 Transfer of a firearm with reasonable knowledge that the firearm will be used to commit a crime of violence or a drug trafficking offense	Transfer	60
15 Distribution of firearms to underage persons, nonresidents, or in violation of state law	Transfer	55
Total		6,838
% possession charges		88.9
% of all charges		95.7

Source: Bureau of Justice Statistics, 2001 (http://www.ojp.usdoj.gov/bjs/).

It appears clear that most of the crimes are of these two types of possession, with other crimes being less common. Because many of the other offenses are defined only in federal law, those two types will also comprise most of the arrests in the states. In 1998, there were about another 140,000 weapons arrests by the states and their subdivisions. It is likely that most of these are of the possession type.

In deciding how many resources to devote to pursuing firearm offenders, it needs to be kept in mind that there are limited resources available to the criminal justice system. Resources have to be allocated to countering other crimes too. The optimal allocation will result in the marginal benefit of each criminal justice activity, relative to its cost, being equal across activities. Important questions to be asked include how much people fear other crimes relative to firearm crimes (which are usually possession), how effective additional enforcement will be in reducing the actual number of such crimes and the attendant fear of those crimes, and how effective firearm enforcement will be in actually reducing other crimes. Until these questions are answered, the question of whether additional enforcement is warranted cannot be answered.

Lawrence Southwick, Jr.

See also Gun Control

For Further Reading:

Becker, Gary S. 1968. "Crime and Punishment: An Economic Approach." *Journal of Political Economy* 76, 2 (March/April): 169–217.

Bureau of Justice Statistics. 2001. Bureau of Justice Statistics home page: www.ojp.usdoj.gov/bjs/.

Ehrlich, Isaac. 1996. "Crime, Punishment, and the Market for Offenses." *Journal of Economic Perspectives* 10, 1 (Winter): 43–67.

General Social Survey. 2000. "Do you happen to have in your home (or garage) any guns or revolvers? If yes, Is it a pistol, shotgun, rifle, or what?" Inter-University Consortium for Political and Social Research. http://www.icpsr.umich.edu/GSS/.

Kleck, Gary. 1986. "Policy Lessons from Recent Gun Control Research." *Law and Contemporary Problems* 49, 1 (Winter): 35–62.

Loftin, Colin, Milton Heumann, and David McDowall. 1983. "Mandatory Sentencing and Firearms Violence: Evaluating an Alternative to Gun Control." *Law and Society Review* 17, 2: 287–318.

Sourcebook of Criminal Justice Statistics, 1999. 2000. Washington, DC: U.S. Department of Justice, Office of Justice Programs, Bureau of Justice Statistics.

Statistical Abstract of the United States, 2000. 2001. Washington, DC: U.S. Bureau of the Census.

Wright, James D., Peter H. Rossi, and Kathleen Daly. 1983. *Under the Gun: Weapons, Crime and Violence in America.* New York: Aldine (especially chapters 13 and 14).

F

Farmer v. Higgins (1990)

After the Bureau of Alcohol, Tobacco, and Firearms (BATF) refused to issue a permit to J. D. Farmer, Jr., to manufacture machine guns, Farmer went to court to seek a reversal of that decision. The federal district court in the northern district of Georgia declared that Farmer had been wrongfully turned down. The BATF appealed that decision and won its case before the United States Court of Appeals for the eleventh circuit (*Farmer v. Higgins*, 907 F. 2d 1041, 1990).

The provision under review appeared in the Gun Control Act of 1968 as amended by the Firearms Owners Protection Act of 1986. The law prevented a private person from legally possessing a machine gun unless the person had the weapon before May 19, 1986, when the amended law became effective. Farmer had sought approval to make and register a machine gun to be part of his personal collection of weapons. He complained that the BATF's decision to disallow his request was "arbitrary, capricious, and an abuse of discretion" (*Farmer*, 1990, p. 1042). The district court had agreed with him that the provision was unreasonable, maintaining that Farmer fell within the law's provision that machine guns could be possessed "under the authority of a governmental unit." If a person complied with the application and registration requirements of the law, then there existed no ground on which to fail to approve his request.

The court of appeals focused its attention primarily on what it saw as the core of the statutory provision, which read as follows: "Applications to make and register machine guns on or after May 19, 1986 ... will be approved if it is established by specific information that the machine gun is particularly suitable for use by Fed-

eral, State or local government entities, and that the making of the weapon is at the request and on the behalf of such an entity."

The district court had maintained that the foregoing statement referred to failure to register the machine gun. Its decision favoring Farmer rested on the somewhat ambiguous additional phrase in the law that specified that machine guns could not be owned except "under the authority of a governmental unit." The court of appeals thought the reasoning of the district court was incorrect. It pointed out that were everybody who had a machine gun to register it, then the law's intent to prohibit further machine gun ownership would be almost totally ineffective.

The eleventh circuit appeals court looked at debates in the Senate during consideration of the law to shore up its position. It quoted the statement of Sen. Frank Lautenberg, who had said that the bill "bars future sales and possession of machine guns by private citizens." Sen. Orrin Hatch had declared that the words in the law "under the authority of a governmental unit" referred to manufacturers of weapons intended for use by subdivisions of government. Sen. Robert Dole had asked what impact the bill would have on a police officer who legally purchased a machine gun under the authority of a law enforcement agency and subsequently retired or left his job. Hatch declared that the police force would then have to make certain that the weapon was returned to it.

The court summed up its decision in these words: "In light of the plain language of [the law], and its legislative history, we hold that [it] prohibits the private possession of machine guns not lawfully possessed prior to May 19, 1986" (*Farmer*, 1990, p. 1045).

Gilbert Geis

See also Bureau of Alcohol, Tobacco, and Firearms; Firearms Owners' Protection Act of 1986; National Firearms Act of 1934

For Further Reading:

Farmer v. Higgins, 907 F. 2d 1041 (11th Cir. 1990). http://www.healylaw.com/case_lst.htm.

Fatalities

See Victimization from Gun Violence

Federal Bureau of Investigation (FBI)

The Federal Bureau of Investigation, as the federal law enforcement agency in charge of the National Instant Criminal Background Check System (NICBCS), plays an important law enforcement role in the regulation of guns in the United States. Federal law requires that any gun buyer be subjected to this instant background check prior to purchasing a firearm. The purpose of the NICBCS is to determine whether a potential gun buyer is complying with the laws that limit which persons may or may not purchase firearms (e.g., persons with a felony record may not purchase firearms).

The FBI also publishes the annual *Crime in the United States,* which is based on its Uniform Crime Reports (UCRs)—information provided voluntarily by police departments throughout the United States. The FBI provides standardized forms for recording the data. The UCRs are the only source of information for deducing trends in crime in the United States as a whole and in localities within the country. They are the primary source of crime statistics for elected officials, criminal justice agencies, administrators, and other policy makers as well as the news media and the general public.

Although the FBI has traditionally played a pivotal role in the enforcement of existing firearm laws, the appointment of John Ashcroft as attorney general of the United States in 2001 altered the enthusiasm with which the bureau has pursued those who are in possession of firearms illegally or attempt to possess them illegally. Ashcroft (2001), in a May 17, 2001, letter to the executive director of the National Rifle Association, made it clear that he interprets the

U.S. Attorney General John Ashcroft (right) with FBI Director Robert Mueller at a press briefing, October 2001. (AFP/Corbis)

Second Amendment's guarantee to a right to bear arms as one that applies to individual citizens rather than organized militias. In response to this letter, others have pointed out that the U.S. Supreme Court has, in fact, consistently ruled that the Second Amendment applies to militias and not to the rights of individual citizens (e.g., *Stevens v. United States,* 1971). It is notable that John Ashcroft's beliefs on gun policy have affected the FBI's activities in the area of gun checks. For example, Ashcroft has proposed that the number of days law enforcement agencies (including the FBI) can hold gun purchasers' instant-background-check records be reduced from ninety days to twenty-four hours. In addition, the *New York Times* reported on December 6, 2001, that Ashcroft barred the FBI from checking records to determine whether any of the people detained after the terrorist attacks on September 11 of that year had bought guns.

While the FBI's role in gun policy has clearly been in the area of law enforcement rather than in forming or advocating policy, the interjection of John Ashcroft's own gun policies has changed the way the FBI does enforce the existing firearm laws.

Elizabeth K. Englander

See also National Instant Criminal Background Check System; Second Amendment; *Stevens v. United States;* Uniform Crime Reports; United States Supreme Court Decisions on Gun Control

For Further Reading:

Ashcroft, John. 2001. "Letter to Mr. James Jay Baker, Executive Director of the National Rifle Association." http://www.nraila.org/images/Ashcroft.pdf.

Cole, George F., and Christopher E. Smith. 2000. *The American System of Criminal Justice.* 8th ed. Belmont, CA: Wadsworth.

FBI's home page: www.fbi.gov.

Federal Firearms Act of 1938 (Public Law No. 75–785)

The Federal Firearms Act of 1938 imposed the first federal limitations on the sale of ordinary firearms. It was aimed at those involved in selling and shipping firearms through interstate or foreign commerce. The law required the manufacturers, dealers, and importers of guns and handgun ammunition to obtain a federal firearms license (at an annual cost of one dollar) from the Internal Revenue Service. Dealers had to maintain records of the names and addresses of persons to whom firearms were sold. Gun sales to persons convicted of violent felonies were prohibited.

However, the legislation was substantially weakened by the National Rifle Association, as it was able to convince Congress to strike a provision that would have empowered the Justice Department to prosecute gun shippers and manufacturers who put guns into the hands of criminals (Carter, 1997, p. 68). They could only be prosecuted if they "knowingly" sold guns to criminals (Spitzer, 1995, p. 140).

Jeffrey Kraus

See also Firearm Dealers; Gun Control; National Firearms Act of 1934

For Further Reading:

Ascione, Alfred M. 1939. "The Federal Firearms Act." *St. John's Law Review* 13 (April): 437–449.

Barnes Company. 1974. *Handgun Laws of the United States.* Fairfield, CT: Barnes Company.

Carter, Gregg Lee. 1997. *The Gun Control Movement.* New York: Twayne Publishers.

Leff, Carol Skalnik, and Mark H. Leff. 1981. "The Politics of Ineffectiveness: Federal Firearms Legislation, 1919–1938." *Annals of the American Academy of Political and Social Sciences* 455 (May): 48–62.

Spitzer, Robert J. 1995. *The Politics of Gun Control.* Chatham, NJ: Chatham House.

Federal Gun Control Act of 1968

See Gun Control Act of 1968

Federal Law Enforcement Officers Association (FLEOA)

Established in 1993, the Federal Law Enforcement Officers Association is a nonprofit organization representing over 19,000 federal law enforcement officers from fifty-seven agencies of the U.S. federal government. Its headquarters are in New York City. The departments represented among its membership include the Bureau of Alcohol, Tobacco, and Firearms; the U.S. Secret Service; the Federal Bureau of Investigation; the Probation and Pretrial Services; the Environmental Protection Agency; and the Bureau of Land Management. The FLEOA is active in legislative affairs in Washington, D.C., and various state capitals. Its bimonthly newsletter, *1811,* informs members of issues of interest to the law enforcement community and reports on activities the FLEOA is engaged in on their behalf.

The FLEOA maintains an active foundation used for charitable purposes. The purpose of the foundation is to "use any contributions made to it or earnings generated to the public welfare for the alleviation of human suffering and the advancement of education" (FLEOA home page). Through the foundation the FLEOA provides assistance to the families of federal law enforcement officers killed in the line of duty. This assistance may last for several years depending upon the circumstances of the surviving family. In addition, disabled members of the federal law enforcement community are also eligible for assistance. A scholarship fund has been established by the FLEOA to assist students majoring in criminal justice, political science, or law.

The FLEOA intersects with the gun debate in at least one important respect: It encourages and works for federal legislation that will allow retired law enforcement officers at all levels—local, state, and federal—to maintain the right to carry concealed firearms. In the words of FLEOA President Richard J. Gallo (1998, p. 1), "After decades of putting their lives on the line, after decades of taxpayer financed firearms and legal training, after decades of walking the streets as a law enforcement officer, the day you trade your active credentials for retired ones you can no longer defend yourself, your neighbors, your family, or your fellow citizens. FLEOA has joined with the Fraternal Order of Police calling for passage of legislation allowing retired federal, state and local law enforcement officials to defend themselves, as well as the American public." No such legislation had yet passed as of mid-2002.

G. Edward Richards

See also Fraternal Order of Police; Right-to-Carry Laws

For Further Reading:

Federal Law Enforcement Officers Association home page: www.fleoa.org.

Gallo, Richard J. 1998. "Statement of Richard J. Gallo, National President, Federal Law Enforcement Officers Association, before the Commission on the Advancement of Federal Law Enforcement on November 12, 1998." http://www.fleoa.org/reports/nov12gallo.htm.

Federalism and Gun Control

The United States is a federal republic, under which the federal government exercises specific powers while the states are free to exercise all powers that do not conflict with federal powers or with rights specified in the federal constitution. The federal government's powers were characterized by James Madison as "few and defined," but they have in recent decades expanded beyond Madison's imaginings. The most dramatic expansion of federal power has been in the area of interstate commerce.

Article 1, Section 8 of the Constitution authorizes Congress to regulate commerce "among the several states." Until the New Deal era, this "commerce clause" power was understood to

have rather sharp limits: Congress could not regulate intrastate activity under the commerce power simply because such activity might have some effect on interstate commerce. Roosevelt's court-packing scheme, however, though unsuccessful, coincided with a string of Supreme Court decisions upholding ever-greater federal authority under the commerce clause. By the 1960s, courts were routinely upholding federal statutes regulating local businesses, on the basis that—if all local business were taken together—there was an effect on interstate commerce. By the 1970s and 1980s, neither the courts nor Congress were even bothering to ask whether there was a connection between a federal statute and the regulation of interstate commerce.

This began to change in 1995, with the Supreme Court's decision in *United States v. Lopez.* Alfonso Lopez, a twelfth-grader at Edison High School in San Antonio, Texas, was caught with a revolver on school property. He was initially charged under Texas law, which (like that of most states) already forbade the carrying of guns at school. Shortly thereafter, though, he was charged under the federal law, and state charges were dropped.

Lopez's conviction was overturned by the U.S. Court of Appeals for the Fifth Circuit on the ground that the statute under which he was convicted was beyond the enumerated powers of Congress. The original statute did not say what power of Congress was being relied upon; in the post–New Deal world, such things appeared unnecessary. But once challenged, the government asserted that the statute represented an exercise of Congress's power to regulate commerce among the several states. The government's argument, in brief, was that (1) the costs of crime are spread through the nation through the mechanism of insurance, so that crime affects interstate commerce, and guns in schools promote crime; (2) crime makes people less willing to travel; and (3) guns in school promote violence, violence promotes poor learning, poor learning produces an undereducated work force, an undereducated work force produces a less productive economy, and a less productive economy naturally produces less commerce among the states (i.e., the "national productivity" argument). Hence, by regulating the possession of guns on school property, Congress was, in essence, regulating commerce among the states.

The Supreme Court rejected this argument. Writing for the majority, Chief Justice Rehnquist noted that under our constitutional system the federal government is intended to have limited and enumerated powers. Under the government's formulation, however, he stated, "it is difficult to perceive any limitation on federal power, even in areas such as criminal law enforcement or education." Thus, the majority held, the acceptance of the government's theory would necessarily mean creating a federal government of general rather than limited powers, with no limits on its jurisdiction beyond those imposed by the affirmative prohibitions of the Bill of Rights.

The *Lopez* decision made clear that Congress lacked the power to regulate the simple possession of firearms absent some clear connection to interstate commerce. This point was further strengthened by the Supreme Court's decision in *Brzonkala v. United States* (2000), which struck down the civil remedy portions of the Violence against Women Act of 1994 as beyond Congress's powers to regulate interstate commerce.

The result is that the federal government's power to regulate simple possession of firearms is sharply limited. Regulation via a tax statute remains possible (the original National Firearms Act, passed in 1934 before the explosion of federal commerce power, was based on Congress's separate taxation power), but regulation via the commerce power is doubtful. On the other hand, the federal government clearly may, under the commerce power, regulate the interstate sale of firearms.

Congress also may not commandeer state officials as part of a federal gun control scheme. In *Printz v. United States* (1997), the Supreme Court struck down a provision of the Brady gun control law that required local law enforcement officials to conduct background checks on gun purchasers. The Court held that Tenth Amendment principles of sovereignty protected the states from having their officials told what to do by the federal government.

State regulation of firearms poses different federalism issues. States are empowered to do anything that their state constitutions permit and that does not conflict with federal powers or with rights protected under the federal constitution. This means that states may (leaving aside issues raised under the Second Amendment or under their own state constitutions, which often contain right-to-arms provisions) ban possession of firearms. Where federalism issues appear is when states attempt to "export regulation" by using lawsuits or statutes to impose limitations not simply on sales within their boundaries but nationwide. Because the Constitution gives the power to regulate commerce among the states to the federal government, a doctrine known as the "dormant" or "negative" commerce clause provides that states do not have the power to regulate interstate commerce, unless Congress affirmatively passes legislation permitting it.

Congress also has some power to affect state regulation of weapons carrying. Under the "Full Faith and Credit" clause of Article 4, Section 4 of the Constitution, Congress could require states to honor one another's concealed weapons permits, though it has not done so.

Glenn Harlan Reynolds

See also Brady Handgun Violence Protection Act; Gun Control; Gun Registration; Gun-Free School Laws; Licensing; National Firearms Act of 1934; *Printz v. United States;* Second Amendment; Tenth Amendment; United States Congress and Gun Legislation; United States Constitution and Gun Rights; *United States v. Lopez*

For Further Reading:

Chamberlin, Carl. 1999. "Johnny Can't Read 'Cause Jane's Got a Gun: The Effects of Guns in Schools, and Options after Lopez." *Cornell Journal of Law and Public Policy* 8 (Winter): 281–346.

Ducoff, John A. 1998. "Yesterday: Constitutional Interpretation, the Brady Act, and *Printz v. United States.*" *Rutgers Law Journal* 30: 209–245.

Jones, Melissa Ann. 1999. "Legislating Gun Control in Light of *Printz v. United States.*" *University of California–Davis Law Review* 32: 455–483.

Kates, Don. 1983. "Handgun Prohibition and the Original Meaning of the Second Amendment." *Michigan Law Review* 82: 204–273.

"Symposium: Reflections on *United States v. Lopez.*" 1995. *Michigan Law Review* 94: 533–831.

Federation for NRA

This is an ad hoc organization formed independently of the National Rifle Association (NRA) in 1977 by disgruntled NRA hard-line members who felt that the NRA's old-guard leadership was insufficiently tough on gun and related political issues. Formed and headed by gun activist Neal Knox and including NRA dissidents Harlon Carter, Robert Kukla, and Joseph Tartaro, the federation became the umbrella group that laid plans to wrest control of the NRA from the old-guard leaders at the NRA's 1977 annual convention in Cincinnati. In what was later dubbed the Cincinnati Revolt, federation members, identifiable by their orange caps, coordinated their activities at the convention using bullhorns and walkie-talkies. They used parliamentary procedures to alter the NRA's by-laws in order to give the members attending the convention greater influence over organizational decisions. They then used these revised procedures to vote out of office the old-guard leaders and to vote in Carter to head the NRA. Federation members were elected or appointed to other NRA leadership posts.

The federation was revived by Knox in 1982 after he was forced to resign as head of the Institute for Legislative Action (ILA) by Carter. By this time, a rift had developed between the two men. Knox believed that Carter had become soft and complacent, corrupted by the authority of his office; Carter believed Knox had become too extremist. Knox objected to Carter's five-year term as president (NRA presidents before and since serve one-year terms) and charged that Carter had interfered with ILA activities. Knox and the federation proposed a return to one-year terms and other procedural changes. At the NRA's 1983 convention these efforts were easily defeated by Carter and his allies, who had led the NRA to a broader membership and financial base. In 1984, Knox became the first NRA Board of Directors member ever voted off that body. In 1991, Knox returned to the board and again gained power in the NRA, only to be thwarted in 1997 by Wayne LaPierre and his candidate for vice president (who became NRA president in 1998), actor Charlton Heston.

Robert J. Spitzer

See also Carter, Harlon; Heston, Charlton; Knox, Neal; National Rifle Association; Revolt at Cincinnati

For Further Reading:

Leddy, Edward F. 1987. *Magnum Force Lobby.* Lanham, MD: University Press of America.
Sugarmann, Josh. 1992. *National Rifle Association: Money, Firepower and Fear.* Washington, DC: National Press Books.
Tartaro, Joseph. 1981. *Revolt at Cincinnati.* Buffalo, NY: Hawkeye.

Feinstein, Dianne (1933–)

A forceful advocate of gun control, Dianne Feinstein has been a Democratic senator from California since winning a special election to that post in 1992. Her Senate career frequently has been marked by her efforts to strengthen the federal role in combating crime. Her efforts have focused particularly on gun control as one approach to reducing the nation's violent crime rate. Feinstein's more prominent federal gun control efforts include her leadership role in winning the passage of two important measures in 1994: the Gun-Free Schools Act and a ban on the sale and manufacture of nineteen semiautomatic assault weapons. Using her membership on the Senate's Judiciary Committee as a platform for her efforts, Feinstein sponsored such additional gun control measures as a proposal to ban the importation of large ammunition clips and magazines.

Feinstein's strong support of gun control was rooted significantly in her experiences in San Francisco city government. In 1978, as president of the city's Board of Supervisors, she was called upon to announce the gunshot murders of Mayor George Moscone and board member Harvey Milk. She made the announcement soon after discovering the two bodies in City Hall. Her experiences in the tragedy were recalled during a noteworthy exchange she had with a fellow senator during a gun control debate. Larry Craig, a Republican senator from Idaho and a member of the National Rifle Association's board, questioned her knowledge of guns. Feinstein replied that she certainly knew of the effects of guns after trying to find Milk's pulse after he was shot fatally. She later became mayor

Dianne Feinstein. (U.S. Senate)

as an amendment to the 1994 crime bill, listed specific types of rapid-fire weapons, partly to separate them from arms commonly used for hunting or target shooting. A key provision of this bill banned the manufacture and sale of ammunition clips carrying eleven or more rounds. Four years later, Feinstein unsuccessfully sought congressional approval of a ban on ammunition clips not covered by the 1994 law.

Robert Dewhirst

See also Assault Weapons Ban of 1994; Craig, Larry E.; Gun-Free School Laws

For Further Reading:

"Dianne Feinstein." 1999. *Congressional Quarterly Weekly Report* 57 (October 30): 54–55.

Roberts, Jerry. 1994. *Dianne Feinstein: Never Let Them See You Cry.* New York: HarperCollins.

Whitney, Catherine. 2000. *Nine and Counting: The Women of the Senate.* New York: HarperCollins.

of San Francisco, where she won approval of a municipal ordinance banning handgun ownership within the city. Then, in a public ceremony, Feinstein surrendered the .38 caliber pistol she had carried in response to death threats, the shooting-out of her windows, and an attempted bombing of her home. Passage of the ordinance greatly angered gun control opponents, some of whom initiated an effort to recall the mayor. Feinstein won the subsequent election by an overwhelming margin, a victory that seemed to solidify her political base in preparation for subsequent statewide contests.

Soon after arriving in the U.S. Senate, Feinstein resumed her anti–violent crime and gun control efforts. The Gun-Free Schools Act, which she cosponsored with Byron Dorgan, a Democratic senator from North Dakota, established uniform nationwide guidelines to make elementary and secondary schools gun-free "safe havens" to protect children and youth from gun-related violence. Feinstein noted that school gun prohibition standards varied enormously among the states; her goal was to ensure that all children would be assured legal protection from gun-related violence.

In 1994 Feinstein also was successful in winning passage of a ban on nineteen forms of combat-type assault weapons. Her proposal, inserted

Felons and Gun Control

Where, how, and why felons obtain, carry, and use guns have been central issues in the gun control debate for decades. One goal of many gun control advocates is to find some mechanism that disrupts the flow of firearms into criminal hands but does not infringe upon the legitimate gun ownership rights of law-abiding citizens. Many recent gun control measures have been enacted with this specific end in mind. Unfortunately, the criminal population has always found it relatively easy to circumvent gun control measures.

The most comprehensive survey of felons and their firearms was undertaken by Wright and Rossi (1986) in the early 1980s and thus is outdated. The study showed that relatively few felons (about one in six) attempted to obtain guns through customary retail channels; the illicit firearm market was dominated by informal purchases, swaps and trades with family members, friends, street sources, drug dealers, and other hard-to-regulate sources. The study also showed that most crime guns (somewhere between half and three-quarters of them) entered the stream of illicit commerce through theft from legitimate gun owners. These results give reason to doubt the efficacy of gun controls imposed at the point of retail sale (e.g., the prohibition in the Gun

Control Act of 1968 against retail sale of firearms to persons with felony records, or the five-day waiting period for new firearm purchases enacted as part of the Brady Handgun Violence Prevention Act of 1993).

The national five-day waiting period was implemented in order to give police departments ample time to undertake background checks on prospective gun buyers. Whether or not a significant number of gun purchases by felons was thwarted by this measure has been a matter of dispute. Proponents cite the number of purchases disallowed because of the background check (some hundreds of thousands over the five years the law was in effect); opponents argue that the principal effect was to divert an even higher proportion of felonious gun acquisitions into the secondary or informal market. Regardless, the most comprehensive evaluation of the effects of the five-day waiting period found no significant effects on rates of homicide and suicide (Ludwig and Cook, 2000).

The five-day waiting period expired in 1998, when it was replaced by the National Instant Criminal Background Check System (NICBCS) managed by the Federal Bureau of Investigation. The heart of the NICBCS is a national database containing information on all felony convictions; in theory, it allows for instantaneous presale background checks of all prospective gun purchasers. A report by the General Accounting Office (2000) on implementation of the NICBCS showed that about three-quarters of all applicants were successfully checked in thirty seconds or less. During the first full year of operation, 8.8 million background checks were processed through the NICBCS. Two percent of these checks resulted in an initial denial; 17 percent of the denials were appealed; and 22 percent of the appeals were successful (that is, the initial denial was reversed).

Restrictions at the point of retail sale, even the NICBCS background checking restriction, are readily circumvented by criminals. Another General Accounting Office (GAO) report released in March 2001 revealed that GAO investigators using fake identification successfully purchased guns from licensed gun dealers in every state they tried. Another easy circumvention is the use of proxy purchasers, associates with "clean" records who purchase guns from retailers in quantity for distribution to their felonious friends. Despite these obvious strategies that allow felons to evade retail-sales controls, the preponderance of evidence continues to show that most felons acquire guns through one-at-a-time off-the-record transactions with friends, family, and other informal sources (Kleck, 1999). Consistent with this conclusion, the Bureau of Alcohol, Tobacco, and Firearms' *Gun Crime Trace Reports* (2000a) that concludes few possessors of crime guns (about 11 percent) purchased their firearms directly from federally licensed gun dealers.

Given the above findings, it is anomalous that most guns used in crimes, confiscated by the police, and traced through the BATF paperwork system prove to be relatively new guns. The elapsed time between a gun's first retail sale and its use in a crime is called "time-to-crime," and numerous BATF reports and other studies have concluded that, on average, time-to-crime is relatively short. This implies a criminal preference for new guns and, perhaps, a larger role for organized gun trafficking in supplying the illicit firearm market than is suggested by the studies reviewed above, a conclusion endorsed by the BATF (Bureau of Alcohol, Tobacco, and Firearms, 2000b). Kleck (1999) resolves the anomaly by noting that criminals are, on average, relatively young and would therefore be expected to own relatively newer firearms. Consistent with this conclusion, one study (Kennedy, Piehl, and Braga, 1996) found that the younger the criminal, the younger his gun.

Among gun owners in general, the secondary or informal market (private purchases or swaps and trades that do not involve licensed gun retailers) accounts for about 40 percent of annual firearm sales (Cook and Ludwig, 1996). The preponderance of evidence is that among felons that fraction is substantially higher. And while it is illegal under federal law to knowingly transfer a firearm to a felon even in a private transaction, this restriction is for all practical purposes unenforceable; as a result, the immense secondary market in firearms is essentially unregulated—a free-market free-for-all that felons can and do exploit to obtain guns of every description in any desired quantity. A serious effort to prevent firearms from falling into felons' hands will require some regulation of this secondary market, and so far no one has come up with a workable strategy to accomplish this end.

James D. Wright
and Teri E. Vail

See also Assault Weapons Ban of 1994; Background Checks; Black Market for Firearms; Brady Handgun Violence Prevention Act; Crime and Gun Use; Enforcement of Gun Control Laws; Gun Control Act of 1968; Gun Shows; National Instant Criminal Background Check System; Youth Crime Gun Interdiction Initiative

For Further Reading:

Allen, John. 1977. *Assault with a Deadly Weapon: The Autobiography of a Street Criminal.* New York: McGraw-Hill.

Bureau of Alcohol, Tobacco, and Firearms. 2000a. *Gun Crime Trace Reports (1999).* Washington, DC: BATF (November).

———. 2000b. *Following the Gun: Enforcing Federal Laws against Firearms Traffickers.* Washington, DC: BATF (June).

Cook, Philip J., and Jens Ludwig. 1996. *Guns in America: Results of a Comprehensive Survey of Gun Ownership and Use.* Washington, DC: Police Foundation.

General Accounting Office. 2000. *Gun Control: Implementation of the National Instant Criminal Background Check System.* Washington, DC: GAO (February).

Kennedy, David M., Anne M. Piehl, and Anthony A. Braga. 1996. "Youth Violence in Boston: Gun Markets, Serious Youth Offenders, and a Use Reduction Strategy." *Law and Contemporary Problems* 59: 147–196.

Kleck, Gary. 1991. *Point Blank: Guns and Violence in America.* Hawthorne, NY: Aldine de Gruyter.

———. 1999. "BATF Gun Trace Data and the Role of Organized Gun Trafficking in Supplying Guns to Criminals." *Saint Louis University Public Law Review* 18: 23–45.

Ludwig, Jens, and Philip J. Cook. 2000. "Homicide and Suicide Rates Associated with Implementation of the Brady Handgun Violence Prevention Act." *Journal of the American Medical Association* 284, 5: 585–591.

Wright, James D., and Peter H. Rossi. 1986. *Armed and Considered Dangerous: A Survey of Felons and Their Firearms.* Hawthorne, NY: Aldine de Gruyter.

Ferguson, Colin

See Long Island Railroad Massacre

Finland, Gun Laws

Finland is a small Nordic country of 5.1 million inhabitants and approximately 3 million firearms. Traditionally, Finland has a strong hunting-related shooting sports culture. It has more firearms per person than most European countries, and the government promotes the idea that maintaining and nurturing the country's strong firearm culture is in the best interests of its citizens.

Legislation on firearms has been collected into a single statute covering all aspects of firearm ownership, commerce in firearms, and punishments for violating the law. This statute was modified in 1998 and 2001 (effective in March 2002) in an effort to promote security and prevention of violence with firearms.

Firearms are highly regulated and the gun statute is very detailed. The more important aspects of the statute follow.

A person must be 18 years old to purchase a firearm. He or she must first submit an application to the police, part of which requires that the reasons for wanting to own the gun must be stated. Accepted reasons include hunting, sport shooting, gun collecting, museum display, security work, and filming. Applicants must back up the reason for wanting to own the gun with some kind of specific evidence—for example, a membership card from a shooting or hunting club or proof of being in the security field. If the application is accepted, the potential gun owner must then apply for a permit for possession.

Out of the approximately 1.7 million gun permits that have been granted, 50 percent have been given for hunting. Hunting is a popular pastime in Finland and there are 300,000 hunters there (6 percent of the population). These figures are the highest in Europe. A small number of these hunters—about 3 percent—are women. The quantity of hunters has remained steady for decades, with approximately 5,000 new hunters taking hunting license tests annually.

The number of applications for gun permits declined slightly during the 1990s. In the early 1990s, 125,000 permits were handled annually, but the number dropped to 55,000 after the stricter firearm law amendments went into effect in 1998. It has been argued that the relatively high number of permits in the early 1990s was due to the government push to control World War II weapons and the belief that gun laws would become stricter.

There are approximately 10,000 new firearms sold annually. Police departments across the country are required to keep records of guns and permits within their area. All such records are classified.

One of the peculiarities of Finnish gun control is the attention paid to vintage World War II weapons. In the aftermath of the war with Russia, many, if not most, males chose to keep both their sidearms and long weapons as war mementos. The trend was replicated by larger unofficial hidings of weapons by private groups and individuals for fear of a Russian invasion. Most of these private firearms were not reported to the police at the time or in the following decades; they were sold illegally or handed over as family heirlooms. In the early 1990s the government wanted to include such firearms in official records and offered amnesty for those who turned in such firearms. Those wishing to keep these historical firearms were offered permits. The police estimate that there are still between 100,000 and 150,000 illegal firearms in Finland, many of which may be old guns, but they also include newer illegal firearms obtained for criminal purposes.

Finnish firearm owners are obligated by law to prevent their firearms from falling into the wrong hands. Thus, for example, if a gun owner has more than five weapons, they must be kept in a locked gun safe or stored with the gun parts separated. In addition, all firearms carried outside the home must be unloaded and—in most cases—disassembled.

Firearm collectors are required to apply for a collector's license. Approximately 1,000 such licenses have been issued. Collectors submit a timetable and collection content outline along with the application. The applicant is furthermore expected to give detailed information about his or her expertise in firearm history and technology. Collectors are required to keep detailed records of their collections.

The European Firearms Pass is used in Finland. This is the identification card for gun owners in which the owner's name, address, identification number, place of birth, and citizenship are displayed along with information about firearm permits and owned firearms both in Finland and in other European Union countries. The European Firearms Pass enables gun owners to transport firearms used for hunting and sport shooting within Europe.

Commerce in firearms is regulated to a high degree by the Ministry of Interior. Gun stores are required to keep detailed records of all firearms held by the store and to provide the police with such records in situations specified by law. All persons working at a gun store need to have a permit to handle firearms.

Finland has its fair share of violent crime, murder, and manslaughter, the rates of which have risen slightly from the beginning of the 1980s through 2000. For example, in 1990 there were 7.8 homicides and attempts per 100,000 people, and this rose to 9.2 by 2000 (though virtually all of the increase was due to attempts, as the actual number of murders was nearly identical—145 in 1990 and 146 in 2000). The rate of actual murders (2.9 per 100,000 people) is about half that of the United States (5.5)—despite the fact that both nations are awash in firearms. Moreover, unlike in the United States, the majority of homicides in Finland are *not* related to firearms, as only around 23 percent of killings are committed with a firearm (compared to 59 percent in the United States). This figure has been extremely steady since 1960. In comparison, over 30 percent of homicides are committed with a sharp instrument and nearly 30 percent are carried out using personal force (Savolainen, Messner, and Kivivuori, 2001, p. 53).

Analyses of the socioeconomic, cultural, and personal attributes of the killers and the types of weapons used reveal that proposed legislative changes that would restrict firearms would not deter homicide or solve many of the other problems surrounding firearms; rather, such analyses find the root causes in broader social problems (such as alcohol abuse and inequality).

Firearms have been noticeably uncontroversial in Finland over the years. Some of the problematic issues in the U.S. gun control debate do not apply to Finland and other countries. For example, "self-protection" is strikingly missing as a right of Finnish citizens. Also, instances where private property has been protected with firearms (against animal rights activists, for example) have been condemned by the authorities. Moreover, unlike in the United States, the majority of Finnish males (due to conscription) and a significant minority of women (due to voluntary military service) have a good deal of familiarity with firearms. Military training not only focuses on the defensive and combat usage of firearms but also highlights safety training.

Tiia Rajala

See also Availability of Guns, Effects on Crime; Russia, Gun Laws; Victimization from Gun Violence

For Further Reading:

Savolainen, Jukka, Steven F. Messner, and Janne Kivivuori. 2001. "Contexts of Lethal Violence in Finland and the United States." Pp. 41–60 in *Homicide in Finland,* ed. Tapio Lappi-Setälä. Helsinki: National Research Institute of Legal Policy.

Firearm Dealers

Virtually all civilian sales of new firearms in the United States are made through federally licensed firearm dealers (FFLs), regulated under a scheme established by the federal Gun Control Act of 1968. Retail dealers range from tiny enterprises, such as mom-and-pop sidelines in rural general stores, to vast specialized emporia with racks of guns and affiliated shooting ranges. Retailers get most of their guns from wholesale distributors, who are also federally licensed. Even so, about 40 percent of all gun sales each year are of used guns bought and sold through unregulated transactions in the secondary market.

Enacted in the wake of the assassinations of President John F. Kennedy, Sen. Robert F. Kennedy, and Dr. Martin Luther King, Jr., the GCA of 1968 is the primary federal law regulating commerce in firearms. The 1968 law created a licensing system aimed primarily at regulating the interstate movement of firearms. By restricting interstate movement of firearms to transactions between FFLs, the law was intended to enhance the ability of the individual states to effectively enforce their own gun laws by barring "gun runners" from buying guns in states with lax laws and transporting them to states with more restrictive laws. The GCA also barred certain prohibited classes of persons, such as convicted felons, from receiving or possessing firearms.

Central to the federal regulatory scheme is the requirement that any person "engaged in the business" of manufacturing, importing, or dealing in firearms obtain a license from the secretary of the treasury, whose authority is delegated in practice to the Bureau of Alcohol, Tobacco, and Firearms. The BATF issues eleven types of licenses, depending on the nature of the licensee's activity. The most common license, Type 01, is issued to retail dealers (70 percent), but some other common licenses include Type 02 for pawnbrokers (10 percent), Type 06 for ammunition manufacturers (2 percent), Type 07 for firearm manufacturers (2 percent), and Type 08 for importers (less than 1 percent).

Possession of a federal Type 01 dealer's license is a powerful tool. It grants the holder the privilege of purchasing and shipping guns in any quantity across state lines to and from other licensees, including retailers, wholesale distributors, and manufacturers. Licensees are required to maintain detailed records of firearm transactions and are subject to periodic inspection by the BATF. Although some states impose their own licensing requirements, most do not, limiting their regulation to collateral matters such as zoning restrictions and generic business licensing and tax collection.

The GCA's original wording limited the BATF's discretion in denying licenses. The law required the BATF to issue a license within forty-five days of an application to anyone who was 21 years old, had business premises, and

A gun dealer in Pittsburgh, Pennsylvania. (Reuters NewMedia Inc./Corbis)

was not prohibited from possessing firearms. The law also failed to define the term "engaged in the business."

As a consequence of these regulatory features, the number of FFLs quickly ballooned. Persons who had no intention of engaging in a full-fledged retail business easily got licenses, issued for three-year periods at an annual fee of only ten dollars. With license in hand, these "kitchen-table" dealers could buy guns out of state, sometimes at wholesale prices, for themselves, their friends, and others, often evading local zoning and tax laws in the process and without undergoing background checks or waiting periods imposed on individual retail customers. By 1992 there were 245,000 licensed gun dealers in the United States—more than the 210,000 gas stations in the country. The sheer number of kitchen-table dealers made meaningful regulation by the BATF impossible and invited criminal abuse. Some dealers purchased large quantities of firearms—thousands in a few cases—for criminal enterprises. By 1993, when the number

of FFLs reached its peak of 286,000, the BATF estimated that 74 percent of FFLs were kitchen-table dealers, and 46 percent conducted no business at all.

Calls for reform brought legislative and administrative changes that significantly tightened the licensing system. For example, the 1993 Brady Bill increased the dealer licensing fee to $200 for the first three years and $90 for each additional three-year period. It also requires applicants to certify that they have notified the chief law enforcement officer in their area of their intent to apply for a license. The 1994 Violent Crime Control and Law Enforcement Act further requires applicants to submit photographs and fingerprints, and to certify that their business complies with all state and local laws, including zoning regulations. Finally, BATF field offices initiated cooperative efforts with state and local authorities to ensure that applicants met all relevant state and local laws.

As a result of these changes, the number of Type 01 FFLs dropped from 245,628 in January

1994 to 66,500 in February 2001, a decrease of 73 percent. Gun rights advocates complained that the reforms infringed on their rights, and the industry complained that the dramatic decrease in dealers hurt sales. But regulators welcomed the drop, arguing that it was easier to supervise fewer dealers and that the drop in casual dealers discouraged criminal gun trafficking. Even so, the BATF reported that in 1998 about 31 percent of FFLs had sold no guns during the preceding year.

Federal law does not require all gun sellers to obtain a license. On the contrary, it exempts from licensing a person who makes "occasional sales, exchanges, or purchases of firearms for the enhancement of a personal collection or for a hobby, or who sells all or part of a personal firearms collection." Although such hobbyists and personal sellers do not enjoy the privilege of interstate sales, they have inspired commercial complaint and regulatory concern, principally in the context of gun shows, venues at which firearms are often sold informally. Forty percent of all gun sales each year are made through such informal secondary market outlets.

Because federal gun control laws have focused primarily on screening gun buyers in an attempt to "keep guns out of the wrong hands," licensed dealers are required to keep specific records on all guns they buy or sell and to initiate background checks on all potential purchasers. Hobbyists and personal sellers are free from these requirements. Licensed dealers complain that this disparity puts them at a competitive disadvantage, especially at gun shows, where the only difference between a licensed dealer and an unlicensed private seller is that a person buying from the latter is free of bothersome paperwork and background checks. Gun regulators argue that unlicensed sellers have become a major source of firearms for felons, juveniles, and others who have been effectively barred from getting guns by the background checks imposed by the Brady Bill. Closing this "gun show loophole" has become a contentious goal of the gun control movement.

Thomas Diaz

See also Assault Weapons Ban of 1994
For Further Reading:
Bureau of Alcohol, Tobacco, and Firearms. 2000. *Commerce in Firearms in the United States.* Washington, DC: U.S. Government Printing Office.
Diaz, Tom. 1999. *Making a Killing: The Business of Guns in America.* New York: New Press.
Violence Policy Center. 2000. *Firearms Production in America: 2000 Edition.* Washington, DC.

Firearm Industry

The modern American firearm industry is shaped by the fact that the United States is the last great civilian firearm market in the world. Foreign commercial interests attracted to this unique market therefore play an important role in the industry.

About 4.5 million new firearms are sold to civilians in the United States each year. Some 2 million of these are handguns. Another 2 million secondhand guns—some 44 percent of all sales—are sold annually in the "secondary market." The U.S. Department of Justice estimated that in 1994 civilians owned 192 million guns, 65 million of them being handguns. These firearms are not uniformly distributed: about one-quarter of the adults in the United States own a firearm, and about one in six own a handgun.

The federal Gun Control Act of 1968 requires that all persons "engaged in the business" of manufacturing, importing, or dealing in firearms obtain a license from the secretary of the treasury. With few exceptions, the law restricts interstate transfers of guns to transactions between license holders. A licensed dealer may sell a long gun (rifle or shotgun) to an unlicensed resident of another state so long as the sale is otherwise legal in both states. But handguns may be sold across state lines only between licensed dealers. On the other hand, persons who manufacture a single gun for personal use, or who engage in casual intrastate sales from their personal collections, are not required to have a federal license.

As a result, new firearms are sold only through the approximately 66,500 licensed retail dealers nationwide. Retail dealers are supplied primarily by wholesale distributors and importers—manufacturers do not as a rule sell directly to retailers. Secondhand firearms, in contrast, are sold in a variety of unregulated venues by an array of unlicensed sources. These range from casual person-to-person sales to large, well-organized gun shows at which unlicensed private sellers sell guns ostensibly from their own collections side by side with licensed retail dealers.

The American gun industry can be said to have been born in 1777, when an arsenal was established in Springfield, Massachusetts, to supply General Washington's army during the Revolutionary War. Although the Springfield Armory continued to make military firearms until the mid-1960s, the industry at large has suffered continuous cycles of boom and bust. Scores of gun makers thrived briefly in "Gun Valley" (as the region in western Massachusetts and Connecticut came to be called), but only a few—buoyed by such clever inventions as Samuel Colt's revolver in the 1830s or timely contracts during major military conflicts such as the Civil War—survived to modern times.

The invention of the revolver, which made firearms convenient to carry on the person, and the Mexican War, Civil War, and frontier expansion—all of which increased mass firearm ownership by an order of magnitude—were the most significant developments in the gun industry before the twentieth century. Otherwise, the history of the industry before World War II is significant more for its role in the mythology of guns in the United States than for its relevance to society today. Almost half of the guns made available to civilians between 1899 and 1993 (46 percent) were produced between 1947 and 1993, and 80 percent of all guns in private hands in 1994 had been acquired since 1974. Moreover, the product mix is significantly different today than it was before World War II, and manufacturing facilities are more widely dispersed—only about 30 percent of guns made in the United States are now manufactured in "Gun Valley."

The 1997 Census of Manufacturers (the latest year available) reported 191 small arms manufacturers, whose combined total product shipments were valued at about $1.2 billion. These gun makers reported 9,907 employees and a combined annual payroll of about $320 million. The value of gun industry shipments in 1997 may be compared to the $28.3 billion in cigarettes and $27.7 billion in alcoholic beverages reported the same year.

Information deduced from the federal excise taxes collected on firearms and ammunition provides a more dynamic perspective over time. The available data show that the wholesale value of firearms and ammunition sold in the United States grew from an estimated total of $846 million in 1983 to a peak of $1.9 billion in 1994, then slipped to $1.5 billion in 1998. This industry is highly concentrated: a few manufacturers make most of the guns. A fluid assortment of other small manufacturers make the rest, some as few as one gun a year.

Firearm industry associations emphasize collateral economic effects of the firearm industry that reach far beyond direct sales of firearms and ammunition. For example, the Sporting Arms and Ammunition Manufacturers Institute claims that hunting and shooting sports generated more than $30.9 billion in economic activity in 1998 and supported more than 986,000 jobs. These estimates include related equipment, clothing, accessories, and trip expenses such as food and lodging.

The uniquely open American civilian firearm market has attracted substantial foreign interest: the United States is a net importer of civilian firearms. Less than 5 percent of all guns brought into the American civilian market between 1899 and 1945 were imported. But foreign companies began heavily exploiting the American gun market in the 1970s, either by exporting guns to the United States or by setting up American subsidiaries. Since the 1990s, between a third and a half of all guns sold in the United States each year have been imported from abroad, with the proportion of imported handguns in the overall handgun market somewhat greater.

The modern gun industry developed in the decades following World War II and its course is marked by three factors: a decided growth spurt in the mid-1960s, a radical change in product mix, and chronic stagnation in the last quarter of the twentieth century (which was marked by cycles of growth and decline).

Firearm sales in the two decades following World War II declined from a high of 2.4 million guns sold in 1950 to a low of 1.4 million in 1958.

But the industry took off in the mid-1960s, surpassing 3.5 million guns in 1968 and hitting an all-time peak of 5.6 million in 1980. Sales declined somewhat in the 1980s, took off again in the 1990s—reaching another peak year in 1994, when 5.1 million guns were sold—and then declined to 3.6 million in 1998.

Analysts attribute the modern industry's spotty fortunes to several unique factors in addition to broader economic cycles. Factors depressing sales include the overall decline of such traditional portals for introduction of youth to firearms and entry into the shooting sports as hunting and military service, an explosion of alternate recreational outlets for youth, and growing social disfavor. Factors boosting sales have been widespread concern for personal safety during periods of apparent social disorder or increasing crime, and the influence of high-visibility gun control legislation such as the 1993 Brady Bill, which appeared to spur sales when it was pending.

The change in the mix of firearm products was dramatic in the last quarter of the twentieth century. Analysts find the growth in handguns significant because two-thirds of all homicides and most gun crimes in the United States are committed with handguns. Prior to the period in question, handguns had been a relatively small proportion of the overall gun market, accounting for about 25 percent of all sales between 1899 and 1945. In 1946 handguns accounted for only 8 percent of firearms available for sale. Beginning in the mid-1960s, however, the firearm product mix changed significantly. Handguns rapidly rose to dominate the civilian market and, with the exception of a brief resurgence of long guns in the mid-1970s, have continued to do so without interruption since 1979. Handguns accounted for 54 percent of domestic firearm production in the peak year of 1994, then declined to 46 percent in 1997 and to 35 percent in 1998 (the last year for which data are available).

Although handgun sales remain at comparatively high levels historically, the decline may be related to falling crime rates. Handgun manufacturers rely heavily on "fear marketing" to sell handguns—three-quarters of handgun owners reported in 1994 that they kept their guns primarily for self-defense (rather than for recreational uses as in the case of long guns). Declining crime rates may have depressed the handgun market.

The gun industry was in turmoil at the beginning of the new millennium. On the one hand, it sought new answers to the marketing problems that have dogged it for decades—how to stimulate sales among its most loyal cadre of aging white male consumers and how to expand into new demographic niches. On the other hand, it was beleaguered by a spate of lawsuits filed by state and local governments seeking to impose on the industry the burden of such costs associated with firearm violence as medical expenses and policing. The industry's answers to its marketing problems were to reach out to new demographic groups such as women, children, and members of racial and ethnic minority groups; emphasize creative sporting uses of firearms such as so-called cowboy shooting and sporting clays competitions; and increase the number of places consumers can shoot by encouraging new shooting ranges. Its answers to the litigation included a dogged defense by most companies and a broad political offensive aimed at enacting laws barring such lawsuits.

Thomas Diaz

See also Browning, John Moses; Civil War and Small Arms; Colt, Samuel; Firearm Dealers; Gun Control Act of 1968; Lawsuits against Gun Manufacturers; Product Liability Lawsuits; Ruger, William Batterman; Smith & Wesson; Winchester, Oliver Fisher

For Further Reading:
Bellesiles, Michael. 2000. *Arming America: The Origins of a National Gun Culture.* New York: Alfred A. Knopf.
Bureau of Alcohol, Tobacco, and Firearms. 2000. *Commerce in Firearms in the United States.* Washington, DC: U.S. Government Printing Office.
Diaz, Tom. 1999. *Making a Killing: The Business of Guns in America.* New York: New Press.
Violence Policy Center. 2000. *Firearms Production in America: 2000 Edition.* Washington, DC.

Firearm Injury Statistical Systems

The first step in addressing any public health problem is collecting data that help describe the extent and nature of the problem. This requires the ongoing and systematic collection of comprehensive health information. Although limited data on firearm *fatalities* are available from vital statistics (e.g., the age and gender of victims) and from crime databases (e.g., on the victim-perpetrator relationship), the United States does not currently have an adequate data system on intentional injury generally and firearm injury in particular. National data are not systematically collected on the circumstances associated with firearm suicides, unintentional gunshot fatalities, or nonfatal firearm injuries, nor on the characteristics of the firearms used to inflict any type of injury.

The enormous benefits that can be provided by a national injury data system are well known from the motor vehicle area. For every motor vehicle fatality, more than a hundred pieces of information are collected—including the make and model of the vehicle, vehicular speed, speed limit, seat belt use, alcohol involvement—consistently across all fifty states. These data are part of the Fatality Analysis Reporting System operated by the National Highway Traffic Safety Administration and are made available to researchers at no cost. Studies using such data have established the effects of driver behavior, vehicle characteristics, and environmental conditions on collision frequency and severity. The data have permitted the scientific evaluation of a wide variety of interventions, including drunk-driver legislation, child restraint laws, mandatory belt-use laws, revised speed limits, vehicle crash survivability standards, motorcycle helmet laws, vehicle inspection laws, minimum-age drinking laws, driver education programs, driver licensing restrictions, no-fault automobile insurance, and right-turn-on-red laws. Recently, the surveillance data have been used to evaluate the effectiveness of driver and passenger-side air bags, resulting in the promotion of rear seating of children, the depowering of airbags, and regulation that allows the disconnection of air bag systems.

In contrast to discussions about U.S. motor vehicle policy, debates about firearm policy are driven more by rhetoric than by fact. In part, this is because comprehensive national information about firearm injuries does not exist, so most policy questions in the firearm area are currently unanswerable. We do not know, for example, whether there are temporal trends in the proportion of gun-related deaths from small, cheap handguns, whether certain types of guns are used preferentially by adolescents to commit crime, or whether there are particular characteristics common to guns involved in unintended shootings of children. A good firearm data system could answer questions like these, plus provide crucial data for the evaluation of child access protection laws, assault weapons bans, one-gun-per-month laws, and other regulations (Barber et al., 2000).

An initial step toward the creation of a national firearm injury data system occurred in 1994 when funding from the Centers for Disease Control and Prevention (CDC) led to the development or enhancement of more than a half dozen firearm surveillance systems, primarily at state health departments. Unfortunately, federal funding for the system was withdrawn in 1997.

As a result, most cities and states do not have a firearm injury data system; those systems that exist are usually rudimentary, and the data collected are not comparable across jurisdictions. Nonetheless, the few states and localities that do have linked, multisource data systems have provided information that would not otherwise have been available. For example, the Massachusetts Department of Public Health surveillance system collects information about injuries caused by guns and knives, using data from hospitals and other sources. Over the ten-year period of 1985–1994 in Massachusetts, there was a dramatic increase in the proportion of firearm injuries associated with semiautomatic pistols, while injuries associated with revolvers, rifles, and shotguns decreased. The dramatic decline in gun violence in Boston in the mid-1990s that followed various innovative police and other initiatives has been called the "Boston Miracle," and Boston has been the model for other cities that are trying to reduce youth gun violence. However, the surveillance system documents substantial declines in firearm injuries in other large Massachusetts cities without such policy initiatives.

The Medical College of Wisconsin's *Firearm Injury Surveillance System* provides another example of a firearm statistical system. Begun in the mid-1990s, it was the first study to link firearm fatality reports from medical examiners, police, and crime labs. Five specific gun makes were identified as accounting for almost 50 percent of the fatalities in the Milwaukee area. These makes accounted for only 6 percent of the guns turned in during the Milwaukee "buy back" program. The buy-back program may have had some beneficial effects, including potentially reducing accidents and suicides, but it did not help rid the streets of the weapons most commonly used in fatal shootings. The Clinton crime bill of September 1994 targeted nineteen specific types of guns. In the Milwaukee area, guns of these types were involved in 9 percent of homicides between 1991 and September 1994. Following the crime bill, between September 1994 and the end of 1996, these types of guns were still involved in 9 percent of homicides, suggesting that the crime bill had little short-run effect.

A trauma center in Maine has linked emergency medical service, emergency department, and hospital data for the entire state. In 20 percent of gunshot wounds, the time between notification of the emergency medical service and arrival at the appropriate hospital is longer than sixty minutes, the so-called golden hour for survival. An improved, integrated trauma system could reduce the time period and save lives.

These existing local systems show the promise of a national firearm injury data system for informing rational gun policy. To help realize this promise, in the late 1990s six foundations funded the Harvard Injury Control Research Center, the coordinating center for a national firearm data system that would promote state-level surveillance efforts and work to ensure that comparable data are collected over time. The foundations hope that their private funding, intended to be short-term only, will spark the development of a federally funded, national reporting system.

The Harvard project has worked with sites around the country to pilot-test a model reporting system. The first year of data focused on gun injuries, both fatal and nonfatal. An assessment of that system by a variety of law enforcement, public health, injury surveillance, and mental health experts led in the second year to the expansion of the fatality component to cover homicides and suicides by all weapon types. The CDC now has plans under way to implement a National Violent Death Reporting System (NVDRS) based on the piloted system. A long-term goal is to expand the system to cover all fatal injuries, including unintentional injuries due to falls, fires, drownings, and other causes. The NVDRS has been endorsed by a wide variety of organizations and its implementation is recommended by the surgeon general's 2001 "National Strategy for Suicide Prevention."

Data collection proved crucial in tracking and eliminating contagious disease epidemics in the United States, and it has been invaluable as a tool for reducing our motor vehicle injury problem. The United States needs better data on the second leading mechanism of fatal injuries—firearms. As the *Milwaukee Journal Sentinel* aptly observed in 1999, "Since 1980, there have been only 137 polio cases in the United States while an estimated 120,000 Americans are injured or killed every year by firearms. Yet government does a better job of tracking polio. That's appalling and must change if this country is going to effectively and fairly address the problem posed by misuse of firearms."

David Hemenway

See also Accidents, Gun; Gun Violence as a Public Health Problem; Suicide, Guns and

For Further Reading:

Azrael, Deborah, Catherine Barber, and James Mercy. 2001. "Linking Data to Save Lives: Recent Progress in Establishing a National Violent Death Reporting System." *Harvard Health Policy Review* 2, 2: 38–42.

Barber, Catherine, David Hemenway, Steven Hargarten, Arthur R. Kellermann, Deborah Azrael, and Susan Wilt. 2000. "A Call to Arms for a National Surveillance System on Firearm Injuries." *American Journal of Public Health* 90: 1191–1193.

Milwaukee Journal Sentinel. 1999. "Another Good Idea on Firearms." February 15.

Firearm Sentence Enhancement (FSE) Laws

Firearm sentence enhancement laws are those criminal laws that impose upon criminal offenders increased penalties if the use of a firearm was involved in the offender's criminal offense. FSE laws, often also called "gun-use laws," typically result in significantly longer terms of imprisonment for perpetrators of crimes committed with guns. By increasing the term of imprisonment, FSE laws were envisioned as a way to decrease violent crimes, including gun assaults and homicides, through deterrence. FSE laws have been assumed by legislators to have a derivative deterrent effect on violent gun assaults and homicides because the potential criminal offender would presumably leave the guns at home to avoid the imposition of greater punishments if apprehended. The arguable assumption behind FSE laws is that the existence of such laws might influence the decision-making process of the criminal offender on whether or not to carry a firearm or to use the firearm during the commission of a felony.

In the gun control and firearm policy areas, few measures have received as much attention at both the state and federal levels as FSE laws. Multiple state statutes and the federal Gun Control Act of 1968 impose increased punishments in criminal cases through the use of FSE provisions. FSE laws have been viewed by state and federal legislators as an attractive means of gun control, as one of their most important expectations is that they will reduce gun-related crime without imposing further constraints on the behavior of "law-abiding" citizens who wish to possess firearms. It is for this reason that interest groups such as the National Rifle Association frequently lend their support to the advancement of FSE laws.

The federal FSE law is contained in section 924(c) of the Gun Control Act (GCA) of 1968. In its original form, the FSE law in the GCA provided a mandatory minimum sentence of between one and ten years for criminals who used or carried a firearm unlawfully during the commission of any federal felony. Since the federal FSE law's original enactment, Congress has amended it many times, including by expanding the coverage to drug crimes, distinguishing among the types of firearms, and raising the penalty to up to thirty additional years if the firearm is a machine gun, an assault rifle, or equipped with a silencer. Congress has also clarified the meaning of "use"

and "possession" of a firearm in the FSE provision in response to several Supreme Court cases restricting the interpretation of the FSE provision. To date, no systematic studies have been published that reveal the effectiveness of FSE laws.

James A. Beckman

See also *Bailey v. United States;* Gun Control Act of 1968; *Muscarello v. United States; Smith v. United States*

For Further Reading:
Hofer, Paul. 2000. "Federal Sentencing for Violent and Drug Trafficking Crimes Involving Firearms: Recent Changes and Prospects for Improvement." *American Criminal Law Review* 37 (winter): 41–73.

Firearm Violence Literature Database

See Pacific Center for Violence Prevention

Firearms Coalition

The Firearms Coalition is almost an organization of one—its founder Neal Knox. The organization is used to channel financial contributions to Knox's political lobbying. The donations are not used to support gun accessories, and in contrast to many other firearm organizations that offer extensive training and merchandise, the Firearms Coalition offers only a bimonthly newsletter.

The Internet is a powerful tool for any advocacy group and many gun organizations have focused on building elaborate websites to gain support and publicize their messages. The Firearms Coalition, which was founded in 1984, at first used phone messages and fax alerts, but it moved quickly to the online format. The Internet not only helps the coalition increase its fund-raising efforts but, more importantly, places the information in the public domain. Members and nonmembers alike are able to view Knox's columns, alerts, and general gun-related news articles via the site. The Firearms Coalition website has also collected gun-related Internet links whose content and quality are briefly described. Interestingly enough, the coalition has also chosen to include a brief message by Knox in Spanish. Latin gun owners are generally not addressed in their own language by gun groups.

Tiia Rajala

See also Knox, Neal
For Further Reading:
Firearms Coalition home page:
http://www.nealknox.com.

Firearms Litigation Clearinghouse

An affiliate of the Educational Fund to Stop Gun Violence and the Coalition to Stop Gun Violence, the Firearms Litigation Clearinghouse is an advocacy group and informational resource created in 1981 to encourage the use of the civil tort system to reduce injuries caused by firearms. According to the clearinghouse's website, the goals of the organization are (1) to disseminate information designed to facilitate successful suits against firearm manufacturers brought by victims of gun violence; (2) to develop legal strategies designed to impose liability on both manufacturers and dealers of firearms; (3) to provide an educational resource for attorneys and citizen activists wishing to bring such suits; (4) to encourage these suits; and (5) to provide legal resources to government entities seeking to recover damages allegedly caused by the manufacture and distribution of firearms.

In particular, the clearinghouse encourages four types of suits that may be brought against the firearm industry: product liability suits against manufacturers for having produced and sold defective products; suits against dealers for negligent sales to persons prohibited from owning guns; suits against manufacturers for intentional shootings; and litigation initiated by cities against manufacturers and distributors to recover costs associated with gun violence, including costs associated with health care or police services. A number of documents related to the municipalities' suits against gun manufacturers are available on the clearinghouse's website.

To further its mission, the clearinghouse offers referrals to local attorneys for those wishing to file suits against gun manufacturers or sellers, and will provide educational support for community leaders and activists wishing to know more about bringing litigation. The clearinghouse also offers plaintiffs' attorneys access to its library of information to assist their litigation efforts, including information on manufacturers,

copies of depositions and pleadings, access to expert witnesses, participation in a network of attorneys, and case consultation with members of the clearinghouse. The clearinghouse also publishes the *Firearms Litigation Reporter,* which digests recent firearm litigation decisions from around the country.

The editor of the *Firearms Litigation Reporter* is the executive director of the Educational Fund to Stop Gun Violence, Joshua M. Horwitz. Formerly a lawyer in private practice, Horwitz joined the Educational Fund in 1989.

Brannon P. Denning

See also Coalition to Stop Gun Violence; *Dix v. Beretta U.S.A. Corp.;* Lawsuits against Gun Manufacturers; Nuisance Law and Gun Suits; Product Liability Lawsuits; Smith & Wesson Settlement Agreement
For Further Reading:
Educational Fund's website: http://www.gunfree.org.
Firearms Litigation Clearinghouse's website:
  http://www.firearmslitigation.org.

Firearms Owners Against Crime (FOAC)

Firearms Owners Against Crime is a nonpartisan political action committee based in Pennsylvania and chaired by Kim Stolfer. The purpose of the organization is to promote the election of legislators and politicians who support unregulated gun ownership. The FOAC is involved at both the state and federal levels in promoting legal gun ownership. The group supports the prosecution of illegitimate users of firearms but does not support the regulation or restriction of gun ownership for legitimate use, "including personal and property protection."

In support of its position, the group cites the Second Amendment to the U.S. Constitution and the first article of the Constitution of the Commonwealth of Pennsylvania. It keeps its membership aware of legislative initiatives and voting records of legislators, which are relevant to its mission. The FOAC publishes voter guides for interested parties who want to support unregulated gun ownership. It only supports candidates who agree with its political positions. The organization features meetings and speakers and provides a website with informational links. The

FOAC does not present alternative views, although it does provide information that it believes supports its positions.

Elizabeth K. Englander

See also Citizens Committee for the Right to Keep and Bear Arms; Gun Owners of America; National Rifle Association; Second Amendment

For Further Reading:
FOAC website: http://www.foac-pac.org/.

Firearms Owners' Protection Act of 1986

This law relaxed several federal gun restrictions that were first enacted in 1968. The move to relax federal gun regulations was a top agenda item of a new and more politically aggressive leadership faction that took control of the National Rifle Association in 1977. Congressional sponsors of the bill were Sen. James McClure (R-ID) and Rep. Howard Volkmer (D-MO). The bill that passed in 1986 (PL99–308, 100 Stat. 449) came to be known as the McClure-Volkmer bill.

As early as 1978, Rep. Volkmer proposed legislation at the behest of the NRA to repeal much of the Gun Control Act of 1968. Sen. McClure joined this effort in the early 1980s. This political drive picked up important momentum from the presidential election of gun control foe Ronald Reagan in 1980 and the more conservative mood of the country, and from the fact that the Republicans won control of the Senate after the 1980 elections.

Earlier versions of the McClure-Volkmer bill had been approved by the Senate Judiciary Committee in 1982 and 1984, but full floor consideration was not obtained until 1985, when at the urging of the bill's sponsors, Senate Majority Leader Robert Dole (R-KS) authorized the unusual move of bypassing the Judiciary Committee and placing the bill directly on the Senate calendar. Once on the floor, the bill was subjected to a barrage of amendments designed to strengthen gun controls; none of these amendments was accepted, however, except for a restriction adopted by the Senate to ban the importation of gun parts for Saturday night specials.

Opponents of the bill, led by Sen. Edward Kennedy (D-MA) and Sen. Howard Metzenbaum (D-OH), threatened a filibuster in June if some of the bill's provisions were not softened. Supporters yielded, and after intense negotiations the bill, S. 49, was passed on July 9, 1985. The final vote for passage of the bill was 79–15. The relatively speedy passage was attributed to the pressure of the NRA and its allies, and to the fact that the Republican-controlled Senate had a sympathetic Judiciary Committee chair, Strom Thurmond (R-SC), and majority leader.

Deliberations in the Democratic-controlled House posed a far greater problem for McClure-Volkmer supporters. House Judiciary Committee Chair Peter Rodino (D-NJ), a staunch gun control proponent, had announced early in 1985 that the bill arrived "D.O.A.—Dead on Arrival." Bill opponents were still confident that Rodino would succeed as he had in the past in keeping the bill bottled up in committee. Yet Rodino was unable to fulfill his prediction. By the fall of 1985, bill supporters had begun a discharge petition that, if signed by a majority of the House membership (218 representatives), would force the bill out of committee and onto the floor. The drastic and unusual nature of the House discharge petition is revealed by the fact that from 1937 to 1986 discharge petitions had succeeded in only twenty instances. Of those, only two such bills were actually enacted into law.

Despite the initial opposition of Rodino and Rep. William J. Hughes (D-NJ), the chair of the Judiciary Subcommittee on Crime, they both realized that unless they formulated a substitute compromise bill the full committee would be forced to report McClure-Volkmer. The committee thus held a markup session on a compromise bill and reported it to the floor by unanimous vote. This remarkable turn of events occurred in March 1986 as the result of a successful discharge petition. By reporting the Rodino-Hughes bill to the floor first (on March 11) before the actual filing of the discharge petition on behalf of McClure-Volkmer (on March 13), gun control supporters hoped to salvage some parliamentary flexibility that would allow priority consideration of the Rodino-Hughes bill. This maneuver failed, however, because Volkmer was able to offer his version of the bill as a substitute for that of the Judiciary Committee in a vote on the floor.

On April 9, Representative Hughes offered a package of law enforcement amendments to McClure-Volkmer, including a ban on interstate sale and transport of handguns and stricter record-keeping regulations. The package was rejected by a wide margin (176–248). During the vote, police officers stood in full uniform at "parade rest" at the entrance to the House floor as a sign of their opposition to McClure-Volkmer. After several other votes on motions to strengthen certain gun control provisions (all were defeated), the House adjourned and then reconvened the next day. On the third try, the House approved (by 233–184) a ban on interstate handgun sales after proponents stressed the difference between sale and transport. A final amendment to bar all future possession and sale of machine guns by private citizens also passed. The bill was approved by a 292–130 vote on April 10. President Reagan signed the measure into law on May 19, 1986.

As passed into law, McClure-Volkmer amended the 1968 act by allowing for the legal interstate sale of rifles and shotguns as long as the sale was legal in the states of the buyer and seller. The act also eliminated record-keeping requirements for ammunition dealers, made it easier for individuals selling guns to do so without a license unless they did so "regularly," allowed gun dealers to do business at gun shows, and prohibited the Bureau of Alcohol, Tobacco, and Firearms (BATF) from issuing regulations requiring centralized records of gun dealers. The law also reduced the penalty for falsifying firearm records from a felony to a misdemeanor. In addition, the act limited to one per year the number of unannounced inspections of gun dealers by the BATF and prohibited the establishment of any system of comprehensive firearm registration. Finally, the act barred future possession or transfer of machine guns and retained existing restrictions (except for transport) on handguns.

In a final move to tighten up elements of the bill that was also a concession to law enforcement groups that had opposed McClure-Volkmer, the Senate passed a separate bill on May 6 that tightened licensing, record-keeping, and interstate transport requirements. That bill easily passed the House on June 24 and was signed into law on July 8, 1986. The passage of McClure-Volkmer represented a high point in the NRA's influence in Washington. In all, the NRA spent about $1.6 million in lobbying and advertising costs to win passage of the bill. At the same time, however, gun control supporters, led by Handgun Control, Inc., also won some concessions in the bill, prompting them to claim victory as well. In addition, this bill marked a public and permanent split between police organizations and the NRA. Formerly, links between the two had been strong. After this, however, most police organizations would side with efforts to strengthen gun control, including the Brady Bill and the assault weapons ban. Despite the NRA's victory, leaders within the organization considered it inadequate, and several dozen NRA employees were fired after the bill's enactment as a consequence.

Robert J. Spitzer

See also Brady Campaign to Prevent Gun Violence; Bureau of Alcohol, Tobacco, and Firearms; Gun Control Act of 1968; National Rifle Association

For Further Reading:

Spitzer, Robert J. 1998. *The Politics of Gun Control.* New York: Chatham House.
Vizzard, William J. 2000. *Shots in the Dark.* Lanham, MD: Rowman & Littlefield.

First Monday: Unite to End Gun Violence, 2000–2001

First Monday is an annual, campus-based organizing campaign that focuses on a different social justice issue each year. The campaign begins each year on the first Monday in October to coincide with the opening of the Supreme Court term. Although First Monday focused on a different social justice issue each year since 1994, in 2000 it decided to focus on gun violence for two years. That decision reflected the organization's view of how critical gun violence is. First Monday 2000 emphasized the victims of gun violence and the importance of gun control laws. The 2001 campaign focused on the gun industry, the gun lobby (especially the National Rifle Association), and how their practices exacerbate gun violence in the United States.

First Monday is a project of the Alliance for Justice in conjunction with Physicians for Social Responsibility. The campaign points out that the United States tolerates levels of gun violence much higher than those in most other industrialized societies, with more than eighty people a day dying from gun violence. Of those eighty people, about twenty-three are 20–30 years of age. The organization suggests that this epidemic of gun violence is a public health issue and developed Unite to End Gun Violence as a broad-based, multifaceted campaign.

First Monday aims to involve students in high schools, colleges and universities, and schools of law, medicine, nursing, social work, and public health in its national education and advocacy campaign. The campaign suggests activities and roles appropriate to different groups of students. For example, high school students could start groups on gun violence prevention in their schools. College students might raise awareness on campuses by distributing information on gun violence or hosting speakers. First Monday suggests that medical, public health, and nursing students should get involved because gun violence is a national public health crisis. Law students could do research on the legal aspects of guns, gun control legislation, and gun violence. Social work departments and students are playing an active role in the campaign, which stresses the importance of education on gun violence for social work practitioners.

First Monday has organized its events around several documentary films. In 2000, the campaign produced *America: Up in Arms,* featuring Martin Sheen. That film examined the public health costs of gun violence. First Monday 2001 produced *Deadly Business,* directed by Glen Pearcy. This film focused on the gun industry, including its marketing practices and product design issues. The film drew close parallels between the gun and tobacco industries. The First Monday website provides extensive information on these films and many other resources for those wishing to participate in the campaign. Over 100 organizations cosponsor First Monday 2001, including the American Academy of Pediatrics, the American Bar Association, the Child Welfare League of America, the National Associ-

ation of School Nurses, the National Education Association, and the Police Foundation.

Although First Monday moved on to a different social justice issue on the first Monday of 2002, the work on gun violence continued through Gun Industry Watch, a new student network that monitors the gun industry and the National Rifle Association. Gun Industry Watch members engage in grassroots activities to expose deceptive advertising by firearm manufacturers, expose and boycott corporate partners and sponsors of the gun lobby, and work toward achieving higher safety standards for firearms.

Walter F. Carroll

See also Accidents, Gun; American Academy of Pediatrics; American Medical Association; Availability of Guns, Effects on Crime; Background Checks; Centers for Disease Control; Consumer Product Safety Laws; Crime and Gun Use; Firearm Injury Statistical Systems; Gun Shows; Gun Violence as a Public Health Problem; Gunshot Wounds; Medicine and Gun Violence; Physicians for Social Responsibility; Suicide, Guns and

For Further Reading:
Cook, Philip, and Jens Ludwig. 2000. *Gun Violence: The Real Costs.* New York: Oxford University Press.
First Monday 2001: Unite to End Gun Violence website: http://www.firstmonday2000.com/about.cfm.
Gun Industry Watch website: http://www.gunindustrywatch.org/.

Fourteenth Amendment

The Fourteenth Amendment granted full citizenship to African Americans and was designed to guarantee the "equal protection" of the law to all citizens. It was one of three amendments passed in the wake of the Civil War. All three were designed to integrate African Americans into the broader spectrum of American politics and to provide full rights of citizenship. Following the 1925 Supreme Court case *Gitlow v. New York,* the Fourteenth Amendment has been used to incorporate the protections of the Bill of Rights at the state and local levels. During the civil rights movement of the 1950s and 1960s, the amendment was used as the basis for efforts to extend basic civil rights and liberties to disadvantaged groups such as African Americans.

The 1857 Supreme Court case *Dred Scott v. Sandford* held that African Americans were not entitled to the full rights of citizenship. Therefore, in the wake of the Civil War, it was necessary to pass constitutional amendments in an effort to guarantee their equality. The Thirteenth Amendment, which was ratified in 1865, outlawed slavery. Passed in 1868, the Fourteenth Amendment is the only component of the U.S. Constitution that specifically addresses the issue of equality by mandating "equal protection of the laws." The Fifteenth Amendment, ratified in 1870, forbade racial discrimination in voting.

Following the Civil War, southern states passed a variety of restrictive gun laws that were designed to prevent African Americans from obtaining guns. Southern elites feared that if African Americans were armed, they would be less compliant, and laws such as the "Black Codes" were passed in order to deny rights to the community. A number of states, including Alabama, Louisiana, and Mississippi, enacted laws that expressly forbade African Americans from acquiring guns. The passage of the Fourteenth Amendment led to the repeal of race-based restrictions on gun ownership. However, these gun laws were often replaced with more restrictive legislation that was race-neutral in language, but its impact was to limit access to weapons. For instance, restrictions on gun ownership were often unequally enforced. While law enforcement vigorously enforced bans on certain weapons in the African American community, the white-dominated police forces ignored possession of guns in the white community.

The disparity of gun ownership and the advent of racially motivated attacks in the South led Congress to debate legislation that would have outlawed southern militias and placed restrictions on the ability of all southerners to possess firearms. However, the majority of members of Congress from both parties ultimately agreed that efforts to ban or prohibit militias would be overturned by the Supreme Court. Since Congress could not limit the ability of whites to acquire weapons, the national legislature concentrated on measures to ensure equal access to firearms. Support for arming African Americans also had an ideological component. Just as

Americans had to resort to force to gain independence from Great Britain and now had to use force to free the slaves, many Radical Republicans envisioned a well-armed African American citizenry as the optimum means to ensure the equality granted under the Fourteenth Amendment and subsequent legislation.

Through the Fourteenth Amendment, the Republican-controlled Congress endeavored to provide African Americans with the means to defend themselves from racist organizations such as the Ku Klux Klan (KKK). The original draft of the act specifically forbade the confiscation of firearms from the newly freed slaves, either from their homes or their persons. Such actions were considered larceny and legally defined as a felony. However, this specific provision was ultimately deleted since it was considered to be redundant in light of the Second Amendment. In response to racial violence, Congress passed the Anti-KKK Act in 1871. Weapons were also seen as a necessary tool to protect African American families from corrupt local law enforcement. The continuing inability of African Americans to gain access to weapons was one of the motivating factors in the passage of the Civil Rights Act of 1875. This act was an effort to bolster the equal opportunity provisions of the Fourteenth Amendment and to ensure that African Americans had the same right to keep and bear arms as whites by defining the militia to include all citizens, including those who were not part of the dominant white community.

In spite of the intentions of the measure, the Fourteenth Amendment initially failed to provide the protections contained within it. A succession of Jim Crow laws were passed in the South that institutionalized segregation. Legal segregation was approved by Supreme Court cases in the 1880s and in the infamous *Plessy v. Ferguson* (which endorsed the concept of "separate, but equal") in 1896. Nonetheless, the amendment would also serve as the basis for later efforts to repeal segregation and ensure political equality.

The Fourteenth Amendment continues to be a core element of the gun control debate in the United States. Contemporary anti–gun control advocates base their arguments against gun regulation on the equal protection clause of the amendment. According to this line of reasoning, all citizens have the right to self-defense since the Fourteenth Amendment guarantees equal protection for all Americans. Currently, the Second Amendment is the only portion of the Bill of Rights in which the Fourteenth Amendment has not been used to extend the protections to include state and local governments. This has led to efforts by anti–gun control groups such as the National Rifle Association to use the Fourteenth Amendment as a means to extend the Second Amendment in such a fashion as to broaden the ability to keep and bear firearms.

Tom Lansford

See also Black Codes; Ku Klux Klan; National Rifle Association; Right to Self-Defense; Second Amendment

For Further Reading:
Bland, Randall, and Joseph V. Brogan. 1999. *Constitutional Law in the United States: A Systematic Inquiry into the Change and Relevance of Supreme Court Decisions.* San Francisco: Austin & Winfield.
George, Robert P., ed. 2001. *Great Cases in Constitutional Law.* Princeton, NJ: Princeton University Press.
Harrison, Maureen, and Steve Gilbert, eds. 1991. *Landmark Decisions of the United States Supreme Court.* Beverly Hills, CA: Excellent Books.
Hoffman, Ronald, and Peter J. Albert, eds. 1997. *The Bill of Rights: Government Proscribed.* Charlottesville: University Press of Virginia.
Mykkeltvedt, Roald Y. 1983. *The Nationalization of the Bill of Rights: Fourteenth Amendment Due Process and Procedural Rights.* Port Washington, NY: Associated Faculty Press.

Fourth Amendment

The Fourth Amendment forbids unreasonable searches and seizures. The amendment was one of the ten original amendments to the Constitution that were collectively known as the Bill of Rights. The Fourth Amendment was designed to protect Americans from general or arbitrary searches by the police or government by requiring a specific warrant to be issued by a judge or magistrate before a search is undertaken. The rise in handgun violence during the 1960s and 1970s led to a gradual erosion of Fourth Amendment rights as the courts granted the police greater latitude in searches for weapons and firearms.

The amendment has its roots in English common law. By the time of the American Revolution, it had become a legal precedent in Great Britain that the police or other forces of the crown needed an official writ before entering a personal home. In fact, one of the factors that created tension between the colonies and Great Britain was the suspension of such protections. Throughout the colonies, royal magistrates and judges issued writs of assistance and general warrants that allowed British soldiers to search houses and seize property without cause or provocation. The lingering resentment against such actions prompted the adoption of the Fourth Amendment in order to prevent government-sponsored intrusions of home and property.

The amendment forbade the government from conducting "unreasonable searches and seizures" and guaranteed the "right of the people to be secure in their persons, houses, papers, and effects." The amendment requires that the police obtain a warrant that specifically describes what place will be searched and what, if any, items are to be seized or people arrested. In order for the police to gain a search warrant, they have to swear under oath that there is "probable cause" for such a warrant.

Since the ratification of the Bill of Rights in 1791, courts have allowed exemptions to the Fourth Amendment. For instance, police are permitted to arrest people who are in the midst of committing a crime. They are also able to arrest people who they have probable cause to suspect are about to commit a crime. In 1912, the Supreme Court began using the exclusionary rule whereby evidence that was seized without a warrant or legally valid probable cause cannot be introduced in a criminal trial. However, this rule initially only applied to federal cases. It was not until 1961 and the Supreme Court case *Mapp v. Ohio* that the exclusionary rule began to be applied to state and local court cases. The Court has allowed some exceptions to the exclusionary rule. In *Nix v. Williams* in 1984, the Supreme Court decided that the police and prosecutors could use evidence, even if it was seized illegally,

Los Angeles police search suspected gang members during a sweep in southern Los Angeles, 1985. (Bettmann/Corbis)

if the discovery of that evidence led police to a discovery that they would have reached without the illegal evidence. That same year, the Court in *United States v. Leon* further expanded the exemptions to the exclusionary rule by finding that evidence could be used for prosecution if it was obtained when the police were acting in "good faith" even if they were mistaken about the scope or breadth of a search warrant.

Critics of some specific gun control efforts claim that these programs violate the Fourth Amendment. For instance, the courts have granted the police wide latitude to search for and seize guns even without probable cause. One result of such latitude has been the police tactic of "profiling" whereby police units stop motorists on the highways or people in certain neighborhoods if they fit a specific set of guidelines, which usually mirror the profiles of those engaged in criminal activity. The police defend these warrantless stops by claiming that they fall under the doctrine of probable cause. Furthermore, many localities have adopted programs that are designed to reduce violence and crime in certain neighborhoods. Central to these programs is the ability of the police to run "sweeps" or warrantless searches of public housing areas to confiscate guns or illicit drugs. For example, in 1988 Chicago began Operation Clean Sweep in which the police randomly "swept" through public housing buildings and seized illegal materials. After the American Civil Liberties Union filed a lawsuit against the tactic, the scope of the sweeps was limited, but they continue. Concern over crime and gun violence in certain urban areas has increased the popularity of these programs that erode an individual's Fourth Amendment protections against unreasonable search and seizure.

Tom Lansford

See also American Civil Liberties Union
For Further Reading:
Bland, Randall, and Joseph V. Brogan. 1999. *Constitutional Law in the United States: A Systematic Inquiry into the Change and Relevance of Supreme Court Decisions.* San Francisco: Austin & Winfield.
George, Robert P., ed. 2001. *Great Cases in Constitutional Law.* Princeton, NJ: Princeton University Press.

Harrison, Maureen, and Steve Gilbert, eds. 1991. *Landmark Decisions of the United States Supreme Court.* Beverly Hills, CA: Excellent Books.

Hoffman, Ronald, and Peter J. Albert, eds. 1997. *The Bill of Rights: Government Proscribed.* Charlottesville: University Press of Virginia.

Monk, Linda. 1991. *The Bill of Rights: A User's Guide.* Alexandria, VA: Close Up Publications.

Fraternal Order of Police (FOP)

The Fraternal Order of Police is the world's largest organization of rank-and-file police officers. After maintaining close relations with the National Rifle Association for many years, the FOP became increasingly troubled by the NRA's opposition to any gun control regulation and in 1994 supported the Brady Bill. The FOP does not have an overall position on gun control; rather, it takes varying positions on gun control legislation based on its assessment of their implications for law enforcement officers and the law enforcement community.

Founded in 1915 by police officers in Pittsburgh as the Fort Pitt Lodge No. 1, the FOP soon spread to other states and in 1955 became a national organization. The FOP now has over 2,000 local and state chapters, or lodges, with over 290,000 members. The national organization, known as the Grand Lodge, maintains an active legislative agenda, lobbying and testifying before Congress on legislation it favors or opposes.

For many years the FOP and other law enforcement associations maintained close ties to the NRA because of the NRA's role in sponsoring firearm safety classes and promoting the responsible use of firearms. However, the NRA's increasing resistance to *any* kind of gun control gradually alienated the FOP and other police organizations, which moved away from it. The NRA opposed regulation of armor-piercing ("cop killer") bullets. Spitzer (1998) suggests the split became final when the NRA began to run advertisements attacking police chiefs who had opposed NRA policies. Carter (1997, p. 103) notes that the passage of the McClure-Volkmer Act in 1986 also contributed to the disaffection of law enforcement organizations—including the FOP—from the NRA. The NRA strongly supported the McClure-Volkmer Act, which "re-moved record-keeping requirements for ammunitions dealers and allowed mail-order sales of rifles, shotguns, and ammunition to resume."

Their estrangement from the NRA led the FOP and other police organizations to ally themselves with Handgun Control, Inc. (HCI, now called the Brady Campaign for the Prevention of Gun Violence). In reaction to the split with the established law enforcement organizations, the NRA supported and subsidized the creation of the Law Enforcement Alliance of America (LEAA) as an alternative to the mainstream law enforcement organizations. LEAA is small, not very influential, and generally takes NRA positions on gun control issues and legislation.

The FOP—and a coalition of other police organizations—supported the Brady Act, allying themselves with HCI. The FOP strongly opposes the 1996 Domestic Violence Offender Gun Ban, also known as the Lautenberg Amendment. This amendment—to a federal spending bill—prohibits anyone with a misdemeanor conviction for domestic violence against a spouse or child from purchasing or owning a handgun. According to the FOP, the amendment has cost some police officers their jobs for having committed one domestic violence infraction in the past. The FOP argues that it is unfair to apply the ban retroactively and supports amending the Lautenberg Amendment so that it would not apply retroactively.

The FOP also supports passage of the Community Protection Act, which Rep. Duke Cunningham (R-CA) introduced in the House of Representatives. The act would allow off-duty and retired police officers to carry concealed weapons, even outside of their jurisdictions. The FOP and the bill's sponsors argue that it would allow those trained in law enforcement to intervene in criminal situations and protect communities. Although several other police organizations also support the bill, the International Association of Chiefs of Police (IACP) opposes it because the federal law would override the concealed weapons laws of seventeen states. The IACP also suggests that the legislation would not contribute to community safety.

The National Legislative Office of the FOP also opposes a wide variety of other handgun control legislation, including legislation to require the licensing and registration of all handguns with the federal government, legislation to require anyone owning a handgun or ammunition to have a license from their state, legislation to prohibit individuals from purchasing more than one handgun in a thirty-day period, and legislation to ban the manufacture of guns that cannot be personalized.

Walter F. Carroll and Robin L. Roth

See also Ammunition, Regulations of; Ammunition, Types of; Brady Campaign to Prevent Gun Violence; Brady Handgun Violence Prevention Act; Concealed Weapons Laws; Domestic Violence and Guns; Firearms Owners' Protection Act of 1986; Gun Registration; International Association of Chiefs of Police; International Brotherhood of Police Officers; Lautenberg, Frank R.; National Rifle Association; One-Gun-per-Month Laws; Safety Courses

For Further Reading:

Carter, Gregg Lee. 1997. *The Gun Control Movement.* New York: Twayne.

Fraternal Order of Police website: http://www.grandlodgefop.org/.

Spitzer, Robert J. 1998. *The Politics of Gun Control.* 2d ed. New York: Chatham House.

Fresno Rifle and Pistol Club, Inc. v. Van de Kamp (1992)

In this case the Fresno Rifle and Pistol Club, along with several other national, state, and local organizations, argued that the federal Civil Marksmanship Program (CMP) took precedence over a 1989 California statute, the Roberti-Roos Assault Weapons Control Act (AWCA), which established rules for the manufacture, sale, transfer, possession, distribution, transportation, and importation without a permit of numerous specified firearms. The AWCA, which had been amended in 1991, now listed as unacceptable assault weapons twenty-one categories of rifles, eight categories of pistols, and three types of shotguns. The legislature declared that "each firearm has such a high rate of fire and capacity for firepower that its function as a legitimate sports or recreational firearm is substantially outweighed by the danger that it can be used to kill and injure human beings" (*Fresno Rifle and Pistol Club, Inc. v. Van de Kamp,* 1992, pp. 723, 724).

The Fresno Rifle and Pistol Club also argued before the appellate courts that the California statute was an unlawful bill of attainder in violation of Article 1, Section 10, Clause 1 of the federal Constitution. That provision disallows the infliction of guilt and punishment on identifiable individuals or groups without a judicial trial. The complainants were the manufacturers of weapons whose use was outlawed by the AWCA statute, thereby, they claimed, unlawfully depriving them of part of their income. The club also maintained that the statute infringed on its members' right to keep and bear arms as guaranteed by the Second Amendment.

The district court ruled against all of these claims and a number of others (*Fresno Rifle and Pistol Club v. Van de Kamp,* 746 F. Supp. 1427, 1990). The Ninth Circuit Court of Appeals supported the district court's judgment.

The Fresno group had argued that the California law had prohibited the use of weapons that the federal program endorsed for instructional and competitive purposes. The circuit court granted that the federal Civilian Marksmanship Program had been established in the early 1990s to encourage interest in shooting skills among persons at an age that would make them eligible for military service. The court concluded, nonetheless, that nothing in the CMP suggested that Congress intended by it to supersede state gun control measures such as the AWCA statute. The judge also declared that shooting competitions with some weapons that were on the AWCA's banned list could go forward, either by arrangements with the army for use of these weapons or by the substitution of similar arms.

In addition, the appellate court ruled against the claim that the California statute violated the bill of attainder clause in the Constitution. It declared that traditional punishments, such as imprisonment and punitive confiscation of property, had not been imposed upon the weapons manufacturers under the AWCA. Nor did the court find in the law any legislative intent to punish the complaining manufacturers; the law's motivation was only a "legitimate desire to protect the health and safety of the citizens of California" (*Fresno Rifle and Pistol Club, Inc. v. Van de Kamp,* 1992,

p. 728). Finally, the Second Amendment challenge was dismissed by the court with the traditional reliance on precedent law that declared that the amendment was binding only on the federal government and not on the states.

Gilbert Geis

See also Roberti-Roos Assault Weapons Control Act of 1989

For Further Reading:

Brady Campaign to Prevent Gun Violence. 2001. "U.S. Supreme Court Rejects Challenge to California's Assault Weapons Ban." February 20. http://www.bradycampaign.org/press/release.asp?Record=53.

Fresno Rifle and Pistol Club, Inc. v. Van de Kamp, 965 F. 2d 723 (9th Cir. 1992). http://www.healylaw.com/case_lst.htm.

Frontier Violence

Many different forms of violence took place on the American frontier. The violence played an important role in creating and shaping the American gun culture. Even today, the effects of the frontier are powerful.

The most common form of frontier violence was hunting. In the British Isles, France, and other parts of western Europe—the sources of almost all of the white population of the British colonies and then the United States before the late nineteenth century—hunting was strictly controlled for the benefit of the aristocracy. A farmer might even be forbidden to kill deer or rabbits that were eating his crops. In theory, all game belonged to the king.

But in the wilds of America, hunting was wide open. Anyone could hunt, and for people living on the frontier—whether in western Massachusetts in the 1670s or Idaho in the 1870s—hunting often made a difference in whether the family would go hungry or not. Even today, there are many poor people in rural parts of the United States for whom the results of the fall hunting season determine how much meat the family will be eating over the winter. The ready availability of hunting gave ordinary people an important reason for owning firearms, and the practical requirements of hunting—such as shooting a squirrel out of a tree dozens of yards away—promoted the development of shooting skills.

Most of the American Revolution and the Civil War did not take place on the frontier, but some important engagements occurred there. The Indian wars took place almost exclusively on the frontier. But perhaps the most important military violence involving the American frontier was the Battle of New Orleans on January 8, 1815. (New Orleans itself was not on the frontier, but the port was the key to the economy of much of the frontier, and frontiersmen played a major role in the battle.) The Treaty of Ghent, signed on December 24, 1814, had officially ended the War of 1812, but news of the treaty had not reached North America. Had the British captured New Orleans—the port through which almost all trade from America's recently acquired Louisiana Territory flowed—it is doubtful that the British would have relinquished it, despite what the Treaty of Ghent required. Indeed, the British had violated the Treaty of Paris, which ended the American Revolution, by refusing to evacuate their forts east of the Mississippi.

The British army was fresh from its triumph over Napoleon, and the forces invading New Orleans were the best in the world—the victors of the Peninsular Campaign in Spain. Against the best-trained, best-equipped army in the world, the Americans did not have enough weapons for their forces. Historian Robert Remini's *The Battle of New Orleans* quotes a contemporary observer: "From all the parishes the inhabitants could be seen coming with their hunting guns" because "there were not enough guns in the magazines of the United States to arm the citizens" (Remini, 1999, p. 45).

The Tennessee militia hardly looked like a professional army, with their rough clothes, unshaven faces, and raccoon caps. The Kentucky militia was even worse, arriving in rags and disappointed to find out that there were no blankets in the city for them. The redcoats called them "dirty shirts." Yet, as Remini explains, "most of these men could bring down a squirrel from the highest tree with a single rifle shot. Their many years living in the Tennessee wilderness had made them expert marksmen" (p. 71).

The Americans who fought at New Orleans were a diverse combination of professional soldiers, militiamen, irregulars, lawyers, privateers,

The Battle of New Orleans: General Andrew Jackson on horseback in the foreground commanding troops against the British, January 8, 1815. (Library of Congress)

farmers, and shopkeepers. They included free blacks, Creoles, Cajuns, Spaniards, Frenchmen, Portuguese, Germans, Italians, Indians, and Anglos. When objections were raised to arming the free blacks of Louisiana, General Andrew Jackson replied, "Place confidence in them, and … engage them by every dear and honorable tie to the interest of the country who extends to them equal rights and privileges with white men."

As the British maneuvered outside the city, nightly raids by the "dirty shirts" killed British sentries, took their equipment, and kept the whole army off balance. During an engagement by the Cypress Swamp on December 28 (eleven days before the main battle), the Tennesseeans waded though the muck and leapt from log to log like cats, driving off the British beefeaters.

In one encounter on the day of the main battle, a dirty shirt took aim at a wounded British officer who was walking back to his camp. "Halt Mr. Red Coat," yelled the American. "One more step and I'll drill a hole through your leather." The officer complied, sighing, "What a disgrace for a British officer to have to surrender to a chimney-sweep."

Although the British greatly outnumbered the Americans, the day of January 8, 1815, turned into one of the worst days in British military history. Over 2,000 British soldiers were killed, captured, or wounded. The Americans lost only 7 killed and 6 wounded, although their total casualties from skirmishes on other days amounted to 333.

As news of the victory spread throughout the United States, the Americans' sense of inferiority to the British began to recede. The Americans had smashed the best that Britain could throw at them. Newspapers quoted Shakespeare's *Henry VI*: "Advance our waving colors to the wall, rescued is Orleans from the English wolves." Jackson's upset victory was as important for America's future as Joan of Arc's was for France.

Until the Civil War, the Battle of New Orleans was celebrated nearly on a par with the Fourth of July. It became a tremendous source of American pride, helping to shape the national identity. The victory also helped propel Jackson to election as president in 1828. The popular song "The Hunters of Kentucky" celebrated the accomplishments of American frontiersmen and their rifles. One version of the song concluded:

> But Jackson he was wide awake,
> And was not scared of trifles,
> For well he knew Kentucky's boys,
> With their death-dealing rifles.
> He led them down to Cypress Swamp,
> The ground was low and mucky,
> There stood John Bull in martial pomp,
> And here stood old Kentucky.
> But steady stood our little force,
> None wished it to be greater,
> For every man was half a horse,
> And half an alligator.

> (chorus) Oh, Kentucky, hunters of Kentucky!
> Oh, Kentucky, hunters of Kentucky!
> And when so near we saw them wink,
> We thought it good to stop them,
> It would have done you good, I think,
> To see Kentuckians drop them.
> And so if danger e'er annoys,
> Remember what our trade is,
> Just send for us Kentucky boys,
> And we'll protect you ladies.

Many of the American rifles at New Orleans were a superbly crafted and effective type originally made by the Pennsylvania Dutch. Thanks in part to the song, though, the Pennsylvania rifles became known as "Kentucky rifles."

The Kentucky rifles were well suited for both hunting and self-defense. In contrast, British guns were more specialized, reflecting who would be using them. Muskets were mass-produced for infantry soldiers, who were not even trained to aim at an individual enemy; but in tightly controlled linear formations, the redcoats could produce massive, devastating firepower. In contrast, British aristocrats hunted on their estates with exquisite shotguns and other firearms tailored for them personally. The way guns were made in America—mass-produced for a mass market and intended for mul-tiple uses—reflected frontier conditions, as "civil and military uses of firearms dovetailed as they had not generally done in Europe" (Kennett and Anderson, 1975, p. 41).

The second great frontier-related military experience that shaped American attitudes toward firearms was the Texas Revolution. As the military dictatorship of General Santa Anna began systematically denying Texans their right to self-government (which the Mexican government had guaranteed to Texan settlers) and other rights guaranteed to all Mexicans by the 1824 Mexican Constitution, Texans began to contemplate a war for independence. At Gonzales, the Mexicans tried to seize a small cannon that the settlers had used to scare away Indians. The Texans were armed only with bowie knives, a few pistols, and flintlock rifles, many of which dated back to the American Revolution. The Texans raised a flag, which dared, "Come and Take It." The Mexicans tried unsuccessfully and then retreated.

At the Alamo, a fort in San Antonio, 136 Texans withstood a siege by the main Mexican standing army from February 23 to March 6, 1836, before finally being destroyed, having refused all demands to surrender. The defenders of the Alamo had bought Sam Houston crucial time to rally the Texan people.

On April 21, 1836, the Texans met the Mexican army at San Jacinto. Although outnumbered two to one, the Texans launched a surprise attack. "Remember the Alamo," they yelled, rushing into battle with their rifles and bowie knives, as a single fife and a single drum played the love song "Will You Come to the Bower?"

In the first hour of battle, the Texans killed 600 Mexicans and captured 200 more. Within a day, the rest of the Mexican army, including Santa Anna himself, had been captured. Texan casualties were 6 dead and 30 wounded. The Mexican standing army was crushed, and although Mexico refused formally to recognize Texan independence, the dictatorship gave up trying to conquer Texas.

The "Texan War Cry"—sung to the same tune as the "Star Spangled Banner"—celebrated the victory of a self-armed people over the professional army of a tyrant:

Oh Texans rouse hill and dale with your cry,
No longer delay, for the bold foe advances.
The banners of Mexico tauntingly fly,
And the valleys are lit with the gleam of their
　　lances.
With justice our shield, rush forth to the field,
And stand with your posts, till our foes fly or
　　yield.
For the bright star of Texas shall never grow
　　dim,
While her soil boasts a son to raise rifle or
　　limb.
Rush forth to the lines, these hirelings to
　　meet,
Our lives and our homes, we will yield unto
　　no man.
But death on our free soil we'll willingly
　　meet,
Ere our free temple soiled by the feet of the
　　foe man.
Grasp rifle and blade with hearts undis-
　　mayed,
And swear by the temple brave Houston has
　　made.
That the bright star of Texas shall never be
　　dim,
While her soil boasts a son to raise rifle or
　　limb.

The frontier attitudes expressed in the "Texan War Cry" and "The Hunters of Kentucky" deeply shaped American culture. Even in the early twenty-first century, these ideas are at the core of the American gun culture: A true man will use a firearm to protect women from predators (the British soldiers had been promised a rape and pillage spree—"beauty and booty"—if they captured New Orleans); the free people of a nation must defend it personally with their own arms; professional soldiers ("hirelings") in the pay of unfree governments are—despite the soldiers' intimidating "martial pomp"—morally and militarily inferior to American soldiers; dying in defense of freedom is better than living under tyranny; and the quintessence of freedom—the precise reason why the stars of liberty shine—is the patriot's rifle.

These attitudes did not start with the frontier, of course. The American Revolution is the most important part of their foundation. And the attitudes were reinforced, with modification, by American participation in World War II. Yet it would be a serious mistake to underestimate the influence of Alamo imagery on almost every generation of American youth until almost the end of the twentieth century. The Battle of New Orleans and the Texan War of Independence helped ensure that the firearms-related "moral lessons" of the American Revolution were not seen as one-time events but recurring facts of the eternal struggle between freedom and tyranny.

In September 2000, Michael Bellesiles's book *Arming America: The Origins of a National Gun Culture* was published with great critical acclaim. Bellesiles, with an obvious eye on the contemporary gun control debate, argued that before the Civil War few Americans owned guns, even on the frontier; that hunting was mostly confined to professionals; and that guns were unimportant in America until the federal government promoted mass armament as a result of the Civil War.

But historians who have investigated Bellesiles's claims have found them to be insufficiently supported by the facts (e.g., Cramer, 2001; Lindgren and Heather, 2001). For example, Lindgren and Heather examined probate inventories to see how often guns were transferred through a will. Bellesiles claimed to have examined a variety of probate records and found that guns were rarely included in wills, which led him to conclude that guns were rare. Lindgren and Heather found that Bellesiles had grossly misrepresented his sources and made assertions that could not possibly be in accordance with the actual probate records. From 1636 to 1810, probate records consistently showed that 50–73 percent of male estates had firearms, as did a significant minority of female estates. Guns were nearly as common as books.

Like Lindgren and Heather, Cramer suggests that the American historical profession, as well as newspaper reviewers, ignored the deficiencies of Bellesiles's book because the book proposed a vision they wished to believe in, even though that vision was at odds with the truth. Bellesiles's book does not contribute to actual understanding of guns and the American frontier, but the book is representative of the continuing desire to imagine a frontier consistent with one's emotional needs.

If some Americans today wish to imagine a "gun-free" America in colonial days and during the early republic, Americans of the late nineteenth century had rather different wishes. For many people in the United States and around the world, knowledge of the American "Wild West" reflects that of the city audiences who attended the enormously popular "Buffalo Bill Wild West Show." The show opened in 1883 and featured a stagecoach robbery, shooting contests, numerous gunfights, and terrifying Indians. In his book *The Mythic West,* Robert Athearn explains how the Wild West, exemplified (or invented) by the Buffalo Bill show, became a symbol of the purest, most rugged form of Americanism. The western frontier, a reasonably calm place in real life, was revered as bloody and heroic.

While the Buffalo Bill show and movie "Westerns" are responsible for popular understanding of the western frontier in the late nineteenth century, the reality was somewhat different. The most thorough investigation of gun ownership and gun violence in the American western frontier is Roger McGrath's *Gunfighters, Highwaymen, and Vigilantes,* an examination of the nineteenth-century Sierra Nevada mining towns of Aurora and Bodie. Aurora and Bodie certainly had as much potential for violence as any place in the West. Their populations were mainly young transient males subject to few social controls. There was one saloon for every twenty-five men; brothels and gambling houses were also common. Governmental law enforcement was ineffectual, and sometimes the sheriff was himself the head of a criminal gang. Nearly everyone carried a gun. Aurorans usually carried a Colt Navy .36 six-shot revolver, while Bodieites sported the Colt double-action model known as the "Lightning," a double-action version of the famous "Peacemaker," or "Frontier," revolver.

The homicide rate in those towns was extremely high, as the "bad men" who hung out in saloons shot each other at a fearsome rate: 64 per 100,000 annually in Aurora, and 116 in Bodie. These rates are comparable to the highest homicide rates in the worst parts of American cities during the late twentieth century. The presence of guns turned many petty drunken quarrels into fatal encounters—as they sometimes do today.

But in Aurora and Bodie other crime was virtually nil. McGrath, writing in 1984, compared the Aurora and Bodie crime rates to the 1980 crime rates in the United States. The per capita annual robbery rate in Aurora and Bodie was only 7 percent of modern New York City's rate. The burglary rate was a mere 1 percent of New York's. Rape was unknown in Aurora and Bodie. Bodie had a robbery rate of 84 per 100,000 persons per year. The rate in 1980 New York City was 1,140; in San Francisco–Oakland it was 521; and in the United States as a whole it was 243. The Bodie burglary rate was 6.4 per 100,000 people per year. The 1980 New York City rate was 2,661; the San Francisco–Oakland rate was 2,267; and the overall rate for the United States was 1,668.

"The old, the weak, the female, the innocent, and those unwilling to fight were rarely the targets of attacks," McGrath found. One resident of Bodie did "not recall ever hearing of a respectable woman or girl in any manner insulted or even accosted by the hundreds of dissolute characters that were everywhere. In part this was due to the respect depravity pays to decency; in part to the knowledge that sudden death would follow any other course." Everyone carried a gun, and except for young men who liked to drink and fight with each other, everyone was secure from crime.

The experiences of Aurora and Bodie were repeated throughout the West. One study of five major cattle towns with a reputation for violence—Abilene, Ellsworth, Wichita, Dodge City, and Caldwell—found that all together the towns had less than two criminal homicides per year (Dykstra, 1983).

During the 1870s, Lincoln County, New Mexico, was in a state of anarchy and civil war. The homicide rate was astronomical, but (as in Bodie and Aurora) it was confined almost exclusively to drunken males upholding their "honor." Modern big-city crimes such as rape, burglary, and mugging were virtually unknown (Utley, 1990).

A study of the Texas frontier from 1875 to 1890 found that burglaries and robberies (except for bank, train, and stagecoach robberies) were essentially nonexistent. People did not bother with locking doors, and murder was rare, except for young men shooting each other in "fair fights" they engaged in voluntarily (Holden, 1940).

John Umbeck's (1981) investigation of the High Sierra goldfields in the mid-nineteenth century yielded similar results. After the Gold Rush brought on by Sutter's Mill in 1848, thousands of prospectors rushed to goldfields in the California mountains. There was no police force. Indeed, there was no law at all regarding property rights, since the military governor of California had just proclaimed the Mexican land law invalid (without offering a replacement). There was intense competitive pressure and greed for gold, and nearly everyone carried firearms. Yet there was hardly any violence. Similarly, when much of the Indian territory of Oklahoma was opened all at once for white settlement, heavily armed settlers rushed in immediately to stake their claims, and the settlers with their guns arrived long before effective law enforcement did. Yet there was almost no violence (Day, 1989).

In sum, historian W. Eugene Hollon (1974) observes that "the Western frontier was a far more civilized, more peaceful, and safer place than American society is today." Americans living in the "Wild West," with its many guns, were far safer than Americans living in many modern cities.

In the modern era, some people argue that the inner cities of the United States constitute a frontier. Sen. Frank Church (D-ID) contended that most people "would not go into ghetto areas at all except in broad daylight under the most optimum conditions—surely not at night, alone or on foot. But some people have no choice. To live or work or have some need to be on this 'frontier' imposes a fear which is tempered by possession of a gun" (Church, 1979).

In contrast, historian Joe B. Frantz (1969) advances the case for the irrelevance of the gun culture to modern problems. He acknowledges that the frontier experience promoted important American values: individualism, mobility (both physical and social), and nationalism. These frontier values, including the attachment to firearms, Frantz continues, are no longer appropriate, for "direct action does not befit a nation whose problems are corporate, community, and complex" (pp. 152–153).

The statements of Church and Frantz encapsulate the competing views about the legitimacy of "direct action" against crime. Is it reasonable for a person who must walk alone in an inner city to carry a handgun for protection, or should she instead rely entirely on community protection and lobby for such things as better streetlights? Whatever the answers to the questions about the modern frontier, it is clear that on the American frontier throughout the seventeenth, eighteenth, and nineteenth centuries, firearms were not only a very important survival tool but also a preeminent symbol of personal and national independence and self-sufficiency.

David B. Kopel

See also American Revolution; Boomtowns, Cowtowns, and Gun Violence; Civil War and Small Arms; Long Rifle (Pennsylvania/Kentucky); Native Americans and Gun Violence; Urbanism and Gun Violence; Vigilantism

For Further Reading:

Athearn, Robert G. 1986. *The Mythic West.* Lawrence: University Press of Kansas.

Bellesiles, Michael. 2000. *Arming America: The Origins of a National Gun Culture.* New York: Knopf.

Church, Frank. 1979. "Foreword." In *Restricting Handguns: The Liberal Skeptics Speak Out,* ed. Don B. Kates, Jr. Croton-on-Hudson, NY: North River Press.

Cramer, Clayton. 2001. *Armed America: Firearms Ownership and Manufacturing in Early America.* http://www.ggnra.org/cramer/ ArmingAmericaLong.pdf.

Day, Robert. 1989. "'Sooners' or 'Goners,' They Were Hell Bent on Grabbing Free Land." *Smithsonian* 20 (November): 192–203.

Dykstra, Robert R. 1983. *The Cattle Towns: A Social History of the Kansas Cattle Trading Centers.* Lincoln: University of Nebraska Press.

Frantz, Joe B. 1969. "The Frontier Tradition." Pp. 127–153 in *Violence in America: Historical and Comparative Perspectives,* ed. Hugh Davis Graham and Ted Robert Gurr. New York: Bantam Books.

Holden, William C. 1940. "Law and Lawlessness on the Texas Frontier, 1875–1890." *Southwestern History Quarterly* 44: 188–203.

Hollon, W. Eugene. 1974. *Frontier Violence: Another Look.* New York: Oxford University Press.

Kennett, Lee, and James LaVerne Anderson. 1975. *The Gun in America: The Origins of a National Dilemma.* Westport, CT: Greenwood Press.

Lindgren, James, and Justin Lee Heather. 2001. "Counting Guns in Early America." *William and Mary Law Review* 43: 1777–1842.

McGrath, Roger D. 1984. *Gunfighters, Highwaymen, and Vigilantes: Violence on the Frontier.* Berkeley: University of California Press.

Remini, Robert. 1999. *The Battle of New Orleans.* New York: Viking Press.

Umbeck, John. 1981. *A Theory of Property Rights: With Application to the California Gold Rush.* Ames: Iowa State University Press.

Utley, Robert M. 1990. *High Noon in Lincoln: Violence on the Western Frontier.* Albuquerque: University of New Mexico Press.

G

General Social Survey (GSS)

The General Social Survey is a rich source of information on attitudes and behaviors associated with gun ownership and gun control. It has several important characteristics that give it a privileged place among the various sources of public opinion data available. Chief among these are the reputation of the National Opinion Research Center (NORC), which conducts the survey; the quality of the data; and the exact replication of questions across three decades of surveys.

While many viewers of national television broadcasts and readers of large daily newspapers may be more familiar with the polls sponsored by those media (and often conducted by equally familiar national polling organizations such as Gallup, Roper, and Yankelovich), the National Opinion Research Center, a not-for-profit facility affiliated with the University of Chicago, is the oldest and arguably the most prestigious of its type in the nation. Although most commercial and media pollsters strive to maintain rigorous controls over procedures to ensure quality data, factors such as newsworthiness, deadlines, and economic bottom lines place constraints on for-profit pollsters that sometimes jeopardize quality. The GSS is conducted over a much longer timeline, which allows leading researchers in many different areas of public opinion research to design and pretest questions. Furthermore, every effort is made to achieve a high response rate from individuals included in the sample, which fosters greater faith in its representativeness.

The emphasis of the GSS on replicating many questions year after year stems from its origins in the social indicators movement of the 1960s. The hope of that movement, which is still reflected in the design of the GSS today, was to create a set of attitudinal and behavioral indicators akin to the economic indicators used to gauge the current status and future direction of the U.S. economy. Beginning from a small set of twenty questions, the GSS database now includes over 3,000 questions, some of which have been asked consistently since 1972. Some of these questions were drawn from earlier surveys dating as far back as the 1930s. (See page 226.)

The GSS has included three broad types of measures directly related to guns and gun control. These are questions on gun ownership, gun permits and gun controls, and gun victimization.

In addition to these questions, the GSS contains many demographic, behavioral, and attitudinal measures that allow exploration of patterns within groups of persons and correlation studies. Much of the data is available at no cost online at the website maintained by the Inter-University Consortium for Political and Social Research at the University of Michigan (http://www.icpsr.umich.edu).

David Russell Harding

See also Attitudes toward Gun Control; Gun Ownership
For Further Reading:
Davis, James A., and Tom W. Smith. 1992. "The NORC General Social Survey." *Contemporary Sociology* 21: 549.
Smith, Tom W. 1983. "The Role of the General Social Survey in the Social Sciences." GSS Project Report no. 9. Chicago: NORC.

Genocide and Guns

For purposes relevant to guns, "genocide" can be included in the broader category of "mass killings by governments of people over whom they have jurisdiction" (Harff and Gurr, 1995, p. 24). This category includes phenomena as diverse as the Belgian destruction of the Congo and the Cambodian killings of those who could read. The costs of mass destruction of one's own

Ownership	Extent of series
Do you happen to have in your home (if house, or garage) any guns or revolvers?	1973, 1974, 1976, 1977, 1980, 1982, 1984, 1985, 1987–1991, 1993, 1994, 1996, 1998
If yes: Is it a pistol, shotgun, rifle, or what?	As above
If yes: Do any of these guns personally belong to you?	As above, 1980 and thereafter

Permits/Controls	
Would you favor or oppose a law which would require a person to obtain a police permit before he or she could buy a gun?	1972, 1973, 1974, 1976, 1977, 1980, 1982, 1984, 1985, 1987–1991, 1993, 1994, 1996, 1998
How important is the gun control issue to you—would you say it is one of the most important, important, not very important, or not important at all?	1976, 1984
How much information do you have about the gun control issue? Do you have all the information you need, most of the information, some information, or very little information?	1984
How firm are you about your opinion on gun control—would you say you are very likely to change your opinion, somewhat likely to change, somewhat unlikely to change, or very unlikely to change?	1984

Gun Victimization	
Have you ever been threatened with a gun, or shot at?	1973, 1975, 1976, 1978, 1980, 1983, 1984, 1986, 1987–1991, 1993
If yes: Did this happen to you as a child or as an adult?	As above; discontinued after 1984
If yes: How many times would you guess this has happened to you?	As above; discontinued after 1984

Source: General Social Survey.

citizens rise in proportion to the costs the targeted citizens are able to impose on the aggressor. Every mass killing in the twentieth century has been preceded, whether by design or for racist or public safety reasons, by a disarming of either the target population or the population as a whole.

Governments disarm their citizens because civilian possession of guns, by virtue of the special defensive properties of firearms, enables a targeted population to impose serious costs on aggressors regardless of disparities in numbers and quality of armaments. The question of how a human right to self-defense against government can be institutionalized rests on the implicit, rather than explicit, right to resist tyranny that a right to bear arms implies. The political issues concerning an armed citizenry include whether armed citizens can effectively resist government and the inefficiencies that accompany civilian arms ownership.

By a large factor, more people were killed in the twentieth century by their own governments than by private agents. If we include only homicides that were clearly unjust, the totals from the Belgian, Turkish, Russian, German, Chinese, Ugandan, Indonesian, Cambodian, Rwandan, and other slaughters sanctioned or administered by governments exceed the totals from the private sector by a substantial factor (Rummel,

1994). As a group, governments are dangerous agents of law and order, more deadly than domestic threats to a government.

The right to resist unjust assaults by legitimate governments is obvious in some cases. In all of the mass killings of the last century, those killed had a right to defend themselves and thus at least a prima facie right to a practical means of defending themselves. Proponents of the right to bear arms as a human right argue that, since defense against aggression is primarily a matter of imposing costs on aggressors, and since firearms are the only effective means by imposing costs on well-armed aggressors, people under any government that might unjustly attack them have a right to own firearms.

As has been amply documented (Simkin, Zelman, and Rice, 1994), every government of the twentieth century that engaged in mass killing either killed a previously disarmed population or took steps to disarm the target population before initiating the destruction of the target group. Such governments accepted the argument that an armed population is costly to destroy.

The question arises: Is there a human right to be prepared to resist one's government by citizen firearm ownership? Many would reply in the negative, claiming that the governments that have not gone bad will intervene on behalf of citizens who are being slaughtered. In fact, that rarely happens, except when outside governments are themselves threatened. Even interventions that would have been cheap, such as in Uganda, were not undertaken in the face of overwhelming evidence that mass killing was going on. Generally speaking, when a government "goes bad" and launches an attack on a portion of its people, those people have only themselves to rely on. When those people are unarmed, they are at the mercy of their government.

A further objection that is raised against citizens being armed is that such armaments are ineffective against modern armies. But this argument overlooks the facts about guerrilla warfare. Furthermore, those defending a right to bear arms assert only that an armed population reduces the chances that a government will become murderous by raising costs. An armed citizenry does not guarantee less-than-totalitarian government, but by raising expected costs of violations of the "social contract" by governments, an armed citizenry makes such violations less likely.

The right to bear arms sidesteps a conceptual difficulty in the notion that a government can recognize a right to resist its unjust coercion. Government claims a monopoly on coercion and the authority to determine when coercion is just. A government that acknowledges that it may coerce unjustly and that citizens can resist it removes its own authority. A right to bear arms implicitly but not explicitly allows effective resistance to government coercion without the government limiting its powers of enforcement and interpretation. Thus, when a government is going bad and a community comes to realize this, those under its jurisdiction are in a position to collectively take up arms, an option that was not available to Ugandans, German Jews, or Cambodians.

There are inconveniences and inefficiencies in a system where citizens can decide to defend themselves against government coercion. Policing will be more expensive and dangerous, since an armed citizenry is more dangerous to coerce than a helpless one. In order to apprehend a lawbreaker who is convinced of the justice of his cause, it will be necessary to send many policemen rather than only the one who would be needed if the lawbreaker was unarmed.

Samuel C. Wheeler III

See also Jews for the Preservation of Firearms Ownership; Racism and Gun Control; Right to Self-Defense; Second Amendment; Self-Defense, Reasons for Gun Use

For Further Reading:
Harff, Barbara. 1992. "Recognizing Genocides and Politicides." *Genocide Watch* 27: 27–41.
———. 1995. "Rescuing Endangered People: Missed Opportunities." *Social Research* 62, 1: 23–39.
Harff, Barbara, and Ted Gurr. 1995. "Victims of the State." *PIOOM Newsletter* 7, 1: 24–38.
Kates, Don B., Jr., and Daniel D. Polsby. 1995. "Review of *Lethal Laws*." *Journal of Criminal Law and Criminology* 86, 1 (Fall): 247–256.
Kopel, David. 1995. "Review of *Lethal Laws*." *New York Law School Journal of International and Comparative Law* 15: 355–398.
Polsby, Daniel D., and Don B. Kates, Jr. 1997. "Of Holocausts and Gun Control." *Washington University Law Quarterly* 75: 237–275.

Rummel, Rupert J. 1994. *Death by Government.* New Brunswick, NJ: Transactions Press.

Simkin, Jay, Aaron Zelman, and Alan M. Rice. 1994. *Lethal Laws.* New York: Jews for the Preservation of Firearms Ownership, Inc.

Wheeler, Samuel C., III. 1999. "Arms as Insurance." *Public Affairs Quarterly* 13, 2: 111–129.

Gottlieb, Alan Merril (1947–)

Alan Merril Gottlieb is a prominent gun rights advocate who oversees a substantial network of gun rights organizations, conservative lobbying organizations, publications, and radio stations. Gottlieb himself also makes regular media appearances and has authored a number of books promoting gun rights and a conservative political agenda. Gottlieb's various enterprises are headquartered in Bellevue, Washington, a somewhat conservative suburb east of Seattle in Jennifer Dunn's (R-WA) congressional district. Gottlieb's wife, Julie, has been involved with his activities, including acting as publisher of *Women & Guns* magazine.

According to Gottlieb's own biography, found on numerous websites related to organizations he leads, he was born in Los Angeles in 1947, spent a portion of his childhood in New York City, and lived in Knoxville, Tennessee, where he earned a bachelor's degree in nuclear engineering from the University of Tennessee. He served in the Army National Guard during the Vietnam War. He also was on the staff of a member of Congress, served as a leader of the Young Americans for Freedom, and was national director of Youth Against McGovern in 1972.

Gottlieb founded both the Citizens Committee for the Right to Keep and Bear Arms and the Second Amendment Foundation in the 1970s. He also founded and still leads the Center for the Defense of Free Enterprise, which promotes "wise-use" environmental positions, and the American Political Action Committee (AmeriPAC), which supports politically conservative candidates. Gottlieb and his organizations own or co-own several radio stations. Gottlieb himself chairs the Talk America Radio Network, claiming over 300 affiliated radio stations.

Gottlieb has authored and coauthored numerous books on gun rights, the environment, and other issues. His books are largely published through his organizations, but distributed nationwide via major booksellers. Titles in print as of 2001 included *Gun Rights Affirmed: The Emerson Case; More Things You Can Do to Defend Your Gun Rights; Politically Correct Guns: Please Don't Rob or Kill Me; Trashing the Economy: How Runaway Environmentalism Is Wrecking America; She Took a Village;* and *Alan Gottlieb's Celebrity Address Book.*

As one might expect, Gottlieb's activities have not been without controversy. He served several months in jail in the mid-1980s for federal income tax evasion from 1970s income earned via his consulting firm. He has also been criticized for receiving an all-expenses-paid trip to a 1983 conference in Jamaica sponsored by a conservative organization with ties to the Rev. Sun Myung Moon and the Unification Church. In the late 1990s, Gottlieb came under additional criticism for supporting a compromise on child safety locks in an editorial written for *Women & Guns.*

Marcia L. Godwin and Christopher Harris

See also Citizens Committee for the Right to Keep and Bear Arms; *Gun News Digest;* Gun Rights Policy Conference; *Gun Week;* Second Amendment Foundation; Trigger Locks; *Women & Guns*

For Further Reading:

American Political Action Committee. P.O. Box 1682, Bellevue, WA 98009. http://www.ameripac.org.

Ballard, Patricia Tsune, ed. 2001. *Encyclopedia of Associations.* 37th ed. Farmington Hills, MI: The Gale Group.

Center for the Defense of Free Enterprise. Liberty Park, 12500 N.E. Tenth Place, Bellevue, WA 98005, (425) 455-5038. http://www.cdfe.org.

Citizens Committee for the Right to Keep and Bear Arms. Liberty Park, 12500 N.E. Tenth Place, Bellevue, WA 98005, (800) 426-4302. http://www.ccrkba.org.

Halpin, Jim, and Paul de Armond. 1994. "The Merchant of Fear." *Eastside Week.* http:// www.nwcitizen. com/publicgood/reports/merchant.htm.

Second Amendment Foundation. Liberty Park, 13500 N.E. Tenth Place, Bellevue, WA 98005. http://www.saf.org.

Utter, Glenn H. 2000. *Encyclopedia of Gun Control and Gun Rights.* Phoenix, AZ: Oryx Press.

Women & Guns. Liberty Park, 13500 N.E. Tenth Place, Bellevue, WA 98005. http://www.womenandguns.com.

Soldier of fortune James "Bo" Gritz at a press conference, 1983. (Bettmann/Corbis)

Gritz, James "Bo" (1939–)

Born on January 18, 1939, in Enid, Oklahoma, James "Bo" Gritz entered military service at the age of 18 in 1957. He served in Vietnam from 1964 to 1969 as a Green Beret commander. During the 1970s, he served at the Pentagon and later as a Delta Force commander in Latin America. Much decorated during his twenty-two years in the armed forces (he received sixty-two citations for valor), Gritz obtained a bachelor of science in law and corrections at the University of Nebraska, and a master of arts in communications at American University during his military career. He also became a certified flight instructor.

Gritz gained media coverage during the 1980s when he searched for American prisoners of war (POWs) thought to have been left behind in Vietnam. He gained even more attention when he helped negotiate the surrender of fellow Green Beret veteran Randy Weaver at Ruby Ridge in 1992. He was also involved in negotiations with the Freemen of Montana (1992) and with abortion clinic bomber Eric Rudolph (1998).

He ventured into politics when he ran for president in 1992 as the Populist Party candidate with the campaign slogan "God, Guns and Gritz." His campaign made it clear that he was strongly against gun control and that he believed individuals resisting the federal government's attempt to enforce gun laws or confiscate firearms—as was attempted against Randy Weaver at Ruby Ridge—were in the right.

Gritz became disillusioned with the government following his unsuccessful POW rescue missions in Southeast Asia, where he allegedly uncovered evidence of CIA involvement in the drug trade. He has been heavily influenced by the Christian Identity movement and has blended its core beliefs into his own message.

In 1989 Gritz founded the Center for Action, an organization dedicated to "putting accountability back into government," and the Fellowship of Eternal Warriors, an organization that combines his paramilitary training with Christian elements. Since 1993 he has offered paramilitary training through SPIKE (Specially Prepared Individuals for Key Events).

Gritz has published *Center for Action* magazine, an autobiography entitled *Called to Serve: A Majority of One,* a video entitled *Nation Betrayed,* several instructional videos related to SPIKE, a short-wave radio call-in program (*Freedom Call*), and a frequent Internet newsletter on his website. Also, in 1994 he established Almost Heaven, a separatist Christian covenant community in Kamiah, Idaho.

Tiia Rajala

See also Ruby Ridge; Survivalism
For Further Reading:
Anti-Defamation League. 2001. "Extremism in America: James Bo Gritz." http://www.adl.org/learn/Ext_US/gritz.asp.
Gritz, James "Bo." 1989. *A Nation Betrayed.* 2d ed. Sandy Valley, NV: Lazarus Publishing Company.
———. 1991. *Called to Serve.* Sandy Valley, NV: Lazarus Publishing Company.
———. 2001. "Colonel Bo Gritz." http://www.bogritz.com.

Guggenheim Foundation, Harry Frank

The Harry Frank Guggenheim Foundation sponsors scholarly research on problems of violence, aggression, and dominance. The foundation and its president, James Hester, focus on guns and gun violence as important dimensions of the problem of violence. The foundation awards research grants and dissertation fellowships, sponsors conferences, and publishes an annual research review.

Harry Frank Guggenheim, founder of *Newsday* and a grandson of John Simon Guggenheim, established the foundation in 1929 to study aggression and violence. Based in New York City, the foundation awards grants of $10,000 to $30,000 to individuals to carry out research on issues related to violence and aggression. The research priorities of the foundation include crime and the relationship between youth homicide and access to guns.

In addition to funding scholarly research, the foundation publishes the annual *HFG Review* to disseminate the results of sponsored research and to link that research to social problems related to violence. The foundation also sponsors conferences to bring together scholars working in areas related to violence, aggression, and dominance. In 1995, the foundation sponsored a symposium to consider policies for reducing serious youth violence by reducing young people's access to guns. The conference papers suggested that "the most important fact about American homicide rates is the role of guns, particularly among young men in the inner city" (Hester, 1997, p. 1). Among the participants were such leading researchers as Philip J. Cook, Colin Loftin, and Franklin Zimring. The Duke University School of Law journal *Law and Contemporary Problems* published the product of the conference, *Kids, Guns, and Public Policy,* as its winter 1996 issue. Cook, who chaired the conference and edited the issue, emphasizes that although homicide rates in general had been falling, homicide rates for youths had increased greatly. All of the increase in youth homicide was due to guns. Other articles addressed ways in which guns have transformed youth violence and suggested appropriate policies for reducing young people's access to guns.

Walter F. Carroll

See also Schoolyard Shootings; Youth and Guns
For Further Reading:
Cook, Philip J., ed. 1996. "Kids, Guns, and Public Policy" special issue. *Law and Contemporary Problems* 59 (winter).
Davis, John H. 1978. *The Guggenheims (1848–1988): An American Epic.* New York: Morrow.
Harry Frank Guggenheim Foundation website: www.hfg.org/.
Hester, James M. 1997. "Introduction: Crimes of Violence." *HFG Review* 2, 1 (Fall). http://www.hfg.org/html.pages/hester2.htm.
Wallman, Joel. 1997. "Disarming Youth." *HFG Review* 2, 1 (Fall). http://www.hfg.org/html.pages/wallman2.htm.

Gun Buyback Programs

Gun buyback programs—in which local governments encourage residents to turn in firearms using cash payments, gift certificates, or merchandise as incentives—became part of law enforcement efforts in the 1990s to reduce gun violence by removing weapons from circulation. However, while the programs have been politically popular, empirical evidence has failed to demonstrate their effectiveness.

The first such program was begun in Baltimore in 1977. During a three-month period, 13,000 guns were collected (Harborview Injury Prevention and Research Center, 1997). The programs became widespread in the early 1990s, as local law enforcement agencies began to employ them as part of their strategy to reduce gun violence that was reaching "epidemic" proportions in many urban areas. In a research brief prepared for Congress, Krouse (2000, p. 15) observes that "gun buy-back programs remove lethal firearms from homes and, therefore, prevent gun violence by removing the possibility that a firearm may fall into the hands of a child (or adult) who may accidentally or intentionally shoot themselves or others … Such programs lend a sense of empowerment to communities seeking to end gun violence."

In 1999, the U.S. Department of Housing and Urban Development (HUD) established a

Washington, D.C., police offficers gather in front of some of the over 2,200 guns turned in to police August 25, 1999, at the Washington Police Academy. (Reuters NewMedia Inc./CORBIS)

$15 million gun buyback program. The program provided grants to local housing authorities and local police agencies to launch community buyback programs. In announcing the program, President Bill Clinton stated that "every gun turned in through a buyback program means potentially one less tragedy" (Bovard, 2000, p. 42).

Krouse (2000, p. 15) also observes that although the programs "usually receive wide acclaim and favorable media coverage, there is little empirical research demonstrating the effectiveness of these programs." Drawing the same conclusion, Sherman (2000, p. 3) notes that the program "that is best known to be ineffective is gun buybacks. In three separate, moderately strong scientific evaluations, there was [found to be] no reduction in gun violence following the purchase of large quantities of guns."

Krouse (2000, p. 15) contends that it is obvious that "persons who are intent on using firearms are unlikely to exchange firearms. If they do exchange a firearm, they may use the money to buy another more lethal firearm." Callahan, Rivara, and Koepsell (1994, p. 474), in their evaluation of Seattle's program, found that 64 percent of sellers had another gun that they did not surrender, and that 3 percent of the sellers reported they would use the money to purchase another gun. Others have suggested that gun buybacks improve public safety if they get guns away from hardened criminals, but that most guns are not turned in by criminals (Dixon, 2000, p. 5).

The Police Executive Research Forum is conducting an ongoing study of the effectiveness of gun buyback programs for HUD.

Jeffrey Kraus

See also Amnesty Programs; Availability of Guns, Effects on Crime; Crime and Gun Use; Guns in the Home

For Further Reading:

Bovard, James. 2000. "Help Promote Fewer Guns—for the Feds." *Los Angeles Times* (May 3).

Callahan, Charles M., Frederick P. Rivara, and Thomas D. Koepsell. 1994. "Money for Guns: Evaluation of the Seattle Gun Buy-Back Program." *Public Health Reports* 109, 4: 470–477.

Dixon, Jennifer. 2000. "Detroit Gun Buybacks Focus on Public Housing." *Detroit Free Press* (July 10).

Harborview Injury Prevention and Research Center. 1997. "Firearm Injury Interventions: Gun Buy-Back Programs." http://depts.washington.edu/hiprc/childinjury/topic/firearms/buyback.html.

Krouse, William. 2000. "Gun Control." Congressional Research Service issue brief for Congress. Washington, DC: Congressional Research Service, Library of Congress.

Plotkin, Martha R., ed. 1996. *Under Fire: Gun Buy-Backs, Exchanges and Amnesty Programs.* Washington, DC: Police Executive Research Forum.

Sherman, Lawrence. 2000. "Reducing Gun Violence: What Works, What Doesn't, What's Promising." Lecture in the Perspectives on Crime and Justice series at the National Institute of Justice, U.S. Department of Justice, April 5.

Van Horn, Dwight. 1992. "What's Wrong with Gun Amnesty Programs." *Law Enforcement Alliance of America Newsletter* 12, 2 (April): 2.

Gun Clubs

Gun clubs, or organizations of shooters, have probably existed since firearms evolved from hand cannons to more manageable and accurate weapons. The nineteenth century saw the formation of national gun clubs, which were sometimes quasi-governmental entities. The primary force behind this development was the perception that long-range marksmanship had become essential to national defense. The replacement of the smoothbore musket with the rifle as the primary infantry arm made marksmanship important, and since a practical machine gun had yet to be invented, laying down long-range fire re-

quired large numbers of men capable of hitting their mark at great ranges. The National Rifle Association of Great Britain was founded in 1860 and given a royal charter in 1890; the National Rifle Association of America was founded in 1871 by retired generals.

In addition to national organizations, there are numerous state and local gun clubs devoted to shooting or collecting firearms. As of 2002, the National Rifle Association of America had 9,200 affiliated gun clubs and 51 associations. Among the largest of these were the California State Rifle and Pistol Association, with 60,000 members; the Texas State Rifle Association, with 45,000 members; and the Ohio Gun Collectors' Association, with 18,800 members.

David T. Hardy

See also Collectors; Gun Culture; Gun Ownership; National Rifle Association

For Further Reading:

Flora, Earl. 1987. "History of the Ohio Gun Collectors Association." Columbus: Ohio Gun Collectors Association.

Gun Control

In its broadest sense, the term "gun control" refers to any government policies that influence the availability and use of firearms among the general public or distinct subsets of the population—such as minors, convicted felons, and the mentally ill. Such policies can affect behavior involving the manufacture of firearms as well as their sale, ownership, importation, and use. Gun control policies may be intended to encourage or discourage the ownership and use of firearms and can influence attitudes toward guns in the general population by granting a certain legitimacy to them or by labeling them suspect products.

Gun control in this wide sense began in colonial America. Bellesiles (2000), in his treatment of the history of firearms in the United States, notes that in the American colonies the possession of firearms was considered a collective duty, not a right. Even privately owned weapons were considered to be ultimately under the control of the state for purposes of maintaining the collective security. In support of local militia units, colonial legislatures passed laws requiring adult white male Protestant property-holders to own guns. Additional measures regulated various aspects of firearms, such as their sale, storage, and where they could be used and by whom. Certain groups of people, including Indians, enslaved persons, indentured servants, and Roman Catholics, were prohibited from owning firearms. As Bogus (1998) has noted, in the southern colonies the possession of firearms and the maintenance of militias were considered crucial to internal security and keeping slave populations under control. Although militia members were required to possess firearms, such legal requirements were often unenforced. Many could not afford to buy firearms and at times colonial governments attempted to subsidize the purchase of weapons. However, gunsmiths were in short supply and the era of interchangeable parts and mass production techniques had not yet begun, so sufficient numbers of firearms were often unavailable.

Bellesiles claims that in the early nineteenth century Americans were generally uninterested in the ownership and use of firearms. Only with the Civil War in the 1860s did a more general distribution of firearms occur, due in large part to government policies encouraging firearm ownership. Following the war, with former Union soldiers keeping their firearms and prices declining because of fewer government contracts, gun ownership in the civilian population became far more widespread. Two Union veterans, William Conant Church and George Wood Wingate, established the National Rifle Association as a means of encouraging more systematic training in marksmanship. From the start, the NRA gained government support for its efforts. In 1871 New York State granted a charter to the organization and provided funds so that land on Long Island could be purchased for rifle practice. In the early twentieth century, government officials began to serve on the organization's board of directors and the organization benefited from discount sales of surplus military firearms and ammunition to gun clubs.

During the twentieth century national and state governments attempted to deal with what were considered the negative consequences of widespread firearm ownership. In 1911, responding to popular reaction against gun violence in New York City, the New York State Legislature passed the Sullivan Dangerous Weapons Law, which required a license to possess or carry a concealable weapon. In 1934, following an attempted assassination of President-elect Franklin Roosevelt in 1933, and in reaction to the use of certain firearms by notorious criminals, Congress passed the National Firearms Act, the first major piece of firearm-related legislation of the twentieth century. This legislation established a tax on the manufacture, sale, and transfer of sawed-off shotguns and sawed-off rifles, machine guns, and silencers. Those purchasing such weapons were required to submit to a background check conducted by the Federal Bureau of Investigation and to acquire approval of such purchases from local law enforcement officers. Four years later, in an effort to bolster the 1934 act, Congress approved the Federal Firearms Act, which required that firearm manufacturers, dealers, and importers be licensed and forbade the sale of firearms to known criminals.

A third piece of gun control legislation was passed thirty years after the Federal Firearms Act, following the assassinations of President John Kennedy in 1963 and Robert Kennedy and Martin Luther King, Jr., in 1968. The Gun Control Act (GCA) of 1968, strongly supported by President Lyndon Johnson, prohibited the purchase and ownership of firearms by certain groups of people, including convicted felons, fugitives, drug addicts, minors, and the mentally ill. The legislation banned mail-order sales of guns and ammunition and required serial numbers on all newly manufactured firearms. Another provision banned the importation of so-called Saturday night specials, cheaply made handguns claimed to be the weapons of choice in criminal activity. The law required federally licensed firearm dealers to keep records of firearm sales and federal agents were authorized to inspect dealers' records and inventory of firearms.

A fourth piece of gun control legislation, the 1986 Firearms Owners' Protection Act, was intended to weaken many of the provisions of the Gun Control Act. The chief sponsors of the legislation, Sen. James A. McClure (R-ID) and Rep. Harold L. Volkmer (D-MO), argued that the 1968 act unfairly penalized law-abiding citizens. Among its provisions, the new legislation permitted the resumption of ammunition sales through the mail, eased the record-keeping regulations for ammunition dealers, and prohibited the Bureau of Alcohol, Tobacco, and Firearms (BATF), which is the enforcement arm for firearm legislation, from centralizing the records of firearm dealers or establishing a firearm registration system. Despite the weakening provisions of the GCA, the legislation also increased restrictions on firearms by prohibiting the future manufacture of machine guns for private sale, banning the importation of barrels for Saturday night specials, and mandating additional penalties for those engaged in drug trafficking who carry firearms.

Just as the Gun Control Act had led to a reaction from gun rights advocates, resulting in legislation that weakened several of its provisions, the Firearms Owners' Protection Act spurred attempts to increase restrictions on firearms, particularly handguns. An assassination attempt on President Ronald Reagan presented the gun control movement with two valuable new allies. By 1989 the president's press secretary, James Brady, who was severely wounded during the assassination attempt, and his wife, Sarah, were actively seeking passage of controls on the sale and ownership of handguns. Sarah Brady became chairperson of Handgun Control, Inc. (now known as the Brady Campaign to Prevent Gun Violence), the leading proponent of what came to be called the Brady Handgun Violence Prevention Act. After several years of struggle, the act finally became law in November 1993. The main provisions of the legislation required a five-day waiting period during which gun dealers in states that had not already instituted such checks were required to provide local chief law enforcement officers with the names of people wishing to purchase handguns and mandated that these officers conduct background checks to determine the eligibility of the purchaser to own a handgun. Although the Supreme Court in *Printz v. United States* (1997) struck down the mandate that law enforcement officers must run background checks, the five-day waiting period was a temporary measure that came to an end in November 1998 when a computerized national instant check system (NICS) went into effect, covering rifle and shotgun as well as handgun sales. Both sides of the gun control issue expressed dissatisfaction with the instant check system. Those supporting stronger controls noted that certain crucial records, such as histories of mental illness, were often not available, while gun rights supporters, such as the National Rifle Association, feared that the BATF would use the computerized system to develop a comprehensive list of firearm owners that would constitute firearm registration.

A sixth case of gun control legislation, the 1994 Violent Crime Control and Law Enforcement Act, banned the manufacture, sale, and possession of nineteen types of semiautomatic assault weapons and other similar firearms. The legislation outlawed magazines holding more than ten rounds of ammunition, prohibited juveniles from possessing a handgun or handgun ammunition, increased the requirements for firearm dealer licenses, and prohibited those people who were under a restraining order involving threats of domestic violence from possessing firearms. In 1996, Sen. Frank Lautenberg (D-NJ) succeeded in attaching an amendment, called the Domestic Violence Offender Gun Ban (also known as the Lautenberg Amendment), to a continuing resolution approving federal spending. This law prohibits anyone convicted of an act of domestic violence against a spouse or child, whether a felony or a misdemeanor, from purchasing or owning a firearm. The measure proved controversial because it was claimed that many police officers and military personnel could be adversely affected due to misdemeanor convictions that may have occurred years earlier; some critics also argued that the legislation amounted to an ex post facto law that increased the penalties for individuals who committed crimes before the law was passed.

Various gun control measures have been passed at the state and local levels. In 1981 the village of Morton Grove, Illinois, gained nationwide attention when local authorities approved an ordinance instituting a general ban on the ownership of firearms. Although the ordinance was upheld in court, it prompted the NRA and other gun rights organizations to lobby state legislatures to pass firearm preemp-

Gun control advocates at a rally against the National Rifle Association (NRA) on the steps of the Colorado State Capitol, May 1, 1999. (Steve Starr/Corbis)

model that should ultimately be followed. Citing Article 4, Section 1 of the U.S. Constitution, which states that "full faith and credit shall be given in each state to the public acts, records, and judicial proceedings of every other state," gun rights advocates encourage the establishment of reciprocity agreements among the states whereby each state will recognize the concealed-carry laws of every other state.

Several municipal governments, including those in New Orleans, Chicago, Boston, and San Francisco, have filed lawsuits against firearm manufacturers and gun dealers to recover the medical and legal costs of violent crimes committed with guns. One basis for such suits is the claim that gun manufacturers and dealers have oversupplied certain markets where gun restrictions are minimal, knowing that guns will be purchased and transported to areas having much stricter firearm regulations. So far, the courts have not been sympathetic to the liability claims made by municipalities, and gun manufacturers and gun rights groups have countered the lawsuit strategy by lobbying state legislatures to limit the authority of cities to file such suits.

Gun control organizations such as the Violence Policy Center (VPC) and the Brady Campaign to Prevent Gun Violence (previously known as Handgun Control, Inc.) have backed several proposals to further restrict the ownership and use of firearms. The VPC supports passage of a Firearms Safety and Consumer Protection Act that would end the exemption of firearms from federal health and safety regulations. Under such legislation, the secretary of the treasury would be given the authority to regulate the design, manufacture, and distribution of firearms and ammunition. Manufacturers would be required to test firearms and firearm products to assure that they meet standards set by the Treasury Department. The VPC also supports an Internet gun trafficking bill that Sen. Charles Schumer (D-NY) introduced during the 106th session of Congress. The legislation would require all gun sales initiated over the Internet to comply with federal and state firearm laws. It would also ban sales by unlicensed dealers and mandate that the BATF be informed of any website that sells firearms. The organization supports

tion laws forbidding local governments from enacting more stringent ordinances than those existing at the state level. Gun rights organizations also petitioned state legislatures to pass liberalized carrying-concealed-weapons (CCW) laws allowing individuals to carry loaded, hidden weapons on their persons. Spurred on in part by Lott's (1998) research indicating that liberalized CCW laws lead to less crime, states with "may-issue" provisions that allow local law enforcement agencies to approve at their discretion applications for CCW licenses were lobbied to pass "shall-issue" laws that require officials to issue a license to anyone who applies, provided the person is not disqualified for a specific reason, such as a felony conviction. By 1998 thirty-one states had adopted shall-issue CCW laws. While many gun rights advocates have supported such liberalization, others point to Vermont, which does not require a license of any kind to carry a concealed weapon, as the a complete ban on the manufacture of Saturday night specials, or "junk guns," as well as additional limitations on the manufacture and purchase of assault weapons. The VPC backs legislation that would allow more efficient monitoring of gun shows by BATF agents, and a measure prohibiting those under 18 years old from possessing rifles and shotguns as well as handguns.

The Brady Campaign has lobbied for several proposals to reduce the perceived dangers of firearms. The organization backs a measure, initiated during President Bill Clinton's administration, to require unlicensed dealers at gun shows to conduct background checks on prospective buyers and to keep records of sales. It also backs legislation that would require locking devices and other technologies to improve gun safety; an increase in the minimum age from 18 to 21 for handgun possession; an expansion of the Brady Act to prevent juveniles convicted of violent crimes from possessing firearms even after they become adults; and a ban on the importation of high-capacity ammunition clips. The Brady Campaign also opposes any legislative efforts to protect the firearm industry from lawsuits brought by victims of violent crime.

Other proposals include a measure that would limit individuals to purchasing one handgun per month in order to discourage persons who are legally qualified to purchase firearms from acquiring a large number of handguns that might be sold to those who would otherwise be prohibited from making such a purchase. In order to keep firearms out of the hands of children and juveniles, gun control advocates in some states have successfully instituted measures making it a crime for an adult to allow youth access to firearms.

Some gun rights supporters consider the vast majority of firearm regulation laws to be violations of the Second Amendment to the Constitution. However, some people who support restrictions argue that the Second Amendment refers to a collective right of state militias, not a right of individuals, and hence limits on individual gun ownership do not run counter to the Constitution. Others contend that even if the amendment can be considered a protection of an individual right, legislatures and the courts need not consider the right to keep and bear arms absolute, and therefore reasonable restrictions may be implemented for the protection of the public safety. While the Second Amendment provides the most emotionally based argument against gun regulation, those opposed to restrictions also argue that gun control legislation has been notably ineffective in its stated goal of keeping firearms out of the hands of those who commit crimes and that the only people adversely affected are law-abiding citizens.

Any attempt to predict the future of gun control depends on consideration of several factors. Although the results of lawsuits so far have not been promising for pro–gun control interests, such suits may still prove to be an avenue for instituting additional controls on the firearm industry, such as more conservative marketing strategies and greater consideration of firearm safety. Although firearms now are exempt from consumer protection laws, efforts to get them covered by such laws may prove successful. Partisan control of Congress, the presidency, and state legislatures will undoubtedly affect the success of lobbying groups on both sides of the issue. Gun rights groups claim to be nonpartisan, but Republicans generally are considered more dependable legislative allies than are Democrats. One of the more emotional arguments for greater control of firearms is the number of gun-related accidental deaths, especially among children. However, although compared to other types of accidents (especially automobile) the rate of gun accidents has increased, the absolute number of accidental deaths over time has decreased. In addition, due to the decrease in the violent crime rate in the last decade, legislators may find any proposals for further legislation less compelling than they had in the past. Yet a renewed increase in the violent crime rate could result in increased pressure for additional legislative restrictions on firearms. A long-term trend that may affect the future of gun control policy is the proportion of Americans owning firearms. Although there is disagreement over when a gun culture arose in the United States, there is little doubt that by the early twentieth century there was a segment of the American population committed to the ownership of firearms that opposed restrictions on the ownership and use of guns. However, General Social Survey (2000) data indicate that in the last twenty-seven years the percentage of households with firearms has declined from over 45 percent to under 33 percent, thus providing evidence for a decline of the gun culture and possibly a weakening of resistance to additional gun restrictions.

Glenn H. Utter

See also Acquisition of Guns; Ammunition, Regulations of; Amnesty Programs; Antiterrorist Legislation; Assault Weapons Ban of 1994; Attitudes toward Gun Control; Bartley-Fox Carrying Law; Black Codes; Brady Campaign to Prevent Gun Violence; Brady Center to Prevent Gun Violence; Brady Handgun Violence Prevention Act; Canada, Gun Laws; Child Access Prevention Laws; Coalition to Stop Gun Violence; Concealed Weapons Laws; Congressional Voting Patterns on Gun Control; Consumer Product Safety Laws; Defensive Gun Use; Democratic Party and Gun Control; Enforcement of Gun Control Laws; Federal Firearms Act of 1938; Firearm Sentence Enhancement Laws; Firearms Owners' Protection Act of 1986; Gun Buyback Programs; Gun Control Act of 1968; Gun Shows; Institute for Legislative Action; Interest Groups and Gun Legislation; Japan, Gun Laws; Lawsuits against Gun Manufacturers; Legal Action Project; Mailing of Firearms Act of 1927; Mexico, Gun Laws; NAACP and Gun Control; National Firearms Act of 1934; National Instant Criminal Background Check System; National Rifle Association; Nuisance Law and Gun Suits; Political Victory Fund; Racism and Gun Control; Republican Party and Gun Control; Right-to-Carry Laws; Second Amendment; Smith & Wesson Settlement Agreement; Sullivan Law; United Kingdom—History of Gun Laws since 1900; United States Constitution and Gun Rights; *United States v. Cruikshank; United States v. Miller;* Waiting Periods; Youth Gun Control Legislation, The Juvenile Justice Bill of 1999

For Further Reading:

Bellesiles, Michael A. 2000. *Arming America: The Origins of a National Gun Culture.* New York: Alfred A. Knopf.

Bogus, Carl T. 1998. "The Hidden History of the Second Amendment." *University of California–Davis Law Review* 31: 311–408.

Carter, Gregg Lee. 1997. *The Gun Control Movement.* New York: Twayne Publishers.

Cook, Philip J., and Jens Ludwig. 2000. *Gun Violence: The Real Costs.* New York: Oxford University Press.

Cottrol, Robert J., ed. 1994. *Gun Control and the Constitution: Sources and Explorations on the Second Amendment.* New York: Garland.

DeConde, Alexander. 2001. *Gun Violence in America: The Struggle for Control.* Boston: Northeastern University Press.

General Social Survey. 2000. "Do you happen to have in your home (or garage) any guns or revolvers? If yes, Is it a pistol, shotgun, rifle, or what?" Inter-University Consortium for Political and Social Research: http://www.icpsr.umich.edu/GSS/.

Kopel, David B. 1992. *The Samurai, the Mountie, and the Cowboy: Should America Adopt the Gun Controls of Other Democracies?* Buffalo, NY: Prometheus Books.

———, ed. 1995. *Guns: Who Should Have Them?* Amherst, NY: Prometheus Books.

Korwin, Alan, with Michael P. Anthony. 1997. *Gun Laws of America.* Phoenix, AZ: Bloomfield Press.

Lott, John R., Jr. 1998. *More Guns, Less Crime: Understanding Crime and Gun Control Laws.* Chicago: University of Chicago Press.

Spitzer, Robert J. 1998. *The Politics of Gun Control.* Chatham, NJ: Chatham House.

Utter, Glenn H. 2000. *Encyclopedia of Gun Control and Gun Rights.* Phoenix, AZ: Oryx Press.

Vizzard, William J. 2000. *Shots in the Dark: The Policy, Politics, and Symbolism of Gun Control.* Lanham, MD: Rowman & Littlefield.

Gun Control Act of 1968

The Gun Control Act (GCA) of 1968 is the foundation for federal gun control laws. Enacted in response to the racial and other unrest of the 1960s, the GCA was the first comprehensive federal gun law. Its most important provisions were sharp restrictions on sales of guns and ammunition across state lines; restrictions on the import of firearms; the "prohibited persons" list of classes of people who are barred from possessing guns; and a point-of-sale system of gun owner registration.

Concerns about abusive enforcement of the GCA eventually led Congress to pass, and President Reagan to sign, the Firearms Owners' Protection Act (FOPA) of 1986, which curtailed some provisions of the GCA while leaving its basic structure intact. Although the GCA was politically important, research does not suggest that it has had a statistically significant impact on U.S. crime rates.

In August 1963, Connecticut Democratic Sen. Thomas Dodd introduced the first version of what would eventually become the Gun Control Act. Connecticut was then the most important state for American gun manufacturing, and American manufacturers had assisted with the drafting of the early versions of the Dodd bill, as they shared Dodd's objective of excluding low-cost imported guns from the American market.

Interest in gun control as a method of crime control rather than a form of protectionism surged in 1966, a year of unrest that frightened much of the American public. For six days in May, Vietnam War protests, sometimes violent, rocked college campuses. On June 7, civil rights leader James Meredith was shot and wounded while leading a march for voter registration. In July and August, city after city suffered race riots, as the contagion of rioting that appeared in the 1965 Watts riot in Los Angeles spread nationwide. "Black power" leaders such as Stokely Carmichael and members of the Black Panthers terrified mainstream America with high-powered rhetoric about violent revolution, as they encouraged blacks to arm themselves against "whitey."

Then, on August 1, 1966, an ex-marine named Charles Whitman who was then an agricultural student climbed to the top of a tower at the University of Texas in Austin. Using a high-powered hunting rifle, he murdered fifteen people and wounded thirty-one before being killed by the police.

In October, the Senate Judiciary Committee convened gun control hearings. Sen. Edward Kennedy (D-MA), serving his first term, called for a ban on mail-order sales of rifles made to military specifications. Gun control advocates were particularly disturbed by the sale of low-priced foreign rifles; as European governments had been replacing their World War II battle rifles, these outdated rifles were being shipped to the thriving U.S. firearms market. The rifles, mostly bolt actions, were available at low prices and were said to be the weapon of choice for urban rioters.

While Senator Kennedy called for giving the secretary of the treasury the discretion to ban the import of firearms not "recognized as particularly suitable" for sporting purposes, Sen. Roman Hruska (R-NE) rejected the idea of giving the secretary of the treasury the power to ban guns. Hruska railed against "the unlikely assumption without evidence that substantial markets for imported products are composed of irresponsible or criminal citizens." Hruska said there was "no justifiable criteria" on which to discriminate among various categories of imported firearms and warned that giving the Treasury Department broad discretion would subject gun owners to the vicissitudes of "domestic politics."

The witnesses who appeared before Congress in 1966 included U.S. Attorney General Nicholas Katzenbach, the attorney general of New Jersey, the chief of police of St. Louis, the chief of police of Atlanta, and representatives of the New York City police bureaucracy, the American Bar Association, and the International Association of Chiefs of Police. Senator Kennedy predicted that adoption of his gun control plan would substantially alleviate the problem of juveniles acquiring guns.

But no federal gun controls were enacted in 1966, and the next year the chaos increased. There were more than 100 riots in the summer of 1967. They erupted in cities such as Boston, Chicago, Cincinnati, Hartford, Minneapolis, New Haven, New York, Philadelphia, Pittsburgh, Tampa, and Washington. The worst riots took place in Detroit and Newark and resulted in seventy-two deaths. Following the Newark riots, the National Guard conducted house-to-house searches for guns in black neighborhoods there.

Senator Dodd had less time to spend on gun control in the summer of 1967, however, as he unsuccessfully attempted to fight off the Senate's move to censure him (by a vote of 92–5) for using tax-exempt campaign funds for personal purposes.

Long before the "long hot summer" of 1968 began, riots erupted again. The Rev. Martin Luther King, Jr., was assassinated by a sniper using a rifle on April 4, and for the next three days riots raged in over 100 cities.

Race riots had not been unknown in the United States in the late nineteenth and early twentieth centuries, but the 1965–1968 riots were unprecedented. Never before 1966 had there been so many riots within a few weeks of each other, and never before 1968 had so many riots erupted all at once. The impact of the riots was magnified by television, which brought the riots into every American living room with an immediacy that made events in one city terrifying to the whole nation. Gun sales zoomed as home owners and store owners prepared to protect themselves in the event of civil disorder. Violent crime rates had been at historical lows when the 1960s began, but they began to surge in mid-decade and every year they got worse and worse.

On June 5, 1968, a young Palestinian male named Sirhan Sirhan used a cheap imported handgun to murder presidential candidate and New York Sen. Robert F. Kennedy. Sirhan was angry with Kennedy's strong support for Israel. Kennedy had just won the California Democratic primary. Although Vice President Hubert Humphrey (who had not entered a single primary) had an insurmountable lead in delegates for the Democratic nomination, Kennedy's idealistic supporters had not been deterred. But now another of their heroes had been killed by gunfire.

Senator Kennedy's assassination galvanized antigun activists more intensely than any event since the assassination of President McKinley in 1901. Immediately after Kennedy's assassination, the Emergency Committee for Effective Gun Control was formed, with former astronaut and future senator John Glenn as chairman. Members included the AFL-CIO, the National Council of Churches, New York Mayor John Lindsay, Johnny Carson, Mississippi newspaper editor (and future White House staffer) Hodding Carter III, Joe DiMaggio, Ann Landers, Green Bay Packers coach Vince Lombardi, and Frank Sinatra. Another member was Paxton Quigley, a young woman who eventually changed her mind on the gun issue and wrote two books urging women to arm themselves for self-protection: *Armed and Female* and *Not an Easy Target: Paxton Quigley's Self-Protection for Women.*

The committee demanded national gun registration, national gun licensing, a ban on interstate gun sales, and a ban on mail-order sales of long guns. (Handguns had been banned from the U.S. mail since the 1920s, but could still be delivered by other carriers, such as UPS.) Many other gun control advocates urged a ban on all small, inexpensive handguns, so-called Saturday night specials (a reference to handgun violence common in poor black neighborhoods on Saturday nights).

On June 24, President Johnson addressed the nation and called for national gun registration. He promised that registration would involve no more inconvenience than dog tags or automobile license plates. "In other countries which have sensible laws, the hunter and the sportsman thrive," he said, urging hunters and target shooters not to oppose the new restrictions.

On June 16, several of the major American long gun manufacturers announced their own gun control plan. A joint statement from Remington, Savage, Olin, Winchester, Mossberg, and Ithaca called for a national ban on mail-order gun sales. (Leading American gun manufacturers had been calling for a mail-order ban since 1958 in order to restrict competition.) Further, the manufacturers suggested that states that wanted additional controls enact gun owner licensing, like the system that Illinois had created in 1966. Three weeks later, in testimony before the U.S. Senate Judiciary Committee, the gun manufacturers demanded that every state adopt the manufacturers' Model Firearms Owner's License Bill. States that did not, the manufacturers said, should be forced to do so by Congress. The National Rifle Association, however, continued to oppose any new federal gun controls, and said that if gun owner licensing were to be done at all, it should be undertaken by the states, not the the federal government.

On August 20, the Soviet Union invaded Czechoslovakia, crushing the "Prague Spring" of liberalization that had been progressing under Czech President Alexander Dubcek. Czech students protested and even rioted, but their efforts were futile against Warsaw Pact tanks and soldiers. Some Second Amendment advocates argued that Czechoslovakia demonstrated the dangers of disarmament. Yet although it was not uncommon for gun control to be described as "a Communist plot," gun control opponents were much more reticent in the 1960s than they are today about defending firearm ownership on grounds of personal safety; then, gun advocates tended to focus on the merits of the sporting uses of guns.

Riots broke out in Chicago the next week when the Democratic convention assembled to nominate Hubert Humphrey. Plans for peaceful protests against the Vietnam War were hijacked by the successful efforts of Yippies and the "Chicago Seven" to promote a riot. The Chicago police, under the command of Mayor Richard Daley, responded with what the National Commission on the Causes and Prevention of Violence later called "a police riot," breaking heads and engaging in indiscriminate violence against rioters, innocent bystanders, and even the media.

In Washington, negotiations continued on the gun control bills. Finally, Senator Dodd and other congressional backers of President Johnson's plan arrived at a compromise with the NRA, leading to the Gun Control Act of 1968. The NRA had fought the GCA at every step of the way, but before the final vote a compromise was reached. The NRA, while not supporting final passage of the GCA, would not score it as an antigun vote. There would be no federal licensing of gun owners. Gun and ammunition sales would be registered, but only by the dealer, not the government. (Registration is done via the 4473 form that the purchaser fills out in gun stores.) Mail-order and interstate gun and ammunition sales were outlawed, except that states could enact laws allowing their citizens to buy long guns in adjacent states.

Ever since the Federal Firearms Act (FFA) of 1938, persons in the business of selling firearms had been required to possess a federal firearms license (FFL). [Federal Firearms Act, Public Law no. 75–785, 52 Stat. 1250, 1938.] The GCA broadened the scope of sellers needing an FFL and imposed various restrictions on FFLs. The FFA had prohibited interstate gun sales to persons with certain types of convictions, but had not applied to in-state sales or to gun possession.

A "prohibited persons" list was established, banning gun possession by anyone with any type of felony conviction no matter how distant or nonviolent, alcoholics, drug users, "mental defectives," fugitives, persons dishonorably discharged from the military, and persons who renounced their citizenship. In the 1990s the list was expanded to include people with any domestic violence misdemeanor conviction and persons sub-

ject to domestic violence restraining orders. The ban on sales, but not possession, was also applied to persons under indictment. In contrast to the laws of many states, the federal prohibited persons list is permanent and retroactive, and applies to all felonies, not just violent ones.

Interstate pistol sales were banned. Interstate long gun sales were also banned, except when contiguous states enacted laws authorizing such sales. Mail-order gun sales were shut down too, as were interstate ammunition sales. People possessing FFLs (including gun manufacturers and wholesalers) were still allowed to sell across state lines to each other and to use the mails. A new class of FFL was created for gun collectors, allowing them to engage in interstate and mail-order transactions for "curios and relics," but requiring them to submit to various registration and paperwork requirements. FFL sales of handguns were banned to persons under 21, as were long gun sales to persons under 18.

In addition, the secretary of the treasury was given the authority to ban the import of any gun not "particularly suitable for or readily adaptable to" sporting purposes. Imports of foreign military surplus were prohibited. This last measure was pleasing to American gun manufacturers, who were tired of losing sales to foreign imports sold at bargain-basement prices. (The surplus ban was later modified to allow curios and relics.) The controls aimed at inexpensive guns led liberal writer Robert Sherrill (1973) to describe the GCA as race control masquerading as gun control.

Most of the Gun Control Act is found at 18 U.S. Code in sections 921–929, and it remains the main federal gun law. New federal gun laws (e.g., the Brady Act, the assault weapons ban) are usually codified as amendments to the GCA statutes.

The GCA also amended a separate federal law, the National Firearms Act (NFA) of 1934. The NFA (U.S. Code, volume 26, section 5801 et seq.) had imposed a taxation and registration system on machine guns, short shotguns, short rifles, and silencers. The GCA amended the NFA by creating a new category of prohibited weapons called "destructive devices" (e.g., mortars and grenades).

Earlier in 1968, in *Haynes v. United States* (390 U.S. 85, 1968), the Supreme Court had ruled part of the National Firearms Act unconstitutional because a particular registration requirement (applying to persons who had acquired the gun illegally, without paying the necessary federal tax) could force a person to incriminate himself in violation of the Fifth Amendment. Congress revised the NFA to make technical changes to the registration mandate, thus complying with the Court's decision.

President Johnson picked up conservative votes for the GCA by agreeing to legislation authorizing federal wiretapping, which he had previously opposed. The GCA was signed into law by Johnson on October 22. (The statutes that are now called the Gun Control Act were actually combined from two different bills. One bill was called the Gun Control Act and the other was called the Omnibus Safe Streets and Crime Control Act, which also had wiretap provisions. Title II of the bill called the Gun Control Act was actually the new version of the National Firearms Act.)

Among the Texas delegation, the only "yes" vote came from a young representative named George Herbert Walker Bush III, who said the GCA was good but that much more needed to be done. In the 1970 Texas Senate race, Democratic candidate Lloyd Bentsen used Bush's vote against him and won the election. In Maryland, Democratic Sen. Millard Tydings made a campaign issue out of his strong support for gun control and wiretapping. He lost the election and thereby frightened many congressmen away from gun control for years to come. Likewise, Connecticut Sen. Thomas Dodd, chief sponsor of the GCA, was defeated by Republican Lowell Weicker, who ran on a progun platform.

The GCA led to the creation of the Bureau of Alcohol, Tobacco, and Firearms (BATF)—upgraded from its previous status as a division—within the Department of the Treasury. The Treasury Department rather than the Justice Department had always had primary authority for enforcement of federal gun laws since the 1934 and 1938 federal laws were enacted under Congress's taxation power. The idea that Congress could use its power "to regulate commerce ... among the several states" to create laws regarding the possession or sale of guns within a single state would have been considered ludicrous before the 1960s.

As with previous federal gun laws, the GCA was part of a self-reinforcing cycle of the expansion of federal power. The National Firearms Act of 1934 (which used the tax power to control machine guns) was patterned after the Narcotic Drug Act of 1914 (which used the tax power to control opiates), and the NFA in turn set the stage for the Marihuana Tax Act (which used the tax power to control marijuana). The GCA of 1968 (which used the interstate commerce power to control noninterstate firearm activity) would not have been possible without the Civil Rights Act of 1964 (which used the interstate commerce power to control in-state racial discrimination). The GCA, in turn, set the stage for vastly expanded federal drug laws and other criminal laws over the following decades.

Many years after resigning the presidency, Richard Nixon revealed that he considered guns an "abomination." The Nixon administration was the first to implement the GCA, and enforcement often appeared consistent with Nixon's view of guns.

Firearm dealers and owners complained that BATF enforcement of the GCA was often lawless and abusive. They alleged that sometimes when gun dealers called BATF for advice about how to comply with the new federal laws, BATF agents would get the caller's name, give him misleading advice, and then arrest him for breaking the law. Allegations of illegal forfeitures, harassment, entrapment, due process violations, and search-and-seizure abuse were common.

With the NRA and other gun rights organizations demanding reform, Congress began to hold hearings. In a 1982 report, the U.S. Senate Subcommittee on the Constitution unanimously concluded that the 1968 Gun Control Act facilitated BATF "conduct which borders on the criminal.... Enforcement tactics made possible by current firearm laws are constitutionally, legally and practically reprehensible.... Approximately seventy-five percent of BATF gun prosecutions were aimed at ordinary citizens who had neither criminal intent nor knowledge, but were enticed by agents into unknowing technical violations" (Senate Committee on the Judiciary, Subcommittee on the Constitution, 97th Congress, 2d sess., Senate document 2807, February 1982, pp. 20–23).

The first version of what would become the Firearms Owners' Protection Act of 1986 was introduced in Congress in 1979 under the title the Federal Firearms Reform Act of 1979. As a candidate for president, Ronald Reagan endorsed the proposal. But when Reagan took office his advisers told the NRA that the economy was the top priority and that gun law reform would have to wait. Although candidate Reagan had endorsed the FOPA without reservation, the Reagan Treasury Department, strongly influenced by career BATF employees, began to insist on major revisions.

The NRA leadership was divided about what to do. Eventually, NRA Institute for Legislative Action head Neal Knox was ousted because of Knox's continued objections to compromising with the White House.

In Congress, the FOPA—also known as "McClure-Volkmer" for its chief sponsors, Sen. James McClure (R-ID) and Rep. Harold Volkmer (D-MO)—was building momentum. Senate Majority Leader Howard Baker (R-TN) had refused to bring the FOPA to the floor, but in the 1985 Congress, Robert Dole (R-KS) became majority leader, and the FOPA was brought to a vote. A modified version of the FOPA that was acceptable to the White House passed the Senate 79–15 in 1985.

The bill then went to the House of Representatives, where House Judiciary Chairman Peter Rodino (D-NJ), a strong gun control advocate, pronounced it "dead on arrival" and refused to schedule hearings. Rep. Harold Volkmer began to circulate a "discharge petition" to bring the bill directly to the floor of the House. When it became clear that Volkmer would obtain the necessary 218 signatures (out of 435 representatives), floor debate was scheduled.

As in the Senate, the NRA prevailed in the House on most recorded votes on amendments. But Rep. William Hughes (D-NJ) offered an amendment to ban the sale of any machine gun manufactured after the FOPA's enactment to any person who was not a government employee. The presiding officer called for a voice vote, pronounced that the "ayes" had it, and refused requests to allow a recorded vote, although opponents insisted that there had been more "no" votes. The NRA decided to accept the FOPA, even with the machine gun amendment, rather than send the bill to a conference committee where House leadership would likely kill it. The FOPA was signed into law by President Reagan on May 19, 1986.

The first provision in the FOPA declared Congress's belief that the Second Amendment guarantees an individual the right to arms. The bulk of the act made technical changes to the GCA. The FOPA prohibited forfeitures on charges for which a defendant had been acquitted; prohibited punishment of unintentional violations of the GCA (by requiring that the government prove that the violation was willful or knowing); clarified what was meant by the GCA requirement that FFLs were necessary for persons "engaged in the business"; allowed people with FFLs to sell guns away from their principal place of business as long as they complied with all relevant laws (thus allowing FFL-holders to sell guns at gun shows); reclassified certain paperwork violations as misdemeanors; limited BATF inspections of gun dealers to one per dealer per year (while still allowing unlimited inspections in the case of a criminal investigation); required the BATF to process FFL applications in a timely manner and not to deny the application without good cause; imposed controls on BATF license revocations; provided for the award of attorney's fees against the BATF if the court found that the case was abusive; prohibited the BATF from creating a national gun registry; removed federal restrictions on interstate ammunition sales; relegalized interstate long gun sales (if the seller was an FFL-holder and the sale was legal in both states); and broadened the scope of firearms that could be imported (Firearms Owners' Protection Act, Public Law no. 99–308, 100 Stat. 449, 1986).

Because of problems experienced by travelers moving through jurisdictions with highly restrictive gun laws (e.g., hunters driving to upper New England via Massachusetts or New York

City), the FOPA exempted interstate travelers from local gun law enforcement if the travel was for sporting gun use and the gun was unloaded and locked in a trunk or similar compartment. The FOPA also modified the National Firearms Act to bring some machine gun parts within the definition of a machine gun.

The GCA had created a mandatory sentence for use of a gun in a federal crime of violence. The FOPA extended this to include drug trafficking crimes and added a thirty-year sentence for use of a machine gun or silencer. As the "war on drugs" developed, these mandatory sentences were used for a far broader range of cases than had been anticipated, including that of the Branch Davidians (one such example was *Muscarello v. United States*).

The FOPA did not end the debate about proper federal implementation of the GCA. The BATF's regulation writing under the GCA and FOPA, as well as enforcement of the two acts, remain objects of great controversy, with allegations that the BATF is implementing the statute too stringently or too loosely.

The GCA and FOPA have been politically important, and of course they have been momentous to some persons directly affected by the acts. But their effect on U.S. crime rates is not clear. During the Carter administration, Professors James D. Wright, Peter Rossi, and Kathleen Daly (1983) were commissioned to produce a comprehensive report on all prior gun control research. Their report was unable to find any statistically significant impact of the GCA on crime, even on interstate criminal acquisition of guns, which had been a major target of the GCA. Subsequent research has not seriously challenged this conclusion.

Today, gun control advocates denounce the GCA as insufficiently strict, whereas gun rights advocates argue that the GCA proves that gun control does not work. Not many people claim that the GCA was a success—other than at laying the foundation for future gun control laws.

David B. Kopel

See also Bureau of Alcohol, Tobacco, and Firearms; Dodd, Thomas Joseph; Federal Firearms Act of 1938; Firearms Owners' Protection Act of 1986; Gun Control; Kennedy, Edward M.; *Muscarello v.*

United States; National Firearms Act of 1934; Omnibus Crime Control and Safe Streets Act; Saturday Night Specials; Texas Tower Shooting

For Further Reading:

Batey, Robert. 1986. "Techniques of Strict Construction: The Supreme Court and the Gun Control Act of 1968." *Boston University Law Review* 13: 123–156. http://www.saf.org/LawReviews/Batey1.html.

Halbrook, Stephen P. 1995. *Firearms Law Deskbook.* New York: Clark Boardman Callaghan.

Hardy, David T. 1986. "The Firearms Owners' Protection Act: A Historical and Legal Perspective." *Cumberland Law Review* 17: 585–682. http://www.hardylaw.net/FOPA.html.

Sherrill, Robert. 1973. *The Saturday Night Special.* New York: Charterhouse.

Vizzard, William J. 1999. "The Gun Control Act of 1968." *St. Louis University Public Law Review* 18: 79–97. http://www.saf.org/LawReviews/Vizzard3.htm.

Wright, James D., Peter Rossi, and Kathleen Daly. 1983. *Under the Gun.* New York: Aldine.

Gun Culture

The American gun culture is a seemingly unified aggregation of individuals, mainly white, small-town males who evidence a longstanding personal attachment to guns, gun ownership, and gun habits, including the use of guns for hunting and sporting purposes. The culture has existed since colonial times. There is considerable diversity among gun owners, but hard-core gun culture adherents are often oriented to single-issue thinking about guns and gun ownership issues.

The gun has played an important role in American history and continues to play a defining role in shaping American values. Yet the gun culture is not defined by guns per se but rather by a number of distinct gun subcultures.

Guns have been part of the American mythos from the very start. Many historical accounts stress the primacy of guns in defending colonial homes from Native Americans, wild animals, and foreign armies. The notion of the militia, the citizen-soldier, successfully and repeatedly rising to the occasion to defend hearth and home from "the other" is a deeply cherished and highly emotionalized aspect of the American historical imagination.

However, recent scholarship questions the efficacy of American militias, in particular their preparedness and the quality and quantity of their arsenals. Local militias were poorly disciplined and insufficiently armed to be of much use (Bellesiles, 2000, p. 151). George Washington's jaundiced view of militias is obvious: "To place any dependence upon Militia is assuredly resting upon a broken staff.... [They] come in, you cannot tell how; [they] go, you cannot tell when; and [they] act, you cannot tell where" (Spitzer, 1999, p. 30). But the myth born at the battles of Lexington and Concord (they were actually defeats, though the British withdrawal to Boston turned into a rout) is indeed potent and pervasive. Reinforced by World War II movies that emphasized the diversity and commonality of foot soldiers—all pulling together to defeat the fascist foe—the idea of the American fighting man as springing spontaneously from the people became an image as solid as the Marine Corps monument commemorating the Battle of Iwo Jima.

The myth of the militia and the American fighting man is predicated on the assumption that, at least in the past, all or most American men owned or had access to firearms and were proficient in their use (the image endures of "ole Betsy" hanging over the mantel). But recent historians point out that most Americans, even on the frontier, did not own guns, nor were they familiar with their use and handling (Bellesiles, 2000, p. 200). As surprising as it may seem, even the denizens of the "Wild West" were not particularly well armed. Even the fast-draw-style gunfight, or "walk down," is largely a creation of the nineteenth-century dime novel and the twentieth-century cinema (Brown, 1994, p. 419). The "gunfight at OK Corral," itself the stuff of epic legend making (and recent demythologizing), was far from a heroic battle of equal forces or one of unmitigated good against the forces of discord and disorder. In reality, it took place at extremely close quarters, was over in a matter of seconds, and was little more than an unexceptional urban shootout between two groups of urban toughs in a boomtown setting.

The problem with guns in early America only erupted with a boom economy, the absence of respectable women, and the presence of under-regulated, armed young men. Almost every "crime wave" in American history, from that in the goldfields of California to the wave spawned by the crack explosion of the 1980s, involves these elements. A "frontier mentality" prevails and violence may occur until the town or area is "civilized"—that is, respectable women arrive in numbers and exert their influence, the men are disarmed, or economic opportunity improves.

The revisionist argument theorizes that in the post–Civil War period, gun manufacturers and well-heeled hunters and target enthusiasts were essential to the formation of a myth of universal firearm ownership in the United States. Firearm advertisements from this period to the present often present a climate of danger and menace and demonstrate the unique "leveling" effect of the firearm. Such ads have sometimes also focused on the aesthetic aspects of the firearms—their fine craftsmanship and materials—but the primary appeal appears to be instrumental, not expressive.

In rural America at least, a culture of gun ownership was ensconced by the 1920s. This condition, coupled with fundamental improvements that had taken place in gun manufacture and in firearms themselves in the previous forty years, led more people to own advanced weaponry than in the past.

Crime waves and accompanying media hysteria in both the 1920s and 1960s increased interest in firearms and gun ownership. Hollywood featured firearms more prominently in its products. Guns came to be viewed as essential to the plots of many television shows and movies—for example, "The Rifleman's" rifle, Paladin's derringer, 007's Walther, and "Dirty Harry's" .44 magnum. A cursory glance at the ads in the movie section in any American newspaper will reveal frequent use of the firearm as a cinematic icon. The gun is almost always presented larger than scale, superimposed on the image, often thrust in an upward Freudian manner. And, of course, advertisements and movies have had some effect on popularizing gun ownership. Ironically, some believe that the growth of popular gun ownership and the gun culture owes much to the climate of menace invoked by media and accompanying cries for gun control.

In other words, the very dialogue over gun ownership issues has stimulated gun sales. Anticipating additional legislation, those who were undecided make the move to get some firearms while they are still available. However, within the context of popular firearm acquisition and interest, a more specialized hard core of gun ownership has flourished.

Features of the Gun Culture

Because gun ownership is so widespread in the United States, generalizations about a monolithic gun culture are risky. Indeed, there are a number of specialized and distinct gun cultures. Examples include the urban minority street culture, Civil War reenactors, rural white male deer hunters, and survivalists. Moreover, individuals own guns for a number of reasons—not just for self-defense but for hunting, collecting, or out of a sense of being linked through the firearm to one's past. There are also subcultures where gun ownership is explained by interests in target shooting or military-type recreation, or devotion to the Second Amendment.

Much of the ideology of these groups overlaps. Committed gun owners, along with other groups recently stigmatized by media and academe, have value systems similar to other "pariah groups." A pariah group is a group whose belief system was formerly dominant or at least respectable but is now considered marginal, unrespectable, and, most significantly, anachronistic.

Like other pariah groups such as cockfighters and Neoconfederates, hard-core gun owners are paternalistic and anachronistic. In general, they long for the "good old days" and ritualistically decry the "mess in Washington." They revere the past, often taking refuge in mythopoeic imagery and notions. Accordingly, the role of women and minorities in gun culture has been insignificant until very recently. In recent decades, firearm manufacturers have aimed their advertisements at these groups (and have been criticized for doing so by gun control advocates), and national groups such as the National Rifle Association have belatedly attempted to broaden their membership base. Yet many local organizations of gun owners and shooters remain white male preserves. It is ironic that while individual

gun owners criticize (sometimes quite viciously) the national government, most profess to be extremely patriotic.

However, the nation that they embrace (however mythical it may be) is that of the period immediately after World War II. Subsequent developments, in the 1960s in particular, are seen as causes of decline in American arms and society. Events such as Waco and Ruby Ridge and FBI blunders—even "Monicagate"—have furthered their estrangement from the national government. The Bureau of Alcohol, Tobacco, and Firearms, the entity charged with enforcement of laws pertaining to firearm commerce, has drawn their special ire.

They venerate more or less uncritically elders of the past, including shooters, writers, and other "great Americans," some of whom have achieved legendary status through their prowess with weapons on the range or "somewhere on the border," serving as lawmen. One consequence of this fixation on the past is a derogation of new ideas, innovations, and technology. In general, gun culture adherents are more likely to be politically conservative and to vote for Republican candidates in national elections; they are frequently "single issue" voters. They are likely to live in the South, West, or Midwest rather than the East (especially the Northeast). Gun owners are likely to say that they are hunters and to live in rural areas and small towns and cities. Typical of "bedrock America," they are generally uncritical consumers of American national mythology.

For them, guns represent both a concrete and a spiritual-emotional link to the heroic past. In this regard, the gun culture, like other anachronistic cultures, may be seen as highly totemistic. Weapons that have been used in combat or that have personal connections to famous figures are especially valued. This is particularly evident in the South, where family heirlooms from the Civil War are venerated and given pride of place in many living rooms. Civil War reenacting, which is especially strong in the South, is also a way of linking to the past, and many reenactors are seriously committed to gun ownership ideology as well.

Little has been written about the aesthetic appeal of guns—the appreciation that many gun collectors feel toward fine craftsmanship and guns as a form of art. One can see the acme of the gunsmith's art in the Musée de la Chasse (Hunting Museum) in Paris and the Imperial War Museum in London, or in the less exotic but more straightforward Sanders-Metzger Collection at Texas A&M University in College Station, Texas. Many gun collectors and recreational shooters focus on a certain type of firearm. For example, a veritable cult of the 1911A Colt .45 automatic, a notoriously powerful but temperamental pistol, has been around for some time. For admirers of this weapon, its replacement in the United States armed forces with the finely crafted and reliable high-capacity Italian-designed Beretta 9 mm was a blow indeed. But the Colt .45 lives on, touted by enthusiasts in the gun media and aided by its own legend as a "man stopper." Similarly, the "broomstick" Mauser in its various configurations attained cult status decades ago and is thus obtainable today only at high prices.

The firearm has been used as a decidedly negative icon in popular culture. A simpleminded plot was repeated throughout the police dramas of the 1970s in which an errant firearm (one seemingly with a will of its own) wreaked havoc among those unfortunate enough to happen upon it. The gun itself was an evil entity and human agency played little part in these melodramas. Similarly, news media typically use a pistol, often a smoking one, as a backdrop for any violent story, whether it involves a gun or not. Finally, some people have attempted to link gun enthusiasts to sexual inadequacy, implying that the bigger the gun (or the more guns the owner has) the more inadequate (or the more latently homosexual) the owner. The firearm, in this context, is a way for the impotent, self-doubting individual to reaffirm his masculinity. This notion, called the priapic theory, is nowhere supported by research, but it is omnipresent in cinema and television entertainment and has become part of popular psychology as well.

One of the most critical factors behind the survival of the gun culture is recruitment and proselytizing. Outdoor and hunting magazines are constantly spreading the gospel of the value of taking a kid hunting or shooting. While in the past these pleas took the form of "take a boy hunting," increasingly one notes in the outdoor press the notion that girls might enjoy the shooting and hunting as well. Daughters, girlfriends, and wives are turning up standing over their fallen quarry grinning proudly at the camera. One critical recruitment venue for gun enthusiasts is reunions, or gun shows. These events, where guns, ammo, literature, technical information, and ideas are exchanged, are critical to the survival of the culture in its present form. Besides being a recruitment site, they are a rare social and expressive opportunity for this ruggedly individualistic group. Crime-control-inspired efforts at ending gun shows through banning them in certain locales or banning specific commercial activities, which are central to the purpose of the show, hurt the gun culture. Attacks by media and politicians on gun shows are seen as a direct attack on the culture.

Young men who enter the gun culture typically come from patriarchal families. Traditionally, the young man gets a BB gun as a child, then somewhat later receives a .22 rifle. Through proper instruction and use of these weapons, he learns about safety, ballistics, and wind drift, not to mention killing small animals and birds. As he becomes an adolescent, he moves on to shotguns, duck and upland game hunting, and deer rifles, and he joins the male world of hunting. But this progression is no longer inevitable; many young men and women never move beyond the video game stage of shooting, or never get practical and ethical instruction in the use of guns and the possible tragedies that careless use can cause. There are fewer places where the young can shoot at beer cans than in the past—a rapidly urbanizing society has placed shooting increasingly out of bounds, legally and morally. The rural gentile "bar mitzvah" that the progression of firearm ownership represents evokes the earlier medieval progression from squire to knighthood. But it is at war with the spirit of the age. Efforts to disarm young men are met with bemusement or anger, although rural folk are increasingly resigned to them. In the past, such efforts would have been seen as bizarre and presumptuous—trusting young men with increasing levels of adult responsibility was the whole point of this progression. To disarm

A father teaches his three-and-a-half-year-old son how to handle a gun. (Bettmann/Corbis)

them, effectively destroying this rite of passage into adulthood, offering nothing in its place but the mall and pop culture, seems excessive and antirural to many in "bedrock" America.

Survival of the Gun Culture

The survival of the gun culture and most forms of gun ownership is problematic. Viewed by policymakers and media as antithetical to progress, and unfairly linked to crime and militia extremists, the gun culture will have to make major efforts to survive as a viable group. Urban, cosmopolitan America sees gun ownership as highly problematic and the gun culture as embodied by toothless "rednecks" easily and deservedly relegated to the margins and legislated into oblivion. On the other side, bedrock Americans see the Second Amendment as a grant from the deity, a right and an obligation, and an exhortation to self-defense. However, as the United States continues its rush toward urbanization, the gun culture may increasingly find its positions eroded and its adherents marginalized. Only a fundamental redirection of the momentum in American media and popular political culture can alter this reality.

F. Frederick Hawley

See also Black Codes; Black Panthers; Civil War and Small Arms; Firearm Industry; Frontier Violence; Gun Clubs; Gun Magazines; Gun Ownership; *Gun Week;* Handguns; Hunting; Ideologies—Conservative and Liberal; Long Gun; Media Violence; Militias; Native Americans and Gun Violence; Oakley, Annie; Safety Courses; Sporting Purposes Test; Vigilantism; Women and Guns; Youth and Guns

For Further Reading:
Bellesiles, Michael A. 1996. "The Origins of Gun Culture in the United States, 1760–1865." *Journal of American History* 83, 2 (September): 425–455.

———. 2000. *Arming America: The Origins of a National Gun Culture.* New York: Knopf.

Brown, Richard Maxwell. 1994. "Violence." Pp. 394–430 in *The Oxford History of the American West,* ed. Clyde A. Milner, Carol A. O'Connor, and Martha A. Sandweiss. New York: Oxford University Press.

Bruce-Briggs, Barry. 1976. "The Great American Gun War." *Public Interest* 45: 37–62.

Carter, Gregg Lee. 2001. "Guns." Pp. 330–335 in *Boyhood in America: An Encyclopedia,* vol. 1, ed. Priscilla Ferguson Clement and Jacqueline S. Reinier. Santa Barbara, CA: ABC-CLIO.

Courtwright, David T. 1998. *Violent Land: Single Men and Social Disorder from the Frontier to the Inner City.* Cambridge, MA: Harvard University Press.

Gibson, James William. 1994. *Warrior Dreams: Violence and Manhood in Post-Vietnam America.* New York: Hill and Wang.

Hawley, Frederick. 1989. "Guns." Pp. 1480–1482 in *The Encyclopedia of Southern Culture,* ed. Charles Reagan Wilson and William Ferris. Chapel Hill: University of North Carolina Press.

———. 1990. "Culture Conflict and the Ideology of Pariah Groups: The *Weltanschauung* of Gun Owners, Southerners, and Cockfighters." Pp. 109–126 in *The Gun Culture and Its Enemies,* ed. William R. Tonso. Bellevue, WA: Merril Press.

Kleck, Gary. 1997. *Targeting Guns: Firearms and Their Control.* Hawthorne, NY: Aldine de Gruyter.

Spitzer, Robert J. 1995. *The Politics of Gun Control.* Chatham, NJ: Chatham House.

———. 1999. "The Gun Dispute." *American Educator* 23: 10–15.

Gun Industry Watch

See First Monday: Unite to End Gun Violence, 2000–2001

Gun Journal

See Gun Magazines

Gun Magazines

All gun magazine writing can be divided into two types: firearms as a hobby and firearms as political and legislative action. The first type includes all columns, articles, and advertising containing information about product reviews, technical comparisons, gun shows, trading, collecting, and practicing. This type of writing is typical of any leisure activity magazine. The amount of space and the types of firearms and accessories featured in each gun magazine vary. But greater differences can be seen in magazine writing about political and legislative action. Guns are legislated and politicized to a degree that necessitates such writing. Gun magazines provide their readers with analysis and interpretation of legal issues, gun control movements, and progun organizations while also offering advice on pro–gun rights activism.

American Rifleman

The *American Rifleman* is the National Rifle Association of America's flagship, members-only magazine. It has the highest number of subscribers—over 1,600,000—of the three official journals. Directed at recreational and professional readers (including competitive shooters) interested in all types of firearms, the magazine features in-depth articles on the technology of firearms, product reviews, and tips on firearm maintenance. Articles on hunting, the outdoor lifestyle, and competitive shooting are frequently published. The *American Rifleman* promotes the NRA's message through several columns. An "Armed Citizen" column (written since 1958) is designed specifically to inform readers of true stories of protective firearm usage. The "President's Column" is a valuable tool of any NRA president for reaching membership. Along with the executive vice president's "Standing Guard" column, these monthly columns offer the best venues for announcements and inspiration. The magazine also features a column tailored to inform members of each region's NRA-affiliated events such as gun shows, shooting competitions, and training events, as well as legislative developments.

Gun Journal

The Collector Arms Dealers Association publishes this monthly journal dedicated to serious gun collectors. Through a focus on the proper maintenance and handling of firearm collections, the magazine promotes firearm safety. Classified ads for antique firearms form the bulk of the content, supplemented by articles on the history of firearms. The natural extension of the classified ads is listings for the nation's gun shows where antique firearms can be purchased, sold, or traded.

Gun collectors are forced to deal with a varying degree of state and federal legislation in pursuing their hobby. The *Gun Journal* explores the limitations that the laws place on collecting and collectors while also commenting on the ever-present gun control debate and its implications for collectors.

Gun Week

Created in 1966 and published by the Second Amendment Foundation since 1985, *Gun Week* is put out three times a month. The newspaper is available by subscription as well as at selected newsstands and stores. *Gun Week* offers up-to-date listings of national gun shows and features the latest product reviews and buying guides. The newspaper covers gun manufacturing, gun rights, gun control, and legislative events with in-depth analysis and discussion.

Gun World

Published twelve times a year by Y-Visionary Publishing, this magazine is directed at both target shooters and hunters with a special emphasis on law enforcement and military developments. Product reviews, how-to articles on shooting a particular firearm, and historical reviews of guns form the core content of this magazine.

Gun policies are an integral part of *Gun World* articles and columns. The editor has a permanent column in which Second Amendment issues are promoted and critiques of infringements are offered. Gun magazines tend to support and publish different gun rights activists, and for *Gun World* the permanent columnist is David Kopel. Kopel's column focuses on gun control efforts and opposition to them by pro–gun rights advocates. Current NRA President Charlton Heston has also frequently written a column for the magazine in which he addresses causes and legislative endeavors promoted by the NRA.

Guns

This magazine follows the standard model of attempting to include all technical aspects of firearms. Hunting and outdoor adventure are covered in monthly columns. Several columns focus on do-it-yourself tips for gun repairs while also offering product evaluations. Many gun magazines have an active readers-write column, and *Guns* magazine's is titled "Crossfire." In this column, readers can offer praise and commentary. *Guns* magazine seems to cover fewer gun policy issues than many of the other gun magazines, yet articles on firearm legislation are frequently featured along with occasional pieces on gun control developments.

Guns & Ammo

Guns & Ammo is one of the most popular gun magazines in the world. It has nearly 600,000 subscribers and boasts over 5.8 million readers each month. According to the magazine's reader profile, 86 percent of its readers are male, which is reflected by the absence of women from the editorial staff.

Guns & Ammo is a traditionalist in the field of gun magazines, having been founded in 1959, and it has been a constant favorite of gun enthusiasts. This California-based publication covers all areas of shooting. The magazine deems hunting important and hence hunting-related articles on firearms, accessories, and outdoor adventure are in each issue. Ample space is given to the self-protective aspect of gun ownership; this is particularly evident in the "Armed Response" column modeled after the "Armed Citizen" column in the *American Rifleman*. The column offers readers the opportunity to post local news stories on how ordinary citizens defend against crime with firearms. New firearms and by-products are reviewed with respect to concealed-carry laws and target shooting. *Guns & Ammo* promotes the safe handling of firearms at all times and includes extensive articles on gun-handling ethics, gun collecting, and the history of firearms.

Guns & Ammo has not become one of the leading gun magazines by ignoring gun policy issues. To the contrary, the "Second Amendment" column features varying authors who respond to challenges to the right to bear arms. The "From the Capitol" column, currently written by NRA head Charlton Heston, covers the latest developments in the nation's capital with a heavy focus on federal gun control measures and attitudes. In "Cooper's Corner," gun guru Jeff

Cooper editorializes on issues of personal importance in American gun cultures. Petersen Publishing publishes twelve issues of *Guns & Ammo* per year.

Handguns

This magazine focuses on handguns and their use in recreational, sports, and self-protective shooting. Handguns form a fairly limited field of firearms and the magazine explores their use by professional as well as recreational shooters. Law enforcement tactics, training classes, and handgun accessories are extensively reviewed for readers. *Handguns* magazine informs readers of correct self-defense tactics for the home while also focusing on concealed-carry etiquette. For history aficionados the magazine frequently offers articles about Cowboy Action Shooting and historical handguns.

Gun control issues are covered in the magazine but are less prominent than in many other gun magazines. Articles and columns deal with legislative issues relevant to handgun ownership and gun control initiatives. *Handguns* magazine has its own celebrity columnist, Don B. Kates, Jr., who regularly writes a column titled "Gun Rights." The magazine's editorial policy is consistent with that of many gun magazines. Around 87 percent of its 3.3 million readers are male. The magazine is published by Petersen Publishing Company, which also publishes *Guns & Ammo.*

Shotgun News

Shotgun News is one of the oldest gun magazines. Founded in 1946, it is primarily a publication for the trading and selling of guns. The magazine offers possibly the widest selection of firearm listings in the world. Gun shows are listed and readers are offered the opportunity to post classified ads to sell or purchase firearms; the magazine also publishes information on federally licensed gun dealers.

Shotgun News touches on gun policy issues through the "Neal Knox Report." The ever-vigilant Knox covers all legislative issues relevant to gun owners in Washington, D.C., and the states. Knox's report is at times highly critical of the NRA while offering evaluations of NRA policies as well as critiques of the gun control movement. *Shotgun News* is published thirty-six times a year and is available by subscription as well as at newsstands.

Small Arms Review

The intent of this magazine is to focus on firearms and accessories regulated by the Gun Control Act of 1968. Such weapons include machine guns, silencers, short-barreled shotguns and rifles, and destructive devices like explosives and poison-gas weapons. *Small Arms Review* describes its readers as collectors, competitive and leisure shooters, law enforcement and military personnel, and firearm industry personnel. The magazine informs readers of gun shows and shooting events not only in the United States but in Europe as well. Legislative aspects of gun ownership are prominently featured in the magazine's articles due to the heavy legislation on ownership and trade of the weapons in question. One of the target audiences for this magazine is firearm industry personnel, for whom the magazine publishes an in-depth column on manufacturing, sales, and gun policies. For enthusiasts of firearm history, *Small Arms Review* evaluates historical weapons and reviews museums and books. Published by Moose Lake since October 1997, *Small Arms Review* is available both by subscription and at newsstands.

Soldier of Fortune

Soldier of Fortune has been an international favorite among gun, adventure, and mercenary enthusiasts since 1975. The magazine's editorial policy is "pro-military, pro–strong U.S. defense, pro-police, and pro-veteran" as well as generally pro–gun rights. Developments within the U.S. military as well as gun control policies and legislation are reviewed with a conservative and heavily pro–Second Amendment stance. Of the gun magazines reviewed here, *Soldier of Fortune* is by far the most global in its content. Each issue contains articles from the world's current hot spots where the magazine's contributors observe or partake in activities. The magazine also offers historical reviews of military actions during wars; successes and mistakes are identified and lessons taught. The reporting is personal and highly in-depth. One of the permanent columns, "World Sitrep," features a compilation of the global military and civil problem areas. In "Command Guidance," the editor and publisher, Robert K. Brown, comments on relevant current events such as elections, gun control measures, and international incidents. The magazine includes a limited number of reviews of firearms and firearm accessories. *Soldier of Fortune* can be purchased by subscription or at newsstands and is published twelve times a year.

Women & Guns

Published by the Second Amendment Foundation every other month and founded in 1989, *Women & Guns* magazine is directed at female gun enthusiasts. The magazine includes all of the familiar product reviews and technical articles of other gun magazines but with a heavy emphasis on self-protection and female-friendly products and accessories. The successful use of weapons for self-protection is featured in the "News" section of the magazine. The magazine also offers interviews of female gun owners and competitive shooters, gun rights news, and legislative information.

Tiia Rajala

See also *American Rifleman; Firearm Industry; Gun Control Act of 1968; Gun News Digest; Gun Shows; Gun Week;* Kates, Don B., Jr.; Knox, Neal; Kopel, David B.; National Rifle Association; Second Amendment Foundation; *Women & Guns*
For Further Reading:
American Rifleman: http://www.mynra.com/frame. cfm?url=http://www.nrahq.org/administration/ publications/tar/index.asp.
Gun Week: http://www.gunweek.com.
Gun World: http://www.gunworld.com.
Guns: http://www.gunsmagazine.com.
Guns & Ammo: http://www.gunsandammomag.com.
Handguns: http://www.handgunsmag.com.
Shotgun News: http://www.shotgunnews.com.
Small Arms Review: http://www.smallarmsreview.com.
Soldier of Fortune: http://www.sofmag.com.
Women & Guns: http://www.womenandguns.com.

Gun News Digest

Gun News Digest is a quarterly magazine of the Second Amendment Foundation and was created in 1995 by publisher Alan M. Gottlieb.

The magazine was established to provide in-depth examination—the "what" and "why"—of firearm issues for the gun community. Executive Editor Joseph P. Tartaro refers to the digest as a "postgraduate" education on trends and concepts affecting firearm owners.

The *Digest* reprints articles from the academic and scholarly press that might otherwise not be readily accessible to the gun community. The quarterly nature of the magazine allows for both a larger and longer-term perspective on topics such as the history of the National Rifle Association, the development of "Clinton compacts" (compact versions of .40 and .45 caliber handguns developed in response to limitations on the size of ammunition magazines established by the 1994 Clinton crime bill), and the global antigun movement. Among magazines aimed at gun owners or gun rights activists, *Gun News Digest* stands at the apex in terms of the length and depth of its articles.

Carol Oyster

See also Gottlieb, Alan Merril; Gun Magazines; Kopel, David B.; Second Amendment Foundation
For Further Reading:
Gun News Digest website: http://www.gunweek. com/subs/gndsub.html.

Gun Owners' Action League (GOAL)

The Gun Owners' Action League promotes public discussion of firearm issues in the state of Massachusetts and also takes part in the national gun control debate. Its aims are lobbying and educating. GOAL actively promotes grassroots political activism in favor of the Second Amendment, interpreting the amendment to protect the *individual* right to keep and bear arms. The organization engages in voter registration, offers evaluations of political candidates regarding their firearm policies, and annually educates state legislators on firearm safety issues. The organization has its own professional lobbyist. Its message is further strengthened through an active grassroots network.

The organization promotes safety and training education for children and youth through the NRA's Eddie Eagle gun safety programs as well as local training courses and visits to schools. Shooting sport enthusiasts and junior Olympic candidates can receive training through the organization. Adults can turn to the organization for extensive information about Massachusetts and U.S. firearm laws. GOAL publishes a monthly newsletter, *The Message,* through which members can receive up-to-date information about developments in legislation. The organization's weekly radio program, *GOAL Line,* discusses issues of interest to most potential groups of firearm owners.

Massachusetts has highly restrictive gun laws that have become progressively more restrictive. GOAL has worked hard and in a professional manner to reverse the trend, but without major political successes.

Tiia Rajala

See also Eddie Eagle; Massachusetts Gun Law
For Further Reading:
GOAL home page: http://www.goal.org.

Gun Owners of America (GOA)

Gun Owners of America is a generally conservative organization of firearm owners. GOA was founded in October 1975 in California by state Sen. Bill Richardson. It presently has about 300,000 members and an annual budget (including that of the affiliated Gun Owners' Foundation) of approximately $4 million. Its official publication is *The Gun Owners,* a monthly member newsletter focusing on firearm legislation and national politics. GOA pioneered the use of member fax and e-mail alerts as a means of targeting specific legislation and quickly generating grassroots opposition.

Parallel organizations include the GOA Political Victory Fund, a political campaign fund that aims to provide heavy support of a relatively few select candidates, and the Gun Owners' Foundation, a tax-exempt organization that supports litigation and educational efforts.

GOA stresses that its objective is the elimination rather than merely the restriction of gun control legislation. It takes a relatively optimistic view of what can be achieved by grassroots opposition and pressure; this results in a more uncompromising position than that held by other firearm groups, including the National Rifle Association. GOA counts among its victories its 1998–1999 opposition to (and eventual defeat of) the Juvenile Justice Bill, which would have banned importation of firearm magazines holding more than ten rounds, forbidden sale of semiautomatic rifles to persons under 21 years of age, and restricted gun show sales. GOA refused to accept the bill after the gun show restrictions were reduced, and the bill ultimately was voted down by an unusual combination of legislators who felt that it went too far and legislators who felt that it did not go far enough.

David T. Hardy

See also National Rifle Association; Pratt, Larry
For Further Reading:
"Who Is Larry Pratt?" 1996. *New Republic* (March 11): 9.
Gun Owners of America website: http://www.gunowners.org

Gun Owners of California (GOC)

Advertised as "attack oriented" and "the toughest, most hard hitting progun organization in the state of California," Gun Owners of California has fought against California's gun control measures since the early 1970s. The organization was founded by H.L. (Bill) Richardson, who served in California's state senate for twenty-two years and also founded Gun Owners of America. Senator Richardson dedicated his political career to progun issues, and upon leaving the California senate he has dedicated his time to progun activism. GOC follows the policy of accepting no compromises and fighting against all gun control measures, whether new or already passed.

Richardson has adopted an interesting strategy for his organization. Many progun organizations compete fiercely for members, but Gun Owners of California openly promotes joining the National Rifle Association of America. Richardson has served on the Board of Directors of the NRA, though this alone does not explain his promotion of the NRA. According to GOC, California's progun organizations have a combined membership of over 400,000, and mobilizing all gun owners, regardless of their organization of choice, is GOC's goal. GOC works entirely in California. It does not attempt to expand beyond the state or gain a more national influence (aspirations that can be fulfilled through Gun Owners of America and the NRA).

GOC's action plan is simple: to find the optimal focus for the organization's efforts. The organization's structure is kept compact, its Board of Directors has five members, support staff work part time, and there are no headquarters or regional/field representatives. Donations collected through the GOC's political action committee are directed toward lobbying, while contributions to GOC, Inc. provide funding for other efforts. Progun candidates are supported not only in senate races but also in local ones; however, the organization has a policy of not financially supporting incumbents unless they are running for a higher office and have proved loyal to progun issues. The gun promotion efforts of GOC are similar to those of other groups and include mail, fax, and e-mail alerts; newsletters; education; recruitment; and contributions to progun candidates.

Tiia Rajala

See also Gun Owners of America; National Rifle Association

For Further Reading:
Gun Owners of California home page: http://www.gunownersca.com.

Gun Ownership

Gun ownership is pervasive in the United States. In 2000, one in three U.S. households reported having one or more firearms, totaling more than 200 million guns in private hands. Demographically, the person most likely to be a gun owner is a native-born, politically conservative white man who is over the age of 40 and lives in a small town in the South or Midwest (see table, p. 254). Conversely, the person least likely to own a firearm is a foreign-born, politically liberal black woman who is under the age of 40 and lives in a big city in the Northeast.

With gun ownership so widespread and gun owners so diverse, it is not surprising that there are many different reasons why people choose to own firearms. Yet it is possible to place most of these reasons in one of three broad categories: recreational ownership, ownership for reasons of personal security, and ownership for political reasons.

Perhaps the least controversial reason people might choose to own guns is recreational, which provides the owner with private enjoyment. Examples of this rationale for gun ownership might include collecting guns as a hobby, target shooting (including skeet shooting and firing at other inanimate objects), and hunting. While it is possible to oppose such activities on grounds like support for animal rights, it seems likely that relatively few Americans would object to recreational gun ownership per se.

Indeed, the relatively low level of opposition to activities such as hunting has often provided opportunities for political candidates and officials to offer apparently nuanced positions on gun control. Many candidates (perhaps especially Democrats) have argued that they have no wish to interfere with "the legitimate rights of hunters," but simply wish to reduce the use of more lethal and dangerous firearms against humans. For example, during his 1992 campaign for the presidency, Bill Clinton was photographed several times in hunting gear, carrying a shotgun in one hand and several recently killed ducks in the other. This sort of symbolic support for firearm-related activity has seemed an attractive option for candidates seeking a moderate position on gun control.

Perhaps unfortunately, such a position does not stand up to close scrutiny. If one understands the notion of a "right" as inalienable, support for freedom to hunt is not an accurate interpretation of the Second Amendment. First, it is difficult to imagine a human activity that is as closely regulated by government as hunting. In most states, hunting requires licenses (which can be withheld) and is limited to narrowly defined seasons and particular species. Also, limits are imposed on the yield of a hunt. Given current practice in most states in which hunting is permitted, it would be difficult to assert that there exists anything approaching a "right" to hunt. Second, the clause with which the Second Amendment begins makes explicit reference to "the security of a free people." If one grants the

General Social Survey Question (2000): "Do you happen to have in your home (or garage) any guns or revolvers? If yes, Is it a pistol, shotgun, rifle, or what?"

	Percentage "Yes"	Pistol	Shotgun	Rifle
National	33	20	19	20
Sex				
Male	42	26	27	27
Female	25	15	12	14
Race				
White	37	23	22	24
Black	14	10	6	4
Age				
40 and over	36	22	22	23
18–39	27	16	14	15
Region				
South	37	23	22	20
Midwest	37	18	26	25
Far West	33	21	13	20
Northeast	18	9	9	12
Foreign Born?				
No	35	21	20	21
Yes	14	8	6	8
Hunter?				
Yes	77	51	60	59
No	24	15	10	12
Political Views				
Conservative	55	25	34	27
Moderate	33	20	19	19
Liberal	22	13	8	12
Urbanization				
Less than 10,000	44	25	30	30
10,000–99,999	31	20	16	18
100,000–500,000	26	18	12	15
More than 500,000	12	8	4	3

Source: Inter-University Consortium for Political and Social Research (http://www.icpsr.umich.edu/GSS/).

(apparently plausible) assumption that threats to security and freedom are more likely to come from other humans and human institutions such as government, it follows that the purpose of the Second Amendment is to allow citizens, under some circumstances, to kill other people.

The second general rationale for gun ownership taps directly the notion of firearms as a source of security. One of the most important reasons people offer for owning guns is that they wish to protect themselves, their families, and their homes from criminals. Some studies have found popular support for extending the right of self-protection to include communities (Spitzer, 1998, p. 173). This sentiment is captured in a popular cliché: "When guns are outlawed, only outlaws will have guns." The perceived importance of firearms as a source of personal security seemed to have increased in the 1990s. Several states (most notably Florida and Texas) have passed laws that would permit people to carry concealed weapons on their persons. The possibility of a potential victim carrying a concealed weapon is thought by some to be a deterrent to potential robbers or muggers.

Finally, some commentators have suggested that gun ownership is an important prerogative of democratic citizens, since the right to bear arms is perhaps the ultimate protection against tyrannical government authority. Again, it is possible to make some distinctions. Some have suggested that equating privately armed citizens with the "well-regulated militia" mentioned in the Second Amendment provides a bulwark against foreign invaders. It is relatively easy to find letters to the editor or discussions on radio talk shows about the "fact" that many formerly "free" nations lost their freedom after the government confiscated firearms from the general public (Fisher, 2001). Regardless of the veracity of such claims, the connection between gun ownership and security from foreign invasion has powerful symbolic value among some constituencies.

Somewhat more controversially, some opponents of firearm regulation have argued that private ownership of guns is necessary to prevent a tyrannical usurpation of liberty by the government of the United States in particular. The most visible manifestations of such sentiments are organized "militias" such as the Aryan Nation, Christian Identity, the Branch Davidians, and other such groups with a secessionist ideology. However, it is occasionally surprising to observe how frequently such sentiments are expressed in the popular culture. Indeed, a recent editorial in the *Las Vegas Review-Journal* contained arguments that free citizens have not only a right but an obligation to bear arms to prevent the imposition of government tyranny. The editorial made reference to the government that had "machine-gunned the babies and nursing mothers at Waco" (site of an FBI raid on the Branch Davidians in 1993), and went on to plug locally run gun shows in which no background check was likely to be imposed on purchasers (Suprynowicz, 2001). While sentiments such as these currently exist on the fringes of American political discourse, they are expressed more frequently in periodicals directed at gun owners and on talk-radio programs. Such attitudes are often couched in the symbols of the American Revolution, which is a powerful rhetorical device in U.S. politics.

Ted G. Jelen

See also Collectors; Concealed Weapons Laws; Defensive Gun Use; Gun Culture; Gun Shows; Hunting; Michigan Militia; Militias; Recreational Uses of Guns; Target Shooting

For Further Reading:

Ellison, Christopher G. 1991. "Southern Culture and Firearms Ownership." *Social Science Quarterly* 72 (June): 267–283.
Fisher, Larry R. 2001. "Communist Threat Remains." Letter to editor. *Putnam County Banner-Graphic* (March 28): 4A.
Jelen, Ted G. 1998. "The Electoral Politics of Gun Ownership." Pp. 224–246 in *The Changing Politics of Gun Control,* ed. John M. Bruce and Clyde Wilcox. Lanham, MD: Rowman & Littlefield.
Kleck, Gary. 1997. *Targeting Guns: Firearms and Their Control.* Hawthorne, NY: Aldine de Gruyter.
Spitzer, Robert J. 1998. "Gun Control: Constitutional Mandate or Myth?" Pp. 164–195 in *Moral Controversies in American Politics: Cases in Social Regulatory Policy,* ed. Raymond Tatalovich and Byron W. Daynes. Armonk, NY: M. E. Sharpe.
Suprynowicz, Vin. 2001. "Are You Shirking Your Duty to Help Keep Us Free?" *Las Vegas Review-Journal* (March 25). http://www.lvrj.com/lvrj_home/2001/Mar-25-Sun-2001/opinion/15716632.html.

Gun Registration
Current Firearm Registration Laws

Registration laws include requirements to register with a governmental authority (1) any possession of a firearm ("possession registration"); (2) any transfer of a firearm, whether from a licensed dealer or from a private person ("transfer registration"); (3) any purchase from a licensed dealer ("purchase registration"); and (4) any importation or transportation into a jurisdiction ("importation registration"). Federal law requires that a purchaser of an ordinary rifle, shotgun, semiautomatic pistol, or revolver from a dealer must fill out a form that discloses, among other things, the identity of the purchaser and the serial number of the firearm ("purchase registration"). The dealer must keep all of these records available for inspection by federal agents. When the dealer goes out of business he must surrender all of his records to the federal Bureau of Alcohol, Tobacco, and Firearms.

Some U.S. states impose some form of registration of pistols and revolvers ("pistol registration"). States that impose pistol possession registration include Hawaii, Michigan, and New York. States that impose pistol transfer registration include New Jersey. States that impose pistol importation registration include California. In addition to registration, New York State imposes licensing to possess a pistol (that is, it requires advance permission to purchase, own, or keep a pistol in one's home or place of business) combined with possession registration. Various cities, such as New York City, impose possession registration of rifles and shotguns. The District of Columbia imposes possession registration of pistols, rifles, and shotguns—while allowing registration of only those pistols that were registered in the district prior to September 24, 1976, and outlawing the possession of all other pistols. Federal and state laws restrict the transfer and possession of fully automatic firearms (machine guns) much more stringently.

Assumed Social Utility of Firearm Registration Laws

Laws requiring registration of firearms are instigated primarily by the hypothesis that such laws will significantly reduce violent crime. For example, as initially proposed, the 1934 National Firearms Act covered taxation and registration of any transfer or interstate transportation of pistols, revolvers, short-barreled shotguns, and high-capacity machine guns. At that time, President Franklin D. Roosevelt's attorney general, Homer Cummings, testified before Congress in support of passage of the bill. He asserted that registration would facilitate the arrest and conviction of gangsters and other career criminals because "the criminal elements are not going to obtain permits" (Cummings, 1934, p. 10). His theory was that although prosecutors could not get quick and easy convictions of criminals for committing violent crimes, they could nonetheless get quick and easy convictions for violations of firearm registration laws. His theory was then questionable, and since then has become more questionable. United States Supreme Court rulings had banned the use of illegally obtained evidence in federal trials since 1914, and they have banned such use in state trials since 1961. Accordingly, the ease of legally arresting career criminals not in the act of committing violent crimes, and then legally searching for, seizing, and using illegally possessed firearms as evidence in criminal trials, is questionable.

Social scientists, including criminologists, who share the hypothesis that registration will reduce crime base their opinions almost universally on mathematical statistical models and methodologies. However, such models are sensitive to the inclusion or exclusion of additional variables. Such models are also probabilistic, and in the case of firearm registration laws the probability of reducing violence through such laws is small. Indeed, the effect of these laws is sometimes in the "wrong" direction (that is, registration is associated with increased violence). In addition, the results of research based on these models depends on the historical period studied, the sample of cases used, and particular mix of variables.

Intuitively, registration of firearms would seem to have little, if any, impact on crime. The vast majority of firearms used in crimes have been stolen from armories or taken during hijackings. Criminals do not register their firearms. Tracing of crime guns through the use of registration lists leads law enforcement back to the last law-abiding person in the chain of possession.

The most reliable raw statistical data on violent crimes are for robbery and murder (in that order). In the two years from 1964 to 1966, the robbery rate in New York City rose by a factor of four. From 1960 to 1970 the robbery rate there increased by a factor of more than ten, the murder rate by a factor of four. During that same decade, the robbery rate in the nation as a whole increased by a factor of four. That was a decade of "rising expectations" associated with passage of the federal Civil Rights Act of 1964 and the Voting Rights Act of 1965. It was also the decade during which the 1968 Gun Control Act passed into law. Canada, following enactment of its 1995 pistol possession registration law, has suffered a markedly rising burglary rate. Few if any social scientists have suggested repeal of the 1964 Civil Rights Act, the 1965 Voting Rights Act, the 1995 Canadian pistol registration law, the 1967 New York City rifle-shotgun registration law, or the 1968 Gun Control Act (or any combination thereof) as crime reduction measures.

One of the most comprehensive comparative studies of the correlation between various firearm control laws and violent crime is found in Kleck (1997). Kleck concludes that the best that can be said about firearm control laws is that requirements for licenses for possession and registration of pistols show the strongest correlation with reduction of firearm ownership by convicted criminals and the mentally ill. Kleck qualifies this conclusion with the cautionary language that research provides "partial support for [this] view" and that the above license requirements "may reduce gun ownership, presumably among 'high-risk' segments of the population" (p. 361). The speculative nature of these conclusions must be balanced by the concomitant reduction of firearm possession among the rest of the population (noncriminals and sane people), faced as it is with onerous requirements of registration or licensing. Kleck estimates that between twenty-five and seventy-five lives are saved by firearms for every life lost to a firearm, and that the medical costs saved by the defensive use of firearms are fifteen times greater than the costs caused by criminal use of firearms. Assuming this estimate to be even approximately accurate, the concomitant reductions in legitimate firearm ownership due to the burdens, hurdles, and delays of firearm registration would significantly contribute to socially harmful effects of this gun control measure.

Constitutional Considerations

At the time of the adoption of the Constitution in 1788, the American people had an absolute, unqualified right to keep ordinary personal firearms and ammunition for defense of home, community, and country. Registration or its equivalent at most was confined to proving that one possessed one rifle or musket for militia purposes; it did not extend to disclosing how many other firearms one possessed, and it did not extend to pistols at all.

Numbers 28, 29, 46, and 60 of the *Federalist Papers* expounded upon the fundamental purpose of private arms-keeping—namely, to deter tyranny and, if necessary, to overthrow it and restore the Constitution. According to Alexander Hamilton in *Federalist* no. 28, either a state or the federal government could become tyrannical. In either case, the armed people would come to the aid of the nontyrannical governmental entity and "infallibly make it preponderate" (p. 179). The suppression of tyranny in the federal government and the foundation and long-term preservation of the Constitution, according to Hamilton, depend

upon the ability of the people at large to conduct "an immediate revolt, headed and directed by the state governments" (p. 404), by virtue of the "people at large [always being] properly armed and equipped [with ammunition]" (p. 184). James Madison, in *Federalist* no. 46, heartily endorsed a similar view of an armed populace, led by their state governments, as a fundamental bulwark for liberty. He deplored the fact that "notwithstanding the military establishments in the several kingdoms of Europe ... the governments are afraid to trust the people with arms" (p. 322). He explained that because of "the advantage of being armed, which the Americans possess over the people of almost every other nation," any federal "schemes of usurpation will be easily defeated by the State governments, who will be supported by the [armed] people" (pp. 321, 322).

Both the Federalists, who advocated ratification of the Constitution, and the anti-Federalists, who opposed it, had intimate familiarity with and glorified the Magna Carta (which was established in 1215). The Magna Carta contained a codification of "the right to control the sovereign by force [that] was merely an application of the general right of revolution under any government" (Adams, 1912, p. 174, n. 26). In this way, the population in arms could rally to duly constituted authority, pursuant to a majority vote of a committee of twenty-five barons that the Magna Carta had established, to compel the government to obey the rule of law and restore the constitution (which was unwritten in England). By analogy, it would take the concurrence of a majority of the American state governments to mobilize their armed populations and conduct a lawful insurrection against a tyrannical federal government for this purpose, and a majority vote of Congress to mobilize the armed nation against a tyrannical state government. The population, being armed, would be better able to contribute to the effectiveness of the National Guard, headed and directed by the states or the federal government, as selected by the people who have the arms, in order to restore the Constitution in accordance with the principle of popular sovereignty.

The Supreme Court's decision in *United States v. Miller* (1939) confirms the unconstitutionality of the registration of ordinary personal arms. In support of its holding that the Second Amendment protects an individual constitutional right to keep those arms that either are suitable for a militiaman to own or the private possession of which "contribute[s] to the common defense" (p. 178), the Court cited but a single precedent or authority, *Aymette v. State* (1840). There the Tennessee Supreme Court had held that "citizens have the unqualified right to keep [suitable arms].... But the right to bear arms is not of that unqualified character" (p. 160). The "unqualified" right to keep arms referred to the individual right to possess suitable arms free from any regulations or restrictions such as registration, licensing, or special taxation. As to special taxation under the First Amendment, in *Grosjean v. American Press Co.* (1938) the Supreme Court held that a tax measure that singles out newspaper publishers and imposes a tax based on the newspaper's circulation was unconstitutional. As to registration under the First Amendment, in *Lamont v. Postmaster General* (1965) the Supreme Court ruled that a federal statute requiring recipients of "Communist political propaganda" mailed from the Soviet Union to register was unconstitutional, because such a registration requirement would impose an inhibition on the right to receive such propaganda. By the same token, the Second Amendment would bar registration or special taxation of ordinary personal firearms. As to what arms are suitable, the *Miller* decision's narration of the development of militia shows that every citizen has the right to keep ordinary personal arms and ammunition. Widespread keeping of these arms would serve as a powerful inducement for government not to transgress its constitutional limitations.

Bearing firearms in the military or militia sense, as opposed to merely keeping them in the private sense, can be strictly limited to governmental sponsorship. Uncontrolled and dangerous arms-bearing by private ragtag militias can be suppressed by law, in the same way that laws suppress anarchy. The authors of the Constitution, including the Bill of Rights, greatly feared and earnestly sought to avoid anarchy.

Registration of firearms by either a state or the federal government undermines the system of checks and balances contemplated by Hamilton and Madison in *Federalist Papers* 28, 29, 46, and 60, as confirmed by the Second Amendment and the *Miller* case. Registration transgresses the absolute, unqualified right to keep socially useful, ordinary personal arms. It makes little, if any, sense for a government to have the unilateral right to know the strength of its potential adversaries. Such knowledge enables any rogue government—aided by its ultrahigh-speed, ultrahigh-storage-capacity computers—to quickly confiscate the people's firearms. During his above-mentioned congressional testimony in 1934, Attorney General Homer Cummings was asked his opinion on the constitutionality of an additional proposal that would require possession registration on the part of those who already owned any firearm included in the classes of firearms covered by the bill. In reply he stated: "I am afraid it would be unconstitutional" (Cummings, 1934, p. 13).

David I. Caplan

See also Ammunition, Regulations of; Anglo-Saxon Tradition of the Right to Keep and Bear Arms; *Cases v. United States;* Gun Control Act of 1968; Magna Carta; National Firearms Act of 1934; Ninth Amendment; *Perpich v. Department of Defense;* Second Amendment; *State v. Kessler;* Tenth Amendment; *United States v. Emerson; United States v. Miller; United States v. Tot*

For Further Reading:

Adams, George B. 1912. *The Origin of the English Constitution.* New Haven, CT: Yale University Press.

Aymette v. State, 2 Humph. 154, 21 Tenn. 119, 124 (1840).

Cummings, Homer S. 1934. Congressional testimony. Pp. 1–31 in *National Firearms Act; Hearings before the Committee on Ways and Means, House of Representatives, Seventy-third Congress, Second Session, on H.R. 9066.* Washington, DC: U.S. Government Printing Office.

The Federalist. 1961. Edited by Jacob E. Cooke. Hanover, NH: Wesleyan University Press.

Grosjean v. American Press Co., 297 U.S. 233 (1938).

Kleck, Gary. 1997. *Targeting Guns: Firearms and Their Control.* Hawthorne, NY: Aldine de Gruyter.

Lamont v. Postmaster General, 381 U.S. 301 (1965).

United States v. Miller, 307 U.S. 174 (1939).

Gun Rights Policy Conference (GRPC)

The Gun Rights Policy Conference is an annual three-day meeting held in the fall, usually in September, by the Second Amendment Foundation (SAF) and the Citizens Committee for the Right to Keep and Bear Arms (CCRKBA). The GRPC is an important tool for educating and training grassroots Second Amendment activists and for networking within the Second Amendment movement.

Every year, the GRPC site changes, usually alternating between locations in the East and the West. A particular city is often selected because holding the conference there will facilitate the progress of gun rights groups that are already active in the area. For example, Seattle (in 1998) and St. Louis (in 1999) were host cities shortly after their states held ballot votes on gun laws.

Speakers at the conferences include U.S. senators and representatives (such as Sen. Ben Nighthorse Campbell [R-CO] and Rep. Bob Barr [R-GA]), other elected officials, media personalities, officials from the NRA, leaders of local gun rights groups, and leaders of the firearm industry. They also include attorneys, scholars, activists, representatives of civil liberties organizations that seek to work with gun owners (such as the American Civil Liberties Union and the National Association of Criminal Defense Lawyers), and, of course, staff from SAF and CCRKBA.

Usually about 400 people attend, some of whom travel cross-country for every annual meeting. Attendees must pay for their own travel and lodging, but the conference itself is free, and the attendees receive large packets of books and other materials. The formal program of speakers aims to improve both the policy knowledge and the political/communication skills of the audience. In addition, a great deal of networking and exchanging of ideas takes place at receptions and in the hallways.

The GRPC was first held in Seattle in 1985. Firearm manufacturers and other companies in the firearm business provide financial support for the event, as do national, state, and local gun rights organizations.

The GRPC is much smaller than the annual convention of the National Rifle Association and the annual Shooting, Hunting, and Outdoor Trades Show (SHOT Show), both of which draw tens of thousands of people. But at the NRA convention and the SHOT Show, political and policy forums are relatively small parts of much bigger events. In contrast, the GRPC is tightly focused and the only people who attend are persons with a high level of interest in Second Amendment activism. Thus, the GRPC is the largest policy-only meeting for gun rights activists. Over the years, the GRPC has developed into an important tool for promoting the success of activists. In recent years, some antigun groups have attempted to create their own events similar to the GRPC.

David B. Kopel

See also Barr, Bob; Citizens Committee for the Right to Keep and Bear Arms; Second Amendment Foundation
For Further Reading:
Second Amendment Foundation website: http://www.saf.org.

Gun Shows

In markets in which collectors and hobbyists play a large role and buyers and sellers have relatively narrow interests, sales volumes may be too small to support traditional stores. Regular fairs or expositions allow buyers and sellers to meet and exchange information without high overheads. As is the case with book fairs, gem and mineral shows, antique expositions, and swap meets, gun shows make transactions less costly for buyers and sellers. To start a gun show, an organizer hoping to make a profit rents a facility and sells booth or table space to people who have items to sell. He or she advertises the event and charges admission. The admission fee ensures that those attending have at least some interest in the wares offered for sale.

The offerings at gun shows typically appeal to hunters, people who shoot for sport, people who collect various classes of weaponry, and those interested in self-defense. In addition to new, used, and antique guns, offerings may include fine knives, bows, specialty clothing, gear,

A gun salesman demonstrates a semiautomatic weapon to a potential customer at the annual Great Western Gun Show, October 1999. (AFP/Corbis)

books, repair services, training programs, hunting expeditions, and vacations. Depending on the size of the show, vendors may include everyone from gun manufacturers to advocates of get-out-the-vote campaigns for various causes.

Since 1938, people engaged in the business of selling firearms have been required to get a federal firearms license. No matter where a sale takes place—in a store, in their home, or at a table in a gun show—dealers are required to check a buyer's background with the FBI on every single sale. As is the case with other consumer products, the government does not attempt to regulate occasional second-hand sales. "Private collectors" may legally sell guns without doing background checks of buyers at a gun show. Such sales are not covered by the Brady Handgun Violence Prevention Act of 1993, which requires licensed gun dealers to perform background checks before selling new or used firearms. Gun control proponents such as the Brady Campaign to Prevent Gun Violence (formerly known as Handgun

Control, Inc.) have labeled the exemption for occasional second-hand sales the "gun show loophole" and have treated it as a major issue in the gun control debate.

The National Rifle Association and others who oppose gun control contend that existing data suggest that the banning of second-hand sales by private citizens at gun shows would increase costs for law-abiding citizens while doing little to limit criminal access to firearms. In the United Kingdom, for example, where private gun ownership is for all practical purposes illegal, thriving black markets supply criminals with firearms of all sorts. In California, where unregulated second-hand sales have recently been outlawed, criminals continue to get their firearms from black markets. According to a U.S. Bureau of Justice Statistics survey of inmates in state prisons, 79 percent of gun-using offenders got their firearms from friends, family, or street or illegal contacts; 8.3 percent purchased them at a retail store; 1 percent got them at a flea market; and 0.7 percent bought them at a gun show (Harlow, 2001).

Linda Gorman

See also Brady Handgun Violence Prevention Act; Collectors; Gun Control

For Further Reading:

Harlow, Caroline Wolf. 2001. *Firearm Use by Offenders.* Bureau of Justice Statistics Special Report, NCJ 189369 (November). http://www.ojp.usdoj.gov/bjs/abstract/fuo.htm.

Kopel, David B., and Alan Korwin. 2002. "Should Gun Shows Be Outlawed?" Issue Paper 1-2002 (January 23), Independence Institute, Golden, CO. http://www.davekopel.com/2A/IP/gunshows2.htm.

Wright, James D., and Peter Henry Rossi. 1986. *Armed and Considered Dangerous: A Survey of Felons and Their Firearms.* Hawthorne, NY: Aldine de Gruyter.

Gun Violence

Literally defined, "gun violence" refers to the use of a firearm to inflict or threaten violent harm. Politically speaking, the term is used by gun control advocates to summarize the harm inflicted by gun misuse. The meaning of the term tends to be determined by the speaker's ideology. Gun violence takes the diverse forms of hunting, "democide," war, crime, self-defense, law enforcement, suicide, and accidents. All of these forms of gun violence (except accidents) are considered legitimate by some people and illegitimate by others, depending upon the context.

The most common form of gun violence in the United States is hunting. Some hunting is purely for sport, some is for putting meat on a family's table, and some is for mixed purposes. Whatever the motivation, millions of animals are killed every year in the United States by firearms (although the number is far smaller than the number killed from factory farming and other meat production).

Throughout human history, hunting has been seen as traditional and respectable, and hunting controversies have involved restrictions on hunting (e.g., the British aristocracy attempting to prevent commoners from hunting) rather than the morality of hunting. Many gun control advocates who disapprove of defensive gun ownership are tolerant of sporting uses of guns such as hunting. In recent decades, however, animal rights advocates and others have argued that hunting is wrong.

For human victims, the most common form of gun violence worldwide is violence perpetrated by governments against civilians. Government is by far the largest cause of premature violent death in the twentieth century. Professor Rudolph Rummel (1994) of the University of Hawaii estimated that from 1900 to 1987, governments killed about 169 million people, and in that same period about 36 million people were killed in combat.

The most famous mass murder by government was the Nazi genocide of European Jews, but in terms of the total number of people killed the Nazis were exceeded by the Chinese and Soviet Communist regimes. When mass murder is directed against a specific ethnic group (e.g., Hitler's attempt to destroy all Jews and Gypsies, or "Romanies"), it is referred to as "genocide." Rummel coins the broader term "democide" for genocide as well as for mass killings not based on ethnicity (e.g., the Khmer Rouge's murder of 2 million people, about a third of the Cambodian population).

Democide may be accomplished directly with firearms, as is especially common in less-developed countries. Less frequently, more sophisticated means may be used (e.g., the Nazi extermination camps, which used poison gas), and very often the victims may be deliberately starved to death, as in the Ukraine in the 1930s. But regardless of the cause of death, firearms play an integral role because governments almost always ensure that the intended victims are disarmed before the democide begins.

Zelman, Simkin, and Rice (1994) examine seven democides in the twentieth century: Turkish killing of Armenians during and after World War I, the Soviet Union, Nazi Germany, Communist China, Guatemala's murder of Indians, Cambodia's killings, and Uganda's murder of non-African immigrants under Idi Amin. In all cases, the authors found, the victim populations had been disarmed first—sometimes through abusive enforcement of firearms laws that had been enacted by democratic governments. A monopoly of force appears necessary for relatively small groups of soldiers to be able to coerce vastly larger civilian populations. As Sachar (1983, p. 60) wrote about the European Jewish holocaust, "The difference between resistance and submission depended very largely upon who was in possession of the arms that back up the will to do or die."

Of course, prohibition of firearms does not inevitably lead to genocide; it is simply one necessary precondition. Zelman, Simkin, and Rice as well as Rummel identify various other conditions (e.g., suppression of a free press, absence of democracy, a government with a need to promote hatred) that also appear to raise the risk of democide.

Democide in the abstract has few defenders, which is one reason governments perpetrating democide squelch press freedom. Nevertheless, ideological allies of particular regimes sometimes do defend particular instances of genocide—as when Stalin and Mao were excused under the theory "You have to break a few eggshells to make an omelet."

Next to mass murder of civilians, war between countries is the largest cause of human deaths from gun violence. While soldiers in the nineteenth century and earlier often used edged or blunt weapons, in the twentieth century firearms emerged as the ubiquitous personal weapon of the soldier. In World War I, crew-served machine guns in trench warfare inflicted a staggering number of casualties; the toll was worsened by the failure of many military leaders to adopt new tactics. Firearms are not, of course, the only military weapon; artillery, bombs, and chemical weapons have also caused many deaths, and edged weapons such as knives may still be used in hand-to-hand combat.

While some pacifists categorically oppose war, the predominant view is that at least some wars are just, and governments are usually successful at convincing their civilian populations of the justness of the war the government is currently waging.

Another form of gun violence is criminal violence. This includes (in decreasing order of frequency) assaults, armed robberies, and homicides. In the United States, firearms are used in the majority of homicides and in a significant minority of serious assaults and robberies. They are rarely used in rape. Annually, the number of violent uses of firearms in the United States amounts to several hundred thousand. Kleck (1997) presents detailed data, and annual updates are available from the FBI's *Uniform Crime Reports* (U.S. Department of Justice, 1930–2003) and from the *National Crime Victimization Survey* (U.S. Bureau of Justice Statistics, 1972–2003). American criminal violence is sometimes defended or excused with the argument that crime is society's fault, not the individual's, or that crime is a legitimate response to social institutions such as racism or capitalism.

Another form of gun violence is the use of firearms for lawful defense against criminal acts. While some countries, such as Great Britain, do not recognize a right to use a firearm for protection against violent crime, all American jurisdictions acknowledge a right to use firearms for defense of self or family against serious violent attacks, such as attempted homicide, rape, or dangerous assaults. American states differ regarding

- the use of firearms for protection of persons not in one's family
- which particular offenses trigger the right to use a firearm for protection
- whether the victim of a felonious attack is required to retreat, if safe retreat is feasible

The earlier entry on "Defensive Gun Use" summarizes research data on the estimated number of defensive gun uses (DGUs) annually in the United States. It is possible that DGUs equal or exceed the number of violent gun crimes.

It should be noted that for both criminal violence and DGUs, the display of guns as a threat or deterrent is much more common than actually firing a gun, and that most times when a gun is fired a fatality does not result (because the shot misses, the wound is not critical, or the person who was shot receives life-saving medical care).

While the American legal system and the majority of the American public approve of defensive gun use, some people, including many gun control advocates, believe that only the police should be allowed to use firearms against criminals. For example, when Jim Brady (1994, p. 18) was asked about whether handgun ownership is legitimate, he replied, "For target shooting, that's okay. Get a license and go to the range. For defense of the home, that's why we have police departments."

Unlike the British, most Americans presume that police officers will be armed and may use deadly force in certain circumstances. Police may use the implied or express threat of gun violence to obtain compliance with their demands. Less frequently, police actually fire their weapons. While the large majority of instances of police gun violence are lawful, unlawful police use of firearms is labeled "police brutality" or "police violence." Unjust police gun violence may be the isolated act of a rogue officer or an authorized (or quietly tolerated) aspect of a policy of oppression by government.

Unlawful police violence, while legally condemned, is sometimes defended as giving criminals or outcast groups what they deserve, or as a necessary fact of life on the street. Lawful police violence, on the other hand, may be condemned as a form of official racism or as another form of abuse of the public. The "war on drugs" has been a major cause of increased police militarization and a concomitant increase in police gun violence such as armed, violent break-ins of homes in order to conduct searches for drugs.

While most gun violence by criminals, citizen defenders, or the police does not result in death, a large majority of attempted firearm suicides do. These suicides are not the only form of suicide with very high "success" rates (hangings, carbon monoxide poisonings, and drownings in large bodies of water also have high completion rates), but firearms are frequently used in suicides by males. In the United States, suicide is the leading cause of firearm death. Suicide is condemned by many with traditional religious views, but it is defended by people in the "right-to-die" movement, among others.

Accidental injury or death from firearms might be considered a form of gun violence—although it would be strange to speak of accidental skiing deaths as "skiing violence" or to describe household drownings as "bathtub violence." As a form of "gun violence," accidents are unique in that no one ever defends them as a public good.

David B. Kopel

See also Accidents, Gun; Defensive Gun Use; Genocide and Guns; Gun Violence as a Public Health Problem; Homicides, Gun; Hunting; Jews for the Preservation of Firearms Ownership; Mass Murder (Shootings); National Crime Victimization Survey; Right to Self-Defense; Schoolyard Shootings; Self-Defense, Legal Issues; Self-Defense, Reasons for Gun Use; Suicide, Guns and; Suicide, International Comparisons; Terrorism; Uniform Crime Reports; Victimization from Gun Violence; Youth and Guns

For Further Reading:
Brady, James. 1994. "In Step with: James Brady." *Parade* (June 26): 18.
Kleck, Gary. 1997. *Targeting Guns: Firearms and Their Control.* Hawthorne, NY: Aldine de Gruyter.
Kopel, David B. 1995. "Review of Aaron Zelman et al., *Lethal Laws.*" *New York Law School Journal of International and Comparative Law* 15: 355–398. http://www.davekopel.com/2A/LawRev/lethal.htm.
Rummel, Rudolph J. 1994. *Death by Government.* New Brunswick, NJ: Transaction Publishers.
———. 2002. Website on democide: http://www.hawaii.edu/powerkills/.
Sachar, Abram L. 1983. *The Redemption of the Unwanted: From the Liberation of the Death Camps to the Founding of Israel.* New York: St. Martin's.
U.S. Bureau of Justice Statistics. 1972–2003. *National Crime Victimization Survey.* Washington, DC: U.S. Government Printing Office.
U.S. Department of Justice. 1930–2003. *Uniform Crime Reports: Crime in the United States.* Washington, DC: U.S. Government Printing Office.
Zelman, Aaron, Jay Simkin, and Alan Rice. 1994. *Lethal Laws.* Milwaukee: Jews for the Preservation of Firearms Ownership.

Gun Violence as a Public Health Problem

Firearm injuries are a major public health problem in the United States. On an average day in the 1990s, firearms were used to kill over 90 people and to wound about 300 more. Each day guns were also used in the commission of about 3,000 crimes.

Compared to those of other developed countries, U.S. rates of property crime and violent crime are unremarkable. What distinguishes the United States is its high rate of lethal violence, most of which involves guns. The U.S. murder rate is typically *five to fifteen* times higher than that of other industrialized nations.

Gun-related deaths are a problem among all age groups in the United States. Of particular concern has been the rise in violent deaths of children. For example, although between 1950 and 1993 the overall annual death rate for U.S. children under age 15 declined substantially due to decreases in deaths from both illness and unintentional injury, during the same period childhood homicide rates tripled and suicide rates quadrupled; these increases were due almost entirely to gun deaths.

A comparison of violent deaths of 5–14-year-olds in the United States and the twenty-six other developed countries in the 1990s shows that the United States has ten times the firearm suicide rate (and the same nonfirearm suicide rate) as these other countries, and seventeen times the firearm homicide rate (and a somewhat higher nonfirearm homicide rate). The U.S. unintentional firearm death rate is nine times higher.

Gunshot wounds can lead to permanent disability. For example, nonfatal gunshot injuries are currently the second leading cause of spinal cord injury in the United States. Spinal cord injuries from gunshot wounds also tend to be more serious than those caused by accidents and other events. Gunshot wounds are more likely to lead to paraplegia and complete spinal cord injury than are traumatic spinal cord injuries caused by accidents (e.g., falls or motor vehicle collisions).

The medical costs of gunshot wounds are estimated to have been $6 million per day in the 1990s. The mean medical cost of a gunshot injury is about $17,000 and would be higher were the medical costs for deaths at the scene not low. Half of these costs are borne directly by U.S. taxpayers. The disability, pain, grief, and fear caused by gun violence in the United States are probably incalculable. The best estimate, derived from asking people how much they would pay to reduce gun violence, is that the cost of gun violence in America is about $100 billion per year.

The psychological costs of firearm trauma can be long-lasting. For example, compared to other traumatic injuries, gunshot wounds are more likely to lead to the development of post-traumatic stress disorder (PTSD). Chronic post-traumatic stress disorder following firearm injury is common: in one study, 58 percent of victims of firearm assault met the full diagnostic criteria for PTSD thirty-six months after their injury.

Even witnessing firearm violence can have serious psychological consequences. In one study, high school students who witnessed a firearm suicide on a school bus were found to be at higher risk than other demographically similar students for developing psychopathology—specifically, anxiety disorders and PTSD.

Through most of the twentieth century, gun assaults were seen almost exclusively as a criminal justice problem, gun suicides as a mental health problem, and unintentional gunshot wounds as a safety issue. Since the mid-1980s it has become increasingly recognized that gun injuries are also a serious public health problem.

Public health involvement in gun issues has many beneficial consequences. First, it broadens the issue from one that is exclusively focused on crime to one that is concerned with all firearm injuries—unintentional as well as intentional, self-inflicted as well as other-inflicted. After all, from the surgeon's perspective, treating a bullet in the head is the same whether the wound occurred during a robbery, a suicide attempt, or adolescent horseplay.

Second, public health adds new data sources (e.g., the National Center for Health Statistics, the National Health Interview survey), new analytic tools (e.g., an emphasis on surveillance data, epidemiological analysis of risk factors, cohort and case-control analyses), and new research professionals from the public health and medical communities. Much of our current scientific knowledge about guns and gun injuries has come from their research.

Third, public health attracts new practitioners and organizations into the arena. Physicians, for example, have first-hand experience concerning the human and medical implications of gunshot wounds and the long-run consequences of injury, and their testimony carries much weight. Public health offers a broader lens to supplement physicians' individual patient focus.

Public health is not merely an academic specialty but a government concern as well. Agencies from the Centers for Disease Control, the National Institutes of Health, and the U.S. Public Health Service as well as state and local health departments have the potential to work to reduce gun violence.

Finally, the public health approach emphasizes that there are many reasonable and beneficial interventions that can reduce gun violence. This perspective takes us past the old sterile debates about guns and gun control. Public health professionals believe that their can-do attitude, as demonstrated by their past successes, inspires hope for fundamentally reducing our firearm injury problem.

David Hemenway

See also Accidents, Gun; Center for Gun Policy and Research; Firearm Injury Statistical Systems; Guns in the Home; Suicide, Guns and; Youth and Guns

For Further Reading:

Cook, Philip J., and Jens Ludwig. 2000. *Gun Violence: The Real Costs.* New York: Oxford University Press.

Hemenway, David. 2001. "The Public Health Approach to Motor Vehicles, Tobacco, and Alcohol, with Applications to Firearms Policy." *Journal of Public Health Policy* 22, 4: 381–402.

Institute of Medicine. 1999. *Reducing the Burden of Injury.* Washington, DC: National Academy Press.

Gun Week

Gun Week is a newspaper published by the Second Amendment Foundation (SAF). For the last several decades it has served as a leading source of information for news about gun policy, the firearm industry, and recreational gun use.

Gun Week was created in 1966, with Neal Knox serving as its first editor. The original publisher was Amos Press in Sidney, Ohio. At the time, Amos Press also published *Linn's Stamp News, Coin World,* and a daily newspaper in Sidney. Its business theory was that the gun field was similar to the stamp and coin collecting fields. *Gun Week* originally earned substantial revenue from classified ads offering guns for sale, but the Gun Control Act of 1968, which banned almost all mail-order sales, ended that.

In 1985, *Gun Week* was acquired by Alan Gottlieb's Second Amendment Foundation. It was the first of what would become a large stable of SAF-owned periodicals. *Gun Week* remains SAF's flagship. At the time of its acquisition, the publication's name was officially changed to *The New Gun Week,* but almost no one uses this title. Currently, it is published on the first, tenth, and twentieth days of each month.

Gun Week's most prominent role on the national political stage came during the 1988 presidential campaign. The same week that the Democratic National Convention was nominating Michael Dukakis for president, *Gun Week* reported that the Massachusetts governor had said on June 16, 1986: "You know I don't believe in people owning guns, only the police and military. And I'm going to do everything I can to disarm this state." Dukakis denied making the remarks, but *Gun Week* had witnesses.

As reports of Dukakis's words spread among gun owners (abetted by the Bush campaign and the National Rifle Association), his support in many rural areas plunged. The gun issue was probably responsible for Dukakis's narrow losses in traditionally Democratic Pennsylvania, Maryland, and Michigan, as well as in Montana, and for Texas voting against Dukakis in a landslide, even though Texas Sen. Lloyd Bentsen was the Democratic vice presidential candidate.

Dukakis had a well-established record on gun control, but the *Gun Week* quote made it very difficult for Dukakis surrogates (such as Bentsen, who was A-rated by the NRA) to convince gun owners that Dukakis was not a serious threat to Second Amendment rights.

A typical *Gun Week* issue of twelve or sixteen pages includes numerous staff-written original articles, as well as summaries of articles from daily newspapers and mainstream magazines. The masthead proclaims that *Gun Week* serves "shooters, collectors, and activists," and the newspaper contains extensive coverage of target matches, hunting news, gun collecting news, firearm business news, and so on. Unlike most monthly gun magazines, *Gun Week* rarely runs how-to articles on hunting tips, self-defense advice, gun cleaning, and so forth.

Gun Week's greatest impact has come from its gun control and gun rights stories. Until the mid-1990s, when e-mail and the World Wide Web became ubiquitous, *Gun Week* was the speediest in-depth source of gun policy news. (The only thing that was faster was the recorded telephone message service from Neal Knox's Firearms Coalition.) For many professionals and serious activists on both sides of the gun policy debate, *Gun Week* was mandatory reading. While *Gun Week* has a very explicit editorial point of view, its stories tend to have much less spin than do the publications from other progun groups or from antigun groups.

Every issue of *Gun Week* contains a list of many of the gun shows that will take place in the United States during the next two months. Executive Editor Joseph P. Tartaro writes a "Hindsight" column (archived from 1994 at http://www.saf.org/hindsight.html) that attempts to provide long-term perspective on current controversies. Robert M. Hausman writes extensively on the firearm industry.

Gun Week has its own website, where, like many periodicals, it makes some but not all of its content available for free. Searchable electronic archives extend from the present back to April 2000.

David B. Kopel

See also Gottlieb, Alan Merril; Knox, Neal; Second Amendment Foundation
For Further Information:
Gun Week, 267 Linwood Avenue, Buffalo, NY 14209, (716) 885-6408. http://www.gunweek.com/.

Gunfighters
See Frontier Violence

Gun-Free School Laws

With the increase in public outrage associated with the perceived unsafe conditions at American schools and in light of recent school shootings, various states and the federal government have enacted laws designed to remove crime and violence from schools by attempting to eliminate the possession of guns and other weapons on or near school property. These laws, frequently called gun-free school laws or weapon-free school laws, mandate both the suspension or expulsion of students who possess weapons on school grounds and the criminal prosecution of any individual who brings a firearm within a certain distance of school property. As of 2002, approximately forty states had enacted laws banning or criminalizing the possession of firearms on or in close proximity to school property. In some states, this ban applies to students and in other states it applies to any individual carrying a firearm or weapon within a certain distance of school property. A few states go even further and specify that the parents of a minor who brings a weapon to school are liable for their child's actions. Depending on the state jurisdiction, the punishments range from suspension or expulsion to actual imprisonment.

The federal government has also adopted multiple measures aimed at ending gun violence in schools. The most expansive attempt by Congress to legislate in this area came with the Gun-Free School Zones Act of 1990, which attempted to prohibit the possession of any firearm within 1,000 feet of any school in the country. This legislation was later held to be unconstitutional by the U.S. Supreme Court in *United States v. Lopez;* the Court ruled that it exceeded the scope of Congress's constitutional powers under the commerce clause. In the aftermath of *Lopez,* Congress amended the Gun-Free School Zones Act in an effort to remedy the original constitutional defects as pointed out by the Supreme Court in *Lopez.* As amended, the Gun-Free School Zones Act currently prohibits the knowing possession or discharge of a firearm within 1,000 feet of a school if the firearm has traveled in interstate commerce. This federal legislation has also been criticized on the grounds that state and local law enforcement officials know their communities far better than the federal government and therefore are in a better position to address school violence and legislate on the subject. Additionally, it is argued, the administration of schools has historically been a state function.

Despite this criticism, Congress has continued to enact other laws aimed at ending gun violence in schools. Under its spending clause powers, Congress enacted the Gun-Free School Act of 1994, which requires each state receiving federal funds under the Elementary and Secondary Education Act to enact laws requiring the expulsion of any student who takes a gun to school. Also under its spending clause powers, Congress has enacted the Safe Schools Act of 1994, offering grants to high-crime school districts that agree to undertake new approaches to decreasing gun violence in schools. In response to these federal legislative actions, state legislators have continued to enact new gun-free school laws penalizing students who are caught with any kind of weapon on school grounds. As the punishment for violating these new laws is immediate expulsion, these laws have also been labeled "zero-tolerance laws." The motivation behind such legislation stems from the hope that school shootings can be significantly reduced and a safer learning environment can be created for our schools. To date, no systematic studies have been published that reveal the effectiveness of gun-free school laws.

James A. Beckman

See also Gun Control Act of 1968; *United States v. Lopez*

For Further Reading:

Bogos, Paul. 1997. "Note: Expelled. No Excuses. No Exceptions. Michigan's Zero-Tolerance Policy in Response to School Violence: M.C.L.A. Section 380.1311." *University of Detroit Mercy Law Review* 74 (Winter): 357–387.

Chamberlin, Carl. 1999. "Johnny Can't Read 'Cause Jane's Got a Gun: The Effects of Guns in Schools, and Options after Lopez." *Cornell Journal of Law and Public Policy* 8 (Winter): 281–346.

Gunpowder

Gunpowder historically falls into two main categories: black powder and smokeless powder. Black powder is a composition of potassium nitrate (saltpeter), charcoal, and sulfur. Smokeless powder is composed of nitrocellulose and various additives.

Black powder was used in China for fireworks over a millennium ago; its use in firearms appears to be a European invention. It is known to have been employed in firearms sometime prior to A.D. 1350. It was initially used in dust form, in which it burned rather slowly when packed into a gun. In artillery, a tight-fitting wooden disk had to be driven atop the powder below the cannonball before the cannonball was loaded in order to permit the powder to burn and gas pressure to build before it began moving the projectile. In the fifteenth century, it was discovered that black powder would burn much more rapidly if the dust powder was moistened, compressed, and driven through screens that formed it into distinct grains.

Black powder had many disadvantages. Each shot was marked by a burst of white smoke, giving away the shooter's position. Also, due to incomplete combustion, tarlike black powder residues built up in the gun's barrel, which slowed loading. And the pressure and thus the power it could develop were limited.

In 1832 nitrocellulose, which was produced by treating cellulose with nitric acid, was discovered. The result was a potent explosive and (when treated with solvents) the first plastic, known as celluloid. In 1884 Paul Vieille, a French ordinance expert, discovered how to tame nitrocellulose's burning rate sufficiently to make a usable powder for firearms, and how to form it into flakes (later it was also produced as tubular and spherical grains). With smokeless powders, the power of firearms, particularly rifles, could be increased. The power was further augmented when it was discovered that the grains could be designed to provide a progressive burning rate—that is to say, the rate of combustion would increase as the grains were consumed, enabling the powder to burn relatively slowly while the bullet was initially being accelerated and increase in burning speed as the bullet accelerated. The result was a revolution in small-arms design as armies switched from .44 and .45 caliber black-powder cartridges to high-velocity rifle cartridges of about .30 caliber.

Today numerous types of smokeless powder with different burning rates are available, so that a cartridge manufacturer or a private individual "handloader" can match the powder to the cartridge and the projectile. A smokeless powder composed solely of nitrocellulose is commonly identified as a single-based powder; one that also contains small amounts of nitroglycerin is identified as a double-based powder. Use of double-based powders is largely confined to pistols, where a very fast burning rate is needed due to the short barrel.

David T. Hardy

See also Ammunition, Types of

For Further Reading:

Davis, Tenney L. 1943. *Chemistry of Powder and Explosives.* Hollywood, CA: Angriff Press.

Delbruck, Hans. 1985. *History of the Art of War.* Vol. 4. Trans. Walter Renfroe. Lincoln: University of Nebraska Press.

Hatcher, Julian. 1962. *Hatcher's Notebook.* Harrisburg, PA: Stackpole Publishing.

Hogg, Ian. 1985. *Jane's Directory of Military Small Arms Ammunition.* New York: Jane's Publishing.

Guns & Ammo

See Gun Magazines

Guns in the Home

At least since the time of the Civil War, many households in the United States have kept firearms. In the last decade of the twentieth century, this practice became the subject of heated debate. The debate concerns the balance between the perceived benefits of keeping guns in the home and the documented risks.

Though many U.S. households have guns, the proportion that keep guns is declining. The Harris poll (2001) found a decrease in gun-owning households from 48 percent in 1973 to less than 39 percent in 2001; the estimates of the General Social Survey (2000) show similar declines and give a recent figure of 33 percent. The estimates of the Gallup poll (2000) fall between these two percentages. Rates of household gun ownership are not uniform across all groups, however; there are lower rates in households with children and higher rates in rural areas and small towns as compared to cities.

Guns in the home vary in type. The majority (66 percent) are long guns (i.e., rifles, shotguns, and so on), which are usually kept for hunting and sporting purposes, particularly in rural areas. Handguns are more often kept for "self-protection" and so are more likely to be kept in a "ready-to-fire" way (such as next to a bed). In a study of households with both guns and children, 43 percent of them had at least one gun

unlocked, and 13 percent had guns stored unlocked, loaded, or with ammunition (Schuster, Franke, Bastian, et al., 2000). Since most handguns can be fired by even young children (Naureckas, Galanter, Naureckas, et al., 1995), this would seem to be a hazardous situation.

Indeed, research confirms that guns in the home are dangerous. In studies of teen suicide by Brent, Perper, Allman, et al. (1991), guns were twice as likely to be found in the homes of suicide victims than in the homes of suicide survivors or members of control groups. The authors summarized their findings this way: "The availability of guns in the home, independent of firearm type or method of storage, appears to increase the risk for suicide among adolescents" (p. 2989).

The risk posed by guns in the home is not only to children. Research on risk factors for homicide in urban areas has shown that guns kept in homes are more likely to be involved in a fatal or nonfatal accidental shooting (four times more likely), criminal assault (seven times more likely), or suicide attempt (eleven times more likely) than to be used to injure or kill in self-defense (Kellermann, Somes, Rivara, et al., 1998). In homes with a gun, the homicide of a household member is three times more likely to occur than in homes without a gun; the risk for suicide is nearly five times greater (Kellermann, Rivara, Rushforth, et al., 1993). Essentially all of the added risk of homicide and suicide in cities is related specifically to handguns. Comparable studies have not yet been done in rural areas, but it is known that long guns cause more of the gun deaths in those areas, most unrelated to sports shooting (Dresang, 2001; Hootman, Annest, Mercy, et al. 2000).

Some studies claim to show that guns are often used in self-defense and that guns that are kept handy reduce crime. These studies are unconvincing to many, however. One study (Kleck and Gertz, 1995) is an analysis of phone surveys, but such surveys are not good at estimating the frequency of very rare events, when small differences can make a big difference in incidence estimates, especially when the respondent's behavior may be socially desirable, as heroic uses of guns may be. The resulting estimate of the number of people shot defensively is implausible, exceeding the number of all those treated for gun injuries (Webster and Ludwig, 2000).

Guns that are kept for use against criminal intruders are actually likely to harm household members, when the guns are used out of anger, depression, or fear. That is because these mental states occur far more frequently than criminal home intrusions. Indeed, using the highest (and implausible) estimates of the frequency of defensive gun use and current estimates of gun ownership and gun deaths, it is clear that on any given day far fewer than 1 percent of all civilian guns are used for self-defense. About half of the adults in the United States (51 percent) believe that guns in the home are hazardous (Gallup News Service, 2000).

One approach to reducing the risk posed by household guns, particularly to children and adolescents, is education on the dangers of guns. But while there is little disagreement with the idea that youth should be taught that guns are dangerous, there is very little evidence to date that such education is effective in preventing young people from firing guns if they happen upon them. Indeed, two recent studies have documented that both preschool and preteen boys will handle and even intentionally fire guns if they find them, even if their parents have taught them otherwise and believe that their sons are "immune" to the temptation of guns (Hardy, Armstrong, Martin, et al., 1996; Jackman, Farah, Kellermann, et al., 2001).

As a result, another focus of gun injury prevention efforts is removal of guns from homes, or at least safer storage of those guns that households decide to keep. Two such initiatives are PAX's "ASK (Asking Saves Kids)" campaign, a national advertising effort developed in collaboration with the American Academy of Pediatrics that urges parents to ask their neighbors if they have a gun in the home before sending their child over to play; and the "Risk: Guns in the Home" public awareness campaign of Physicians for Social Responsibility, which is designed to educate Americans about the dangers of having a handgun in the home where children are present, and to encourage them to make informed decisions about their guns, safety, and health.

These campaigns are consistent with the policies of most medical organizations. Organizations with formal statements on gun ownership in the home that promote removal of guns and/or physician education of patients about the risks of guns include the American Academy of Child and Adolescent Psychiatry, American Academy of Pediatrics, American College of Emergency Physicians, American College of Physicians, American Society of Internal Medicine, and American Medical Association. Many other organizations take similar positions, promoting public gun safety/education programs and specific actions to reduce risks. These include, for example, the American Psychological Association, American Public Health Association, and the Presbyterian Church (USA).

Other approaches to reducing the risk of guns in the home are also being developed, such as encouraging families to safely dispose of unwanted guns. This generally involves calling the police to take the guns away. Jurisdictions vary as to whether they then melt the guns down or offer them for repurchase in the community. Gun buyback programs, run in collaboration with the police, are another way to assist families that seek to remove guns from their homes. These are popular means of public education and do get guns out of some homes. However, the net effect on home arsenals has so far been very small. Further, in the United States, where it is extremely easy to replace a discarded gun with a new model, the effect on injuries is not likely to be large; thus far it has not been demonstrated. (In other regions of the world, where transportation and gun purchases are more difficult, this approach may hold more promise.)

Other approaches to reducing the risk of guns in the home seek to reduce access to the guns that are kept there. This can involve the use of trigger locks or gun lock boxes (Denno, Grossman, Britt, et al., 1996). Recent information about defective trigger locks highlights the need for testing and regulation of such devices (U.S. Consumer Product Safety Commission, 2000). Evaluation of safer gun storage approaches is currently under way.

Another approach to reducing access to guns in the home involves developing guns that are "personalized"—so-called smart guns equipped with mechanical or electronic devices that would prevent firing by unauthorized users (Vernick, Meisel, Teret, et al., 1999). While there are now prototypes of such weapons, they are not yet available for purchase, so it remains to be seen how quickly such novel weapons might reduce the accessibility of guns in the home and thereby reduce firearm injuries and deaths.

Katherine Kaufer Christoffel
and Jennifer Hurtarte

See also Accidents, Gun; American Academy of Pediatrics; American Medical Association; Defensive Gun Use; Gun Buyback Programs; Gun Violence as a Public Health Problem; HELP Network; Kellermann, Arthur L.; Medicine and Gun Violence; PAX; Physicians for Social Responsibility; Presbyterian Church (USA); Smart Guns; Straight Talk About Risks

For Further Reading:

Brent, David A., Joshua A. Perper, Christopher J. Allman, et al. 1991. "The Presence and Accessibility of Firearms in the Homes of Adolescent Suicides: A Case-Control Study." *Journal of the American Medical Association* 266: 2989–2995.

Denno, Donna M., David C. Grossman, John Britt, et al. 1996. "Safe Storage of Handguns: What Do the Police Recommend?" *Archives of Pediatric and Adolescent Medicine* 150: 927–931.

Dresang, Lee T. 2001. "Gun Deaths in Rural and Urban Settings: Recommendations for Prevention." *Journal of the American Board of Family Practice* 14: 107–115.

Gallup News Service. 2000. "About Four in Ten Americans Report Owning a Gun." October 5. Princeton, NJ: Gallup Organization.

General Social Survey. 2000. "Do you happen to have in your home (or garage) any guns or revolvers? If yes, Is it a pistol, shotgun, rifle, or what?" Inter-University Consortium for Political and Social Research. http://www.icpsr.umich.edu/GSS/.

Hardy, Marjorie S., F. Daniel Armstrong, Breta L. Martin, et al. 1996. "A Firearm Safety Program for Children: They Just Can't Say No." *Journal of Developmental and Behavioral Pediatrics* 17: 216–221.

Harris Poll. 2001. "Gun Ownership: Two in Five Americans Live in Gun-Owning Households." May 30. New York: Louis Harris and Associates, Inc.

Hootman, Jennifer, Joseph L. Annest, James A. Mercy, et al. 2000. "National Estimates of Non-Fatal Firearm Related Injuries Other Than Gunshot Wounds." *Injury Prevention* 6: 268–274.

Jackman, Geoffrey A., Mirna M. Farah, Arthur L. Kellermann, et al. 2001. "Seeing Is Believing: What Do Boys Do When They Find a Real Gun?" *Pediatrics* 107: 1247–1250.

Kellermann, Arthur L., Frederick P. Rivara, Norman B. Rushforth, et al. 1993. "Gun Ownership as a Risk Factor for Homicide in the Home." *New England Journal of Medicine* 329: 1084–1091.

Kellermann, Arthur L., Grant Somes, Frederick P. Rivara, et al. 1998. "Injuries and Death Due to Firearms in the Home." *Journal of Trauma* 45: 236–267.

Kleck, Gary, and Marc Gertz. 1995. "Armed Resistance to Crime: The Prevalence and Nature of Self-Defense with a Gun." *Journal of Criminal Law and Criminology* 86: 150–187.

Naureckas, Sara M., Cathryn Galanter, Edward T. Naureckas, et al. 1995. "Children's and Women's Ability to Fire Handguns." *Archives of Pediatric and Adolescent Medicine* 149: 1318–1322.

PAX's "ASK" campaign website: www.askingsaveskids.com/ask.html.

Physicians for Social Responsibility's "Risk: Guns in the Home" campaign website: www.psr.org/riskguns.html.

Schuster, Mark A., Todd M. Franke, Amy M. Bastian, et al. 2000. "Firearm Storage Patterns in U.S. Homes with Children." *American Journal of Public Health* 90: 588–594.

Senturia, Yvonne D., Katherine Kaufer Christoffel, and Mark Donovan. 1994. "Children's Household Exposure to Guns: A Pediatric Practice-Based Survey." *Pediatrics* 93: 469–475.

U.S. Consumer Product Safety Commission. 2000. "CPSC, Master Lock Co. Announces Recall to Replace Gun Locks." July 24. http://www.cpsc.gov/CPSCPUB/PREREL/prhtml00/00149.html.

Vernick, Jon S., Zachary F. Meisel, Stephen P. Teret, et al. 1999. "I Didn't Know the Gun Was Loaded: An Examination of Two Safety Devices That Can Reduce the Risk of Unintentional Firearm Injuries." *Journal of Public Health Policy* 20: 427–440.

Webster, Daniel, and Jens Ludwig. 2000. "Myths about Defensive Gun Use and Permissive Gun Carry Laws." Berkeley, CA: Berkeley Media Studies Group.

Guns Magazine

See Gun Magazines

Gunshot Detection Technologies (GDTs)

Gunshot detection technologies are designed to detect the sound of a muzzle blast from a gun within seconds of the shot being fired, pinpoint the location from which the shot was fired, and then alert the police about the shot. Gunshot detection technologies seek to identify the location and time of gunfire in a specified target area through a series of acoustic sensor modules. Some companies have produced acoustic sensors that are about the size of a videocassette and battery powered. The battery-powered units comprise an acoustic sensing element, gunshot identification electronics, and a transmitter. About eighty-five battery-powered units are needed to adequately cover a one-square-mile area. By contrast, other companies have developed acoustic sensors that transmit muzzle blast sounds via telephone lines. These acoustic sensors include microphones, acoustic sensing elements, and gunshot identification electronics that are approximately one cubic foot in size. These larger sensors can be disguised as birdhouses or heating vents. About eight acoustic sensors that transmit sounds via telephone lines are needed to cover a one-square-mile area.

The acoustic sensors transmit information about the gunshot location and time to a personal computer located in the police department's dispatch center. The information is transmitted in under two seconds from when the shot is fired and the information about the gunfire is displayed on a computerized map, enabling dispatchers to relay the information to officers on the street if and when they choose. GDT "triangulates" gunfire alerts such that information from responding acoustic sensors is used to pinpoint the precise location from which the shot was fired. Triangulation procedures can pinpoint 99 percent of shots within a 65-foot radius of the event; 88 percent of shots within 30 feet; 63 percent of shots within 20 feet; and 35 percent of shots within 10 feet (Mazerolle, Watkins, Rogan, and Frank, 1999).

Parameter settings in the GDT software determine the system's level of sensitivity: if the thresholds are set quite high, then background noise is less often identified as gunfire. Conversely, if the thresholds are set quite low, then more background noise could be detected as gunfire, increasing the potential for incorrectly identifying extraneous noises as gunfire. Once the sensors detect a sound and transmit the information to the central computer, the software discriminates against most other community sounds (such as car backfires, jackhammers, thunder, and barking dogs) and pinpoints the location of gunfire and explosions. The computer map distinguishes property boundaries including front or side yards, curbsides, or street corners.

Some GDTs store all waveforms for every detected gunfire event and six seconds of audio from each detecting acoustic sensor (2.3 megabytes each). A significant amount of system memory is required when numerous gunfire events occur simultaneously or when many noises are relayed to the system in quick succession (such as on New Year's Eve or the Fourth of July). Once the GDT detects a shot and reports the location on the computer screen, dispatchers can play back the six-second snippet of sound from any sensor to assist them in determining what they believe to be the true source of the sound: firecracker string, multiple gunshots, shotgun blast, or, say, backfire from a vehicle. The ability to play back the sound of the apparent gunfire alert offers the police the opportunity to determine whether or not they think the sound is, in fact, gunfire.

Do They Work?

Gunshot detection technologies identify about 80 percent of shots fired when the path of the muzzle blast is not blocked by walls or other physical impediments. Hence, shots that are fired indoors or in alleyways are typically not detected. Shotgun blasts are more easily detected by GDTs than assault rifle or pistol rounds, which raises issues for the police in determining how useful GDT would be in most high-gun-crime urban areas.

Police Response to GDT Alerts

Citizen reporting of a shot is typically dependent on (1) the citizen hearing the shot; (2) the citizen being able to discern the noise as gunfire; (3) the citizen making the decision to call the police within a reasonable time frame of the shot being fired; and (4) the citizen being able to tell the police exactly where the shot was fired from. The introduction of gunshot detection technology removes the citizen contingencies that influenced random gunfire reporting. The technology also challenges police departments to carefully consider the manner in which they mobilize police resources in response to gunfire detection system alerts.

Gunshot detection systems present the police with four possible outcomes: (1) when the device is neutral no warning is produced (true negative) and no evasive actions by the police need be taken; (2) when shots are fired one expects the device to activate an alarm (true positive) and some type of corrective action will be taken (whether as an immediate, delayed, or problem-solving response); (3) when the device fails to activate when gunfire is present (false negative) evasive actions cannot be considered, leaving open the possibility of an escalating problem; and (4) a potential waste of scarce police resources may occur when the device reacts without the presence of gunfire (false positive) if evasive action is needlessly undertaken. Gunshot detection systems thus provide police departments with great potential to discern the extent, nature, and specific locations of outdoor gunfire problems beyond what they already know from citizen calls for police service. Yet, the technology also poses challenges to police departments to determine how, when, and under what circumstances they want to mobilize police resources in response to gunfire alerts.

A recent evaluation of GDT found that the technology will identify three times as many gunshot incidents as are typically reported to the police by citizens (Mazerolle, Watkins, Rogan, and Frank, 1999). Indeed, the evaluation suggests that large numbers of random gunfire incidents typically are not detected by the police when they rely entirely on citizen calls.

The increase in random gunfire alerts is somewhat of a double-edged sword: On the one hand, the gunshot detection system provides police with much more information about the extent, nature, and location of random gunfire problems than previously known through citizen calls to the police. This additional information about random gunfire provided by the gunshot detection system could give the police important insights as to the nature, extent, and locations of random gunfire problems. On the other hand, the increase in random gunfire alerts has the potential to cripple the delivery of police services. The threefold increase in radio dispatches following the implementation of GDTs under field trial conditions represents a significant increase in police workload for a very small geographic area (less than one square mile).

Police departments need to think very carefully about the policy implications of utilizing gunshot detection systems. On the positive side, the technology can help identify random gunfire hot spots and shape police problem-solving responses to these locations. On the negative side, gunshot detection systems are unlikely to result in arrests of shooters; they can also significantly increase police workloads and potentially reduce the amount of time patrol officers have available to deal with citizen complaints about random gunfire events.

Police Views of Gunshot Detection Systems

Surveys have been conducted with patrol officers from cities that have tried using GDTs to assess their perceptions of the impact of gunshot detection systems on their work routine, their confidence in the technology to report incidences of gunfire, and their perceptions of the ability of the technology to improve police effectiveness in handling incidents when random shots are fired (Mazerolle, Watkins, Rogan, and Frank, 1999). The findings reveal that patrol officers do not have a great deal of confidence in the ability of the gunshot detection systems to identify and locate gunfire. They worry most about false alerts and express concern about their time spent responding to gunfire alerts with a low likelihood of catching or arresting the shooters.

Officers also believe that they tend to respond more quickly to gunshot-detection-system calls than to citizen-generated calls. Some officers explain that they merely want to clear the call quickly and move on to the next call. Officers generally feel that they are more likely to talk to citizens on citizen-generated calls than on gunshot-detection-system calls and that they make more problem-solving progress on citizen alerts than on technology alerts. Generally, officers feel that citizen calls about gunfire give them a focal point in responding to the call. They can ask the citizen about what they heard and they can glean some context on the shot fired. By contrast, officers explain that the gunshot detection system provides no details about the apparent shot, leaving them without any guidance to pursue an investigation. They have no specific citizen to talk to and they have no details about the context of the shot being fired from which they can begin their investigation.

Gunshot detection systems seem to offer the most potential as a problem-solving tool. Gunshot detection systems would fit nicely with the emerging problem-oriented policing paradigm, as they could be used to scan for hot and cold gunfire spots and then track the success of problem-solving interventions by depicting the changes in the number of shots fired in targeted locations.

Lorraine Mazerolle

See also Crime and Gun Use
For Further Reading:

Egan, Timothy. 1996. "Police Surveillance of Streets Turns to Video Cameras and Listening Devices." *New York Times* (February 7).

Mazerolle, Lorraine Green, Jan Roehl, and Colleen Kadleck. 1998. "Controlling Social Disorder Using Civil Remedies: Results from a Randomized Field Experiment in Oakland, California." Pp. 141–160 in *Civil Remedies and Crime Prevention,* Crime Prevention Studies, vol. 9, ed. Lorraine Green Mazerolle and Jan Roehl. Monsey, NY: Criminal Justice Press.

Mazerolle, Lorraine Green, R. Cory Watkins, Dennis Rogan, and James Frank. 1998. "Using Gunshot Detection Systems in Police Departments: The Impact on Police Response Times and Officer Workloads." *Police Quarterly* 1, 2: 21–49.

_____. 1999. "Random Gunfire Problems and Gunshot Detection Systems." Research in Brief. Washington, DC: National Institute of Justice, U.S. Department of Justice.

Watkins, R. Cory, Lorraine Green Mazerolle, and Dennis Rogan. 2000. "The Spatial Distribution of Random Gunfire: A Block-Level Investigation of Physical and Social Structural Conditions." *American Journal of Criminal Justice* 24, 2 (Spring): 217–233.

Gunshot Wounds (Wound Ballistics)

Ballistics is the study of the motion of projectiles, specifically bullets, after leaving the gun muzzle. This includes both the path of the bullet in the air and the results of a bullet's impact on its targets. Bullet trajectory is affected by bullet design and by the gun that launches it. In the air, a bullet accumulates kinetic energy, which is an important concept as it is the transfer of kinetic energy to the target that causes damage on impact. A bullet's size and speed determine its kinetic energy. The proportion of this energy that is transferred from the bullet to the target tissue depends on characteristics such as the bullet's shape and fragmentation, the firing distance of the gun, and the properties of the target itself. Wound ballistics studies the patterns of damage inflicted on a target once a bullet hits it. Modifications can be made to bullets to increase their target damage based on such principles of ballistics. Knowledge about ballistics permits a gun user to tailor his gun and ammunition to specific purposes. It also has relevance in the vast field of medical forensics, where the path is traced backwards from the wound to describe the bullet.

Bullet Ballistics

As suggested, the damage that a particular bullet can inflict is related to the amount of kinetic energy it obtains. A bullet's kinetic energy is described in physics as $E = 1/2\ mv^2$, where E is kinetic energy, m is bullet mass, and v is bullet velocity. Therefore heavier bullets accumulate more kinetic energy in flight. Likewise, the speed of a bullet has a squared effect on the amount of energy it carries, with faster bullets building exponentially greater damaging potential. Kinetic energy alone does not determine target damage. Rather, other factors such as shape and fragmentation dictate the proportion of this kinetic energy that is actually transferred as damage to the target.

Size: A bullet's size is described by its caliber and weight. Caliber refers to a bullet's circumference. It is measured in either inches or millimeters. Bullets are commonly referred to by their caliber; for instance, the familiar 16 mm or .45 (forty-five hundredths of an inch). Bullet weight is described in grains per pound (gr/lb), a unit that is internationally standardized. The greater the caliber or weight of a bullet, the greater its mass, and the greater the kinetic energy it possesses.

Velocity: A bullet's velocity refers to the speed it is capable of gathering within the gun muzzle. Velocity is measured in terms of feet per second (ft/sec) or meters per second (m/sec). Low-velocity bullets move at less than 600 m/sec, or approximately 1,900 ft/sec. Higher-velocity bullets exceed a critical velocity of greater than 600 m/sec, or 1,900 ft/sec. Handguns fire bullets of lower velocity, while rifle ammunition is usually of high velocity. Modifications can be made to increase a bullet's velocity. A full metal jacket is a lining of copper around a lead bullet, the stronger copper protecting the bullet from heat and allowing it to travel faster. Magnum bullets have more gunpowder, which launches a bullet at higher velocities. The higher the velocity, the greater the kinetic energy a bullet gathers.

Shape and Configuration: The most common bullet has a round-shaped nose with a solid core of lead or steel. Bullets can undergo profile modification that alters this basic shape, affecting their ballistics. For instance, a hollow-point bullet has a cavity carved into the nosetip of its presenting surface. This hole becomes a heat-trapping cavity. As the bullet accelerates, hot gas accumulates in the hollow point, causing the bullet to flatten and mushroom, giving it a larger area of impact. By increasing the bullet's forward area of contact, there is increased energy transfer and greater damage.

Fragmentation: Bullets can be made to fragment by packaging them into shot. Shot consists of numerous small lead or steel pellets packed together in a plastic casing. The casing then fragments after being fired, scattering the tiny bullets and increasing the area impacting a target. Bird shot often has many small light pellets, permitting a wider area of impact but with each small projectile still potent enough for the target. Buckshot is used for hunting larger animals and contains less numerous but heavier shot.

Yaw and Tumble: A bullet does not always travel in a straight line. Its path can be altered by air, tissue, or other objects. Yaw is a term used to describe the natural dipping and rising of the nose of any projectile, altering its perfectly linear or curvilinear path. Tumble describes when a bullet begins to cartwheel down its forward path. Both of these are natural phenomena. The yaw and tumble of a bullet before reaching its target can reduce a bullet's accuracy. On impact, though, yaw and tumble may result in greater tissue damage, as they multiply the area of contact and injury.

Wound Ballistics

Wound ballistics involves the damage inflicted on a target once a bullet hits it.

Crush and Cavitary Injury: A bullet damages its target by transferring its kinetic energy into crush and deforming forces. When a bullet hits, it causes direct tissue damage at points of contact. It also creates a ring of cavitary injury surrounding its direct path. Greater kinetic energy increases the depth of this ring. Once entering tissue, the bullet's path is distorted and subject to yaw and tumble. Such nonlinear pathways in addition to bullet fragmentation and mushrooming can multiply the degree of cavitary injury.

Firing Distance: The proximity of the gun to its target can sometimes be determined by examining markings at a bullet's entrance site into a target. When a gun is in direct contact with its target, the heat from the gunpowder can cause an actual flame, burning the entrance wound and leaving a sear mark. Contact wounds are also close enough that the still-expanding gas from gunpowder detonation distorts the tissue at the entrance-wound edges, causing a muzzle contusion and a stellate-shaped wound. The exception is tight contact wounds that retain a more circular contour. Guns that are fired in contact can also force clothing and other material into the wound, another identifying clue.

At close but not contact firing ranges of 6–12 inches, there is a soot pattern left on the wound edges by discharge of the gun. The distribution and concentration of these soot marks leave footprints. Guns fired at an intermediate range of 1–2 feet are too distant to leave soot deposition. Instead, they leave characteristic wound tattoos. These are indelible marks caused by micro-impregnation of the nearby skin by pellets of unburned gunpowder. Guns fired at distant ranges of greater than 10 feet leave no soot residue or tattooing around the bullet entrance, as these are too distant for gunpowder to reach the wound. These instead have abrasion collars—bruises from the force of bullet impact in contrast to close-range markings that are burns from the heat of combustion.

Entrance and Exit Wounds: An exit wound often has everted, irregular edges and should have no soot markings or gunpowder tattooing. Entrance and exit wounds, however, are not always clearly distinguishable. Not all entrance wounds are smaller than their exit wounds. For instance, a contact entrance wound may have the large stellate pattern from the nearby gunfire but retain a small exit wound if the bullet maintains a straight path. The damage inflicted by a bullet is not necessarily proportional to its visible entrance and exit wounds. Wounds from bullets that fragment or that have a high degree of yaw and tumble can have deceptively greater internal tissue damage, despite seemingly small external wounds.

Target Properties: Properties of the target tissue affect the amount of damage that a bullet can cause. The elasticity of the tissue can affect entrance and exit wounds; for instance, bullets entering the elastic palm surface may appear slit-like, since the tissue contracts the wound. Elastic tissues are also more resilient to cavitary injury, given their greater capacity to stretch and contract and retain less permanent damage. Target tissues that are denser (for instance, bone) suffer greater damage when hit by a bullet. This is because in a given surface area there are more particles to accept the transfer of kinetic energy.

Winny W. Hung

See also Accidents, Gun; Gun Violence as a Public Health Problem
For Further Reading:
Bartlett, Craig S., David L. Helfet, Michael R. Hausman, and Elton Strauss. 2000. "Ballistics and Gunshot Wounds: Effects on Musculoskeletal Tissues." *Journal of the American Academy of Orthopedic Surgery* 8, 1 (January/February): 21–36.
Naudé, Gideon, Demetrios Demetriades, and Fred Bongard. 1999. *Trauma Secrets.* Philadelphia: Hanley and Belfus.
Rosen, Peter, et al., eds. 1998. *Emergency Medicine Concepts and Clinical Practice.* Vol. 1. 4th ed. St. Louis: Mosby.
Sellier, Karl G., and Beat P. Kneubuehl. 1994. *Wound Ballistics and the Scientific Background.* Amsterdam: Elsevier.
Yee, Doreen A., and J. Hugh Devitt. 1999. "Mechanisms of Injury: Causes of Trauma." *Anesthesiology Clinics of North America* 17, 1 (March): 11–14.

H

Stephen P. Halbrook. (Courtesy of author)

Halbrook, Stephen P. (1947–)

Over the last quarter century, Stephen Halbrook has become one of the most important attorneys and legal scholars on the Second Amendment and firearm law. Winner of three Supreme Court cases, Halbrook is a prolific scholar of legal history. He has written extensively about the original meanings of the Second Amendment and the Fourteenth Amendment (the latter as applied to Second Amendment rights). He has also become an expert on the effects of firearm laws during World War II—in particular, the effect of the universal militia system in Switzerland in keeping that nation free,

and the effect of German firearm laws in facilitating the oppression and murder of Jews.

After earning a Ph.D. in philosophy in 1972 from Florida State University, Halbrook taught philosophy for the next nine years at the Tuskegee Institute, Howard University, and George Mason University. Tuskegee and Howard are both historically black universities, and in times when many universities would not admit blacks, Tuskegee and Howard were among the most important educational institutions for American blacks. Later, when Halbrook began to write on firearm issues, civil rights would be one of his major topics.

Halbrook's work continues to reflect his background in philosophy: his writing eschews quantitative material (e.g., how often guns are used for self-defense or committing crimes) and instead focuses on pure law and history.

While teaching philosophy, Halbrook earned his J.D. from the Georgetown University Law Center in 1978. By the early 1980s, he had emerged as a leading attorney and scholar on Second Amendment issues. As an attorney, Halbrook has participated in dozens of important federal and state cases involving constitutional law and firearm statutes or regulations. He has taken three cases to the United States Supreme Court, and won them all.

The first Supreme Court case was *United States v. Thompson/Center Arms Co.* (504 U.S. 505, 1992). The issue was the interpretation of a complex federal statute involving a kit that was intended for the home assembly of a rifle that could be lawfully converted into a handgun (but which also could be used to unlawfully assemble a handgun with an illegal rifle shoulder stock). If the gun were assembled illegally, it would be the type of gun that is subject to a special federal tax and regulatory system (National Firearms Act,

Stephen P. Halbrook arguing before the Supreme Court. (Courtesy of author)

U.S. Code, volume 26, section 5801, et seq.). The Court agreed 5–4 with Halbrook that the tax was not applicable to the manufacturer, who sold the kit for lawful purposes.

The second case was Halbrook's most famous. In *Printz v. United States,* a sharply divided Supreme Court ruled 5–4 that Congress did not have the authority to compel local law enforcement agencies to conduct the federal background check on retail handgun purchasers (521 U.S._, 117 S. Ct. 2365, 138 L. Ed. 2d 914, 1997). The mandatory federal check, which had been created by the 1993 Brady Act, was set to expire in 1998 anyway, so the case did not have a drastic impact on firearm policy.

Printz's long-term impact, however, was enormous. First of all, the case foreclosed the proposed "Brady II" congressional gun control legislation, which would have ordered state governments to set up handgun licensing and registration systems according to a federal scheme.

Even more significant, *Printz* was one of a series of Supreme Court cases, beginning with *New York v. United States* in 1991, in which the Court began paying renewed attention to federalism and states' rights and enforcing constitutional limits on congressional power. (Another case in this series was *United States v. Lopez* [514 U.S. 549, 1995], in which the Court held 5–4 that Congress lacks authority to create "gun-free school zones.")

Halbrook's third Supreme Court case, *Castillo v. United States,* grew out of the invasion by the Bureau of Alcohol, Tobacco, and Firearms (BATF) of the Branch Davidian compound in Waco, Texas, on February 28, 1993. A gun battle had erupted between the Branch Davidians and the BATF. When several Branch Davidians were put on trial later, they were acquitted of all charges of murder, aiding and abetting murder, and conspiracy to commit murder. For those charges, the judge had told the jury that it could consider whether the Branch Davidians had been acting in self-defense. But the judge did not allow the jury to consider self-defense for the lesser charge of aiding and abetting voluntary manslaughter (defined as a homicide resulting from "adequate" provocation). Several Branch Davidians were convicted of this charge; although the jury expected that the Branch Davidians would be sentenced only to time served, the federal statute provides a penalty of up to ten years.

Federal law provides an additional penalty of up to five extra years when a gun is used in a federal violent crime, and up to thirty additional years when the gun is a machine gun (18 U.S. Code, § 924, c, 1). Although the indictment had never charged the Branch Davidians with using machine guns, and although the jury had never been asked to make any findings about whether any of the Branch Davidians had used machine guns, federal District Judge Walter Smith sentenced several Branch Davidians to the maximum term of forty years: ten for manslaughter, plus thirty for using a machine gun.

Unlike in the *Thompson* and *Printz* cases, Halbrook had not participated in the Branch Davidian cases from the beginning. Rather, he volunteered to serve pro bono as an appellate attorney for Jamie Castillo, one of the convicted Davidians.

Federal circuit courts of appeal were split on whether the issue of machine-gun use in a federal crime was to be determined unanimously by the jury, based on a finding beyond a reasonable doubt, or decided by a judge based only on the preponderance of the evidence.

Unanimously, the Supreme Court ruled that the jury must make the finding about the machine gun (*Castillo v. United States*, 2000). The case was one of several in the late 1990s in which the Court resolved ambiguous statutes in favor of the constitutional presumption that a person should only be sentenced to time in prison based on what a jury had determined that the person actually did.

Halbrook has also been on the losing side of a variety of cases, including *Fresno Rifle and Pistol Club, Inc. v. Van de Kamp* (746 F. Supp. 1415, E.D. Cal., 1990; *affirmed* 965 F. 2d 723,

9th Cir., 1992), which was an unsuccessful challenge to California assault weapon law; and *Quilici v. Village of Morton Grove* (695 F. 2d 261, 7th Cir., 1982; 464 U.S. 863, 1983), in which Halbrook filed an amicus brief unsuccessfully arguing against the city's handgun ban. Halbrook's clients include the National Rifle Association, firearm businesses, and individuals.

Based on his extensive litigation experience, Halbrook was asked to write the *Firearms Law Deskbook: Federal and State Criminal Practice*, published annually by West Group. The book is the leading guide for attorneys in firearm litigation.

Halbrook's greatest influence, however, has been as a scholar. Had Halbrook lived in the nineteenth century, his research would have appeared as merely a restatement of the obvious. All legal scholars of the nineteenth century, and every judge (with a single exception) who wrote about the Second Amendment during the nineteenth century, regarded it as an individual right (Kopel, 1998). But by 1975, the once-obvious Second Amendment had become obscure, at least to the legal community. While polls showed that the American public continued to regard the Second Amendment as protecting an individual's right to keep and bear arms, legal scholars paid virtually no attention to the amendment, and there was almost no awareness of its original meaning.

Halbrook first appeared on the Second Amendment scene with a 1981 article in the *George Mason University Law Review*, arguing that the Second Amendment guaranteed an individual right to arms, and that the Fourteenth Amendment was intended to make that Second Amendment guarantee enforceable against the states. Halbrook elaborated on this thesis in a 1982 report for the United States Senate Subcommittee on the Constitution. The subcommittee unanimously adopted a report ("The Right to Keep and Bear Arms," reprinted in Cottrol, 1993) agreeing with both of Halbrook's claims.

Halbrook's most important scholarly contribution, however, was the book *That Every Man Be Armed*, originally published in 1986. The book was the most thorough analysis of the legal history and original intent of the Second Amendment. Since then, virtually every subject addressed by Halbrook (e.g., the American Revolution and British efforts to disarm the colonists, proposals for a Bill of Rights, nineteenth-century legal history, Reconstruction and its aftermath, twentieth-century cases) has been analyzed in much greater detail, sometimes by Halbrook himself. Even so, the book remains a starting point for many readers investigating the Second Amendment. The book is characteristic of Halbrook's general scholarly style, in that the research is meticulous, and careful review of Halbrook's sources virtually never reveals a conflict between the claim in Halbrook's text and the cited source. But, as noted in Malcolm's (1986) review of the book, Halbrook treats sources that do not fully support his thesis too gingerly rather than confronting them head-on.

Other scholarship by Halbrook has studied the origins and legal history of the right to arms in many of the eastern seaboard states, and in Texas and West Virginia. His book *Freedmen, the Fourteenth Amendment, and the Right to Bear Arms, 1866–1876,* is the most detailed examination of congressional Reconstruction, the Civil Rights Act, and the passage of the Fourteenth Amendment as they relate to Second Amendment rights. Through quote after quote, Halbrook shows that the Congress that carried out Reconstruction and sent the Fourteenth Amendment to states for ratification understood the Second Amendment as an individual right to firearms for personal protection, and voted for the Fourteenth Amendment in part to keep southern states and local governments from infringing that right.

In an article on the 1886 U.S. Supreme Court case *Presser v. Illinois,* which upheld a ban on armed public parades, Halbrook shows that the origin of the antiparade law was a determination by Illinois' governing class to suppress demonstrations by working people.

More recently, Halbrook has turned much of his research attention to European history. In *Target Switzerland,* which has been translated into French and German, Halbrook examines the impact of the Swiss militia system on World War II. He shows how the universal armament policy of the Swiss deterred (if only barely) a German invasion at various stages during the war. He also points out that because control of the Swiss army was widely distributed (in the sense that all able-bodied adult males were active members of the militia), Switzerland was not vulnerable to the problems of France, the Low Countries, or other European nations that had centralized standing armies, and whose national elites quickly surrendered the army to advancing Nazi forces.

Currently, Halbrook is researching German and Nazi firearm laws and how they were implemented to disarm Jews and other opponents of Hitler. This research reflects Halbrook's longest-running theme: gun control is used by dominant groups to suppress their victims. These victims range from colonial Patriots to ex-slaves to workingmen to Jews, depending on the time and place.

Both in print and in oral argument, Halbrook's style is methodical and straightforward rather than flashy or brilliantly creative. His contribution has not been to create new Second Amendment theory but rather to return scholarly attention to matters that had been familiar in their own time but have since been neglected.

Halbrook has twice won first place in revolver shooting in the National North-South Skirmish Association, a competitive shooting association that uses Civil War–era firearms. His law practice is located in Fairfax, Virginia.

David B. Kopel

See also *Fresno Rifle and Pistol Club, Inc. v. Van de Kamp; Presser v. Illinois; Printz v. United States; Quilici v. Village of Morton Grove;* Switzerland, Gun Laws

For Further Reading:

Cottrol, Robert J., ed. 1993. *Gun Control and the Constitution: Sources and Explorations on the Second Amendment.* New York: Garland.

Halbrook, Stephen P. 1995. *Firearms Law Deskbook: Federal and State Criminal Practice.* Deerfield, IL: Clark Boardman Callaghan.

———. 1998. *Freedmen, the Fourteenth Amendment, and the Right to Bear Arms, 1866–1876.* Westport, CT: Praeger.

———. 2000a. *That Every Man Be Armed.* Oakland, CA: Independent Institute.

———. 2000b. *Target Switzerland: Swiss Armed Neutrality in World War II.* Rockville Centre, NY: Sarpedon.

———. 2001. Website: http://www. stephenhalbrook.com/.

Kopel, David B. 1998. "The Second Amendment in the Nineteenth Century." *Brigham Young University Law Review* 1998: 1359–1545.

Malcolm, Joyce. 1986. "Review of *That Every Man Be Armed.*" *George Washington University Law Review* 54: 582.

Hamilton v. Accu-Tek

See Lawsuits against Gun Manufacturers

Hammer, Marion P. (1939–)

Marion Hammer is executive director of Unified Sportsmen of Florida, a position she has held since 1978. She is past president of the National Rifle Association of America (NRA), the first woman in the NRA's history to hold that office.

She learned to shoot and hunt at age 5, taught by her grandfather, who helped raise her after her father was killed in action at Okinawa during World War II. She was elected to the NRA's Board of Directors in 1982, to its vice presidency in 1992, and to its presidency in 1996 and 1997. She currently serves on its board and its Executive Committee and was elected for life to its Executive Council. The NRA Foundation honored her by naming its award for distinguished philanthropy by a woman the Marion P. Hammer Award. At the NRA, she emphasized the education of youth in firearm safety and use, and during her presidency she broke ground for construction of the NRA National Firearms Museum.

In 1993 the National Safety Council presented her with its Outstanding Community Service Award for creating the NRA Eddie Eagle gun safety program. In 1997, she received the Outstanding Woman Achievement Award from the Florida secretary of state and in 1985 she became the only woman to win the Roy Rogers Man of the Year award. In 1996, the American Legion presented to Hammer its National Education Award for the Eddie Eagle program.

In Florida, Hammer was the force behind passage of Florida's landmark right-to-carry law, which provided for liberal issuance of concealed-firearm-carry permits to law-abiding citizens, and which became a model for legislation in dozens of other states.

A public speaker and media spokesperson for the NRA, Hammer has been featured in many profiles in newspapers and national magazines, including *People* and *George*. On television, she has been prominently featured on A&E's *Biography*, CBS's *60 Minutes*, ABC's *Nightline*, NBC's *Today Show*, the *Oprah Winfrey Show*, and CNN.

David T. Hardy

See also Eddie Eagle; National Rifle Association; Right-to-Carry Laws

For Further Reading:

Howard, Susan. 2001. "In Search of Remarkable Women." http://www.obrpc.org/women/remarkable_women.htm.

"Marion P. Hammer." 2001. http://www.nrawinningteam.com/hammer.html.

Handgun Control, Inc.

See Brady Campaign to Prevent Gun Violence

Handguns

A handgun is a short firearm that can be held and fired with one hand. The two main types are revolvers and semiautomatic pistols. According to the National Survey of Private Ownership of Firearms, handguns make up about one-third of the privately owned firearms in the United States and are present in about one-quarter of households. Most owners cite self-defense as their primary reason for owning a handgun. Other reasons for handgun ownership include target shooting and job-related needs. A relatively small number of people also collect handguns or hunt with them (Cook and Ludwig, 1996).

The distinctive feature of handguns is their small size, which makes them handy, concealable, and portable. Compared to rifles, handguns gain the advantages associated with small size at the expense of range, accuracy, and lethality. Although many rifles are accurate to ranges of 300 yards or more, it is difficult to hit targets with even the most accurate handguns beyond about 50 yards. Also, although all handgun cartridges have the potential to cause lethal injury, handgun rounds cause less damage than most rifle rounds.

Advertisement in the Saturday Evening Post, *1912, showing a woman with a pistol and purse and a man holding a pistol in his vest. (Library of Congress)*

A deer hunter wears his handgun while playing poker at hunters' camp. (National Archives)

The same features that make handguns useful for self-defense also make them useful in criminal acts. In the late 1990s, approximately 65 percent of murders were committed with firearms, and approximately 80 percent of those (or half the total number of murders) were committed with handguns (Federal Bureau of Investigation, 2000).

The main parts of a handgun are the frame, to which the other parts are attached and which may be made of polymer, steel, or other metal; the barrel, which is made of steel; the grip, where the gun is held and which may be made of polymer, plastic, or wood; the sights, used to point the weapon at the intended target; and the action, which causes the weapon to fire when the trigger is pulled and which includes the slide on semiautomatic pistols and the cylinder on revolvers. In modern handguns, as well as rifles and shotguns, a cartridge (which consists of a bullet mounted in a case—usually brass—with gunpowder and a primer) is inserted in the firing chamber at the breech, or rear end of the barrel. When the trigger is pulled, the firing pin is allowed to strike the primer, igniting the powder, which propels the bullet down the barrel. In almost all modern small arms except shotguns, the barrel is rifled with spiral grooves running its entire length to make the bullet spin. This prevents the bullet from tumbling in flight, increasing accuracy over longer distances.

Handgun Types

The three main varieties of modern handguns are single-shot pistols, revolvers, and semiautomatic pistols. (Although revolvers are frequently called pistols and semiautomatics are sometimes called automatics, neither usage is technically correct.) Single-shot pistols find specialized use in target shooting, hunting, and as very small self-defense weapons, and are much less common than revolvers or semiautomatics. Revolvers hold several rounds—usually six—in chambers bored in a rotating cylinder located at the breech of the barrel. Before each shot is fired the cylinder is rotated to bring the next chamber in line with the barrel for firing. Cylinder rotation is accomplished by cocking the hammer. This can be done manually or, in double-action revolvers (see below), merely by pulling the trigger. Semiautomatic pistols hold rounds in a magazine inside the butt, or handle. Magazine capacities vary, but most hold between seven and seventeen rounds. When the pistol's slide is pulled back and allowed to move forward under spring pressure, the action advances a round from the magazine into the firing chamber and the pistol is ready to fire. When a round is fired, energy from the shot pushes the slide back, ejecting the empty cartridge that was just fired; the spring then pushes the slide forward again and loads the next cartridge.

Since the ammunition magazine of most pistols fits in the butt (or handle), revolver butts can be smaller than pistol butts, making them more comfortable for shooters with small hands to grasp. Revolvers have an edge in reliability and often are easier for beginners to use because of their simplicity. Semiautomatics have greater magazine capacity, are easier for most shooters to reload quickly, can be fired a little bit faster than revolvers, and, depending on configuration, may have a lighter trigger. Shooters who wish to maximize simplicity and reliability usually opt for a revolver; those who wish to maximize the number of rounds available to fire usually will choose a semiautomatic.

Triggers
Handguns are available with three main types of triggers: single action (SA), double action (DA), and double action only (DAO). An SA trigger does one thing: it releases the hammer, causing the bullet in the firing chamber to fire. However, in order for the hammer to be in position to strike, it must first be cocked. On a single-action revolver, the hammer must be cocked by hand before firing each round. On a single-action semiautomatic pistol, the gun must be cocked by hand before the first round is fired (which can be accomplished by working the slide to chamber the first round). When the gun is fired the semiautomatic action will load the next round and cock the weapon. Double-action triggers perform two functions: they cock the gun and release the hammer to fire it. On a DA revolver, the trigger cocks the hammer, rotates the cylinder, and releases the hammer. On a DA semiautomatic pistol, when a round is fired the mechanism automatically loads the next round and cocks the hammer, so after the first round the trigger functions as single action. This is significant because the single-action trigger pull is lighter than the double-action trigger, so DA pistols have relatively

heavy trigger pulls on the first shot and lighter pulls on subsequent shots. For example, while a double-action trigger might require 6 to 12 pounds of pressure to fire, a single-action trigger might require only 3 to 5 pounds of pressure. Some shooters who prefer a consistent trigger pull for all shots opt for a DAO trigger, which provides the convenience of double action along with the consistency of uniform trigger weight.

A lighter trigger makes it easier to shoot accurately because light pressure on the trigger makes it less likely that the gun will be pulled off aim while firing, so single action is preferred for target pistols. However, lighter triggers may also increase the chance of an accidental discharge, and single action is sometimes more cumbersome to operate, so double action is often preferred for defensive weapons.

Ammunition
Ammunition is described in terms of its caliber, which is approximately equal to the diameter of the bullet and of the inside of the barrel from which the bullet is intended to be fired. The 9 mm, the .38 Special, the .357 Magnum, and the .380 ACP all fire bullets approximately 9 mm (or .355 inch) in diameter from barrels of approximately the same diameter. Ten-millimeter ammunition is about 10 mm in diameter, .22 caliber ammunition is about .22 inch in diameter, and so forth. Whether caliber is expressed in British or metric units merely reflects the decisions of the designers.

One of the most common types of ammunition is the .22 Long Rifle (which, despite its name and despite its use in long guns, is a low-power handgun cartridge). The .22 is well suited for target shooting because it is inexpensive, accurate (when used in an accurate firearm), and generates very little recoil. It is generally considered a poor choice for defensive use because of its small size. Among the most popular cartridges for defensive use are the 9 mm Parabellum (also known as the 9 x 19 mm and 9 mm Luger, or simply the 9 mm), the .38 Special, the .357 Magnum, the .40 Smith & Wesson, and the .45 ACP. All of these cartridges have adequate penetration and bullet diameter to provide a reasonable chance of promptly incapacitating an attacker. Other common cartridges include the .25 ACP, the .32 ACP, and the .380 ACP, which, along with the .22, are frequently used in Saturday night specials and other relatively compact handguns but are less effective for self-defense use than the larger calibers.

Lethality

When a weapon is used in self-defense, the shooter's goal is to promptly incapacitate an assailant. Contrary to the images of handgun use frequently portrayed in entertainment media, handgun bullets generally do not cause incapacitation by knocking people down and killing them instantly. Incapacitation occurs as a result of blood loss, central nervous system damage (when bullets hit the brain or spinal cord), and psychological factors, and the first and last of these may take considerable time. Bullets also do not knock people backwards to any significant degree. They could not be expected to, since they deliver approximately the same amount of momentum to the target as the shooter experiences as recoil. (The momentum of a 9 mm bullet is roughly equal to the momentum of a 10-pound weight dropped from a height of three-quarters of an inch, hardly enough to knock people down regularly.) Although all handgun rounds have the potential to cause lethal injury, most people who are shot with handguns survive. That said, of the 12,658 murders committed in the United States in 1999, more than half (6,498) were carried out with a handgun (51 percent). The second most common choice of weapon, a long gun (rifle or shotgun), was relatively rare in comparison—with 890 murders committed with long guns (7 percent).

Matthew DeBell

See also Long Gun; Saturday Night Specials; TEC-DC9 Pistol; Uniform Crime Reports

For Further Reading:

Cook, Philip J., and Jens Ludwig. 1996. *Guns in America: Results of a Comprehensive National Survey on Firearms Ownership and Use.* Washington, DC: Police Foundation.

Ezell, Edward C. 1981. *Handguns of the World.* Harrisburg, PA: Stackpole Books.

Federal Bureau of Investigation. 2000. *Crime in the United States, 1999.* Washington, DC: Federal Bureau of Investigation.

Handguns Magazine

See Gun Magazines

Health Care Professionals

It is difficult if not impossible and inappropriate to make broad assumptions about any group defined by one characteristic, particularly in the field of employment. Health care professionals (HCPs) are a diverse lot. They include physicians, dentists, nurses, scientists, technicians, and others. Also, the demographic makeup of these groups varies substantially, including by race and ethnicity, education, sex, and income.

Health care employees also have varying opinions on many if not most important topical issues (not just on firearms), and probably are as susceptible to media influence as the general population. Although many of the professional organizations to which HCPs belong have taken antigun positions, the levels of agreement between the members and the organizations are not known.

There is a surprising lack of information and knowledge about gun-related attitudes among HCPs, but some data are available on the prevalence of firearm ownership. Cassel et al. (1998) interviewed 915 members of the American College of Physicians (ACP) and the American College of Surgeons (ACS). Most of the respondents accepted the dominant epidemiological paradigm (DEP) related to firearms and most agreed that firearm violence was a public health issue. Support for the DEP was greatest among respondents who had little exposure to guns and who belonged to gun control organizations. These people tended to be female, younger, and currently practicing in large cities. Those who accepted the DEP tended to believe that it is appropriate to offer counseling on firearm safety, to believe the medical literature on guns, to think that physicians should be involved in firearm injury prevention, and to think that violence prevention should be a priority for physicians. This concern was not reflected in actual practice, however, as few of these HCPs currently include firearm safety counseling in their clinical practice. Not surprisingly, most thought that gun control legislation will reduce the risks of injury and death from firearms. Restricting access to high-capacity, rapid-fire weapons, dangerous new forms of firearms and handguns, and registration of handguns were favored.

Guglielmo (2000) published a survey of gun ownership among physicians, reporting that 32 percent of the respondents owned a gun. This estimate for physicians is identical to that for the general population (General Social Survey, 2000). The level of ownership varied by a number of factors: it was higher among males and married physicians than among females and single physicians; it increased with age; and it was highest among Protestants and Catholics. Medical specialty was also associated with gun ownership: it was highest among orthopedic surgeons and lowest among pediatricians.

Several other studies have examined the prevalence of gun ownership among physicians and other health care workers, and they report levels of ownership that are quite high. Fargason and Johnston (1995) found that 50 percent of surveyed pediatricians reported owning a gun, and that 34 percent had a handgun in their household. They also surveyed trauma center workers (Fargason and Johnston, 1994) and found that 65 percent owned a gun and 56 percent owned a handgun. Goldberg, Whitlock, and Greenlick (1996) surveyed 6,436 nonphysician employees of a large health maintenance organization and asked two questions about firearm ownership and storage practices. Forty-two percent of those surveyed reported keeping a firearm in their home. Price and Oden (1999) surveyed health directors in cities with populations greater than 60,000 and were surprised to find that 34.8 percent owned firearms.

In short, in spite of the antigun positions taken by many medical associations and organizations, members of the professions own firearms at levels similar to, and in some cases even higher than, the general U.S. population. The implications of this are not clear, but it may be that the organizations do not reflect the true beliefs and attitudes of the members. If this is the case, then antigun positions taken by such organizations should not necessarily be considered an accurate reflection of the opinions of members of the profession.

David Cowan

See also American Academy of Pediatrics; American Medical Association; Association of American Physicians and Surgeons; Centers for Disease Control; Doctors for Integrity in Policy Research; Gun Violence as a Public Health Problem; Hemenway, David; Kellermann, Arthur L.; Medicine and Gun Violence; Motor Vehicle Laws as a Model for Gun Laws; Physicians for Social Responsibility; Victimization from Gun Violence

For Further Reading:
Cassel, Christine K., Elizabeth A. Nelson, Tom W. Smith, C. William Schwab, Barbara Barlow, and Nancey E. Gary. 1998. "Internists' and Surgeons' Attitudes toward Guns and Firearm Injury Prevention." *Annals of Internal Medicine* 128 (February 1): 224–230.

Fargason, Crayton A., Jr., and Carden Johnston. 1994. "Gun Safety Practices of Trauma Center Workers in a Southern City." *Southern Medical Journal* 87, 10 (October): 965–970.

_____. 1995. "Gun Ownership and Counseling of Alabama Pediatricians." *Archives of Pediatric and Adolescent Medicine* 149, 4 (April): 442–446.

General Social Survey. 2000. "Do you happen to have in your home (or garage) any guns or revolvers? If yes, Is it a pistol, shotgun, rifle, or what?" Inter-University Consortium for Political and Social Research. http://www.icpsr.umich.edu/GSS/.

Goldberg, Bruce W., Evelyn Whitlock, and Merwyn Greenlick. 1996. "Firearm Ownership and Health Care Workers." *Public Health Report* 111, 3 (May–June): 256–259.

Guglielmo, Wayne J. 2000. "How Many Doctors Own Guns?" *Medical Economics* 19 (October 9): 151. http://Me.pdr.net/be_core/search/show_article_search.jsp?searchurl=/be_core/content/journals/m/data/2000/1009/0l_guns.html&navtype=m&heading=m&title=How@many@doctors@own@guns?

Price, James H., and Lorette Oden. 1999. "Reducing Firearm Injuries: The Role of Local Public Departments." *Public Health Reports* 114: 533–539.

HELP Network

The Handgun Epidemic Lowering Plan (HELP) Network is an international group of medical and allied organizations formed in 1993 for the purpose of reducing firearm-related deaths and injuries, especially from handgun use. HELP has over 100 organizational members that include the American Academy of Pediatrics, the American College of Physicians, the American Society of Internal Medicine, the American Academy of Child and Adolescent Psychiatry, the Child Welfare League of America, and the American Medical Association. Members also include a variety of local medical groups and numerous antigun lobbying and educational organizations.

HELP believes that deaths and injuries from handgun use have reached epidemic proportions in the United States. It views this situation as a "man-made plague" and a major public health emergency, no less threatening than any medical disease. According to HELP, the best available evidence shows that guns endanger their owners and those around them far more often than they protect them. Furthermore, guns are not only a crime problem but cause mental and physical harm, lead to the expenditure of large amounts of medical resources, and are the most dangerous of products—yet they remain unregulated.

Among HELP's policy goals are reducing civilian access to handguns and handgun ammunition; developing tracking systems for handgun injuries and the firearms used in crimes; and mandating personalized gun technology (designed so that guns can only be fired by their owners).

HELP also works to support the research and prevention activities of the National Center for Injury Prevention and Control of the Centers for Disease Control (CDC), and CDC speakers sometimes appear at HELP events. In 1996, the CDC rescinded a grant that it had given HELP after CDC critics in Congress pointed out that the money had been used to produce a newsletter that urged readers to lobby for gun control.

HELP believes that certain strategies are useful in reducing the public health toll from firearm injuries: mobilization of health professionals to provide clinical counseling, advocacy, and public education on the "gun epidemic"; the use of litigation to target the design and distribution of firearms; and the mobilization of survivors of firearm-related incidents to keep public attention focused on the need to prevent future incidents.

HELP's medical director is Dr. Katherine Kaufer Christoffel, a pediatrician. Christoffel believes that firearm injuries can be reduced through a variety of measures, including requiring waiting periods for gun purchases; placing restrictions on purchases of assault weapons (guns that look like military weapons); making the use of trigger locks and other safety devices mandatory; increasing taxation on firearms and ammunition; requiring firearm registration and licensure of gun owners; modifying ammunition to reduce its lethality and the severity of nonfatal injuries; adding safety features to handguns such as triggers that require greater force to activate them, highly visible loaded-gun indicators, and automatic safety locks on triggers; and banning the possession of all handguns in locations where children live and visit.

In a 1994 interview with *American Medical News,* Christoffel stated: "Guns are a virus that must be eradicated.They are causing an epidemic of death by gunshot, which should be treated like any epidemic—you get rid of the virus.... Get rid of the guns, get rid of the bullets, and you get rid of the deaths."

However, the parallel made between firearm-related violence and medical disease by Christoffel and others in the HELP Network has been criticized as an illogical extension of the disease model. The criticism is based on the fact that firearm-related violence does not meet the criteria of a true disease, susceptible to treatment using epidemiological methods.

The pathogen model of disease was first put forth by German bacteriologist Robert Koch (1843–1910). "Koch's postulates" establish the relationship between a microorganism and a disease: (1) the microorganism must be regularly isolated from cases of the specific illness; (2) the microorganism must be able to be grown in a culture medium outside the diseased host; (3) the susceptible host must be inoculated with the microorganism that has been isolated from the culture medium, and the disease must result; (4) the microorganism must be able to be again isolated from the inoculated host. (Koch's postulates were later modified for other infections, particularly viral diseases, but the principles remain essentially the same.)

Critics of the "guns are a virus" theory argue that if a scientist "inoculates" a host with a firearm (e.g., gives someone a gun), the "host" may come down with the "disease" of "violence." But the vast majority of gun owners do not perpetrate gun violence. Most gun owners who commit violence showed signs of the "disease" of "violence" prior to being "inoculated" with a firearm. If one gives a violence-prone person a baseball bat, a knife, or a gun, the person might use any of the weapons to commit violence; although the weapon would be a tool of violence, it would not be the "cause" of violence. A germ or virus causes an otherwise healthy person to become sick; a gun (or knife or bat) does not cause an otherwise peaceful person to become violent.

To take the analogy further, as Professor Max von Pettenkofer proved when he drank a cup of cholera germs, germs can only cause infection if there is a susceptible population and a suitable environment. HELP's critics contend that the group pays far too little attention to factors that make some people—but not the majority of the American population—susceptible to violence. The critics argue that if guns were truly disease agents like deadly viruses, we could expect tens of millions of America's gun owners to be dead or dying because of the guns in their homes. Instead, almost all of the more than 70 million gun owners escape injury because they are responsible and safety-conscious stewards of a tool that can be used for good purposes, not only for bad ones. Critics suggest that a better analogy would be to consider private firearm ownership a vaccine against violent crime because of its protective and deterrent value.

HELP provides a variety of publications for both its members and the public (especially health professionals, the media, and policymakers), such as newsletters, fact sheets, and brochures. The HELP Network holds a national conference every twelve to twenty-four months for the purpose of devising strategies for reducing firearm injuries, as well as for sharing new research on public health approaches to firearm injury prevention. Since its inception, it has held seven such conferences, most recently in October 2002. Among the speakers at HELP events have been various officials from the Centers for Disease Control.

Paul Gallant and Joanne D. Eisen

See also American Academy of Pediatrics; American Medical Association; Centers for Disease Control

For Further Information:

Children's Memorial Hospital, HELP Network, 2300 Children's Plaza, #88, Chicago, IL 60614, (773) 880–3826. http://www.helpnetwork.org.

For Further Reading:

Christoffel, Katherine K. 1991. "Toward Reducing Pediatric Injuries from Firearms: Charting a Legislative and Regulatory Course." *Pediatrics* 88, 2: 294–305.

Doctors for Responsible Gun Ownership, Claremont Institute, 250 W. First Street, Suite 330, Claremont, CA 91711, (909) 621–6825. http://www.claremont.org/1_drgo.cfm.

Kates, Don B., Henry E. Schaffer, and William C. Waters. 1997. "Sick of Guns: The Centers for Disease Control's Campaign against Gun Ownership." *Reason* (April): 24–29.

Marwick, Charles. 1999. "HELP Network Says Firearms Data Gap Makes Reducing Gun Injuries More Difficult." *Journal of the American Medical Association* 281, 9: 784–785.

Suter, Edgar A., William C. Waters, George B. Murray, et al. 1995. "Violence in America: Effective Solutions." *Journal of the Medical Association of Georgia* (June): 253–263.

Hemenway, David (1945–)

David Hemenway is a professor of health policy at Harvard's School of Public Health. A major exponent of the public health approach to reducing injury, he is helping to lead the efforts to create a National Violent Death Reporting System for the United States, a system that will provide consistent, comparable, and detailed information about every suicide, homicide, and accidental gun death.

Hemenway received his Ph.D. in economics at Harvard in 1974 and has since written four books and ninety journal articles. His injury research includes work on falls and fractures, fires, drownings, motor vehicle crashes, child abuse, suicides, and homicides.

His career in the injury field began more than three decades ago when he worked for Ralph Nader and Consumers Union. In the early 1980s he started the first class at Harvard on injury prevention. He has won more teaching awards at the Harvard School of Public Health than any other faculty member.

Hemenway is currently director of both the Harvard Injury Control Research Center and the Harvard Youth Violence Prevention Center. He has been head of the Injury Council of the National Association of Public Health Policy and is past president of the National Association of Injury Control Research Centers. He was a Pew Fellow on Injury Control and a Soros Senior Justice Fellow, and he received a Robert Wood Johnson Investigator Award to study firearm violence.

His research on fatalities shows that the developed countries with higher levels of firearm ownership have higher rates of homicide for both men and women due to higher rates of firearm homicide. His U.S. studies show that states with higher rates of household gun ownership have substantially higher levels of suicides, homicides, and accidental firearm fatalities. These findings also hold separately for females, children, the middle-aged, and the elderly.

Some of his research findings come from surveys of students, criminals, and the general U.S. population. From national surveys, he discovered that many gun owners report storing their firearms loaded and unlocked, and that firearm training is associated with an increased likelihood of such storage practices. He found that the vast majority of Americans, including the majority of gun owners and National Rifle Association members, favor many reasonable gun policies, which have yet to be enacted. He found that respondents to national surveys report feeling less safe as other people obtain or carry firearms, and that less than 10 percent of the population wants regular citizens to be able to carry guns into bars, restaurants, sports stadiums, hospitals, or government buildings.

Some of his best-known and contentious findings deal with self-defense gun use. He has shown that criminal gun use is far more common than self-defense gun use, and that self-defense gun use is often aggressive gun use in an escalating argument. Purported self-defense gun uses have been assessed by criminologists and criminal court judges as usually being illegal acts that harm the social welfare. Hemenway has argued that the methodology used to claim that more than a million Americans use guns each year in actual self-defense could also be used to claim that almost a million Americans have personally been in contact with aliens from other planets.

Roseanna Ander

See also Defensive Gun Use; Gun Violence as a Public Health Problem; Kellermann, Arthur L.; Kleck, Gary; Medicine and Gun Violence; Victimization from Gun Violence

For Further Reading:

Hemenway, David. 1997. "Survey Research and Self-Defense Gun Use: An Explanation of Extreme Overestimates." *Journal of Criminal Law and Criminology* 87: 1430–1445.

———. 2002. "The Public Health Approach to Motor Vehicles, Tobacco and Alcohol, with Applications to Firearm Policy." *Journal of Public Health Policy* 22: 381–402.

Hemenway, David, Deborah Azrael, and Matthew Miller. 2001. "U.S. National Attitudes Concerning Gun Carrying in the United States." *Injury Prevention* 7: 282–285.

Hemenway, David, and Matthew Miller. 2000. "Firearm Availability and Homicide Rates across 26 High-Income Countries." *Journal of Trauma* 49: 985–988.

Hemenway, David, Matthew Miller, and Deborah Azrael. 2000. "Gun Use in the United States: Results from Two National Surveys." *Injury Prevention* 6: 263–267.

Hemenway, David, Deborah Prothrow-Stith, Jack M. Bergstein, Roseanna Ander, and Bruce Kennedy. 1996. "Gun Carrying among Adolescents." *Law and Contemporary Problems* 59: 39–53.

Hemenway, David, Sara J. Solnick, and Deborah Azrael. 1995. "Firearm Training and Storage." *Journal of the American Medical Association* 273: 46–50.

Miller, Matthew, Deborah Azrael, and David Hemenway. 2002. "Firearm Availability and Unintentional Firearm Deaths, Suicide and Homicide among Women." *Journal of Urban Health* 79: 26–38.

Herbert, Henry William (1807–1858)

Henry William Herbert, the grandson of an English earl, became the great popularizer of sport hunting in antebellum America. Prior to Herbert, the term "sportsman" smacked of card playing and horse racing, but after him the term was applied to respectable professionals and businessmen who practiced "the wholesome, exhilarating excitements" of hunting and fishing, his friend and biographer, Thomas Picton, commented (Picton, 1882a, p. 10).

Upon immigrating to New York in 1831, Herbert became one of the so-called remittance men who received regular funds from their families in England. Because of his birth, his accomplishments in Greek and Latin, and his love of field sports, Herbert was soon befriended by young New Yorkers from elite families. Herbert meanwhile sought to make a name for himself by writing historical romances and poetry. Though he failed to achieve his goal of becoming a respected litterateur, he soon gained fame as a chronicler of sport. Under the pseudonym "Frank Forester," Herbert wrote numerous articles for William Trotter Porter's *Spirit of the Times* as well as for other periodicals. In the early 1840s, Herbert collected a number of his hunting sketches in *The Warwick Woodlands, or Things as They Were Ten Years Ago* (1845). The book sold well and was followed by other titles, including *Frank Forester's Field Sports of the United States and British Provinces of North America* (1849), *American Game in Its Seasons* (1853), and *The Complete Manual for Young Sportsmen ... With Directions for Handling the Gun, the Rifle, and the Rod* (1856).

What gave Herbert a wide readership among the middle and upper classes of the United States was his identification of hunting and field sports with virtue. Herbert argued that hunting would prevent "the demoralization of luxury" and "the growth of effeminacy and sloth" and ensure "the maintenance of a little manhood in an age, the leading characteristics of which are fanaticism, cant, and hypocrisy" (Herbert, 1849, pp. 26–27). Hunting, argued Herbert, had made English aristocrats strong of body and mind. The propensity to hunt, indeed, was a genetic trait of the "warrior and hunter races" of northern Europe whose descendants had populated North America. "Wherever a drop is to be found of that fierce Northern blood surviving in people's

Henry William Herbert, c. 1844–1860. (Library of Congress)

veins," wrote Herbert, "there you will find, and in no other land, the passion for the chase alive and dominant" (Herbert, 1865, p. 22).

In earlier decades, as Herbert noted, many middling and elite Americans (at least in the North) had frowned on sport hunting because it reeked of both Indian savagery and aristocratic luxury. Herbert's hyperbole, however, was welcomed by a new generation of Americans who were annexing a continent and engaging in a market revolution and yet leaving behind the old Jeffersonian virtues of a nation of small farmers. The secret of Herbert's success—though he may not have recognized it—was that he gave American men a dual identity. Through hunting and through reading about the hunting exploits of others, Herbert's readers could identify both with backwoodsmen like Daniel Boone and with sons of aristocracy like Henry William Herbert. They could be, in short, both egalitarian and elitist; both traditional and modern; both rough and genteel. Through hunting, moreover, Herbert's admirers surmounted the fears of "effeminacy" that plagued men who worked with pen rather than plow.

Herbert's love of hunting, however, did not save him from tragedy. After being abandoned by his second wife (his first wife had died decades earlier), Herbert shot himself in a New York hotel room in 1858. Though his suicide cast a pall on his reputation, many of his works were reprinted throughout the second half of the nineteenth century. By associating hunting with manly virtues, Herbert helped make sport hunting both ubiquitous and beloved among American men of the upper and upper-middle classes in the late nineteenth and early twentieth centuries.

Daniel Justin Herman

See also Hunting
For Further Reading:

Herbert, Henry William [Frank Forester, pseud.]. 1849. *Frank Forester's Field Sports of the United States and British Provinces of North America.* Vol. 1. New York: Stringer & Townsend.

———. 1853. *American Game in Its Seasons.* New York: Charles Scribner.

———. 1865. *The Complete Manual for Young Sportsmen: With Directions for Handling the Gun, the Rifle, and the Rod.* New York: Stringer & Townsend.

Herman, Daniel Justin. 2001. *Hunting and the American Imagination.* Washington, DC: Smithsonian Institution Press.

Hunt, William Southworth. 1933. *Frank Forester [Henry William Herbert]: A Tragedy in Exile.* Newark, NJ: Carteret Book Club.

Newark Herbert Association. 1876. *Newark Herbert Association to "Frank Forester." In Memoriam, May 19, 1876.* Newark, NJ: Newark Herbert Association.

Picton, Thomas. 1882a. "Henry William Herbert [Frank Forester]: The Story of His Life." In *Life and Writings of Frank Forester (Henry William Herbert.),* vol. 1, ed. David W. Judd. New York: Orange Judd Co.

———. 1882b. "Herbert's Personal Characteristics." In *Life and Writings of Frank Forester (Henry William Herbert.),* vol. 1, ed. David W. Judd. New York: Orange Judd Co.

Smith, Harry Worcester. 1930. "Henry William Herbert. Frank Forester." In Henry William Herbert [Frank Forester, pseud.], *The Deerstalkers, The Hitchcock Edition of Frank Forester,* vol. 4. New York: Derrydale Press.

Van Winkle, William Mitchell, comp., with David A. Randall. 1971. *Henry William Herbert (Frank Forester): A Bibliography of His Writings, 1832–1858.* New York: Ben Franklin.

White, Luke. 1943. *Henry William Herbert and the American Publishing Industry, 1831–1858.* Newark, NJ: Carteret Book Club.

Heston, Charlton (1923–)

Academy Award–winning actor, star of over 100 films and theatrical productions, former president of the Screen Actors Guild, and civil rights activist, Charlton Heston was elected president of the National Rifle Association at its 1998 convention. Since then, Heston has been the NRA's public face, championing the right to keep and bear arms and presenting the NRA as a mainstream, all-American organization.

Heston was born John Charlton Carter on October 4, 1923, in Evanston, Illinois, but he spent his formative years in Michigan after his mother divorced Heston's father and married Chester Heston, a timber mill owner. Heston attended Northwestern University in Evanston on an acting scholarship, and there he majored in speech and drama. At Northwestern he met Lydia Clarke, whom he married in 1944. He served in the Army Air Corps during World War II. Heston then went to Hollywood, where he enjoyed immense success as an actor. Among Heston's most notable films were *Ben-Hur,* for which he won the Academy Award for Best Actor in 1959, and *The Ten Commandments,* in which he portrayed Moses.

Though Heston is today closely identified with conservative causes and groups, such as the NRA, he, like fellow actor Ronald Reagan, began as a Democrat. Heston was a strong supporter of the civil rights movement and participated in Dr. Martin Luther King's 1963 March on Washington. Perhaps more surprisingly, Heston once publicly supported federal gun control legislation. In 1968, when President Lyndon Johnson was trying to push gun control legislation through Congress (a compromise version of which became the Gun Control Act of 1968), the White House enlisted the support of various "cowboy" actors to endorse gun control. Among the actors who endorsed the White House gun control proposal was Charlton Heston. Years later, when asked about his support for gun control, Heston said that he had changed his mind

NRA President Charlton Heston raises a Revolutionary War–era musket at the 2000 annual NRA meeting. (Getty Images)

about gun control after he became a supporter of Barry Goldwater's presidential campaign. Goldwater, however, was the Republican presidential nominee in 1964, four years before Heston endorsed the White House gun control plan.

Already an Honorary Life Member of the NRA, Heston became an NRA officer against the backdrop of a political struggle within the group. The NRA's chief operating officer, Executive Vice President Wayne LaPierre, was being challenged by Neal Knox, who was then serving as the NRA's second vice president. As second vice president, Knox was in line to become first vice president and eventually president of the National Rifle Association. (The first and second vice presidents and the president are unpaid positions. The executive vice president is a full-time, salaried staff position.) In an early 1997 NRA board meeting, LaPierre's group narrowly turned back a challenge from Knox supporters. The Knox group had argued that LaPierre's financial management of the group was deficient and that LaPierre was sometimes too willing to compromise on gun rights issues.

At the 1997 NRA convention, Heston was a candidate for the seventy-sixth director position and won the race overwhelmingly. (Under the NRA's bylaws, one member of the seventy-six-member Board of Directors is elected by all members who attend its annual convention.) Shortly thereafter, the Board of Directors met and elected Heston first vice president over Neal Knox. Subsequently, Heston was elected president of the National Rifle Association. In 2001, the organization modified its bylaws to allow Heston to exceed the ordinary term limits. He was elected to a third one-year term in 2001 and to a fourth term in 2002. Heston used his presidential authority, such as the power to appoint committee members, to remove Knox supporters from positions of power. Within the NRA, Heston has played an important role in solidifying Wayne LaPierre's day-to-day control of the organization.

As the NRA's most visible spokesman, Heston has played a major role in LaPierre's campaign to present the NRA as a mainstream organization. Heston has campaigned tirelessly for NRA-supported candidates, usually attracting large crowds. In addition, he speaks frequently on college campuses, urging students to stand up for their free-speech rights and not to be afraid to be vocal when speaking their minds.

His campus speeches are sometimes met with efforts by school administrators or campus groups to prevent the speech from taking place, such as at Brandeis University, where the administration imposed requirements on Heston that had not been required for other controversial speakers.

Heston's celebrity status allows him to raise issues to a much higher degree of visibility than the NRA could ordinarily achieve. For example, when Heston challenged gun control advocate Barbra Streisand to a debate on the Second Amendment, the challenge was reported in newspapers nationwide (Streisand declined the invitation). On another occasion, early in 2000, the NRA ran a series of paid advertisements featuring Heston accusing then-President Clinton of lying when he accused the NRA of being unconcerned with public safety.

A common theme in Heston's writings and speeches is that gun ownership by law-abiding citizens helps reduce crime. Instead of enacting more gun control laws that don't work, Heston argues, we should seek solutions to broken families and a flawed criminal justice system. He is also seeking to increase the NRA's membership among women and minorities.

Heston's critics fall into two major camps. Within the gun rights movement, some activists criticize Heston for not being fully informed on issues—especially in appearances on Sunday morning television interview programs and the like—and for making misstatements as a result. Most of these critics, however, concede that when delivering a speech, Heston is probably unsurpassed as a defender of Second Amendment rights. Gun control advocates, well aware of Heston's role in presenting the NRA as a core element of the American mainstream, have conducted their own countercampaign to portray Heston as an extremist.

Thus far, criticism of Heston from either perspective does not appear to have made a great impact. Heston has played a significant role in the NRA's membership growth to a new high of over 4 million members. He also played a major role in the NRA's successful political efforts in the 2000 elections. In the late 1980s and early 1990s it could be said that Sarah Brady was indispensable to the gun control cause, as she led her organization, the Brady Campaign to Prevent Gun Violence (formerly known as Handgun Control, Inc.), to new levels of political achievement and public support. The Brady Handgun Violence Prevention Act of 1993 (originally named for Sarah Brady, then later named for her husband, Jim Brady) was well titled, for without Sarah Brady as the public face of the gun control movement, the movement would not have achieved nearly as many victories as it did. Charlton Heston has performed a similar role for the NRA and the gun rights movement. As the Associated Press noted, to the public at large, Heston and the NRA have become synonymous.

Heston is the author of an autobiography, *In the Arena,* and an essay collection, *The Courage to Be Free*, on, among other things, the Second Amendment and the virtues of an armed populace. In September 2002 he announced that he was in the early stages of Alzheimer's disease; he wanted to make the announcement while still mentally clear. He stated his intention to complete the final months of his fourth term as NRA president.

Brannon P. Denning

See also Defensive Gun Use; Enforcement of Gun Control Laws; Knox, Neal; LaPierre, Wayne R., Jr.; National Rifle Association

For Further Reading:

Heston, Charlton. 1995. *In the Arena: An Autobiography.* New York: Simon & Schuster.
_____. 2000a. *The Courage to Be Free.* Kansas City, KS: Saudade Press.
_____. 2000b. "Our First Freedom." *Saturday Evening Post* 272, 1: (January/February): 42–43.

Hickok, James Butler ("Wild Bill") (1837–1876)

James Butler Hickok is best remembered by the sobriquet "Wild Bill," which he reportedly earned in 1862 by stopping a lynching of a bartender in Independence, Missouri. During his thirty-nine-year life span, Hickok served as a scout and spy for the Union army during the Civil War, as a law enforcement official (deputy U.S. marshal, acting sheriff, and marshal of Abilene, Kansas), as an entertainer (giving shooting exhibitions in "Buffalo Bill Cody's Wild West Show"), and as a professional gambler. Hickok became a legendary gunfighter who was popularized in *Harper's* magazine and in dime novels. Many of the facts of Hickok's life have been obscured by the legends that were created in his name. He was killed during a poker game in Deadwood, South Dakota, on August 2, 1876.

Hickok was born on May 27, 1837, in Homer, Illinois, one of seven children (five boys, one of whom died in infancy, and two girls). He left home with his brother, Lorenzo, in June 1856, heading for the Kansas Territory. A hunter from childhood, Hickok was already known as a remarkable shot. In 1861, Hickok joined the Union army in a civilian capacity. During his time with the army, Hickok served as a wagon master, a scout, and a spy. In 1867, he served as an Indian scout for General George Custer and the 7th Cavalry, where he remained until 1869.

Hickok's military career overlapped with his career in law enforcement. In 1858 he was one of four constables elected to magistrate in Johnson County, Kansas. He left that position in 1859. In 1864, he served as a provost on the marshal's staff in Springfield, Missouri. He ran for election as marshal of Springfield in 1865 and was defeated. In 1867 he was appointed a deputy U.S. marshal, a position he held intermittently until 1870. In August 1868, the commissioners of Ellis County held a special election at Hays City, Kansas, in which Hickok was elected acting sheriff. In the November elections for the position of sheriff, Hickok was defeated. Hickok's final stint in law enforcement took place between April 15 and December 13, 1871, as marshal of Abilene, Kansas. During his law enforcement career, Hickok was known for his matched pair of ivory-handled Colt model 1851 Navy revolvers.

Hickok joined "Buffalo Bill Cody's Combination"—the official name of the Wild West show—in 1872 and performed with the "Wild West" show until 1874. When he left the show he was given $1,000 and a pair of .44 caliber Smith & Wesson revolvers. Documents from this period show that Hickok was not comfortable in the role of performer and was known for playing pranks on other members of the company.

During his life, Hickok was a media darling. The nickname "Wild Bill" appeared in print for

"Wild Bill" Hickok. (Mercaldo Archives)

the first time in an article in the *Weekly Patriot* in Springfield, Missouri, on July 27, 1865. The legends of Hickok's career as a gunfighter and lawman were presented to the public in magazine and newspaper articles, such as in a piece in *Harper's* by George Ward Nichols in 1867 and in one in the *Saint Louis Weekly Missouri Democrat* by Henry M. Stanley on April 16, 1887 (in which he reported the account of the first time Hickok killed a man). Hickok was also the hero of dime novels such as *Wild Bill the Indian Slayer, Wild Bill: The Pistol Prince,* and *Wild Bill's Last Trail.* Long after his death, Hickok was portrayed in plays and movies, including *Wild Bill Hickok* (1923), *The Great Adventures of Wild Bill Hickok* (1938*), Young Bill Hickok* (1940), *Wild Bill Hickok Rides* (1941), *Adventures of Wild Bill Hickok* (1951), and *I Killed Wild Bill Hickok* (1956).

After leaving law enforcement, Hickok supported himself through gambling. It was during a poker game on August 2, 1876, in Nuttall and Mann's Saloon #10 in Deadwood, South Dakota, that he was shot through the head and killed instantly by John (Jack) McCall. Hickok usually preferred a seat where his back was against a wall, but for this game he lost the seat to Charlie Rich, who refused to move. When Hickok was shot, he was holding what has come to be known as the "deadman's hand"—which consisted of two aces (hearts and clubs) and two eights (clubs and spades). The fifth card is a matter of controversy. The term "deadman's hand" was coined by Ellis T. Pierce in Frank Wilstack's 1926 book, *Wild Bill Hickok: The Prince of Pistoleers.*

Carol Oyster

A self-portrait of John Hinckley, 1982. (Bettmann/Corbis)

See also Boomtowns, Cowtowns, and Gun Violence; Cody, William "Buffalo Bill"; Dime Novels and the Sensationalization of Frontier Violence; Frontier Violence

For Further Reading:

Eisele, Wilbert. 1931. *The Real Wild Bill Hickok.* Denver, CO: W. H. Audre.

O'Connor, Richard. 1959. *Wild Bill Hickok.* New York: Curtis Books.

Rosa, Joseph G. 1994. *The West of Wild Bill Hickok.* Lawrence: University Press of Kansas.

———. 1996. *Wild Bill Hickok: The Man and His Myth.* Lawrence: University Press of Kansas.

"Wild Bill Hickok." 2002. http://adamsmuseumand house.org/wildbill.htm.

High Schools and Gun Violence

See Schoolyard Shootings

Hinckley, John Warnock, Jr. (1955–)

On March 30, 1981, John Warnock Hinckley, Jr., attempted to assassinate President Ronald Reagan as Reagan left the District of Columbia Hilton Hotel after speaking to the AFL-CIO. Hinckley opened fire with a .22 caliber pistol and fired six shots in three seconds. One of the bullets ricocheted off the presidential limousine and wounded Reagan, entering under his arm and penetrating to his lung. Also wounded were Presidential Press Secretary James Brady, police officer Thomas Delahanty, and Secret Service agent Timothy J. McCarthy.

Hinckley was born on May 29, 1955. He was 25 years old at the time of the assassination attempt. He had developed an obsession with ac-

tress Jodie Foster—having viewed Martin Scorsese's movie *Taxi Driver* over a dozen times. Hinckley had contacted Foster at Yale University twice and had written to her that he would prove his love for her through a "historic act."

Hinckley was brought to trial and found not guilty by reason of insanity on June 21, 1982. He was committed to Saint Elizabeth's Hospital in Washington, D.C. The verdict resulted in changes in a number of states' insanity defense laws, while Montana and Idaho eliminated the defense entirely. Hinckley was awarded supervised visits outside the hospital in 1999 and unsupervised outside visits in 2000. The outside privileges were revoked when a book about Foster was found in Hinckley's room. (He had been prohibited from having any materials about Foster.) In the early 1990s, Hinckley had attempted to win his release so, he said, he could lobby for gun control.

When lobbying for the Brady Bill—enacted in 1993 as the Brady Handgun Violence Prevention Act and named in her honor—Mrs. Sarah Brady stated, "Had a waiting period been in effect seven years ago, John Hinckley would not have had the opportunity to buy the gun he used" (Meddis, 1988, p. A6).

It seems doubtful, however, that the Brady Bill would have had such an effect. Hinckley had no public record of mental illness, and thus there was no record that could be discovered by a mental records check.

As for criminal records, a police background check was run on Hinckley a few days before he bought the gun, and nothing turned up. Hinckley was caught trying to smuggle a gun aboard a plane on October 9, 1980, in Nashville. His name was run through the National Crime Information Center, which reported, correctly, that he had no felony convictions in any jurisdiction. He was promptly released after paying a fine of $62.50 and pleading guilty to a misdemeanor.

On October 13, 1980, John Hinckley walked into Rocky's Pawn Shop in Dallas, Texas, and walked out shortly thereafter with two .22 caliber RG revolvers. As with the retail purchase of any firearm, the gun dealer was required to complete federal form 4473, which listed Hinckley's address. Because Hinckley was buying two handguns in the same five-day period (in fact, at the same moment), the dealer also filled out another federal form. That federal form was sent to the local office of the Bureau of Alcohol, Tobacco, and Firearms. At the time, the bureau reportedly ran name checks as standard procedure.

By federal law, the dealer was required to verify that Hinckley was a resident of Texas, the state in which he was buying the handgun. When asked for identification, Hinckley offered his valid Texas driver's license. The Lubbock, Texas, address he listed on his federal gun form (the address for a rooming house) was different from both his driver's license address and his address in the Lubbock phone book. Because the only use of the driver's license (for a gun purchase) is to prove a person's identity and residence in the state, there is no federal requirement that a handgun purchaser reside at the street address shown on his license, as long as the address is in the same state. Thus, whatever the other benefits of the Brady Bill, it does not appear that the bill would have affected John Hinckley.

Carol Oyster
and David B. Kopel

See also Brady Handgun Violence Prevention Act; Brady, James S.; Brady, Sarah Kemp; Reagan, Ronald Wilson

For Further Reading:
Carter, Gregg Lee. 1997. *The Gun Control Movement.* New York: Twayne.
Kopel, David B. 1995. "Background Checks and Waiting Periods." Pp. 53–126 in *Guns: Who Should Have Them?*, ed. David B. Kopel. Buffalo, NY: Prometheus Books.
Meddis, Sam. 1988. "Petitioners Taking Aim at Gun Laws." *USA Today* (July 20): A6.

Homicides, Gun

The U.S. property crime rate matches those of most other industrialized countries, but its homicide rate exceeds that of western Europe (by four to one) and Japan (by seven to one). When people commit murder in the United States, the weapon of choice is a gun in the majority of cases. This pattern clearly existed between 1976 and 1999. Statistics from the U.S. Department of Justice indicate that in cases of murder in the United States, guns are most commonly used. The use of such weapons first increased and then declined slightly between 1976 and 1999 and was very popular between 1989 and 1994. This pattern has remained constant into the twenty-first century.

Americans are more likely than Europeans and Japanese to murder and to do so with weapons. This disparity is most often attributed to the unique history of firearms in the United States. Part of this history involves a long romance with guns in the country as well as the gradual development of easy-to-use firearms. The American attitude toward firearms is rooted in British North America, where all freemen were required to carry arms for protection against the Native Americans, the French, and others. The colonial era's long guns and dueling pistols were expensive and difficult to handle. In 1840 came the more efficient, cheaper, and easily concealed Colt revolvers, and with them an increase in homicide rates.

In the United States, there are approximately 230 million firearms; 76 million of the firearms in circulation are handguns. The United States has the highest rate of gun homicide in the industrialized world. Approximately 80 percent of gun murders today involve a handgun. Rates of murder involving guns are higher in southern

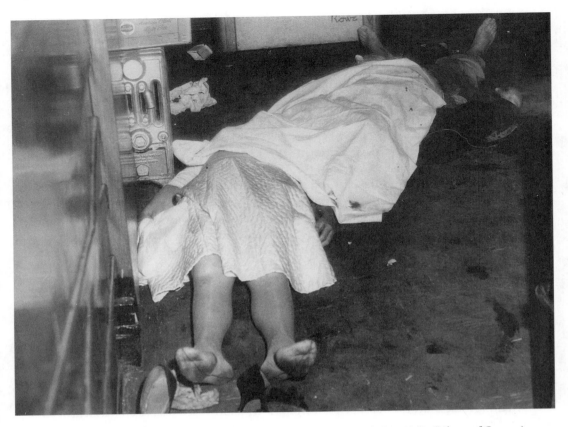

The bodies of two people killed by gunfire lie on the floor of a tavern in New York City, 1960. (Library of Congress)

regions of the United States. Relatively low rates of murder involving guns exist in New England and the Midwest.

Today the proportion of homicides involving guns differs by circumstance. Gun involvement in gang-related homicides increased after 1980. Gun involvement in homicides resulting from arguments remains relatively constant. In fact, the presence of a firearm increases the risk of homicide in the home almost threefold. A gun in the house where a homicide occurs is much more likely to be the cause of death than any other method of homicide. Most homicides by juvenile offenders (over three-fourths) involve guns. Most law enforcement officers are killed with firearms, particularly handguns.

Duggan's (2000) research conducted under the auspices of the National Bureau of Economic Research has found that increases in gun ownership lead to a higher gun homicide rate and that legislation allowing citizens to carry concealed weapons does not reduce crime. His research suggests that declines in gun homicides in the United States may be related to reductions in firearm ownership.

Kim A. Mac Innis

See also Availability of Guns, Effects on Crime; Concealed Weapons Laws; Crime and Gun Use; Gun Violence; Gun Violence as a Public Health Problem; Guns in the Home; Justifiable Homicides; Lott, John R., Jr.; Mass Murder (Shootings); Victimization from Gun Violence; Youth and Guns

For Further Reading:

Doyle, Roger. 2000. "By the Numbers: The Roots of Homicide." *Scientific American* 283, 4 (October): 22.

Duggan, Mark. 2000. "More Guns, More Crime." National Bureau of Economic Research Working Paper no. W7967 (October). http://papers.nber.org/papers/w7967.

Fox, James Alan, and Marianne W. Zawitz. 2001. "Homicide Trends in the United States." http://www.ojp.usdoj.gov/bjs/homicide/homtrnd.htm.

Homicides by Weapon Type

Year	Handgun	Other Gun	Knife	Blunt Object	Other Weapon
1976	8,651	3,328	3,343	912	2,546
1977	8,563	3,391	3,648	900	2,618
1978	8,879	3,569	3,685	937	2,490
1979	9,858	3,732	4,121	1,039	2,710
1980	10,552	3,834	4,439	1,153	3,061
1981	10,324	3,740	4,364	1,166	2,927
1982	9,138	3,501	4,381	1,032	2,957
1983	8,473	2,794	4,214	1,098	2,730
1984	8,183	2,835	3,956	1,090	2,626
1985	8,164	2,973	3,997	1,052	2,795
1986	9,054	3,126	4,235	1,176	3,018
1987	8,781	3,094	4,076	1,169	2,980
1988	9,375	3,162	3,978	1,296	2,869
1989	10,225	3,197	3,923	1,279	2,877
1990	11,677	3,395	4,077	1,254	3,037
1991	13,101	3,277	3,909	1,252	3,161
1992	13,158	3,043	3,447	1,088	3,024
1993	13,981	3,094	3,140	1,082	3,233
1994	13,496	2,840	2,960	963	3,071
1995	12,069	2,671	2,735	974	3,162
1996	10,731	2,531	2,692	917	2,778
1997	9,706	2,631	2,363	832	2,678
1998	8,813	2,160	2,249	893	2,796
1999	7,950	2,168	2,049	903	2,460

Source: Bureau of Justice Statistics, U.S. Department of Justice. http://www.ojp.usdoj.gov/bjs/.

Huddleston v. United States (1974)

The Gun Control Act of 1968, an amendment to the Omnibus Crime Control and Safe Streets Act of 1968, specifies that it is unlawful to knowingly make a false statement in connection with the "acquisition" or "sale or other disposition" of a firearm. The false statement has to be intended to or likely to deceive the dealer and has to be relevant to the legality of the transaction. The question before the Supreme Court in *Huddleston v. United States* (415 U.S. 814, 1974) was straightforward: Did this requirement apply to a transaction in which a man redeemed from a pawnbroker guns that had been purchased at an earlier time? Eight justices ruled that it did, upholding the split judgment of the United States Court of Appeals for the Ninth Circuit (*United States v. Huddleston*, 472 F. 2d 529, 1973).

Supreme Court Justice William Douglas dissented from the majority opinion. "A person who took his gun to a pawnshop for a loan undoubtedly had 'acquired' the gun prior to that time," Douglas insisted. "It is therefore odd to think of the 'acquisition' occurring when he reclaimed his own gun from the pawnbroker" (*Huddleston,* 1974, p. 834).

The defendant, William C. Huddleston, Jr., had pawned three weapons in Oxnard, California, during October 1971 and redeemed them the following February and March. He had checked "No" in response to the following question on the form he signed: "Have you ever been convicted in any court of a crime punishable by imprisonment to a term exceeding one year (note: The actual sentence given by the judge does not matter—a yes answer is necessary if the judge could have given a sentence of more than one year)."

The year before this transaction, Huddleston had been convicted for writing checks without sufficient funds, an offense that carried a possible maximum sentence of fourteen years. His actual penalty was a thirty-day jail term.

The Supreme Court placed little credence in Huddleston's testimony that he was not aware of the possible length of imprisonment for his offense, and that he regarded it as a misdemeanor.

The Court found that his dealings with the pawnbroker fell under the "sale or other disposition" clause in the Gun Control Act. It noted that the aim of the act was to limit access to guns by people with criminal histories and cited testimony before Congress about a 20-year-old in St. Paul, Minnesota, who had severely wounded a teller during a bank robbery. The offender had committed the crime with a revolver that he had redeemed from a pawnbroker on the day of the robbery.

For denying his previous conviction, Huddleston was sentenced to concurrent three-year terms, but the sentence was suspended and he was required to serve twenty weekend days in jail.

Gilbert Geis

See also Gun Control Act of 1968; United States Supreme Court Decisions on Gun Control

For Further Reading:

Ballinger, Jacqueline. 1995. "Torts: Torts and Gun Control: Sealing Up the Cracks and Helping Licensed Dealers Avoid Sales to Unqualified Buyers." *Oklahoma Law Review* 48: 593–625.

Hunting

Historically, hunting for many American males has been an affirmation of masculine identity. This has often brought derision from antihunters, who depict hunters as developmentally arrested males, perpetually adolescent misogynists who must project phallic extensions of their psyches—namely, guns—to capture their lost manhood. In their own terms, males who hunt have defined their ideal of manhood by the local standards of hunting prowess, sportsmanship, and reputation. In certain subcultures, the single most important coming-of-age rite was young males' killing of their first deer, duck, grouse, rabbit, or other prey. Many an American male dated his manhood from such events. In some rural regions, schools still virtually shut down in hunting season to permit adolescents to hunt and then reopen to find "blooded" young males returning triumphant. Of course, the fact that some women have hunted enthusiastically (as Mary Zeiss Stange details in *Woman the Hunter*) blurs this category of masculine affirmation, but mostly hunters have overlooked the female "intrusion" and preserved hunting as a male bastion.

Many hunters have argued that hunting was one of the first cooperative ventures that protohistoric societies accomplished, that it is timeless, traditional, and atavistic. To antihunters who charge that hunting is a barbaric holdover from pagan centuries, hunters cheerfully respond that it is just that anachronistic quality of hunting that validates the sport as a necessary connection with nature. Paul Shepard, in his *The Tender Carnivore and the Sacred Game* and other writings, and José Ortega y Gasset, in his *Meditations on Hunting*, made the strongest case for the persistence of hunting in human cultural patterns. Some anthropologists and feminist scholars have challenged these assertions recently, positing instead that female-oriented gatherings were more important than hunting, but the verdict is far from clear. Hunters have maintained that hunting is an effective form of environmental perception and immersion in ecological processes. To many hunters, antihunters seem well-meaning but essentially voyeurs of nature, refraining from participating honestly in the cycles of death and regeneration that inform natural processes.

Hunters have also asserted that they have been very important influences in American conservation and environmental movements. As predators, hunters have claimed that they control overpopulated herds and flocks whose irruptions threatened those species with mass starvation. As purchasers of hunting licenses and contributors to game preservation organizations such as Ducks Unlimited, hunters have argued that they have been the primary economic backers of game and nongame conservation efforts. As John Reiger has conclusively shown in *American Sportsmen and the Origins of Conservation,* American hunters and fishers led the crusade for conservation starting in the 1860s, antedating the nongame wildlife enthusiasts and antihunters by two or three decades. Indeed, it was two figures who were hunters, one part time, Henry David Thoreau, and the other full time, Aldo Leopold, who provided much of the germinal thought for twentieth-century environmentalism.

In folklore and literature in America, hunting has held an important status. Frontier legend is full of the Daniel Boones, Davy Crocketts, Jim Bridgers, Jedediah Smiths, and other buckskin hunters who trod the woods or prairies. The fact that the sagas and tales embellished or falsified their exploits did not lessen their hold on the American imagination. Americans looked to the mythic hunter for national self-identification and proof of American exceptionalism, as a long line of scholars, most recently Daniel Herman in *Hunting and the American Imagination,* have illustrated. Folktales about hunting relayed information about geography, nature lore, and danger, and served as vehicles for class or group reaffirmation or resentment. They also attempted to resolve the tension between angel and animal in the human personality. American writers have always been quick to seize upon the literary potential of the hunter and the hunt. From James Fenimore Cooper to modern novelists such as Norman Mailer, American literature abounds with hunting stories. Washington Irving, the "southwestern" humorists such as Thomas Bangs Thorpe and Mark Twain, as well as Henry David Thoreau, Francis Parkman, Herman Melville, Jack London, Stephen Crane, Ernest Hemingway, William Faulkner, A. B. Guthrie, Vardis Fisher, Frank Waters, Jean Stafford, Walter van Tilburg Clark, and Wallace Stegner, are a few of the many writers who have employed hunting as a metaphor for environmental perception, social differentiation, and nature.

Although hunters have used other weapons than guns to kill or capture their quarries, hunting and firearms are inextricably associated. For decades, the term "gunning" was a synonym for hunting. From colonial muskets to muzzleloaders and Pennsylvania long rifles to Henry and Sharps buffalo guns to twentieth-century .22s and 30.06s, .410s and 12 gauges, American hunters went to the woods and prairies well armed, at least according to tradition. In hunting art and photography, the gun is an omnipresent fixture, an icon nonchalantly propped at the shooter's side or fixed in his grip. Prize guns, such as Purdys and Parkers, have long been family treasures. In hunting humor, husbands routinely complain that their wives will not let them upgrade or add to the gun closet. Although his book *Arming America* has at-

A duck hunter in a blind. (Library of Congress)

tracted a crossfire of controversy, historian Michael Bellesiles (2000) has forced Americans to reexamine just how many Americans had firearms before the Civil War and the extent of their competency and gun knowledge. Even he, however, acknowledges the powerful appeal of the image of the hunter sighting his or her prey and squeezing off the lethal shot, the cool blue steel emitting smoke from the barrel, gun and shooter merged as extensions of the other.

In recent decades, hunting has declined in scale and overall importance in American society. There are fewer hunters percentage-wise today than even thirty years ago. The General Social Survey (2000) found a drop of households in which there was at least one adult hunter from 29.3 percent in 1977 to 17.6 percent in 1998. This still means, however, that there are tens of millions of Americans who hunt.

Why the drop? The reasons are numerous. Other sports and forms of recreation compete with hunting for limited expenditures and leisure time. Landowners who are antihunters or nonhunters have closed off land to hunters.

Suburban sprawl has taken its toll on wildlife habitat, although it has ironically created some thriving edge communities for such opportunistic species as white-tailed deer and raccoons. Many hunters find that the best available hunting is on private club land or in commercial hunting preserves that rig the hunt for the shooters. Vivid antihunting programs such as the 1975 CBS show "The Guns of Autumn," which depicted hunters as heartless butchers and bullies, alienated many nonhunters. Countering such criticism of hunting, hunters in a few states have pushed for "right to hunt" constitutional amendments and the enactment of hunter harassment laws to prevent obstruction of hunting. The sporting press sounds off glumly about the end of hunting in America. Probably Americans will continue to hunt, in whatever numbers, for many of the reasons explored above, but today's hunters feel more endangered than at any time in the nation's history.

Thomas Altherr

See also Boone, Daniel; Long Rifle (Pennsylvania/Kentucky)

For Further Reading:

Altherr, Thomas L. 1976. "'The Best of All Breathing': Hunting as a Mode of Environmental Perception in American Thought and Literature from James Fenimore Cooper to Norman Mailer." Ph.D. dissertation, Ohio State University.

Bellesiles, Michael A. 2000. *Arming America: The Origin of a National Gun Culture.* New York: Knopf.

General Social Survey. 2000. "Do you or your (husband/wife) go hunting?" Inter-University Consortium for Political and Social Research. http://www.icpsr.umich.edu/GSS/.

Herman, Daniel J. 2001. *Hunting and the American Imagination.* Washington, DC: Smithsonian Institution Press.

Marks, Stuart A. 1991. *Southern Hunting in Black and White: Nature, History, and Ritual in a Carolina Community.* Princeton, NJ: Princeton University Press.

Miller, John M. 1992. *Deer Camp: Last Light in the Northeast Kingdom.* Cambridge, MA: MIT Press.

Mitchell, John G. 1981. *The Hunt.* New York: Penguin Books.

Ortega y Gasset, José. 1972. *Meditations on Hunting.* New York: Charles Scribner's Sons.

Petersen, David, ed. 1996. *A Hunter's Heart: Honest Essays on Blood Sport.* New York: Henry Holt.

Proper, Datus C. 1990. *Pheasants of the Mind: A Hunter's Search for a Mythic Bird.* New York: Prentice-Hall.

Reiger, John F. 2001. *American Sportsmen and the Origins of Conservation.* 3rd ed., rev. and exp. Corvallis: Oregon State University Press.

Shepard, Paul. 1973. *The Tender Carnivore and the Sacred Game.* New York: Charles Scribner's Sons.

Stange, Mary Zeiss. 1997. *Woman the Hunter.* Boston: Beacon Press.

Swan, James A. 1995. *In Defense of Hunting.* New York: HarperCollins.

Henry Hyde. (U.S. House of Representatives)

Hyde, Henry J. (1924–)

Rep. Henry Hyde chaired the House Judiciary Committee after the Republicans took control in 1995 and in that capacity played a key role in the discussions on gun control. Hyde proposed a compromise between the position of progun Republicans such as Majority Leader Richard Armey and that of gun control advocates such as John Conyers, but ultimately his proposal was defeated by an amendment backed by Democratic Rep. John Dingell. Hyde continued to serve on the committee in 2001 (though no longer as chair) and is likely to continue to play a key role in gun control legislation in the U.S. House.

Hyde received a law degree from Loyola University in 1949 and served in the Illinois House from 1967 to 1974. He was elected to the U.S.

House in 1975, part of a large freshman class dominated by liberal Democrats. Working in the minority party in a chamber where the majority dominates the agenda, Hyde's major claim to public attention in the 1980s was his sponsorship of what became known as the Hyde Amendment, which barred the use of federal funds to pay for abortions through the Medicaid program. The amendment remains in effect today, although in 1993 the House permitted national funds to pay for abortions in the case of rape or incest and to save the life of the mother. Unlike many prolife conservatives, Hyde supported a consistent pro-life ethic, including emergency food aid for pregnant women without access to other government programs and additional pregnancy health care for poor women who do not qualify for Medicaid. This is but one example of a more general pattern of Hyde's legislative activity—he defies simple ideological labels.

Hyde is widely respected in the House as intellectually honest and fair-minded, and he has proven to be an eloquent advocate for his ideas. Hyde's stint as chair of the Judiciary Committee included the impeachment of Bill Clinton. Hyde initially sought to structure a bipartisan approach, but perhaps inevitably the entire process became deeply partisan. Hyde was the chief impeachment manager in the House, but despite his eloquent summation of the case, the Senate voted to acquit Clinton on all charges. Hyde asked the GOP caucus to extend his term as chair of the Judiciary Committee because of the interruption in the committee's work that impeachment caused, but the caucus did not permit him to serve past the common term limit

for chairs. Hyde assumed the chairmanship of the International Relations Committee in 2001.

Hyde's record on gun control is typically complex and nuanced. Initially a strong backer of gun rights who applauded citizens who used guns to defend their property in times of disaster, Hyde changed his position to support the ban on assault weapons in 1994 and became a cosponsor of the Brady Bill. In 1999, Hyde sought to pass gun control over the fierce opposition of key Republicans, proposing a compromise on the "gun show loophole" that would have asked law enforcement officials to conduct their background check in twenty-four hours but would have permitted them to take three days if necessary. Like many compromises, his proposal was not greeted warmly by either side, and eventually it was defeated by an amendment offered by John Dingell that scuttled the bill.

As of 2002 Hyde remained on the House Judiciary Committee, where he was likely to be a critical player in any future legislation. Although he no longer chaired the committee, his eloquence, intellectual honesty, and willingness to work hard to broker compromises made him one of the most important figures in the House on gun control issues.

Clyde Wilcox

See also Assault Weapons Ban of 1994; Brady Handgun Violence Prevention Act; Conyers, John; Dingell, John D.; Gun Shows

For Further Reading:

Barone, Michael, and Grank Ujifusa. 1999. *The Almanac of American Politics, 2000.* Washington, DC: National Journal.
Hyde, Henry J. 2001. "Biography." http://www.house.gov/hyde/bio.htm.

Ideologies—Conservative and Liberal

A political ideology is a system of beliefs about the political world. Fundamental to all ideologies are questions of power, freedom, and the role of individuals and collectives (especially governments) in a society. Public policies and public debate about the place of guns and gun control in American society are intimately bound up with these questions.

Because it is a system, we expect the individual components of any ideology to somehow relate to each other or to be organized around one or more unifying dimensions. Components of ideologies include beliefs about what politics is (the substance of politics), how politics is organized and carried out (the procedures of politics), as well as what these things should be and how they should be done. This latter, prescriptive aspect of the system is most often the focus of discussions about political ideologies.

The particular mix of beliefs, attitudes, and emotional responses to political matters produces a wide range of ideologies from totalitarianism to anarchism. In the United States, ideology is almost exclusively thought of in terms of liberalism and conservatism. Moreover, the two are often treated as the defining poles of a single dimension. This view is somewhat misleading for two related reasons. First, liberalism itself has two strands. Classic liberalism, which can be traced to the ideas of John Locke, whose ideas strongly influenced the debate among the authors of the U.S. Constitution, emphasizes personal liberty and freedom from government intervention, especially in economic policy. Positive liberalism, which developed during the nineteenth century in response to the excesses of the industrial revolution, casts government and freedom in a much different light. The power of government, in this view, is to be used in a positive or constructive fashion to provide a socioeconomic environment that allows each person to develop to his or her potential. The difference between the two strands of liberalism is often cast as the difference between "freedom to" (work, worship, own a gun) and "freedom from" (poverty, hunger, discrimination). Furthermore, positive liberals, in their emphasis on the development of human potential, tend to be opposed to government interference in matters of personal choice outside of economics (i.e., morality issues such as abortion and civil liberties, especially of minority groups).

Today, adherents of classic liberalism have come to be known as conservatives. This brings us to the second confusing aspect of modern political discourse concerning ideologies: there is a distinct ideological system of organic conservatism whose adherents find themselves both at odds with and in sympathy with classic liberals. Whereas a classic liberal holds government in low esteem, conservatives tend to have a negative view of human nature and of individuals. The organic conservative emphasizes morality and social control. Rather than wishing to free the individual to do or to be something, conservatives hope to use the coercive power of government to restrain the individual for the benefit of society as a whole. This is not to say that conservatism espouses a pervasive or invasive government; indeed, quite the opposite is true. Governments themselves, because they are the creations of fallible humans, should also exercise restraint, working to preserve traditional institutions and values and avoiding grand schemes and revolutionary departures from the status quo. Because the classic liberal tends to give less emphasis to social and moral issues, and the organic conservative is not primarily concerned with economic issues, a coalition of the two is possible.

The fundamental value conflicts that shape the battle lines on gun control policy tend to cut across these ideological groups. One of the primary arguments cited by gun control advocates is based on the widely held but often criticized notion that the purpose of the Second Amendment's "right to keep and bear arms" was to enable a free citizenry to protect itself from its own government. Such a notion certainly fits with the overall belief system of those in the conservative coalition who subscribe to the tenets of classic liberalism. It requires some effort, however, to place it inside a conservative system of beliefs, which is usually profoundly antirevolutionary and founded on government control of individuals for the greater good.

The reconciliation is accomplished on two fronts. First, the focus is placed on the problem of crime, criminals, and gun violence, deemphasizing the role of guns and of ordinary law-abiding gun owners. Gun violence is a moral issue and an area in which conservatives are anxious to impose governmental controls. Conservative anticontrol groups therefore advocate "people" control rather than gun control, calling for harsher penalties and stricter enforcement of existing laws. This still leaves the problem of the purported revolutionary origins and purpose of the Second Amendment, which, as the literal battle cry of the anticontrol movement, cannot simply be ignored. The resolution of the dilemma is found in the organic conservative's distaste for revolution in any form. By portraying the government, especially federal law enforcement agencies such as the Federal Bureau of Investigation and the Bureau of Alcohol, Tobacco and Firearms, as agents of a conspiracy to overthrow existing institutional arrangements and traditional rights and values, conservatives can find a way to make progun sentiments fit into an antirevolution world view. That these strategies do not completely heal the rift in the traditional conservative coalition can be seen, for example, in the split between anticontrol organizations such as the National Rifle Association and police and law enforcement organizations.

The high ground on the anticrime theme is hard to hold and groups on the left have been eager to exploit the split among conservatives. For example, victim-rights organizations on the "liberal" side have been able to commandeer the themes of crime and violence as often as not. Perhaps the best example of this is the Brady Handgun Violence Prevention Act of 1993, more popularly called the Brady Bill. Another example is the Omnibus Violent Crime Control and Prevention Act of 1994, more popularly referred to as the assault weapons ban, which included a ban on certain firearms defined as having "assault weapon" characteristics. The cause of victims is a good fit with the positive liberal ideology in that it calls for government intervention to produce an environment in which individuals are safe to live up to their potential.

Polling data gathered as part of the General Social Survey confirm the meager fit of the gun control issue with traditional ideological positions. For example, throughout the 1980s and 1990s, a majority of Americans of all political stripes supported purchase permits. While those who considered themselves to be political conservatives were less likely than liberals to favor such laws, the differences were negligible, considering that support levels topped 75 percent even among conservatives. The most recent General Social Survey (2000) data reveal that 79 percent of conservatives, 84 percent of moderates, and 87 percent of liberals would "favor" a law that "would require a person to obtain a police permit before he or she could buy a gun."

David Russell Harding

See also Attitudes toward Gun Control; Congressional Voting Patterns on Gun Control; General Social Survey

For Further Reading:

Converse, Philip E. 1964. "The Nature of Belief Systems in Mass Publics." Pp. 202–261 in *Ideology and Discontent,* ed. David E. Apter. New York: Free Press.

Freeden, Michael. 1996. *Ideologies and Political Theory.* Oxford: Clarendon Press.

General Social Survey. 2000. "Would you favor or oppose a law which would require a person to obtain a police permit before he or she could buy a gun?" Inter-University Consortium for Political and Social Research. http://www.icpsr.umich.edu/GSS/.

Jacoby, William G. 1995. "The Structure of Ideological Thinking in the American Electorate." *American Journal of Political Science* 39: 314–335.

Independence Institute

The Independence Institute in Golden, Colorado, is one of the oldest state-based, free-market think tanks in the United States. Founded in 1986, it seeks to increase public acceptance of free-market, profreedom public policy ideas through a variety of publications, public debates, and conferences.

In 1999, the *Nation* called the Independence Institute one of the four most visible state-based think tanks in the United States. Former Colorado Governor Roy Romer bemoaned the institute's influence on the Colorado legislature. The governor who succeeded him, Bill Owens, has praised it as a leading source of free-market ideas. When serving in the Colorado Senate, Owens convinced the Senate to pass a resolution honoring "the Institute's public policy research."

The institute's primary issue has always been education reform. Its "Parent Information Center" was the first organization in the nation to provide parents with free report cards listing standardized test scores for every public school in the state. Tax reform, health care, and transportation are also major subjects of attention. While the institute's main focus is state-level policy, it is also involved in local, national, and international issues.

With David B. Kopel as research director since 1992, the institute has special expertise in firearm issues and the Second Amendment of the U.S. Constitution. Its Second Amendment Project maintains a website housing one of the most extensive collections of articles on firearm issues available today.

The institute's former staff, senior fellows, and trustees include numerous elected and appointed public officials. Its founders were the late David S. D'Evelyn, the father of Colorado's charter school law, and John Andrews, who serves as a minority leader in the Colorado State Senate. Tom Tancredo, its president from 1993 to 1998, was elected to the U.S. House of Representatives. Before being elected attorney general of Colorado in 1990, Gale Norton served as a senior fellow at the Independence Institute. She became a trustee of the institute in 1999 and was appointed secretary of the interior by President Bush in 2001. After serving as chairman of Denver's Regional Transportation District, Jon Caldara became president of the institute in 1998. Caldara is also a talk radio host on Colorado's largest radio station, KOA, and the host of a weekly PBS television program, *Independent Thinking*, on KBDI channel 12 in Denver.

Linda Gorman

See also Kopel, David B.
For Further Reading:
Independence Institute website: http://www.IndependenceInstitute.org.
Kopel's Second Amendment website: http://www.davekopel.com/2dAmendment.htm.

Injuries, Gun

See Accidents, Gun; Gun Violence as a Public Health Problem

Institute for Legislative Action (ILA)

The political arm of the National Rifle Association (NRA), the Institute for Legislative Action (ILA) spearheads the organization's political activities. Since the 1970s, the ILA has been the largest division in the NRA and its center of power.

The NRA's explicit involvement in politics dates back to the 1930s, when the predecessor of the ILA, the NRA's Legislative Division, was formed in 1934. The NRA exercised great influence over the two primary gun control laws enacted in the 1930s, the National Firearms Act of 1934 and the Federal Firearms Act of 1938, but unlike its political posture in later decades, the NRA was willing to accept some gun controls, including waiting periods and taxes on firearms. For the most part, however, the NRA's main focus was on sporting, marksmanship, and hunting activities. This began to change in the 1960s, when national outrage over rising violence and the assassination of political leaders sparked calls for stronger gun laws. This, in turn, roused opposition from the NRA, which opposed enactment of the Gun Control Act of 1968. Even at this point, however, NRA opposition was not as unyielding as it would become later.

In the late 1960s and early 1970s, the NRA focused political efforts for the first time on specific legislative races, claiming credit for defeating two gun-control proponents in the Senate, Joseph Clark (D-PA) in 1968 and Joseph Tydings (D-MD) in 1970. Buoyed by these victories and persuaded to make politics a higher priority, the NRA reconstituted and concentrated its lobbying activities in 1975 with the creation of its ILA. Focusing primarily on legislative efforts in the states and in the nation's capital, the ILA has become the primary power center in the NRA. The elevation of political activities was pushed further by the NRA's new president, Harlon Carter, who led the hard-line faction that overthrew the NRA's old-guard leadership in 1977. The hard-line faction believed that the old guard did not place a high enough priority on political action and was too willing to compromise. In recent years, the ILA has consumed 25 percent or more of the NRA's total budget. In 1988, the ILA spent $20.2 million on political activities. By 1992, its spending had risen to $28.9 million. In 1994, ILA spending was $28.3 million, which, in combination with previous ILA spending, accounted for about 70 percent of the NRA's fiscal deficit. In the 2000 election, the ILA raised an estimated $30 million.

The NRA, through its ILA, is widely known for its unyielding, uncompromising insistence on 100 percent support among its friends and its willingness to oppose those who fail to meet this standard. In 1994, for example, the ILA turned its political resources against one of its longest and strongest supporters in Congress, Rep. Jack Brooks (D-TX). Brooks vigorously opposed the assault-weapons ban that eventually passed that year, but the NRA turned on him in the belief that he did not do enough to try to defeat the bill. This, plus other factors, contributed to Brooks's defeat. In 2000, the ILA turned its resources against another longtime ally, Rep. Bart Stupak (D-MI). Stupak was a consistent NRA ally and previous recipient of NRA contributions. But in 1999, Stupak supported some limited gun control measures in the House of Representatives, which prompted the NRA to launch a campaign to defeat him. Despite that, Stupak was reelected.

Beyond its lobbying activities, the ILA has become the primary means through which the NRA mobilizes political support among NRA membership and sympathizers. In 1991, for example, the NRA spent about $10 million on "legislative alerts," fund-raising, and mass mailings. The alarmist tone of the politically charged mailings has been labeled by journalist Osha Gray Davidson the "Armageddon Appeal." As a former NRA head said, "You keep any special interest group alive by nurturing the crisis atmosphere. 'Keep sending those cards and letters in. Keep sending money.'" In one instance, the NRA ran afoul of the law when it printed on the outside of one of its mailings: "If you fail to respond to this letter you could face a jail term." The New York State attorney general's office charged the NRA with fraud. After resisting investigative efforts by New York to examine other NRA mailings for two years, the NRA finally complied. The matter was resolved when the NRA promised to avoid such tactics in the future. A study of NRA advertising conducted by the Congressional Research Service found numerous inaccuracies in the way NRA literature described gun bills before Congress.

Even though the NRA's ILA is by no means the largest lobbying group in the country, its belief in membership mobilization for political purposes is most clearly reflected in its spending on internal communications designed not only to buttress support for the NRA agenda, but to rally support for political candidates sympathetic to the NRA perspective. In most years since the end of the 1970s, the NRA has spent more money on internal communications than any other comparable group. During the 1991–1992 election cycle, for example, the NRA spent $8.4 million on political mail and other related internal political costs aimed at members and others. This level of spending represented a 90 percent increase over its spending for the same purpose four years earlier. Unlike donations to candidates' fund-raising committees, there are no federal spending limits on such internal communications.

The NRA ILA has expanded its political efforts to the international stage. It joined with gun manufacturers and gun groups from eleven countries in 1997 to fight international efforts at gun control, including enactment of tougher gun laws in such countries as Great Britain, Australia, Canada, and New Zealand. The NRA also obtained "advocacy" (comparable to lobbyist) status at the United Nations (UN) in 1997. The following year, it unsuccessfully fought a UN resolution to curb illicit international firearm trading.

Despite the vast resources funneled to its political efforts, and the zeal with which it promotes its anti–gun control cause, the ILA's successes are relatively limited. In the 2000 elections, for example, it launched an all-out effort to swing key states to Republican presidential candidate George W. Bush. Despite the fact that Bush won the election, battleground states with large gun-owning populations—like Pennsylvania, Michigan, and Iowa—all went to gun control supporter and Democratic presidential candidate Al Gore. At the congressional level, NRA successes have also been limited, given that most such elections are not determined by a single issue; that gun control is not a top issue concern of most voters; and that NRA political activities are, to some degree, counterbalanced by other groups seeking to influence the same pool of voters.

Robert J. Spitzer

See also *American Rifleman;* Carter, Harlon; Eddie Eagle; Federation for NRA; National Rifle Association; Political Victory Fund
For Further Reading:
Bruce, John M., and Clyde Wilcox, eds. 1998. *The Changing Politics of Gun Control.* Lanham, MD: Rowman & Littlefield.
Spitzer, Robert J. 1998. *The Politics of Gun Control.* Chatham, NJ: Chatham House.

Instrumentality Effect
See Weapons Instrumentality Effect

Intelligence Project
See Klanwatch Project

Interest Groups and Gun Legislation

Interest group participation in the congressional politics of gun control began in the early 1960s, when the National Rifle Association became interested in Sen. Thomas J. Dodd's (D-CT) proposed legislation to ban mail-order sales of pistols and revolvers. Although initially supportive of the measure, the National Rifle Association became the preeminent and staunch foe of it and other gun control legislation since 1965. For a number of years, no organized and powerful pressure group existed to offset the NRA's impressive political might. In the mid-1980s, the Brady Campaign to Prevent Gun Violence (then known as Handgun Control, Inc.) and law enforcement groups became involved in successful lobbying efforts in opposition to the NRA.

Until well after World War II, the NRA paid little attention to Congress. Firearm regulation proposals were rare and the group concerned itself largely with gun safety and training. But in the mid-1960s the NRA began setting itself up to be what would become the most vociferous and powerful opponent of federal gun control legislation in the nation. In 1965 it urged its 700,000-plus members to write letters strongly opposing President Lyndon B. Johnson's tough crime and gun control proposal. Over the next decade, the NRA's positions and tactics toughened. And by the late 1970s the group branded all congressional gun control supporters as extremists and all gun control proposals as schemes designed to lead to the abolishment of private gun ownership. Since then it has continued playing hardball, relentlessly opposing any federal proposal to regulate guns.

For many years the NRA functioned as the only organized and powerful interest group in the congressional arena of gun control politics. The NRA's power grew as its lobbying activities expanded. In 1967 it spent only $131,000 on legislative activities, and in 1968 it had a membership of 900,000. By 1992, NRA expenditures on political activities swelled to nearly $30 million, and they have remained there since. The group's membership has been uneven but was nearly 4,000,000 in 2001.

In the late 1960s, police groups, city officials, and the American Bar Association made attempts to counter the political power of the NRA, but they typically consisted of endorsements that did little to offset the NRA's organized lobbying. Gun control advocates attempted to form groups and coalitions, and through petition drives and advertising they fought for passage of the Gun Control Act of 1968. The act became law, but this served to energize and expand the membership of the NRA, and opposition groups were not organized for long-term pressure politics. Thus in 1986 the NRA successfully weakened the provisions of the 1968 act by spearheading the passage of the Firearms Owners' Protection Act. The key to the NRA's success has not changed since the "Revolt at Cincinnati" in 1977, when NRA hard-liners took over the leadership positions of the organization at its annual meeting. The group's ability to keep its membership alert and informed about gun control bills and to provoke them allows it to bring considerable pressure upon members of Congress to oppose gun control.

The NRA has acquired political power for a number of reasons. First, it has been in existence for many years and has gained a great deal of political experience and expertise. It has had close ties with powerful leaders in government and the gun industry, and it has used these advantages to benefit itself financially and politically. NRA board members and executives have consisted of Pentagon officials and congressional leaders. Also, the NRA motivates its membership by fostering an "us-versus-them" attitude and characterizing any gun control legislation as leading to inevitable government confiscation of guns. In addition, the NRA membership core consists of individuals who share a common culture of fierce passion for guns. In contrast to gun control supporters who may consider a variety of issues when voting for members of Congress, NRA members often vote solely on the issue of gun control. The group has been credited with defeating a few incumbent legislators as well as creating major headaches for those it targets.

However, some of the NRA's traditional hard-line tactics that were effective in the short term may be causing long-term political difficulties. The group's zero-tolerance approach, bitterly opposing even modest gun control proposals, is based on the belief that there are gun control supporters who will keep pushing more and more controls until firearms are completely abolished. The NRA's approach has caused some difficulties for the group's public image. For example, in the mid-1980s the NRA initially opposed the ban of what gun control advocates skillfully coined "cop-killer bullets"—bullets that could pierce an officer's protective armor. This stance, along with other rigid positions against the Brady Bill and assault weapons ban, has created a public perception of the NRA as an extremist organization. This perception has somewhat weakened the NRA's might in the congressional arena.

Pro–gun control groups, such as the Council for a Responsible Firearms Policy and its Emergency Committee for Gun Control, emerged to mobilize support for firearm regulation after the assassinations of President John F. Kennedy, the Rev. Martin Luther King, and Sen. Robert F. Kennedy in the 1960s. However, these groups were no match for the political clout and staying power of the NRA in the congressional battleground. The NRA lacked strong rivals until Sarah Brady joined Handgun Control, Inc. (HCI) in the mid-1980s. HCI was originally founded as the National Council to Control Firearms, a more radical organization whose goal was the abolition of all handguns. In 1981 the group changed its name to Handgun Control, Inc. and changed its agenda to include the promotion of more modest and incremental firearm regulation. Today the group, which is known as the Brady Campaign to Prevent Gun Violence, has the stated goal of keeping guns out of the wrong hands. With this more moderate approach the group became more in line with American public opinion and was able to increase significantly its political capital.

Sarah Brady is the wife of James Brady, the former presidential press secretary who became well known after being critically wounded during the assassination attempt on President Ronald Reagan by John W. Hinckley, Jr. Once Sarah Brady joined the board of HCI, the group gained credibility and notoriety and its membership and resources grew tremendously. And with Brady's solid conservative reputation, the group could no longer be labeled an extreme or liberal organization. In 1981, HCI's membership was approximately 100,000. In the mid-1990s the group reached an annual membership of over 400,000. Today the Brady Campaign to Prevent Gun Violence is the leading gun control organization in the nation. The group's success is partly a result of its tactics, which are strikingly similar to those of its archenemy, the NRA. The Brady Campaign, like the NRA, strives to build an ever-expanding grassroots membership. The group also tends to mimic the NRA's reliance on polemical and alarmist rhetoric to motivate its membership and discredit those on the other side. The Brady Campaign works with smaller state and local gun control advocacy groups.

Though the Brady Campaign still lacks the tremendous resources of the NRA, it proved itself to be David to NRA's Goliath in its successful seven-year struggle to enact the Brady Bill. But it did so with some help from unlikely allies—law enforcement groups. Traditionally, law enforcement had a cozy relationship with the NRA because of the group's focus on gun safety and training. However, once the NRA transformed its focus to political opposition to gun control legislation, the relationship began to sour. The International Association of Chiefs of Police joined forces with the Brady Campaign in lobbying for the enactment of the Brady Bill. Although the Brady Bill has been criticized by some as having limited effectiveness, the Brady Campaign has been racking up victories on small legislative measures. The Brady Campaign has been behind the enactment of federal laws banning so-called cop-killer bullets, plastic guns, and certain assault weapons.

Keith Rollin Eakins

See also Brady Campaign to Prevent Gun Violence; Brady Center to Prevent Gun Violence; Brady, Sarah Kemp; Hinckley, John Warnock, Jr.; Institute for Legislative Action; International Association of Chiefs of Police; National Rifle Association; Orth, Franklin L.; Revolt at Cincinnati

For Further Reading:

Brady Campaign to Prevent Gun Violence. 2001. "Brady Campaign to Prevent Gun Violence." http://www.mynra.com/.

Brady Center to Prevent Gun Violence. 2001. "Brady Center to Prevent Gun Violence." http://www.bradycenter.org/.

Carter, Gregg Lee. 1997. *The Gun Control Movement.* New York: Twayne.

Davidson, Osha Gray. 1993. *Under Fire: The NRA and the Battle for Gun Control.* New York: Henry Holt.

Jelen, Ted G. 1998. "The Electoral Politics of Gun Ownership." Pp. 224–246 in *The Changing Politics of Gun Control,* ed. John M. Bruce and Clyde Wilcox. Lanham, MD: Rowman & Littlefield.

Lambert, Diana. 1998. "Trying to Stop the Craziness of This Business: Gun Control Groups." Pp. 172–195 in *The Changing Politics of Gun Control,* ed. John M. Bruce and Clyde Wilcox. Lanham, MD: Rowman & Littlefield.

Langbein, Laura I. 1993. "PACs, Lobbies, and Political Conflict: The Case of Gun Control." *Public Choice* 77, 3: 551–572.

National Rifle Association. 2001. "My NRA." http://www.mynra.com/.

O'Connor, Karen, and Graham Barron. 1998. "Madison's Mistake? Judicial Construction of the Second Amendment." Pp. 74–87 in *The Changing Politics of Gun Control,* ed. John M. Bruce and Clyde Wilcox. Lanham, MD: Rowman & Littlefield.

Patterson, Samuel C., and Keith R. Eakins. 1998. "Congress and Gun Control." Pp. 45–73 in *The Changing Politics of Gun Control,* ed. John M. Bruce and Clyde Wilcox. Lanham, MD: Rowman & Littlefield.

Spitzer, Robert J. 1995. *The Politics of Gun Control.* Chatham, NJ: Chatham House.

Sugarmann, Josh. 1992. *National Rifle Association: Money, Firepower and Fear.* Washington, DC: National Press Books.

Yassky, David. 2000. "The Second Amendment: Structure, History, and Constitutional Change." *Michigan Law Review* 99, 3 (December): 588–668.

International Association of Chiefs of Police (IACP)

The 18,000-member International Association of Chiefs of Police was founded in 1893. According to the organization's website, the IACP's goals are to "advance the science and art of police services; to develop and disseminate improved administrative, technical and operational practices and promote their use in police work; to foster police cooperation and the exchange of information and experience among police administrators throughout the world; to bring about recruitment and training in the police profession of qualified persons; and to encourage adherence of all police officers to high professional standards of performance and conduct."

Professional programs that the IACP takes pride in initiating or supporting are the Federal Bureau of Investigation's Identification Division and the Uniform Crime Records reporting system. The IACP was also one of the first law enforcement organizations to appreciate fingerprinting as a viable means of identification.

Current programs that the IACP is involved in promoting include child safety seat enforcement, crime-gun interdiction, radar testing, and management analysis of police agencies. The organization also seeks to influence legislation through lobbying, expert testimony, and letter-writing campaigns to Congress. Importantly, the organization supports gun control. For example, the IACP "strongly supports provisions that would require the performance of background checks prior to the sale or transfer of weapons at gun shows, as well as extending the requirements of the Brady Act to cover juvenile acts of crime" (Neubauer, 1999, p. 1).

G. Edward Richards

See also Federal Law Enforcement Officers Association; Fraternal Order of Police; International Brotherhood of Police Officers; Law Enforcement for the Preservation of the Second Amendment; National Association of Police Organizations; National Sheriffs' Association; National Troopers' Coalition; Police Executive Research Forum
For Further Reading:
Carter, Gregg Lee. *The Gun Control Movement.* New York: Twayne.
International Association of Chiefs of Police website: http://www.theiacp.org.
Neubauer, Ronald S. 1999. "Letter to Juvenile Justice Conferees Supporting Senate-Sponsored Firearms Provisions." September 14. http://www.theiacp.org/documents/index.cfm?fuseaction=document&document_id=76.

International Brotherhood of Police Officers (IBPO)

Founded in 1964 with the officers of the Cranston, Rhode Island, Police Department comprising the first local, the International Brotherhood of Police Officers is the largest police union in the United States. The IBPO is affiliated with the AFL-CIO and offers its membership numerous benefits and services. The IBPO provides free legal services on all work-related matters, including worker's compensation, suspensions, dismissals, and grievances. It also assumes a portion of the cost during arbitration proceedings. To provide effective stewards at the workplace, the IBPO offers steward training seminars. Other member benefits include term life insurance, a home mortgage program, and a subscription to the IBPO quarterly newspaper, *Police Chronicle.*

In order to promote the interests of police officers and their families, the IBPO maintains a powerful lobby in Washington, D.C. IBPO lobbyists were instrumental in the Senate's passage of legislation in 1976 providing for an initial $50,000 in death benefits for police officers killed in the line of duty. This has since been increased to $250,000. Sen. Edward Kennedy credited the IBPO as being the most influential organization in the passage of the legislation. The IBPO also seeks to influence legislation at the state level through lobbying efforts in state capitals.

As with the comparable union for federal law enforcement agencies, the Federal Law Enforcement Officers Association, the IBPO supports legislation—such as Gary Cunningham's (R-CA) proposed H.R. 218 bill—that would allow active and retired law enforcement officers to carry their firearms across state lines and that would give retired officers in general the right to carry concealed guns. However, in general the IBPO has been an ally of the gun control movement since the mid-1980s, and it supports legislation restricting the possession of armor-piercing ammunition.

G. Edward Richards

See also Federal Law Enforcement Officers Association; Fraternal Order of Police; International Association of Chiefs of Police
For Further Reading:
Carter, Gregg Lee. 1997. *The Gun Control Movement.* New York: Twayne.
International Brotherhood of Police Officers home page: http://www.ibpo.org.

Intervention Effects

Intervention effects refers to techniques of assessing the societal impact of some firearm-related law or policy change. Examples of interventions would include

- the passage of a "shall-issue" concealed-carry law that would enable law-abiding citizens to carry concealed handguns in their jurisdiction without many legal impediments
- a ban on specific weapons such as the federal assault weapons ban (Title XI, Subtitle A of the Violent Crime Control and Law Enforcement Act of 1994), or similar and more comprehensive bans on such weapons in New York, California, Connecticut, and Massachusetts
- ammunition restrictions in California, Illinois, Massachusetts, or New Jersey
- laws mandating weapons ownership such as those passed in Kennesaw, Georgia, in 1982 and in Virgin, Utah, in 2000

An example of a possible intervention effect would be that burglaries showed a dramatic decrease after passage of the Kennesaw, Georgia, law, as some claimed.

As Kleck (1997) points out, two major strategies are used to evaluate intervention effects. The first is time-series analysis. Data are collected on some indicator related to firearm issues for a period of time predating the effective date of the intervention. Similar data are collected for a period of time after the intervention. For example, Loftin et al. (1991) report that the Firearms Control Regulations Act implemented in 1997 in Washington, D.C., significantly decreased firearm suicides and homicides.

The second strategy is to use cross-sectional analyses to compare different localities, which hopefully are similar in characteristics but have different gun laws or policies. Statistical analyses are used to see if the intervention produces a significant change in the indicator. For example, Lott (1998) reports significant drops in state crime rates after passage of a shall-issue concealed handgun law.

These types of studies are controversial, with both defenders and opponents of gun rights as well as scholars finding problems with their methodologies. The studies lack randomized controls. Communities can differ in terms of the control variables used in a particular cross-sectional study; similarly, time-series studies have failed to consider other forces that covaried with the intervention. To wit, a good economy can decrease crime rates, and one has to separate this effect out. Studies that are supportive of gun ownership (Lott, 1998; though see criticisms in Black and Nagin, 1998) and those that are critical of it (Loftin et al., 1991; though see criticisms in Kleck, 1997) are both subject to these criticisms.

It is also the case that intervention studies conducted by criminologists, sociologists, and economists do their analyses based on population-sized units. Rarely are the effects assessed on the level of the individual to see whether the intervention has impacted their behavior or consciousness.

In sum, intervention effects are controversial. In 1997, the Harborview Injury Prevention and Research Center at the University of Washington concluded that the findings of intervention-effects studies are unclear and often contradictory. Nevertheless, recent work does clearly indicate that the passage of shall-issue concealed-carry laws have not produced a Wild West–style shooting rampage as predicted by opponents of such laws. Also, it is now clear that the federal assault weapons ban has had minimal effects on gun trafficking and gun violence (Koper, 2001).

Glenn E. Meyer

See also Assault Weapons Ban of 1994; Concealed Weapons Laws; Gun Control; Kennesaw, Georgia; Lott, John R., Jr.

For Further Reading:
Black, Dan A., and Daniel S. Nagin. 1998. "Do Right to Carry Laws Deter Violent Crime?" *Journal of Legal Studies* 27: 209–219.

Kleck, Gary 1997. *Targeting Guns: Firearms and Their Control.* New York: Aldine de Gruyter.

Koper, Christopher 2001. "A Follow-Up Assessment of the Federal Assault Weapons Ban: Impact on Gun Markets and Gun Violence." Paper presented at the meeting of the American Society of Criminology, Atlanta, GA.

Loftin, Colin, David McDowall, Brian Wiersema, and Talbert J. Cottey. 1991. "Effects of Restrictive

Gun Licensing on Homicide and Suicide in the District of Columbia." *New England Journal of Medicine* 325: 1615–1620.

Lott, John R. 1998. *More Guns, Less Crime: Understanding Crime and Gun Control Laws.* Chicago: University of Chicago Press.

Izaak Walton League of America (IWLA)

Named for the seventeenth-century English angler who wrote *The Compleat Angler,* the Izaak Walton League of America is among the nation's oldest conservation organizations and was the first to focus on effecting environmental protection through changes in public policy. The IWLA identifies hunting as a major component of wildlife conservation and consequently takes a positive and constructive stance toward firearm use and ownership. The league places heavy emphasis on ethical behavior in the field and has traditionally been in the forefront in advocating hunter ethics and gun safety education.

Founded by a small group of hunter-conservationists in Chicago in 1922, the IWLA was initially formed to combat water pollution and other environmental abuses that interfered with wildlife-related recreational activities. Over the ensuing years the IWLA expanded its interests beyond water quality to include soil conservation, air pollution, forestry issues, the protection of wildlife habitat and endangered species, outdoor recreational opportunities (particularly hunting and fishing), and sustainable resources. The league has lobbied for initiatives as diverse as the 1972 Clean Water Act, the creation of the National Elk Refuge in Wyoming and Everglades National Park, the 1976 Federal Land Policy and Management Act, and the federal agricultural Conservation Reserve Program. Major themes running through all of IWLA's work are outdoor ethics and public environmental education. Headquartered today in Gaithersburg, Maryland, the IWLA claims a national membership of 50,000 in 330 chapters nationwide. It publishes the quarterly magazine *Outdoor America.*

The IWLA has an official policy on firearm use. It supports the individual constitutional right to keep and bear firearms and generally opposes any legislation that would impede or restrict the lawful activities of private gun owners, firearm professionals like gunsmiths, and firearm dealers or manufacturers. It opposes legislative initiatives that fail to make meaningful distinctions between "assault weapons" and other semiautomatic firearms and would thereby limit or ban the legitimate use of semiautomatic sporting arms. The IWLA supports the Pittman-Robertson tax on firearms and ammunition, but opposes any tax on firearms that diverts revenues away from conservation initiatives or research.

The league is opposed to the registration of firearms. At the same time, it supports those laws already on the books that prevent firearm sales to, or possession by, convicted felons, individuals found by courts to be mentally incompetent or insane, and individuals under the age of 18. The IWLA also supports the legislation of severe and mandatory penalties for gun-related crimes, and it opposes any attempts to classify crimes involving the use of firearms as public health issues.

Finally, the IWLA supports legislation to protect privately operated shooting ranges from "nuisance" lawsuits or civil liability arising from natural or foreseeable risks, and urges the creation of state commissions that would set the standards for ranges and define range liability. Nationally, approximately one hundred shooting ranges are operated by local IWLA chapters.

In 1978, the IWLA established its Outdoor Ethics Program to act as a clearinghouse for information on outdoor ethics and to promote responsible behavior among hunters and other outdoor recreationists. The program has sponsored several major events, including a 1987 International Conference on Outdoor Ethics that brought together academics and wildlife professionals from a variety of disciplinary and organizational contexts. It also sponsored a 1994 survey on "Hunter Behavior in America" involving state fish and game agencies and hunter organizations. Both the conference proceedings and the published survey results indicate that hunter behavior, while apparently improving as a result of increasing emphasis on hunter ethics education, remains an issue of concern both for wildlife professionals and for the general public. However, in neither the conference proceedings nor the survey did firearm abuse (with the exception of hunters shooting too close to roads) appear to figure prominently in unethical hunter behavior, which had more to do with trespassing on private lands and violation of various state hunting regulations.

Mary Zeiss Stange

See also Gun Violence as a Public Health Problem; Hunting; Second Amendment; Semiautomatic Weapons

For Further Reading:
Izaak Walton League of America. 1987. *Proceedings of the International Conference on Outdoor Ethics.* Arlington, VA: Izaak Walton League of America.
Izaak Walton League of America. N.d. "History of the Izaak Walton League of America." http://www.iwla.org/history/.
Ruh, Glen B. 1994. *Hunter Behavior in America: A Survey of State Fish and Wildlife Agencies Conducted by the Izaak Walton League of America.* Arlington, VA: Izaak Walton League of America. http://www.iwla.org/policies/ch15.html.

J

Japan, Gun Laws

Japanese law prohibits the ownership of pistols while imposing a very strict licensing system on shotguns and air guns, as well as an even more severe licensing for rifles. The firearm law appears to be both a cause and a consequence of the relatively authoritarian nature of Japanese society. Starting in the 1990s, Japan began to work to impose its firearm policies on other nations.

Japanese gun law (like New Jersey gun law) starts with prohibition as the norm: "No one shall possess a firearm or firearms or a sword or swords." From there, some exceptions are made. Japanese sportsmen are permitted to possess shotguns for hunting and for skeet and trap shooting, but only after submitting to a lengthy licensing procedure. Air rifles (but not air pistols) are also allowed for sporting purposes.

A prospective gun owner must first attend classes and pass a written test. Shooting-range classes and a shooting test follow; 95 percent pass. After the safety exam, the applicant takes a simple "mental test" at a local hospital to ensure that the applicant is not suffering from a readily detectable mental illness. The applicant then produces for the police a medical certificate attesting that he or she is mentally healthy and not addicted to drugs. The police investigate the applicant's background and relatives, ensuring that both are crime-free. Membership in "aggressive" political or activist groups disqualifies an applicant. The police have unlimited discretion to deny licenses to any person for whom "there is reasonable cause to suspect [he or she] may be dangerous to other persons' lives or properties or to the public peace."

Gun owners must store their weapons in a locker and give the police a map of the apartment showing the location of the locker. Ammunition must be kept in a separate locked safe. The licenses also allow the holder to buy a few thousand rounds of ammunition, with each transaction being registered.

Civilians can never own handguns. After possessing a shotgun license for ten years, a person may receive a rifle license for calibers .25 through .40. Rifles in .22 caliber are allowed only to elite target shooters such as Olympic hopefuls. Matchlock guns do not require any license. Hunting is allowed only with modern shotguns and rifles, not with bows or with antique guns such as muzzleloaders.

The severe controls on gun ownership in Japan are consistent with Japanese practices on other matters that are guaranteed by the Bill of Rights in the United States, but which are subject to extensive control in Japan. For example, Japan has no meaningful limits on police search and seizure. A person who is arrested may be held incommunicado for long periods of time, and, according to the Tokyo Bar Association, police torture of suspects is routine. Compared to trials in the United States, criminal trial procedures are much more heavily tilted toward the government, and acquittals are extremely rare. Trial by jury has been abolished. Restrictions on speech and the press are much broader than in the United States.

Guns first arrived in Japan along with the first trading ships from Portugal in 1542 or 1543. The Portuguese had landed on Tanegashima Island outside Kyushu. One day the Portuguese trader Mendez Pinto took Totitaka, Lord of Tanegashima, for a walk. The trader shot a duck. The Lord of Tanegashima made immediate arrangements to take shooting lessons, and within a month he bought both Portuguese guns, or *Tanegashima,* as the Japanese soon called them.

The *Tanegashima* caught on quickly among Japan's feuding warlords. The novelty of the guns was the main reason that the Portuguese were treated well. The Japanese rapidly improved their firearm technology. They invented a device to make matchlocks fire in the rain (the Europeans never figured out how to do this), refined the matchlock trigger and spring, developed a serial firing technique, and increased the matchlock's caliber. The Arabs, Indians, and Chinese had all acquired firearms long before the Japanese, but only the Japanese mastered large-scale domestic manufacture.

By 1560, firearms were being used effectively in large battles. In 1567, Lord Takeda Harunobu declared, "Hereafter, guns will be the most important arms." Less than three decades after Japan saw its first gun, there were more guns in Japan than in any other nation on the planet. Several Japanese feudal lords had more guns than the whole British army.

It was Lord Oda Nobunaga whose army truly mastered the new firearm technology. At Nagashino in 1575, 3,000 of Nobunaga's conscript peasants with muskets hid behind wooden posts and devastated the enemy's cavalry charge. Feudal wars between armies of samurai knights had ravaged Japan for centuries. Nobunaga and his peasant army, equipped with matchlocks, conquered most of Japan and helped bring the feudal wars to an end.

Guns dramatically changed the nature of war. In earlier times, after the introductions fighters would pair off and go at each other in single combat—a method of fighting apt to let individual heroism shine. Armored, highly trained samurai had the advantage. But with guns, the unskilled could be deployed en masse and destroy the armored knights with ease. Understandably, the noble *bushi* class thought firearms undignified.

Starting out as a groom for Lord Nobunaga, a peasant named Hideyoshi rose through the ranks to take control of Nobunaga's army after Nobunaga died. A brilliant strategist, Hideyoshi finished the job that Nobunaga began and reunified Japan's feudal states under a strong central government. On August 29, 1588, Hideyoshi announced "the Sword Hunt" (*taiko no katana-gari*) and banned possession of swords and firearms by the nonnoble classes. He decreed: "The people in the various provinces are strictly forbidden to have in their possession any swords, short swords, bows, spears, firearms or other arms. The possession of unnecessary implements makes difficult the collection of taxes and tends to foment uprisings.... Therefore the heads of provinces, official agents and deputies are ordered to collect all the weapons mentioned above and turn them over to the Government."

Although the intent of Hideyoshi's decree was plain, the Sword Hunt was presented to the masses under the pretext that all the swords would be melted down to supply nails and bolts for a temple containing a huge statue of the Buddha. The western missionaries' *Jesuit Annual Letter* reported that Hideyoshi "is depriving the people of their arms under the pretext of devotion to religion." Once the swords and guns were collected, Hideyoshi had them melted into a statue of himself.

According to historian Stephen Turnbull (1977, p. 190), "Hideyoshi's resources were such that the edict was carried out to the letter. The growing social mobility of peasants was thus flung suddenly into reverse.... Hideyoshi had deprived the peasants of their weapons. Ieyasu [the next ruler] now began to deprive them of their self respect. If a peasant offended a samurai he might be cut down on the spot by the samurai's sword."

The inferior status of the peasantry having been affirmed by civil disarmament, the samurai enjoyed *kiri-sute gomen,* or permission to kill and depart. Any disrespectful member of the lower class could be executed by a samurai's sword. Hideyoshi forbade peasants to leave their land without their superior's permission and required that warriors, peasants, and merchants all remain in their current posts.

After Hideyoshi died, Ieyasu founded the Tokugawa Shogunate, which would rule Japan for the next two and a half centuries. Peasants were assigned to a "five-man group," headed by landholders who were responsible for the group's behavior. The groups arranged marriages, resolved disputes, maintained religious orthodoxy, and enforced the rules against peasants possessing firearms or swords. The weapons laws clarified and stabilized class distinctions. Samurai had swords; peasants did not.

The Japanese experience was consistent with the belief of Aristotle and Plato that deprivation of a role in the armed defense of a society would lead to deprivation of any role in governing that society. Historian Mary Elizabeth Berry (1982) explains: "The mounted magistrates who rounded up everything from muskets to daggers changed men's thoughts about themselves. Farmers had borne arms for centuries and taken part in the contests that helped fix the rights of lordship. Their military role brought political influence and obscured class boundaries. A pivotal member of his community by the warring-states era, the armed peasant symbolized opportunity. The confiscation of his weapons, far more than a 'hardship,' altered a condition of life."

Historian Noel Perrin (1979) offers five reasons why Japan was able to renounce the gun while Europe was not, despite the fierce resistance to guns by the European aristocracy. First, the samurai warrior nobility, who hated guns, amounted to 6–10 percent of the population, unlike in Europe, where the noble class never exceeded 1 percent. Second, the Japanese islands were so hard to invade and the Japanese were such formidable fighters that swords and bows sufficed for national defense. Third, according to Perrin, swords were what the Japanese truly valued. Guns depreciated the importance of swords, so a policy of protecting swords by eliminating guns was bound to be popular, at least with the classes who carried swords. Fourth, the elimination of guns was part of a xenophobic reaction against outside influences, particularly Christianity. Finally, writes Perrin, in a society where aesthetics were prized, swords were valued because they were graceful to use in combat.

During the early twentieth century, the gun controls were slightly relaxed. Tokyo and other major ports were allowed to have five gun shops each and other prefectures were allowed three. Revolver sales were allowed with a police permit, and registration of every transaction was required.

In the 1920s and 1930s, the military came increasingly to control civilian life. Historian Hidehiro Sonoda (1985, p. 200) explains: "The army and the navy were vast organizations with a monopoly on physical violence. There was no force in Japan that could offer any resistance."

Although the Japanese devastated much of the U.S. Navy's Pacific Fleet with the Pearl Harbor attack, seized some islands in Alaska, and conducted a few raids on the West Coast, the Japanese Imperial Navy and Army never seriously contemplated a full-scale invasion of the American mainland—in part because they believed that the American population was well armed and well practiced in firearm use.

After World War II ended with Japan in ruins, the military was reviled by the Japanese people and abolished by General MacArthur's occupation government. The MacArthur government also dismantled centralized national control of the police. In 1946, it ordered the Japanese police to begin carrying guns; upon finding out that this edict was still being ignored in 1948, the American occupation forces distributed revolvers to the Japanese police.

Today, the police have reverted to central national control, and many of the American-style restrictions on police power that the occupation government wrote into the new Japanese constitution are ignored. The American-imposed policy of police armament remains in place, however.

But unlike in the United States, police regulations and culture do not glorify police gun ownership and use (and therefore, unlike in the United States, do not promote a broader gun culture by example). Japanese police carry only .38 special revolvers, not the high-capacity 9 mm handguns often toted by the U.S. police. No officer would ever carry a second smaller handgun as a backup, as many American police do. Policemen may not add individual touches, such as pearl handles or unusual holsters, to dress up their guns. While U.S. police are often required to carry guns while off duty, and almost always are granted the privilege if they wish (even when retired), Japanese police must always leave their guns at the station. Unlike in the United States, desk-bound police administrators, traffic police, most plainclothes detectives, and even the riot police do not carry guns.

One poster on Japanese police walls ordered: "Don't take it out of the holster, don't put your finger on the trigger, don't point it at people." Shooting at a fleeing felon is unlawful under any circumstance, whereas U.S. police and civilians are both allowed to use deadly force to stop certain types of escaping felons. Japanese police and civilians can both be punished for any act of self-defense in which the harm caused was greater than the harm averted. In an average year, the entire Tokyo police force only fires a few shots.

The Japanese gun suicide rate is one-fiftieth of the rate in the United States, but Japan's overall suicide rate is nearly twice as high. Teenage suicide is much more frequent in Japan. Japan also suffers from double or multiple suicides (*shinju*). Parents bent on suicide often take their children with them (*oyako-shinju*).

Of the many reasons suggested by researchers for the high Japanese suicide rate, one of the most startling is weapons control. Japanese scholars Mamon Iga and Kichinosuke Tatai (1975) argue that one reason Japan has a suicide problem is that people have little sympathy for suicide victims. Iga and Tatai suggest that the lack of sympathy—and hence the lack of social will to deal with a high suicide rate—is based in Japanese feelings of insecurity and a consequent lack of empathy. They trace the lack of empathy to a "dread of power." That dread is caused in part by the awareness that a person cannot count on others for help against violence or against authority. In addition, say Iga and Tatai, the dread of power stems from people being forbidden to possess swords or firearms for self-defense.

In 1999, there were 1,265 murders reported to the police in Japan—not counting cases of parents killing children, which are often classified as suicide rather than murder. That same year, 4,237 robberies were reported. Some scholars argue that Japanese crime reporting rates are unusually low, because victims fear retaliation from the organized criminal gangs (*yakuza*) who perpetrate much of the crime. Even so, gun crime is rare, and violent crime is much lower than in the United States.

To gun prohibition advocates, Japan represents the ideal, with its near-prohibitory controls and nearly no gun crime. Skeptics argue that Japan's low crime rates are mainly due to cultural factors. Skeptics also point out that the crime rate of Japanese Americans (who have just as much access to guns as do other Americans) is actually lower than the crime rate of Japanese in Japan.

It is also argued that Japanese-style gun laws, whatever their efficacy, are particularly unsuited to the United States, since American ownership of guns is deeply tied to American concepts of individualism, self-protection, and freedom from oppressive government. To many in Japan, where the focus is on the group rather than the individual, the American attitude seems absurd and barbaric.

On the evening of October 17, 1992, in Baton Rouge, Louisiana, a Japanese exchange student named Yoshihiro Hattori and a teenager from his host family, Webb Haymaker, entered a carport, mistakenly thinking that the home was hosting a Halloween party. The teenagers had the wrong address. Frightened by the rapidly approaching young males, Bonnie Peairs screamed for help, and her husband, Rodney, came running with a .44 Smith & Wesson revolver. He yelled, "Freeze!" Haymaker retreated and tried to get Hattori to stop, but Hattori, apparently not understanding that "Freeze!" can mean "Don't move or I'll shoot," advanced toward Peairs, who pulled the trigger and shot him dead.

Rodney Peairs was acquitted of manslaughter in a criminal trial, partly because Haymaker testified that, in the dark, Hattori's camera might have looked like a gun, and that Hattori waved his arms at Peairs.

While the incident initially attracted only brief attention in the national American press, the shooting horrified Japan, where television networks devoted massive coverage to "the freeze case." In July 1993, President Clinton apologized to Hattori's parents, Masaichi and Mieko. At Yoshi's funeral, the parents stated, "The thing we must really despise, more than the criminal, is the American law that permits people to own guns."

Over the next several months, 1.7 million Japanese and 150,000 Americans signed Mrs. Hattori's "Petition for Removing Guns from Households in the United States." Working with the Coalition to Stop Gun Violence, the Hattoris delivered the petitions to President

Clinton personally on November 16, 1993, a few days before final Senate passage of the Brady Bill. President Clinton told the Hattoris that he believed that only police and the military should have handguns.

Mrs. Hattori tells Japanese audiences that the petitions led to the passage of the Brady Bill. Mr. and Mrs. Hattori filed a civil suit against Peairs, won $653,000, and used part of the money to set up foundations that award money to antigun groups in the United States and that bring an American student to Japan each year to experience gun-free life.

Spurred in part by the Hattori tragedy, in the 1990s Japan began funding gun surrender programs in South Africa, pushing the United Nations to act against private gun ownership, and supporting gun prohibition around the world. Although the core of the gun prohibition campaign is a belief that Japan's policy is culturally superior, another basis is that, according to the Japanese National Policy Agency (NPA), handguns are smuggled into Japan from the United States, China, the Philippines, Thailand, Russia, Brazil, Peru, and South Africa. The NPA reports that the main techniques are spot-welding guns to cars imported to Japan, smuggling guns aboard fishing boats, concealing them in sea or air cargo, and hiding them in hand-carried luggage inside items such as electric appliances.

Ironically, Japan has a large firearm manufacturing industry geared toward the export market. Browning firearms are manufactured there, by the Miroku Firearms Manufacturing Company, as are several other well-respected brands of shotguns.

David B. Kopel

See also Canada, Gun Laws; Gun Control
For Further Reading:

Berry, Mary Elizabeth. 1982. *Hideyoshi.* Cambridge, MA: Harvard University Press.
Iga, Mamon, and Kichinosuke Tatai. 1975. "Characteristics of Suicide and Attitudes toward Suicides in Japan." Pp. 255–280 in *Suicide in Different Cultures,* ed. Norman Farebrow. Baltimore: University Park Press.
Kopel, David B. 1992. *The Samurai, the Mountie, and the Cowboy: Should America Adopt the Gun Controls of Other Democracies?* Buffalo, NY: Prometheus.
_____. 1993. "Japanese Gun Control." *Asia-Pacific Law Review* 2: 26–52. http://www.davekopel.com/2A/LawRev/Japanese_Gun_Control.htm.
Perrin, Noel. 1979. *Giving Up the Gun: Japan's Reversion to the Sword, 1543–1879.* Boston: David R. Godine.
Sonoda, Hidehiro. 1985. "Seventy-Seven Keys to the Civilization of Japan." In *Seventy-Seven Keys to the Civilization of Japan,* ed. Tadao Umesao. Union City, CA: Heian International.
Turnbull, Stephen R. 1977. *The Samurai: A Military History.* New York: Macmillan.
Yoshi Coalition. http://www.tcp-ip.or.jp/~hatmi/english.html.

Jefferson, Thomas (1743–1826)

Thomas Jefferson was one of the intellectual leaders of the American Revolution. He was the author of the Declaration of Independence, the nation's first secretary of state, and its third president. Throughout his political career, Jefferson was a staunch advocate of limited government and a champion of individual rights. His faith in the capacity of the people to govern themselves and his distrust of government led the Virginia statesman to be a proponent of an armed citizenry. Jefferson's writings and papers have subsequently been used as an intellectual foundation for opponents of gun control.

Jefferson was born on April 13, 1743, in Albemarle County, Virginia. His parents were among the Virginia elite and Jefferson grew up in a culture of wealth and privilege. In 1769, Jefferson entered the College of William and Mary. While at William and Mary, Jefferson studied under some of the greatest scholars in the British North American colonies and became a devotee of the European Enlightenment. After graduation, Jefferson studied law and was admitted to the Virginia Bar in 1767. Following the death of his father, Jefferson inherited a sizable estate. In 1770, he began construction of his homestead, known as Monticello. When completed, the estate became noted for its architectural innovations, style, and grace. In 1772, Jefferson married Martha Wayles Skelton.

Jefferson became a noted lawyer, but his real interest was politics. In 1769, the 25-year-old Virginian was elected to the colony's legislature,

Thomas Jefferson. (Library of Congress)

the House of Burgesses. In the legislature, Jefferson developed a reputation for brilliance with the pen, but also for poor oratorical skills. After the British disbanded the colonial legislature in 1774, Jefferson remained active in politics as one of the foremost advocates of American independence. He was one of the founding members of the Virginia Committee of Correspondence and worked to foster a recognition of the natural rights of people, including the right of self-government. Jefferson's position and influence led to his election to the First Continental Congress in 1775. The following year, Jefferson worked to draft the first constitution for the state of Virginia. In his draft, Jefferson wrote that "no freeman should ever be disbarred the use of arms." This statement reflected Jefferson's belief in the necessity of a well-armed citizenry in order to fight the British and any other future despots. It also reflected the political reality of the day, when firearms were an essential part of society and widely used for hunting and self-defense.

In 1776, Jefferson was designated one of four members charged to draft a declaration of independence from Great Britain. Jefferson himself penned the first draft. It was accepted with only

minor revisions. In its final form, the Declaration of Independence detailed the basic principles of the American Revolution, including the notion of universal rights, and listed the specific grievances that the colonists had against the British monarchy. Three years later, Jefferson was elected governor of Virginia. As governor, he wrote the Bill for Establishing Religious Freedom. This measure was the model for the religious freedoms contained in the First Amendment of the Constitution. As governor, Jefferson became firmly convinced of the need for a well-armed militia. British troops invaded the state and Jefferson became the focal point for blame because of the ineffectiveness of the state's troops.

Jefferson served in a variety of political posts in the government of the new nation. He was elected to Congress again in 1783 and then appointed minister to France. Jefferson was absent during the debate over the Constitution and the Bill of Rights. Nonetheless, from France he expressed his support for the right of individuals to possess arms as a means to counter tyranny. He envisioned a well-armed citizenry as the most effective means to prevent the national government from transgressing on the rights of individuals and the states. He also perceived that a well-armed population could negate the need for a regular standing army. Since armies were often used as tools of oppression, Jefferson hoped that the nation could rely on well-regulated state militias for defense instead of a large military. In 1789, President George Washington asked Jefferson to become the country's first secretary of state. Jefferson disagreed with Washington and other Federalists, including Alexander Hamilton, who championed a strong central government. Tensions between Secretary of State Jefferson and Hamilton, who was secretary of the treasury, led Jefferson to resign in 1793.

The growing power of the federal government led Jefferson to run for the presidency in 1796. He lost to John Adams, but under the system at the time the second-place finisher became vice president. Jefferson ran successfully for the presidency in 1800. He served two terms as president. His tenure was notable for the Louisiana Purchase in 1803, which doubled the size of the United States, and for his use of military force to end tribute payments to the Barbary pirates. When he left office in 1809, Jefferson was succeeded by his friend and political protégé, James Madison, who had served as Jefferson's secretary of state. For the remainder of his life, Jefferson remained active in politics and was instrumental in the establishment of the University of Virginia in 1819. He died at Monticello on July 4, 1826, only hours after the death of his friend and political opponent John Adams.

Jefferson's mistrust of large government has been embraced by opponents of gun control. Groups such as the National Rifle Association view government efforts to restrict access to firearms or proposals to register weapons as steps toward an eventual confiscation of all individual weapons. Like Jefferson, they suggest that a well-armed citizenry is the best check on government despotism.

Tom Lansford

See also American Revolution; Anglo-Saxon Tradition of the Right to Keep and Bear Arms; National Rifle Association
For Further Reading:
Eicholz, Hans L. 2001. *Harmonizing Sentiments: The Declaration of Independence and the Jeffersonian Idea of Self Government.* New York: P. Lang.
Ferling, John. 2000. *Setting the World Ablaze: Washington, Adams, Jefferson, and the American Revolution.* New York: Oxford University Press.
Read, James H. 2000. *Power versus Liberty: Madison, Hamilton, Wilson, and Jefferson.* Charlottesville: University Press of Virginia.
Skarmeas, Nancy. 1998. *Thomas Jefferson.* Nashville, TN: Ideals Publications.

Jews for the Preservation of Firearms Ownership (JPFO)

Jews for the Preservation of Firearms Ownership is a civil rights organization focused on firearm ownership as a fundamental right. JPFO believes that citizens have the right to own firearms primarily to resist aggression, oppression, and genocide, and only secondarily for hunting, sport, or collecting.

JPFO membership is open to all who share its views. The organization publishes books, booklets, the *Bill of Rights Sentinel* journal, articles, and other educational materials. Some of its publications are aimed at the general reader,

while others are designed to influence people who ordinarily do not read books. JPFO publications often present scholarly research that is unavailable elsewhere. Its book *"Gun Control": Gateway to Tyranny* (1993) argued that there are direct parallels between the Nazi Weapons Law of 1938 and the U.S. Gun Control Act of 1968.

Death by Gun Control (2001) draws upon that book as well as *Lethal Laws* (1994) and newer sources to argue that gun control laws render citizens defenseless against aggression by criminals or governments. By compiling the relevant gun laws and examining the history of several twentieth-century genocides and recent mass murders, *Death by Gun Control* argues that disarming a targeted population makes genocide possible. This thesis makes a priori sense, given that any regime with a political goal would prefer to achieve that goal as cheaply as possible, and that an armed and resisting target population is either impossible or relatively expensive to eliminate.

JPFO also distributes *Dial 911 and Die* (1999), which collects laws from all fifty American states to show that the government and police have no legal duty to protect individual citizens from crime or criminal attack, and *The Mitzvah* (1999), an action novel of ideas that examines the prejudices of some Jews against firearm ownership and self-defense. Other publications include the popular "Grandpa Jack" series of small-format illustrated pamphlets that make arguments from the history of gun control, the role of firearms in defeating oppression, and especially the firearm-control aspects of the Third Reich. The pamphlets argue that the motivations of gun prohibitionists are racist, elitist, and dangerous.

Samuel C. Wheeler III

See also Genocide and Guns; Racism and Gun Control; Second Amendment
For Further Reading:
Jews for the Preservation of Firearms Ownership home page: http://www.jpfo.org.
Kates, Don B., Jr., and Daniel Polsby. 1995. "Review of *Lethal Laws.*" *Journal of Criminal Law and Criminology* 86, 1 (Fall): 247–256.
_____. 1997. "Of Holocausts and Gun Control." *Washington University Law Quarterly* 75, 3: 1237–1275.

Simkin, Jay, Aaron Zelman, and Alan M. Rice. 1994. *Lethal Laws.* Hartford, WI: JPFO Publishing.

Stevens, Richard W., and Aaron Zelman. 2001. *Death by Gun Control.* Hartford, WI: JPFO Publishing.

John Birch Society

The John Birch Society was founded by Robert Welch as a means to counter what some conservatives perceived to be a vast Communist conspiracy to undermine the United States and western ideals. The organization is rooted in conservative religious values and broadly opposes government efforts to restrict gun ownership. The power and influence of the society reached their peak in the 1960s, when it emerged as one of the nation's most visible right-wing groups.

The John Birch Society was named after missionary John Morrison Birch (1918–1945), who was killed by Chinese Communists on August 25, 1945, just ten days after the end of World War II. A wealthy Boston candy magnate, Robert H. W. Welch, Jr. (1899–1985), thought that Birch was the first casualty in the struggle between the forces of communism, as represented by China and the Soviet Union, and the forces of freedom, as represented by the United States. Welch was convinced that the American way of life was under attack by subversive elements in the United States. Welch supported Sen. Joseph McCarthy's efforts to expose known and suspected Communists in the United States during the 1950s. The society also opposed the candidacy of Dwight D. Eisenhower in 1952, because the former general was perceived as being too moderate and "soft" on communism. Welch founded the John Birch Society in 1958 in an effort to combat what he perceived to be an attack on American politics and culture.

The society's main principles were based on conservative religious beliefs, anticommunism, and fear of the pervasive nature of both state and national governments. The fall of Cuba to Communist forces led by Fidel Castro in 1959 seemed to confirm for Welch and the leadership of the society the corruption of the Eisenhower administration. In order to promote the society, Welch wrote a number of works, including a biography of Birch, *The Life of John Birch.* Meanwhile, the society became noted for its numerous pamphlets and books, including the regular journals *American Opinion* and *The New American.* The ultraconservative message of the organization appealed to some Americans who mistrusted the central government. This message centered around the idea that there was a vast left-wing conspiracy of American liberals, international Communists, and moderate American Republicans who worked together to undermine the Christian values and individual liberties of Americans.

Efforts by the national and state governments to restrict access to guns or to register weapons were seen by the society as part of a larger conspiracy to ensure the complacency of the citizenry by depriving them of the ability to resist government excesses and defend their property and families. Soon the society had branches in all fifty states and its membership rose into the hundreds of thousands. The society organized broad letter-writing campaigns and organized grassroots efforts to defeat various candidates and legislation (including gun control legislation). The visibility of the society eventually harmed mainstream conservative groups and the Republican Party by enhancing the perception in the 1960s that conservatives were extremists. For instance, the 1964 defeat of Republican presidential candidate Barry Goldwater was partially attributed to this image.

By the 1980s, the society began to decline dramatically in both membership and influence. The death of Welch in 1985 and the collapse of communism at the end of the decade led to a deep decline in membership. On the domestic level, the organization continues to oppose gun control legislation. Meanwhile, on the international level, the society continues to work for the withdrawal of the United States from the United Nations.

Tom Lansford

See also United Nations
For Further Reading:
Broyles, J. Allen. 1964. *The John Birch Society: Anatomy of a Protest.* Boston: Beacon Press.

Himmelstein, Jerome L. 1990. *To the Right: The Transformation of American Conservatism.* Berkeley: University of California Press.

Schomp, Gerald. 1970. *Birchism Was My Business.* New York: Macmillan.

Johns Hopkins Center for Gun Policy and Research
See Center for Gun Policy and Research

Johnson, Lyndon B. (1908–1973)

As the thirty-sixth president of the United States, Lyndon Baines Johnson fought for and signed America's first comprehensive national gun control legislation. Johnson took office in November 1963 following the assassination of President John F. Kennedy. From 1965 through 1968, the United States suffered through a devastating series of urban summer riots, primarily involving blacks who destroyed and looted small businesses in their neighborhoods. In March 1968, Martin Luther King, Jr., was assassinated, sparking a new round of riots. In June 1968, Sen. Robert F. Kennedy was assassinated the night he won the California presidential primary. The growing sense of national lawlessness and disorder helped spur President Johnson to make a major speech to promote comprehensive gun registration a few weeks later.

Calling for every gun and every gun owner to be placed on a government list, President Johnson argued that "in other countries which have sensible laws, the hunter and the sportsman thrive." Johnson's speech provided important support for antigun legislation—which had long been endorsed by the Johnson administration—and which was being pushed in Congress by Sen. Thomas Dodd (D-CT).

The Johnson administration included individuals with a wide variety of opinions on gun rights. On the one hand, Vice President Hubert Humphrey had told *Guns* magazine in 1960 that "certainly one of the chief guarantees of freedom under any government, no matter how popular and respected, is the right of citizens to keep and bear arms.... The right of citizens to bear arms is just one guarantee against arbitrary government, one more safeguard against the tyranny which now appears remote in America but which historically has proven to be always possible."

On the other hand, Johnson's attorneys general, Nicholas Katzenbach and Ramsey Clark, were strong opponents of Second Amendment rights. Indeed, Clark's position on gun prohibi-

Lyndon B. Johnson. (Library of Congress)

tion, expressed after he left the Johnson administration, showed him to be an even more determined opponent of guns than President Clinton's attorney general, Janet Reno.

After a summer of political struggle in Washington, a compromise version of the Dodd bill was passed as the Gun Control Act of 1968 and eagerly signed into law by President Johnson. As president, Johnson ranks second only to William J. Clinton in using the presidency as a platform to push for extensive gun controls.

David B. Kopel

See also Dodd, Thomas Joseph; Emergency Committee for Gun Control; Gun Control Act of 1968; Gun Registration
For Further Reading:
President Johnson's June 24, 1968, speech, *Congressional Record,* June 24, 1968: H5371–5372.

Justifiable Homicides

The term "justifiable homicide" has a variety of technical meanings. As used here it covers two overlapping circumstances in which crime victims use force likely to cause death or great bodily injury: (1) the victim reasonably believes the use of such force is necessary to avert a threat of immediate and unlawful infliction of such force against her or another innocent; and (2) the victim's use of such force is necessary to prevent the commission of an atrocious felony (rape, robbery, arson, or the like). A person lawfully killed is called a "decedent." The person who killed him is called a "victim" because she generally is a crime victim (and referred to as "she" to further distinguish her from the decedent, who in a lawful civilian homicide is virtually always male).

Legal Doctrine: The Anglo-American law of deadly force rests on concepts of proportion and reasonability. Continental European legal theory is very different as exemplified by a 1920 German case in which the owner of an orchard shot a fleeing child, that being the only way to prevent the child from escaping with some of his fruit. Such a killing would have been illegal under English law even in medieval times. But the German court exonerated the owner using Kantian categorical reasoning: the owner was in the right and the child in the wrong, and the right need never yield to the wrong (Fletcher, 1985, p. 952).

Under Anglo-American law, deadly force may be used only to preserve personal safety and not for the protection of mere property (except when it is inextricably linked to safety). Thus the reason a householder may shoot a burglar who broke into her home is not to protect the property but because of the inherent threat such a situation poses to her safety. But if upon looking out a window a householder sees her car being stolen from her driveway, she is not privileged to shoot, for the theft poses no danger to her safety (Kates and Engberg, 1982, pp. 874–888).

Likewise the victim is privileged to shoot a rapist or robber because she is not required to submit to his demands and he is explicitly or implicitly threatening her safety unless she submits. But a storekeeper is not privileged to shoot to prevent the escape of a mere shoplifter, for the shoplifter is only threatening her property, not her safety.

Empirical Findings: Justifiable civilian homicide (JCH) has received little attention as a criminological phenomenon. The most complete treatment is found in MacDonald and Tennenbaum (1999), which also reviews other treatments. There is less than perfect understanding as to how often JCHs occur and in what circumstances. National (though partial) data available from the FBI's unpublished supplementary homicide reports include only such JCH data as local police choose to report to the FBI. MacDonald and Tennenbaum's (1999) analysis of a fifteen-year set of these FBI data, as well as of a few city-level data sets with more detail, suggests the following tentative generalizations:

(1) In the great majority of JCHs the weapon involved is a firearm, with 68.2 percent being handguns. The obvious reason for this is that victims of criminal attack are usually weaker than attackers and also are taken by surprise. Unless the victim has a firearm, when a death occurs in such an unequal confrontation it will usually be hers, even if the attacker has no weapon. Tellingly, firearms are significantly more often used in JCHs (up to 92 percent) than they are in criminal homicides (68 percent).

(2) JCHs are concentrated in the areas of the country that also have most criminal homicides; indeed, the six cities with populations of over a million people have roughly 22 percent of American criminal homicides and 40 percent of JCHs. A narrow majority of JCH decedents are white, as are a narrow majority of the victims who killed them.

(3) The great majority of both decedents and victims are male, the decedent being in his early 20s and the victim 15–20 years older. Most of the decedents have criminal records, while the victims do not.

(4) A large majority of the decedents are strangers to the victim and are killed in her home or business, which they have entered or broken into.

Data Gaps and Bias: The last two generalizations above may, however, be misleading results of problems and biases in the FBI data. Those data cover only 20 percent or less of JCHs while the other 80 percent may have very different circumstances (Kleck, 1991, pp. 112–113). An unknown number of JCHs occur on the streets and the victim just walks away without reporting the JCH to police, who later misclassify the death as a murder. Some such incidents involve ordinary people who flee because, even though they legally shot a mugger, they had no license and so were committing a crime by carrying the gun. Other JCH perpetrators are criminals, such as a drug dealer who defends himself against a robber and walks away because reporting the killing would mean admitting his own illegal drug dealing. Another reason the FBI files undercount JCHs is that if the police classify a homicide as a JCH they may put little effort into pursuing it and may not bother including it in their report to the FBI.

Far more important lacunae that bias reported JCH cases are caused by the FBI reporting protocol. It requires that homicides be reported to the FBI as the police initially classified them. A JCH will, therefore, be reported to the FBI as a murder if the police initially classified it as possibly unlawful—even though the coroner, prosecutor, or court eventually determined it to be a lawful defensive homicide.

This FBI protocol severely restricts how many and what kind of JCHs get reported to the FBI. Police agencies have a very strong disincentive to initially classify a JCH as such even if they think it eventually will be so classified by the prosecutor. From the police viewpoint there is no harm in initially classifying a killing as possibly unlawful since it will not be prosecuted if the prosecutors later decide it was a JCH. On the other hand, if the police initially call it a JCH that will severely reduce the likelihood of conviction if prosecutors later decide to try it as an unlawful homicide: defense counsel will seize on the initial police finding of a JCH as proving there is reasonable doubt.

The following examples suggest contrasting factors that might move police to initially classify a homicide as a JCH or otherwise:

Example 1: The decedent, a man with a long record of burglaries, is shot dead after breaking into the victim's home. The victim has no record and no prior acquaintance with the decedent. Though the police may hesitate to initially classify even such a clear case as a JCH, they may nevertheless do so because there seems to be no other plausible explanation of the facts.

Example 2: The decedent, a man with a long record of physically abusing his wife, is shot dead by her in their home. She claims he was advancing on her holding a knife and screaming that he was going to kill her this time. A knife is found in his hand. If he actually was approaching her this way, this is a JCH. But there are at least two other possibilities: (1) they got into an angry but nonphysical quarrel, she killed him, and then she planted the knife in his hand; (2) he was threatening to hurt her and was approaching her, but without a weapon, when she shot him and then planted the knife. Note how the fact of his previous abuse cuts both ways. While it shows he is violent and abusive, it also shows that he had never previously inflicted the kind of extreme violence the law requires to justify the defensive use of deadly force. (It should be noted, however, that domestic homicides are usually preceded by multiple prior assaults by the male partner on the female.) The police may well deem it premature to initially classify the death as a JCH because investigation might develop facts that crucially bear on whether the killing was justifiable or not. For instance, scientific comparison of the position of the bullet hole in the victim with its position in his clothing may show that the clothing was not stretched upward as it would be if his arm was upraised. So the police will probably initially classify the killing as possibly criminal, even though they think the wife is telling the truth and that the eventual decision will be to not prosecute her.

The severe bias caused by the FBI protocol is illustrated by comparison to a data set of JCHs that were later so classified by the coroner's office rather than by the police. If only those JCHs initially so classified by the police are counted, JCHs comprise less than 1.7 percent of all homicides (MacDonald and Tennenbaum, 1999, table 18.1). But in Challener, Adelson, and Rushforth's (1987) analysis of twenty-five years of homicides in Cleveland, JCHs so classified by the coroner constituted 11.2 percent of the total; indeed, in this sample, JCHs accounted for over three times more dead criminals than police had killed. And unlike the JCHs in the FBI sample, the Cleveland JCHs were not virtually limited to cases involving men killing other men whom they had never previously met.

Detroit data also show how different the characteristics of JCHs are when the sample is not arbitrarily limited to the few initially so classified by police. More wives kill husbands in Detroit than vice versa, yet far more husbands are convicted of spouse killing, as even if police initially classified their killings as unlawful, three-quarters of the wives were not charged because prosecutors eventually classified their killings as lawful, having been necessary to preserve their lives or those of their children (Daly and Wilson, 1988, p. 15 and table 9.1).

The FBI protocol is likely to produce a severe underestimate of the number of JCHs committed by women; for although women kill far less often than men, when women do kill the decedent is almost always a man, generally one with whom they have had a relationship and who has abused them (Daly and Wilson, 1988, p. 278). These facts mean that the police are very unlikely to initially classify a killing by a woman as a JCH, even though the killing may eventually end up being so classified. Thus MacDonald and Tennenbaum's finding that the killer in most JCHs was a man and that the decedent was a stranger who had invaded the man's home or business may simply be an artifact of an FBI reporting protocol that severely minimizes the number of JCHs.

Don B. Kates

See also Average-Joe Thesis; Defensive Gun Use, Legal Issues; Right to Self-Defense; Self-Defense, Reasons for Gun Use

For Further Reading:

Challener, R. C., L. Adelson, and N. B. Rushforth. 1987. "Justifiable Homicide: A Study of the Application of Nonculpable Deadly Force in Cuyahoga County (Cleveland), Ohio, 1958–1982." *Journal of Forensic Sciences* 32: 1389–1402.

Daly, Martin, and Margo Wilson. 1988. *Homicide.* New York: Aldine de Gruyter.

Fletcher, George P. 1985. "The Right and the Reasonable." *Harvard Law Review* 98: 949–982.

Kates, Don B., and Nancy J. Engberg. 1982. "Deadly Force Self-Defense against Rape." *University of California–Davis Law Review* 15: 873–906.

Kleck, Gary. 1991. *Point Blank: Guns and Violence in America.* New York: Aldine de Gruyter.

MacDonald, John M., and Avraham Tennenbaum. 1999. "Justifiable Homicide by Civilians." Pp. 463–491 in *The Criminology of Criminal Law,* ed. William S. Laufer and Freda Adler. New Brunswick, NJ: Transaction.

K

Don B. Kates. (Courtesy of author)

Kates, Don B., Jr. (1941–)

Don Kates's scholarship and litigation have played important parts in the modern renaissance of the Second Amendment. More importantly, Kates has played a major role in bringing together scholars and opinion leaders. Along with Stephen Halbrook, Kates deserves the primary credit for making Second Amendment scholarship an important topic of scholarly interest.

After growing up in the San Francisco Bay Area, Kates matriculated at Reed College. He then attended Yale Law School and served as a law clerk for the famous radical attorney William Kunstler. Kates spent one summer during law school in the South as a civil rights worker. Like many other civil rights workers, he carried firearms for personal protection against the Ku Klux Klan and other violent white supremacists whose attempts to murder civil rights workers were tacitly supported by local sheriffs.

After graduating from Yale, Kates went to work for California Rural Legal Assistance and the San Mateo Legal Aid Society. In 1969, he was awarded the Reginald Heber Smith Medal by the National Legal Aid and Defender Association as poverty lawyer of the year. The award was partly based on his work in the case of *Damico v. California* (389 U.S. 416, 1967), in which the United States Supreme Court ruled that persons wishing to sue under Section 1983 of the federal civil rights law do not need to pursue administrative remedies first. (Kates's name does not appear on the brief in the case because he had only been practicing law for six months, and the Supreme Court Bar requires five years of practice before an attorney is admitted.)

Kates has litigated scores of firearm law cases. His most notable victory was in *Doe v. San Francisco* (136 Cal. App. 3d 507, 1982), in which the California Supreme Court ruled that San Francisco's handgun ban was contrary to a state law restricting local firearm ordinances. He is a founding partner of Benenson & Kates, a bicoastal law firm that is the first national law firm specializing in firearm law.

Kates served as a professor at St. Louis University Law School from 1976 to 1979, where he taught classes on federal courts, criminal law, criminal procedure, constitutional law, and other subjects. More recently, Kates has served as an adjunct professor at Stanford Law School, where he cotaught a class on firearm law and policy. He is currently a fellow at the Pacific Research Institute for Public Policy, a San Francisco think tank.

Opinion editorials by Kates have appeared in the *New York Times, Wall Street Journal,*

Christian Science Monitor, and many other newspapers. He has edited two books: *Restricting Handguns: The Liberal Skeptics Speak Out* (1979), and *Firearms and Violence: Issues of Public Policy* (1984). Along with Gary Kleck, he coauthored *The Great American Gun Debate: Essays on Firearms and Violence* (1997).

But Kates's most significant writings are his law review articles. In 1983, the *Michigan Law Review* published his "Handgun Prohibition and the Original Meaning of the Second Amendment," which was the first in-depth treatment of the Second Amendment to appear in a major law review. When Attorney General John Ashcroft announced in May 2001 that the Second Amendment guarantees an individual the right to arms, the Kates article was among those he cited.

The article was a well-written synthesis of work by other scholars, but its importance derived mainly from the prestige of the *Michigan Law Review.* Kates's greatest theoretical contribution to Second Amendment scholarship was "The Second Amendment and the Ideology of Self-Protection," which appeared in *Constitutional Commentary* in 1992. Drawing on numerous sources from the founding era, Kates provided the first in-depth scholarly exposition of the Second Amendment as a guarantee of the right of personal protection against criminals. Citing American founders and other sources, Kates argued that the framers of the Second Amendment saw no distinction between resistance to a lone criminal and resistance to a large army controlled by a criminal government. The difference was only quantitative (more criminals to resist) rather than qualitative; good people had a right to use arms against criminal violence, he argued, no matter whether the perpetrator was a lone criminal or a despot with many accomplices. Hence, the Second Amendment (originally described mainly as a right to resist tyranny) encompassed a right to resist more mundane criminals.

Kates's other notable contribution to Second Amendment theory is "The Second Amendment and States' Rights: A Thought Experiment," coauthored with Glenn H. Reynolds in the *William and Mary Law Review.* Kates and Reynolds explored the "states' rights" theory of the Second Amendment (that the amendment is only a guarantee of a state government's power to maintain a state militia), and argued that the theory is internally incoherent and leads to dangerous policy results.

Kates has also written extensively on criminological issues related to firearms. By far the most important of his policy articles is "Guns and Public Health: Epidemic of Violence or Pandemic of Propaganda?," which appeared in a symposium issue of the *Tennessee Law Review* in 1994. Along with several coauthors from medical and related disciplines, Kates surveyed the "public health" scientific literature on guns and delivered a scathing critique accusing the public health authors of fraud, extreme carelessness, willful blindness, and a host of other errors. Defenders of the public health literature have tended to acknowledge the accuracy of Kates's claims about the articles he critiques, but have argued that other articles are not so flawed.

Media treatment of the gun issue is another of Kates's recurring topics, most recently in *The Great American Gun Debate: Essays on Firearms and Violence* (1997). He argues that media bias against gun owners poisons the political debate and frightens many gun owners into a "no compromise" mentality.

Kates's greatest significance, however, has been in his tireless work as a behind-the-scenes advocate of the Second Amendment. Scores of professors and journalists have changed their minds on the Second Amendment and gun control after being contacted by Kates and reading his research.

Scores of academics and other writers have also been brought into the gun issue (or brought along on it) by Kates and his incessant networking. From the late 1970s through the mid-1990s, there were very few scholars who looked favorably on the right to arms who were not connected in some way to the Kates network. More recently, Kates's work has slowed down, however, and the number of firearm law and policy researchers has grown beyond the size of a manageable network. But this very growth is a testament to the effectiveness of Kates's work in prior decades.

While vigorously opposed to the prohibition of any type of firearms, Kates differs from many so-called Standard Model scholars (those who believe the Amendment grants the absolute right of the *individual* to bear arms) in that he finds no constitutional impediment to many regulatory forms of gun control. Stephen Halbrook has denounced Kates's defense of certain gun controls as "Orwellian newspeak."

Because Kates (in sharp contrast to John Lott) tends to avoid electronic media (including the Internet), he has not created the kind of high profile that attracts personal attacks from gun control groups. Contributing to Kates's relatively low public profile is his utter lack of interest in working with grassroots gun rights activists and his noninvolvement in politics.

David B. Kopel

See also Academics for the Second Amendment; Halbrook, Stephen P.; Kleck, Gary; *Quilici v. Village of Morton Grove*

For Further Reading:
Don Kates's website: http://www.donkates.com/.
Kates, Don B., Jr. 1983. "Handgun Prohibition and the Original Meaning of the Second Amendment." *Michigan Law Review* 82: 204–273.
———. 1992. "The Second Amendment and the Ideology of Self-Protection." *Constitutional Commentary* 9: 87–104.
Kates, Don B., Jr., and Glenn H. Reynolds. 1995. "The Second Amendment and States' Rights: A Thought Experiment." *William & Mary Law Review* 36: 1737–1768.
Kates, Don B., Jr., Henry E. Schaffer, John K. Lattimer, George B. Murray, and Edwin H. Cassem. 1995. "Guns and Public Health: Epidemic of Violence or Pandemic of Propaganda?" Pp. 233–308 in *Guns: Who Should Have Them?*, ed. David B. Kopel. Amherst, NY: Prometheus Books.
Kleck, Gary, and Don B. Kates, Jr. 1997. *The Great American Gun Debate: Essays on Firearms and Violence.* San Francisco: Pacific Research Institute for Public Policy.

Kellermann, Arthur L. (1955–)

Arthur L. Kellermann is director of the Center for Injury Control at the Rollins School of Public Health, and professor and chairman of the Department of Emergency Medicine at the Emory University School of Medicine. He is best-known for his research on firearm-related injuries and deaths and has been one of the most controversial scholars in this area. The focus of Kellermann's research has been whether the benefits of keeping a firearm in the home are worth the risks.

Kellermann received his M.D. degree from Emory University School of Medicine in 1980 and his M.P.H. degree from the University of Washington in 1985. He has published over fifty papers on various aspects of emergency cardiac care, health services research, and the role of emergency departments in the provision of health care to the poor.

At the Rollins School, Kellermann coteaches a course on legislative advocacy for public health. He has received the Hal Jayne Academic Excellence Award from the Society for Academic Emergency Medicine and was also awarded the Excellence in Science Award from the Injury Control and Emergency Health Services section of the American Public Health Association.

Kellermann's first study that gained widespread attention was published in 1986 in the *New England Journal of Medicine* (NEJM). Analyzing firearm-related deaths in the home in Kings County (Seattle), Washington, Kellermann and Reay found forty-three "suicides, criminal homicides, or accidental gunshot deaths involving a gun kept in the home for every case of homicide for self-protection" (1986, p. 1560). They concluded that "the advisability of keeping firearms in the home for protection must be questioned" (1986, p. 1557).

Their finding that suicides, criminal homicides, and accidental gunshot deaths were forty-three times more likely to occur than was a homicide for self-protection may be the most widely quoted factoid in the American gun control debate. It has been criticized for many reasons, including that it counts only deaths as the measure of the protective benefits of a firearm and ignores nonlethal defensive uses, and that it lumps together high-risk homes (e.g., homes with alcoholics or people with violent felony convictions) with ordinary homes.

In another study coauthored by Kellermann, this one published in the July 1992 issue of the *Journal of Trauma,* the authors concluded:

"When women kill, their victim is five times more likely to be their spouse, an intimate acquaintance, or a member of the family.... In light of these data, the wisdom of promoting firearms to women for self-protection should be seriously questioned" (Kellermann and Mercy, p. 5). Dr. Edgar A. Suter (1994) retorted, "Most women kill in defense of themselves and their children. In these common circumstances, lawful self-defense by women against their attackers [even self-defense against a violent ex-husband] is not 'murder' in any jurisdiction" (p. 140).

In 1993, Kellermann again sought to demonstrate that a gun in the home presents a greater risk to its owner than to a criminal, and specifically to address the issue of "whether keeping a firearm in the home confers protection against crime or, instead, increases the risk of violent crime in the home." In the October 7 issue of the *New England Journal of Medicine,* Kellermann and his coauthors concluded that "rather than confer protection, guns kept in the home are associated with an increase in the risk of homicide" (p. 1091). In fact, claimed the authors, the risk for homicide by a family member or acquaintance was 2.7 times higher if a gun was kept in the home than if one was not.

Among the criticisms leveled at this study were its failure to account adequately for false denials of gun ownership (in other words, telling a pollster that one does not own a gun when, in fact, one does) by some of the control population, and its failure to connect the victim's gun with any role in most of the homicides.

Because some of Kellermann's firearm research has received extensive and highly favorable media attention, other scholars have requested that Kellermann make his data sets available for study. In response, Kellermann has slowly made some, but far from all, of the requested data available. Much of Kellermann's research was funded by taxpayer funds through the Centers for Disease Control and Prevention (CDC), which did not require its researchers to reveal their data as a condition for funding.

More than any other CDC grant recipient, Kellermann's work sparked congressional interest in the CDC's gun control agenda. This was because Kellermann's research was of great value to gun control advocates—in part because of his knack for distilling the results of a study into a single, easily remembered numerical factoid. After U.S. House of Representatives hearings in 1996, where Kellermann's work received both scathing attacks and passionate defenses, Congress prohibited the CDC from spending any funds in order to "advocate or promote gun control."

Upon rejection of his subsequent application for additional grant money from the CDC, Kellermann stated that "this will be the first time in my career that I won't be funded by the CDC. I will look elsewhere." He soon began to receive research support from the National Institute of Justice, which is part of the U.S. Department of Justice.

Paul Gallant and Joanne D. Eisen

See also Centers for Disease Control; National Institute of Justice

For Further Information:

Center for Injury Control, Rollins School of Public Health, 1518 Clifton Road N.E., Atlanta, GA 30322, (404) 727-9977. http://www.sph.emory.edu/CIC.

Faria, Miguel, Jr. 2001. "Public Health and Gun Control—A Review." *Medical Sentinel* 6, 1: 11–18.

Kates, Don B., et al. 1995. "Guns and Public Health: Epidemic of Violence or Pandemic of Propaganda?" *Tennessee Law Review* 62, 3: 513–596.

Kellermann, Arthur L., and James A. Mercy. 1992. "Men, Women, and Murder: Gender-Specific Differences in Rates of Fatal Violence and Victimization." *Journal of Trauma* 33: 1–5.

Kellermann, Arthur L., and Donald T. Reay. 1986. "Protection or Peril? An Analysis of Firearms-Related Deaths in the Home." *New England Journal of Medicine* 314: 1557–1560.

Kellermann, Arthur L., et al. 1992. "Suicide in the Home in Relationship to Gun Ownership." *New England Journal of Medicine* 327: 467–472.

———. 1993. "Gun Ownership as a Risk Factor for Homicide in the Home." *New England Journal of Medicine* 329, 15: 1084–1091.

Suter, Edgar A. 1994. "Guns in the Medical Literature—A Failure of Peer Review." *Journal of the Medical Association of Georgia* 83 (March): 133–148.

U.S. House of Representatives, Committee on Appropriations, Subcommittee on the Departments of Labor, Health and Human Services, Education, and Related Agencies. 1996.

Departments of Labor, Health and Human Services, Education, and Related Agencies' Appropriations for 1997. Part 7, "Testimony of Members of Congress and Other Interested Individuals and Organizations." Washington, DC: GPO.

Kennedy, Edward M. (1932–)

Sen. Edward M. "Ted" Kennedy (D-MA) has served in the U.S. Senate since 1962, when he was elected to finish the term of his brother John Kennedy, who had been elected president. Kennedy lost two brothers—John and Robert—to assassins' bullets, and this may well be the inspiration for his ardent and forceful advocacy of gun control. His political career has been handicapped by personal scandals, including the drowning death of a young woman when his car plunged off a bridge in Chappaquiddick, Massachusetts, in 1969. Yet Kennedy has been a workhorse in the Senate, often forging compromises with unlikely collaborators such as Sen. Orrin Hatch (R-UT). Kennedy is one of the most liberal members of the Senate; his principal achievements have been in the area of health care.

Kennedy was 30 years old when elected to the Senate, and after the deaths of John and Bobby Kennedy it was assumed that he would run for the presidency. The Chappaquiddick incident put his political ambitions on hold, and Kennedy emerged as a key player on health care in the Senate in the 1970s. In 1980 he challenged incumbent Jimmy Carter for the Democratic nomination for president, and although initial polls showed him far ahead, he was unable to articulate a coherent message and eventually lost to Carter. His lukewarm endorsement of the Democratic winner is seen by some as a factor in Carter's defeat by Ronald Reagan in the general election.

While in the Senate, Kennedy has been a strong supporter of labor, social welfare spending, affirmative action, and abortion rights. His major legislative focus has been health care. A strong advocate of national health insurance, Kennedy has been able to compromise effectively with moderate Democrats and Republicans. He was a sponsor of the Family and Medical Leave Act, which was signed by Clinton in 1993. He

Edward Kennedy. (U.S. Senate)

pushed hard for portable health insurance for those who lose or leave their jobs, which culminated in legislation in 1996, and was a principal player in the expansion of the Children's Health Act of 1977. In 2001, Kennedy remained active in support of a Patient's Bill of Rights.

Kennedy has long been a proponent of gun control. He has often linked his support to his family tragedies, and his speeches on the topic often carry substantial emotional intensity. Kennedy was a strong backer of the Gun Control Act of 1968, although the assassination of Bobby Kennedy that spring kept him away from much of the action. During the 1970s and early 1980s, Kennedy successfully thwarted efforts to weaken gun control measures, using Senate rules skillfully, including the filibuster and the "disappearing quorum." In 1986, as the Senate reversed course with the McClure-Volkmer bill, Kennedy and Howard Metzenbaum threatened filibusters and negotiated changes in the bill.

In the 1990s, Kennedy was a strong supporter of the assault weapons ban, the various incarnations of the Brady Bill, and many other gun control provisions. He sponsored a number of bills that would have limited gun purchases to one per month, mandated trigger locks and other child-protection measures, and supported "smart gun" technology. In the summer of 2001, Kennedy opposed proposals by Attorney General John Ashcroft to shorten the period for background checks in the Brady Bill. Kennedy remains one of the staunchest supporters of gun control in the Senate.

Clyde Wilcox and
Benjamin Webster

See also Assault Weapons Ban of 1994; Brady Handgun Violence Prevention Act; Firearms Owners' Protection Act of 1986; Gun Control Act of 1968; Smart Guns

For Further Reading:

Barone, Michael, and Grant Ujifusa. 1999. *The Almanac of American Politics, 2000.* Washington, DC: National Journal.

Patterson, Samuel C., and Keith R. Eakins. 1998. "Congress and Gun Control." Pp. 45–73 in *The Changing Politics of Gun Control,* ed. John M. Bruce and Clyde Wilcox. Lanham, MD: Rowman & Littlefield.

Spitzer, Robert J. 1995. *The Politics of Gun Control.* Chatham, NJ: Chatham House.

Kennedy-Rodino Handgun Crime Control Act

See Kennedy, Edward M.

Kennesaw, Georgia

In 1982, government officials in the small town of Kennesaw, Georgia, passed a local ordinance requiring that all heads of households own a firearm and ammunition. This ordinance was passed in response to ordinances in other small towns banning gun ownership—most particularly in the Village of Morton Grove in Illinois.

Although the ordinance clearly was intended to demonstrate to the world the town's support for gun ownership, it was not intended to coerce individuals who did not want to own guns into doing so. There was no provision in the ordinance for enforcement, and the provision itself included several clauses "excusing" those who did not want to own a gun for moral or religious reasons, or because they were a convicted felon or mentally or physically disabled.

The apparent intention of the ordinance was twofold: to generate publicity for the support of gun ownership rights and to promote gun ownership itself.

Since the ordinance was passed in 1982, those who support unregulated gun ownership in the United States have pointed to Kennesaw's subsequent decline in crime rates as proof that gun ownership can, in fact, deter crime. It is indisputably true that Kennesaw's already low crime rate became somewhat lower following enactment of this ordinance. However, the interpretation of this decline is open to question. While some point directly to the notion that criminals avoid Kennesaw due to fear of universal gun ownership, others suggest that the publicity generated by the ordinance itself had the effect of deterring criminals. A more systematic analysis of the crime rates in Kennesaw (and other towns promoting gun ownership) was published in the journal *Criminology* in 1991 by McDowall, Lizotte, and Wiersema. They found that the crime reduction noted in Kennesaw was more likely part of a normal crime fluctuation than a real response to the ordinance. Crime rate reductions were also found in towns banning guns. In addition, other experts have noted that crime was very low in Kennesaw before the ordinance and that since the entire United States experienced a reduction in crime rates in the mid-1990s, it is difficult to gauge the long-term consequences of enforced gun ownership. Civil libertarians have found themselves as dismayed by mandatory gun ownership laws as they are by mandatory gun bans.

Elizabeth K. Englander

See also Availability of Guns, Effects on Crime; *Quilici v. Village of Morton Grove*

For Further Reading:

McDowall, D., A. J. Lizotte, and B. Wiersema. 1991. "General Deterrence through Civilian Gun Ownership: An Evaluation of the Quasi-Experimental Evidence." *Criminology* 29: 541–559.

Kentucky Long Rifle

See Long Rifle (Pennsylvania/Kentucky)

Officials remove bodies from Luby's Cafeteria, Killeen, Texas, October 16, 1991. (AP Photo/Ron Heflin)

Killeen, Texas, Massacre

On October 16, 1991, in Killeen, Texas, George Hennard, Jr., drove his pickup truck through the plate-glass window of a Luby's Cafeteria. Using a pair of handguns, Hennard murdered twenty-three people and then killed himself. Among the victims were the parents of chiropractor Suzanna Gratia, whose handgun had been left in her car in the parking lot, in conformance with Texas law prohibiting the carrying of concealed handguns. Dr. Gratia became a crusader for reform of handgun-carry laws, both in Texas and nationally. Although there are many mass murderers who have killed more people, either all at once or over a long period of time, Hennard killed more people with firearms on a single day than any other murderer in American history.

It was at about 12:40 P.M. on a Wednesday afternoon that Hennard, then age 35, rammed his truck into the cafeteria. Killeen, Texas, is located in Bell County in east Texas, southwest of Waco. The Luby's Cafeteria, located near Interstate 190, was part of a ten-state chain of 175 restaurants. Four months earlier, Hennard had been arrested at the Lake Mead National Recreation Area on charges of drunk driving and carrying loaded weapons. Pursuant to a plea bargain, he pled guilty and paid a fine of $170. Unemployed, Hennard lived in Belton, Texas, east of Killeen.

When Hennard's truck broke through the plate glass, many diners were sprayed with glass fragments, and one man was caught underneath the truck. Hennard exited the truck, shouting, "This is for what the women of Bell County did to me!" It was later revealed that Hennard considered his mother a "viper" who had ruined his childhood. Most, but not all, of his victims were women.

The man under the truck pulled himself out and was immediately shot in the head. Hennard was armed with a Glock 17 and a Ruger P-89 pistol. Both pistols are self-loading and use detachable magazines. The Glock and the Ruger are generally considered to be excellent handguns, similar to the Colt .45 (but less powerful). The Glock is carried by many police officers, while the Ruger is a favorite of target shooters. Neither firearm is considered an assault weapon. The Ruger's magazine holds fifteen rounds, while the Glock uses seventeen-round magazines.

Hennard had a large supply of reserve magazines, and as one magazine was emptied he would quickly pop in a replacement. There were 162 people in the restaurant, but (with one exception detailed below) no one offered any resistance. The last victim to die was Kitty Davis, who died from chest wounds three days later. In the course of seventeen minutes, Hennard fired sixty-one rounds from the Ruger and forty-one from the Glock—killing 23 people and wounding 21.

A police training class was taking place at a hotel near the cafeteria, and when police arrived on the scene a marksman wounded Hennard. Hennard retreated and fatally shot himself through his left eye. As medical personnel and ambulances arrived, a refrigerated lorry was brought to the scene. It served as a temporary morgue so that the corpses would not begin to rot in the hot Texas sun.

A search of Hennard's home turned up a revealing videotape in his VCR: a documentary about the 1984 mass murder at a McDonald's in San Ysidro, California. In that case, James Huberty had walked out of his home and announced that he was going "to hunt humans." He entered the McDonald's and opened fire with a shotgun. When the shotgun jammed, he switched to his backup (a Browning Hi-Power pistol), and when it jammed he turned to an Uzi carbine. A police SWAT team sped to the restaurant and swiftly had Huberty in their sights. But the SWAT team did not open fire. Instead, they watched Huberty as he methodically reloaded, strolled over to victims who lay wounded, and shot them in the head. Huberty carried only a single twenty-round magazine and had no speed loader for his shotguns. Yet he was able to fire over 150 shots with deliberation. The SWAT team was under strict orders not to fire until their lieutenant arrived on the scene. The lieutenant was stuck in a traffic jam.

The Killeen Luby's reopened in 1992, after spending $350,000 on repairs and security features. The cafeteria closed in 2000 due to declining customer visits.

A 1994 study in the *American Journal of Psychiatry* reported that nearly a third of the survivors appeared to suffer from posttraumatic stress disorder. Almost all of the survivors had at least some symptoms.

The Killeen murders ended up aiding the passage of both assault weapon prohibition and "shall-issue" concealed handgun laws. The U.S. House of Representatives had been scheduled to vote on an assault weapon ban the next day. Sponsored by Reps. Charles Schumer (D-NY) and Richard Gephardt (D-MO), the bill would have given the Bureau of Alcohol, Tobacco, and Firearms the administrative authority to outlaw any self-loading rifle or pistol that accepts a detachable magazine. Magazines of over seven rounds would also have been outlawed. The massacre turned out to have little impact on the vote, however, as the bill was defeated 247 to 177. The one vote that did switch to the pro-ban side was that of Democrat Chet Edwards, whose district included Killeen.

In 1992, when the Democratic Party nominated Bill Clinton for president, its platform called for various gun controls, including a ban on large magazines; this portion of the platform specifically mentioned Killeen. In May 1994, a tremendous lobbying effort by President Clinton pushed a milder assault weapon bill to passage by a one-vote margin. Although Representative Edwards's vote appeared essential, House Speaker Tom Foley (D-WA) would have voted in favor of the ban had the vote been tied, and two other Democratic representatives (Jolene Unsoeld of Washington and Blanche Lambert Lincoln of Arkansas) would have switched their votes and supported the ban if their votes had been needed. Enacted into law in September 1994 as part of a comprehensive crime bill, the law also outlawed new production of magazines holding more than ten rounds of ammunition (U.S. Code, volume 18, section 921).

Shortly after the Killeen massacre, Killeen's police chief suggested that citizens ought to be able to carry guns for protection. Earlier that year in Texas, the senate had passed a bill to allow trained, licensed adults to obtain permits to carry concealed handguns for lawful protection. There were enough votes to pass the bill on the floor of the Texas House. The House Rules Committee, acting in secret, killed the bill by keeping it from coming to the House floor for a vote.

Even if the bill had passed the legislature, however, Governor Ann Richards would have vetoed it, as she did when a handgun-carry bill passed the next legislature. That veto played a major role in Richards's 1994 election defeat by Republican George W. Bush. In 1995, Bush signed a concealed-carry bill nearly identical to the one vetoed by Richards.

The Killeen massacre played a major role in influencing the political climate, both nationally and in Texas, in favor of concealed carry. Two months after Killeen, a pair of criminals with stolen pistols herded twenty customers and employees into the walk-in refrigerator of a Shoney's restaurant in Anniston, Alabama. Hiding under a table in the restaurant was Thomas Glenn Terry, armed with the .45 semiautomatic pistol he carried legally under Alabama law. One of the robbers discovered Terry, but Terry killed him with five shots to the chest. The second robber, who had been holding the manager hostage, shot at Terry and grazed him. Terry returned fire and mortally wounded the robber. Advocates argued that in Alabama, where concealed carry is lawful, only the criminals died, but in Texas, where concealed carry was prohibited, twenty-three innocents died.

But much more influential than the Anniston incident was the personal testimony of Suzanna Gratia. Along with her parents, Gratia, it will be recalled, was in the Luby's Cafeteria when Hennard opened fire, and her Smith & Wesson .38 Special was in her car in the parking lot, because Dr. Gratia had been afraid that if she were caught carrying a gun she could lose her chiropractor's license. She later testified to the Missouri legislature that after Hennard drove in and opened fire,

My father and I immediately put the table up in front of us and we all got down behind it. Your first opinion is, is this guy robbing this place? What's the deal?

And then you're realizing that all he's doing is simply shooting people. As he was working his way toward us, I reached for my purse, thinking, "Hah! I've got this son of a gun." Now, understand, I know what a lot of people think.… They think, "Oh, my God, then you would have had a gunfight and then more people would have been killed." Unhunh, no, I was down on the floor; this guy is standing up; everybody else is down on the floor. I had a perfect shot at him. It would have been clear. I had a place to prop my hand. The guy was not even aware of what we were doing. I'm not saying that I could have saved anybody in there, but I would have had a chance. My gun wasn't even in my purse … it was a hundred feet away in my car!

My father was saying, "I gotta do something! I gotta do something! This guy's going to kill everyone in here!" So I wasn't able to hold him down and when my father thought he had a chance, he went at the guy! The guy turned, shot him in the chest and my dad went down. It made the guy change directions and he went off to my left. Shortly after that somebody broke out a window in back and I saw a chance to get out. I grabbed my mother and tried to get her up, hoped she was following me, and I grew wings on my feet. As it turned out, my mother crawled over to my father and stayed with him; and this—I'm trying to think of a civil word to use—this person eventually came around and shot her also.

Police told Dr. Gratia that they had seen her mother cradling her father's head in her lap. She looked up at Hennard, then bowed her head just before he shot her in the head.

Over the next decade, Dr. Gratia testified to legislatures all over the United States, as the number of states with concealed-handgun-permit laws grew from fourteen to thirty-two. Among those states was Texas.

Now married and a mother of two boys, Suzanna Gratia Hupp has been elected as the Republican state representative in Texas for the district that includes Killeen. In the Texas legislature, she is a strong proponent of Second Amendment rights. She applauds the Texas concealed-carry licensing law, but favors replacing it with a law patterned after Vermont's law, under which adults who do not have criminal records can carry firearms without needing to obtain a permit.

David B. Kopel

See also Assault Weapons Ban of 1994; Concealed Weapons Laws; Defensive Gun Use; Mass Murder (Shootings); Right-to-Carry Laws

For Further Reading:

Hupp, Rep. Suzanna Gratia Hupp. 2002. "State Representative Suzanna Gratia Hupp, District 54." http://www.house.state.tx.us/house/bios/dist54b.htm.

Kuempel, George. 2000. "Despite Tragedy, Many Sad to See Killeen Luby's Go." *Dallas Morning News* (September 8).

Morello, Carol. 2000. "A Daughter's Regret: After Massacre, a Vow to Shoot Back." *Washington Post* (May 13): A1.

North, Carol S., Elizabeth M. Smith, and Edward L. Spitznagel. 1997. "One-Year Follow-Up of Survivors of a Mass Shooting." *American Journal of Psychiatry* 154: 1696–1702.

Klanwatch Project

The Klanwatch Project was an operation of the Southern Poverty Law Center (SPLC), which is based in Montgomery, Alabama, and headed by attorney Morris Dees. Klanwatch has been merged into the SPLC's "Intelligence Project," which keeps tabs on "hate groups" and the "patriot movement." The SPLC is a widely quoted source for journalists and has a very strong base of donors. Critics, such as the authors of a two-year investigation for the *Montgomery Advertiser,* charge that the SPLC is a cynical fund-raising machine that terrifies donors about nonexistent threats and that the SPLC dishonestly maligns people for political gain.

The Southern Poverty Law Center was founded in Montgomery in 1971 by Dees. Dees, a direct-mail entrepreneur, sold cookbooks, birthday cakes, tractor seat cushions, and rat poison. Dees became a national figure when he applied his direct-mail skills to George McGovern's successful insurgent campaign for the Democratic presidential nomination. Dees made McGovern the first major presidential candidate to raise large sums from small donations solicited by direct mail.

Direct-mail political fund-raising was in its infancy when Dees used the 700,000 names on the McGovern mailing list to begin raising funds for the SPLC. But Dees proved himself a great master of the new art. The SPLC's endowment stands at approximately $120 million in 2002, far larger than the endowments of better-known groups such as the National Association for the Advancement of Colored People and the American Civil Liberties Union. In 1998, Dees was inducted into the Direct Marketing Association's Hall of Fame.

More recently, Dees has applied his skills to the Internet. The SPLC's website has offered visitors the opportunity to buy $30 "Teaching Tolerance" kits, which the website promised were actually valued at $325. In 2000, the SPLC and several Internet search engines implemented a plan by which web surfers who searched for certain intolerant key words would be redirected to a website run by the SPLC.

In 1999, the SPLC earned $17 million in income from its investments and raised $27 million from donors. The same year, the SPLC spent $13 million on its programs, approximately half of which was spent on producing direct-mail solicitations and paying for postage. The American Institute of Philanthropy gives the SPLC a "D" rating because of the SPLC's large excess of income over program expenditures, and because of the SPLC's refusal to disclose basic financial information.

During the 1970s, the main focus of the SPLC was litigation, and the SPLC won some notable cases, including forcing the Alabama state troopers to adopt an affirmative action program, requiring cotton mills to institute better working conditions for employees with brown lung disease, and changing the tax structure in Kentucky.

In 1981, the SPLC began its Klanwatch Project, which was later expanded to cover a variety of different targets. In 1986, the Southern Poverty Law Center's entire legal staff quit, upset that the SPLC was no longer practicing poverty law but was instead focused on the Ku Klux Klan.

Although the SPLC did death penalty legal work in the 1970s and still touts its "innovative" work in that field, the SPLC no longer takes death penalty cases. Critics charge that the SPLC's abandonment of such cases is meant to avoid scaring off the SPLC's mostly white donor base. The Southern Center for Human Rights, an Atlanta group specializing in death penalty defense, is one of a number of poverty law organizations that are upset with the SPLC for raising so much money and doing so little (in their view) for poor people and people of color. In 1996, the group's director, Stephen Bright, denounced Dees as "a fraud and a con man."

In 1994, the SPLC created a separate militia-watch unit, dedicated to the militia movement and the patriot movement. Today, these SPLC units have been merged into the Intelligence Project. The Klanwatch Project had proven to be a tremendous revenue center for the SPLC, but even greater fund-raising success resulted from the rise of the militia movement and from the Oklahoma City bombing.

The Intelligence Project publishes a quarterly *Intelligence Report* magazine of information about its target groups. Staff members conduct training for police, schools, and local groups. The Intelligence Project reports that its staff has collected "dossiers" on thousands of suspected militia members or militia sympathizers, and has placed infiltrators in the militia movement. The Intelligence Project supplies information to the FBI and other law enforcement agencies.

Intelligence Project staff also lobby state and federal lawmakers in support of a variety of laws, such as "militia training" bills to prohibit group firearms training or use accompanied by political discussion. The Intelligence Project is frequently quoted in American and foreign media as an expert source on the patriot movement, militias, hate groups, and others. The project's periodic reports on such groups often attract substantial media coverage. As an expert source in reported stories, as a background influence on media attitudes, and through direct-mail communication with a large donor base, the SPLC has played a very major role in shaping what much of the American public believes about the militia movement and the patriot movement.

Dees is the author of three books. *A Season for Justice: The Life and Times of a Civil Rights Lawyer* is a 1991 autobiography. The same year, Dees received the Martin Luther King, Jr., Memorial Award from the National Education

Association. *Hate on Trial: The Case against America's Most Dangerous Neo-Nazi,* coauthored with Steve Fiffer, tells the story of a civil lawsuit that the SPLC brought against Tom Metzger.

Highly publicized anti-Klan and anti-Nazi suits are the SPLC's most prominent legal work. The most famous suit came in 1987, when the SPLC recovered $51,875 for Beula Mae Donald, the mother of a black man who had been lynched by two members of the United Klans of America. The SPLC garnered $9 million from fund-raising related to the case and has been criticized by some people for not sharing any of the fund-raising revenue with Donald. The SPLC's direct-mail letters touted the size of the verdict awarded by the jury—a spectacular $7 million—but did not mention that the Klans' seizable assets amounted to less than 1 percent of the verdict.

Dees's third book is *Gathering Storm: America's Militia Threat,* coauthored with James Corcoran. Dees warned that the militia movement "could lead to widespread devastation or ruin." The book argued that the militia movement is the creation of Ku Klux Klan leader Louis Beam, although Dees also wrote that most militia members were not racists but rather dupes of Beam's conspiracy. The book claimed that the "citizens' militia movement ... led to the most destructive act of terrorism in our nation's history"—the April 1995 Oklahoma City bombing. Fund-raising appeals from the SPLC have continued to tie bomber Timothy McVeigh to the militia and patriot movements, although no evidence has ever been produced that he was part of either one. Dees did present what he regards as circumstantial evidence, such as the fact that after being arrested, McVeigh only supplied his name and no other information. This conduct, Dees noted, is consistent with instructions for members of the Militia of Michigan if they are captured. Dees did not note that the instruction is also given to all soldiers of the United States Army, in which McVeigh served.

Gathering Storm also promotes gun control and argues that the Second Amendment guarantees no individual right. The book was heavily praised by *New York Times* columnist Abe

Rosenthal, President Jimmy Carter, Arthur M. Schlesinger, Jr., and indeed by most reviewers.

Mainstream press coverage of the SPLC has generally been extremely favorable. Dees was the subject of an admiring made-for-television movie biography, *Line of Fire*. The SPLC was, however, sharply criticized in an award-winning investigative series in the *Montgomery Advertiser* in 1994. The series accused the SPLC of taking in far more than it spends, enjoying lavish offices, benefiting from high salaries, and consistently exaggerating its need for money in direct-mail fund-raising. The *Advertiser* suggested that the SPLC preyed on gullible northern donors by creating vastly exaggerated pictures of the prevalence and danger of barely viable groups like the Ku Klux Klan.

According to the *Advertiser*, many nonwhite former employees of the SPLC complained about racial discrimination, racial slurs, or condescension within the organization. Laird Wilcox (2002, p. 308), a scholar who studies political extremist organizations of both the right and left and the organizations that oppose them, offers a different critique: "Dees is the classic example of an apparently unprincipled opportunist waging a holy war against an unpopular foe and profiting from it, both financially and ideologically." The SPLC's annual lists of hate groups, militias, and patriot movement groups and leaders have not always been accurate in their characterizations. For example, Bob Glass, a Jewish owner of a gun store in Longmont, Colorado, was labeled an anti-Semite. Groups interested in Norse mythology have been labeled neo-Nazis; groups interested in promoting southern culture and romantic views of the Confederacy have been called racist. Militia and patriot groups—and even mainstream political conservatives—have been subjected to repeated innuendo claiming that they are violent or that they promote violence.

Barbara Dority, who is the president of Humanists of Washington, the executive director of the Washington Coalition Against Censorship, and the founder and cochair of the Northwest Feminist Anticensorship Taskforce, has criticized the SPLC for using guilt by association and for reporting its ideological opponents to law enforcement agencies while simultaneously proclaiming its belief in "tolerance" (Dority, 1995).

David B. Kopel

See also Ku Klux Klan; McVeigh, Timothy; Militia Watchdog Groups; Militias

For Further Reading:
Dees, Morris. 1997. *Gathering Storm: America's Militia Threat*. New York: HarperCollins.
Dority, Barbara. 1995. "Is the Extremist Right Entirely Wrong?" *Humanist* (November/December): 12–15.
Jaffe, Greg, and Dan Morse. 1994. "Rising Fortunes: Morris Dees and the Southern Poverty Law Center." *Montgomery Advertiser* (November).
Silverstein, Ken. 2000. "The Church of Morris Dees." *Harper's* (November): 54–57.
Southern Poverty Law Center home page: http://www.splcenter.org/.
Wilcox, Laird. 2002. "Who Watches the Watchdogs?" Pp. 290–333 in *The Cultic Milieu: Oppositional Subcultures in an Age of Globalization*, edited by Jeffrey Kaplan and Helene Loow. Walnut Creek, CA: Alta Mira Press.

Kleck, Gary (1951–)

Gary Kleck is a professor of criminology and criminal justice at Florida State University. His extensive research on violence, crime control, and the impact of firearms and gun control on violence established the figure of 2.5 million defensive gun uses (DGUs) in the United States per year. His research also contributed to his move from a self-described believer in the contribution of firearms to violence in the United States to one who argues that the best possible evidence available indicates that guns do not measurably contribute to increased rates of homicide, suicide, robbery, assault, rape, or burglary. Kleck asserts that while gun ownership is related to the rates of gun violence, the total rates of violence in the United States are not affected by gun availability.

Before 1995, about a dozen social science polls had attempted to estimate the frequency of armed self-defense in the United States. The results suggested that there were hundreds of thousand of instances of armed self-defense. The U.S. government's National Crime Victimization Survey (NCVS), which does not directly ask about armed self-defense but does allow people to volunteer that they used a firearm for self-defense against a crime, found about a hundred thousand instances annually.

Kleck's 1995 survey was designed to avoid

flaws in the methodologies of previous surveys. For example, when a respondent indicated that he had used a firearm for self-defense, Kleck's pollsters were required to ask a detailed series of follow-up questions designed to weed out persons who might be inventing an incident. Kleck and Gertz's polling indicated that there were probably 2.5 million or more defensive uses of firearms every year in the United States. The vast majority of uses involved merely brandishing a gun, or referring to a gun, with no shots fired.

Kleck's position, which is so diametrically opposed to the beliefs that are the foundation for antigun organizations such as the Brady Campaign to Prevent Gun Violence, the Coalition to Stop Gun Violence, and the Violence Policy Center, has attracted much criticism. Kleck's research methodology has been attacked by a number of scholars, most notably Cook and Ludwig (1997, 2000). Hemenway (1997) has also criticized the Kleck DGU data on a variety of grounds, including arguments that the number of real-world events that would be correlated with DGUs (e.g., hospital admissions of criminals with gunshot wounds) are not as frequent would be implied by Kleck's DGU figures. Kleck responds that DGU skeptics are merely speculating and that they have failed to produce actual data to refute his figures. In support of Kleck, the prominent criminologist and gun control advocate Marvin Wolfgang (1995, p. 188), in a discussion of the research on which Kleck bases his estimates, has admitted, "I do not like their conclusions that having a gun can be useful, but I cannot fault their methodology."

Kleck is the author of many scholarly articles and books on the gun control debate, including *Point Blank: Guns and Violence in America* (1991), which won the 1993 Michael J. Hindelang Award from the American Society of Criminology as the year's most outstanding contribution to criminology.

Carol Oyster and David B. Kopel

See also Availability of Guns, Effects on Crime; Cook, Philip J.; Defensive Gun Use; Hemenway, David; Lott, John R., Jr.; National Crime Victimization Survey

For Further Reading:

Cook, Philip J., and Jens Ludwig. 1997. "Guns in America: National Survey on Private Ownership and Use of Firearms." Research in Brief report no. NCJ165476. Washington, DC: National Institute of Justice, Office of Justice Programs, U.S. Department of Justice.
———. 2000. *Gun Violence: The Real Costs.* New York: Oxford University Press.
Hemenway, David. 1997. "Survey Research and Self-Defense Gun Use: An Explanation of Extreme Overestimates." *Journal of Criminal Law and Criminology* 87: 1430–1435.
Kates, Don B., Jr., and Gary Kleck. 1997. *The Great American Gun Debate: Essays on Firearms and Violence.* San Francisco: Pacific Research Institute for Public Policy.
———. 2001. *Armed: New Perspectives on Gun Control.* Amherst, NY: Prometheus Books.
Kleck, Gary. 1991. *Point Blank: Guns and Violence in America.* Hawthorne: NY: Aldine de Gruyter.
———. 1997. *Targeting Guns: Firearms and Their Control.* Hawthorne, NY: Aldine de Gruyter.
Kleck, Gary, and Marc Gertz. 1995. "Armed Resistance to Crime: The Prevalence and Nature of Self-Defense with a Gun." *Journal of Criminal Law and Criminology* 56: 150–187.
Wolfgang, Marvin. 1995. "A Tribute to a View I Have Opposed." *Journal of Criminal Law and Criminology* 86, 1: 188.

Knox, Neal (1935–)

Neal Knox is one of the most vocal U.S. advocates of the individualist interpretation of the Second Amendment (that is, that the amendment guarantees the right of individuals to keep and bear arms). Knox has associated with many of the important players in debate over gun rights in the United States. He took part in founding *Gun Week, Handloader,* and *Rifle* magazine and is a frequent contributor to newspapers and gun magazines. *Shotgun News* magazine features the "Neal Knox Report," in which Knox tackles issues surrounding the gun control debate and often critiques other progun organizations' policies.

Knox has had long-standing relations with the National Rifle Association. He was executive director of its Institute for Legislative Action (ILA) from 1977 to 1982. Under Knox's leadership, and following the directions of then NRA President Harlon B. Carter, the ILA effectively established a strong political lobbying presence on Capitol Hill. During the 1980s Knox and Carter assisted in the crafting of the McClure-

Volkmer Act (the Firearms Owners' Protection Act of 1986), which weakened the 1968 Gun Control Act. Despite this success, the NRA chose to replace Knox with the more flexible Warren J. Cassidy as a result of Knox's unwillingness to negotiate and compromise.

Knox's NRA affiliations have been highly controversial throughout the years. Among the most important was his participation in the "Revolt at Cincinnati" at the NRA national meeting in 1977. The "revolt" was a watershed event in the NRA's history, taking it from an organization that was willing to compromise on selected gun control measures to one that would fight any and all such measures at local, state, and national levels of government.

Knox has served on the NRA's Board of Directors on several occasions. After being ousted in the mid-1980s, Knox staged a comeback in 1991. Eventually he rose to the position of first vice president only to face another ousting when Charlton Heston was elected to that NRA position on a "Stop Knox" ticket in 1997.

Knox has been a vocal critic of the NRA not only in his own newsletters but also in columns and articles written for *Guns & Ammo* and other gun magazines. Knox wrote his own column, "Knox's Notebook," for the *American Rifleman* magazine from 1994 to 1997. However, his column in the *American Rifleman* refrained from any critique or self-promotion. Knox has generally believed the NRA is stepping away from the important issues and not being confrontational enough.

Knox's attitude and manner have often been criticized as confrontational and extreme. To paraphrase him, the Second Amendment is about the fundamental human right to defend self, family, home, and country. Knox believes the Second Amendment does not permit any legislation that limits the availability and ownership of firearms. Each piece of gun control legislation is met with severe opposition by him, and in this capacity Knox has testified before Congress on several occasions. He has founded a fund-raising organization, the Firearms Coalition, to help in his work to protect Second Amendment rights.

Tiia Rajala

See also Carter, Harlon; Firearms Coalition; Firearms Owners' Protection Act of 1986; Gun Magazines; *Gun Week;* Heston, Charlton; Institute for Legislative Action; National Rifle Association; Second Amendment

Kopel, David B. (1960–)

The research director of the Independence Institute since 1992, David B. Kopel is an internationally respected expert on the Second Amendment, international firearm law, and firearm policy. An associate policy analyst with the Cato Institute and a director of the Center on the Digital Economy at the Heartland Institute, he received the American Society of Criminology's 1992 Book of the Year award for *The Samurai, the Mountie, and the Cowboy,* a landmark examination of the international evolution of firearm laws. Editor-in-chief of the *Journal on Firearms and Public Policy,* he is also a contributing editor for *Gun Week, Gun News Digest,* and *Liberty,* as well as a columnist for *National Review Online* and the *Rocky Mountain News.* He has also edited a number of books, been a prolific contributor to scholarly journals, and taught a course entitled "Gun Control and Gun Rights" at New York University School of Law. He publishes regularly in a variety of newspapers and magazines and appears frequently on television.

Kopel has received a number of awards for his steadfast defense of civil liberties. They include the 1999 Gun Rights Defender of the Year award from the Citizens Committee for the Right to Keep and Bear Arms, the 1997 Bill of Rights Award, and the 1995 and the 1989 James Madison Award from the Second Amendment Foundation. In 1997 he received the Thomas S. Szasz Award for Outstanding Contributions to the Cause of Civil Liberties from the Center for Independent Thought for his book *No More Wacos,* a lucid examination of the constitutional and public safety issues raised by the growth and inappropriate use of heavily militarized, federally controlled law enforcement agencies.

A graduate of the University of Michigan

Law School and Brown University, Kopel has also served as an assistant district attorney in New York City and an assistant attorney general for the State of Colorado specializing in environmental law.

Linda Gorman

See also Citizens Committee for the Right to Keep and Bear Arms; Gun Magazines; *Gun News Digest; Gun Week;* Independence Institute; Second Amendment Foundation

For Further Reading:

Bijlefeld, Marjolijn. 1999. *People for and against Gun Control.* Westport, CT: Greenwood Press.

David Kopel's website: http://www.davekopel.org.

Kopel, David B. 1992. *The Samurai, the Mountie, and the Cowboy: Should America Adopt the Gun Controls of Other Democracies?* Buffalo, NY: Prometheus Books.

_____. 1995a. *Guns: Who Should Have Them?* Buffalo, NY: Prometheus Books.

_____. 1995b. "Guns, Germs, and Science: Public Health Approaches to Gun Control." *Journal of the Medical Association of Georgia* 84: 269.

_____. 2000. "Treating Guns like Consumer Products." *University of Pennsylvania Law Review* 148: 1701. http://i2i.org/SuptDocs/ Crime/LawReviews/TreatingGunsLikeCars.htm.

———. 2001a. "Comprehensive Bibliography of the Second Amendment in Law Reviews." Bellevue, WA: Second Amendment Foundation. http://www.saf.org/AllLawReviews.html.

_____. 2001b. "Lawyers, Guns, and Burglars: Why Mass Tort Litigation Fails to Account for Positive Externalities and the Network Effects of Controversial Products." *Arizona Law Review* 43, 2: 345.

Kopel, David B., and Paul H. Blackman. 1997. *No More Wacos: What's Wrong with Federal Law Enforcement, and How to Fix It.* Buffalo, NY: Prometheus Books.

———. 2000. "Firearms Tracing Data from the Bureau of Alcohol, Tobacco and Firearms: An Occasionally Useful Law Enforcement Tool, but a Poor Research Tool." *Criminal Justice Policy Review* 11: 44.

Kopel, David B., and Joseph Olson. 1999. "All the Way Down the Slippery Slope: Gun Prohibition in England, and Some Lessons for America." *Hamline Law Review* 22: 399. http://www.keepandbeararms.com/files/ slope.htm.

Members of the Ku Klux Klan burn a cross in Swainsboro, Georgia. (Library of Congress)

Ku Klux Klan

The Ku Klux Klan is the nation's best-known and most visible racial hate group. The white supremacist organization actively opposes ethnic and religious minorities. The Klan—or KKK, as it is commonly known—has a history of violence and was originally founded to prevent African Americans from achieving full equality. For most of the 1800s and well into the 1900s, the KKK utilized a near-monopoly on gun ownership in certain regions of the nation to suppress minorities.

The Klan was established in 1866 in the aftermath of the Civil War. A group of former Confederate soldiers formed the secret organization in an effort to undermine Reconstruction governments and suppress African Americans. The name of the organization was based on the

Greek word "kuklos," or circle. The majority of the first members of the Klan were former Confederate soldiers and white landowners. The first leader, or "Grand Wizard," of the Klan was Confederate General Nathan Bedford Forrest. The KKK was organized into local units, known as "klaverns." In order to hide their identities and cover their operations, members of the Klan wore robes and hoods and usually operated at night. Hence, members were often known as "nightriders" and the organization as the "invisible empire."

During the Reconstruction Era, African Americans had a difficult time obtaining weapons because of local and state ordinances. These laws were part of the "black codes" that endeavored to overturn the newly won political freedoms of African Americans. This gave the Klan a virtual monopoly on firearms. The group used its superior firepower to target Reconstruction officials and African Americans in the southern states. The Klan flogged, shot, or lynched targeted individuals. Often, a cross would be burned as a warning to people that they faced increasing levels of violence from the Klan.

Within a few years after its formation, Klan violence was widespread throughout the South. Congress responded with legislation designed to suppress the organization. These laws included the Force Bill, which authorized the use of federal troops to quell the violence. The passage of various civil rights acts and the ratification of the Fourteenth Amendment in 1868 further increased legal pressure to end the campaign of violence. The Civil Rights Act of 1866 specifically forbade state laws that prohibited African Americans from possessing firearms. The federal pressure led Forrest to officially disband the Klan in 1869. However, many individual klaverns continued their operations throughout the nineteenth century.

Individual state governments enacted legislation that benefited the Klan. For instance, many states passed laws that banned the sale of inexpensive handguns. These laws affected only the purchase of new weapons, not the possession of existing guns. Hence members of the Klan were able to keep their weapons, many of which were acquired through service during the Civil War,

while African Americans were unable to obtain new guns. States including Alabama, Arkansas, Tennessee, and Texas passed such legislation. In 1875, the Supreme Court ruled in *United States v. Cruikshank* that the federal government did not have the authority to prevent the KKK from disarming African Americans. The Court ruled that African Americans had to rely on local and state agencies to protect them from the Klan. Since these government bodies were dominated by whites, there was little real enforcement of federal equal-protection laws during the 1800s and early 1900s.

The Klan's power and size peaked during the first decades of the twentieth century. Col. William J. Simmons revived the Klan in Atlanta in 1915. Simmons sought to recast the Klan as a legitimate conservative political organization in order to broaden the appeal of the secret society beyond the South. The renewed Klan portrayed itself as a faith-based conservative Protestant group that sought to promote traditional American values. It took advantage of the growing anti-immigrant sentiment in the nation and came to oppose not just African Americans but also religious minorities, especially Jews and Roman Catholics. At its height in the 1920s, Klan membership reached almost 4 million and the organization had klaverns in states ranging from Oregon to Indiana to Maine. The KKK even fielded candidates for local and state offices with some electoral success. The Klan had its greatest political success in opposing the presidential candidacy of Alfred E. Smith, a Roman Catholic, in the 1928 election.

However, the new Klan continued to utilize the same violent tactics that it had in the past. During the 1920s, there was a renewed wave of racially motivated shootings and lynchings throughout the country. The Great Depression of the 1930s and the onset of World War II led to the demise of the new Klan. By the end of World War II, Klan membership had declined significantly and KKK activity was mainly concentrated in the South and some midwestern states, primarily at the local and state levels.

In 1946, Samuel Green, an Atlanta physician, endeavored to once again revive the Klan as a national organization. But Green died in

1949 and the national Klan split into a number of factions. Klan membership and activity increased dramatically in the 1950s in response to the civil rights movement. A new wave of violence swept across the South and resulted in the murder of several civil rights workers and leaders. The Klan was also involved in numerous bombings, including the infamous bombing of a Birmingham church. These acts led the Federal Bureau of Investigation to undertake a concentrated campaign to suppress the illegal activities of the KKK. Numerous Klansmen were arrested and a number of klaverns were broken up. By the mid-1970s, Klan membership had fallen below 5,000.

Klan membership briefly expanded during the 1980s. By 1985 there were approximately 10,000 members. The KKK actively sought to include women and children and to once again promote itself as a religious-based organization. Some Klan groups also moderated their anti-Catholic positions. Nonetheless, this resurgence was short-lived. By the mid-1990s membership in the Klan had fallen to around 6,000.

Tom Lansford

See also African Americans and Gun Violence; Black Codes; NAACP and Gun Control; Racism and Gun Control; *United States v. Cruikshank;* Vigilantism
For Further Reading:
Davidson, Osha Gray. 1996. *The Best of Enemies: Race and Redemption in the New South.* New York: Scribner.
Nelson, Jack. 1993. *Terror in the Night: The Klan's Campaign against the Jews.* New York: Simon & Schuster.
Quarles, Chester L. 1999. *The Ku Klux Klan and Related American Racialist and Antisemitic Organizations: A History and Analysis.* Jefferson, NC: McFarland.
Ruiz, Jim. 1998. *The Black Hood of the Ku Klux Klan.* San Francisco: Austin & Winfield.

L

Wayne LaPierre, executive vice president of the NRA, speaking at a news conference in Washington, D.C., 1999. (AFP/Corbis)

LaPierre, Wayne R., Jr. (1950–)

Wayne LaPierre is the executive vice president and chief executive officer of the National Rifle Association. Along with the NRA's board, LaPierre is responsible for overseeing and implementing the NRA's nationwide policies and supervising the administrative aspects of the NRA's nationwide operations.

LaPierre joined the NRA in 1978 as a lobbyist responsible for a ten-state area; he was named director of state and local affairs in 1979. In 1980, LaPierre was promoted to director of federal affairs, the lobbying arm responsible for overseeing the organization's congressional and executive branch relations. Six years later, LaPierre was named director of the NRA's Institute for Legislative Action and assumed responsibility for superintending all of the NRA's lobbying efforts at the federal, state, and local levels.

He accepted his current position as NRA executive vice president (the chief operating officer) in 1991, replacing J. Warren Cassady. LaPierre's accession to the position of executive

vice president was generally regarded as moving the NRA in a direction of taking a firmer stance on Second Amendment rights issues.

When LaPierre became executive vice president, NRA membership was 2.5 million. As of early 2001, it had risen to 4.3 million. In the interim, membership had surged to over 3 million in 1994 (when President Clinton made gun control a top priority) but had declined in 1995, after the Republican takeover of Congress reduced gun control fears.

Within the NRA, LaPierre's position as executive vice president was challenged in 1996–1997 by longtime gun rights activist Neal Knox, who argued that LaPierre was mismanaging the group's finances. LaPierre narrowly survived an NRA board of directors vote in early 1997; then, at the NRA's annual meeting in the spring, he brought in Charlton Heston as a director and officer and proceeded to purge Knox's supporters from the board.

Although LaPierre is a consummate Washington professional, he has not shied away from using rhetoric. In an early 1995 fund-raising letter, he asserted that some Bureau of Alcohol, Tobacco, and Firearms agents behave like "jack-booted thugs." Several weeks later, the Oklahoma City bombing took place. (Timothy McVeigh had once belonged to the NRA, but quit in disgust over the group's moderation.) Shortly thereafter, former President George Bush publicly announced that he was resigning from the NRA because of the fund-raising letter. (Bush had joined the NRA in January 1988, just before he began to run for president. The NRA spent $6 million in support of Bush in 1988, but refused to endorse him in 1992 because he supported gun control when he was president, in contravention of promises he had made in 1988.) The Bush resignation over the "jack-booted thugs" letter was a major public relations disaster for the NRA.

In 1999, LaPierre again was the source of controversy. On a Sunday morning television program, he claimed that President Clinton accepted a certain amount of gun violence in the United States in order to further his political agenda. LaPierre argued that Clinton barely enforced the many federal gun laws already on the books. LaPierre further pointed out that Clinton had recently refused to accept legislation containing certain gun controls that the NRA said it would accept, because Clinton preferred to make extreme gun control demands so as to preserve the gun control issue for the 2000 election.

The White House fired back, and President Clinton himself spoke out in response to LaPierre. The LaPierre-Clinton showdown garnered significant media attention for over two weeks. Although the media reports at the time were generally supportive of Clinton, analysts later suggested that the public showdown had exposed the American people to LaPierre's message that Clinton was interested in politicking about new gun control laws rather than enforcing existing laws.

As executive vice president of the NRA, LaPierre has overseen both the best of times and the worst of times for the group. In 1993–1994, the NRA suffered by far its worst two years ever in Congress, with the passage of the Brady Handgun Violence Prevention Act in 1993 and the assault weapons ban and a host of other gun controls in the 1994 Clinton crime bill.

But the NRA's tenacious opposition to the assault weapons ban (which nearly derailed the entire Clinton crime bill) set the stage for the greatest election in NRA history in November 1994. That December, President Clinton said that the NRA was the reason the Republicans now controlled Congress. Progun candidates also swept to victory in a wide variety of state legislative races all over the country. Despite LaPierre's fund-raising gaffe noted above, 1995 was the greatest year in the organization's history, as progun laws were enacted or expanded in dozens of states and many gun control laws were rolled back or repealed.

The most notable of these were "shall-issue" concealed-handgun-licensing laws, which establish objective criteria for issuing permits to carry a concealed handgun for lawful protection to adults who pass a background check (and, in many states, a safety class). When LaPierre became head of the NRA's Institute for Legislative Action in 1986, only a few states had such laws. The 1988 enactment of a shall-issue law in Florida started a national trend, putting shall-issue laws on the books in thirty-three states (including Vermont, which does not require a permit).

On April 20, 1999, two young men murdered twelve students and a teacher at Columbine High School near Littleton, Colorado. The NRA and LaPierre were sent reeling by the shooting. LaPierre told the NRA to maintain public silence until the NRA's annual meeting a week and a half later, which by terrible coincidence (from the NRA's viewpoint) was scheduled for Denver. LaPierre canceled all of the annual meeting events except for the formal membership meeting required by the group's bylaws.

About a month later, the U.S. Senate passed a draconian juvenile crime bill, which included various gun controls, the most significant of which was a highly restrictive provision on gun shows, which the Senate adopted after Vice President Gore cast the tie-breaking vote. The NRA was plainly in retreat, and many commentators expected that the retreat would become a rout.

But by the time the action shifted to the House of Representatives in June, LaPierre had rallied his forces. Working closely with the Republican leadership, LaPierre acceded to a variety of compromise gun controls and gained the leadership's support in standing firm against more extensive proposals. Relying on support from moderate and conservative Democrats, especially those in rural districts, the NRA was able to pick its battles in the House, and it emerged tactically victorious—although it still had to surrender ground.

The next year and a half saw the greatest gun control showdown in American history, with groups such as the "Million Mom March" threatening that they would turn support for gun rights into a political liability, not an asset, all over the country. LaPierre, meanwhile, kept hammering at his theme that the problem was lack of enforcement of existing gun laws, and that there was no need for more laws. The NRA's vaunted grassroots network was sent into action with its greatest intensity and size ever—aided in significant part by LaPierre's use of the Internet to communicate directly with gun rights supporters, thus bypassing the traditional media. (The NRA even has a daily short television program that it broadcasts over the web.)

By August 2000, Democratic presidential candidate Al Gore was running from the gun issue, and in January 2001 departing President Clinton credited the NRA with delivering five southern and border states to Bush (thereby electing Bush president) and being the main reason that Republicans retained control of the House of Representatives. In May 2000, *Fortune* magazine's annual ranking of lobbying strength named the National Rifle Association the most powerful lobbying group in Washington.

LaPierre's most enthusiastic supporters—who include a number of powerful Republican senators—credit LaPierre with a brilliant political sense of when to hold firm on principle and when to compromise out of necessity. On the other hand, LaPierre's critics within the gun rights movement complain not only about his willingness to compromise but also about his penchant for lending NRA support to Republicans with weak records on the gun issue in order to cultivate favor with the Republican hierarchy.

Gun control advocates call LaPierre an uncompromising extremist who has pulled the NRA from its sport-shooting roots. Indeed, LaPierre, unlike many previous NRA leaders, comes from the world of Washington lobbying, not the rural world of sport shooting. But except when LaPierre ratchets up his rhetoric, it has been difficult for the gun control lobbies to make an issue out of LaPierre personally.

Whatever one thinks of LaPierre's policy positions, it does not seem unreasonable to call him a political genius. He has mastered the Byzantine world of internal NRA politics and

now holds more real power within the NRA than anyone in decades, perhaps even ever. He has also mastered American politics and brought his organization to the pinnacle of American political power.

In 1994, LaPierre published *Guns, Crime, and Freedom,* in which he set forth a full-scale defense of the individual right to keep and bear arms. He concluded not only that the framers of the U.S. Constitution intended the Second Amendment to guarantee such an individual right to arms, but also that arming the populace was good public policy—that it was a hedge against an out-of-control or tyrannical government and provided individuals with the ability to protect themselves from criminals. The book was a *New York Times* best-seller, and it has been reprinted in paperback and issued in audio.

As executive vice president of the NRA, LaPierre is responsible for overseeing a staff of 500 people with a $200 million annual budget.

Brannon P. Denning

See also Assault Weapons Ban of 1994; Brady Handgun Violence Prevention Act; Bush, George H. W.; Clinton, William J.; Columbine High School Tragedy; Concealed Weapons Laws; Enforcement of Gun Control Laws; Gun Shows; Heston, Charlton; Institute for Legislative Action; Knox, Neal; Million Mom March; National Rifle Association; Republican Party and Gun Control; Second Amendment

For Further Reading:
LaPierre, Wayne D., Jr. 1994. *Guns, Crime, and Freedom.* Washington, DC: Regnery.

Lautenberg Amendment
See Lautenberg, Frank R.

Lautenberg, Frank R. (1924–)
A three-term Democratic U.S. senator from New Jersey from 1982 through 2000, Frank R. Lautenberg remained a strong advocate of gun control throughout his career on Capitol Hill. He was best known as the author of and primary force behind a major federal gun control provision—the Lautenberg Amendment to the 1997 Transportation Appropriations bill. The amendment barred anyone convicted of domestic violence

against a spouse or child from buying or owning a firearm.

The Lautenberg Amendment, also called the Domestic Violence Offender Gun Ban, closed what gun control advocates considered a loophole in federal regulations. The amendment expanded the prohibition of gun purchases, ownership, or possession to include persons convicted of misdemeanor offenses. Previously such bans covered only convicted felons. Lautenberg won passage of his proposal over the intense opposition of the National Rifle Association, the Gun Owners of America, and other prominent anti–gun control organizations.

Lautenberg and his supporters also overcame the opposition of House Republicans, led by Speaker Newt Gingrich of Georgia, and several law enforcement organizations. House Republicans blocked passage of the overall appropriations bill while seeking to weaken Lautenberg's amendment by limiting the ban to cover only persons convicted by judges. Because most misdemeanor convictions were made by juries, the Republicans' proposal would have greatly reduced the number of persons covered by the ban. However, fearing a political backlash for delaying passage of the appropriations measure, the Republicans withdrew their proposal after Lautenberg, supported by President Bill Clinton, declined to compromise.

Following its passage, the amendment came under fire from some law enforcement organizations. Leaders of these groups were responding to complaints from members who were now prohibited from carrying firearms because of previous misdemeanor domestic violence convictions.

Throughout his Senate career Lautenberg waged a continuous campaign to expand federal control of the sale of firearms. In 1997 he won passage of a measure to establish security regulations to protect stores selling guns. The proposal, which Lautenberg cosponsored with Joseph Biden, a Democrat from Maryland, sought to direct the Treasury Department to establish minimum gun safety and security standards governing federally licensed firearm dealers. However, in the 106th Congress (1999–2000) Lautenberg's gun control efforts, while often successful in the Senate, were stifled in the Republican-controlled House of Representatives. In 1999 Lautenberg played a prominent role in winning Senate passage of his amendment to mandate background checks of customers buying weapons at gun shows. In addition, working with Sen. Barbara Boxer, a Democrat from California, Lautenberg worked tirelessly for such gun control reforms as banning the importation of high-capacity ammunition clips and mandating that all handguns be sold with child safety trigger locks or safety storage boxes.

In sum, Lautenberg established a place for himself in the leading ranks of public officials pressing for increased federal government gun control efforts. He accomplished this through his votes on the chamber floor, in committee and subcommittee deliberations, and by sponsoring notable gun control amendments to other legislation. He often used his position as the ranking Democrat on both the Senate Transportation and Budget committees and his seat on the Appropriations Committee as platforms for launching his gun control efforts.

Robert Dewhirst

See also Boxer, Barbara; Gun Shows
For Further Reading:
Carney, Dan. 1999. "Gun Control Backers Get Upper Hand as Senate Passes New Restrictions." *Congressional Quarterly Weekly Report* 57: 1204–1207.
Duncan, Philip D., and Brian Nutting, eds. 1999. "Sen. Frank R. Lautenberg." Pp. 849–851 in *Politics in America 2000: The 106th Congress.* Washington, DC: Congressional Quarterly Press.

Law Enforcement for the Preservation of the Second Amendment (LEPSA)

Founded in 1989, Law Enforcement for the Preservation of the Second Amendment began as a "grassroots, pro–Second Amendment police organization," according to the group's website. The founder of the LEPSA, Thomas J. Aveni, a former police officer in New Jersey, created the LEPSA in an effort to prevent legislation to ban most semiautomatic rifles and shotguns in the state. Within a short period of time, the LEPSA garnered the signatures of over 3,000 New Jersey police officers and presented this petition to members of the state's legislature. Although unsuccessful in this initial attempt to influence gun control legislation, the organization grew to over 5,000 members in its first year.

The attitudes of the LEPSA's membership are reflected in the organization's philosophy that disarming honest citizens of firearms that may protect them and their loved ones is unfair. In the opinion of the LEPSA, gun control laws are specifically designed to control people, not crime. Based on surveys of its membership, the LEPSA argues that national police organizations such as the Fraternal Order of Police (FOP) do not speak for the bulk of their membership on Second Amendment issues. However, most mainline police organizations—such as the FOP, the International Brotherhood of Police Officers, the International Association of Chiefs of Police, the Police Executive Research Forum, the National Organization of Black Law Enforcement Executives, the National Troopers' Coalition, the Federal Law Enforcement Officers Association, the National Sheriffs' Association, and the National Association of Police Organizations—have been on the side of the gun control movement since the mid-1980s (Carter, 1997, pp. 103–104).

The LEPSA prides itself on accepting no donations. It does not want to be viewed as the tool of any other organization. Consequently, it does not want to be at the financial mercy of individuals with other agendas. The organization is supported through sales of merchandise from the LEPSA's "Cop Shop." The merchandise includes books, auto parts and accessories, and apparel. The apparel, mainly T-shirts, is emblazoned with particularly conservative slogans.

G. Edward Richards

See also Federal Law Enforcement Officers Association; Fraternal Order of Police; International Brotherhood of Police Officers; National Association of Police Organizations; National Sheriffs' Association; National Troopers' Coalition; Police Executive Research Forum

For Further Reading:
Carter, Gregg Lee. 1997. *The Gun Control Movement.* New York: Twayne.
Law Enforcement for the Preservation of the Second Amendment home page: http://www.lepsa.org.

Lawsuits against Gun Manufacturers

Since the late 1970s, victims of gun violence increasingly have turned to the judicial system to seek redress against gun manufacturers and sellers, drawing on traditional legal principles applied in other contexts to argue that the gun industry should bear some responsibility for the damage its products cause. These victim suits, in turn, have laid the groundwork for a significant new development in gun litigation: suits by municipalities against the gun industry that seek to recover the public costs associated with gun violence.

Some victim suits have involved allegations of irresponsible sales practices by gun retailers, targeting such practices as selling to buyers acting as "straw purchasers" for persons legally prohibited from buying guns, sales to persons who may be mentally impaired, and sales in violation of regulatory requirements. In these cases, victims typically rely on theories of negligence, negligent entrustment, or, in the case of regulatory violations, negligence per se. Although some courts have rejected such suits on the ground that the shooting of the victim was a superseding cause of the injury, cutting off the dealer's liability, other courts have imposed liability where the shooting was a foreseeable result of the dealer's negligence. In *Kitchen v. K-Mart Corp.* (697 So. 2d 1200 Fla. 1997), for example, the Florida Supreme Court unanimously held that a gun dealer could be liable for selling a gun to a visibly intoxicated buyer who then used the gun to shoot his estranged girlfriend. The court reversed a lower court ruling that had dismissed the suit on the ground that Florida law did not prohibit gun sales to intoxicated persons. The Supreme Court held that a cause of action for negligent sale did not require that the sale violate statutory law where the injury inflicted was the foreseeable result of the negligence. The court held that because guns involve "such a high degree of risk of serious injury or death," gun sellers owe a duty to exercise the "highest degree of care" in their activities.

The general duty to exercise care to avoid increasing the risk of gun violence also has been invoked by gun violence victims in lawsuits against gun manufacturers. The two most noteworthy victim cases alleging negligence by gun manufacturers leading to criminal violence are *Hamilton v. Accu-Tek* (62 F. Supp. 802 [E.D. N.Y., 1999]), which was vacated (*Hamilton v. Beretta U.S.A. Corp.* [264 F. 3d 21 (2d Cir., 2001)]); and *Merrill v. Navegar, Inc.* (89 Cal. Rptr. 2d 146 [Cal. Ct. App. 1999]), which was reversed (28 P. 3d 116 [Cal., 2001]).

Hamilton v. Accu-Tek was a lawsuit against twenty-five major gun manufacturers by victims of shootings by juveniles. The suit alleged that the manufacturers had fueled the illegal market by "oversupplying" the legitimate handgun market in southern states with weak gun laws, knowing that the guns would be trafficked into the illegal market in states like New York with strong gun laws. The suit also charged that the manufacturers impose no control over their distributors and sellers to prevent the diversion of guns to the illegal market. In February 1999, *Hamilton* produced the first jury verdict against gun makers for negligent conduct leading to violence, as a New York jury found fifteen gun manufacturers had negligently distributed their products and awarded damages to one of the victims against three defendant manufacturers.

After federal judge Jack Weinstein refused to overturn the verdict, on appeal the U.S. Court of Appeals for the Second Circuit referred to the highest state court two legal questions: (1) whether the defendant manufacturers owed plaintiffs a duty to exercise reasonable care in the distribution of handguns, and (2) whether liability may be apportioned among the manufacturers on a market share basis. In April 2001, the New York Court of Appeals answered both questions in the negative. However, as to the duty issue, the court emphasized that its answer was based only on the evidence presented in this case, observing that "whether, in a different case, a duty may arise remains a question for the future." The court suggested, for example, that a stronger case could be made by showing that the manufacturers sold guns through particular dealers that they knew or had reason to know were disproportionate sources of guns for the illegal market. The court also cited the absence of proof that the particular guns used to inflict the plaintiffs' injuries (which were not recovered) were sufficiently connected to the defendants' alleged negligence in distribution. On the basis of the Court of Appeals' answers to the certified questions, the Second Circuit overturned the verdict.

Merrill v. Navegar produced the first appellate court ruling that a gun manufacturer could be liable for the criminal use of a gun. The suit was brought in 1994 by several victims of a 1993 multiple shooting in a San Francisco office building against Navegar, Inc., the manufacturer of the two TEC-9 semiautomatic assault weapons used in the shooting. The suit alleged that the TEC-9 was designed for use in close combat, with maximum firepower to efficiently kill large numbers of people very quickly, but that it had little or no legitimate sporting or self-defense uses. The TEC-9 had been banned in California since 1989 as a threat to public safety (the shooter, Gian Luigi Ferri, had acquired his TEC-9s in Nevada shortly before the shooting). The plaintiffs alleged that it was negligent to have sold such a gun to the general public without safeguards to prevent misuse, instead of confining sales to the military, the police, and shooting ranges. In September 1999, in a landmark ruling, the California Court of Appeals reversed a lower court ruling dismissing the suit, holding that a gun manufacturer owes "a duty to exercise reasonable care not to create risks above and beyond those inherent in the presence of firearms in our society." The California Supreme Court later reversed the decision 5–1, but on other grounds: A 1983 California statute which immunized gun manufacturers in product liability actions based on an assessment of the risks of guns versus their benefits precluded the plaintiffs' suit. Only the dissenter, Justice Werdegar, who found the statute inapplicable to claims of negligent marketing and distribution, reached the underlying tort issues. She concluded that manufacturers owed the public "a duty of care in the conduct of their design, distribution and marketing activities." Public outrage about the decision led the California legislature to repeal the immunity statute in 2002.

Gun violence victims also have invoked the public nuisance doctrine to seek the liability of the gun industry for distributing guns in a manner that fuels the illegal market. *Young v. Bryco Arms* (2001 WL 1665427 [Ill. App. Ct., December 2001]) is the first appellate court opinion recognizing that a gun maker may be liable under the public nuisance doctrine to an individual shooting victim. In *Young* the Illinois Court of Appeals held that the plaintiff victims had stated a cause of action for public nuisance against various gun manufacturers, distributors, and dealers by alleging that the defendants had designed and marketed weapons targeting criminals, flooded the handgun market in the Chicago suburbs knowing that the excess supply would be trafficked into the illegal market in Chicago, and intentionally created and maintained an underground market for handguns.

Gun manufacturers also have faced suits grounded in strict product liability. Most such cases have involved accidental shootings that allegedly were caused by specific manufacturing or design defects in guns. During the 1980s, more potentially far-reaching cases were brought seeking to make manufacturers of handguns, or particular kinds of handguns, strictly liable for criminal acts committed with their products, even though no claim was made that the guns could have been made safer. These suits charged that manufacturers were liable because the risks to society posed by their guns outweighed the benefits. This theory generally was rejected by the courts on the ground that the plaintiffs had made no allegation of a true defect in the gun's design. However, the Maryland Court of Appeals in *Kelley v. RG Industries, Inc.* (497 A. 2d 1143 [Md. 1985]) recognized a new strict liability cause of action against manufacturers of Saturday night special handguns characterized by short barrels, easy concealability, poor quality, and special appeal to criminals. The *Kelley* cause of action, however, was superseded by legislation in Maryland that banned the guns at issue.

Strict liability causes of action have been recognized in cases involving unintentional shootings that could have been prevented through the installation of specific safety devices in guns. For example, in *Hurst v. Glock* (684 A. 2d 970 [N.J. Super. Ct. App. Div. 1996]) a New Jersey appeals court held that a gun maker could be liable for failing to install a magazine safety to prevent a pistol from firing with the magazine out of the gun. In the most extensive discussion of the pertinent legal principles, the New Mexico Court of Appeals in *Smith v. Bryco Arms* (33 P. 3d 638 [N.M. Ct. App. 2001]), which was denied certiorari (34 P. 3d 610 [N.M. 2001]), held that a teenage victim of an unintentional shooting had stated a valid strict liability claim that the gun manufacturer "could have—and therefore should have—incorporated long-known design features which would have helped prevent this shooting and others like it." The *Smith* appeals court ruling reversed a lower court's dismissal of a lawsuit asserting that the manufacturer's failure to use a magazine disconnect safety or a chamber-loaded indicator rendered the handgun at issue defective in design.

In October 1998, the City of New Orleans inaugurated a new era in the history of gun litigation by filing the first lawsuit ever brought by a public entity against the gun industry. Inspired by state and city suits against the tobacco industry, New Orleans sought to recover the public costs of gun violence, including the costs associated with law enforcement, criminal prosecution, increased school security, and medical treatment of victims in public hospitals. The New Orleans case focused on the industry's sale of guns without safety mechanisms to prevent unintentional shootings and unauthorized use. Chicago followed with its own suit two weeks later, charging that the industry had contributed to a public nuisance by maintaining a distribution system that ensures the easy flow of guns into the illegal market. Eventually, over thirty cities and counties, and the State of New York, filed suit. Most of the suits adopted elements from both the New Orleans and the Chicago approaches.

The New Orleans case eventually was dismissed by the Louisiana Supreme Court, relying on the retroactive application of a Louisiana statute legislature barring cities in that state from suing the gun industry (*Morial v. Smith & Wesson Corp.,* 785 So. 2d 1 [La. 2001]); certiorari denied, 122 S. Ct. 346 [U.S. 2001]). In cases not controlled by such statutes, courts have reached varying results. Although appeals courts have affirmed dismissals in some cases (e.g., Bridgeport,

Miami/Dade County, Camden County, and Philadelphia), other cases have survived industry motions to dismiss them, including those brought by Boston, Cleveland, Newark, Wilmington, and twelve California cities and counties, including Los Angeles and San Francisco. In perhaps the most far-reaching court ruling on gun industry liability, in June 2002 the Ohio Supreme Court reinstated Cincinnati's case against the industry, reversing its dismissal by a lower court. The Supreme Court held that the city has stated proper legal claims of negligence, public nuisance, and product liability against the industry. As of this writing in 2002, other municipal cases are on appeal.

Dennis A. Henigan

See also California Street (101) Massacre; Firearms Litigation Clearinghouse; *Merrill v. Navegar, Inc.;* Nuisance Law and Gun Suits; Product Liability Lawsuits; Smith & Wesson Settlement Agreement; TEC-DC9 Pistol

For Further Reading:
Firearms Litigation Clearinghouse home page: http://www.firearmslitigation.org.
Legal Action Project home page: http://www.gunlawsuits.org/.
Lowy, Jonathan E. 2000. "Litigating against Gun Manufacturers." *Trial* 36, 12 (November): 42–48.
Siebel, Brian J. 1999. "City Lawsuits against the Gun Industry: A Roadmap for Reforming Another Deadly Industry." *St. Louis University Public Law Review* 18, 1:247–290.

Lawyer's Second Amendment Society (LSAS)

The Lawyer's Second Amendment Society was formed in 1994 by a small number of pro–gun rights lawyers. The society seeks to advance the individualist interpretation of the Second Amendment, expressed by the organization as "a personal right to bear arms." The organization also maintains a legal defense fund for actions against gun control laws and those prosecuted under them, and publishes a newsletter, *The Liberty Pole,* to promote its ideas. The position of the LSAS stands in opposition to that of the American Bar Association, which has endorsed the "collective" or militia-based interpretation of the Second Amendment since the 1970s.

Robert J. Spitzer

See also Second Amendment; United States Supreme Court Decisions on Gun Control

For Further Information:
Lawyer's Second Amendment Society, Inc., 18034 Ventura Boulevard, #329, Encino, CA 91316.
For Further Reading:
Spitzer, Robert J. 2002. *The Right to Bear Arms.* Santa Barbara, CA: ABC-CLIO.

League of Women Voters and Gun Control

The League of Women Voters (LWV) is a nonpartisan political organization that encourages informed and active participation in government. LWV works to increase understanding of major public policy issues and to influence public policy through education and advocacy. The league has always taken a strong stand on gun control, with an emphasis on protecting "the health and safety of citizens through limiting the accessibility and regulating the ownership of handguns and semiautomatic assault weapons."

Founded by Carrie Chapman Catt in 1920 as an outgrowth of the suffragist movement, LWV has over 130,000 members and supporters. It operates at local, state, and national levels, with over 1,000 local and 50 state leagues.

At its 1990 convention, the league adopted its comprehensive "Statement of Position on Gun Control." The 1994 and 1998 conventions amended the statement. According to the LWV, the proliferation of handguns and semiautomatic assault weapons in the United States is a major health and safety threat. Because of that threat, the league supports (1) strong federal measures to limit the accessibility and ownership of those weapons by private citizens; (2) the regulation of firearms for consumer safety; (3) licensing procedures for gun ownership by private citizens, including a waiting period for a background check, personal identity verification, gun safety education, and annual license renewal; (4) banning Saturday night specials; (5) enforcement of strict penalties for the improper possession of and crimes committed with handguns and assault weapons; and (6) allocation of resources to improve regulation and monitoring of gun dealers. The league takes the position that the Second Amendment does not confer on private citizens the right to keep and bear arms.

After adopting this gun control position in 1990, the league wrote to all members of Congress to inform them of the league's position and to urge passage of federal legislation to control the proliferation of handguns and semiautomatic assault weapons. The league strongly supported passage of the Brady Bill and legislation to ban semiautomatic assault weapons. The league joined other organizations in 1995–1996 to lobby against efforts to repeal the Brady Bill and the assault weapons ban.

Walter F. Carroll

See also Assault Weapons; Brady Handgun Violence Prevention Act; Consumer Product Safety Laws; Interest Groups and Gun Legislation; Second Amendment

For Further Reading:

League of Women Voters website: http://www.lwv. org/where/promoting/guncontrol_read.html.

Stuhler, Barbara. 2000. *For the Public Record: A Documentary History of the League of Women Voters.* Westport, CT: Greenwood Press.

Young, Louise Merwin, with Ralph A. Young. 1989. *In the Public Interest: The League of Women Voters, 1920–1970.* New York: Greenwood Press.

Legal Action Project (LAP)

The Legal Action Project of the Brady Center to Prevent Gun Violence (the sister organization of the Brady Campaign to Prevent Gun Violence) is a public-interest law program at the forefront of legal initiatives to reform the gun industry and establish far-reaching judicial precedents to reduce gun violence. From its headquarters in Washington, D.C., the LAP provides pro bono legal representation and advice to victims of gun violence as well as to public entities throughout the United States. The LAP has been involved in groundbreaking lawsuits against gun manufacturers and sellers and has successfully helped to defend gun laws, including state and federal assault weapons bans, from legal challenges. LAP attorneys also have authored numerous law review articles and special reports on a range of liability and constitutional issues related to gun violence.

Lawsuits brought by the LAP have charged gun manufacturers and sellers with negligent gun distribution, unsafe gun designs, deceptive gun advertising, and creating a public nuisance to health and safety. Several of these suits have garnered national attention.

In the California case of *Merrill v. Navegar,*

LAP attorneys achieved the nation's first appellate court ruling that a gun manufacturer can be liable for negligent conduct that increases the risk of criminal violence. In *Merrill,* the LAP represented the relatives of four victims of the July 1993 mass shooting at 101 California Street in San Francisco. The LAP argued that Navegar, the manufacturer of the assault pistol used in the killings, should be held liable for negligently selling to the general public an assault weapon that had no legitimate self-defense or sporting value and that was particularly well adapted for a military-style assault. In a September 1999 decision, the California Court of Appeals for the First Appellate District held that gun manufacturers have a common-law duty to avoid creating "risks above and beyond those [that] citizens may reasonably be expected to bear in a society in which firearms may legally be acquired and used and are widely available." This decision later was reversed by the California Supreme Court on the ground that a California statute gave gun makers immunity from certain common-law negligence claims. Largely as a result of that decision, the gun industry immunity statute was repealed by the California legislature in 2002.

In 1995, the LAP brought the first case ever filed against a gun manufacturer for failing to "personalize" guns to prevent their use by children. The suit was filed in a California superior court by the parents of 15-year-old Kenzo Dix, who was shot with a Beretta 9 mm pistol in 1994 while playing at a friend's house. The friend took the gun from under his father's bed, removed a full ammunition magazine, replaced it with an empty magazine, and fired without realizing that a bullet was still loaded in the chamber. In *Dix v. Beretta U.S.A. Corp.,* the LAP argued that the pistol was defective because the manufacturer failed to equip the gun with childproof safety features and an adequate indicator that the chamber was loaded. In *Smith v. Bryco Arms,* LAP secured a July 2001 ruling by the New Mexico Court of Appeals that a gun manufacturer could be held liable for failing to include safety features, like chamber-loaded indicators or magazine safeties, on their handguns.

The LAP also is leading the effort by urban cities and counties to hold the gun industry legally accountable for the public costs of gun violence. In 1998, the LAP represented the City of New Orleans in filing the first lawsuit by a U.S. city against the gun industry. Over thirty cities and counties, as well as New York State, brought similar lawsuits against gun manufacturers and sellers, seeking compensation for the costs of gun violence to their communities or injunctive relief. The LAP serves as cocounsel for most of these public entities. The lawsuits charge that the industry has failed to use feasible safety systems to protect against use of guns by children and other unauthorized users, and has helped to create and maintain the illegal gun market by distributing guns without adequate controls.

In addition to directly representing victims of gun violence, the LAP has worked to defend gun laws and regulations by filing amicus curiae briefs in virtually every major lawsuit challenging the constitutionality of gun laws. The LAP's amicus briefs have helped secure favorable rulings upholding local and state gun control laws in Ohio, Colorado, Oregon, New York, Connecticut, Arizona, and California.

Outside the courtroom, LAP attorneys have had a significant impact on the legal and policy debate surrounding the gun issue through numerous publications and special reports. In 2001, the LAP released its report *Targeting Safety: How State Attorneys General Can Act Now to Save Lives,* detailing how Massachusetts Attorney General Scott Harshbarger pioneered the regulation of the gun industry under state consumer protection laws and arguing that attorneys general in at least twenty other states could establish similar firearm safety standards. The LAP's March 2000 report, *The Enforcement Fable: How the NRA Prevented Enforcement of the Nation's Gun Laws,* detailed the National Rifle Association's work to weaken the enforcement power of the Bureau of Alcohol, Tobacco, and Firearms. In 1998, the LAP issued *Guns & Business Don't Mix,* which encouraged businesses to restrict the carrying of concealed weapons on their property. Law review articles by LAP attorneys on liability and constitutional issues frequently have been cited by courts and legal scholars.

Dennis A. Henigan

See also Brady Center to Prevent Gun Violence; California Street (101) Massacre; *Dix v. Beretta U.S.A. Corp.;* Lawsuits against Gun Manufacturers; *Merrill v. Navegar, Inc.;* Smith & Wesson Settlement Agreement

For Further Reading:

Legal Action Project home page: http://www.gunlawsuits.org/.
Lowy, Jonathan E. 2000. "Litigating against Gun Manufacturers." *Trial* 36, 12 (November): 42–48.
Siebel, Brian J. 1999. "City Lawsuits against the Gun Industry: A Roadmap for Reforming Gun Industry Misconduct." *St. Louis University Public Law Review* 18, 1: 247–290.

Legal Community Against Violence (LCAV)

The Legal Community Against Violence is a San Francisco–based organization that enlists attorneys and legal professionals in violence prevention and gun control efforts. LCAV has assisted with the preparation of gun control ordinances, tracked the adoption of local ordinances, and provided legal assistance to organizations and governments. In recent years, LCAV has taken a more national focus by expanding its network of volunteer attorneys and launching an education project on the Second Amendment.

LCAV was formed after the shootings at 101 California Street in San Francisco in 1993, when eight people were killed at a law firm by a disgruntled client. The San Francisco area has been the site of other high-profile shootings, including the 1978 assassinations of its mayor and a supervisor, which generated support for gun control measures. The California Street shootings increased support for gun control among the public, attorneys, and elected officials; a friend of Sen. Barbara Boxer's son was among those killed.

LCAV initially focused on a lawsuit against the manufacturer of the assault weapons used in the shooting. The California Supreme Court ultimately ruled in 2001 that the California Civil Code provided immunity to the weapons manufacturer (*Merrill v. Navegar,* 26 Cal. 4th 465). While appeals were pending, LCAV began expanding its activities and offered free legal assistance to a number of California cities and counties in the development and defense of local gun control ordinances. Although another state law appears to restrict local government regulations on gun control activity (a so-called preemption law), most of the local ordinances have been upheld through state courts. With financial support from a number of California-based foundations, including the California Wellness Foundation and the David and Lucille Packard Foundation, LCAV formalized its activities as the Local Ordinance Project. LCAV tracked the adoption of local ordinances, disseminated a comprehensive annual *Legal Resources Manual,* sponsored legal workshops, and testified before local and state officials.

LCAV is now expanding its activities nationwide. Following a 1999 federal district court decision in *United States v. Emerson* that apparently interpreted the Second Amendment in favor of gun rights advocates, LCAV began its own Second Amendment Education Campaign. LCAV argues that the Second Amendment allows for reasonable restrictions on firearms. LCAV participated in a 2000 open letter to Charlton Heston and ad in the *New York Times* calling for an end to misrepresentation on the meaning of the Second Amendment. LCAV is also extending its volunteer attorney network nationwide and as of 2001 was developing a strategic plan to provide legal assistance outside of California.

Marcia L. Godwin

See also Boxer, Barbara; California Street (101) Massacre; Feinstein, Dianne; *Merrill v. Navegar, Inc.;* Preemption Laws; *United States v. Emerson*

For Further Reading:

Godwin, Marcia L., and Jean Reith Schroedel. 2000. "Policy Diffusion and Strategies for Promoting Policy Change: Evidence from California Local Gun Control Ordinances." *Policy Studies Journal* 28, 4: 760–776.

Legal Community Against Violence, 268 Bush Street, #555, San Francisco, CA 94104. http://www.lcav.org.

Legal Community Against Violence. 2000. "Addressing Gun Violence through Local Ordinances: A Legal Resource Manual for California Cities and Counties, 2000 Supplement." San Francisco: Legal Community Against Violence.

Fans hold up signs during a vigil in New York for the slain John Lennon, 1980. (Corbis)

Lennon, John (1940–1980)

Born on October 9, 1940, John Lennon gained international recognition as a musician, poet, and humanitarian before he was fatally shot on December 8, 1980. A native of Liverpool, England, Lennon was influenced by the music of Elvis Presley and Jerry Lee Lewis. When he was 17, he started his first band, known as the Quarrymen, with Paul McCartney, George Harrison, and Ringo Starr. These four young men became better known as the Beatles.

Lennon was considered to be the most intellectual and socially driven of the Beatles. He was credited with influencing the members of the band to experiment with psychedelic drugs and the political activism that characterized the late 1960s. The Beatles' last album, *Abbey Road,* was released in 1969.

Living in New York City at the time of his death, Lennon was shot outside his apartment building by Mark David Chapman. Chapman had conducted surveillance of the Dakota apartment building where Lennon lived with his wife, Yoko Ono, and son Sean the weekend prior to the shooting. On the evening of December 8, 1980, as Lennon and his wife approached the building, Chapman called out to the musician. When Lennon turned, the former security guard went into a combat shooting stance and shot Lennon five times. Lennon was pronounced dead at a local hospital, where his death was attributed to a loss of blood.

Lennon's murder served as a vehicle for the gun control lobby to demand greater restrictions on weapons. The Lennon murder weapon, a Charter Arms .38 caliber handgun, was considered a Saturday night special because of its low cost, ready availability, and ease of concealment. The murder also boosted interest in the foremost gun control organization, Handgun Control, Inc. (renamed the Brady Campaign to Prevent Gun Violence in 2001), taking the organization from 5,000 to 80,000 dues-paying members in a matter of weeks (Carter, 1997, p. 83).

G. Edward Richards

See also Brady Campaign to Prevent Gun Violence; Saturday Night Specials

For Further Reading:

Carter, Gregg Lee. 1997. *The Gun Control Movement.* New York: Twayne.

Hamilton, Sue L., and John C. Hamilton. 1989. *The Killing of a Rock Star: John Lennon.* New York: Abdo and Daughters.

Jones, Jack. 2000. *Let Me Take You Down: Inside the Mind of Mark David Chapman, the Man Who Killed John Lennon.* New York: Random House.

Lethality Effect of Guns

Assumptions and assertions about the comparative lethality of various potentially deadly weapons have been critical in the debate over gun policy. Zimring's influential study (1968) asserted that gun wounds are five times more lethal than knife wounds and that homicide would decline substantially if outlawing guns caused the less deadly knife to become the primary weapon used in assaults (p. 728). A flaw in this argument is that attackers who would have inflicted a gunshot wound would presumably substitute a very large, very dangerous knife if a gun were not available. Zimring's data do not, however, focus on large knives but rather on an undifferentiated sample of wounds inflicted with knives defined to include any edged or pointed weapon (e.g., hairpins, fingernail files, forks, safety razors, etc.) as wounding agents. A comparison of wounds inflicted by such trivial weapons with lethal gunshot wounds does not tell us how much more lethal guns are than long-bladed knives. A nearly contemporary medical study of victims hospitalized with penetrating abdominal wounds showed the following death rates: 16.8 percent for those shot with handguns, 14.3 percent for those stabbed with ice picks, and 13.3 percent for those stabbed with large knives (Taylor, 1973). A review of several studies suggests that gunshot wounds are 1.3 to 3 times deadlier than knife wounds (Wright, Rossi, and Daly, 1983, pp. 199–209).

The major reason guns in general are so much deadlier than even large knives is that rifles, and particularly shotguns, are so much deadlier than either knives or handguns (Fackler, 1987; Kleck, 1984). Long-gun wounds may be as much as fifteen times deadlier than knife wounds, which would make long guns five to eleven times deadlier than handguns, depending on the calibers involved (Kates, 1989, p. 205).

All this reflects negatively on "handgun-only controls"—that is, controls aimed at reducing handgun ownership without imposing the same politically unpalatable restrictions on long-gun ownership. For the sake of argument, assume a ban made it impossible for criminals to obtain handguns. That would only reduce the number of homicides if the great majority of those criminals, upon being deprived of handguns, switched to using knives when committing their crimes. If instead any substantial number of criminals began using the much more deadly sawed-off shotgun, homicide would actually increase. What would happen if a handgun ban caused 50 percent of woundings that now occur with handguns to occur with sawed-off shotguns instead, while the other 50 percent of woundings were inflicted with knives instead of handguns? Given comparative lethality figures like those set out in the last paragraph, the number of murders would double from the shotgun woundings alone—even if none of the 50 percent of woundings caused by knifing resulted in death.

A hypothetical 50–50 shotgun-knife substitution is realistic. "Anywhere from 54 percent to about 80 percent of homicides occur in circumstances that would easily permit the use of a long gun," Gary Kleck has observed (1984, pp. 186–194). Indeed, if a handgun-only ban actually kept handguns from criminals, long guns might be substituted by far more than 50 percent of those criminals. In a National Institute of Justice survey of 2,000 felons in ten prisons across the country, 82 percent agreed that "if a criminal wants a handgun but can't get one he can always saw off a long gun." Further, according to 87 percent of those felons who had often used handguns in crime and 89 percent of those who had often used shotguns, it would be "easy" to do this (Wright and Rossi, 1986, p. 221, table 11.3). Based on these responses, Lizotte (1986) calculated that the current handgun death toll could more than triple if a handgun ban led to long-gun substitution at the rates indicated.

Two caveats to the foregoing must be noted. First, Col. Martin Fackler, M.D., an experienced battle surgeon who founded and for a decade directed the U.S. Armed Services Wound Ballistics Laboratory and who is a leading technical expert on woundings, discounts all the precise comparison figures given above (including Zimring's) because no study compares wounds and deaths with all these weapons based on tracing actual wound paths. Fackler does nevertheless agree that, all other things being equal, a knife wound is less likely to kill than a handgun wound, which, in turn, is less deadly than one inflicted with a long gun, particularly a large-gauge shotgun. Second, the fact that knives are short-range weapons while guns allow killing at a distance has little practical import because the great majority of shootings occur at very short range.

In sum, a fundamental principle of gun policy should be to avoid any legislation that would drive criminals to use more deadly weaponry rather than less deadly weaponry. This principle counsels against banning Saturday night specials (SNSs) instead of, or without, banning all other handguns or firearms in general. The controversy over SNSs is an odd one in which each of the opposing parties holds a position that is difficult to square with their general views. The NRA exalts the important defensive value of guns: so why does it not endorse banning SNSs as a consumer-protection measure? If the SNS label is strictly limited to apply only to cheap, low-caliber handguns, such guns have far less "stopping power" (ability to disable an attacker rapidly) than larger-caliber handguns. On the other hand, the antigun lobby denies the defensive value of guns and sees handguns as tools for crime: so why would it lobby for banning SNSs, with the inevitable result of driving criminals to obtain larger-caliber, more deadly handguns?

As for the defensive utility of firearms, several other points require clarification because they have been the subject of so much mythology. Movie portrayals create the false impression that bullets can pick shooting victims up and throw them backwards. If firing a gun actually released that much energy, Newton's third law ("equal and opposite reaction") would mean the shooter would concomitantly be knocked backwards. In fact, shooting victims usually fall forward in whatever direction they were traveling. If victims exhibit violent body motion at all, it is not from the physical force of the bullet but from neuromuscular reaction. That does not necessarily cause the victim to move backwards, but rather may impel the body in any number of directions.

Similarly, gun owners' faith in the efficacy of their firearms is often highly exaggerated. It is nonsensical to suggest that a victim could be knocked down by being hit in the finger with a .45 caliber gun. Indeed, the supposedly definitive military testing establishing the .45's "stopping power" was a farce: the experts doing the testing began with a strong bias favoring the .45 and manipulated a wholly inadequate testing program to support that result. Incidentally, though most any rifle bullet will penetrate the Kevlar vests police wear under their shirts, neither .45s nor other handguns will reliably do so.

By the same token, the idea of a single hit, particularly with a handgun, physically incapacitating an attacker is also largely a myth. With the exception of shots that penetrate the brain, anyone who immediately falls down after being shot only once has been mentally rather than physically incapacitated (i.e., he has lost the will to continue). Even a shot through the heart does not physically incapacitate the victim for ten or more seconds; persons shot through the heart have been able to continue strenuous activities for that long, including returning fire. There are many verified instances of persons continuing to attack, fight, or flee for short periods after being shot multiple times in vital areas.

This is not to deny that firearms represent the only or most practical resort for victims who are likely to be both taken by surprise and physically weaker than criminal attackers. This is effectively conceded even by opponents of defensive gun use when they suggest that, rather than using any other weapon, "the best defense against injury" for victims facing robbers or rapists "is to put up no defense—give them what they want or run" (Shields, 1981, pp. 124–25; Zimring and Zuehl, 1986; Yeager, Alviani, and Loving, 1976). And in instances when criminal attackers are killed by victims, the weapon is generally a handgun and almost always a firearm of some kind (MacDonald and Tennenbaum, 1999).

The point, however, is that though comparatively powerful, firearms are still not as effective a weapon as many owners think they are. Victims who pull a gun on an attacker are fortunate that in the great majority of cases that suffices to frighten criminals into flight rather than provoking a gunfight in which both sides might suffer severe injury or death (Kleck, 1997, pp. 162–163).

Don B. Kates

See also Gunshot Wounds; Saturday Night Specials; Weapons Instrumentality Effect

For Further Reading:

Fackler, Martin. 1987. "Physics of Missile Injuries." Pp. 25–41 in *Evaluation and Management of Trauma*, ed. Norman E. McSwain, Jr., and Morris D. Kerstein. Norwalk, CT: Appleton-Century-Crofts.

Kates, Don B. 1989. "Firearms and Violence: Old Premises and Current Evidence." Pp. 197–215 in *Violence in America*, vol. 1, ed. Ted Robert Gurr. Beverly Hills, CA: Sage Publications.

Kleck, Gary. 1984. "Handgun-Only Control: A Policy Disaster in the Making." Pp. 167–200 in *Firearms and Violence: Issues of Public Policy*, ed. Don B. Kates. Cambridge, MA: Ballinger.

———. 1997. *Targeting Guns: Firearms and Their Control*. New York: Aldine de Gruyter.

Lizotte, Alan J. 1986. "The Costs of Using Gun Control to Reduce Homicide." *Bulletin of the New York Academy of Medicine* 62: 539–558.

MacDonald, John M., and Abraham N. Tennenbaum. 1999. "Justifiable Homicide by Civilians." Pp. 463–491 in *The Criminology of Criminal Law*, ed. William S. Laufer and Freda Adler. New Brunswick, NJ: Transaction Press.

Shields, Pete. 1981. *Guns Don't Die—People Do*. New York: Arbor House.

Taylor, Frederic W. 1973. "Gunshot Wounds of the Abdomen." *Annals of Surgery* 177, 2: 174–177.

Wright, James D., and Peter H. Rossi. 1986. *Armed and Considered Dangerous: A Survey of Felons and Their Firearms*. New York: Aldine.

Wright, James D., Peter H. Rossi, and Kathleen Daly. 1983. *Under the Gun: Weapons, Crime and Violence in America*. New York: Aldine.

Yeager, Matthew G., Joseph D. Alviani, and Nancy Loving. 1976. *How Well Does the Handgun Protect You and Your Family?* Handgun Control staff technical report no. 2. Washington, DC: U.S. Conference of Mayors.

Zimring, Franklin E. 1968. "Is Gun Control Likely to Reduce Violent Killings?" *University of Chicago Law Review* 35: 721–737.

Zimring, Franklin E., and James Zuehl. 1986. "Victim Injury Death in Urban Robbery: A Chicago Study." *Journal of Legal Studies* 15: 1–40.

Lewis v. United States (1980)

This Supreme Court case upheld the Gun Control Act of 1968 under the due process clause of the Fifth Amendment and reaffirmed the Court's 1939 decision on the Second Amendment as previously set forth in *United States v. Miller*. The *Lewis* case is the only case in which the Court has addressed the meaning of the Second Amendment in the over half century since *United States v. Miller*. In doing so, albeit in a perfunctory fashion, the Court concluded that "restrictions on the use of firearms are neither based upon constitutionally suspect criteria, nor do they trench upon any constitutionally protected liberties." The Court further expressed its view that "the Second Amendment guarantees no right to keep and bear a firearm that does not have 'some reasonable relationship to the preservation or efficiency of a well-regulated militia.'" Since the Court also cited its 1939 decision in *Miller* as support, the Court's underlying Second Amendment analysis in *Miller* arguably remains good law today.

In *Lewis,* the Court addressed the case of an individual who was convicted of a felony in Florida in 1961, whose conviction for the offense was never overturned, but whose original felony conviction was nonetheless unconstitutionally obtained under the Sixth and Fourteenth Amendments. Specifically, the petitioner had been convicted of burglary in Florida in 1961 and was not provided with counsel to assist in his defense. Thus, his conviction was invalid under the retroactive rule regarding the right to counsel as put forth by the Supreme Court in *Gideon v. Wainwright.* Rejecting the petitioner's claim, the Court held that the constitutionality of the petitioner's conviction had no bearing on his liability under the Gun Control Act of 1968. The Court held that an offense under the Gun Control Act may be predicated upon a prior state court felony conviction, even though the conviction would be subject to a collateral attack by the person convicted as being in violation of the Sixth and Fourteenth Amendments. That is, the Court concluded that Congress could rationally conclude that any felony conviction, even an allegedly invalid one that could be collaterally attacked, is a sufficient basis on which to prohibit possession of a firearm.

James A. Beckman

See also Fourteenth Amendment; Gun Control Act of 1968; Second Amendment; *United States v. Miller*
For Further Reading:
Kopel, David. 1999. "The Supreme Court's Thirty-Five Other Gun Cases: What the Supreme Court Has Said about the Second Amendment." *Saint Louis University Public Law Review* 18: 99–187.
Lewis v. United States, 445 U.S. 55 (1980).

Liability of Gun Manufacturers

The societal value and fairness of holding gun manufacturers liable for accidental or intentional injuries or homicides caused by misuse of firearms that have no inherent defects have been much debated. The law on the patentability of the Colt revolver furnishes an instructive

starting point for discussion of these issues. In 1961, the Court of Customs and Patent Appeals decided a patent case titled *In re Anthony.* The court recognized that a revolver is "an instrument of death" (*In re Anthony,* p. 1395). Moreover, the court cited approvingly a 1903 patent case that had identified three social disadvantages of a revolver: (1) it enabled private revenge; (2) it was capable of fatal accidental discharge; and (3) it facilitated private warfare among frontiersmen. Thus in *Anthony* the court reasoned that a revolver may well have been "injurious to the morals, and injurious to the health, and injurious to the good order of society" (p. 1395). Nevertheless, in *Anthony* the court hastened to add, "On the other hand, the revolver, by furnishing a ready means of self-defense, may sometimes have promoted morals and health and good order" (p. 1395). Therefore, the court approved the 1903 case's opinion that Colt's revolver could receive patent protection because a revolver possessed occasional good uses and hence occasionally promoted public morals, health, and order. The court added that courts are in no position to reliably balance the good and evil functions of the revolver. Courts lack the machinery to make such value judgments.

The *Anthony* court noted that the noblest inventions—such as steam engines, dynamos, electric railroads, automobiles, tires, power tools, and drugs—likewise could be injurious to morals, health, and the good order of society. Nevertheless, they too could be patented because of their socially redeeming utility.

Inherent in the court's approach was the unfairness of holding an inventor or manufacturer responsible for the misuse by others of defectless products. Another consideration was that the existence of any social advantage of a product, even if it was manifested on only relatively few occasions, inherently outweighed the disadvantages. And by virtue of its self-defense function, Colt's revolver is the great equalizer of the physically weak and the strong.

Increasingly, many scholars as well as federal and state courts are coming to the recognition that the Constitution protects an individual right to keep ordinary personal firearms in the home. This recognition furnishes all the more reason not to burden that right with costly liability suits against innocent manufacturers of defectless personal firearms.

In 1964, the U.S. Supreme Court freed the press from the burden of costly libel and slander suits by laying down strict standards for winning such suits: the defamatory statement had to be made "with knowledge that it was false or with reckless disregard of whether it was false or not" (*New York Times v. Sullivan*, 1964, p. 280). By the same token, some argue that a manufacturer of ordinary personal firearms should be free from the burden of costly tort liability lawsuits unless it distributed a mechanically defective firearm knowing that it was mechanically defective or with reckless disregard of whether it was mechanically defective or not.

David I. Caplan

See also California Street (101) Massacre; *Dix v. Beretta U.S.A. Corp.;* Lawsuits against Gun Manufacturers; Second Amendment; Smith & Wesson Settlement Agreement; *United States v. Emerson*

For Further Reading:

In re Anthony, 414 F. 2d 1383 (1969), 56 C.C.P.A. 1443.

New York Times v. Sullivan, 376 U.S. 254 (1964).

Liberalism and Support for Gun Control

See Ideologies—Conservative and Liberal

Licensing

Licensing is a method of control employed by the government to regulate behavior through the granting of permission to engage in some behavior or activity. With respect to guns, the states or federal government have considered or enacted systems of licensing pertaining to gun manufacturers, gun dealers, and gun owners. Licensing is defended on up to four grounds: it prevents certain categories of individuals, including criminals, children, and those considered mentally incompetent, from gaining easy access to guns; it ensures that those having guns demonstrate some degree of competency (though not all states impose this as a require-

ment); it facilitates criminal prosecutions; and it restricts the accessibility of an inherently dangerous commodity based, for example, on the needs of one's occupation.

Gun and ammunition manufacturers are required to have a federal license and to pay annual fees ($50 for gun manufacturers, $10 for ammunition makers), according to the Gun Control Act of 1968. Manufacturers of armor-piercing ammunition or "destructive devices" (such as land mines, bombs, and hand grenades) pay annual fees of $1,000.

Since enactment of the Federal Firearms Act of 1938, gun dealers have been required to have a federal firearms license (FFL) if they buy or sell firearms across state boundaries. The Gun Control Act of 1968 tightened some of these regulations. The license fee of $1 set in the 1938 law was increased to $10 in 1968. The act also banned the interstate shipment of most guns and ammunition to private individuals and strengthened dealer record-keeping requirements. Because of the small fee, relative ease of acquisition, and limited enforcement, many private individuals acquired FFLs in order to receive discounted prices or make gun shipments easier rather than to set up a retail or wholesale business. Up until the early 1990s, about 80 percent of all FFLs went to such individuals. The Firearms Owners' Protection Act of 1986 relaxed interstate regulations, allowing for interstate sales of long guns. Gun dealers were also allowed to conduct sales in locations other than their stores; restrictions were placed on the ability of the Bureau of Alcohol, Tobacco, and Firearms (BATF) to regulate dealers; and record-keeping requirements were reduced. The Violent Crime Control and Law Enforcement Act of 1994 tightened certain regulations, requiring licensees to be photographed and fingerprinted, and requiring that they cooperate with firearm trace requests and report any thefts to the BATF. License fees were also increased to $200 per year, with annual renewal fees of $90. This plus stricter regulation prompted a dramatic drop in the number of FFLs, from just under 300,000 in the early 1990s to under 80,000 by 2000.

Calls to enact a national system of licensing for gun owners date to at least the 1930s, but no such national system has been enacted yet. In recent years, the subject has not been discussed much at the national level. During the 2000 presidential elections, however, both of the Democratic candidates for president, Vice President Al Gore and former Sen. Bill Bradley, endorsed licensing. Gun owners are licensed in some states. Handgun owners must obtain licenses in Hawaii, Illinois, Iowa, Kansas, Massachusetts, Michigan, Minnesota, Missouri, Nebraska, New Jersey, New York, North Carolina, and Ohio. Permits for long-gun purchases are required in Hawaii, Illinois, Massachusetts, and New Jersey. Handgun ownership is barred in the District of Columbia.

Robert J. Spitzer

See also Assault Weapons Ban of 1994; Bureau of Alcohol, Tobacco, and Firearms; Federal Firearms Act of 1938; Firearms Owners' Protection Act of 1986; Gun Control Act of 1968

For Further Reading:

Henderson, Harry. 2000. *Gun Control.* New York: Facts on File.
Vizzard, William J. 2000. *Shots in the Dark.* Lanham, MD: Rowman & Littlefield.

Long Gun

A long gun is a long firearm that is fired from the shoulder. Most long guns owned by civilians are rifles, carbines (short-barreled long guns, often using pistol-caliber ammunition, which for most purposes may be considered a variety of rifle), or shotguns. According to the National Survey of Private Ownership of Firearms, Americans own a total of about 70 million rifles (including 28 million semiautomatic rifles) and 49 million shotguns. Most owners cite hunting as their primary reason for owning a long gun. Other reasons include self-defense and target shooting. A relatively small number of people also collect long guns or own them because of job-related needs (Cook and Ludwig, 1996).

Several features distinguish rifles from handguns. Rifles fire higher-power ammunition, which makes them more lethal at greater distances. They have longer barrels and a longer sight radius, which make them more accurate at greater distances, and they are brought to the shoulder to fire, which helps shooters to manage recoil and to aim accurately. While it is difficult to hit targets with handguns at ranges of 50 yards, rifles can do so at 300 yards or more. Rifle bullets can kill game or humans more reliably and quickly at long range. (Despite this fact, handguns are much more commonly used in the commission of murder in the United States—in the year 1999, 51 percent of all murders were committed with handguns compared to only 7 percent with long guns.)

Dozens of rifle cartridges are available with different ballistic and wounding properties. For casual plinking, competitive target shooting, or hunting small animals such as squirrels, a rifle chambered for the .22 long-rifle cartridge is often used. Military assault rifles and civilian rifles used to hunt small vermin (usually called "varmints" by hunters) at long range usually use relatively small-caliber, high-velocity bullets. The 5.56 mm round used in the military M-16 assault rifle is also used as a civilian "varmint" cartridge. Heavier, larger-diameter bullets are used to hunt larger animals such as deer; the .308 Winchester and .30–06 (pronounced "thirty aught six") are venerable deer-hunting cartridges. The most powerful ammunition, such as the .458 Winchester Magnum, is demanded for large, dangerous game.

Shotguns are smoothbore weapons that are usually used to fire shells containing small balls called "shot." Unlike the caliber designations of other firearms and ammunition, shotgun shells are designated by gauge and shot type. The most common type of shotgun is 12-gauge, meaning that twelve lead balls of the diameter of the shotgun bore would weigh one pound. (The bore diameter of a 12-gauge shotgun is .73 inch, or about 18.5 mm.) Large gauge numbers indicate smaller bore size, so a 20-gauge shotgun is smaller than a 12-gauge. Shot types vary the size and number of balls for different purposes. Small numbers of relatively large balls (about .33 inch for 00 buckshot) are used for deer hunting or self-defense. Larger numbers of smaller pellets (about .12 inch for #5 birdshot) are used to hunt smaller game such as ducks, squirrels, and wild turkeys.

The shot from a shotgun begins spreading or dispersing as soon as it leaves the barrel. At short ranges the shot remains in a dense cluster and will make one large hole in the target. At longer ranges the shot disperses in a pattern that makes it easier to hit small moving targets such as birds. The extent of dispersion at a given range can be adjusted by means of a choke, which is a tubular barrel insert. By narrowing the barrel with a choke, the shot can be made to disperse less rapidly, producing denser shot patterns at longer ranges, increasing the effective range. By leaving the barrel open, the shot can be made to disperse more rapidly, making hits easier at close range and allowing game at close range to be taken without an overly dense shot pattern destroying an excessive amount of meat.

Shot dispersion varies with ammunition and gun selection, but generally a full choke will put about 70 percent of the shot in a 30-inch circle at 40 yards. A modified choke will put about 60 percent of the shot in the same circle, while an improved cylinder places about half in the circle and a cylinder bore places about 40 percent in the circle.

There are six main types of modern long-gun action. The *break-open* action, more often used with shotguns than rifles, consists of a barrel on a hinge that allows the gun to "break" so that the shooter can insert or remove single cartridges from the breech. Two barrels may be used to allow two shots. Double-barrel shotguns are often much more expensive than single-barrel shotguns because of the difficulty of aligning two barrels precisely so that they fire to the same point of aim. *Lever action* is used in rifles but not shotguns. The lever-action rifle is often chambered for pistol cartridges such as the .44 Magnum and usually holds cartridges in a tube magazine under the barrel. A lever behind the trigger is moved down to eject a spent cartridge and back up to reload the chamber. *Pump action,* also called slide action, is more often seen on shotguns than rifles. It requires that a handle under the barrel be pulled back to eject a spent cartridge and pushed forward to load a new cartridge. *Bolt action,* which is a common action on high-power hunting rifles because it is strong, reliable, and accurate, requires that the firer pull back the bolt handle to eject a spent cartridge and return the bolt handle to the forward position to load a new cartridge. Some bolt-action weapons are single shot, but most feed between three and ten rounds from an internal magazine. In *semiautomatic* weapons some of the energy from the cartridge's expanding gas is used to eject the spent cartridge and load a new one without any action by the shooter. Each time the trigger is pressed this process is repeated. Fully *automatic* weapons repeat this process continuously as long as the trigger is held and the ammunition supply is not exhausted.

Matthew DeBell

See also Assault Weapons; Handguns; Uniform Crime Reports

For Further Reading:

Cook, Philip J., and Jens Ludwig. 1996. *Guns in America: Results of a Comprehensive National Survey on Firearms Ownership and Use.* Washington, DC: Police Foundation.

Ezell, Edward C. 1984. *Small Arms Today.* Harrisburg, PA: Stackpole Books.

Long Island Railroad Massacre

The Long Island Railroad massacre took place in December 1993, when an armed man boarded a crowded train filled with commuters and Christmas shoppers and opened fire, killing six and wounding nineteen. On December 7, as the 5:33 P.M. train out of New York's Pennsylvania Station pulled into the Merillon Avenue Station in Garden City, New York, Colin Ferguson shot twenty-five people at point-blank range. More people might have been shot if two passengers had not subdued Ferguson as he stopped to reload.

Ferguson, an African American, claimed that he was the victim of a racist society that had caused him to take action. He also said that he had decided to open fire on the train after it left New York City so as not to embarrass Mayor David Dinkins, an African American who was completing his term after being defeated for reelection by Rudolph Giuliani. Dinkins described Ferguson's remarks as "nonsense" (Moore, 1993, p. 177).

Ferguson was found competent to stand trial and was permitted to act as his own attorney. He invoked a "black rage defense," claiming

Colin Ferguson in police custody. (Reuters NewMedia Inc./Corbis)

that he should not be held responsible for his actions since they had been triggered by the racism he experienced in American society. In February 1995 Ferguson was convicted of twenty-five counts of murder and attempted murder and sentenced to life imprisonment (the most severe sanction available in New York at the time). Subsequent appeals, including one that argued that Ferguson's conviction should be overturned because he was not competent to defend himself, were rejected by the courts.

Carolyn McCarthy, whose husband was killed and whose son was seriously injured by Ferguson, ran for the U.S. House of Representatives in 1996 after her congressman, Dan Frisa, voted to repeal an assault weapons ban. McCarthy, who was a registered Republican, was elected as a Democrat on a gun control platform. Her campaign victory was later the subject of a made-for-television movie produced by Barbra Streisand.

In January 1997, a multimillion-dollar lawsuit brought by the families of the victims against the Long Island Railroad was dismissed, when a judge ruled that the railroad was not liable for Ferguson's actions.

In August 2000, New York Governor George Pataki stood at the site of the massacre to sign what was described as the "nation's toughest state anti-gun bill" into law (Gearty and Goldiner, 2000, p. 6). The law mandated background checks for gun buyers at gun shows; required child safety locks on all guns; outlawed assault weapons; raised the minimum age to buy guns from 18 to 21; ordered gun makers to equip handguns with unique ballistic markers; and ordered the state police to combat gun trafficking.

As of this writing in 2002, Ferguson remains in the custody of the New York State Department of Correctional Services.

Jeffrey Kraus

See also Columbine High School Tragedy; Mass Murder (Shootings); Stockton, California, Massacre; Texas Tower Shooting

For Further Reading:

Gearty, Robert, and Dave Goldiner. 2000. "Pataki Signs Tough Gun Bill." *New York Daily News* (August 10).

Moore, Colin. 1993. "Mayor Rips Suspect's 'Nonsense.'" *Newsday* (December 9).

Schuler, Christine. 1996. *The Long Island Railroad Massacre.* New York: A&E Home Video. Written and produced by Christine Schuler; narrated by Bill Kurtis.

Long Rifle (Pennsylvania/Kentucky)

The Pennsylvania long rifle represents a unique American technological development, one that enthusiasts sometimes claim is the first distinctly American invention. If such a claim has real merit, it shows just how closely tied the Pennsylvania rifle is to the history of the first trans-Appalachian settlements.

The Pennsylvania long rifle—also commonly known as the Kentucky rifle—resulted from a set of very specific technological adaptations in the design of firearms. The design made the weapon particularly suited to the frontier conditions prevalent in the eastern mountains and hardwood forests of Kentucky, Tennessee, and the Ohio River Valley. The Pennsylvania rifle's importance to the early trans-Appalachian explorers and pioneers quickly gave it a prominent place in the lore and legends popular among Americans. As a design, the first Pennsylvania rifles appeared clearly only in the 1760s. Yet by the time of the American Revolution the image of the hawkeyed, buckskinned sharpshooter from the frontier was already established in the American consciousness. Armed with the Pennsylvania rifle, this frontiersman of late-eighteenth-century lore became one of America's most enduring icons.

The Pennsylvania rifle was an adaptation, or hybrid, a cross between two earlier firearm technologies: the German jaeger rifle and the English fowling piece. The jaeger was a short (relatively) heavy-looking rifle of large caliber (over .60). These rifles were adapted for hunting large game in the forests of northern and central Europe. They were expected to hit hard and accurately,

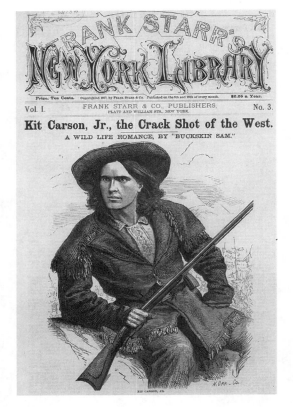

Kit Carson portrayed on the cover of Frank Starr's New York Library, *1877, holding a long rifle. (Library of Congress)*

bringing an animal down immediately. The English fowling piece was, in effect, a flintlock shotgun with a relatively long barrel. These fowling pieces were expected to deliver a very small-caliber projectile, or buckshot, that would do minimal damage while killing very small game. The resulting technological merger brought together the rifling and accuracy of the German big-game weapon with the lightness, delicacy, and small bore of the English fowling piece. The "invention" took place in the purchase of guns from immigrant gunsmiths who worked on the western frontier of the 1750s and 1760s.

At that time, the westernmost fringe of frontier settlements was still on the eastern slopes of the Appalachians, in the areas around York, Lancaster, and Reading, Pennsylvania. The German immigrant communities in and near these settlements provided the gunsmiths who were familiar with rifling technology and the techniques for fabricating rifled barrels. The explorers and pioneers who planned to cross the mountains placed the orders for weapons that drove the development of the new and highly specialized design that became known as the Pennsylvania rifle.

The eastern hardwood forests of the Ohio River Valley and the mountains of Kentucky contained few animals that posed any serious threat to men. Firearms were seldom needed for defense from animals, and in those few cases where there was such a need, nothing called for a weapon as heavy as the German hunting rifle. More importantly, the long treks required for penetration of the forests and wilderness placed a premium on the weight of equipment and supplies. A smaller-caliber weapon offered real advantages. Likewise, in this frontier world, where one might live for months at a time without visiting any settlement capable of providing supplies, a very accurate weapon that wasted little lead or powder would be highly prized. The Pennsylvania rifle was born out of such considerations. These were small-caliber weapons (usually in the range of .45 to .50 caliber) with an exceptionally long barrel and a characteristically strong curve to the butt stock.

Daniel Boone's long rifle can provide a point of comparison to illustrate the economies of the Pennsylvania rifle. His weapon was 5 feet, 3 inches long. The barrel itself was over 4 feet long. Boone's gun was .44 caliber and fired a ball that weighed 130 grains, which is equivalent in weight to the bullet fired from a modern .32 caliber weapon. It weighed eleven pounds. The length and weight of the weapon gave it stability and significantly helped steady the aim. Using round shot of such small caliber, Boone could expect to fire fifty-five rounds from a pound of lead. Each shot would require no more than a thimble full of gunpowder. On the other extreme, the standard Brown Bess musket of this era was bored at .75 caliber, which meant that its shot was molded at the rate of sixteen per pound. The standard charge was the equivalent of the ball in weight—one ounce. Boone's rifled barrel would have allowed fairly reliable aim at distances in excess of 200 yards. The smooth bore of the Bess and the windage (or gap between the ball and the walls of the barrel) facilitated rapid loading, which meant that a marksman would

not have been able to hit a human-sized target at much beyond 50 yards.

The Pennsylvania rifle and the eighteenth-century musket were very different weapons intended for very different purposes. The long rifle was a precision device intended to make carefully aimed shot count at relatively long range. The primary incentives for accuracy and range were the practicalities of long treks and distant supply. Survival in the forest often depended on hunting. Husbanding supplies of powder and shot as much as possible only made sense. The gun that resulted was heavy but fragile. It was very accurate, but required very careful loading. Even an expert marksman needed two to three minutes between shots. The shot was sufficient for hunting the game of the eastern forests, but its small size meant that it lacked stopping power. Large game, such as deer, commonly bled to death while running away, but that mattered less than other considerations. Finally, its small shot could go wildly astray in even a mild crosswind.

Despite the mythologies that surround the long rifle, it was not a weapon well suited for military use or even for fighting the Indian wars in which it played such a prominent role. The long rifle was most particularly suited to woodland hunting. After initially being enthusiastic about forming companies of riflemen in the Continental army, George Washington and most other military leaders quickly came to the point of disbanding such units. Critics of the frontiersman mythology often point to the independent and undisciplined ways of the frontiersmen as a cause for the military's disenchantment, but it is just as valid to point to the technological limitations of their rifles as a cause for the difficulties these units faced during the American Revolution. This point can be illustrated by recalling the tactics the Native Americans developed for dealing with small groups of frontiersmen armed with Pennsylvania rifles. The most effective ploy was very simple: first to draw fire and then to charge all out with tomahawk, knife, or club. No rifleman—not even the best—could fire and reload quickly enough to stop a determined charge. The range of the weapon, the speed of a runner, and the time required for reloading meant almost certain death or capture for the rifleman. If the rifleman fired and then turned to run, the Native Americans simply followed and ran him down. The lore and legends of the frontier are full of stories of frontiersmen on the run after they fired their one shot. Few eluded their pursuers, and when they did they became the stuff of frontier legend. Even fewer, including the likes of Simon Kenton, Lewis Wetzel, and Daniel Boone, ever mastered the trick of reloading a long rifle on the run. According to the legends, that skill was an almost certain lifesaver. It countered the Native Americans' skills in distance running and use of hand weapons. According to the legends, the pursuers always gave up the chase when their quarry managed the second shot from a long rifle.

The same vulnerabilities that limited the long rifle's effectiveness in the Indian fighting of the eastern forests also followed riflemen onto the battlefields of the American Revolution. Riflemen could never match the volume of fire possible with the massed infantry tactics based on the flintlock musket. The rifles were most effective at "picking off" selected targets at long distances. This tactic could be used to some effect in eliminating the officers who were so critical to the effectiveness of massed infantry. Logical as the idea seems, however, such sharpshooting found remarkably little effective use. The best-known instance was at the Battle of Saratoga, where the colonials did make very effective use of sharpshooters.

There are a number of technical reasons for the problems sharpshooters faced on the battlefields of the eighteenth century. First and foremost, black-powder weapons produce very thick clouds of smoke. Except in the earliest stages of a battle, a pall of smoke typically disrupted the opportunities for any kind of systematic sharpshooting. Under normal circumstances, battlefield conditions simply did not lend themselves to effective use of rifles. Beyond the inherent limitations of the visibility on an eighteenth-century battlefield, the rifle-equipped sharpshooter would face the same problem he found facing Native Americans in the forest—a determined charge could cover a great deal of ground during the time required for reloading. Once again, given the density of fire that a formation

of riflemen could generate, the tactical advantage on the battlefield lay with the determined charge—not with the rifle. The determined charge was especially effective when carried out by infantrymen whose muskets mounted bayonets. The bayonet charge usually put the riflemen to flight quite easily. Moreover, troops particularly resented the sharpshooting tactics that made their officers the riflemen's particular targets. Riflemen put to flight could expect no quarter from British troops, and there are numerous stories recounting the grisly slaughter of frontiersmen who fell into the hands of the troops they had tormented with their sharpshooting.

The Pennsylvania rifle was too delicate to accept a bayonet. It broke easily when used as a club. The soft wrought-iron barrels bent easily in rugged use. All in all, it was a weapon poorly suited for the battlefield. Nevertheless, the effectiveness of the American sharpshooter during the Revolution and the War of 1812 has been firmly established in the myth and lore of American history. Certainly, the sharpshooters existed and they fought. Saratoga during the Revolution and the Battle of New Orleans were sites of the two most widely recognized battlefield triumphs for the long rifle. In each of those cases, the rifles did make important contributions to the victory. In both cases, however, it is important to note that the sharpshooters were heavily supported by troops using conventional arms to prevent the riflemen from being overrun. At Saratoga it was infantry armed with muskets who protected the sharpshooters; at New Orleans it was massed artillery. The rifles were important for picking off officers—disrupting command and control—but conventional arms inflicted the heavy casualties.

Eyewitness accounts, especially those of the British, make it clear that the American artillery batteries took the heaviest toll among the British troops at New Orleans. Nevertheless, in the American consciousness, when Packenham's 93rd Regiment threw itself vainly against the redoubt south of New Orleans, it was the long rifle that turned the tide. The event was quickly celebrated in a popular song entitled "The Hunters of Kentucky." This song clearly credited the victory at New Orleans to the riflemen from Kentucky:

For we with rifles ready cock'd,
Thought such occasion lucky,
And soon around the general [Andrew
    Jackson] flock'd
The Hunters of Kentucky....
We did not choose to waste our fire
So snugly kept our places,
But when so near we saw them wink,
We thought it time to stop 'em,
And it would have done you good, I think,
To see Kentuckians drop 'em.

"The Hunters of Kentucky" had two significant effects in American popular culture. First, it interpreted the victory at New Orleans entirely as a clear and unequivocal triumph of sharpshooting woodsmen over the British regulars. This interpretation has long endured in the historical consciousness of Americans. Second, it changed the name of the long rifles made in Pennsylvania. From 1815 on, these rifles became almost universally known as "Kentucky long rifles."

Actually, there have been numerous names applied to these distinctive long rifles, depending on where they were used and for what purpose. Nevertheless, whether called Kentucky rifles, Tennessee rifles, barn guns, southern poor boys, the Schimmel, or the Pennsylvania long rifle, the manufacturing of these guns has consistently been centered in Lancaster County, Pennsylvania. Even when gunsmiths turning out long rifles appeared on the frontier in Kentucky, Tennessee, or the Carolinas, the origins of their skills can be traced to apprenticeships or contacts in the Lancaster County region of Pennsylvania.

The Pennsylvania rifles were particularly well adapted to the geography and the kinds of game found in the Ohio Valley and the eastern woodlands. Their use was very widespread, a fact that is lost in focusing on the surviving models that exhibit intricately grained maple stocks, beautifully polished brass furniture, and silver chased inlays on the stock. Such examples were the showpieces of a culture; the plain walnut-stocked barn gun or southern poor boy was the rifle that actually did the daily work of hunting and protecting the homestead. The plain, unadorned Pennsylvania rifle was a working gun, which is illustrated by the fact that many of the plain barn guns continued in daily use in remote areas of the Carolinas, Kentucky, and Tennessee well into the twentieth century. The same qualities that recommended them to the likes of Daniel Boone continued to recommend them to people living in these areas: great accuracy and range, sufficient caliber for the local game, and excellent economy of shot and powder.

The heyday of the Pennsylvania rifle ended in the 1820s as the frontier moved west. As the line of settlements crossed the Mississippi River, the particular conjunctions of geography, distributions of game, and challenges to survival that had called forth the Pennsylvania rifle simply disappeared. Very quickly, the much heavier Hawken and Henry rifles supplanted the light-caliber weapons appropriate in the eastern woodlands. These new rifles were designed for the Great Plains. The Hawken and Henry were altogether sturdier and more rugged weapons, firing projectiles that could stop a grizzly, drop a buffalo, or stand up to the confrontation with the Native Americans of the Great Plains.

The Pennsylvania rifle does provide an early instance in which the specific circumstances of the American frontier experience called forth a very particular technological response. The Pennsylvania rifle achieved almost universal adoption among arms-bearing frontiersmen and pioneers of the regions west of the Appalachians in the period from the 1760s to about 1820, but the same weapon has never been found in common usage outside the original areas of its use. The Pennsylvania rifle is widely known and admired by gun aficionados around the world, yet the need for its particular combination of accuracy and extreme economy was clearly bounded by geography and historical circumstances.

David S. Lux

See also American Revolution; Boone, Daniel; Brown Bess
For Further Reading:
Brown, M. L. 1980. *Firearms in Colonial America.* Washington, DC: Smithsonian Institution Press.
Wilkinson, Frederick. 1977. *The World's Great Guns.* London: Hamlyn Publishing Group.

Lott, John R., Jr. (1958–)

John R. Lott is the author of *More Guns, Less Crime,* a study that concludes that concealed-carry laws deter violent crime. Lott's research also indicates that waiting periods for gun purchases and the passage of gun storage laws increase some types of crimes. Lott's work has been widely cited by gun rights advocates, but strongly criticized by gun control proponents.

Lott was born in 1958 in Detroit and received his bachelor's, master's, and Ph.D. degrees in economics from the University of California, Los Angeles. The bulk of his research has been in the areas of law, economics, public choice, and public finance. Lott's choice of research topics, as with many scholars, reflects his views about the political system. Lott's research shows a politically conservative and libertarian view of government regulation, leading some critics of his work on gun laws to argue that his findings are biased; Lott vigorously refutes this criticism.

Lott served as chief economist for the United States Sentencing Commission in the late 1980s and has held academic and research fellowships at a number of prominent academic institutions, including Texas A & M, Rice, Stanford, the University of Pennsylvania, and the University of Chicago. Lott was a senior research scholar in the School of Law at Yale University as of 2001 and an adjunct scholar of the American Enterprise Institute, a conservative think tank. These affiliations have been the subject of additional criticism; the Violence Policy Center has called Lott an "avid proponent" of the Chicago School that espouses "extreme points of view." Other critics have erroneously linked Lott's acceptance of a John M. Olin Foundation fellowship at the University of Chicago with research bias. By coincidence, the foundation was originally established by an ammunition manufacturer.

Lott's research on the defensive use of weapons contains very complicated statistical analysis, by county, on how the number of weapons and the passage of concealed-carry laws impact crime rates, types of crimes committed, and the use of firearms for self-defense. In the second edition of his book *More Guns, Less Crime,* Lott extends his research to include additional years, analyzes city-level data, and incorporates additional variables that may contribute to crime rates. Lott is also continuing his research on multiple-victim shootings, laws on safe storage of weapons, and police policies.

The basic premise behind Lott's research is quite straightforward: as the number of concealed weapons held by law-abiding citizens increases, potential criminals will be less likely to directly confront victims and violent crime rates will decline. Lott generally finds evidence consistent with this proposition, although there are a number of potential problems with his research methodology. Critics have pointed out the difficulty of proving that one factor causes another in time-series analysis. Crime rates declined across the country at the same time that many concealed-carry laws were adopted. It is possible that other factors that reduced crime rates were not accounted for in Lott's research. The choice of more local-level data rather than statewide data also creates some problems in analyzing the effectiveness of state laws. And there may be other possible problems with the actual data, since some survey data were used.

Lott responds to criticisms of him and his research at length in *More Guns, Less Crime.* He admits to being surprised at the level of controversy that his research has generated. As is common with peer-reviewed academic research, Lott has consistently made his data set available to other researchers for replication. In a more unusual step, Lott responds to over twenty different questions about his research in a chapter in the first edition of *More Guns, Less Crime* and to an additional sixteen questions in the second edition.

Marcia L. Godwin

See also Defensive Gun Use; Hemenway, David; Self-Defense, Legal Issues; Self-Defense, Reasons for Gun Use

For Further Reading:

Brady Campaign to Prevent Gun Violence. 2001. "John Lott's *More Guns, Less Crime:* An Alternative Q & A." http://www.bradycampaign. org/facts/research/lott.asp.

Lott, John R., Jr. 2000. *More Guns, Less Crime: Understanding Crime and Gun-Control Laws.* 2d ed. Chicago: University of Chicago Press.

Lott, John R., Jr., and David Mustard. 1997. "Crime, Deterrence and Right-to-Carry Handguns." *Journal of Legal Studies* 26, 1: 1–68.

Violence Policy Center. 1999. "Who *Is* John Lott and Why Is He Claiming That More Guns Mean Less Crime?" http://www.vpc.org/fact_sht/wholott.htm.

Ludwig, Jens Otto (1968–)

Jens Otto Ludwig, an associate professor of public policy at Georgetown University, has made important contributions to the debate on gun violence and policy. In addition to studying crime and gun violence, he has written on education and urban poverty. With Philip J. Cook he has carried out a comprehensive survey of private gun ownership in the United States, examined underground gun markets, evaluated the effects of various gun policies and legislation, contributed to the debate on defensive gun use (DGU), and coauthored *Gun Violence: The Real Costs* (Cook and Ludwig, 2000).

Ludwig received his B.A. from Rutgers College and his Ph.D. in economics in 1994 from Duke University. In graduate school he worked with Cook. Ludwig has received numerous grants and academic honors and has published extensively. He has been the Model-Okun Visiting Fellow in Economic Studies at the Brookings Institution and is a research affiliate of the Northwestern University/University of Chicago Joint Center for Poverty Research, an affiliated expert of the Johns Hopkins Center for Gun Policy and Research, and a member of the National Consortium on Violence Research at Carnegie Mellon University. The Smith Richardson, Joyce, Spencer, Annie E. Casey, and William T. Grant Foundations, along with the National Institute of Justice (NIJ) and the U.S. Department of Housing and Urban Development, have funded his research.

In 1994, Ludwig and Cook carried out the National Survey of Private Ownership of Firearms (NSPOF), the most comprehensive overview of the gun inventory and gun ownership in the United States. The survey, which was funded by an NIJ grant to the Police Foundation, provided data on the size, composition, and ownership of the nation's gun inventory; the methods of and reasons for firearm acquisition; the storage and carrying of guns; and DGUs (Cook and Ludwig, 1997). The survey indicated that in 1994, 44 million Americans owned 192 million firearms, of which 65 million were handguns. This research also documented the concentration of gun ownership, with 74 percent of gun owners owning two or more guns.

Ludwig has also made additional important contributions to the debate over DGUs in the United States. Kleck and Gertz (1995; Kleck, 1997) have suggested that there may be as many as 2.5 million DGUs a year. Ludwig and his colleagues have argued that Kleck and Gertz's estimate is much too high, referring to it as "the gun debate's new mythical number" (Cook, Ludwig, and Hemenway, 1997). The estimate of 2.5 million DGUs emerged from a survey of 5,000 people, in which only 1 percent of the respondents reported a defensive gun use. With such a small number of respondents, small errors in reporting by those respondents could lead to major inaccuracies in the estimate of the number of DGUs (Webster and Ludwig, 2000).

Webster and Ludwig (2000) also dispute John Lott's (1998) conclusion that permissive carry laws lead to lower overall rates of violent crime, as conveyed by the title of his book *More Guns, Less Crime*. They argue that Lott does not control for important confounding factors and suggest that Lott's research establishes correlation but not causation between permissive carry laws in some states and lower rates of violent crime.

In *Gun Violence: The Real Costs,* Ludwig and Cook (2000) estimate the real costs of gun violence in the United States. They develop an economic-cost framework to calculate the full costs of handgun violence "to document how gun violence reduces the quality of life for everyone in America" (p. viii). They estimate that gun violence costs about $100 billion per year. Ludwig and Cook largely base their estimate on respondents' answers to questions in the 1998 General Social Survey, which asked how much it would be worth to them to reduce violent crime in their community. Ludwig and Cook suggest that all Americans are potential victims of gun violence.

Walter F. Carroll

See also Acquisition of Guns; Availability of Guns, Effects on Crime; Concealed Weapons Laws; Cook, Philip J.; Crime and Gun Use; Defensive Gun Use;

General Social Survey; Gun Ownership; Gun Violence; Gun Violence as a Public Health Problem; Kleck, Gary; Lethality Effect of Guns; Lott, John R., Jr.; National Institute of Justice

For Further Reading:

Cook, Philip J., and Jens Ludwig. 1997. *Guns in America: National Survey on Private Ownership and Use of Firearms.* Research in Brief. Washington, DC: U.S. Department of Justice, National Institute of Justice (May).

———. 2000. *Gun Violence: The Real Costs.* New York: Oxford University Press.

Cook, Philip J., Jens Ludwig, and David Hemenway. 1997. "The Gun Debate's New Mythical Number: How Many Defensive Gun Uses per Year?" *Journal of Policy Analysis and Management* 16: 463–469.

Kleck, Gary. 1997. *Targeting Guns: Firearms and Their Control.* New York: Aldine de Gruyter.

Kleck, Gary, and Marc Gertz. 1995. "Armed Resistance to Crime: The Prevalence and Nature of Self-Defense with a Gun." *Journal of Criminal Law and Criminology* 86: 150–187.

Lott, John R., Jr. 1998. *More Guns, Less Crime: Understanding Crime and Gun-Control Laws.* Chicago: University of Chicago Press.

Webster, Daniel, and Jens Ludwig. 2000. "Myths about Defensive Gun Use and Permissive Gun Carry Laws." Berkeley, CA: Berkeley Media Studies Group. http://support.jhsph.edu/departments/gunpolicy/documents/myths.pdf.